Measuring Instructional Results

or Got A Match?

*How to find out if
your instructional objectives
have been achieved*

Third Edition

Robert F. Mager

BOOKS BY ROBERT F. MAGER

Preparing Instructional Objectives, *Third Edition**

Measuring Instructional Results, *Third Edition**

Analyzing Performance Problems, *Third Edition**
(with Peter Pipe)

Goal Analysis, *Third Edition**

How to Turn Learners On ... without turning them off, *Third Edition**

Making Instruction Work, *Second Edition**

Developing Vocational Instruction (with Kenneth Beach)

Troubleshooting the Troubleshooting Course

The How to Write a Book Book

What Every Manager Should Know About Training

* Sold as a six-volume set (The Mager Six-Pack)

WORKSHOPS BY ROBERT F. MAGER

Criterion-Referenced Instruction (with Peter Pipe)

Instructional Module Development

The Training Manager Workshop

For more information, contact:
The Center for Effective Performance, Inc.
4250 Perimeter Park South, Suite 131
Atlanta, GA 30341
(770) 458-4080 or (800) 558-4237

ISBN 1-879-618-16-8 (PREVIOUSLY ISBN 1-56103-340-5)
ISBN 1-879-618-15-X (SIX-VOLUME SET)

Library of Congress Catalog Card Number: 96-072448
Printed in the United States of America

05 04   10 9 8 7 6 5 4

Contents

Preface

Once upon a time, as the crow flies, the king of Hairmania decided to shave off his beard.

"It is an event that will bring attention and fame—not to mention tourists," he beamed. "Bring the Royal Barber."

"But sire," lamented his advisor, "there are none left in Hairmania. No one has been allowed to shave for a hundred years."

"Hairesy!" exploded the king. "No wonder we're so crowded. Sally ye forth, therefore, and find me the best in all the land."

Which he did. And when at last the most famous barber was found, he was sent to the Royal Three Committees for the Royal Testing.

"Tell us about the history of barbering," asked the first committee.

And he did.

"Tell us about the importance of barbering," asked the second committee.

And he did.

"Tell us what instruments you would use to shave the king," asked the third committee.

And he did.

Whereupon they draped his neck with their Medallion of Approval and led him before the king. Wasting no time, the barber prepared his tools and spread his cloth. But when he picked up his razor with a swirling flourish—he accidentally sliced a piece off the king's ear.

"Gadzooks!" cried the king. "You've cut off my royal ear!"

"Oops," chorused the nine voices of the Royal Three Committees.

"*Oops?*" astonished the king. "I ask for *skill* and you give me *oops?*"

"We're very, very sorry," apologized the Royal Three Committees. "We must have lost our heads."

"A capital idea," rejoiced the king, and sprang himself forth to make it decidedly so.

And ever since and forever more,
There hang nine heads on the Royal Door.
For this was the fate of the Committees Three . . .
May it never befall such as me . . . or thee.

And the moral of this fable is that:

**HE WHO ASKS WRONG QUESTIONS MAY LOSE
MORE THAN FACE**

—RFM

Unlike the Committees Three, we would never think to measure barbering skill by asking about the history of barbering . . . would we? Neither would we weigh steam with a yardstick or evaluate music with a bathroom scale. Similarly, we shouldn't measure the results of our instruction with instruments (i.e., test items) that are inappropriate for the task at hand.

The Focus

There are any number of things that might be useful to know about the effects of one's instruction. For example:

- Did the students *like* the instruction?
- Would they recommend the instruction to others?
- Did the students experience obstacles to learning?
- Did the instruction do what it was supposed to do?
- Do the students use what they learned on the job, in their daily lives, or during subsequent courses?
- Can the instruction be delivered more smoothly, i.e., are there opportunities for improvement?

These and other questions are all legitimate subjects of inquiry. Only one, however, is the direct focus of this book— whether the instruction did what it was supposed to do. There is good reason for this emphasis. Until you know how well your instruction is doing what it is supposed to be doing, there is little reason to evaluate anything else. Why? Regardless of the eloquence of the instructor or the cleverness of the procedures used, instruction is of little value unless its objectives are achieved—unless students depart the instruction able to perform at least as well as the objectives require.

That's why the focus of this book is on learning how to find out whether instruction has accomplished its purpose. It's the most important thing to know about a piece of instruction.

This book is therefore designed to provide you with the basic tools through which to measure instructional success.

The Objective

Specifically, the objective of this book is this:

> Be able to discriminate (select, point to) test items that are appropriate (i.e., items that match the objective in performance and conditions) for testing the achievement of an instructional objective, when given (1) an objective, (2) one or more allegedly suitable test items, and (3) the Objective/Item Matching Checklist.

In short, this book is about how to find out whether your instruction has succeeded as you intended.

Robert F. Mager

Carefree, Arizona
January 1997

1

What It's All About

Suppose you worked hard to achieve this objective handed you by the instructor on the first day of the course:

On a level paved street, be able to ride a unicycle one hundred yards without falling off.

Suppose you had strengthened your thighs with deep-knee bends and had practiced riding until you could mount and ride with relative ease for at least two hundred yards. And suppose that when testing time came around, your instructor asked you to get out pencil and paper and answer the following questions:

1. Define *unicycle*.

2. Write a short essay on the history of the unicycle.

3. Name at least six parts of the unicycle.

4. Describe your method of mounting a unicycle.

What would be your reaction? How would you feel if you had been told to learn one thing and were then tested on another? And how would the instructor ever find out whether the objective had been achieved?

Suppose the instructor "justifies" this situation to you with one or more of the following comments. How would (did) you feel?

"We don't have the facilities to give performance tests."

"We don't have enough unicycles to go around."

"This is an educational institution, not a training institution."

"It doesn't matter how well you can ride; if you don't know anything about the unicycle, you can't really appreciate it."

"I'm teaching for transfer."

"It's too easy to learn to ride a unicycle; I have to add some harder items so I can grade on a curve."

"If everybody learned to ride, I'd have to give everybody an A."

"I like to vary the type of items I use to make my tests interesting."

"I want my tests to be a learning situation."

"I'm teaching creativity and insight."

"I have to design my tests so they can be machine scored."

"Students should learn by discovery."

Regardless of the truth or falsity of the comments listed above, the fact remains that you *cannot* find out whether a person can ride a unicycle unless you or someone else watches that person ride one. In other words, you cannot find out if the objective is achieved unless you use test items that ask the student to do whatever the objective is about. If you use items that aren't "right" for an objective, not only will you *not* find out if your objective has been achieved, you may fool yourself into thinking it has. That can make a person feel pretty silly and unprofessional to students who know an irrelevant, unrealistic, unfair test item when they see one.

That's not so bad when an objective isn't very important, but when there are significant consequences for achieving or not achieving an objective, you'd better take appropriate steps to *find out* whether it has been achieved. If it matters whether the patient's temperature is less than 100 degrees, you'd better use a thermometer to measure temperature rather than a yardstick . . . or a multiple-choice exam. If it matters whether a student pilot can react quickly and accurately in a stall emergency, then you'd better use a reaction-producing item rather than a thermometer . . . or an essay. If it matters whether a student is able to read at least two hundred words per minute, then you'd better find out if that skill can be performed. You'll then be able to respond with more instruction when it can't or with applause when it can, rather than with merely a label (i.e., a grade).

The View From the Top

Unless they are talking about instruction, most people have no difficulty whatever in deciding how to measure results. Ask them how they would find out whether a cake is any good, and most will reply, "Taste it." It is unlikely that anyone would suggest that you should measure the characteristics of the cook or that you should evaluate the *process* of baking.

Similarly, if you asked people how they would find out whether someone could write an essay, they would have no trouble responding, "Well, I'd have them write an essay." It wouldn't even occur to them to respond, "Well, I'd ask the students to describe the characteristics of an essay," or, "I'd give the students an essay and ask them to edit it (or correct it, comment on it, etc.)."

Only when we enter the instructional world do we seem to have difficulty in making the connection between the accomplishment we want to measure and the means of measuring it; between what we want to know and what we should do to find it out.

Measuring the accomplishment of an objective isn't hard.

One merely has to prepare test items that ask students to demonstrate the performance called for by the objective, i.e., to demonstrate the point of the objective. In other words, one prepares items in which the performance and conditions match those of the objective to be assessed. In practice, it's only a little more difficult than the telling. (Those who have well-stated objectives derived from analyses may well wonder what the fuss is all about; they already follow this procedure as a matter of course.)

> **NOTE:** A performance will be judged according to the criteria stated in an objective, of course, but it isn't necessary to include those criteria in the test items. Why not? Often there are several criteria by which the performance will be judged and to include them in a test item would serve only to confuse the student. Also, when more than one item is used, the criteria by which the performance will be judged are applied collectively to all the items; it would make no sense to include criteria in each. It is usually enough for the item simply to tell the student what to do, as well as where and with what (or without what) to do it.

Obstacles

The difficulties experienced while writing items seldom are caused by an inability to craft suitable test items. Instead, they are caused by poorly written objectives. When people try to test the accomplishment of vaguely-written objectives, they find it impossible to decide what type of measuring instrument to use. And no wonder. If you're not clear about what you want to measure, it's not possible to decide intelligently how to measure it.

Another important obstacle to easy preparation of suitable test items arises from the tendency of instructors to consider the student fair game for almost any kind of test. This tendency somehow gives instructors a feeling of uneasiness when they construct test items strictly according to the objective. "These items don't cover enough ground," the feeling says. "These items are too easy," it tells them; and it makes them conveniently forget that the object is not to develop a variety of items that only half the students can master, but to prepare items that will reveal which students can perform as desired. And the feeling goes on to say, "Well, maybe students can perform as well or better than expected, but they won't really understand it unless . . ." and then urges instructors to add items having little or no relation to the objective. Finally, this funny feeling, in a last desperate bid for survival, says, "Well, maybe all the students have achieved the objective, but I need to add some harder items so I can spread them out on a curve."

I can help you avoid that feeling by describing the rationale for the procedure described in this book and by helping you develop skill in implementing that procedure. After all, people who know how to do something are more likely to do it than those who don't know how! And if they know why they are doing it, they may feel more at ease when following the more productive path.

> **NOTE:** The use of inappropriate test items is a widespread phenomenon and is a practice (malpractice?) most urgently in need of jettisoning. When we deceive students by teaching one thing and testing another, we lose and the students lose. Putting it more plainly, when we cheat students, they generally find a way to cheat back. Everyone associated with education and training need to know how to avoid that.

What's to Come

So that words won't get in our way, the next chapter will describe a few distinctions in terms. Following that, there will be discussion and practice in interpreting—decoding—the key characteristics of an objective. That will prepare us for discussion and practice in matching potentially useful test items to objectives.

Then, before practicing the entire skill, you can practice repairing some items to match the objectives they are supposed to be related to. Finally, a set of items is provided with which you can test your skill.

> **NOTE:** Because the actual objectives we see and use vary considerably in the clarity with which they are stated, I will use similarly imperfect statements in the examples that follow. After all, we need to learn to handle the world as it is, rather than to practice only on well-stated objectives that you may seldom encounter.

2
Distinctions

Barriers to communication arise when words have different meanings to different people. To avoid this possibility, a few definitions and distinctions are in order. If we both use words in the same manner, they won't get in the way of our ideas.

Items and Tests

It is useful to be able to tell the difference between tests and test items. If you've ever spent much time in a school, you couldn't avoid either one, so this distinction may appear obvious. Then again, maybe not.

Item: A test item calls for a single response or set of responses to a single stimulus or stimulus pattern. It asks for one sample of a behavior. That performance may be simple, as when asking someone to write the answer to an addition problem, or it may be complex, as when asking someone to perform an appendectomy, analyze a problem, compose a sonata, fly a plane, or operate a computer.

Test: A test is an event during which someone is asked to demonstrate some aspect of his or her knowledge or skill. Though a test can consist of a single test item, a test generally consists of several items.

NOTE: Because of the uncomfortable emotional baggage often associated with the word "test," tests (especially in industry) are referred to as "skill checks" or "performance checks." These are especially appropriate terms in environments where the purpose of the exercise is to find out whether someone can now perform as desired, rather than to collect information on which to base a grade.

Measurement, Evaluation, and Grading

Measurement: The process of measurement determines the extent of some characteristic associated with an object or person. For example, when we determine the length of a room or the weight of an object, we are measuring.

Evaluation: The act of evaluation compares a measurement with a standard and passes judgment on the comparison. We are making evaluations when we say things like—it's too long, it's too hot, he's not motivated, she's too slow. To arrive at these evaluations we have noted the extent of some characteristic, compared it with some standard, and then passed judgment on the comparison.

When we then say things such as:

"She passed."
"He flunked."
"She's not working up to her potential."
"He's competent."

we are making *evaluations*. We have compared the results of the measurement with some standard (real or imagined, stable or floating, visible or invisible) and have made a judgment.

The difference between measurement and evaluation can be illustrated by this example:

Measurement: "These watermelons are three feet long."

Evaluation: "Wow!"

Or by this example:

Measurement: "This student can type 30 words per minute."

Evaluation: "That's too slow."

Grading: A grade is a label representing an evaluation. When you note that your cow has been stamped "U.S. Choice," you know that it has been given a grade. (What the cow had to do to deserve such a grade is another matter.)

Sometimes an evaluation is based on measurement and sometimes on guesses, intuition, expectation, or bias. Traditionally, a grade says something about how well a student has performed *in relation to his or her peers;* the student is very good, pretty good, about the same as, not as good as, or much poorer than those who happen to be his or her classmates. Also traditionally, the student is seldom informed of the precise basis for the grade.

Norm-Referenced and Criterion-Referenced Evaluations

Norm-referenced evaluation: When the performance of one student is compared with that of other students, and a judgment is made on the basis of that comparison, a norm-referenced evaluation has been made.

Thus, when we say that Student X is above average and that Student Y is below average, we are rank-ordering students on the basis of their performance *in reference to each other,* and therefore we are making a norm-referenced evaluation.

Grading on a curve is such an evaluation. So is the assignment of IQ.

For example, if we have five automobiles, and none of them runs, we might measure the extent of their defects and say "Automobile B 'doesn't run' the best. None of them goes at all, but B is the best of the non-goers." We've just made a norm-referenced evaluation. If we then said, "Give that car an A+," we would have assigned a grade on the basis of a norm-referenced evaluation.

Criterion-referenced evaluation: When we make a judgment based on a comparison of a measurement with an objective standard, we make a criterion-referenced evaluation.

If, for example, we evaluate our automobiles and say "None of them runs," we've compared the state of each car with a standard that says, "It has to move to be acceptable," and judged that none meets this criterion. We have made a criterion-referenced evaluation.

Here's another example. Suppose students are expected to accomplish this objective:

Within three minutes, be able to solve fifty addition problems, without the use of a calculator.

Suppose further that one student solves only 35 problems within the time allowed. There are two kinds of evaluation that can follow this measurement:

Norm-referenced: "Gee, this performance is the best in the class. Give this student an A."

Criterion-referenced: "Oops. This performance did not meet the criterion. Give this student more instruction and/or practice."

The Coffee-Pot Caper

The difference between the norm-referenced and criterion-referenced methods of evaluation was beautifully illustrated some years ago by an example that went like this: Imagine that an objective called for a student to be able to make a pot of coffee, when given all the necessary tools and equipment. A checklist of each of the steps in the process is prepared, and the student's performance is then scored on both a norm-referenced and a criterion-referenced basis. Note the difference between the two methods of scoring:

Checklist for Making a Pot of Coffee

	Norm-referenced Scoring	Criterion-referenced Scoring
Disconnects coffee pot	10	✓
Disassembles coffee pot	10	✓
Cleans components and pot	10	✓
Inspects components	10	✓
Fills pot with water	10	✓
Reassembles components	10	✓
Fills basket with coffee	0	✗
Reconnects coffee pot	10	✓
Sets dial on coffee pot	10	✓
Turns coffee pot on	10	✓
SCORE	90%	Not yet competent

Note that a norm-referenced approach would allow a student to accumulate a score of 90 percent, *even though the student failed to make a pot of coffee.* Using a criterion-referenced approach, on the other hand, the same student would receive a score of zero. By failing to accomplish the objective of being able to make a pot of coffee, the student must be judged to be "not yet competent." (Just last week I failed to put the little coffee pot under the spout of our espresso maker. I made coffee, all right, all over the kitchen counter . . . but my wife refused to give me 90% for my effort. Never mind what she did give me.)

Though there are some uses for norm-referenced evaluation, our attention will be focused on criterion-referenced evaluation. When we want to know *whether* an expectation (objective) or criterion has in fact been achieved, only criterion-referenced procedures are appropriate.

Criterion Items and Diagnostic Items

Criterion item: An item designed to help determine whether some criterion has or has not been achieved.

Diagnostic item: An item designed to reveal *why* a criterion was NOT achieved.

For example, if we want to find out if someone could bake a pie that met certain standards, we would use *criterion items* designed for that purpose. Simply, we would ask someone to bake a pie. If that person could do it, and if the pie met the standards set for it, we would say that the criterion had been met. He or she could bake a pie.

If, however, the pie did not get made at all, or if the finished pie oozed to the floor in a puddle, we would say that the would-be baker did not meet the criterion. When this is the case, we may want to know *why* the person did not meet the criterion—why the task wasn't performed as required. Items designed to find out *why* a criterion was *not* achieved are called *diagnostic* items.

The distinction is important. A test often contains both criterion items and diagnostic items; many contain *only* diagnostic items. If we don't know the difference between the two, we might decide *whether* a student has achieved a criterion by evaluating performance on a diagnostic item. Thus, if we want to know if a student can peel an orange, we should make that judgment on the basis of the criterion item, (e.g., "Peel that orange") rather than on the basis of diagnostic items (e.g., "Tell me *how* you would peel that orange," or "Is this an orange?" or "Whose team wears orange jerseys?").

The criterion item provides the proof of the pudding but doesn't help much with the recipe. A simple depiction of the uses of the two types of items is shown in the sketch below.

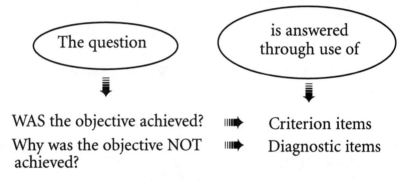

The question	is answered through use of
WAS the objective achieved? ➠	Criterion items
Why was the objective NOT achieved? ➠	Diagnostic items

Although some criterion items can be useful for diagnostic purposes, the emphasis here is with using them to find out whether an objective has been accomplished. More on this in Chapter 6.

End-of-Course and On-the-Job Evaluations

Instructional effects can be assessed at several points along the instructional road. For example:

- **End-of-unit:** Criterion and diagnostic test items (skill checks) are used to determine whether a student has accomplished the objective of an instructional unit, so that remedial action can be taken when needed (e.g., additional practice).

- **End-of-course:** Skill checks (tests) are used to find out whether a student can be judged "competent" or "not yet competent." (It's risky to rely solely on end-of-course evaluations, of course, because there no longer is any time left to provide remedial help when a student is not yet competent.)

- **On-the-job:** Performance of the job incumbents (the former students) is assessed to determine whether they actually use what they were taught.

The end-of-unit and end-of-course evaluations tell us whether or not the instruction works; that is, whether it accomplished what it set out to accomplish. These are the assessments that will tell you whether a student can or cannot be judged competent.

On-the-job evaluations can tell you many things, but they cannot tell you whether the instruction was successful. Such evaluations, in fact, aren't *instructional* evaluations at all. If, for example, it is discovered on the job that people *don't know how* to do what they're supposed to do, it's possible that the instruction was somehow defective. However, when people don't perform their jobs right even though they know how to do so, it can't be legitimately inferred that the instruction was at fault. Why not? Too many variables interfere with such a conclusion; there are many reasons why people don't perform as expected, and a lack of know-how is only one of them. For example:

- They may not have the authority.
- They may not have the tools, space, equipment.

- They may not know what they're expected to do.
- They may get punished when they do it right.
- They may get rewarded for doing it wrong.

And more. When people are not performing on the job as expected, therefore, it is simply wrong to conclude that the training didn't work. In most situations, what isn't working right is management. Those interested in guaranteeing that their instruction does what it was designed to do will make sure their students can perform according to the objectives before they leave the instructional environment.

And Now?

Now that we've sorted out a few distinctions, it's time to plunge into the purpose of it all, that of selecting or writing test items that will measure accomplishment of an objective. To do that, though, we've got to be able to figure out what those objectives are saying. In other words, we need to be able to decode an objective so we can answer the eternal question, "Where's the beef?"

3
Decoding the Objective

$\mathbf{M}$any procedures take longer to explain than to perform. Tying a shoelace, adding a column of numbers, and playing a sonata are examples. In each case, the skill can be performed faster than it can be explained—once the skill has been learned.

So it is with writing or selecting test items relevant to assessing an objective. The explaining takes longer than the doing, long enough to make the point worth mentioning. In practice, the drafting of a suitable test item will take but a minute or two. Only a small percentage of your items will take longer to think through and draft.

The Goal

We're seeking to be able to write or select items that will test achievement of an objective, that will help us decide whether our instruction actually accomplished what it was intended to accomplish. That means writing or selecting test items that ask students to:

(a) do what the objective asks them to be able to do,

(b) under the conditions described by the objective.

The objective wants students to be able to give speeches? Fine. We'll write a test item that asks them to give a speech. The objective wants the speech-giving to occur under water? OK, we'll add that condition to the test item. And that's that. Well, it would be that—if every objective were clear and contained the information you need to help you with your decision-making and if you didn't sometimes have to test under conditions different from those desired. Unfortunately, as the old song says, "It Ain't Necessarily So."

Why not? Simply because many objectives either don't tell you what you need to know, or they make you guess at what they really mean. Some "objectives" don't state a performance; those that do may still leave you wondering what the objective really is. Some will tell you how a performance should be measured without giving you a clue about what you're supposed to be measuring.[1]

If we didn't encounter so many objectives that don't do what they're supposed to do (some of which we write ourselves), we'd have no need to learn to decode an objective (that is, noting the presence or absence of key characteristics) and could go directly to the business of building measuring instruments to test their achievement. But because reality requires us to "Get real!" we need to take a little time out to make sure we can squeeze the information we need from an objective, even when it isn't cleanly stated.

What You Need to Know

To carry out the decoding procedure, you need to be able to recognize the difference between:

1.　Performances and abstractions,

1. For more help in understanding objectives, read *Preparing Instructional Objectives*, Third Edition, R. F. Mager (The Center for Effective Performance, Atlanta, GA, 1997).

2. Main intents and indicator performances, and

3. Overt and covert performances.

Once you know how to make these distinctions, you'll not only be able to deal with well- and poorly-stated objectives, you'll find the decoding procedure a piece of cake. Of course, if you already can make these discriminations, it would be a waste of your time to have to read the sections that deal with them. Therefore, you have a choice. Turn to the page number shown beside the statement that best describes your decision.

I can already make these distinctions.   *Turn to page 33.*

I could use a quick review.   *Turn to page 20.*

Performances and Abstractions

Performances: Performances are things that people say and do. They sing, write papers, type, hit golf balls, solve problems, give speeches, make discriminations, and point to things. Performances are what objectives are about.

Abstractions: Sometimes, however, people use words that describe a state of being. For example, someone lying on a desk may be described as "lazy." But lazy isn't a performance. It's a word describing an alleged state of being. Words like nice, genial, and studious, as well as expressions such as "they have a poor attitude" and "he's not motivated" refer to people, rather than describe something that they are doing.

For instance, all of the items in this list qualify as performances:

- Add these numbers
- Ride this bike
- Solve this problem
- Edit this speech
- Play this song
- Divide these numbers
- Draw a duck

These would not qualify as performances:

- Internalize a growing awareness
- Be happy
- Think clearly

- Demonstrate an understanding
- Be safety-conscious
- Have empathy for browbeaten husbands
- Understand physics
- Be concerned with the bottom line
- Be empowered

Here's a little practice. Circle the performance, if any, mentioned in these statements:

1. Without a musical score, sing any of the songs on the following list (list would be added here).

2. Be able to know the principles of behavior modification.

3. Be able to demonstrate an understanding of the principles of aerodynamics.

4. Be able to record blood pressure for an adult patient of any size or weight.

5. Be able to describe verbally the procedure for completing a ballot used in a national election.

Check your responses on the next page.

1. Without a musical (score) sing any of the songs on the following list (list would be added here).

2. Be able to know the principles of behavior modification.

3. Be able to demonstrate an understanding of the principles of aerodynamics.

4. Be able to (record blood pressure) for an adult patient of any size or weight.

5. Be able to (describe verbally) the procedure for completing a ballot used in a national election.

The performance mentioned in the first item is *sing*, but no performances are stated in Items 2 and 3. Items 4 and 5 state performances; you can tell whether someone is recording blood pressure or describing verbally.

Indicators and Main Intents

Until you know what an objective is really about—its reason for being—you can't select items that will help you find out whether it's been achieved. While the performance stated in the objective is often its main intent, this isn't always the case. Sometimes the objective will state a performance, but it won't be the main intent. Instead, it will describe a way to find out whether the main intent has been accomplished. These performances are called indicator behaviors, because they are intended to indicate whether the main intent was achieved. Here are the definitions of main intents and indicator behaviors:

> **Main intent** (primary intent, principal purpose) is the performance that is the purpose of the objective, i.e., what you want people to be able to do in the real world after they've left the instruction.

> **Indicator behavior** is a visible or audible activity through which the existence of the main intent will be inferred.

Consider this example:

Given a fully equipped surgery, be able to perform a lobotomy on any breed of cockroach.

First question: What's the performance mentioned in the objective? *Perform a lobotomy.* That's what it *says*.

Next question: What's the point (main intent) of the objective? What is the objective mainly about? Why, it is about being able to perform a lobotomy. There is no reason to suspect otherwise. Lobotomizing is the skill the learner is expected to develop.

In this example, the performance stated in the objective is the main intent of the objective. Knowing that, we also know that the only way we can find out if someone has accomplished the objective is to ask that person to perform a lobotomy.

Now let's ask the same two questions of this statement:

Given a series of pictures depicting animals and non-animals, be able to color all the animals.

First question: What's the performance stated in the objective? *Coloring.* That's what it *says.*

Next question: What's the main intent? Why, the objective wants performers to be able to tell the difference between animals and non-animals. It doesn't say so, but in this case it is clear this is the main intent. So the answer to "What is the main intent?" here is "Discriminate *(recognize, differentiate)* between animals and non-animals." How did we know that coloring is an indicator behavior and not a main intent? We asked ourselves whether coloring is what the objective writer wants students to be able to do in the real world after leaving the instruction. It's unlikely that the point of the objective is for students to be able to trundle through life coloring animals.

Why does the objective say *color* when it wants learners to be able to discriminate? Simply because in this case the objective writer decided to state an indicator rather than a main intent. So the stated performance is an indicator, and the main intent is implied.

There is nothing wrong with having an objective state an indicator behavior and not the main intent, *so long as the main intent is clear.*

In this example, you are told to infer from the performers' coloring behavior whether they can tell the difference between animals and non-animals. Because the main intent is clear, you know you are not going to teach the student to color simply because coloring is the performance stated in the objective. You also know that you will not evaluate or grade the student on his or her coloring ability (i.e., you would never say a thing such as "Yes, yes, you can tell the difference between animals and non-animals, all right, but you did a sloppy job of coloring so I'll have to take 10 points off."). The objective isn't about coloring; it is about discriminating. Since the main intent is clear, I wouldn't bother to rewrite the objective; I'd leave it as is and simply make sure I didn't accidentally evaluate the quality of the coloring when evaluating achievement of the main intent.

One more example:

Given a collection of business letters, be able to make a check mark on those conforming to company policy as outlined in the Perfect Policy Manual of 2093.

What performance is actually stated? Make a check mark. That's what it *says*. But is *checkmarking* the point (main intent) of the objective? Does the objective writer expect people to wander through life making check marks? Not likely. So what is the objective really about? What is the main intent? Discriminating, that's what. It's about being able to tell the difference between letters that do, and don't, meet the standards stated in the manual. Though the objective doesn't actually say that, you can be pretty sure that's what it is by reading the indicator behavior.

So again a performance is stated, but it isn't the main intent of the objective. The main intent is discriminating, and the visible behavior selected as the means by which to indicate presence of the intended skill is checkmarking. Whenever you're not sure about whether the performance is an indicator or main intent, ask the objective writer. If that's you, fix the objective.

To check your skill at identifying main intents and indicators, try the items on page 27.

Here's What To Do:

Circle the performance stated, and then check (✓) the appropriate column to the right. Is the *stated* performance an indicator or a main intent?

	MAIN INTENT	INDICATOR
1. Be able to identify the verb in any sentence.	_____	_____
2. Be able to circle a verb in any sentence.	_____	_____
3. Given any number of one-dollar bills, be able to mark those that are counterfeit.	_____	_____
4. Given a group of essays and a set of standards, be able to evaluate the essays according to the standards.	_____	_____

Check your responses on the following page.

	MAIN INTENT	INDICATOR

1. Be able to (identify the verb) in any sentence.   ✓

2. Be able to (circle a verb) in any sentence.   ✓

3. Given any number of one-dollar bills, be able to (mark) those that are counterfeit.   ✓

4. Given a group of essays and a set of standards, be able to (evaluate the essays) according to the standards.   ✓

1. This statement asks learners to be able to *identify* verbs. That is the main intent. There is no indicator, and so you don't know how you will know that the identifying was accomplished. Even so, it seems pretty clear that identifying is the main intent.

2. The stated performance is *circling*. But is that the main intent of the objective? No, circling is an indicator by which you will find out if the main intent, probably recognizing, has been accomplished. (It's doubtful that many people earn their living at verb-circling.)

3. This item says *mark,* but it is clear that the main intent is for someone to be able to recognize a counterfeit one-dollar bill.

4. The performance stated is *evaluate.* That's what it says. It doesn't state, or even hint, at what visible behavior might be acceptable as evidence of evaluating, but it seems clear that evaluating is the main intent. If you think evaluating is an abstraction rather than a performance, follow the rule; i.e., either fix the objective yourself or get its writer to do so.

Overt and Covert

The third and final distinction you need to be able to make is between performances that are visible (overt) and performances that are invisible (covert). Why is this distinction important? Because that's how you will know when to look for indicator behaviors in the objective.

For example, suppose an objective says that someone needs to be able to identify, and that identifying is the main intent. So far, so good. But identifying is a covert (invisible) activity. You could stand perfectly still at an airport while identifying all the brown bags that walk by, and no one would ever know you were doing it. For someone to find out that you're identifying, you'd have to do something visible, such as pointing. Pointing is an indicator behavior through which someone could infer that you did your invisible identifying correctly or incorrectly.

The rule here is simple: When the objective states a covert performance, make sure it also states an indicator. If it doesn't, then someone will have to repair the objective before you can match test items to it.

For a bit of practice in distinguishing between overt and covert performances, look at the next page.

Below are a few words describing various actions. Some are directly visible and some are not. Check (✓) those that are directly visible or audible, those about which you can say, "When people are doing that, I can see or hear them doing it."

1. State   _____

2. Acquire   _____

3. Write   _____

4. Draw   _____

5. Recognize   _____

6. Solve   _____

7. Recall   _____

Check your responses on the following page.

1. **State.** Overt. You can tell if someone is stating something.

2. **Acquire.** Covert or overt, depending on what is being acquired. Acquiring a concept is covert; acquiring a wallet is overt. (Words can be sneaky, can't they?)

3. **Write.** Overt. You can tell directly when someone is writing.

4. **Draw.** Overt or covert. Drawing a picture is overt; drawing a conclusion is covert. (Don't blame me for the fact that words don't always have a single meaning or implication.)

5. **Recognize.** Covert. For you to be able to tell whether someone *recognized*, he or she would have to do something other than recognize—such as point a finger, say something, or write a note.

6. **Solve.** Covert. Similar to adding. Both can be done invisibly.

7. **Recall.** Covert. I can recall all sorts of things and easily hide the fact that I am doing it. If you want to know if someone has recalled something, you need an indicator—an overt behavior that will signal the recalling.

Continue to the next page.

Now it's time to attack the objective/item matching procedure directly.

How To Do It

NOTE: When decoding an objective, the quickest and surest way is to use a pencil to draw a circle around the "doing" word and then to underline any conditions that may be stated.

STEP ONE. Circle the performance stated in the objective.

This means no more than noting the word or phrase that tells what students will be doing when demonstrating their achievement of the objective. Most of the time this is easy to do. When it is more difficult, it is because of a gray area between performances and abstractions or because the "objective" doesn't state any performance at all.

Let's look at a few simple examples, just to be sure we are thinking about the same thing.

Here's What To Do:

Draw a circle around the explicit *performance* (the doing word), if any, mentioned in the following statements:

1. Be able to write the symbols for any twenty electronic components.

2. Be able to demonstrate an understanding of modern poetry.

3. Be able to multiply pairs of two-digit numbers.

4. Be able to show a knowledge of the basic elements of a contract.

Turn the page to check your responses.

1. *Be able to write the symbols for any twenty electronic components.*

   The performance stated is write the symbols. That's what it says. Never mind for the moment whether writing is what the objective is really about. For the moment we are only concerned with whether any kind of performance is stated at all.

2. *Be able to demonstrate an understanding of modern poetry.*

   No performance is stated. The word demonstrate doesn't qualify. What would someone be doing when demonstrating an understanding? Running? Jumping? Writing? Explaining? We can't tell. The word demonstrate sounds like a performance, but that's all.

3. *Be able to multiply pairs of two-digit numbers.*

   This item asks students to multiply. Multiplying qualifies as a performance (as would similar intellectual skills), because we can determine directly whether the multiplying occurred.

4. *Be able to show a knowledge of the basic elements of a contract.*

   No performance is stated. What would someone be doing when "Showing a knowledge of . . ."? Delivering a speech? Writing an essay? Describing contracts? It doesn't say.

   To recap, the first step in selecting test items appropriate for measuring accomplishment of an objective is to note the performance mentioned in the objective. When no performance is stated, the statement isn't an objective, and you must either get clarification from whomever wrote the statement, clarify it yourself, or throw it away. Without a performance, there is little sense going on to the next step.

Step One.   Circle the performance stated in the objective.

STEP TWO. If the performance is an indicator, identify the main intent.

If the main intent is clear, then that's all there is to this step. If not, you will need to ask the objective writer for clarification. For example, in the following statement it is clear that the performance called for is an indicator. But what is the main intent?

Given any page of non-technical prose, be able to circle dangling participles.

Why should one be able to circle these things? Surely a person won't be expected to go through life circling danglers. Circling is just an indicator that shows a learner can do something meaningful. But what? Perhaps he or she is expected to be able to recognize or identify dangling participles. That would be my guess. But I could be wrong. It may be that the objective writer wants students to be able to write grammatically correct sentences and is using circling (incorrectly) as a means of finding out whether they can do so. The point is simply that we are not sure. When you can't easily tell what the objective is all about, ask or fix. The example on dangling participles might be rewritten as follows:

Given any page of non-technical prose, be able to identify (circle) dangling participles.

Step One.   Circle the performance stated in the objective.

Step Two.   If the performance is an indicator, identify the main intent.

STEP THREE. If the stated performance is the main intent, note whether it is overt or covert.

If the main intent is a visible or audible performance, you're finished decoding for now. If, on the other hand, the main intent is covert, you'll have to make sure an indicator is stated and that the indicator is the simplest available.

Figure 1 on the opposite page offers a visible picture of the situation. It shows that a performance can be:

1. An **overt main intent** (visible or audible).

   (Examples: writing, marking, singing, kicking, and screaming.)

2. A **covert main intent** (invisible).

   (Examples: identifying, recalling, solving, adding.)

3. An **overt indicator** (visible or audible).

   (Indicators are always overt.)

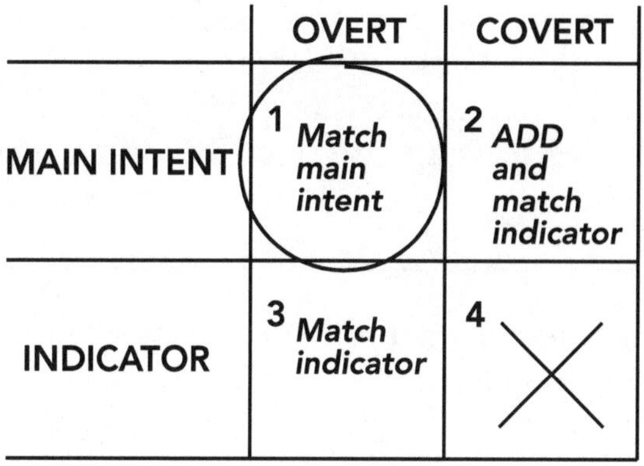

	OVERT	COVERT
MAIN INTENT	1 *Match main intent*	2 *ADD and match indicator*
INDICATOR	3 *Match indicator*	4

Figure 1

In Figure 1, the box representing "covert indicator" is crossed out because that category is an absurdity. An indicator can't indicate anything if it's invisible. Here's what to do for each of the three situations:

Visible (overt) main intent. When the performance stated in an objective is a main intent and is observable (visible or audible), then you've finished decoding the objective. Test items will be selected that ask students to accomplish the stated main intent.

Invisible (covert) main intent. When, instead, the main intent is *not* visible—that is, when the main intent is covert (cognitive, internal, or mental)—add a suitable indicator. Always. The indicator must be added because you can't match test items to something that is invisible. The easiest way to do that is simply to add an indicator behavior in parentheses after the performance, like this:

Given a list of statements describing goals and performances, be able to identify (circle) the performances.

Indicator behavior. When the performance stated is an indicator, make sure it is appropriate for testing the main intent, because it's possible to select indicators that are wrong for the task they are expected to perform. How do you tell whether an indicator is a good one? By testing the indicator. That's the next step.

Step One.   Circle the performance stated in the objective.

Step Two.   If the performance is an indicator, identify the main intent.

Step Three. If the stated performance is the main intent, note whether it is overt or covert.

STEP FOUR. For objectives containing an indicator, test the indicator.

To *test the indicator* simply means to answer this question:

Is this indicator the simplest and most direct available and well within the repertoire of the student?

If the answer is "Yes," then the indicator behavior is probably acceptable, and you've finished decoding the objective. If the answer is "No," the indicator needs to be simplified.

Let me illustrate the point with this example, borrowed from an English teacher. The objective was stated like this:

Demonstrate an understanding of the difference between a limerick and a sonnet by writing one of each.

Now watch closely (there's nothing up my sleeve, and at no time do my fingers leave my hands).

First question: What's the performance stated in the objective? *Writing.* That's the doing word.

Second question: What is the main intent of the objective? It's about being able to *recognize the difference* between limericks and sonnets. That's what it says. It's about discrimination. (It doesn't say *what kind* of difference the student should be able to discriminate, but it clearly implies that "being able to tell the difference" is the main intent.)

Third question: If the main intent is to find out whether students can tell the difference between limericks and sonnets, how does the instructor intend to find out if they can do it? Why, the instructor will ask them to *write* one of each. It is clear that writing a limerick and a sonnet is the indicator by which the objective writer intends to tell if the main intent is achieved.

Asking students to *write* sonnets and limericks to find out whether they can tell them apart seems a bit much, don't you think? Many students may be unable to write poems, yet be able to tell the two apart. Surely you can think of an easier, more direct indicator than writing. What will tell us whether students can recognize limericks and sonnets when they see them and that will not require students to do more than tell us which poem fits each category? There are several alternatives.

We could give students a pile of pages, each of which has a limerick or sonnet on it, and ask students to *sort* the pages into two piles—one pile for limericks and one for sonnets. *Anyone* ought to be able to sort pages. Or, we could ask them to poke a pencil through the limericks. Or, we could ask them to make a check mark on the sonnets. Or ask for any number of simple, direct actions (behaviors) that *anyone could be expected to perform.* Each of these indicators would tell us whether the desired discrimination is taking place; each of them would directly assess the main intent, without making it easy to assess something *other* than the main intent.

"Well," you might hear an instructor say to a student, "Sure, you can tell the difference between limericks and sonnets, but you write a lousy sonnet and so I'm going to have to take 20 points off." Or, "OK, you can tell one from another, but you don't *really understand* the difference until you can write one." Balderdash! When the indicator isn't the simplest, most direct one available, and if it isn't well within the present capability of the student, the evaluation of the main intent of the objective will almost invariably be confounded with an evaluation of the student's ability to perform the indicator. How often have you heard things like this:

> "Well, you got the problems right, but your handwriting is terrible."

> "Your essay said all I wanted it to, but I'll have to mark you down for grammar."

Each such sentiment suggests that academic sneakery has been perpetrated. And that's why it is important to test an indicator—to make sure your test items will test the main intent rather than the indicator.

NOTE: Any indicator will do if it is simple, direct, and well within the ability of the student. In the example of the limericks and sonnets, checkmarking sonnets would be as direct as circling limericks. Each of these indicators is a simpler behavior from which we can directly infer whether the covert main intent has been achieved.

Let's nail down Step Four with a few practice items. On the next right-hand page are some objectives with covert main intents and some form of indicator. To ease your reading burden, I've left off detailed conditions and criteria.

Here's What To Do:

1. For each objective, circle the indicator behavior.

2. If it's the simplest possible, check YES.

3. If not, then check NO and write a better one.

OBJECTIVE	Is the indicator simple and direct?		
	YES	NO	WRITE A BETTER INDICATOR
1. Demonstrate an ability to recognize a user-friendly web page by creating one.	⎯⎯	⎯⎯	⎯⎯⎯⎯⎯⎯
2. Be able to identify sentences that are statements of bias, assumption, generalization, or conclusion by writing sentences illustrating those categories.	⎯⎯	⎯⎯	⎯⎯⎯⎯⎯⎯
3. Be able to compute the solution to binary addition problems.			

3. Be able to compute the solution to binary addition problems.

Sample test item:
Describe the steps for solving each of the following binary addition problems:

11000	0101		
+11000	+0011	⎯⎯ ⎯⎯	⎯⎯⎯⎯⎯⎯

Turn the page to check your responses.

| | Is the indicator simple and direct? | | |
OBJECTIVE	YES	NO	WRITE A BETTER INDICATOR
1. Demonstrate an ability to recognize a user-friendly web page by creating one.		✓	Point to
2. Be able to identify sentences that are statements of bias, assumption, generalization, or conclusion, by writing sentences illustrating those categories.		✓	Circle the category
3. Be able to compute the solution to binary addition problems. *Sample test item:* Describe the steps for solving each of the following binary addition problems: 11000 0101 +11000 0011		✓	Write the solution

See explanation on the following pages.

Here's the explanation.

1. *Main intent:*   Recognize.

   Indicator: Create.

   Simplest, most direct indicator? No.

The indicator is more complex than required, requiring more skill than called for by the main intent. A better indicator would be to have students point to suitable web pages or to write their initials on them.

2. *Main intent:*   Discriminating statements of bias, etc.

   Indicator: Writing sentences.

   Simplest, most direct indicator? No.

In this example, the indicator would tell you whether the objective has been achieved. But the indicator is by no means the simplest possible; it asks students to do more than needed to indicate their ability to recognize the types of sentences listed. It asks students to *write* a sentence when the objective only wants to know if they can *recognize* a sentence. Several indicators would be less bulky and less demanding of student time. For example, four columns could be drawn to the right of the sentences to be judged, each headed with one of the four judgment categories (i.e., bias, assumption, generalization, conclusion). Students could be asked to read each sentence presented and to check the appropriate column or columns.

3. *Main intent:*   Solving problems.
   Indicator: Describing solution steps.
   Simplest, most direct indicator? No.

(continued on page 46)

Here the main intent and the indicator clearly do not match. It is not possible to determine whether students can solve problems by asking them to describe the steps they would follow in solving the problems. Oh, sure, if they can't describe the steps, you might conclude with some confidence that they can't solve the problems. But if they *can* describe the steps, you cannot conclude that they *can* solve the problems. Describing isn't the same as solving.

What would be a more appropriate indicator? Ask performers to tell or write the solution. Either indicator would be appropriate—more direct and simpler. If you were interested in *how* they arrived at their solution, some other indicator would be called for. The objective, however, relates to outcomes rather than processes.

Caution

Be watchful when the word *identify* is used in an objective; it's a slippery one. You may not be aware that other people are using a different meaning for the same word. For example, *identify* is sometimes used to mean "point to," as in "Identify the bones of the body." This could mean to point to bones on a diagram or to point to the real thing.

Sometimes *identify* means to select a verbal description of the real thing, as in "Identify the correct answers in each of these multiple-choice questions." The word is also used to mean describe or tell, as in "On the paper provided, briefly identify the causes of bankruptcy." Finally, it is sometimes used to mean list, as in "Identify the steps in cashing a check." With all these possible meanings floating around, *identify* should be accompanied by a simple indicator when used as a main intent.

Where We Are

At this point, you should be able to carry out the steps associated with decoding an objective. You should be able to:

1. Identify (circle) the performance stated.

2. When the stated performance is an indicator, identify the main intent.

3. When the main intent is covert, add a suitable indicator behavior.

4. Test the indicator to ensure that it is the simplest and most direct one possible and well within the repertoire of the students.

Now that you can decode objectives, you're ready to begin drafting or selecting test items that will tell you whether your objective has been achieved as you intended.

So let's get to it.

4
Matching the Performances

"So the way you find out how many cows are in the pasture is to count the number of legs and divide by four."

"Why not just count heads directly?"

"Because if you're off just a few legs, you won't be off that many cows."

Dumb, isn't it? And about as useless as my trying to find out how well you write by asking you to answer some multiple-choice questions about writing. About as useless as trying to find out if students can interview by asking them to point to errors in other peoples' interviews. Unless the measuring instrument matches the thing to be measured, we haven't got a chance of learning what we want to know, i.e., whether a student can do whatever an objective requires. To do that, we make sure that each and every item asks for the same performance as the objective, under the conditions described in the objective. This chapter is about matching performances.

Most of the time performance matching takes only a second or so, provided the objective is well stated. It takes a little longer only when the objective is poorly stated. Here's the procedure:

When the performance stated in the objective is:

1. **Main intent and overt**

   Only one type of test item will do. *Ask the student to do that which is called for by the indicator.*

2. **Main intent and covert**

   Add an indicator to the objective: Test to make sure it is simple, direct, and well within the repertoire of the student. *Write or select test items that call for the same or equally simple and direct indicator behavior.*

3. **Indicator and overt**

   Check the main intent. If unclear, fix or discard the objective. If clear, make sure that the indicator is appropriate—simple, direct, and well within student capability. *Write or select test items that call for the same or equally simple and direct indicator behavior.*

4. **Indicator and covert**

   There's no such thing. *Say something tart to the objective writer. Get the objective fixed or discarded.*

Let's explore each of the first three possibilities.

1. **The performance stated in the objective is the main intent and overt.**

	OVERT	COVERT
MAIN INTENT	1 Match main intent	2 ADD and match indicator
INDICATOR	3 Match indicator	4 ✕

When the performance stated in the objective is the *main intent* of that objective, and *visible,* prepare or select test items that *ask* students to *perform the main intent of the objective.* No indicator is needed; when the main intent is visible, it is its own indicator. Whatever the main intent, the item must ask students to do it. No other form of the item is acceptable. For example, if the objective says:

Be able to ride a unicycle 100 yards on a level, paved surface without falling off,

the performance stated is *ride a unicycle.* The performance of riding is visible (overt) and is the main intent of the objective. Therefore, the only way to find out if learners have achieved the objective is to ask them to ride. No other form of test item is appropriate, regardless of the "difficulty level." Questions that ask about the history of spokes, a request for an essay on seat appreciation, or multiple-choice questions on nomenclature won't do. The only way you can find out if they can ride is to watch them ride.

Of course, you may want them to ride successfully three times out of four before you will say the objective is achieved (provided that's the criterion stated in the objective), in which case you would have four items or behavior samples. But each and every one of them MUST ask students to ride. If it asks them to do anything else, you will *not know* whether the objective is achieved. Consider this example:

> *Be able to pick open at least four five-pin tumbler locks within twenty minutes.*

What's the performance stated? Picking locks. Is the performance visible? Yes, you can see people picking locks. What is the main intent? Why, lock picking. The objective wants students to be able to open locks of a certain kind by picking them. Would any of the following items be appropriate for assessing the objective?

1. Draw a diagram of a typical pin tumbler.

2. For a five-pin tumbler lock, name the picks you would use in picking it open.

3. Name three people important to the history of the pin tumbler.

4. For each of the locks named on the list below, write the name of the picks most appropriate for speedy opening.

5. Write a short essay on the history of keyholes.

No, not one of those items is appropriate if you want to find out whether students can actually pick. Items such as these may be useful as *diagnostic* items designed to tell you why an objective was not accomplished, but they are useless for telling you whether the objective has been accomplished. To include items like these just because they may make the test more interesting is not playing fair with students. It is simply no good to have items that ask them to pick a little, talk a little. It's got to be pick, pick, pick, or you will never know if the objective has been achieved. And if you don't know whether it has been achieved, you won't be able to show that your instruction is as successful as you believe it is.

NOTE: When the performance mentioned in the objective is OVERT and at the same time the MAIN INTENT, the test item looks almost identical to the objective; the objective describes what students should be able to do, and the test item says, "Do it." But this is true *only* when the main intent is overt. Unfortunately, it is this category of objective that causes some people to mistakenly conclude that there is no difference between objectives and test items. Now you know what to say to such people. Tactfully, of course.

2. **The performance stated in the objective is the main intent, and covert (internal, invisible, mental).**

	OVERT	COVERT
MAIN INTENT	1 *Match main intent*	2 *ADD and match indicator*
INDICATOR	3 *Match indicator*	4 ✕

(continued on page 54)

When the main intent stated in the objective is covert, do this:

1. If the main intent of the objective isn't clear, fix it or junk it.

2. Add an indicator behavior by which accomplishment of the objective can be assessed.

3. Make sure the indicator is the simplest and most direct indicator possible.

4. Note the performance called for by the test item.

5. If that performance is the same, or same type, as the indicator stated in the objective, the performances match and the item is potentially useful. If not, modify or discard the test item.

Let's look at an example. Originally, the objective read like this:

Objective: *Be able to identify verbs in a series of sentences.*

The main intent is "identify," but since there are so many possible meanings, an indicator was added, like this:

Objective: *Be able to identify (underline) the verb in a sentence.*

A test item was drafted to read like this:

Test item: *There are ten sentences on this page. Circle the verb in each.*

First question: What's the *visible* performance stated? *Underlining.*

Second question: Is that the simplest, most direct indicator? Yes. It's one of several that might be used, but it is simple, direct, and well within the student's ability.

Third question: What's the performance called for in the test item? *Circling.*

Last question: Is that the same, or the same *type* of, performance as underlining? Yes. Underlining and circling are two simple ways to *point to* the verbs. Each requires the same amount of skill (or lack of it.)

In this example, therefore, the performance called for by the test item is the "same" as that of the objective, and the item is a good candidate for assessing achievement of the objective. All that remains is to make sure the conditions match, which we'll do in the next chapter. Here's another example:

Objective: *From an array of watchmaking tools, be able to identify those used for winding mainsprings.*

Test item: *Each of the tools laid out on Table 2 has been tagged with a number. On your answer sheet, write the tag number of each of the tools used for winding mainsprings.*

First question: What's the *visible* performance stated in the objective? *There isn't any.* Identifying is a covert performance. So before proceeding, we must add an indicator. After a second or two of thought, we revise the objective as follows:

Objective: *From an array of watchmaking tools, be able to identify* (point to) *those used for winding mainsprings.*

Notice how easy it is to improve the objective by adding a word or two in parentheses, rather than by rewriting the entire statement? Now we have a visible performance and can go on to the next question.

Second question: Is this a simple, direct indicator? Yes. Everybody has *something* they can point with.

Third question: What's the performance called for in the test item? *Writing* a number.

Last question: Is that the same, or same type of, performance as pointing? Close, but no cigar. *If* the target audience (students) can write numbers easily and legibly, then writing numbers would be OK as an indicator behavior. Can you think of an even simpler indicator to use? One that wouldn't require a writing skill? How about the following as possibilities:

- Put the tools used for mainspring winding in the green tray, or

- Remove the tags from the correct tools and hand them to the instructor, or

- Point to the tools used for mainspring winding.

3. **The performance stated in the objective is an indicator.**

	OVERT	COVERT
MAIN INTENT	1 *Match main intent*	2 *ADD and match indicator*
INDICATOR	3 *Match indicator*	4

When the stated performance is an indicator (and necessarily overt), you'll need to be sure of the main intent before you can successfully decide whether a given test item will be useful. For example:

Objective: *Given completed employment application forms, be able to checkmark those that meet the standards listed in the Guide to Quality Employees.*

Test Item: *List characteristics an applicant must have to meet the standards described in the Guide to Quality Employees.*

What's the point (main intent) of the objective? What does the objective writer actually want people to be able to do once the instruction is over? Probably identify. So let's modify the objective:

Objective: *Given completed employment application forms, be able to identify (checkmark) those that meet the standards listed in the Guide to Quality Employees.*

Now we can try to match the item to the objective.

First question: What's the *visible* performance stated in the objective? *Checkmarking.* That's what it says.

Second question: Is that a simple, direct way to indicate identifying? Yes.

Third question: What's the performance called for in the test item? *List characteristics.*

Last question: Is listing the same as check-marking? Not even close. The item is therefore unacceptable in its present form.

"But," you will hear people say, "If students don't know what characteristics are relevant, they won't be able to select the forms that meet the standards." Probably true. But that's irrelevant, isn't it? The point is that if you want to find out whether students have accomplished the objective, you have to ask them to perform as the objective describes, not to demonstrate what they would need to know *before* performing as desired. In this example, then, the performances called for in the test item and the objective do not match. One or the other needs to be fixed, or the item discarded.

You should now be ready for some practice in matching per-formances, and so some guided practice is coming up. To help you with your matching, I'll offer three kinds of aids. Take your pick.

A brief summary of what to do in
response to each kind of stated
performance.   *Page 60*

A checklist to remind you of the
steps to follow in matching
item to objective.   *Page 61*

A flowchart that shows the
relationship between the steps
of the matching procedure.
(WARNING: If you are not used to
using flowcharts as a thinking
tool, don't even look at it.)   *Page 62*

The guided practice begins on   *Page 64*

What-To-Do Summary

	OVERT	COVERT
MAIN INTENT	1 *Match main intent*	2 *ADD and match indicator*
INDICATOR	3 *Match indicator*	4 ✕

When the performance stated in the objective is:

1. **Main intent and overt** . . . Ask the student to perform the main intent.
2. **Main intent and covert** . . . Add an indicator to the objective, and test to make sure it is simple, direct, and well within the repertoire of the student. Write or select test items that call for the same or equally simple and direct indicator behavior.
3. **Indicator and overt** . . . If the main intent is unclear, fix or discard the objective. If clear, make sure that the indicator is appropriate — simple, direct, and well within student capability. Write or select test items that call for the same or a similar indicator behavior.
4. **Indicator and covert** . . . No such thing. Sneer at the objective writer (tactfully, of course). Get the objective fixed or junked. (How would you like to have to evaluate someone's accomplishment of this "objective," for example? "Be able to demonstrate an ability to think by recalling the parts of a syllogism." Lotsa luck.)

Objective/Item Matching Checklist*

1. What is the performance stated in the objective?
   - If there isn't any, repair or discard the objective.

2. Is the performance a main intent or an indicator?
   - If you can't tell, revise or discard the objective.

3. If it is an indicator, can you identify the main intent?

   NO . . . revise or discard the objective.
   YES . . . test the indicator against the main intent.

4. If the performance is a main intent, is it overt or covert?

   COVERT . . . add an indicator and test it for simplicity.
   OVERT . . . go to 5.

5. If the performance is overt, does the item performance match?

   YES . . . go to 7.
   NO . . . revise or reject the item or the objective.

6. If the performance in the objective is an indicator, does the performance in the test item match?

   YES . . . go to 7.
   NO . . . revise or reject the item.

7. Do the conditions described in the item match those of the objective?

   NO . . . revise the conditions in the item.
   YES . . . the item is potentially useful for testing accomplishment of the objective.

*A removable copy of this checklist is inserted between the last page and back cover of this book.

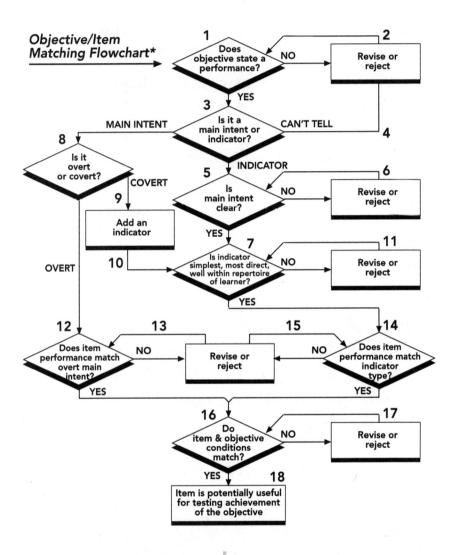

Objective/Item Matching Flowchart*

* *A removable copy of this flowchart is inserted between the last page and back cover of this book.*

GUIDED PRACTICE

Here are some practice items that will let you try your hand at matching performances.

Each pair of statements that follows consists of an objective and a test item. Decide YES or NO, according to whether the performance called for by the test item matches that called for by the objective. If you CAN'T TELL whether there is a match because the objective or item doesn't call for a performance, check (✓) the CAN'T TELL column.

> **NOTE:** You will find it easier to decode the objective and item pairs if you *circle the performances* with your pencil as you go. If there is no performance to circle in the objective, it doesn't matter how profound the statement sounds; check CAN'T TELL and go on to the next item.

On the chance that you will be able to move through the practice in a more sprightly manner if I model the procedure, I will invite you to peer into my stream of consciousness as I work through the first practice item.

Turn the page for the practice item and explanation.

Do the performances match?
YES   NO   CAN'T
                 TELL

1. *Objective:* Given a customer's deposit to either a savings or checking
   account, be able to verify the deposit.
   (Verify means compare the cash with
   amount shown on deposit slip, check
   deposit slip calculations for accuracy,
   stamp and initial deposit slip after
   verification.)

   Test Item: Describe how you would
   respond to this customer comment:
   "I'd like to make a deposit to my
   checking account, but I don't know
   how to fill out these new deposit slips.
   What do I have to do to deposit
   $20.00 in cash and a check for   ✓
   $14.79?"   _____ _____ _____

Thoughts While Matching. "Let's see, now. What's the performance called for by the objective? Well, it says *verify the deposit.*
I'll circle that so it won't get away. Is that the main intent or an
indicator? Looks like the performance is a main intent. Is it
overt or covert? Hmm. I could watch someone verifying
deposits directly—counting money, stamping and initialing
deposit slips—so I'll say the performance is overt.

"Okay, the performance stated in the objective is an overt
main intent. That tells me that there is only one kind of item
that will do—one that asks the student to verify deposits. So
let's look at the test item. What does it ask the student to do? It
says *describe a response to a customer comment.* Oh, oh.
Describing a response isn't the same as verifying a deposit. The

performances don't match, so I'll put a check in the NO col-umn." (In real life, you would discard or repair the item rather than check a column.)

Now it's your turn.

Do the performances match?
YES   NO   CAN'T
TELL

1. *Objective:* Be able to construct a staircase according to a blueprint and specifications.

   Test Item: Inspect the blueprints and specifications in Envelope A and decide whether they were properly followed in the construction of the staircase labeled Staircase 3.   _____ _____ _____

2. *Objective:* Support a candidate of your choice in his or her campaign for election to a public office.

   Test Item: Prove that you have supported a candidate of your choice in his or her campaign for election to a public office.   _____ _____ _____

3. *Objective:* Be able to carry out the booking procedure for an adult violator of any section of the Penal Code that requires taking the subject into custody.

   Test Item: George Spelvin, age 23, male, has been caught in the act of setting fire to an office building (Section 448a, PC). Complete all the steps needed to book the subject.   _____ _____ _____

Do the performances match?
YES   NO   CAN'T
TELL

4. *Objective:* Given poorly-stated objectives, be able to reword them so that they include a performance, conditions under which the performance will occur, and a criterion of acceptable performance.

Test Item: The objectives below are in need of work. Reword them so that they meet the criteria of well-stated objectives.

_____ _____ _____

5. *Objective:* Be able to sort accident reports into two piles; those that are complete and those that are incomplete.

Test Item: Sort the accident reports in Envelope B into "complete" and "incomplete" piles, and circle the missing information on those reports that are incomplete.

_____ _____ _____

Do the performances match?
YES   NO   CAN'T
TELL

---

6. *Objective:* Understand how statistics are used to determine risk and probability.

   Test Item: Describe at least three ways that statistics may be used to determine risk and probability.   _____   _____   _____

7. *Objective:* Given wiring diagrams, be able to identify (name) the item represented by each symbol.

   Test Item: Locate the laminated wiring diagram labeled "Test Diagram D," and write the name of each symbol on the diagram.   _____   _____   _____

Turn the page to check your responses.

Do the performances match?

YES   NO   CAN'T
TELL

---

1. *Objective:* Be able to construct a staircase according to a blueprint and specifications.

   Test Item: Inspect the blueprints and specifications in Envelope A and decide whether they were properly followed in the construction of the staircase labeled Staircase 3.

   _____ ✓____ _____

2. *Objective:* Support a candidate of your choice in his or her campaign for election to a public office.

   Test Item: Prove that you have supported a candidate of your choice in his or her campaign for election to a public office.

   _____ _____ ✓____

3. *Objective:* Be able to carry out the booking procedure for an adult violator of any section of the Penal Code that requires taking the subject into custody.

   Test Item: George Spelvin, age 23, male, has been caught in the act of setting fire to an office building (Section 448a, PC). Complete all the steps needed to book the subject.

   ✓____ _____ _____

1. No match. Inspecting a staircase is not the same as constructing one. If you want to know if students can construct a staircase, then you must ask each of them to construct one. There is no other way to determine whether they can do it. If it is impractical or impossible to have them do it, have them do the next best thing, perhaps build models of a staircase, and then *infer* whether students have achieved the objective.

   Remember that inferences are risky; they are even more risky if the consequences of not achieving the objective are perilous. (Your students may be able to build models of a staircase but may not be able to build one of actual size that meets safety specifications.)

2. Can't tell. Neither the objective nor the test item describes a performance. What is someone doing when supporting a candidate? Propping the person up? Contributing to the campaign fund? Speaking in the candidate's favor? Unless you know the performances that define *supporting,* you can't decide how to test the objective.

3. A match. The objective wants trainees to be able to carry out the booking procedure, and that's what the item asks them to do. The item is appropriate for finding out if the objective has been achieved. Will one item be enough? Should several similar items be used? This, and similar issues, will be discussed in Chapter 6.

Do the performances match?

	YES	NO	CAN'T TELL

---

4. *Objective:* Given poorly-stated objectives, be able to reword them so that they include a performance, conditions under which the performance will occur, and a criterion of acceptable performance.

   Test Item: The objectives below are in need of work. Reword them so that they meet the criteria of well-stated objectives.   ✓

5. *Objective:* Be able to sort accident reports into two piles; those that are complete and those that are incomplete.

   Test Item: Sort the accident reports in Envelope B into "complete" and "incomplete" piles, and circle the missing information on those reports that are incomplete.   ✓

6. *Objective:* Understand how statistics are used to determine risk and probability.

   Test Item: Describe at least three ways that statistics may be used to determine risk and probability.   ✓

7. *Objective:* Given wiring diagrams, be able to identify (name) the item represented by each symbol.

   Test Item: Locate the laminated wiring diagram labeled "Test Diagram D," and write the name of each symbol on the diagram.   ✓

4. A match. The objective asks that students be able to re-word objectives, and that's exactly what the test item asks them to do. So the performances match.

5. The objective says sort, but it's clear that the (unstated) main intent is to be able to recognize complete and incomplete reports. The test item also asks for sorting. So far, so good. But the item *also* asks for students to circle missing information. Hmm. How can you circle information if it's missing? So the item asks for more in the way of skill than does the objective (and more than is humanly possible).This is like those situations where you're told, "Oh, sure. You got the right answers, but you didn't show your work." No match.

6. Can't tell. Until a performance is stated in the objective, there's no way of knowing whether "describing" is a suitable way to find out whether the non-stated performance has been achieved. The correct response here is to fix the objective or throw it away.

7. A match. The objective states the main intent (identify) and adds an indicator by which you can tell whether the identifying was done (name). But the test item asks the student to "write the name" on the diagram, and the objective just says "name." So the item asks for more skill (writing) than does the objective, but writing is a skill that the student knows.

Now that you've had practice in matching performances, it's time to move on to the second part of the process, that of matching the conditions. This is where you'll get to smite, smote, and skewer another potential source of instructional sneakiness.

Go get 'em !

5
Matching the Conditions

Suppose you are enrolled in a penmanship course and are working to accomplish the objective of writing capital letters that conform to a specified size standard. You practice diligently on all the scratch paper you can find and begin to feel pretty confident with the grand flow of your letters. Then, when exam time comes around, you are handed the following test item:

> Write the letters of the alphabet in capital letters. Write them on the slab of butter placed beneath 6 inches of water in the bottom of Sink 3. Write with the wooden stylus provided.

The ensuing conversation with the instructor might sound something like this:

> "Wait a minnit. The objective said I need to be able to write capital letters."
> "Correct. And that's precisely what the test item asks you to do."
> "But it says I gotta do it on a slab of butter *under water!*"
> "Come now. *Anybody* can write letters on *paper.* You don't

really understand how to do it unless you can do it under water. That's the *real* test."

"But the objective didn't say anything about water."

"It doesn't have to. It's obvious that I should be allowed to ask you to write on any surface I select. Besides, I'm testing for transfer."

Having decided that the job market for underwater writers is probably limited, you now register for a course in TV repair. During this course you are expected to accomplish the following objective:

With all parts, tools, and diagrams available, be able to assemble any antenna found in the 1999 Bleak and Dreary catalog.

After properly shredding your fingertips and dripping solder on your lap, you finally feel ready to show what you have learned. When you announce your readiness to demonstrate your skill, you are given a piece of paper that says:

On the lab table you will find a package labeled "A," containing the parts and diagram needed to assemble a common TV antenna. Using any tools of your choice, assemble the antenna on the roof of the shop garage and mount it on top of the 50-foot tower.

The ensuing discussion might go something like this:

"Now, see here, kind sir, this test item appears not to be consistent with the objective."

"Oh?"

"Yes, indeed. It appears that the objective tells me to be able to assemble an antenna ..."

"And that's *exactly* what the test item asks you to do."

"Please, sir, but I beg to differ. The item says I must do the assembling on the roof of the garage, which, as we all know, slopes."

"So?"

"Well, sir, I did all my assembly practice on the floor of the shop. Quite different conditions, you know."

"Oh? Do you think you're going to have a nice level shop floor handy every time you want to put an antenna together?"

"Of course not, sir . . ."

"Well, then, what're you complaining about?"

"Simply that I was not apprised of the conditions under which I would be ultimately expected to perform. Unless you tell me what you, as the expert, think I should be able to do, how will I know what to practice?"

"How could you get this far in the course without knowing that you put antennas together on roofs and not on shop floors?"

"Easily, sir."

"Oh, how?"

"I just believed what I read in the objectives you gave me."

Clearly, the conditions called for in the test item were different from those called for in the objective. And readers of this scenario must admire your restraint in not mentioning to the instructor that the test item actually asked for a skill in addition to the one stated in the objective. The objective asked you to assemble, and the item asked you to *assemble* and *mount*.

Though these examples may seem rather bizarre (they were chosen for that purpose), you will probably remember even stranger ones as you think back over your years as a student— if you ever saw an objective at all.

Matching Conditions

So far, you have seen that to find out whether students have achieved an objective, your test items must ask them to do what the objective asks them to do.

The item must also ask students to perform under the same conditions the objective prescribes. If it doesn't, you may learn that students can do *something*, but you will not learn whether they have achieved the objective. If, for example, you want to know if students can make change in the presence of harried customers, you will never find that out if you ask them to make change only in a quiet classroom. You might *predict* that skills learned under quiet conditions will transfer to those of turmoil and anxiety, but you won't know for sure.

Thus, the conditions under which testing is performed should be the same as those called for in the objective.

What's a Condition?

A condition is anything that will impact on the shape of a performance, anything that will make a difference in how the performance is executed. For example, if a student is given a set of tools or instruments to aid the performance, that's a condition that would influence the way the performing is done. People who are making sales presentations with the aid of a sales outline and/or an actual product would make the presentations differently than if these conditions were not present.

Conditions, therefore, are the things that competent performers have available to them while they are performing, as well as environmental features that might influence the nature of the performance. (Students should have the same conditions while learning and demonstrating their competence.) The objective should state all the conditions that might have a significant impact on how the performance is carried out. If there is any sort of "trick" to deciding which conditions to provide while testing, do it by answering this question: "What things and environmental features will I have to provide before the student can practice the objective?"

How To Do It

1. Read the conditions stated in the objective.

2. Arrange for the test item to be administered under the same conditions, or under conditions as close to the objective as you can manage.

For example, consider the following objective:

Given an automobile that has just received scheduled maintenance, be able to road test the car and complete road test report RTR-3A. Criteria: The tested car is not damaged or the interior soiled; the road test report is complete and legible.

You already know how to identify (circle) the performance. In this case there are two: road testing and report completion. So the test item will ask for road testing and report completion. What about the conditions? Well, you'll need to provide the testee with an automobile and a copy of report RTR-3A. So your test item might look like this:

Test item: *Envelope D contains a copy of RTR-3A. Road test the black 1929 Ford Sedan in stall 12, and complete the road test report. Make sure you refrain from soiling the car interior in any way and that your completed report is legible.*

The rule for matching conditions is the same as for matching performances: *Make sure that the test items are administered under the same conditions (no more, no less) as are called for by the objective.*

NOTE: Notice that the criteria stated in the objective are included in the above test item. Should test items *always* state criteria? No. You may want to include them as reminders, but most of the time it would make the item too wordy.

Here are a few practice items. First you'll practice detecting whether conditions in test items and objectives match, after which we'll consider what to do when it's not possible to provide test conditions that exactly match those of the objectives.

Practice Items

Below are pairs of statements, each consisting of an objective and a potential test item. Check (✓) the appropriate column to the right, depending on whether the conditions in the item match conditions in the objective:

Do the conditions match?

	YES	NO

1. *Objective:* Be able to introduce yourself to a peer in a suitable manner (i.e., look the person in the face, offer a firm handshake, give your name, repeat his or her name when it is given, express pleasure at making his or her acquaintance).

    Test Item: The instructor will point to various members of the class. Introduce yourself to them in a suitable manner.

2. *Objective:* Given each of the following products (list attached), be able to describe to an uninterested prospective customer the features and benefits of each product.

    Test Item: Here's what to do:

    1. Read the product literature in Envelope A.

    2. Describe the features and benefits of each product to your classroom partner.

3. *Objective:* Given a person with a first-degree burn on any part of his or her body, be able to apply first aid using the steps outlined in the Red Cross manual for treatment of first-degree burns.

    Test Item: Instructor points to patient lying on table with midsection exposed and says, "This patient has a first-degree burn on her posterior. Treat it according to the Red Cross manual."

Turn the page to check your responses.

Do the conditions match?

              YES   NO

---

1. *Objective:* Be able to introduce yourself to a peer in a suitable manner (i.e., look the person in the face, offer a firm handshake, give your name, repeat his or her name when it is given, express pleasure at making his or her acquaintance).

   Test Item: The instructor will point to various members of the class. Introduce yourself to them in a suitable manner.

           ✓ _____ _____

2. *Objective:* Given each of the following products (list attached), be able to describe to an uninterested prospective customer the features and benefits of each product.

   Test Item: Here's what to do:

   1. Read the product literature in Envelope A.

   2. Describe the features and benefits of each product to your classroom partner.

           _____ ✓ _____

3. *Objective:* Given a person with a first-degree burn on any part of his or her body, be able to apply first aid using the steps outlined in the Red Cross manual for treatment of first-degree burns.

   Test Item: Instructor points to patient lying on table with midsection exposed and says, "This patient has a first-degree burn on her posterior. Treat it according to the Red Cross manual."

           ✓ _____ _____

1. A match. The performances match—both test item and objective ask the student to exhibit the same performance. And the condition? Well, the objective just says the student is expected to be able to introduce himself or herself to peers. It doesn't specify any special or unusual conditions under which the introducing is to occur. The test items ask for the performance in a classroom. That is acceptable, inasmuch as there is nothing in the objective to suggest otherwise.

2. No match. First, the objective says you will have each of the products available while describing their features and benefits. The test item provides only literature about the products.

    Second, the objective says you need to be able to do your describing to an uninterested prospective customer. The test item asks you to do your describing to your partner.

    Thus, the item describes what might be a useful practice situation in the classroom, but it does not describe a situation that will tell you whether the objective has been achieved.

3. A match. Both objective and test item ask for application of first aid to a person with a first-degree burn. The question of how many items of this type may be needed to adequately test for competence will be discussed a little later.

Turn the page for three more practice items.

More Practice Items

Do the conditions match?

YES   NO

4. *Objective:* Given any model of Disaster Master aircraft, be able to remove and replace any engine part.

   Test Item: On Table 3 are engines from three different Disaster Master aircraft and a new engine part for each. For each engine, remove the old part and replace it with the new.   _____   _____

5. *Objective:* For a blouse made of any material, be able to repair bad stitches or skipped stitches.

   Test Item: Inspect the pile of clothing on Table 4 and repair any incorrect work.   _____   _____

6. *Objective:* Be able to multiply correctly any pair of two-digit numbers.

   Test Item: Without using a calculator, multiply the following pairs of two-digit numbers (numbers added).   _____   _____

Do the conditions match?

	YES	NO

4. *Objective:* Given any model of Disaster Master aircraft, be able to remove and replace any engine part.

   Test Item: On Table 3 are engines from three different Disaster Master aircraft and a new engine part for each. For each engine, remove the old part and replace it with the new.   ✓

5. *Objective:* For a blouse made of any material, be able to repair bad stitches or skipped stitches.

   Test Item: Inspect the pile of clothing on Table 4 and repair any incorrect work.   ✓

6. *Objective:* Be able to multiply correctly any pair of two-digit numbers.

   Test Item: Without using a calculator, multiply the following pairs of two-digit numbers (numbers added).   ✓

4. No match. The objective says the student needs to be able to do something to an *aircraft;* specifically, to take out and replace engine parts. The item asks the student to take out and replace parts in engines that are *sitting on a table.* If you have ever looked under the hood of a car or tried to work on an engine there, you know that working on an engine mounted in a car is quite different from working on one sitting on a table. So the performances match, but the conditions don't.

5. No match. There are two problems with this pair of statements. First, though both the objective and test item ask the student to be able to repair, the objective expects to see the skill of "repairing bad or skipped stitches," while the test item asks to see the skill of "repairing *any* incorrect work." Thus, though both use the word "repair"—thereby lulling us into thinking the performances match—the test item asks for more skill than the objective.

   Second, the conditions don't match. The objective wants the student to be able to apply his or her skill to blouses; the test item, to unspecified types of clothing. You may think the difference trivial, but only if you've never been faced with test items that ask for something different from what you were led to expect.

6. No match. The objective is concerned with correct multiplication, rather than with the means by which the multiplication is done. The test item provides a restriction (no calculator) not required by the objective.

   Again, this pair exemplifies that all-too-common situation in which a test requires more, or different, skills than called for by the objective. Don't put up with it. It's not a professional practice.

Approximations

Sometimes the *"match the conditions in the items with the conditions in the objective"* rule must be bent, and, occasionally, twisted literally out of shape.

Consider this objective, from a course on how to repair atomic bombs at Hypothetical U (now known as Crater Lake II):

> *When faced with a malfunctioning atomic bomb of 10 kilotons or less, and shown one symptom, be able to repair the malfunction. Repair must be completed within 45 minutes, and the bomb must function within manufacturer's specifications.*

As you must guess, it might be somewhat impractical to create a test in which the student is given a live bomb with a "bug" in it. Making the conditions on the test match the conditions of the objective might be somewhat foolhardy. The consequence of an error is just potentially too great. After all, this doesn't seem to be a situation in which a serious error is likely to be followed by little more than an embarrassed "Oops."

It's clear what the objective wants—it wants students to be able to fix troubles in real bombs. So far, so good. And to find out if students can fix troubles, you must ask them to fix troubles. That's clear, too. But in this case it's too dangerous to let them demonstrate their skill on the real thing (the students might get a little testy). What can you do?

You can simulate. You can approximate. You can give the students some sort of pretend bomb and ask them to do what the objective wants them to do. If they can do it with the pretend bomb, you will have to *assume* they can do it with the real thing. Is that a safe assumption? Depends on how closely your conditions match those of the objective. If you only have to *approximate* one condition, your guess as to whether they will be able to perform under the real conditions will be better than if you have to approximate two or more. If, for example, bomb repair is done under stressful conditions and you watch students repair in the cool, cool, cool of the evening, you should be less confident of their ability to do it "out there" than if you had provided some real stress during the performance on the pretend bomb.

Two points. First, *never* simulate *performance*. Always ask your students to do that which the objective asks them to do, even though you must provide simulated conditions. Second, remember that when you simulate or approximate conditions, you will have to make *inferences* about whether students will be able to do the "real thing" asked for by the objective. You will have to make an educated guess about whether the objective has been achieved, after watching performance under other-than-appropriate conditions.

Sometimes we can provide conditions close to those called for by the objective, and sometimes the conditions will be considerably different from those called for by the objective. Suppose, for another example, that the objective says something like this:

Be able to rescue a drowning person.

If you want to find out whether the objective has been achieved, it's pretty clear that you will have to simulate the conditions. I suppose you and your students could hang around the beaches waiting for the right moment, but that would be inefficient—not to mention dangerous if your students aren't very competent yet. So some approximation would have to do. What kind of approximation? The closest approximation to the real thing that you can arrange. Multiple-choice questions on the history of drowning won't work, nor will having them describe how they would save an unfortunate drowning person. You can do better than that. You could provide them with someone pretending to need help and ask each student to perform the desired task. That is, wherever possible, ask students to perform the *main intent,* even though the conditions under which the performance is exhibited are somewhat different from those that represent the real thing.

Consider poor Dr. Harry Lymph, professor of medicine, who wants to know if his students can perform an appendectomy. He can't just run down to the street and accost strangers with, "Hi, there. Mind having your appendix out?" If he doesn't have enough patients to go around, he must do some approximating.

As one alternative, he could find out if students can perform each of the sub-skills separately. For example, he could ask each student to show on a real person where the incision would be made, show and describe how to use retractors, how to tie the knots, and so on. But while that would tell him whether subordinate objectives were achieved, it wouldn't tell him if students could actually perform an appendectomy. It would not qualify as a simulation or an approximation of an appendectomy, because the skills called for in any of the items testing a piece of the performance is not the same as that called for in the objective. *Unless performances match, you can't conclude you are approximating.*

So what can the poor professor do? Well, he could use one of the mannequins that have been created for use in surgery simulations, asking each student to remove the appendix of the mannequin. Learners would be demonstrating the desired skills, but under conditions somewhat different from those faced with a live patient.

He might also ask each student to remove the appendix from a cadaver. Here again, learners would be performing the relevant skills, but under conditions different from those faced with live patients. Then, after observing the performance of students in the simulation situation, he would *infer* what each student will be able to do with real patients. Since he hasn't observed students performing the objective, he wouldn't *know* for sure they can perform as desired, but the basis of his inferences would be much more sound than if they were based on the answers to multiple-choice or true-false test items.

When it is a small approximation—that is, when conditions are very close to those called for in the objective—it is a small inference, a small leap. For instance, if the objective says:

> *Be able to select (collect) from the storeroom those instruments and equipment needed to perform anappendectomy,*

and if the test item says:

> *From the array of instruments located on Table 5, collect the instruments used in the performance of an appendectomy and put them into the green tray marked "A",*

the performances match, but the conditions don't. Selecting tools from a table is not the same as selecting them from a storeroom. The difference is so small, however, that you aren't taking much of a risk in using this type of item. That is, if students can select tools from a table, it is a pretty small risk to assume they can select them from a storeroom. The inference is a small one.

But suppose the test item said:

> *On the following page are sketches of a variety of surgical instruments. Check those that are used in the performance of an appendectomy.*

Again, the performances match (both objective and item ask learners to select instruments from "givens"), but the conditions don't. The objective says select from a storeroom, and the item says select from sketches. The inferential leap is larger. The hope is that if students can recognize sketches on paper, they can also recognize the real thing in a storeroom. But the leap from sketches on paper to instruments in storeroom is larger than the leap from instruments on table to instruments in storeroom. Why? Because sketches of instruments are not the same as the instruments themselves. Sketches are only representations of that which students are expected to recognize. As the conditions become less and less like those described in the objective, the size of the inferential leap increases.

Perhaps I can clarify this point with Figure 2. Shown on the far left is the performance called for by the objective. If a test item asks for that performance directly, under the conditions described in the objective, there is no simulation or approximation, and one can decide directly whether the objective has been achieved.

The boxes behind the left-hand box show conditions progressively *less* like that called for by the objective.

- Selecting instruments from a table is a little less like selecting them from a storeroom;
- Selecting instruments from a virtual-reality display of a storeroom is a little less like selecting real instruments from a table;
- Selecting sketches of instruments is still less direct than selecting the real thing;
- Selecting verbal descriptions of instruments is considerably different from selecting the real thing;
- Selecting codes or symbols of the real thing (such as a verbal description written in Morse code) is about as far from the intention of the objective as I can imagine.

The farther one moves to the right in Figure 2, the greater the difference between *observed* performance and *intended* performance (as described by the objective). Thus, the farther one moves to the right, the greater the inference from the performance you see to the performance you *want*.

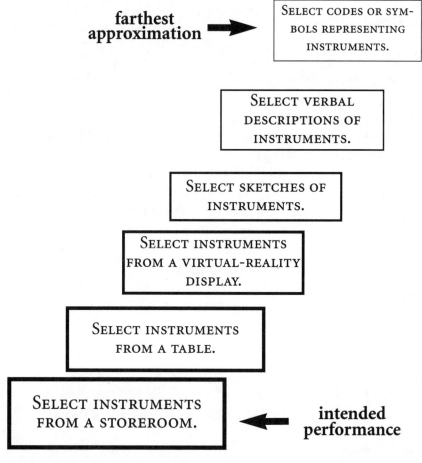

Figure 2. As approximations increase, the "size" of the inferential leap increases.

Consequence of an Error

How large an inference can you tolerate? *It depends on the consequence of an error.* If the consequence of *not* performing as desired is tolerable, then a larger inference is tolerable. If the consequence of not performing as desired is *serious,* then a large inference (large difference between conditions in item and objective) is risky and should not be tolerated.

In the present example, the consequence of not being able to perform an appendectomy properly can be as large as the loss of a life. While such a loss is not nearly as great as the consequence of a commercial pilot's inability to land a planeload of passengers safely, the loss of life is always a serious consequence. When the potential consequence can be this large, it is important to have students demonstrate their achievement of the objective before certifying them to perform on their own.

If the objective describes an ability to add, on the other hand, and the consequence of an error is only that a little time will be lost or that inappropriate change will be made, you wouldn't have to be excruciatingly diligent in making the test conditions match those of the objective.

So whenever you are unable to make the conditions in the test item match the conditions in the objective, ask yourself:

How serious is the consequence of an error?

The seriousness of the consequence(s) of poor performance will tell you how much energy and budget to invest in matching the test-item conditions to those of the objective.

Dodge City

Some people use some strange dodges or arguments to justify use of items that don't match their objectives. It doesn't seem to matter that by doing so they prevent themselves from finding out whether their objectives are achieved. Here are some common examples:

"But I like my tests to be interesting."

"I like to use a *variety* of items in my tests."

"Well, sure the objective says learners need to be able to DO it, but they don't really understand it unless they can _____ (define it, describe it, tell the history of it, write an essay on it, teach it, etc.)."

"I don't have time to test."

"I don't have the budget needed to arrange real conditions."

"My company has a policy against testing."

My reply to these attempts to weasel is simple and persistent: *If the items don't match the objective, you won't know if the objective has been achieved.* Moreover, if the consequence of an error is serious, you can run some pretty big risks with the lives of your students, as well as those of innocent bystanders. Make your test as interesting as you want, but not at the expense of items that match.

What's Your Pleasure?

You have now practiced all the pieces of the objective/item matching skill. Now you'll be offered some guided practice to put it all together (i.e., you've practiced the steps—now it's time to practice the entire dance).

In addition to the practice, there are two other options I'd like to offer. Though the purpose of the book is to consider only the issue of how to recognize test items relevant to assessing achievement of an objective, there are some related questions buzzing around that I'd like to discuss. Though I may not answer the one(s) distressing you the most, I'd like to try my hand at three or four of them. These are covered in Chapter 6, "Peripheralia."

The other option is to go directly to the skill check (criterion test) in Chapter 8, "Got a Match?" What's your pleasure?

6
Peripheralia

No matter how we try to confine ourselves to a specific topic, there are always loose ends, related issues, and questions. It's rather like trying to explain in detail the workings of some part of the body. Invariably there are questions about how a particular part connects to, interacts with, and influences the functioning of other parts. Though I would like to simply fold up my keyboard at this point and send you off into the exciting practice chapter, I feel a need to deal with a few pieces of peripheralia—oddments that have something to do with testing. They're important issues, but they're not strictly related to the task of matching items to objectives.

How Many Items?

A question that arises when drafting skill checks is "How many items should I use?"

The short answer is, "It depends."

Range of Conditions

The number of times you will need to ask students to perform (i.e., the number of test items you will need) will depend on the range of conditions under which the performance will be expected to occur. If there is only one condition, one or two items should suffice. If, on the other hand, the objective asks for performance under a range of conditions, more items may be needed. The rule is:

Use as many test items as you need to sample the range of conditions.

When should you do that? Whenever the student is expected to (a) use the same things under different conditions when performing or (b) use different things under the same or different conditions when performing. For example, suppose the objective says:

Be able to ride any unicycle 100 yards on a level surface without falling off.

And suppose that "Pedals" Purplin brings her own unicycle to the test situation and rides up a storm. Would you agree that she has achieved the objective? If you said "No," you are right. For one thing, one of the conditions requires her to be able to ride any unicycle, and so far, she's only shown that she can ride one kind. How many kinds would she have to ride before you would be willing to agree that she can ride "any" kind?

The answer is, as many as it takes to sample the range of conditions. There are tall unicycles and squat ones. Some with large wheels and some with small ones. You might say to yourself, "If she can ride a tall one and a short one, I'd be willing to judge that she can ride everything else in between." In this case, you would use two test items to sample the range of conditions. On the other hand, you might say, "Wait a minute. If I have to certify her as being able to ride any unicycle, I would want to see her ride a wider variety than just a tall one and a short one." In that case you would use more items to sample the range of conditions. But each and every such item would ask her to ride a unicycle.

Here's another example. Suppose the objective says:

Given a customer attempting to return merchandise, be able to complete the merchandise return procedure without irritating the customer.

Would one demonstration of the performance suffice to tell you whether someone had achieved the objective? Again, no. Why not? Because customers vary greatly. Some are calm, some are angry. Some speak clearly, some don't. Some have accents, and some have chips on their shoulders. Knowing that, how many customers would students have to deal with to cause you to conclude that they've achieved the objective? Enough to sample the range of conditions. (In this instance, three or four should do.)

Police officers have to learn when to shoot and when not to shoot. But there are many different kinds of situations in which they might find themselves. What would it take to convince you that a given police officer knew when to shoot and when not to shoot? (You can answer that question only if you know the range of possible conditions and which of those conditions are most common.)

Suppose an objective wants students to be able to land a plane on any serviceable airstrip. (Hooray for simulators, wherein faulty performance doesn't kill the student or the customer.) How many test items would you need? Enough for you to sample the range of serviceable airstrips. If students were expected to make those landings in a variety of weather conditions, then different weather conditions would have to be sampled as well. During each test item the student would be doing the same thing, i.e., landing a plane, but the conditions would vary from item to item.

Here is one final example of an objective that contains a range of conditions.

*Given a soldering gun, solder, and flux, be able to replace
any given component in the Model 10 Brainwasher.*

In this case students would be using the same tool no matter
which component they were replacing. But there are undoubtedly differences in the conditions under which the replacement
must be accomplished. If you have never seen the Model 10
Brainwasher, I can assure you that some components need to
be replaced in tight spaces, and some components need to be
replaced while the replacer is almost standing on his or her
head. So to find out if the objective is achieved, you would
need to ask students to replace components in as many parts of
the machine as are needed to represent the range of conditions
under which the replacement is expected to be done.

It wouldn't be necessary, or practical, to ask for performance
under *all* possible combinations of conditions, of course.
That's why you are urged to sample the *range* of conditions.
Just make sure that each and every item used matches the
objective.

What Would Satisfy You?

If, even with an infinite number of perfectly elegant items,
you *still* wouldn't be willing to certify as competent each student who performs well on those items, there is something
wrong either with your objective or your items. It's no good to
say, "Even if students perform well on these ten items, I still
wouldn't be willing to say they've achieved the objective." If
that's your feeling, your test construction isn't finished. Take
another look at the objective, especially at its main intent,
because the trouble is likely to be there. The trouble is probably
that the objective doesn't accurately describe what it is you
really want students to be able to do. If there is something *more*
you want students to do than is expressed by your items, it is
likely that the objective needs revision.

The Rule of Reason

While we're on the subject of "how many items make a test," it would be well to mention the rule of reason relating to item range. It is terribly tempting to create bizarre or improbable items when an objective describes a range of givens or conditions. "Oh, well," the argument often goes, "they don't really understand those problems unless they can solve them while being strung up by their toes," or "they can't really be said to know how to diagnose illness unless they can recognize symptoms of Martian malady and Diddlefinger's disease," or "they really don't know how to troubleshoot unless they can solve problems that may occur only once in a lifetime."

Sometimes items calling for performance with highly improbable givens are created solely to keep the instructor amused. After all, it can get rather boring to test students over and over with items that are reasonable and practical. But the result of all this is that the instructor doesn't learn how well students are likely to do that which is expected of them. (The instructor also gains a well-deserved reputation for capriciousness, arbitrariness, unprofessionalism, and maybe even stupidity among his/her students.) In this case the rule of reason says:

When a range of stimuli and/or conditions is to be used in a series of test items, use only those stimuli and conditions that students will encounter within six months of the time they are tested.

This rule means simply that the items should match the objective in performance and that the givens and conditions should be reasonable. What's reasonable? Well, it's reasonable to prepare students to handle situations they will run into within the immediate future. It is not reasonable to insist that they be able to handle situations that are known to be highly improbable. There is nothing magical about six months; it is merely a guide. If, in your situation, three or nine months make more sense, then that is the guide to use. If you are an expert in your subject, you will either know what is and is not probable, or you can find out. If you can't find out, then don't write test items.

Remember, there's no test that will guarantee that the skill needed to handle a rarely occurring situation will still be there when needed, because unused skills deteriorate. They leak away—in short, they atrophy. So if it is important that students be able to handle a situation that may occur only rarely, and if the consequence is dire (e.g., "If you don't push the panic button as soon as the red light comes on, the sky will fall."), then give them refresher training often enough to warrant confidence that the skill will be there if needed.

Item Difficulty

It has been common practice to try to arrange the difficulty of a test item so that just about half the students get it right. Difficulty indices are often computed for each item, on the grounds that an item must not be too easy or too hard.

This is a norm-referenced practice and has nothing to do with the practice of finding out if objectives have been achieved. The practice is perfectly defensible when one wants to know how well a given student can perform in relation to his or her peers or when testing the *extent* of someone's content knowledge in a given area. But when you want to know *whether or not* people can do something you want them to do, what's the sense of being arbitrarily devious by making items easier or harder? Ask them simply and directly to do the thing you are after.

The expression "the item was too easy" implies a terrible thing about the nature of education. It implies that rather than work to help as many students as possible to achieve important objectives, many educators act instead to *limit* the amount of instructional success they will tolerate. It implies that if too many students are able to perform as desired, rather than jump up and down with joy at such success, many educators will arbitrarily make the test more difficult.

> "Everybody accomplished all the objectives, so I'm going to have to make the test harder."

Unfortunately, there is substance to these implications. Education is *not* yet designed to be totally successful; many educators do limit the amount of success they will allow. As mentioned earlier, the use of the normal curve is evidence of such limitation. No matter how well the students perform, no matter how many meet or exceed the instructor's expectations, only a portion of them will be allowed to think of themselves as competent. Conversely, no matter how poorly a group of students performs, those who perform the best will be given a label (grade) signifying success.

There is further evidence to support the allegation that education is not designed to tolerate total success. Ask yourself and your colleagues what would happen to them if their instruction *were* totally successful and that, as a result, they gave every student an A and could prove the grades were deserved. Would this result in a banquet in their honor? Applause from their peers? A raise from the administration? Seldom. Though there are now a few institutions that will tolerate total instructional success, the majority still seem bent on fulfilling the prophecy of the "normal" curve.

The message is this: don't worry about item difficulty. Make the items clear and make them match the objective. If everyone performs perfectly, shout with joy. Or with Mary, if you prefer. But in any case, rejoice.

Grading

Another question that often oozes to the surface has to do with that weird practice called grading. The issue shows itself in a variety of forms.

"But if all the students get it right, how can I give grades?"

"If the items are too easy, everybody will get them right."

"Gee, I'm not allowed to give everybody an A, no matter how well they can perform. It just isn't done."

"What about the students who try hard but don't quite make the criterion? Surely you don't expect me to fail them?"

"What about the students who do ten times more than I ask for—surely I can't give them the same grade as the ones who just barely squeak through?"

Each of these sentiments arises from a concern caused by the shift from the old norm-referenced way of grading to the criterion-referenced method of grading. It used to be acceptable to grade students by comparing them with one another. It didn't seem to matter whether the best students could actually do what instructors wanted them to be able to do; if they were better at something than anyone else in the class, they got the highest grades.

"Nobody in this class accomplished any of the objectives, but since Jack and Jill didn't accomplish them with the most style, I'm going to give them each an A."
Or . . .

"Make sure that some of our products are defective when they leave the factory. I don't want to be known as a manager who runs a 'Mickey Mouse' operation because all the products work perfectly."

The practice of giving the "best-in-class" the highest grades can lead to dire consequences. Imagine you are flying along in a jumbo jet when the pilot announces, "Ladies and gentlemen, we are about to begin our descent. There is absolutely nothing to worry about." And then adds, condescendingly, "I got perfect scores on almost all my exams . . . I only flunked landing."

(The Nuclear Regulatory Commission requires nuclear-power-plant operators to get 80% right on multiple-choice exams to be certified. Does that make you feel secure?)

The norm-referenced system is simply not appropriate when you have important objectives for students to achieve. Regardless of how hard students try, or how close they are to reaching competence, if they *can't* perform they *mustn't* be certified as being able to perform. You'll want to know *why* a student failed to achieve an objective, of course, so you can provide the necessary instruction and practice. But until that student *can* perform, you shouldn't pretend that he or she can.

And when you discover that all your students can perform according to the objectives, should they not be certified as being able to perform as desired?

"Oh, but I couldn't give everybody an A," is a comment often heard. But why not? If an A means that a student is able to perform each of the objectives, why would you not be willing to certify that he or she can perform? What does it mean to say you are "not allowed to give everybody an A"? If it means that your institution or school system isn't designed to cope with that much success, then some serious changes are in order. If it means that there would be adverse consequences to you because too many of your students were successful, then again, some serious changes are in order, because the implication is that your job is to produce failures. And that's obscene. Whenever the normal curve is used as a basis for grading, the user is legislating *in advance* the amount of success he or she will tolerate. With the curve system, one is saying to the students, "It doesn't matter how well you can perform . . . only a certain percentage of you will be allowed to think of yourselves as successful" (i.e., we'll only admit that a certain percentage of you are any good).

Some schools have adopted a pass-fail grading arrangement. But what does *pass* mean? Without well-stated objectives, nobody knows. In some courses it means that a minimum score on an exam has been made. In others, that attendance was adequate. In still others it means that students have completed all the assignments. But "pass" is little better than a letter grade unless the nature and the number of the objectives that are represented by the pass or the grade are made public.

A more meaningful reporting system lists the competencies accomplished by individual students. Such a list, in effect, says, "These are the things this student can do," and is a much better indicator of achievement than either a letter grade or a "pass."

"Affective" Objectives

You may have noticed that all the examples used so far have dealt with knowing and doing performances. Nothing whatever has been said about "affective" objectives (those that describe feeling states). That's because there is no such thing as an "affective objective." That's an oxymoron—a contradiction in terms. By the time you have described what students will have to do to convince you that an "affective" state has been accomplished, those descriptions will be written in performance terms and thus can be turned into objectives. And if they are objectives, they won't include "affective" words. Though the objectives may have been derived from definitions of affective states, they won't look any different than other objectives.

There is no question that issues such as attitudes, motivation, growth, and development are important. You should indeed concern yourselves with how students feel about the instruction you offer them and about their values and aspirations. But statements that describe abstract states or intentions (e.g., "Be able to value free enterprise" and "Have a love of learning") contain no "doing" words and so are not objectives. You can't match test items to statements that don't include performances.

If you have a special interest in the "affective" area, I'd like to refer you to two small books that address this topic in some detail.[2]

What Next?

The next chapter offers some guided practice. If you don't feel the need for more practice, then go directly to the skill check of Chapter 8, called "Got a Match?" Your choice.

I'd like a little practice.   *page 111*

I'm ready to test my skill.   *page 145*

2. Read *How to Turn Learners On . . . without turning them off,* Third Edition, R.F. Mager (The Center for Effective Performance, 1997) and *Goal Analysis, Third Edition,* R.F. Mager (The Center for Effective Performance, 1997).

7

A Pride of Items

A common instructional error is to send students away without their having had practice doing that which is the object of the instruction. A widely practiced variation is that of giving students practice in performing as desired and then testing more complex concepts and skills than were practiced. Not wishing to be guilty of such deviousness, I present in this chapter some optional exercises containing the same kinds of items you will find on the skill check (criterion test) in Chapter 8. Keep the removable Objective/Item Matching Checklist card handy as you proceed (it's located between the last page and the back cover of this book); it will remind you of the key steps of the matching procedure.

Three kinds of practice will be presented, followed by information with which you can check your own responses.

1. *Yes or no.* Each practice item will consist of an objective and a criterion item. Your task will be to say whether the item is appropriate for assessing achievement of the objective. While you may rightly feel that *several* items would be needed to determine if the objective has been accomplished, you will be asked only to say whether the presented item matches the objective.

2. *Which, if any.* Each practice item will consist of an objective and a series of items, each allegedly appropriate for

assessing achievement of the objective. Your task will be to review each item and say whether it is or is not appropriate for testing the objective.

3. *Fix it.* Each practice item will consist of an objective and an allegedly appropriate item. But something will be wrong. Either the objective will need some repair, or for some reason the item won't match. Your task will be to repair things so that the item will be satisfactory as a test of the objective. If you apply the step-by-step procedure for checking the appropriateness of an item, you shouldn't have any trouble.

"Wait a minute," I hear you screaming. "How come the objective of the book asks me to be able to identify items that match objectives, and now you want me to do a repair job?" And a very astute question that is. You're right, of course; the objective is for you to be able to recognize test items that do or don't match an objective, and that is exactly what you will be asked to do in Chapter 8. By asking you to repair a few objectives and/or items, however, you will be more likely to attend closely to the critical characteristics of each. But the fixing is just for practice; it wouldn't be correct to ask you to fix objectives and items on the skill check merely because it was "covered" in the instruction. In Chapter 8, you will only find items that match the objective of the book.

Working Through the Matching Task

One of the testers of the draft manuscript suggested that before sending readers off to practice the entire matching procedure, another example or two showing how I work through the matching task would be helpful. So I'll show you an objective and an item and then offer the stream of thought that ekes forth as I work my way through the matching process.

Example 1

Objective: *Given a group of numerical expressions, be able to circle examples of the commutative property of addition.*

Criterion Item: *Underline the numerical expressions that are examples of the commutative property of addition.*

$$(a)\ 3 + 7 = 2 + 8 \qquad (d)\ 5 + 2 = 2 + 5$$

$$(b)\ 4 + 5 = 5 + 4 \qquad (e)\ 9 + 1 = 5 + 5$$

$$(c)\ 0 + 4 = 4 + 0 \qquad (f)\ 6 + 2 = 2 + 6$$

Thoughts While Matching. I'll begin with the objective. What's the performance called for in the objective? "Circle examples." I'll circle it so it won't escape. Now what's the main intent? Well, the objective wants students to be able to recognize examples of the commutative property (whatever that is) when they see them. That means the stated performance (circling) is an indicator. Is it the simplest, most direct indicator I can think of? Not bad. Circling is easy to do and the quality of the circling is not likely to be confused with the quality of the recognizing. Is circling well within the repertoire of the students? I can't tell for sure unless I know exactly who the target audience is, but unless it is a group that doesn't know how to, or cannot, use a pencil, the indicator should be just fine.

Now for the item. The item wants students to underline numerical expressions. I'll circle that. Do the performances match? Well, circling isn't exactly the same behavior as underlining, but both can be used to indicate whether students can recognize the desired property, and they are both simple and direct. So the performances match.

What about the conditions? The objective says students are to be given some numerical expression to work with, and the item does just that. The objective asks them to indicate examples of the commutative property, and the item does, too. So the item matches the objective and would be useful for finding out if the objective has been achieved.

Example 2

Here's an example of the same process when the objective exists and an item needs to be drafted to test it.

> **Objective:** *At the end of the course, the student should be familiar with the process of joining and splitting given cells in the Spiffy Spreadsheet program, using the Eunuch terminal provided.*

Thoughts While Drafting. Let's begin with the objective. Good grief! That's awful. I can't draft an item until I have a decent objective, so either I'll have to rewrite it or get its author to do it.

> **Objective:** *Given a Eunuch terminal and Spiffy Spreadsheet software, be able to join and split given cells.*

That's better. No criterion, so I'll have to talk with the objective writer. Now then. The performance is to be able to join and split cells. Is that the point of the objective (main intent)? Sure looks like it. So in this case the main intent is visible, and therefore it is its own indicator. So the test item must ask for splitting and joining of spreadsheet cells. What about conditions? Well, the performer will be provided with a terminal and software, as well as with some specific cells to join or split asunder. OK, let's draft an item.

Criterion Item: *Go to Eunuch terminal #3. The terminal has been booted and a Spiffy Spreadsheet file has been opened. Do two things to the spreadsheet:*

    1. Join cells B23 and C23.

    2. Split cells A19 and A20.

Save your changes and ask an instructor to check your work.

There's a draft. The item asks for the same performance as does the objective, under the conditions specified. I'll have the objective writer check this to make sure I haven't distorted the intent of the objective.

You can see that though I appeared not to have followed each of the checklist items in the precise order given, I did ask the relevant questions. And now it's your turn.

Practice Items

YES OR NO

Each item below consists of an objective and a test item. If the item matches the objective—that is, if the item is suitable for testing achievement of the objective—check (✓) the YES column to the right. If the item is not suitable, for whatever reason, check (✓) the NO column.

	A match?	
	YES	**NO**

1. *Objective:* Given Sunday comics, be able to list all of the individual strip titles within the classifications of dry humor, light humor, romance, mysteries, detective stories, adventure, sociology, and religion.

   Criterion Item: Name three comic strips that deal with light humor. ____ ____

2. *Objective:* Be able to list five major pieces of legislation that were passed in the United States during the Progressive Era (1900-1917).

   Criterion Item: Underline five of the following pieces of twentieth-century legislation that were passed during the Progressive Era (1900-1917).

   (a) Pure Food and Drug Act

   (b) Federal Reserve Act

   (c) Underwood Tariff

   (d) Hepburn Act

   (e) Prohibition Act

   (f) Social Security Act ____ ____

3. *Objective:* Given ten minority groups in the United States, list at least eight of them in order according to total population.

   Criterion Item: What are eight of the largest minority groups in the United States? ____ ____

Turn to the next page to check your responses.

	A match?	
	YES	**NO**

1. *Objective:* Given Sunday comics, be able to list all of the individual strip titles within the classifications of dry humor, light humor, romance, mysteries, detective stories, adventure, sociology, or religion.

   Criterion Item: Name three comic strips that deal withlight humor. _____ ✓

2. *Objective:* Be able to list five major pieces of legislation that were passed in the United States during the Progressive Era (1900-1917).

   Criterion Item: Underline five of the following pieces of twentieth-century legislation that were passed during the Progressive Era (1900-1917).

   (a) Pure Food and Drug Act

   (b) Federal Reserve Act

   (c) Underwood Tariff

   (d) Hepburn Act

   (e) Prohibition Act

   (f) Social Security Act _____ ✓

3. *Objective:* Given ten minority groups in the United States, list at least eight of them in order according to total population.

   Criterion Item: What are eight of the largest minority groups in the United States? _____ ✓

1. No match. The objective asks the student to list (main intent is recall); the test item also asks the student to recall, but to recall something different from the demands of the objective. So the performances don't match.

   The objective provides the student with comic strips to review; the test item does not, so the conditions don't match.

2. No match. The objective says list (recall) and the item says underline (recognize).

3. No match. The performances don't match. The objective says the learner will be given something and he or she is to rearrange them. The item asks the learner to recall. Moreover, the objective asks for an arrangement in order according to population; the item only asks for a list of the largest. The item therefore tests for something different than does the objective.

More Practice Items

A match?

	YES	NO

4. *Objective:* Given the original price and the sale price of an article, be able to compute the rate of discount of the article to the nearest whole percent.

    Criterion Item: A boat normally selling for $1,500 is on sale for $1,200. What is the rate of discount to the nearest whole percent? _____ _____

5. *Objective:* Be able to perform a neurological examination using proper techniques and equipment.

    Criterion Item: Describe the equipment and procedures used to conduct a neurological examination. _____ _____

6. *Objective:* For each of these procedures (craniotomy, laminectomy), describe the locations and functions of the scrub nurse and assistants.

    Criterion Item: Describe the locations and functions of the scrub nurse and assistants for each of these surgical procedures:

    (a) Craniotomy

    (b) Laminectomy _____ _____

A match?

	YES	NO

7. *Objective:* Having written a broad intent (goal) you feel worthy of achievement, be able to list the performances which, if achieved, will cause you to agree that the goal is also achieved. (That is, write the operational definition of a goal you consider worthy of achievement.)

   Criterion Item: Which of the following goals do you feel is most worthy of achievement in today's society?

   (a) Good citizenship

   (b) Population reduction

   (c) Law and order

   (d) Honest government   _____   _____

8. *Objective:* Be able to list four possible elements of kidnapping that are outlined in the Penal Code, Section 208.

   Criterion Item: Joe has taken Tom across the state line against his will. Which section of the Penal Code outlines this action as a kidnapping?   _____   _____

   Refer to the next few pages to check your responses.

| | A match? | |
	YES	NO

4. *Objective:* Given the original price and the sale price of an article, be able to compute the rate of discount of the article to the nearest whole percent.

   Criterion Item: A boat normally selling for $1,500 is on sale for $1,200. What is the rate of discount to the nearest whole percent?   ✓

5. *Objective:* Be able to perform a neurological examination using proper techniques and equipment.

   Criterion Item: Describe the equipment and procedures used to conduct a neurological examination.   ✓

6. *Objective:* For each of these procedures (craniotomy, laminectomy), describe the locations and functions of the scrub nurse and assistants.

   Criterion Item: Describe the locations and functions of the scrub nurse and assistants for each of these surgical procedures:

   (a) Craniotomy

   (b) Laminectomy   ✓

4. A match. Both objective and item ask the student to find the rate of discount, and the item asks for that performance under the same conditions described by the objective. Additional items might be used in a complete performance test, of course, but each would need to be of this type.

5. Not on your life. Describing equipment and procedures is not at all the same as performing an examination. No match.

6. A match. The item matches the objective in every way. Notice that you didn't have to be big in medical knowledge to tell whether the item matches the objective. This isn't always true, but it should be comforting to know that you can spot good or bad items in fields other than your own.

	A match?	
	YES	**NO**

7. *Objective:* Having written a broad intent (goal) you feel worthy of achievement, be able to list the performances which, if achieved, will cause you to agree that the goal is also achieved. (That is, write the operational definition of a goal you consider worthy of achievement.)

   Criterion Item: Which of the following goals do you feel is most worthy of achievement in today's society?

   (a) Good citizenship

   (b) Population reduction

   (c) Law and order

   (d) Honest government   ✓

8. *Objective:* Be able to list four possible elements of kidnapping that are outlined in the Penal Code, Section 208.

   Criterion Item: Joe has taken Tom across the state line against his will. Which section of the Penal Code outlines this action as a kidnapping?   ✓

7. No match. The objective calls for deriving a list of performances, and that appears to be the main intent. The item clearly does not ask for the same thing. To be suitable, the item would have to ask the student to derive a list of performances that define a goal. No other type of item form would suffice.

8. No match. The objective says to list (recall) four elements. The item offers a situation and asks the student to recall a section that applies.

More Practice Items

WHICH, IF ANY

Following are three objectives and a set of test items for each. If an item matches the objective, check the YES column to the right. If not, check the NO column.

	Is the item appropriate?	
	YES	**NO**

Objective #1: Be able to construct a parallelogram of any given dimensions that is accurate to within 1.5 cm.

Test Items:

1. Define parallelogram. _____ _____

2. Describe the difference between a parallelogram and a rectangle. _____ _____

3. Look at the following figures and draw a circle around the one that is a parallelogram. _____ _____

4. Draw a parallelogram whose sides are 11 cm and 13 cm in length. _____ _____

5. Construct a parallelogram whose sides are 5 cm and 7 cm in length, accurate to ± 1.5 cm. _____ _____

Turn the page to check your responses.

	Is the item appropriate?	
	YES	NO

Objective #1: Be able to construct a parallelogram of any given dimensions that is accurate to within 1.5 cm.

Test Items:

1. Define parallelogram. _____ ✓_____

2. Describe the difference between a parallelogram and a rectangle. _____ ✓_____

3. Look at the following figures and draw a circle around the one that is a parallelogram. _____ ✓_____

4. Draw a parallelogram whose sides are 11 cm and 13 cm in length. ✓._____ (?)_____

5. Construct a parallelogram whose sides are 5 cm and 7 cm in length, accurate to ± 1.5 cm. ✓_____ _____

1. One of the least appropriate items imaginable (though popular). "But students don't really understand parallelograms unless they can define one," one might cry in anguish. All right. But if you feel that way about it, either teach your students the definition as enrichment or background and don't test on it, or write an objective that reflects your intent.

2. No match. This item might be useful for finding out why a student has *not* achieved the objective—but it is not appropriate for finding out if he or she *has* achieved it.

3. Not appropriate. Again, this item might be good for discovering that students had not achieved the objective because they couldn't recognize a parallelogram when they saw one, but it won't tell whether they can construct one.

4. Well, if you are non-mathematical like me, this item would be okay. A mathematician, however, makes a distinction between drawing and constructing. Drawing is what one does when sketching freehand; constructing is what one does when drawing accurately with the use of instruments.

5. Appropriate. Finally. Use as many such items as you feel are necessary to sample the stimulus range, ensuring that each item asks students to construct a parallelogram.

More Practice Items

Objective #2: Be able to read a domestic electric-power meter correctly to the nearest unit, and record your readings on the appropriate page of the meter reader's log.

Test Items:

1. Record on the appropriate page of your log the readings of each of these ten domestic meters to the nearest unit.   _____ _____

2. Of the five dials on the domestic meter, which records "thousands of units"?   _____ _____

3. Look at this picture of a dial. What is the reading?   _____ _____

4. Look at the dials on these domestic meters. What are the readings?   _____ _____

5. Define kilowatt-hour.   _____ _____

Turn the page to check your responses.

	Is the item appropriate?	
	YES	NO

Objective #2: Be able to read a domestic electric-power meter correctly to the nearest unit, and record your readings on the appropriate page of the meter reader's log.

Test Items:

1. Record on the appropriate page of your log the readings of each of these ten domestic meters to the nearest unit. ✓ ____ ____

2. Of the five dials on the domestic meter, which records "thousands of units"? ____ ✓ ____

3. Look at this picture of a dial. What is the reading? ____ ✓ ____

4. Look at the dials on these domestic meters. What are the readings? ____ ✓ ____

5. Define kilowatt-hour. ____ ✓ ____

1. An appropriate item. The objective says "read and record" to the nearest unit, and the test item says "record" to the nearest unit. Presumably meter readers can't record what they haven't read, so I would consider this item a match. If you think I am assuming too much, then a small modification of the test item would be in order.

2. This might be a good diagnostic item and useful for determining whether a person who had not achieved the objective was having trouble because he or she didn't know which dial was showing what, but it is not adequate for finding out whether one can read and record complete readings in a book.

3. This one tests for *part* of the objective, to be sure, but not for the entire objective. You may learn that a person can read the dials properly, but you won't find out if he or she can read and then record to the nearest unit.

4. Same problem as Item 3. If an item is not appropriate for testing achievement of an objective, adding several more items of the same type will not improve matters.

5. Not appropriate. What is the main intent of the objective? Read and record. What does the test item ask for? A definition. They are not the same.

More Practice Items

This one is a little more subtle than it may appear. Follow the checklist and you shouldn't have any trouble.

	Is the item appropriate?	
	YES	**NO**

Objective #3: Be able to type a business letter in accordance with the standards described in Company Manual 12-21.

Test Items:

1. Describe the five basic elements of a business letter.   _____ _____

2. Sort the ten sample letters into piles representing those that are written in accordance with Company standards and those that are not.   _____ _____

3. On the five sample letters given, circle any errors or items not in accordance with standards of good grammar.   _____ _____

4. Describe in a paragraph the rationale for the business letter standards currently in effect.   _____ _____

5. From the handwritten copy given, type a business letter in the form set out by manual 12-21.   _____ _____

Turn the page to check your responses.

	Is the item appropriate?	
	YES	**NO**

Objective #3: Be able to type a business letter in accordance with the standards described in Company Manual 12-21.

Test Items:

1. Describe the five basic elements of a business letter.   _____   ✓

2. Sort the ten sample letters into piles representing those that are written in accordance with Company standards and those that are not.   _____   ✓

3. On the five sample letters given, circle any errors or items not in accordance with standards of good grammar.   _____   ✓

4. Describe in a paragraph the rationale for the business letter standards currently in effect.   _____   ✓

5. From the handwritten copy given, type a business letter in the form set out by manual 12-21.   _____   ✓

1. The objective says *type,* and the test items says *describe.* Not the same, so you needn't even bother to look at the conditions.

2. Not appropriate. Typing is not the same as sorting. During instruction, sorting might be a useful activity to sharpen the ability to recognize letters written according to company standards. Or, it might be a good diagnostic item for finding out why a student *cannot* type letters as desired. But it is not appropriate for testing achievement of the objective.

3. Not appropriate. Same comment as for Item 2.

4. Neither the performance nor the conditions match. (To chant "I like to vary the type of test items I use to make my tests more interesting" doesn't make this item any more acceptable.)

5. Here's the sticky one. The performances match. Right? Both objective and item ask students to type a letter. So far, so good. But the test item asks for typing under conditions *different* from those called for by the objective, i.e., typing from *handwritten* copy. If you don't type much, this point could easily slip by; but typists know that it can be very difficult to have to type from scraggly handwritten copy. The objective or the item needs to be changed to match the other.

More Practice Items

FIX IT

Below are pairs of statements, each pair consisting of an objective and a test item allegedly appropriate for testing whether the objective has been achieved. Edit (fix, repair) either the objective, the item, or both, so that there is a match.

1. ***Objective:*** Given a recipe, all necessary utensils, and ingredients, be able to bake a cherry pie. Criteria: (a) the crust is brown but not burned, (b) the cherry juice has not run out of the pie, and (c) the instructor did not die immediately after tasting it.

   Test Item: Following is a recipe for cherry pie. In the space below, describe (write) the steps you would follow in baking a cherry pie.

2. ***Objective:*** Be able to describe to a customer the primary services provided by the bank.

   Test Item: Circle the services that are available to bank customers.

   (a) Checking accounts   (d) Manicures

   (b) Savings accounts   (e) Loans

   (c) Neck massages   (f) Mortgages

Check your fixes on the next page.

1. *Objective:* Given a recipe, all necessary utensils, and ingredients, be able to bake a cherry pie. Criteria: (a) The crust is brown but not burned, (b) the cherry juice has not run out of the pie, and (c) the instructor did not die immediately after tasting it.

   Test Item: Following is a recipe for cherry pie. In the space below, describe (write) the steps you would follow in baking a cherry pie.

   This one is easy. The main intent of the objective is to bake a cherry pie. The item asks someone to describe the steps. Baking and describing are not the same, so something has to change. If we assume that the objective is correct, then we have to make the item match. Something like this:

   Objective: Given a recipe, all necessary utensils, and ingredients, be able to bake a cherry pie. Criteria: (a) the crust is brown but not burned, (b) the cherry juice has not run out of the pie, and (c) the instructor did not die immediately after tasting it.

   Test Item: Go to Cookspace #3, where you will find a recipe for cherry pie, along with all the utensils and ingredients you will need. Bake a cherry pie. Your finished pie will be accepted when it is determined that the crust is brown but not burned, the juice didn't run out, and it didn't immediately kill the instructor who tasted it.

2. *Objective:* Be able to describe to a customer the primary services provided by the bank.

   Test Item: Circle the services that are available to bank customers.

   (a) Checking accounts   (d) Manicures

   (b) Savings accounts   (e) Loans

   (c) Neck massages   (f) Mortgages

Here you'll need to match performances; the objective asks for a verbal performance (describe to a customer), and the item merely asks for recognition (identify by circling). I would make the objective and item read as follows, though your own version is acceptable if the performances and conditions match.

Objective: Using the list of services provided, be able to describe verbally each of the bank services that is available to the customer. For each service, present the following information: (a) what the service is and what it provides, (b) how the service may be obtained, and (c) the cost of the service to the customer.

Test Item: Using the tape recorder provided and a list of bank services, record your description of each service. Include in each description (a) the extent of the service, (b) information on how it may be obtained, and (c) cost.

More Practice Items

FIX ONE MORE

3. ***Objective:*** Given a functioning computer terminal and a word processing program with which you are familiar, be able to draft and print a business memo. Criterion: The memo meets the standards described on pp. 45-46 in the Corporate Policy Manual.

   Test Item: Draft a business memo on a topic of your choice. The memo should conform to the Corporate Policy Manual, pp. 45-46. Use your own terminal and the word processing software of your choice.

Turn the page to check your revision.

3. **Objective:** *Given a functioning computer terminal and a word processing program with which you are familiar, be able to draft and print a business memo. Criterion: The memo meets the standards described on pp. 45-46 in the Corporate Policy Manual.*

Test Item: *Draft a business memo on a topic of your choice. The memo should conform to the Corporate Policy Manual, pp. 45-46. Use your own terminal and the word processing software of your choice.*

This pair is pretty good. Both call for the same performance (writing a business memo). The objective, however, calls for a printed memo and the item doesn't. One or the other has to be changed. If you change the item, it might look like this:

Test Item: *Draft a business memo on a topic of your choice, and print out a hard copy of the memo. The memo should conform to the Corporate Policy Manual, pp. 45-46. Use your own terminal and the word processing software of your choice.*

That should be enough practice to enable you to whiz through the skill check (Chapter 8) in blazing glory. Have at it.

8
Got a Match?

It's time to discover whether you are able to recognize criterion (test) items suitable for assessing achievement of an objective. How shall this be done? Shall I ask you to trace the history of testing or to write an essay on the significance of the multiple-choice item? Mmmm. I've got it! I'll write an item that asks you to compare and contrast norm-referenced with criterion-referenced testing. If you can do that, I can conclude that you really understand the subject. Right?

Oh. I can see you're going to be fussy about it, so I'd better try to practice what I've been trying to get you to practice. On the other hand, the temptation is great to slip in a few items that test the limits or breadth of your understanding. You know how it is—if I just use items that test for the objective, you might get them all correct. And then where would I be? I'd have to write some "harder" items so you didn't get the idea the "course" was too easy. Right? All right, enough is enough, but I just couldn't resist one last chance to make the point that it isn't exactly being honest with students to tell them you want them to be able to do one thing and then test their ability to do something else.

So let's get on with it. Here are some criterion items, each of which is appropriate for testing the objective of this book which is, you'll recall:

*Be able to discriminate (select, point to) test items that are
appropriate for testing the achievement of an instructional
objective, when given*
   (a) An objective
   (b) One or more allegedly suitable test items
   (c) The Objective/Item Matching Checklist

Section I. Yes, No, or Can't Tell

The following 10 pairs of statements each consist of an
objective and a test item. If the test item is appropriate for testing achievement of the objective, check the YES column to the
right. If the item is not appropriate, check the NO column. If
you can't apply the matching procedure because the objective
is too fuzzy (i.e., doesn't state a performance), check the
CAN'T TELL column.

Is the item suitable?
YES   NO   CAN'T
TELL

1. *Objective:* Given a performance of an
   instrumental or vocal melody containing
   a melodic or rhythmic error, and given
   the score for the melody, be able to point
   out the error.

   Criterion Item: The instructor will play
   the melody of the attached musical score
   on the piano and will make an error
   either in rhythm or melody. Raise your
   hand when the error occurs.   ____ ____ ____

(continued on next page)

Is the item suitable?
YES   NO   CAN'T
TELL

2. *Objective:* Given mathematical equations containing one unknown, be able to solve for the unknown.

   Criterion Item: Sam weighs 97 kilos. He weighs 3.5 kilos more than Barney. How much does Barney weigh? _____ _____ _____

3. *Objective:* Be able to demonstrate familiarity with sexual anatomy and physiology.

   Criterion Item: Draw and label a sketch of the male and female reproductive systems. _____ _____ _____

4. *Objective:* Given any one of the computers in our product line, in its original carton, be able to install and adjust the machine, preparing it for use.

   Criteria: The machine shows normal indication, and the area is free of debris and cartons.

   Criterion Item: Select one of the cartons containing one of our Model XX computers, and install it for the secretary in Room 45. Make sure it is ready for use and the area is left clean. _____ _____ _____

(continued on next page)

Is the item suitable?
YES   NO   CAN'T
                TELL

5. *Objective:* When given a set of para-
    graphs (that use words within your
    vocabulary), some of which are missing
    topic sentences, be able to identify the
    paragraphs without topic sentences.

    Criterion Item: Turn to page 29 in your
    copy of *Silas Marner*. Underline the topic
    sentence of each paragraph on that page.   —— —— ——

6. *Note:* Not every objective comes in a sin-
    gle sentence. Many objectives that
    describe a complex or higher-order skill
    need several sentences, as the following
    one illustrates. Use your checklist, and
    the objective should fall easily into place.

    Objective: Given a chapter in a textbook,
    be able to derive and draw a hierarchy of
    the objectives accomplished by the chap-
    ter. Each objective must state the action
    required of the student and any impor-
    tant conditions under which the action is
    to be performed.

    Criteria need not be specified. The pyra-
    mid should extend through at least two
    levels of subordinate objectives or to the
    assumed entry-level skills of the target
    population, whichever chain is longer.

(continued on next page)

Is the item suitable?
YES   NO   CAN'T
TELL

Criterion Item: Refer to Chapter 7 in the textbook, *Nuclear Physics for Fun and Profit.* Derive and state the objectives actually accomplished by the chapter, and then draw a hierarchy of the objectives. Each objective must state the action required of the student and any important conditions under which the action is to be performed. Criteria need not be specified. The pyramid should extend through two levels of subordinate objectives or to the assumed entry-level skills of the target population, whichever chain is longer.

⎯⎯ ⎯⎯ ⎯⎯

7. *Objective:* Given live or video demonstrations of various actions, be able to tell which actions are in violation of Section 415, Disturbing the Peace.

    Criterion Item: Check each of the following actions that represent a violation of Section 415, Disturbing the Peace.

    (a) Helen fires a pistol into the ground in her own back yard.
    (b) Hal and Joe are having a fistfight in the corner bar.
    (c) Sarah, wanting to sleep, asks her neighbor to turn down a noisy TV. The neighbor turns it up to full volume.

⎯⎯ ⎯⎯ ⎯⎯

(continued on next page)

Is the item suitable?
YES NO CAN'T
TELL

8. *Objective:* Be able to taxi any C-series aircraft, according to criteria stated in the Flight Crew Checklist, without performing steps that are unnecessary or a danger to the aircraft, its crew, or other aircraft in the area.

   Criterion Item: Following is a list of steps to be completed before taxi of the C-124A aircraft. Check (✓) those that are correct, and "X" those that are unnecessary or incorrect.

   ___ (a) Hydraulic pressure "WITHIN LIMITS"

   ___ (b) Brakes "CHECKED"

   ___ (c) Flight instruments "CO-PILOT'S CHECKED" (CP), "PILOT'S CHECKED" (S)

   ___ (d) Scanner's report "ENGINE CHECKED" (S)

   ___ (e) CHECK COMPLETED (CP)   ___ ___ ___

9. *Objective:* Be able to observe any patient and tell which of the patient's characteristics should be responded to and which should be ignored (i.e., not responded to).

   Criterion Item: Describe to your instructor any five patient characteristics that should be responded to and at least five characteristics from which you should withhold a response.   ___ ___ ___

(continued on next page)

Is the item suitable?
YES   NO   CAN'T
TELL

10. *Objective:* Given a Model 31 Brain-washer, a standard tool kit, a standard spares kit, test equipment, and at least one symptom of a common malfunction, be able to return the system to normal operation.

Criteria: The system functions within specifications. There is no cosmetic or structural damage to the system or to the immediate area. No more than one unnecessary spare part is used. All paperwork is completed correctly, and no complaints are filed by client personnel.

Criterion Item: The model 31 Brain-washer in the test room can be turned on, but the washing fluid leaks onto the brain-removal mechanism during the wash cycle. Return the machine to normal operating condition. The tool kit, spares, and test equipment beside the machine are available as you need them. Call the instructor when you have finished.

Section II. Which, If Any

Following are four objectives and a set of test items for each. If an item is appropriate for testing the objective, check the YES column at the right. If not, check the NO column. If an item is in some way obscure so that you can't apply the matching procedure, check the CAN'T TELL column.

Is the item suitable?
YES   NO   CAN'T
TELL

A. *Objective:* When approached by a prospective customer, be able to respond in a positive manner (with a smile, a suitable greeting, and a pleasant tone of voice).

Criterion Items:

1. Describe the three basic characteristics of a positive response to the approach of a prospective customer.   _____ _____ _____

2. Watch the following ten film clips and write down the numbers of those that represent a correct response to the approach of a prospective customer.   _____ _____ _____

3. When the instructor hangs the "customer" sign around his neck and approaches you, make the positive response to the approach of a prospective customer.   _____ _____ _____

4. When approached by each of five students selected by the instructor, make the appropriate (positive) response to customer approach.   _____ _____ _____

Is the item suitable?
YES   NO   CAN'T
TELL

B. *Objective:* Given the stock-market quotations from recent news-papers for two different dates and a schedule of brokerage fees, be able to compute the profit or loss resulting from the "buy" of a given number of shares on the earliest of the two dates and a "sell" on the latest.

Criterion Items:

1. In Packet A are stock-market quotations from newspapers of different days and a schedule of brokerage fees. For each of the five stocks circled, calculate the profit or loss that would result from buying 12 shares of the stock on the earlier date and selling them on the later date. Write the profit or loss in the spaces provided.   ____ ____ ____

2. In Packet A are stock-market quotations from newspapers of different days and a schedule of brokerage fees. Describe in writing how brokerage fees are applied to any stock sale.   ____ ____ ____

3. Using the schedule of brokerage fees pro-vided, write an example to illustrate how profit and loss are computed for sale of stocks.   ____ ____ ____

4. Explain the meaning of each of the entries shown for the stock circled on the newspa-per stock pages attached.   ____ ____ ____

5. Describe the procedure for buying and sell-ing a stock.   ____ ____ ____

Is the item suitable?
YES   NO   CAN'T
TELL

C. *Objective:* Given a malfunctioning amplifier of any design, one symptom, reference materials, and tools, be able to repair the unit so that it functions within design specifications.

Criterion Items:

1. Design an amplifier that meets the specifications shown on the attached sheet. Show the values and tolerances for each component.   ____   ____   ____

2. List the three most common troubles to be expected from each of the amplifier designs contained in Packet A.   ____   ____   ____

3. Attached to this sheet are the schematic diagrams for three different kinds of amplifiers. A red circle is drawn around one component of each amplifier. On the bottom of the page, write the symptom(s) that would show up if the circled components were malfunctioning.   ____   ____   ____

4. At Stations A, B, and C are three amplifiers. The tag on each amplifier describes one symptom of the trouble that has been inserted. Using the tools and references provided at each station, repair each amplifier.   ____   ____   ____

5. At Stations A, B, and C are three amplifiers. The tag on each amplifier describes one symptom of trouble that has been inserted. On the page provided, describe the steps you would take to clear the trouble and put the amplifier back into operation.   ____   ____   ____

Is the item suitable?
YES   NO   CAN'T
TELL

D. *Objective:* Given a set of diagrams or slides of correctly angled periodontal probe calibrations, write the correct probe reading of each, rounded to the next highest millimeter.

Criterion Items:

1. On a periodontal probe, which marks are missing?   ____ ____ ____

2. Look at the slides in Envelope D, and write down the probe reading shown in each. Round your answer to the next highest millimeter.   ____ ____ ____

3. In Envelope E are slides showing probes that have been inserted into the sulcus. For each slide, tell whether any precautions have been overlooked, and if so, which ones.   ____ ____ ____

RESPONSES

Here is how I would respond to the items on the previous pages. Perhaps you would like to compare your responses with mine.

Turn to the next page.

Responses to Section I. Yes, No, or Can't Tell

Is the item suitable?

	YES	NO	CAN'T TELL

1. *Objective:* Given a performance of an instrumental or vocal melody containing a melodic or rhythmic error, and given the score for the melody, be able to point out the error.

   Criterion Item: The instructor will play the melody of the attached musical score on the piano and will make an error either in rhythm or melody. Raise your hand when the error occurs. ✓ ___ ___

2. *Objective:* Given mathematical equations containing one unknown, be able to solve for the unknown.

   Criterion Item: Sam weighs 97 kilos. He weighs 3.5 kilos more than Barney. How much does Barney weigh? ___ ✓ ___

3. *Objective:* Be able to demonstrate familiarity with sexual anatomy and physiology.

   Criterion Item: Draw and label a sketch of the male and female reproductive systems. ___ ___ ✓

4. *Objective:* Given any one of the computers in our product line, in its original carton, be able to install and adjust the machine, preparing it for use.

   Criteria: The machine shows normal indication, and the area is free of debris and cartons.

   Criterion Item: Select one of the cartons containing one of our Model XX computers, and install it for the secretary in Room 45. Make sure it is ready for use and the area is left clean. ✓ ___ ___

1. The item is suitable. The objective wants students to be able to recognize errors in the performance of a piece of music for which they are given the score; it wants them to detect (*discriminate, locate, spot*) errors between the rendition and the score. The item asks for the same. True, the indicator stated in the objective is "point out," and the test item asks for hand-raising. Since hand-raising is a simple and direct method for indicating the main intent, the item is a match.

2. No match. This one represents a common mismatch between teaching and testing. Students are expected to be able to solve a given type of mathematical equation. Not only does the item not provide an equation to solve, it asks for a different skill. Solving an equation is not the same as setting up an equation from a word problem. Neither the performance nor the conditions match.

3. Can't tell. What is someone doing when demonstrating his or her familiarity with sexual anatomy? Don't answer that! But unless the objective answers it, there is no way to tell if the item is appropriate for checking out success at achievement of the objective.

4. A match. The objective asks someone to install and adjust, as does the test item. The conditions also match.

Is the item suitable?
YES   NO   CAN'T
TELL

5. *Objective:* When given a set of paragraphs (that use words within your vocabulary), some of which are missing topic sentences, be able to identify the paragraphs without topic sentences.

   Criterion Item: Turn to page 29 in your copy of *Silas Marner.* Underline the topic sentence of each paragraph on that page.   ✓

6. *Objective:* Given a chapter in a textbook, be able to derive and draw a hierarchy of the objectives accomplished by the chapter. Each objective must state the action required of the student and any important conditions under which the action is to be performed. Criteria need not be specified. The hierarchy should extend through at least two levels of subordinate objectives or to the assumed entry-level skills of the target population, whichever chain is longer.

   Criterion Item: Refer to Chapter 7 in the textbook, *Nuclear Physics for Fun and Profit.* Derive and state the objectives actually accomplished by the chapter, and then draw a hierarchy of the objectives. Each objective must state the action required of the student and any important conditions under which the action is to be performed. Criteria need not be specified. The hierarchy should extend through at least two levels of subordinate objectives or to the assumed entry-level skills of the target population, whichever chain is longer.   ✓

5. No match. The objective asks students to identify paragraphs without topic sentences; the item asks them to identify (by underlining) topic sentences. Not the same.

6. A match. The objective asks that learners to able to construct a hierarchy of objectives derived from a chapter in a textbook; the item asks for the same. And though the wording is slightly different between objective and item, the conditions match as well.

   Why does the item look so much like the objective? You know the answer to that. When the performance stated in the objective is mainly overt and at the same time the main intent, there is only one type of item suitable for assessing achievement of the objective—the type that asks learners to do just what the objective says. Only in this instance do the objective and test items look similar; whenever the objective main intent is covert, an indicator must be used, regardless of whether that covert main intent is mainly cognitive or "affective." In those instances the test items look noticeably different from the objective.

Is the item suitable?
YES   NO   CAN'T
TELL

7. *Objective:* Given live or video demonstrations of various actions, be able to tell
   which actions are in violation of Section
   415, Disturbing the Peace.

   Criterion Item: Check each of the following actions that represent a violation of
   Section 415, Disturbing the Peace.

   (a) Helen fires a pistol into the
       ground in her own backyard.

   (b) Hal and Joe are having a
       fist fight in the corner bar.

   (c) Sarah, wanting to sleep, asks
       her neighbor to turn down a
       noisy TV. The neighbor turns it
       up to full volume.   ✓
                                              ____ ____ ____

7. No match. Both objective and item want students to be able to identify actions that are violations of Section 415. The objective, however, wants them to be able to do their identifying in response to live or video demonstrations; the item asks for the identifying in response to verbal descriptions of situations. Not the same. If a learner responded well to the item as written, would you be able to conclude that he or she could handle real situations as well? I'm not sure. What is clear is that the item demands an inference about whether the objective has actually been accomplished.

Is the item suitable?
YES   NO   CAN'T
TELL

8. *Objective:* Be able to taxi any C-series aircraft, according to criteria stated in the Flight Crew Checklist, without performing steps that are unnecessary or a danger to the aircraft, its crew, or other aircraft in the area.

   Criterion Item: Following is a list of steps to be completed before taxi of the C-124A aircraft. Check (✓) those that are correct, and "X" those that are unnecessary or incorrect.

   __ (a) Hydraulic pressure "WITHIN LIMITS"

   __ (b) Brakes "CHECKED"

   __ (c) Flight instruments "CO-PILOT'S CHECKED"(CP), "PILOT'S CHECKED" (S)

   __ (d) Scanner's report "ENGINE CHECKED" (S)

   __ (e) CHECK COMPLETED (CP)   ✓
                                              ____ ____ ____

8. No match. Taxiing an aircraft and recognizing written steps to be completed before taxiing are not the same.

   Again, the item might be useful as a diagnostic item to reveal one of the reasons the taxiing was not accomplished as desired.

   Or it might be useful as a preflight checkout to find out if a student is ready to try taxiing. After all, you wouldn't let any student taxi an expensive aircraft (they all are) unless you felt confident that he or she knew what to do. But that doesn't slice any bananas. If you want to find out if students can taxi, ask them to taxi.

Is the item suitable?
YES   NO   CAN'T
TELL

9. *Objective:* Be able to observe any patient and tell which of the patient's characteristics should be responded to and which should be ignored (i.e., not responded to).

   Criterion Item: Describe to your instructor any five patient characteristics that should be responded to and at least five characteristics from which you should withhold a response.   NO ✓

10. *Objective:* Given a Model 31 Brainwasher, a standard tool kit, a standard spares kit, test equipment, and at least one symptom of a common malfunction, be able to return the system to normal operation.

    Criteria: The system functions within specifications. There is no cosmetic or structural damage to the system or to the immediate area. No more than one unnecessary spare part is used. All paperwork is completed correctly, and no complaints are filed by client personnel.

    Criterion Item: The model 31 Brainwasher in the test room can be turned on, but the washing fluid leaks onto the brain-removal mechanism during the wash cycle. Return the machine to normal operating condition. The tool kit, spares, and test equipment beside the machine are available as you need them. Call the instructor when you have finished.   NO ✓

9. Same as Number 8. Not appropriate. The item asks students to recall some characteristics, while the objective asks them to describe characteristics of real patients. Not the same.

10. Close, but no bell ringer. The performances match, both objective and item ask students to repair a machine when shown at least one symptom of malfunction. And some of the conditions match. But the objective asks that paperwork be completed; the test item asks that the instructor be called when the task is completed. The objective asks that no complaints be filed by client personnel; the test is clearly conducted in a classroom rather than on client premises.

    Of course, it may be necessary or practical (convenient) to do the testing in a classroom instead of on client premises. If that is the case, that wouldn't change the fact that the conditions don't match. If this test item were used as the means of finding out whether the objective was achieved, the evaluators could only infer—make an educated guess—whether the objective was achieved. It might be a pretty good inference about whether a student could repair the machine, but it would be a poor inference about whether a student could work correctly on client premises or complete the necessary paperwork.

Responses to Section II. Which, If Any

Is the item suitable?
YES   NO   CAN'T
TELL

A. *Objective:* When approached by a prospective customer, be able to respond in a positive manner (with a smile, a suitable greeting, and a pleasant tone of voice).

Criterion Items:

1. Describe the three basic characteristics of a positive response to the approach of a prospective customer.   ____ ✓ ____

2. Watch the following ten film clips and write down the numbers of those that represent a correct response to the approach of a prospective customer.   ____ ✓ ____

3. When the instructor hangs the "customer" sign around his neck and approaches you, make the positive response to the approach of a prospective customer.   ✓ ____ ____

4. When approached by each of five students selected by the instructor, make the appropriate (positive) response to customer approach.   ✓ ____ ____

A.

1. No match. Describing characteristics is not the same as responding in a positive manner. Neither performances nor conditions match.

2. No good. Recognizing proper approaches in a film is not the same as responding to a prospective customer. Items 1 and 2 may provide some good practice in developing parts of the desired skill, but they are not useful for finding out if the skill has been developed.

3. Pretty good. The item asks for a response to an instructor who is pretending to be a prospective customer, and so the item is asking for a simulation of the desired performance. Or is it? Maybe the instructor is a prospective customer. You would need to know more about the actual situation to be sure. I would accept this item as suitable, but if you feel the urge to revise it, I will be happy to cheer you on.

4. This one is very similar to the one above, except that it asks for the response to be made five times instead of one and asks that the response be made to students instead of the instructor. The performances match, and the conditions seem very close. If you would not be willing to accept the item, how would you change it?

Is the item suitable?
YES   NO   CAN'T
TELL

B. *Objective:* Given the stock-market quotations from recent newspapers for two different dates and a schedule of brokerage fees, be able to compute the profit or loss resulting from the "buy" of a given number of shares on the earlier of the two dates and a "sell" on the later date.

Criterion Items:

1. In Packet A are stock-market quotations from newspapers of different days and a schedule of brokerage fees. For each of the five stocks circled, calculate the profit or loss that would result from buying 12 shares of the stock on the earlier date and selling them on the later date. Write the profit or loss in the spaces provided.   ✓ ___ ___ ___

2. In Packet A are stock-market quotations from newspapers of different days and a schedule of brokerage fees. Describe in writing how brokerage fees are applied to any stock sale.   ___ ✓ ___ ___

3. Using the schedule of brokerage fees provided, write an example to illustrate how profit and loss is computed for sale of stocks.   ___ ✓ ___ ___

4. Explain the meaning of each of the entries shown for the stock circled on the newspaper stock pages attached.   ___ ✓ ___ ___

5. Describe the procedure for buying and selling a stock.   ___ ✓ ___ ___

B.

1. Item is suitable. The main intent of the objective is that students be able to compute profit and loss on a stock sale. Though the objective doesn't state an indicator, you can safely assume that writing down the result of the calculation is the simplest and most direct indicator that would tell you if the computation is correct. If you don't think you can so assume, I would be happy to support your urge (is that a performance?) to modify the item a little.

2. No good. Describing a procedure is not the same as carrying out the procedure.

3. No good. Writing an example is not the same as calculating profit or loss.

4. Not adequate. But students couldn't calculate profit or loss unless they knew the meaning of the newspaper stock entries, could they? Of course not. But that's not the point, is it? If your intent is for students to be able to describe entries, then that is what the objective should say.

5. Not adequate. Describing a procedure is not the same as carrying out a procedure.

Is the item suitable?
YES NO CAN'T
TELL

C. *Objective:* Given a malfunctioning amplifier of any design, one symptom, reference materials, and tools, be able to repair the unit so that it functions within design specifications.

Criterion Items:

1. Design an amplifier that meets the specifications shown on the attached sheet. Show the values and tolerances for each component. — ✓ —

2. List the three most common troubles to be expected from each of the amplifier designs contained in Packet A. — ✓ —

3. Attached to this sheet are the schematic diagrams for three different kinds of amplifiers. A red circle is drawn around one component of each amplifier. On the bottom of the page, write the symptom(s) that would show up if the circled components were malfunctioning. — ✓ —

4. At Stations A, B, and C are three amplifiers. The tag on each amplifier describes one symptom of the trouble that has been inserted. Using the tools and references provided at each station, repair each amplifier. ✓ — —

5. At Stations A, B, and C are three amplifiers. The tag on each amplifier describes one symptom of trouble that has been inserted. On the page provided, describe the steps you would take to clear the trouble and put the amplifier back into operation. — ✓ —

C.

1. No match. The objective wants students to be able to repair, and the item asks for design. Not the same thing at all. What would you say to someone who said, "But students don't really understand how to fix one unless they can design one"? (Now don't be too nasty.) Hopefully, you would remind that person that while his or her comment has a grain of truth, it is not relevant to the point. If you want to know if learners can fix, ask them to fix.

2. Not adequate. Listing (recalling) common troubles is not the same as repairing an ailing amplifier.

3. Sounds good, but it won't do. Actually, the item is backwards from the objective, in the sense that the objective asks students to go from symptom to trouble, and the item asks them to go from trouble to symptom.

4. A match (at last). But where does the item writer get off asking for three repair jobs? Why not only one? Or ten? I dunno. The item writer may have asked for three because with three he or she could sample the range of amplifiers and troubles that learners will be expected to handle in the immediate future.

5. Not adequate. Talking a good job isn't the same as doing a good job.

Is the item suitable?
YES   NO   CAN'T
TELL

D. *Objective:* Given a set of diagrams or slides of correctly angled periodontal probe calibrations, write the correct probe reading of each, rounded to the next highest millimeter.*

Criterion Items:

1. On a periodontal probe, which marks are missing?   _____ ✓ _____

2. Look at the slides in Envelope D, and write down the probe reading shown in each. Round your answer to the next highest millimeter.   ✓ _____ _____

3. In Envelope E are slides showing probes that have been inserted into the sulcus. For each slide, tell whether any precautions have been over-looked, and if so, which ones.   _____ ✓ _____

*Objective and criterion items courtesy of Pipe & Associates

D.

1. Not adequate. Even though you may not know what a periodontal probe is, you can see that telling which marks are missing is not the same as writing correct probe readings. (If a dentist could peer through a periodontal probe, would that make it a perioscope? No ... Don't throw it!)

2. Suitable. Both item and objective ask learners to write correct probe readings. What's that you say? You don't know that the slides in the envelope show correctly handled insertions? Ahh, you are getting to be the sly one. You are correct, of course; we have to assume that the slides represent the objective conditions to call it a match.

3. No again. Describing precautions is not the same as writing correct probe readings.

How'd You Do?

How is your skill at recognizing items relevant to objectives? Are you as good at it as some, better than most? By now you know my answer to this question is that it doesn't matter. What matters is whether you can or cannot perform the skill with adequacy. What's adequate? Well, if I were to have to decide whether you had met my criterion of success, I would do so on this basis:

At least 8 of 10 items correct from Section I, including items 1, 3, 5, 7, 8, and 10,

and

at least 15 of 17 items correct from Section II, including items A3 or A4, B1, C4, and D2.

A final word about the matching of test items to objectives:

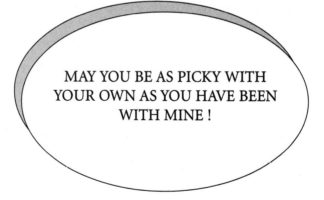

MAY YOU BE AS PICKY WITH
YOUR OWN AS YOU HAVE BEEN
WITH MINE !

Useful References

1. Mager, R.F. *How to Turn Learners On . . . without turning them off,* Third Edition, 1997.

2. Mager, R.F. *Goal Analysis,* Third Edition, 1997.

3. Mager, R.F. *Preparing Instructional Objectives,* Third Edition, 1997.

4. Schrock, Sharon A., and Coscarelli, William C. C. *Criterion-Referenced Test Development,* 1996. ISBN: 0-9616690-22-0.

References 1–3 are available from:
    The Center for Effective Performance
    4250 Perimeter Park South, Suite 131
    Atlanta, GA 30341
    (800) 558-4237

Trial Summary

Trial was held on January 17, 1984, in Superior Court of World Opinion, Judge Kang A. Roo presiding. After all were seated and the gavel banging had subsided, the judge turned to the plaintiff, Robert F. Mager, and asked that the charges be summarized.

"They're all guilty, your honor," he said.

"Yes, yes, I know," replied the judge impatiently. "But I think we should at least identify the defendants and read the charges before we pass sentence. In the interests of justice, that is. Read the charges."

"Oh, all right," grumbled Mager. "But they're all guilty of tampering with the subject manuscript or its packaging in one way or another.

"The usual meliorists helped with the initial continuity check, making sure there was some sort of coherence or flow from start to finish. They insisted on wholesale changes of the first draft, leading to a lot of work. They are David Cram and John Warriner."

"Scoundrels," said the judge. "We'll deal with them later."

"Those who badgered me on aspects of technical consistency, leading to additional anguished effort, are Bill Deterline, Peter Pipe, Maryjane Rees, and Paul Whitmore."

"A devious sounding lot," snorted the judge.

"A whole basketful of people tested for content to make sure the desired outcome was achieved. They are Norman Carter, Ray Dargus, Margo Hicks, Jane Kilkenny, Dan McCampbell, Tim Mossteller, Dick Niedrich, Peter Selby, Nancy Selden, Andy Stevens, and Eileen Mager."

"Incredible," eyebrowed the judge.

"A number of souls checked to make sure there were no unnecessary turnoffs. These attitude checkers demanded changes to things that slowed them down, turned them off, or rubbed them the wrong way. They are Dale Ball, Tom Frankum, Don DeLong, and Pam Varga."

"You have my complete sympathy," sighed the judge. "Is there more?"

"Yes, your honor," replied Mager. "There are the jargon checkers who pointed to words that were longer or more obscure than necessary, the ones who carried out my poor man's readability test: Joanne Lackey and Katia Prozinski."

"Such impudence will not go unvarnished. Carry on."

"There is a clump of folks who did the title check, poking and picking at words, inferences, and implications. They are Max Forster, Mary Hurley, Dick Lewis, Jeanne Mager, Laura Newmark, Charles Selden, Bill Shanner, Jim Shearer, Charlie Spears, Hal Chitwood, Carol Valen, Casey Williamson, Eileen Mager, Robert Lowe, Linda Marsh, Bill Valen, Stuart Burnett, Susan Klein, Herb Goodyear, JoAnn Egenes, Sally Livingston, Bruce Fredrickson, and Laura Mandel. They are particularly guilty."

"Oh? Why izzat?" queried the judge.

"Because they didn't like MY title and made me give it up."

"Never mind. Justice will triumph."

"Then, your honor, there are those who hooted and hollered and stomped all over the cover designs, trying to make sure that something agreeable to folks other than myself would be used. They are Marshall Arky, Pete Burt, Jim

Edwards, John Feldhusen, Ollie Holt, Roger
Kaufman, Kathy Keeler, Brad Mager, Sue Markle,
Rosalind Kuhl, Harry Shoemaker, Miriam Sierra-
Franco, Randy Mager, Bob Snyder, Wanda Sterner,
Barbara Wachner, John Welser, Dee Williams, C.
Glenn Valentine, and Lori Vanderschmidt. Those
who tested the second edition cover designs
were Johan Adriaanse, Gérard Conesa, Paul Guer-
sch, David Heath, Eileen Mager, Clair Miller,
Fahad Omair, Dan Piskorik, Phil Postel, Jim
Reed, Ethel Robinson, Bill and Carol Valen, Bob
White, and Letitia Wiley."

"There can't be more," incredulated the pon-
tiff.

"Oh, yes. There are those who hooted and
hollered at boo-boos they found in this third
edition: David Cram, Carl Winkelbauer,
Albro Wilson, Eileen Mager, Verne Niner,
Seth Leibler, and Paul Whitmore."

"Well," exclaimed the keeper of the scales.
"I never! What I mean is—I never! Whatever
shall we do with them?"

"Why, we should expose them for what they
are," replied Mager while fervently waggling a
straightened finger. "We should place them in
the pillory of public perception. We should
place their names in posterity where all will
be reminded of their deeds, where all will be
required to note just who was responsible for
the shaping of the innards and the outards of
subject manuscript. The world should know how
helpful they were and that their help was
appreciated."

"So ordered," gaveled the judge. "And let
this be a lesson to everyone. Court's
adjourned."

And it was, too.

Index

Criterion test items, 12–13. *See also*
    Test items

Definitions, testing on, 129, 133
Description
    as an objective, 85
    testing for, 140
Diagnostic test items, 12–13, 52,
    133, 137, 163
Difficulty indices, 104–105
Discrimination, as a main intent,
    24–25, 41, 157
Drawing, versus constructing, 129

Education, success and, 105.
        See also Instruction, value of
End-of-course evaluations, 14
End-of-unit evaluations, 13–14
Environmental features,
    as conditions, 80
Errors
    consequences of, 90, 96, 97
    recognizing, 157
Evaluation. *See also* Measurement
    basis for, 9
    criterion-referenced, 10, 11–12
    defined, 8
    end-of-course, 14
    of indicator behaviors, 43–46
    of main intents, 42
    norm-referenced, 9–10, 11–12,
        104
    on-the-job, 14
    of process, 3
    rationale for, vii
    types of, 13–15

Failure, producing, 108
Feeling states, objectives that
        describe, 109–110
"Fix It" matching practice,
    139–144
Flowchart, of performance-matching
    steps, 62

Goal Analysis (Mager), 110
Goals, matching performance with,
    124, 125. *See also* Objectives
Grading, 106–109. *See also* Normal
    curve
    basis for, 9
    consequences of, 108
    on a curve, 5, 9–10
    defined, 9
    pass-fail, 109
    performance and, 105
    versus performance evalua-
        tion, 8
Guided practice. *See* Practice

Hierarchy of objectives, 148, 149,
    159
Higher-order skills, objectives with,
    148
*How to Turn Learners On . . . without
    turning them off* (Mager), 110

Identification skills, testing, 161
Identifying
    as a covert performance, 55
    as a main intent, 54
    used in an objective, 46
Improbable conditions, 103–104
"Indicator and covert" perfor-
    mances, 50
"Indicator and overt" performances,
    50, 56–58, 60
Indicator behaviors, 23–29, 40
    ability to perform, 42
    appropriate, 40
    covert performance and, 30
    evaluating, 43–46
    identifying, 27–29
    simplicity of, 41, 42, 43–46, 54
Indicators
    adding to objectives, 60
    appropriate, 60
    identifying, 113

MORE GREAT BOOKS FROM DR. ROBERT F. MAGER!

Dr. Robert F. Mager has authored one of the most extensive and renowned collections of books and resources on issues of human performance in existence today. These books are considered to be *the* reference library for anyone serious about educating others and improving human performance. You'll find everything you need to learn how to:

- develop successful instruction,
- find realistic solutions to performance problems,
- measure the results of your instruction,
- generate positive attitudes in learners,
- and much more!

Order your copies today and get resources you'll use for a lifetime.

	Quantity	x Price=	Total
Measuring Instructional Results *How to determine whether your instructional results have been achieved*		x $19.95=	
Preparing Instructional Objectives *A critical tool in the development of effective instruction*		x $19.95=	
How to Turn Learners On... without turning them off *Ways to ignite interest in learning*		x $19.95=	
Analyzing Performance Problems *How to figure out why people aren't doing what they should be, and what to do about it*		x $19.95=	
Making Instruction Work *A step-by-step guide to designing and developing instruction that works*		x $19.95=	
Goal Analysis *How to clarify your goals so you can actually achieve them*		x $19.95=	
The How to Write a Book Book		x $17.95=	
Troubleshooting the Troubleshooting Course		x $17.95=	
What Every Manager Should Know About Training		x $17.95=	
Subtotal			
Shipping & Handling*			
GA residents add 5% sales tax to the subtotal plus shipping and handling			
Total Order			

* Please add $4.50 for the first book, plus $1.50 for each additional book. Please allow four weeks for delivery by UPS Ground Service.

Name _____

Phone _____ Fax _____

Organization _____

Address _____

City _____ State _____ Zip _____

- My check or money order for $ _____ is enclosed

Charge my • Visa • Mastercard • AmEx   Exp. Date _____

Card Number _____

Name on Card _____

Please send this form and your check, money order, or credit card number to:

CEP
P.O. Box 102462
Atlanta, GA 30368-2462

Call 1-800-558-4CEP for volume discount information.

Call for shipping charges on international orders.

For credit card orders, fax this order for faster delivery:
(770) 458-9109

Analyzing Performance Problems

or You Really Oughta Wanna

How to figure out why people aren't doing what they should be, and what to do about it

Third Edition

Robert F. Mager
Peter Pipe

CEP PRESS
A wholly owned subsidiary of
The Center for Effective Performance, Inc.
Atlanta, Georgia

BOOKS BY ROBERT F. MAGER

Preparing Instructional Objectives, *Third Edition**

Measuring Instructional Results, *Third Edition**

Analyzing Performance Problems, *Third Edition**
(with Peter Pipe)

Goal Analysis, *Third Edition**

How to Turn Learners On . . . without turning them off, *Third Edition**

Making Instruction Work, *Second Edition**

Developing Vocational Instruction (with Kenneth Beach)

Troubleshooting the Troubleshooting Course

The How to Write a Book Book

What Every Manager Should Know About Training

* Sold as a six-volume set (The Mager Six-Pack)

WORKSHOPS BY ROBERT F. MAGER

Criterion-Referenced Instruction (with Peter Pipe)

Instructional Module Development

The Training Manager Workshop

BOOKS BY PETER PIPE

Developing Performance Aids

Decision Table Algorithms

For more information, contact:
   The Center for Effective Performance, Inc.
   2300 Peachford Road, Suite 2000
   Atlanta, GA 30338
   (770) 458-4080 or (800) 558-4237

ISBN 1-879-618-17-6 (PREVIOUSLY ISBN 1-56103-336-7)
ISBN 1-879-618-15-X (SIX VOLUME SET)
Library of Congress Catalog Card Number: 96-72446
Printed in the United States of America

05 04 03 02   10 9 8 7 6 5 4

Contents

Introduction
Considering the Whole

People do things for the strangest reasons. For equally strange reasons, they also don't do things. Looking at society as a whole, at other people both old and young, in the world of work and elsewhere, and noting their apparent shortcomings, we are tempted to conclude:

"They don't have the right attitude . . ."

"They don't understand. We've got to teach them to . . ."

"They're just not motivated . . ."

"We've told them and told them, and they still don't . . ."

"We've got a training problem. . ."

Each of those statements, and many more like them, express discontent with what someone is doing. Each comments on what is perceived to be a problem in need of a solution. And each, because of the way it's phrased, suggests something about what the solution should be.

It would be a mistake, though, to take these comments at face value and, in particular, to think that a solution to the problem has been found. That's a rush to judgment, because people don't do what's expected of them for many reasons. Unless steps are taken to understand the problem before solutions are applied, substantial resources might be committed while at the same time leaving the problem unsolved.

If we label others as having *poor attitude* and *lack of motivation,* we are finger-pointing, naming a culprit and hinting at a solution instead of probing for the problem by asking, "Why is this so? What causes it?" Similarly, we jump the gun if we look at inadequate performance and declare, "We've got a training problem." Again, this confuses problem and solution. Training isn't a problem; it's just *one of the solutions* used to solve problems that arise *when people truly cannot do* what is expected of them.

The danger in leaping from apparent problem to apparent solution is that large amounts of time and money can be spent in throwing training at a problem that training cannot solve. Similarly, if you leap to a conclusion that someone's attitude needs to be "fixed" and that what it takes is "training" and perhaps a "good talking to," you can end up blue in the face and with nothing much changed. You need to dig a little deeper.

This is why a procedure like performance analysis is important to those who actually want to solve problems—rather than just talk about them.

Analyzing Performance Problems will show you how to seek out the real reasons why people don't perform the way they should, the true problems, and then help you match solutions to those problems. Mainly, we will discuss this in the context of the world of work, but, as you will see, these same ideas also apply anywhere that people are not doing what they should.

The procedure to be described is not unlike the quest for the villain in a mystery story, wherein the detective sorts through a collection of clues—some useful, some not—to discover the perpetrator of the dastardly deed. But rather than solving crimes, we'll work with problems in which what someone is expected to do is not the same as what that person is *actually* doing. Or, saying that another way, we'll be dealing with *performance discrepancies.*

Note that word *discrepancies.* We are being careful at this stage not to talk about performance *deficiencies.*

- If we say that someone's performance is *deficient,* it implies that there's something "wrong" with the individual whose performance doesn't match what we want. It also implies that something about the individual is what must be changed.
- On the other hand, when we talk of a *discrepancy,* we are simply recognizing that a difference exists between the performance we have and the performance we want; the two are simply not in balance. And if we could weigh them on a scale, we could bring them into balance by either subtracting weight from one side of the scale or by adding to the other, thereby increasing our options for solutions.

That last point about increasing options is important because (as we'll try to show you):

- People don't perform as desired for many reasons; for example,

    (a) they don't know what's expected;

    (b) they don't have the tools, space, authority;

    (c) they don't get feedback about performance quality;

    (d) they're punished when they do it right;

    (e) they're rewarded when they do it wrong;

    (f) they're ignored whether they do it right or wrong; and

    (g) they don't know how to do it.

- Often, what is identified as "the problem" isn't the problem at all.
- Proposing a solution before the problem is understood is

just shooting from the hip. (Taking action before the problem is understood can lead to unnecessary waste of time and effort, to unsolved problems, and to embarrassment.)
- The best solutions are not always found in the obvious places and often can be a blend of several solutions.

What's In It For Me?

Once you've learned to apply the performance analysis procedure you'll be able to solve the "mysteries" of performance problems in an orderly way. You'll be able to:

- Identify the causes of the problems,
- Decide which problems are worth solving,
- Describe solutions which will help you solve the problems, and
- Decide which solutions will be both practical and economically feasible.

By the time you are done, your new X-ray vision will help you see where expensive misfits exist between problems and solutions. You will see that some problems cost millions and others cost no more than the annoyance of the person perceiving the discrepancy as a "problem." You will find that sometimes providing information really is the answer; other times you will reach solutions that are too massive to put into practice and, maybe more often than you might think, you will find solutions that are easy to apply and cost only pennies or even nothing at all.

From Here to Mastery

To help develop your new X-ray vision, we'll describe and illustrate each of the steps of the procedure. So that you can see the sequence of steps and also keep track of where you are, we will center our discussion on a flow diagram (opposite). This is just a "map" that will remind you of where you are in the process. (Though it may look a bit formidable when you first

Performance Analysis Flow Diagram*

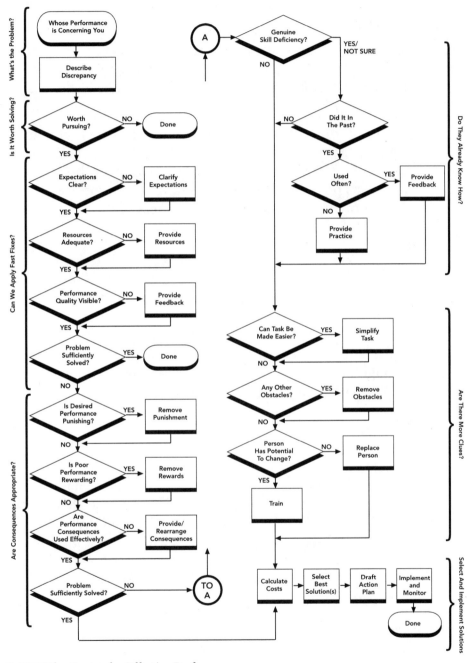

© 1997 The Center for Effective Performance
* An insert of the Performance Analysis Flowchart is found at the back of the book.

look at it, rest assured that it will quickly become as familiar and as easy to use as your favorite can opener.)

Caution: The diagram makes it look as if everything is neatly welded into place, each step leading inevitably to the next. *Don't be deceived by appearances. The formula is not that rigid.*

As you become skilled in using it, you may find that you can leap a step here and there. That's fine; our whole approach is designed to help solve your problem as quickly as possible. At first, though, you'll get more complete, more innovative, and more successful results if you stay fairly close to the steps as given.

Another caution: Beware the hazards of considering only one possible solution to any problem. That's only one stage better than viewing all performance discrepancies as problems of training—or attitude. To avoid this trap, you'll find the flow diagram, and the reminder questions at the end of each chapter, useful. Run your problem through all the steps before you decide that your analysis is complete.

What Now?

Because "you can't fix it if you can't recognize it," we'll begin by learning how to recognize and describe performance discrepancies. Before we do, however, we'd like to offer this happy thought: It will take a lot longer to describe and illustrate the performance analysis procedure than it will take you to apply it.

Part I
They're Not Doing What They Should Be Doing

We think we've got a training problem.

The procedure we are about to describe is one that shows you how to analyze the nature, the importance, the causes, and the solutions to things called performance discrepancies. Since you can't analyze one unless you know how to recognize one when you see one, we'll begin there.

1
What Is the Performance Discrepancy?

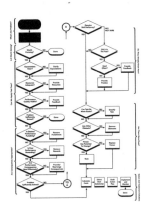

WHERE WE ARE

Someone has identified a "problem," and we are trying to determine the nature of the performance discrepancy.

A discrepancy is a *difference*, a mismatch, between *what is* and what *should* be. And our focus here is on *human* performance discrepancies, those differences between what *people* are actually doing (or not doing) and what they should be doing. As we proceed, we'll want to identify those discrepancies large enough to warrant action, collect clues that will lead us to one or more solutions, and select among those solutions those which are the most powerful, practical, and economical.

Performance discrepancies come in many shades. They may be tiny, mere pinpricks of irritation to someone, or they can be big enough to have significant impact on life and limb, or anywhere in between. They can exist in:

- *Personal interactions.* For example, the parent wants dirty clothes in the laundry hamper; the child leaves clothing in a pile on the floor.

- *Clashes with policy.* For example, the instructor wants assignments turned in on time; students offer excuses for bringing them in late.

- *Unacceptable work practices.* For example, workers are expected to follow safety rules; they find shortcuts around the rules.

All of those are performance discrepancies, differences between what someone is expected to do and is actually doing. All are what one might call "sins of omission," or perhaps "sins of substitution," costing somebody grief, discomfort, or money, or worse. Sometimes, discrepancies are caused by *too much* performance. You may have read about or even have encountered cases such as:

- The social worker too quick to destroy a family member through unwarranted accusations of child abuse.
- The editor who inserts his/her own thought here and there in an attempt to "improve" the manuscript.
- The truck driver who has too many accidents.

What Is the Performance Discrepancy?

Faced with problems like those above, the first thing to realize is that it's not useful to start out proposing an answer, as in "We've got to train/teach/motivate . . ." Nor is it helpful to lay blame, as in "These people are lazy/not motivated/careless . . ." Not one of these comments says anything about people performance; not one describes a performance that is or is not satisfactory. In each case, we need more information if something useful is to be done about the alleged "problem."

What you have to do is ferret out the discrepancies between what *is* (the actual performance) and what *ought to be* (the expected performance). Do that by asking questions about why someone believes there is a problem to be solved. For example:

Him: We've got a training problem.
You: Oh? Why do you say you have a training problem?
Him: Well, our welders are having too many accidents.
You: So what you want is for welders to have fewer accidents?
Him: Exactly.

With the discrepancy identified in terms of what people are or aren't doing, we can go on to find out how many accidents are "too many." Then, we can plan a course of action to reduce the discrepancy between what is and what is desired. And that may or may not call for training. Another example:

Her: These students just aren't motivated.
You: Ah. And what do they do that causes you to say that?
Her: For one thing, they don't come to school on time, and when they do show up, they rarely have what they need to get to work.
You: So what you would like to do is to increase the number of students who show up on time?
Her: Yes.
You: And you would like to increase the number who come prepared to work?
Her: Definitely.

What started out as a finger pointed at the students' motivation was clarified as a desire for them to start in timely fashion and ready to work. With the true discrepancy revealed, we can now explore why this state of affairs exists. Is it because the bus breaks down a lot, because the students can't tell time, or is it something else? Once the reason(s) for the tardiness are revealed, thoughts can be turned toward solutions. Similarly for the preparedness issue. Here is yet another example:

> *Mgr:*   I want you to teach these supervisors to be motivated.
>
> *You:*   Mmm. Just what is it they're doing that causes you to say that?
>
> *Mgr:*   Doing? It's what they're not doing that's the problem.
>
> *You:*   And what is that?
>
> *Mgr:*   Well, for one thing, they aren't managing. They spend too much time running the machines they used to run before they were promoted. They shouldn't be doing that. They should be managing.
>
> *You:*   So what you want is for them to spend less time operating machines?
>
> *Mgr:*   Absolutely! When they're operating, they're not managing.

The complaint was about motivation, but at least one of the performance discrepancies comes down to this:

> *Actual performance:*   Time spent operating machines

> *Desired performance:*   Little or no time operating machines

Whose Performance Are We Talking About?

You need to be specific about which person or persons are being discussed. Why? Because:

First, it helps ensure that you are dealing with a "people performance problem," not some other kind of problem.

If the problem has to do with something other than people's performance, it follows that an analysis of someone's performance is not likely to be useful.

Second, the answer to "Whose performance?" is likely to influence the selection of workable solutions. Take, for example, this statement:

"They need to be taught the right attitude about safety."

You don't have to be a rocket scientist to see that what will improve "safety" in the chemistry lab could well be different from what will improve safety in a foundry or an office. So you need to identify the target of the complaint, like this:

Mgr: They need to be taught to have the right attitude about safety.
You: Who does?
Mgr: Everybody working in the chem lab.

Now you're ready to start pinning down what the discrepancy is:

You: Why do you say they don't have the right attitude about safety?
Mgr: Because instead of washing their used beakers and putting them back where they belong, they just shout, "Prosit," and throw the beakers into the fireplace.

You can see that had we been dealing with bookkeepers or, say, musicians, not only would an apparent "attitude problem" take a different form, but the solutions would also be different, as in:

Mgr: They just don't have the right attitude about their jobs.
You: Who doesn't?
Mgr: Our sales people.

You: What makes you say they don't have the right attitude?

Mgr: Because they refuse to use the sales aids that we provide them.

In this instance, the quest will be to find out why the sales aids are not used, and then, if the aids really would be of value, to find ways of encouraging their use. But suppose the dialogue had played out this way:

Mgr: They just don't have the right attitude about their jobs.

You: Who's "they"?

Mgr: Our legal staff.

You: Oh. Why do you say they don't have the right attitude?

Mgr: All they want to do is litigate, no matter how trivial the issue. It seems that the only tool in their legal toolbox is litigation. They drive us nuts.

Again, the initial complaint was about attitude. But because different people were involved, the discrepancies were different, which means that the solutions would be different. And even if the issue for the chem-lab folks, the accountants, the sales people, and the lawyers was safety, it would require different remedies, because "safety" means different things in different circumstances. So before you even ask about the discrepancy, find out whose performance is at issue.

Summing Up

A performance discrepancy is a difference between what is and what should be. These discrepancies can exist in personal interactions, clashes with policy, and unacceptable work practices. We must first identify the discrepancy before attempting a solution.

What to do

First, identify the person or persons whose performance is said to be lacking. Then describe the perceived performance discrepancy in terms of (a) what is actually happening, and (b) the desired performance.

How to do it

Ask these questions:

- Whose performance is at issue?

- Why do I (or someone else) think there's a problem?

- What is the actual performance at issue?

- What is the desired performance?

2

Is It Worth Pursuing?

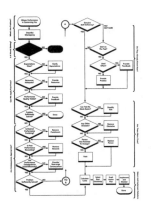

WHERE WE ARE

A performance discrepancy has been identified. Before we do anything else, we want to verify that it is worth continuing the analysis.

What Would Happen if We Let it Alone?

Different people see things in different ways. A situation causing some to just shrug their shoulders is seen by others as a Big Deal. The joke that tickles our funnybone may leave you wondering what the guffawing is all about. What to one is a spectacular sunset is to someone else just the end of another day. (Which is why the ancient Romans said, "One man's meat is another's poison.")

So when you first encounter a performance that seems to be pinching somebody, it's always appropriate to wonder if you are dealing with just a point of view that sees the "problem" as considerably larger than it actually is. The question to ask is: "What would happen if we let it alone?" If serious consequences would follow, then you have a discrepancy calling for further analysis. But if the only consequence of ignoring the "problem" is that it annoys the person describing it, then it probably isn't worth pursuing. Here's an example of just such a situation.

The Case of the Longhairs

Back in the days when the Baby Boomers were beginning to test their wings, the Beatles arrived in the USA to immediate success despite (Gasp!) long hair. Suddenly long hair was "in" for young males, not to mention some folks older than the Boomers. And equally suddenly parents and bosses began to sound off. "They oughta be ashamed of themselves," they said. "We've got to *teach* them not to look like bums." (Translation: They oughta wanna look like *me*.)

What was the discrepancy? About three inches of hair. Which led to this conversation with one manager:

"You are unhappy about the length of the new employees' hair?"

"Yes. It's disgraceful."

"Aside from your displeasure with long-haired males, what would be the consequence of ignoring it?"

"What do you mean?"

"What would happen if you let it alone?"

"Well, it probably wouldn't make much difference to business, but they ought to have more respect for the company. They ought not to want to look so sloppy."

In other words, the company would suffer no serious consequences. It just meant that some of the shorthairs would continue to be made uncomfortable (for awhile) by the presence of the longhairs. Hardly a reason for mounting a serious effort to eliminate the discrepancy, wouldn't you think? (Historical note: The world did not come to an end.)

But other companies had a different answer to the same question. To quote one machine-shop foreman: "Nobody in my shop wears long hair, or long *anything.* People with long hair, long ties, or loose clothing are a menace to themselves and maybe to others, because they can easily get caught in the rotating machinery."

Another manager said: "Most of our customers are shorthairs. If we send them a longhair sales rep, we just might put ourselves out of business."

So here, in two different settings, we have the same set of facts as before, but this time the response is not "Let it alone." In these settings, there is a consequence of some importance, and this time it looks as if the problem is worth pursuing.

Are Our Expectations Realistic?

Even if a problem cannot simply be dismissed (thereby saving yourself valuable time), one more step is needed before you commit to completing the entire analysis. The big question remains, "Should we ignore this discrepancy?" but this time the issue is, "Are our expectations realistic? What would happen if we succeeded?" Sometimes a little probing will show that it is less costly to ignore the discrepancy than to do something about it.

A Case of Success Would Kill Us

A sales manager with a force of more than a hundred people complained that they didn't heed his memo exhorting them to turn in a monthly article for the internal newsletter. The conversation went something like this:

Manager: "I've asked each person to send in a short article each month . . . less than a page . . . describing success stories or other interesting items. But only a few of them do it."

Analyst: "What happens as a result of your not getting articles from each person every month?"

Manager: "We don't hear about what they've been doing, and they don't get a chance to tell of their successes."

Analyst: "How much do you suppose that's costing in terms of dollars?"

Manager: "Dollars? That's hard to say. Nothing directly, of course, but we may be losing something in terms of motivation."

Analyst: "What would happen if everyone did as you asked?"

Manager: "What?"

Analyst: "What would happen if everyone sent in an article every month, just as you expect them to do?"

Manager: "Hmm. Then I'd have 112 articles for the monthly newsletter . . . ahh . . . gee . . . I see I'd have to hire another typist . . . and then I'd need another word processing terminal . . . uhh . . . we'd have to add a hundred more pages to our 12-page newsletter. That's a lot more than we can afford!"

Very quickly it became clear that the cost of eliminating the discrepancy would have been too heavy to bear. The solution? The sales manager readjusted his expectations, and the problem evaporated.

Summary So Far

When a performance discrepancy raises its head, it doesn't necessarily follow that you should rush into a full-blown search for solutions. Instead, follow these steps:

1. Ask: "What would happen if we ignored it?"

    If the answer is, "Nothing much," then the problem is trivial and can be set aside.

2. Ask: "What would happen if we succeeded?"

    If the problem cannot be easily set aside, then take a look at "the world as you would like it to be" and do a reality check.

    If it's plain that the cost of having the world as you would like it to be would be too high, that is, if the cost of "success" would be prohibitive, then stop.

On the other hand, if the problem's not trivial and the expectations are not unrealistic, then it's time to put on your Sherlock Holmes hat, get out your magnifying glass, and start digging (!). To solve the problem, you'll need to:

- find out more about the cost of the discrepancy,
- ferret out the causes and possible solutions, and then
- compare the cost of the problem against the cost of a potential "cure."

That will tell you whether it's time to act and, if so, what needs to be done.

How Big Is It?

Determining the "size" or "cost" of the discrepancy may not be a simple matter of adding up a few numbers. In some cases, direct costs are readily calculated—people are hurt, machinery is damaged, materials are wasted, or time is lost. Other times, the calculation is more obscure, as in lost sales, increased insurance premiums, or reduced production or quality. And sometimes, costs are intangible, such as loss of good will or morale or a tarnished company image. Yet all of these factors may be important in arriving at an estimate of discrepancy costs vital to deciding how much time and money a solution is worth.

But the moment you get away from direct costs and enter the realm of guessing about "what might happen if," move with care, because an attempt to assign costs to *potential* consequences can open a Pandora's box. In a paper mill, for example, workers were exhorted to replace the covers on fast-moving pulleys after working on them. But they weren't replacing them, and management said, "That's one of our problems. They should be putting the covers back on, but they *don't*. And that's dangerous. *Could* lead to serious accidents."

It *could*. But it never had. A check of the files showed that in the entire history of the company, not a single accident had been attributed to this "discrepancy." The maintenance people, apparently, were more careful than they were being given credit for (as is often the case). As a result, the *actual* "cost" of the discrepancy was zero.

But what about potential costs? Well, one might *speculate* that government safety inspectors, noting uncovered moving parts, might feel inclined to impose a penalty of a size clearly specified in such-and-such a regulation. Or that one or more employees might decide to sue because of an alleged exposure to potential harm. Or that an overzealous reporter might write a hand-wringing piece about the "dangers" of working for this company, thereby reducing the number of qualified job applicants and increasing the cost of insurance. Or . . . any of a thousand other "maybes."

The issue here is not whether hypothetical, as well as actual, costs should be considered when estimating the cost of a performance discrepancy, but whether such hypotheticals represent real and reasonably likely hazards. In the case in point, the coverless pulleys represent a known hazard; they are *known* to cause harm—even though they haven't yet done so in this company setting. Jaywalking also has been *known* to cause harm, so can be considered a likely hazard, even though only a hypothetical one to anyone not yet a casualty of this risky behavior.

Note that *potential* costs cannot be assigned only to performance discrepancies. One can catastrophize even about performance that is exactly correct, legal, moral, and ethical. The troubleshooter who performs according to all written policies and professional standards of conduct may still be fired, demoted, or even sued, over some alleged infraction. Physicians are routinely sued for malpractice, whether or not their performance has been exemplary. The hapless homeowner who damages an armed burglar in self-defense *could* find the cost of subsequent legal action running into the thousands of dollars. Driving legally along the highway *could* lead to loss of one or more lives in the case of an accident. (As our colleague Bonnie Abney points out, "You can be a terrific driver and still get pushed against a guard rail by a falling boulder.") And so on. Potential costs simply cannot be confined to performance discrepancies; *any* course of action could lead to any number of unexpected costs.

What to do? Add to the actual cost of the discrepancy the estimated cost of potential consequences, but only of those you can defend as being reasonably probable. Then, take remedial action to prevent the discrepancy from even happening, especially when such remedies are inexpensive and easy to apply. For example, in the case of the coverless pulleys, one might devise an inexpensive interlock that would prevent the machinery from turning on when the covers were not in place.

Possible Costs Arising from a Discrepancy

To get you thinking, here's a list of likely sources of costs. Usually, it makes sense to project such costs over a period of a year, so that you can report, "This discrepancy is costing us the whopping amount of _____ per year." If the project lasts less than a year, calculate the costs of the discrepancy over the lifetime of the project so that you can report, "This discrepancy will cost us _____ before this project is concluded."

Money. Is money lost directly (as when tellers or salesclerks give out more money in change than they should)? Are goods or materials lost (as through theft or accident)? Calculate the amount lost per year or the amount that would be lost per year if the discrepancy were allowed to persist.

Time. Do people waste time as a result of the discrepancy? Do they lose time because of materials shortages or lateness, because services are slow, or because defective work has to be redone? Is time lost because you or someone else worries about the discrepancy? If so, calculate the amount of time lost and its cost for a whole year.

Material Waste (Scrap). Is more scrap generated than is acceptable? How much more? What is the value of that scrap? What's the annual cost of having it hauled away or burned or remelted?

Equipment Damage. What is the cost of equipment damage resulting from the discrepancy? What's your estimate of the annual cost if the discrepancy continues?

Amount of Work Completed. Is there less production because of the discrepancy? What's the cost of the difference between the amount of completed work you are getting and the amount you should be getting?

Accuracy of Work Completed. Is the quality of the work suffering because of the discrepancy? How? And how much is it costing?

Insurance Premiums. Has the discrepancy led to increases in insurance premiums (as when drivers or others have too many accidents)? How much more per year are you paying?

Accidents. Does the discrepancy increase the frequency of accidents? Accidents can be costly, and most of the costs can be calculated. Add up the cost of workdays lost, hospital stays, damaged or destroyed equipment, and increased insurance premiums.

Even if the probability of an accident seems remote, the potential damage from an accident needs to be considered. When you can't accept the consequences of an accident, a potential cost needs to be assigned. Particularly when loss of life is more than a remote possibility, and particularly when someone may be legally held to blame, you are dealing with a potentially serious problem that cannot be dismissed as "not worth pursuing."

Lost Business. This one may be harder to quantify, but if someone says that a discrepancy is resulting in lost business, it is fair for you to ask "How much?" The answer may be only an approximation based on a review of sales records, but even an estimate provides better guidance than a mere guess.

Does the discrepancy require customers to spend more time waiting in line, filling out forms, waiting for the doctor, or returning items for repair? If so, there is a negative effect on the customer. Check to see whether the impact is resulting in lost business.

Duplicated Effort. Does it now take two people to do what one did before the discrepancy occurred? Are two departments now doing what only one did before? How much is that duplication costing?

Extra Supervision. Does the discrepancy mean that more supervision is needed than before? Do you need more guards, more security equipment, more monitoring time, or more monitoring equipment? Does someone spend more time overseeing? Does the supervisor end up doing the job himself/herself?

Other Costs. Will the discrepancy, or possibly the elimination of the discrepancy, lead to lawsuits? To sexual-harassment charges? To EEO complaints?

Multipliers Are Important

Earlier, we suggested that typically you should project the costs of a discrepancy for a year or some other significant period. In other words, don't look just at a single occurrence of the problem. Multiply it by the number of times it happens over a reasonable cycle. You need to determine: How many people are involved? How often? In how many places? You may find that what is judged to be a small problem can escalate enormously. Here's an example.

The Case of Late Displays

A young man working for one of Europe's biggest supermarket chains was learning to complete this kind of analysis. The only kind of problem he could think of, he said, was too trivial to bother with. As he explained, "Each week we send out displays for the weekly loss-leader items. And as often as not, a display sits in a market's warehouse and isn't set up until a couple of days into the week."

He estimated the amount of business lost through failure to "highlight the special" to be the equivalent of $100—too little, he thought, to make an examination worthwhile.

PP: Isn't there more than one loss-leader display sent out each week?

YM: Yes. And the people in the stores are sloppy about displaying them.

PP: Every week?

YM: Yes.

PP: How many stores are affected?

YM: Several hundred.

PP: So one hundred dollars lost per week per store, times several hundred stores . . .

YM: Wow! That could add up to as much as fifty thousand dollars a week!

You see the point. By the time we had multiplied all the various dimensions, this "trivial" problem was estimated to cost the equivalent of two million dollars a year!

———————

But let's not get too pushy about the two million dollars. These were estimates, and although we tried to be conservative, perhaps the numbers were inflated. But even if the scale of the problem were only a tenth of what was estimated, that's still a lot of problem. If the true extent of the problem were only ten percent of the estimate, there's still a problem worth a substantial amount of a problem-solver's time.

When you have located and listed as many results or consequences of the performance discrepancy as you can think of, calculate, as best you can, the annual cost of each. When you add all costs together you will have quantified the total cost of the discrepancy and assessed its importance. Even though you may not be able to put a dollar amount on each of the costs, you will have a reasonably objective basis for deciding how much you can reasonably invest in a solution. In other words, you will be in a good position to compare the cost of potential solutions to the cost of the problem.

Summing Up

In deciding whether or not a solution to a performance discrepancy is worthwhile, we must determine what would happen if we let it alone and what could happen if we solved it. The costs and benefits of solving the discrepancy must be weighed against the costs and benefits of leaving it alone.

What to Do

Having identified a performance discrepancy that you or someone else feels is important to eliminate, check to see that the problem is truly a problem and not just an opinion, bias, or unrealistic expectation not worth pursuing. Reject if the problem is trivial.

If the problem is not plainly trivial, check that the expectations ("What we want to be happening") are reasonable, and reject the problem if they are not.

If the problem still survives this screening, find out what the discrepancy is costing. To estimate the size or value (and thus the importance) of the discrepancy:

- List all the consequences (outcomes) caused by the discrepancy.

- Calculate the cost of each outcome wherever possible.

- Total the costs.

How to Do It

Ask these questions:

- "What would happen if I let it alone?" If the answer is "Nothing much," the problem can be ignored. You're done.

- "Are our expectations reasonable?" If success in eliminating the discrepancy seems unlikely to achieve anything worthwhile, revise your expectations.

- "Does the discrepancy still survive?" If so:

  a. List all the consequences caused by the discrepancy.

  b. Calculate the cost of each outcome wherever possible. Use multipliers if appropriate (number of times the discrepancy is repeated over a period of, say, a year; number of sites; and so on).

  c. Total the costs.

  d. Do a final reality check by answering the question, "Is the cost of the discrepancy high enough that it seems worth pursuing a solution?"

Part II
Explore Fast Fixes

*Are there obvious solutions
that will help?*

You intend to complete the entire analysis before selecting
a course of action, of course; but before you do, you want
to know whether you can apply some obvious "fast-fix"
solutions that can make the performance discrepancy
smaller or even go away.

3

Can We Apply Fast Fixes?

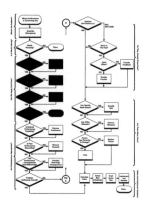

WHERE WE ARE

We have a performance discrepancy to eliminate, and the cost indicates that it's worth pursuing. Before going further with the analysis we want to see if we can end or reduce the discrepancy by a simple, easy-to-apply remedy.

Now that a performance discrepancy has been identified, and we have verified that the problem is big enough to warrant action, you may feel that it would make sense to move in with a complete analysis in the hunt for solutions. Not yet. Experience shows that many discrepancies are readily eliminated with little effort or expense. And even when you can't take care of the entire problem this way, you may solve enough of it to be hailed as a hero (after which you can belt out a lusty chorus of: *Put'cher finger in the dike, Mabel, before we spring another leak*).

Invisible Expectations

The first place to look for fast-fix possibilities is under a rock labeled "invisible expectations." When people don't know what they're expected to do or to accomplish, it is unlikely that their performance will meet expectations. You know you're in the presence of this category when you hear, "Nobody told me."

The Case of the Befuddled Draftees

Come with us to an aircraft builder's drafting department. Engineers were using the same symbols on drawings that they had used for their last employer. The situation looked like this:

Who?	Engineers
Actual Performance:	Using "wrong" notation on blueprints
Desired Performance:	Use notation prescribed by company

You ask a simple question ("Do they know what's expected of them?") and find that nobody has ever told these engineers what the desired notation was. They never were issued a copy of the notation policy, let alone a reminder sheet to hang over their desks. You might say to yourself, "Wait a minute. They're not doing what they're supposed to be doing—because nobody ever *told* them what they were supposed to be doing. We could solve this thing in a minute simply by letting them in on the secret." And you'd be right. All it took to put things right was to let them in on the secret of what was expected.

The clues that you may be dealing with invisible expectations sound like this:

"You never told me you wanted me to do it."

"You never said you wanted it done like *that.*"

"How was I supposed to know you wanted it today?"

"They may have changed it in the spec book, but nobody told *us* about the change."

———————

The Case of the Secret Agenda

The secret agenda is too common in industry. It often shows up in discussions with the bewildered employee who has just been demoted or booted clear off the payroll, particularly in these days of "downsizing."

"What did you do that got you fired?" one might ask.

And you might receive a reply like this: "I don't know! I honestly don't know. My performance reviews were all favorable . . . and my boss kept telling me I was doing a good job. Then, all of a sudden, I was fired. I honestly don't know why."

———————

Although it is probably true that some employees pretend ignorance of the reason for their sudden separation, it would be foolish to assume that all of them are being deceitful. More likely it never occurred to anyone to tell the employees what was expected of them; or perhaps those in charge were not mature enough (i.e., no backbone) to inform them of what they were doing to cause the displeasure of the establishment.

Remember when you were in school and the test papers came back? How often have you heard or said, "Gee. He/she never told us that grades were going to be based on the footnotes (or the lab work, or neatness, or any number of other things). If we had known what he/she wanted, we could have done a lot better."

It's easy for invisible expectations to creep into the equation. Jobs change, quality and output expectations change, and often the communication of those changes to those involved is slow to catch up. So always look to see whether performance expectations are known and clearly understood.

Inadequate Resources and Other Obvious Obstacles

Physical obstacles are often not hard to see. If your car won't move, and you discover that the emergency brake is still on, or that a rock is blocking the front wheel, you disengage the brake, move the rock, and get on with life. Same thing in the workplace. Suppose, for example, you find a discrepancy like this:

Who?	Supermarket shelf stockers
Actual performance:	Stocking 100 cases per hour
Desired performance:	Stocking 150 cases per hour

You look around and find that this stocker spends a lot of time walking between the stockroom and the shelves, struggling with one case at a time. A simple question reveals that he lacks a basic tool, namely a dolly that will carry several cases at a time. Provide a dolly and you'll have eliminated a big obstacle to performing as desired, not to mention making the job easier.

The Case of the Tool Crib

Here is another example, taken from life, but with a different kind of obvious obstacle.

Who?	Machinists
Actual performance:	Don't return expensive, specialized tools to the tool crib after use
Desired performance:	Check tools back in when job is completed

Important? Yes. The tools are very expensive, not readily replaced, and in short supply within the shop. Sometimes work is delayed while chasing down a needed tool which is not in its place in the tool crib. Do all concerned know this? Yes. So why don't they follow the rules? Because the tool crib is likely to be temporarily closed when the machinists try to return tools. Seems the person in charge of the crib takes frequent breaks and, like a diligent cribkeeper, locks the crib rather than leave it unattended. The result, however, is that the attempt to return tools is often frustrated. After a few such frustrations, the machinists find they waste less time if they just leave the tools where they are.

Inadequate Feedback

The third place to look for "miracle fixes" is in the area of feedback—information about the quality of performance. If you aren't getting regular information to answer the "How am I doing?" question, you don't have a basis for improving performance. Practice alone, without feedback, is not enough to "make perfect." In fact, performance is as likely to get worse as it is to get better when feedback is absent.

Often, of course, we can generate our own feedback. But that only works once we have learned how to recognize good from bad performance. If you know that in planting a rose the hole needs to be twice the size of the football, then you can decide (that is, provide yourself with feedback) when the hole is big enough. But if, say, you're practicing shooting at a hidden target, with no way of telling where the bullets are flying, how can you improve your aim? Or if nobody, not even you, tastes the food you have prepared, how can you tell whether it needs more salt?

(Pause for thought: When was the last time you received any feedback regarding the quality of your telephone-answering performance? Do you know anyone who needs such feedback?)

The Case of the Dancing Smiles

Consider this example: A dance coach wants your help in training dancers to smile whenever they're on stage. To observe the situation for yourself, you go to the theater and sit in the fifth row with the coach while the dancers run through their routines.

Who?	Dancers
Actual Performance:	Not smiling when dancing
Desired Performance:	Smiles on dancers' faces

Whenever one of the dancers drops her smile, the coach leans over to you and says, "See? She's not smiling." So you ask, "Why don't you tell that to the dancer you're pointing at?" You're thinking, "It doesn't do the dancers any good if I'm the only one getting the feedback." The coach replies, "I can't do that. Interruptions like that would completely ruin their timing."

So here is a situation in which *you* got feedback, but the *dancers* didn't. They obviously don't need training; they already know how to smile. Apparently, the dancers were concentrating so hard on counting the beat that they forgot to smile. Suppose the coach had them face their mirrored wall as they practiced; then they would be able to see when they were doing things right (when they weren't watching their feet, that is).

NOTE: You say that dealing with dancers isn't a part of your job description? How about other people for whom smiling might be said to be part of the job—receptionists, flight attendants, store clerks; or managers and trainers?

If you need further examples of performance that suffers from lack of feedback, you need look no further than the institution of marriage. If you have ever heard anyone say things such as:

> "Every once in awhile she just clams up. She won't talk to me, and she won't tell me what's bothering her."

> "Whenever I try to tell him what he did that upset me, he just walks away."

you're listening to situations wherein feedback is being withheld. The clammer-upper is missing an opportunity to communicate (provide feedback), as is he who walks away. Until the situation changes, it will be difficult for the relationship to improve.

When, for whatever reason, people cannot generate feedback for themselves and there's no outside source of feedback for expected performance, you have to expect the desired performance to be less than adequate. Turning that around, always make sure that a feedback source exists for what you or someone else expects people to do.

Summing Up

When an identified performance discrepancy warrants action, we should explore fast fixes before spending time and resources on further analysis. We may find that all that is required is a quick-and-easy remedy such as uncovering invisible expectations, providing proper resources, and supplying feedback.

What to Do

Before plunging into the serious analysis of a discrepancy, check to see whether there are one or more obvious impediments to performance that can be readily eliminated or lessened.

How to Do It

Ask these questions:

- Do the performers know what's expected of them? Have they been told or otherwise notified, or is it assumed that "everybody knows?" Are any written standards incomplete or unclear?

- Can the performers tell you what they're expected to do? To accomplish?

- Are there obvious obstacles to performance? Are all needed tools available? Is something missing or inadequate in the work environment? Do they have everything they're supposed to have for doing their job?

- Do performers find out how well they're doing? How do they find out?

Part III

Are the Consequences Right-Side Up?

*Does desired performance
lead to consequences favorable
to the performers?*

A fertile area for clues about how to fix the problem is that of performance consequences. Because upside-down consequences are such a common source of the problem, they should be addressed before moving to more familiar causes.

4

Is Desired Performance Punishing?

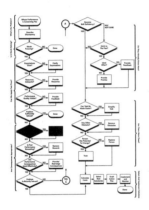

WHERE WE ARE

An important discrepancy in someone's performance needs to be eliminated. We need to check to see whether desired performance is being punished.

Actions lead to results. Sit on a hot stove, and the consequence of doing so will make it much less likely that you'll do it again. Recognize someone's good work with attention or favorable comments, and it's more likely that the person will continue to do good work.

Actions produce consequences; those consequences, favorable or unfavorable, shape how we will act in the future. Favorable consequences make it more likely that actions will be repeated. Unfavorable consequences work the other way, decreasing the likelihood of repeated performance. We need to be sure that this linkage of actions and consequences is not working against us, with punishing consequences following desired actions.

The last thing we want to do is to punish good performance. Yet strange to say, one of the most common reasons why people don't do what we'd like them to do is that the desired "doing" is seen as punishing by the performer(s). Their world becomes somehow dimmer as a result of what they did, and so they seek (consciously and otherwise) other ways to go. Here are several examples we've encountered over the years.

Actual Cases

The following real cases demonstrate how desired performance can be punishing.

A Case of Musical Madness

A college music student had the chance to play with his city's symphony orchestra. For a student who had not yet completed his training, this was a rare opportunity. Since he needed both the money and the experience, he asked his music teacher if something could be worked out.

"I think so," replied the teacher. "There is no reason why you shouldn't take the job, provided you make up the school work you miss on the days you are absent."

So, the student threw himself into both tasks. He did well with the symphony and earned "As" and "Bs" on all his make-up work. But when grading time arrived, he found himself with a "C" for the course. Astonished, he asked his teacher why he was given only a "C" after receiving "As" and "Bs" for all his work.

She replied: "Well, you're getting entirely too much experience and not enough learning."

If you were the student, how would you feel in such a situation? No matter how you slice it, this is a situation in which desirable activity was followed by an unpleasant consequence (punishment). If, as a result of this dampening, the student were to perform his school work with less enthusiasm, one can imagine the teacher telling her colleagues, "You know, we've got to teach him to be more motivated about his studies. He oughta wanna have more interest."

A Case of Attitude

Some time ago one of us was assigned the task of "fixing the doctors' attitudes" at a large hospital. The hospital had just installed a computer, and physicians were now expected to *type* their medical orders into a terminal twice a day, instead of scribbling them on a pad.

"But they're not doing that," explained management. "Instead, they're grumbling about it, doing it wrong, or trying to get the nurses to do it for them." Asked, "Why should the physicians do it willingly?" management replied, "Because it's good for the hospital—and for the patient. The labs get the medication orders a lot faster, inventory can be kept up more easily, and the billing is more accurate."

In other words, lots of good consequences for the hospital, but what about the physicians? For the physicians, desired performance was punishing—in spades.

After two days of on-site observation, here is what was found. The terminals had been placed in the nursing stations—very busy, public, and crowded places. As a result, there was no place to put a piece of paper down to the left or right of a terminal; and as each terminal top was "modern-designed" to slope downward, any paper placed there would slither to the floor. Now, physicians tend not to be a typing population. Some type competently, but most don't; and many think of typing as somewhat demeaning "clerk's work." The result was that most physicians would sit at terminals, notes in one hand, with the "proctological" finger of the other hand laboriously "hunting 'n' pecking" away at their medical orders.

The nurses, who had banded together to agree not to take over this chore, would tend to stand in the background and snicker. After all, they typed on the terminals regularly and were pretty good at it.

There's more. The terminals were mounted on tables 30 inches high. That's no problem for you with your perfect vision, but those of us who wear bifocals find ourselves sitting at terminals with our heads tilted back and our necks getting stiff. The same thing happened to many of the physicians. Had you observed them you would have noticed that after a short while of sitting with heads bent back, some would (unconsciously, it seemed) slide out of their seats, push the chairs to the tables, and then look *down* at the screens. This was far more comfortable for the necks and eyes, but action led to yet another source of punishment. When they picked up light pens to touch the screens and thus enter their orders into the computer, they sometimes hit the "Erase" spot rather than the "Enter" spot and wiped out all their hard work. You see, the computer programmer had put the "Enter" code on the screen right next to the "Erase."

Finally, to add insult to injury, because the physicians were looking *down* at the computer screen at an angle (because they were standing rather than sitting), they were likely to touch *another* wrong place with their light pens because of the parallax problem (the bending of light by the thickness of the glass screen, much as water bends light and makes a partially submerged stick look bent), and get whooshed to the other end of the program.

Adding it all up, desired performance (typing orders into a computer terminal) was mildly painful, humiliating, frustrating, and exasperating. Should anyone be surprised that there was some grumbling and a reluctance to perform as requested?

The solution was simple. Two terminals were installed on low tables in the physicians' office complex. There, each physician could enter medical orders at his or her convenience, in private and in relative comfort.

The Case of the Reluctant Readers

Examples of instances in which desired performance is punished are everywhere, but sometimes the source(s) of punishment are less visible than in the examples above.

"Trainees just won't read the material they are assigned before coming to the course," instructors will complain.

But why should they? What happens to them if they *do?* Well, the instructor goes over the same material anyhow, thus creating a boring time for those who did as requested.

What happens to the trainees who *don't* do the reading? Nothing. The reading is covered anyway. So desired performance is punishing, and undesired performance is largely ignored. Is it any wonder people don't do the reading assignments? Listen to this story.

A Case of Welfare Woes

In one welfare office the supervisors complained that social workers were closing fewer cases than they should.

"Not everyone stays on welfare for generations," a supervisor explained. "Social workers should be helping people to establish objectives and to accomplish them, and then the workers should close those cases."

But consider the consequences to the *social workers* who did what was expected of them. If they *closed* cases, they had, in their own words, to open other cases. And that took a lot of legwork until each case "settled down." By "settle down" they meant that in time, cases usually become routine and can be handled with periodic phone calls or visits. In other words, the consequence of desired performance was more work.

What happened to them if they *didn't* close cases? The supervisors complained . . . among *themselves*. Why? Because the supervisors preferred that their social workers produce fat reports with lots of psychiatric language, rather than good records for closing cases.

The Case of the Reluctant Manager

An insurance company had a policy of trying to recruit upper-level managers from the ranks of its field agencies. But the agency managers resisted the promotions. One of them described the situation this way:

"They tell me it would be good *for the company* if I accepted the promotion and moved to corporate headquarters back East. But why would I want to do that? The raise doesn't mean that much. Besides, I'm my own boss here. I do the hiring and firing; I set the working hours. I know everybody in town; I belong to the club and play golf with my friends. Why should I give up all this just to sit in a concrete blockhouse back East?"

From this agency manager's point of view, the performance desired by head-office management (accepting the promotion) would definitely make his world dimmer. And if a consequence makes someone's world dimmer, less pleasant, or less interesting, you can consider that a punishing consequence. In this example not only was desired performance punishing, but *non*-performance (staying on as agency manager) was highly rewarding. In situations such as these, it is folly to expect that "inspirational lectures" or exhortation will do much good.

The Case of the Empowerment Trap

In these days when empowerment of the workforce is such a popular business practice, it is common for managers to "empower" employees to make decisions and take actions previously reserved for managers. So far, so good. Unfortunately, however, the empowered employees aren't told specifically what they are empowered to do now that they weren't empowered to do yesterday. As a result, they are reluctant to behave any differently than before the empowerment policy went into effect.

In addition, managers themselves sometimes get no training in how to handle this new-style management. In particular, they don't get information and practice in dealing with employees who *do* behave as they're expected to. The result? Employees who behave in the expected empowered ways can get dumped on by managers who don't know how to recognize empowered actions when they see them. Would you be surprised to learn that "punishment for empowered behavior" often leads to less of it?

Consequences Work at Home, Too

Punishment for desired or superior performance is so common that one may overlook it in an area where it frequently occurs—the family. Yet punishment is plain to see in what we call the "anti-intellectual family." Think about the consequence to sons or daughters who aspire to rise above the intellectual level of their relatives, or who set their sights on occupations different from those pursued by relatives, or who raise their conversations above the level of the family "norm." Are they applauded or revered or urged to greater heights? Seldom. More likely, they are insulted and stung with ridicule so that they lose their motivation to escape their mental ghettos.

In many more cases around the home, desired performance is withheld because of its unfavorable consequence. Parents complain, "I don't know what they teach 'em in school these days, but our kids don't come to us with their questions and problems like they used to." Observe these same parents interacting with their children, however, and it quickly becomes apparent that the parents are causing the problem.

> *Kid:* Hey, Mom 'n' Dad! Look what I made in school today!
>
> *Parent:* Wipe ... your ... mouth!

Little wonder the kids behave as they do. The parents, unintentionally perhaps, have engineered it that way. And usually they couldn't have done a better job if they had been trying.

These examples are here to remind you of a simple truth about human behavior:

People learn to avoid the things they are hit with!

It doesn't matter whether they are hit with a club, an insult, humiliation, repeated failure, frustration, boredom, or an increased workload of uninteresting tasks. If people feel they will be punished, or even that there is a risk of being punished when they perform as you desire, they will avoid doing it your way whenever they can. People don't often purposely do things that will lead to their world being dimmer than it is.

Spotting Ill-Placed Punishment

A classic example from industry is the comparative emphasis on safety and production. Management says, "Safety is our top priority. Right after it comes productivity."

But what does a supervisor's reputation depend upon? Production. You'll rarely hear, "Great supervisor. Tremendous safety record. This is the person we'll promote."

Safety managers complain that as long as nothing goes wrong—as long as people "get away with it"—nobody cares about safety.

Production is seen as the result that counts. And despite the lip service, safety takes a second (or third or fourth) seat in the perception of those affected.

And so, when people aren't performing as desired, one thing to explore is whether or not it is unnecessarily punishing to perform as desired. Do they see desired performance as being geared to penalties? If so, you have probably located a strong reason why you aren't getting the results you would like.

We must emphasize, however, that it is not *your* view of the outcome that is important here. You must try to see the situation through the eyes of the performers themselves and ask yourself, "What is the result to them for doing as I desire? How might *they* see the consequences of doing it?" What may strike you as a favorable consequence could be seen as *un*favorable by them.

On occasion, this can be subtle. Sometimes it may strike you as ridiculous. No matter. Listen to what the performers say.

The employer complains, "I don't see why they won't work overtime—they make good money on it." But the employees say, "What's the good of overtime? Anything you earn, they take away in taxes."

The parent says, "I don't see why she won't take math. It will get her a better job when she's grown." But the student says, "Math is for those who want to follow the establishment road. I'm interested in *people*. Besides, the math teacher is the least liked guy in the whole school."

Or consider the case of "rate busters" in school or industry—those who turn out more work than anyone else. Do colleagues revere these people for their skill or industriousness? More likely, the group's attitude will be perceived as punishment for performance, and the person will slow down to the level of the group . . . or be pushed out of it.

ann landers

Dear Ann Landers: I have never written to you before but after I read the letter signed "Lonesome" I knew my time had come.

My in-laws are also "Lonesome"—or at least that's what they tell everybody.

We hear from many people that they complain constantly about how we ignore them and how hurt they are. It burns me up.

Last Sunday my husband and I and the kids went to see them and it was the same old story.

Grandma and Grandpa talked about nothing but how sick they are, how much they suffer (she with backaches and he with rheumatism in his legs). It is a real contest to see who is in worse shape.

Then they tell us for the 50th time about how bad their operations were. (Hers two years ago for a tumor, his five years ago for a hernia.)

They are so self-centered it is awful. Never a question about the children or my husband's job or my interests.

All they want to do is talk about themselves and their sicknesses.

Also, whenever we go to see them they greet us with, "We didn't think you were coming."

I wonder how many other "Lonesome" parents there are around? If so, maybe there's a good reason their children don't visit them more often. —Cause and Effect

Dear Cause: There are plenty around, and I hear from dozens of them. Your signature was most appropriate.

Whenever you get an "effect" like the one described in your letter there's got to be a "cause." Thanks for writing.

Reprinted by permission: Ann Landers, Field Newspaper Syndicate

Did you ever attend a school where the consequence of knowing your subject or of showing your intelligence was ridicule from other students? Where the "in" thing was not to do homework and not to make good grades? Where diligent students were dismissed as "nerds," "eggheads," and "brains," or worse? (By the way, so far as we know, *all* the terms used by students to describe their diligent colleagues are disparaging or insulting.)

Or consider the eight-year-old girl who avoided playing with kids her age, preferring to hang around with adults. Why? Because to the adults she was intelligent, smart, creative, and well-behaved. She felt accepted. What happened when she played with kids her own age (the desired performance)? She was made fun of because of her haircut, her weight, her eyeglasses, her failure at sports, and because she excelled at her school work. Upside-down consequences are everywhere.

You hear teachers and administrators complain of students who don't do their homework. "They oughta wanna do their homework. If they don't, they will be doomed to a lifetime of mediocrity." And then, because teachers and administrators fail to look at the problem from the students' viewpoint, they make new policies that only aggravate the situation.

This can be doubly punishing for the students. They perceive homework first as an onerous duty that replaces more pleasant activities. If, despite this, they do the homework, the lumps they take from their peers may outweigh more positive outcomes, such as good grades and teacher approval. So next time, they don't do their homework. So the school invents new punitive policies, and more threat of failure is laid on. Now the students perceive yet another reason to beat the system. (One can't help thinking of two gladiators beating each other to death with bloodied clubs, each telling the other he oughta wanna be the first to stop.)

The situation is even worse when homework is used as the actual instrument of punishment. It goes like this: "All right! Just for *that* you can do *fifty* math problems for homework rather than the ten I was *going* to assign!" When you punish others that way, you may leave them hating the very thing you want them to "learn to love."

A more effective way to break the miserable chain of events would be to make the consequence of studying more immediately favorable than it currently is, so that those who study successfully will have reason to be envied rather than ridiculed. Rather than complain that students "oughta wanna" study *for their own good,* make desired privileges dependent upon the performance wanted.

More Actual Cases

The following cases demonstrate additional ways that desired performance can be punishing.

The Case of the Dental Dance

Several years ago the clinical faculty of a dental school complained that students were putting in too little laboratory time on dentures they were making for their patients. The situation was this. Students treated their patients in the clinic. When adjustments were needed in the fitting of dentures, the student would go to the laboratory to make adjustments and then return to the patient in the clinic to try again. The complaint of the faculty was that the students were not as painstaking as they should have been and as they knew how to be in getting dentures to fit. "We've got to teach them to be less careless," was the cry. "We've got to teach them to have the right attitude." (What would they put in such a curriculum—molar appreciation?)

When the question, "What is the consequence of performing correctly?" was finally asked, the nature of the problem became obvious. The laboratory was one floor up and at the other end of the building from the clinic. Obviously, it was less punishing to cut a few corners than to run up and down every few minutes. When the lab was finally moved next to the clinic, the quality of the dentures improved miraculously—without any added instruction or exhortation—and the faculty ceased to complain about students' attitudes toward dentures.

The Case of the Call-Button Caper

The hospital provides another example of how it is possible to design *against* the results one wants. Patients who cannot get out of bed have a call button with which to summon help. Mostly, the system works quite well. Occasionally, however, a patient will resist pressing the call button for long periods of time even though in great distress.

Why would a patient not press the call button when he or she is in need? What consequence of pressing might cause the patient to suffer? Is it possible that button-pushing can be punishing?

You bet it can! It can be embarrassing, even upsetting. Occasionally, pushing the button summons a grouch who bursts into the room with a "What now?" or a "Not *you* again?" After only a few such experiences, the weakened patient finds it easier to tolerate distress than to press the "Help" button.

A Case of Unsafe Safety

Industry, too, has its situations in which desired performance is punishing. For example, the flouting of safety regulations despite "safety training" is a familiar problem. Though people know how to recognize and report a safety hazard, often they don't. Why not? It may not be safe.

In some places, reporting safety hazards is looked on as "rocking the boat." (It usually implies that someone has been sloppy or irresponsible.) In others, it's considered "chicken" to use protective goggles or a saw guard. Regardless of the reason, the consequence of hazard reporting is punishment. The person reporting may be looked down on or insulted by peers and may have to bear the brunt of insults. Sometimes, the "rules" of the department may even be "explained" with a fist. It's not unheard of for someone to be fired for calling attention to hazards—after being accused of "whistleblowing," of course!

When a problem arises because performance is punishing, plainly the answer is not the usual "Train 'em." Desirable consequences have to follow desirable performance. Better solutions have included recognition, even bonuses, to individuals and departments with good safety records.

A Case of Meeting Madness

For another common, if less important, example, take meeting-attending behavior. Time is wasted waiting for latecomers. But late-coming persists no matter how often instructions are given or exhortations are delivered. Plainly, this isn't a miniature training problem. To get at the true problem, you have to ask: "What's the consequence of performing as desired?"

What happens if you arrive *on time?* Well, you have to sit around and wait for latecomers. That can be punishing, especially if you have work to do.

What's the result of being *late?* The meeting starts almost as soon as you arrive.

Thus, punctuality is punished and tardiness is rewarded, precisely the opposite of what is intended. The solution is to reverse the "polarity" of the consequences; make it rewarding to be on time, and punishing to be late. How? Here are some suggestions:

- Start the meeting on time.
- Make something pleasant happen at the start of the meeting.
- Present information at the start of the meeting that the late-comers will miss.
- Hand out the plum assignments at the start of the meeting.
- Save less attractive assignments for the latecomers.

The Case of the Reluctant Loaners

Another interesting problem of this sort arose when a bank decided, "We've got to teach our branch managers to be a little less conservative about making loans." The remainder of the conversation with management went like this:

"Do these managers know how to be riskier about making loans?"

"Yes. They merely have to accept those loan applications closest to the top of the reject pile."

"Do they know you want them to be less conservative?"

"Oh, yes. We have been sending them corporate memos for the past six months, but it doesn't seem to do much good."

"What happens to managers who take a conservative stance?"

"All their loans are paid back and they are looked at favorably by their superiors."

"What happens if they take the riskier stance, as desired?"

"Well, if some of their loans default, their superiors rate their performances down."

The Case of the Reluctant Tellers

Another example of the double-bind of upside-down consequences, again from the world of banking: Tellers were urged to sell the bank's extra services, such as special accounts and rentals of safe-deposit boxes. At the same time, the tellers were expected to keep the lines of waiting customers short. Since service-selling takes time, it tends to keep the lines longer. As long lines are more visible and their consequences more immediate than the selling or non-selling of services, service-selling tends to get the short end of the pickle.

Or consider this common situation:

>*Mgr:*   That's right, boss. It wasn't easy, but I managed to get my division in $50,000 under budget this year.

>*Boss:*   (Beaming.) That's great! Now I can reduce your budget by that amount for next year.

Notice what's happening here. Two different people are reading the same event in different ways. For bosses, coming in under budget is rewarding. For managers, a cut in next year's budget may be perceived as anything but rewarding. Bosses who want to encourage getting under budget need to pump some sunshine toward their managers, not kick them in the financial butt.

Perception is important here. Whenever people aren't doing what they should be doing, look for consequences that the *performer* sees as punishing. Eliminating or diminishing the sources of that punishment will make it more likely that people will perform as desired.

Summing Up

When faced with a performance discrepancy, suspect that, no matter what else may be contributing to the problem, desired performance is being punished.

Upside-down consequences, beating people down when they should be built up, are common. When you find such negative (aversive) effects, eliminate them or reduce their effect and do all you can to create or strengthen positive or desired consequences. And be sure that those new consequences are considered favorable by the performers.

As we said, people learn to avoid the things they are hit with.

What to Do

Determine whether desired performance leads to unfavorable consequences.

How to Do It

Ask these questions:

- What is the consequence of performing as desired?

- Is it punishing to perform as expected?

- Does the person perceive desired performance as being geared to penalties?

- Would the person's world become dimmer by doing it the expected way?

5

Is Undesired Performance Rewarding?

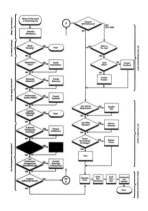

WHERE WE ARE

We are dealing with a discrepancy needing elimination, and we want to know whether the "wrong" or undesired performance accidentally leads to one or more forms of reward.

In the last chapter, we examined the fact that sometimes people don't do what they're expected to do because doing it the expected way leads to unpleasant results.

There is another side to this issue. Performance may not be as expected because some other way of performing is actually *rewarding*. That is, whether or not desired performance has favorable consequences, they are not as favorable as those of an *other*-than-desired performance. Thus, another place to look for causes of undesired performance is in the consequences of that undesired performance. In other words, find out what happens *to them* when they don't do it the way they're expected to do it.

Actual Cases

Here are some examples of situations in which undesirable performance was rewarding—where doing it "wrong" led to more favorable consequences than doing it "right."

A Case of Preventive Maintenance

An office equipment manufacturer maintains a large staff of people whose task it is to repair customers' equipment when it goes belly-up. Their work is usually satisfactory, but at one point, management noticed what was said to be a performance discrepancy.

"They just aren't doing their pm's," they said. A "pm" is a preventive-maintenance routine involving dusting, adjusting, oiling, and replacement of suspiciously worn parts.

"We've sent them several memos, but they just don't do a pm when they should—which is every time they service a machine," said management.

It was puzzling, especially since "doing a pm" was good for the machine, good for company image, and thus good for sales, and even good for the maintenance people. (pm's helped avoid the embarrassment of repeat calls.) The source of the problem was revealed when questions were asked about consequences.

"What happens if they *don't* do their pm's?" Well, the machine works just as well as it would otherwise, for the moment, and the service call takes less time.

"What happens if they *do* the pm as desired?" Well, then the service call takes a little longer. And though top management wanted the pm's done, the service managers were evaluating performance mainly by counting the number of minutes spent on a service call. So to do the pm's (the desired performance) was to risk losing out on pay raises and promotions.

Remedy? Find one or more ways to make undesired performance (NOT doing pm's) less rewarding than doing them. This was done by describing the accomplishments expected of the technicians and then rewarding them for the quality of the service calls. This meant, among other things, rewarding them more highly for service calls that didn't require callbacks (repeat visits to correct earlier mistakes or things overlooked) rather than for the time taken to complete the call.

A Case of "I Don't Make the Rules"

Examples of people performing in ways that are other than desirable are not hard to find. There's the maternity ward receptionist who makes you fill out a dozen documents when it's obvious that the arrival of your child is imminent, and there's the emergency room receptionist who makes you provide documentation proving that you're rich enough to pay, even though it's obvious that you are bleeding to death or that your nose is about to fall off. Then there's the petty bureaucrat who counters all of your attempts to get something done with a regulation that says you can't, but who never offers a hint of the right course to follow.

If you take the view that these people are supposed to facilitate rather than obstruct, you have to conclude that they are performing in an undesirable manner. Obstructive behavior must be more rewarding than facilitating behavior, probably because of the "attention" they get from their frustrated petitioners for the former, even though the formal rewards of the job (pay, promotions) are apparently tied to the latter.

Push back at one of these functionaries and you will quickly be told, "I'm just doing my job. I don't make the rules."

Some of these misguided souls, finding no other satisfaction in their work, get satisfaction (attention?) from exerting petty tyranny over others. Others may be speaking the literal but partial truth when they say, "I'm just doing my job." They should add for the sake of accuracy," . . . in a way that I perceive that my superiors want it done." Their perceptions may be far from accurate.

In all cases, something positive can be done. For petty tyrants, one has to find a way to make their world brighter when they perform in the desired way. (And since this may be hard to do, one may have to fall back on the last-but-not-least alternative: Change the job or change the person.) For those who have an inaccurate picture of what their superiors want, there's plainly a need to spell out the true intent—ensuring that they know what is to be done and can recognize when it has been done properly.

A Case of Keeping Subordinates Uninformed

Here's a similar example: "We've got to teach Mary to train her staff." (It's the production manager of a manufacturing company speaking about one of the "leads.") "Training is her responsibility."

The lead knew what her people needed to know, all right, but didn't tell them, so production suffered.

Why didn't she do what needed to be done? What did she get out of keeping her staff ignorant?

Status! Anyone who wanted to know what was going on had to talk to her. The lead saw herself as the queen bee. Keeping subordinates uninformed, she thought she would keep things that way. It was more rewarding not to perform as expected.

Solution? Not training. Make it *matter* to perform as desired.

The Case of All Is Not Gold

In one of the large gold mines of Africa, the management once decided that they had a training problem involving African underground workers who operated the drilling rigs on the mine face. "We've got to teach these men to wear their earplugs," they said. The discussion with one of the managers went something like this:

"What happens if these men don't wear their earplugs?"

"Why, they go stone deaf from the unbelievable noise."

"Do they know that they're expected to wear earplugs?"

"Of course they do."

"Do they know *how* to wear their earplugs?"

"Of course. All they have to do is stick them into their ears."

"Do they have the plugs handy?"

"Yes. They carry them in their pockets. In fact, they are checked when they enter the mine to make sure they *do* have their earplugs with them."

"I see. So they know how to wear the plugs, and the plugs are always available?"

"That's right. But they don't wear them, and they really should."

"Why?"

"Why, to keep from going deaf, of course."

"Do you have any idea why they *don't* wear their earplugs?"

"You know why they don't wear their earplugs? They don't wear their earplugs because this is the highest job an African can have in this mine . . . and he wears his deafness like a *status symbol*."

Well, that put a new light on the problem. Then it was seen for what it was, a problem where performing as desired wasn't nearly as rewarding as performing otherwise. Loss of hearing was more desirable than loss of status. Notice again that all the training in the world is not likely to get those earplugs worn.

And before you conclude that this example is cultural, think about all the people who would rather suffer pain or disfigurement for similar status reasons: women of the world who suffer pain from shoes that are too tight, the millions who risk disease and early death rather than quit smoking, athletes who continue playing with painful injuries rather than sit on the sidelines. And what about those who endure pain or ill health because they believe they are avoiding even greater pain— those who endure a painful toothache rather than go to a dentist, or chance getting measles or mumps rather than tolerate the needle in a simple inoculation?

No doubt you can think of several possible solutions if the problem is posed this way: How can we make "being a driller" more visible to the outside world than deafness? Give them a special uniform? Stripes on their sleeves, or gold braid on a cap? Some symbol, like the physician's stethoscope, to hang around their necks?

Not as Rare as You Might Think

Situations like this aren't as rare as you might think. Though you may think it "unbelievable" that people would rather go deaf than wear earplugs, you can find similar examples if you just look around you.

The Case of Old Leatherlung

In working with a group of firefighters on performance analysis issues, we learned of this little gem:

"They're supposed to wear their breathing apparatus when they go into a hot fire, but often they don't."

"What happens if they wear it, as they're supposed to?"

"Well, they complain that it's heavy, hard to see through the eyepieces, and clumsy to work with."

"And what happens if they don't wear the breathing apparatus?"

"If they don't wear it they have more mobility and can see better. And if they don't wear it, and live, they get to be known as 'old leatherlung', and that's real hero stuff."

Clearly that was a case where undesirable performance (not wearing the apparatus) was more rewarding than performing as desired. Keep in mind that people respond to consequences whether they are aware of them or not. In other words, in most instances people don't *deliberately* non-perform. They simply do it because their world is more comfortable or pleasant that way than it is if they do it the way someone else says is the desired way.

It's a fact that there's a whole world out there just filled with people who are not doing as you would like. Not all are acting against your wishes because they don't know any better or because they don't know how to do differently. Most behave the way they do because they feel that *their* way leads to more favorable consequences for them than does *your* way. If you want them to do differently, you will have to invent an approach where doing it right feels better than doing it their way.

This is an appropriate point to note that problems of this kind do not always fall so neatly into categories (desired performance punished; undesirable performance rewarded) as do our examples. Typically, problems have elements of more than one of the categories we have discussed, or they can move from one category to another.

In this chapter we have looked at cases where the consequences of *un*desired performance were more favorable than those that followed desired performance. Now consider this case.

The Case of "Ol' Boney"

"Our department has a dozen truck drivers. They're all safe drivers, except one, and he costs about two thousand dollars per year in property damage and ill will. We never know when he's going to hit somebody. And he's also erratic in his private driving, as his record shows. He's run over a gas pump, run over a customer's wet concrete, and so on."

"Is it a skill deficiency, do you think?"

"No, because most months his driving is perfect."

"Hmm. What happens when he does have an accident?"

"Then he gets a lot of attention from his cronies. They gather around him and ask him to recount the episode while they chuckle. 'Ol' Boney's done it again,' they'll say, and he gets to tell it again."

"By the way, what happens to your good drivers?"

"What do you mean?"

"What is the consequence of having a good driving record?"

"We don't do anything special for good drivers; that's what we expect of them."

"Oh."

Even our educational establishment is loaded with examples of conditions or consequences that make someone's world brighter for *not* performing as you wish.

Water the What?

Let's begin with an analogy. Suppose that while walking in the park you come upon a man standing in front of two plants and muttering to himself. He is using a watering can to water one of the plants. You ask him what he is doing.

"I'm trying to make *that* one grow," he replies, and points to the *other* one.

"Well," you might ask, puzzled, "if you want *that* one to grow, why are you watering *this* one?"

"Because the other one oughta wanna grow anyhow! It's the plantlike thing to do."

Wacky? Of course. Yet this is very much like the way our school system is operated.

The chief goal of a school is alleged to be to help students' capabilities grow—to change their state of knowledge, skill, and understanding. Thus, the measure of success is the degree to which the students' capabilities are increased. Since student performance is what is desired, one would think that the rewards of the system (money, raises, position, status) would be strongly tied to teaching excellence. Yet this appears not to be the case. Look at the salary schedule of nearly every school and you will find that the rewards (favorable consequences) of the system have little direct relationship to effective teaching. Raises and promotions are based almost exclusively on the number of months served and the number of academic credit hours earned. There is as yet little or no attempt to tie these rewards for the teacher to the quantity and quality of student performance.

In these circumstances, to say that teachers oughta wanna teach more effectively is to behave like the nut with the watering can—it is demanding one kind of performance while rewarding another. (To improve the situation, of course, would require examining the forces that are opposed to judging teachers on the basis of their ability to teach.)

The situation is even more bizarre at the university level. Here, professors get promotions and raises not on how well they succeed with students, but on the basis of how much they publish, how many government grants they are able to garner, and the number of committees on which they serve. Again, they are exhorted to do one thing while being rewarded for another.

Since people tend to do those things that brighten their world, the moral is:

Water the performance you want to grow.

Think for a moment about the expression "resistance to change." It's a judgment often made about people who don't perform as desired. But the expression is misleading, because it puts a derogatory emphasis where it doesn't belong. When people oppose the introduction of some new idea or thing, there usually isn't an *active* resistance in force. Often, people cling to the old because there is *no real reason,* no favorable consequence to *them,* for doing it the new way. It is more comfortable, more pleasant, more rewarding to stay with the old. So here again, simply plying people with information about the new thing or exhorting them that they oughta wanna be in favor of newness may not change much. The desired performance (the new thing) will be more readily adopted (and made to work during any "teething troubles") if it is plain to the doer how it will make his or her world brighter.

In much the same way, the teacher passes the blame for his or her own failure to be interesting by complaining about students' "short attention spans." It would be much better if he or she approached the problem by asking, "What's the consequence to the student who *does* pay attention?" If the honest answer is "boredom," then there isn't much doubt where the remedy lies.

One more type of situation. Let's call it the "don't-let's-stick-our-necks-out-more-than-we-have-to" category. It's found at many levels in the working world and in private life, and can be found under at least two subheadings—the mental version and the physical version.

A typical instance of the first is found in people who apparently "don't like to take responsibility." These are often people who have discovered that when they make a wrong decision, they get it in the neck. And if they get it in the neck often enough and hard enough, they're going to conclude that one way of shutting off aversive consequences is to make *fewer* of these decisions. Eventually, they establish an equilibrium, making as few decisions as it is possible to make without getting genuine complaints that they're loafing.

You can think of your own examples of students who try but get poor grades, and children who seem reluctant to do chores.

That's the mental aspect of the problem. The physical aspect is similar. Some activities are physically exacting; the more a person does, the more tired he or she gets. When getting excessively tired leads to no positive consequence, the doer finds a point of equilibrium.

When someone is exhibiting these symptoms, mental or physical, people may say, "He's a good man, but. . . ." Or, leaping sprightly to conclusions, they judge: "She's not ambitious." "He doesn't care." "She procrastinates." Or worst of all, "He's lazy."

The people judged may not like to act this way. But, as they see the world, the less they do, the less they have to answer for or the less they suffer. The consequence—or, more accurately in most cases, the sum of the consequences—for doing more is not worth the effort.

Maybe they don't have the mental or physical stuff to perform as you would like. But if you're the one in charge of the consequences that come to them as a result of action or non-action, maybe you should take a close look at those consequences to make sure they are worthy of the effort you are expecting.

Summing Up

The cause of the performance discrepancy may be the favorable consequences that follow undesired performance. If the analysis reveals that poor performance is being rewarded, the incentives for performing poorly must be removed.

What to Do

Determine whether undesired performance or other performance leads to more favorable consequences than desired performance does.

How to Do It

Ask these questions:

- What is the result of doing it the present way instead of my way?

- What does the person get out of the present performance in the way of reward, prestige, status, comfort?

- Does the person get more attention for undesirable rather than for desirable performance (for misbehaving than for behaving)?

- What event in the world supports (rewards) the present way of doing things? (Are irrelevant behaviors inadvertently rewarded while crucial behaviors are overlooked?)

- Is this person "mentally inadequate," doing less so that there is less to worry about?

- Is this person "physically inadequate," doing less because it is less tiring or less painful?

6

Are There Any
Consequences at All?

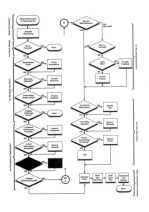

WHERE WE ARE

*We are analyzing a performance
discrepancy worth doing something
about, and want to know whether
appropriate consequences
are in place.*

Sometimes a performance discrepancy continues to exist, not because the consequences of performing are upside-down, but because it simply makes no difference whether people perform or not. There are no meaningful consequences to *them* if they take the trouble to perform, and no consequences to them if they don't.

The laws of nature tell us that unless a performance is followed at least periodically by an event considered favorable by the performer, that performance tends to disappear. Saying it another way, if there is no consequence to make something worth doing, it will tend not to get done.

An important point (because few people seem to grasp it): Wagging your forefinger at someone and telling him or her, "You oughta wanna," does *not* qualify as a universal incentive to action.

A common instance of a performance that dwindles in the absence of a consequence comes from the chore known as paperwork. Managers complain, "Reports just don't get in on time," or "Those reports are haphazardly done." In such instances, the conversation often tends to go like this:

"The reports are sloppily done?"

"They certainly are. And they don't come in on time."

"Why not, do you suppose?"

"Staff members just don't seem to care!"

"What happens if the reports are late?"

"Well, then I have to explain to my superiors why I am late with *my* reports."

"No, no. What happens *to the people who submit the reports?*"

"Well, nothing, I guess. But they oughta wanna get them in on time."

"What happens if the reports are sloppily done?"

"Disaster! My poor secretary works like mad trying to get them cleaned up in time to attach to my own report."

"Yes, of course. But what happens to the people who send in the sloppy work?"

"Well, nothing, I guess."

"You don't phone them or drop them a memo to tell them they have not met expected standards?"

"No."

"You don't send the reports back for *them* to correct?"

"Heavens, no. There's never *time.*"

"So it doesn't really matter *to the staff members* whether their reports are well done and on time?"

"No, I guess not. But they oughta wanna do them right."

Let's not get caught up in a debate about the importance of paperwork. The point is that you're less likely to see desired performance when that performance does not "matter" to the performer—that is, when the performance does not lead to consequences considered favorable by the performer.

Actual Cases

The following cases demonstrate discrepancies when there are no consequences for either good or bad performance.

The Case of the Bopping Sticks

Police departments seem to be as good a source of "no-consequence" examples as business and industry. In one department, patrol teams were required to take their batons (bopping sticks) with them whenever they got out of the patrol car. Apparently this wasn't happening all the time, and so the captain asked the trainer to add something to the instruction that would "teach patrol officers to have the right attitude" about baton handling.

The officers, however, already *knew* they were to take their batons with them. So why didn't they do it? Well, a baton is a stiff, hard item that can cause pain if not removed from the belt ring before entering a patrol car (or any other car, for that matter). As a result, there is a tendency to remove the baton from the belt ring and place it on the seat. On leaving a car, officers may have to take their hats, a clipboard, or perhaps a shotgun, and once in a while there is a tendency to forget the batons.

But consider the consequences to the officers. If they took their batons with them (the desired performance), what happened to them? Nothing much. They had them when they needed them, but that was seldom. What happened if they left them in the car most of the time? Nothing much. Besides, if the radio call described a situation that sounded like a potential head-thumper, they didn't forget to take them along. So there were no consequences for the desired performance either way.

The solution? Well, if it is truly important that batons be in their rings whenever police officers step out of a patrol car, management can inform officers of the expectation and then provide a variety of demerits (that would be recorded on personnel records) for instances in which they are observed to be "out of uniform." Can you think of other possible remedies?

––––––––––

A Clean Case of Dirty Cars

In yet another department, drivers were expected to keep their own patrol cars clean. Because of the "hassle," though, they weren't too diligent about that chore, and management would periodically complain and tack memos onto the bulletin board. When the performance expectation was looked at in terms of consequences, though, favorable responses were again lacking. If drivers went to the trouble of keeping the cars clean, nobody said anything. If the drivers didn't, management nagged. As most people learn to tune out nagging, it hardly qualifies as a meaningful consequence. Without consequences, why should anyone expect the performance to be different from what it is?

The solution to this "problem" was simple. The police department contracted with a local car wash to clean patrol cars whenever they appeared. Drivers were told to run through the car wash whenever they had a little spare time. As that was easy to do, the problem was solved.

––––––––––

The Case of Taking Orders—or Not

In this next example, a manager is discussing the people who work at the serving window of a fast-food chain.

> "When taking orders, these window people are supposed to ask whether the customer wants any of the various extras. But most of the time they forget."

> "What's the result?"

"The result is that our sales are less than they might be, and customers aren't reminded about items they may really want."

"Yes, but what's the result to the *window people*? What happens to *them* if they forget to tout the extras?"

"Well, we can't afford to stand over their shoulders and tell them every time they forget."

"Does anything *ever* happen to them when they don't do as you want?"

"No, I guess not."

No consequence for doing it right, and none for doing it wrong—and thus, no real urgency for behaving differently. Solution? List all the possible ways of making the order-takers' world a little brighter when performing as desired. Then select one or more that are practical and less expensive than the problem and that would also be seen as favorable by the recipients of the consequence(s).

The Case of You Really Oughta Wanna Sit Down Front

And here's a common "problem" solved by ingenuity. A professor kept urging his students to "sit down front" when attending lectures in the tiered classroom, but students continued to sit in the back. "If you sit in the front," the professor would tell the students, "I won't have to talk so loudly." But still they sat in the back.

Someone finally hit on an idea—it was adopted and the problem was solved. The solution? The first five rows of seats were upholstered; the remaining rows were left with hardwood seats. After that, almost everyone tried to get to class early so they could sit down front.

The Case of Nothing Like Attention and a Kind Word

Here's another success story, engineered by a Midwestern florist who noticed that many hospital nurses frequently went without recognition of any kind for their efforts, whether perceived as helpful or not. Whenever he sent flowers to a hospital patient, he always enclosed a single, separate carnation with a card saying, "For your favorite nurse."

Nurses who received them (including the men) pinned them on their uniforms, and in the cafeteria there was always conversation about "Whose favorite nurse are you?"

As one of the nurses explained, "Usually, the only way for a patient to express gratitude is with a 'Thank you' at the end of a stay. This way, everybody was a winner. Nurses got recognition. The patient was still around to receive more of the TLC. And it didn't hurt the florist's business, either."

The Case of Pick It Up!

Meanwhile, nearer home, you have undoubtedly heard your neighbor complain that her daughter simply will not pick up after herself, no matter how often she is told. If you were to listen to a conversation between this parent and someone skilled in the use of our checklist, you might hear:

"She doesn't pick up after herself, even though you've made it clear you expect her to?"

"I've told her and I've told her, but it doesn't do any good."

"And she knows where to put the clothes?"

"Of *course* she does. She isn't stupid, you know."

"Sorry. Ah, tell me—what is the result of her not picking up after herself?"

"The result? The result is that I spend half *my* time picking up after her. *That's* the result!"

"I understand. But what's the result to *her*?"

"I nag."

"And how about if she does pick up?"

"What do you mean?"

"Does something favorable happen if she picks up after herself for a certain period of time—like an extra movie, or a round of applause from the family, or a favorite meal, or something else she might like to have?"

"Certainly *not!* You don't think I'm going to *bribe* her to do something she oughta wanna do anyhow, do you?"

NOTE: *Bribe* is a loaded word, implying something illegal or designed to make someone do something against his or her will. But bribery is a *legal* concept, pure and simple. Bribery means to offer inducement to someone to do something illegal—fix a parking ticket, throw a race, award a contract, etc. What we're talking about is a *positive consequence* that, if you like loaded words, could as well be called a *reward.* By providing a positive consequence, you increase the probability that behavior will occur. Even when you do something you don't like to do (when, say, you submit to surgery), you do it because you expect that life will be improved as a result. But you don't look on "getting better as a result of surgery" as a bribe. When a mother says to her child, "If you pick up your clothes for a week, I'll take you to a movie," it is not bribery. It is the offer of an incentive (a consequence desired by the child) in return for performance desired by the mother. If it were *illegal* to pay people to pick up their clothing, *then* you could rightfully call it bribery. But only then.

In this case, the performance discrepancy is that the youngster doesn't pick up her clothes in the desired manner with the desired regularity. She knows how to do it, but doesn't. Thus, the discrepancy is not likely to be eliminated by training or instruction. Her world doesn't get brighter if she does as expected; and, since she's so used to being nagged that she doesn't even hear it, her world doesn't get dimmer if she doesn't. In effect, nothing meaningful happens one way or the other. In the absence of a consequence meaningful to her for performing as desired, she tends not to perform.

Again, it is easy to say that she should pick up after herself because it is the adult thing, the right thing, the moral thing, the mother-saving thing, etc. And some day, probably, she *will* pick up after herself, because it will matter to her self-concept or her convenience or her marriage to do so. But right now there are none of these *internal* consequences. If the mother expects her daughter to perform, then she must see to it that the child's performance is followed by an *external* consequence that has value for the child.

A Case of How Smooth Is It?

Another interesting example is found in the inspection department of a manufacturing company where one of the duties is to inspect incoming materials. The features to be evaluated include the smoothness of various metal surfaces. The inspector checks to see if the smoothness meets or surpasses specifications. If it does, the material is accepted and sent on to the production department. If not smooth enough, the material is returned to the vendor.

It was noticed that inspectors were rejecting material that was, in fact, smooth enough to be accepted. "We have a training problem," said a manager. "We need to teach these inspectors to be more accurate in their smoothness judgments."

To the question, "What is the consequence of performing as desired?" a double answer appeared. To the inspectors, the result of rejecting a good batch was nothing. The batch went back to the vendor; and the vendor, knowing the game, probably let it sit in the warehouse for a month or so and then resubmitted it. On the other hand, accepting a bad batch brought the wrath of the production department down on an inspector's head. Right now.

So now we have: No noticeable consequence for rejecting a good batch of material (undesirable performance); punishment for accepting a bad batch of material (also undesirable performance). The result was that the inspectors, without even realizing it, gradually rejected more and more good batches in order to avoid the punishment that came with accepting a bad one. This was not a conscious action; it just happened.

Several options might serve for correcting this kind of problem. Management could act to make both undesirable alternatives equally undesirable to the inspectors. Since the inspectors *want* to perform well, one could also make the accuracy of their performance more

© King Features Syndicate, Inc., 1973

immediately visible to them. If inspectors knew they were making a bad decision, they wouldn't make it. In this case, performance feedback would probably do the trick.

Actually, however, a third alternative was selected, mostly because of the awkwardness and time needed in providing immediate feedback during inspection. Since this situation combined both a need for skill maintenance and a no-consequence problem, a little device was constructed with which the inspectors could periodically check their smoothness perceptions. The device provided a number of graded-samples for inspectors to judge, and then told them whether they were right or wrong. They weren't learning anything they didn't already know, but they *were* keeping their skill sharpened. It would also have helped to equalize the consequence for either of the undesired performances (accepting a bad batch or rejecting a good one) or to have increased the consequence of good performance. But to our knowledge this was not arranged.

As mentioned elsewhere, many discrepancies have elements of more than one cause; this was one such example.

Examples of "no-consequence" situations are all around us:

"The manager is not walking the store."

"The manager isn't delegating."

"Employees don't show enough courtesy to customers."

"Meat cutters aren't cutting the meat right."

In every one of these examples (from our files) the answers to the consequence questions were negative. It didn't matter whether a performance was done in the desired manner or in some other manner. Oh, it mattered to *somebody*, all right, or the problem wouldn't have become visible. But even though performance mattered a great deal in some of these cases, the mattering didn't consist of consequences that impinge on the performers themselves. Whenever you hear any of the following:

"They should do it because it's good for the company,"

"Our image will suffer if they don't _____,"

"What will the neighbors think if you don't _____?"

"All hell breaks loose here when you don't _____,"

"It's the patriotic thing to do,"

"It's the professional thing to do,"

"It's the adult thing to do,"

"It's the Christian thing to do,"

"They just don't seem to realize how their actions affect others,"

you are hearing descriptions of situations in which the consequences or results, large though they may be to someone, are probably not having any effect on those at whom the finger is being pointed.

The Case of the Delicious Duplication Caper

During a workshop on performance analysis, two pleasant women recounted an experience they described as "delicious." They began:

"Among other things, we're responsible for duplicating professors' tests by the deadlines set for the examinations. Most of the professors bring in their items in enough time for us to do the duplication without any trouble. Only one was always late."

"What happened when he was late?"

"Oh, then we had to drop everything at the last minute, and we had to be late with some of our other work. It was very exasperating."

"But what was the consequence to the professor?"

"Ahh, but *that's* the *point*. We finally figured out that we were experiencing all the consequences. So the very next time he brought his items in late, we said, 'Sorry, professor, but your items are too late to include in the test,' and went on about our business. Well, you should have seen him! Practically had a tantrum. Ranted and raved, got all flushed in the face. But you know what?"

"No. What?"

"He has *never, ever* been late since!"

Once they understood the problem (no consequences *to the professor* for undesired performance), the solution was clear. Make it matter *to the performers;* arrange consequences.

When hunting for consequences that follow desired and undesired performance, be sure to keep in mind that it is the consequences to the performers that matter rather than the consequences to the boss, the parent, the organization, or the economy. It is the perception of the performers that matters; how they see it is what controls the outcome.

The Case of the Perfectly Puzzled Lecturer

That important point was brought home to us again during a discussion with the chief neurosurgeon of a large hospital. He was describing the time he had decided to offer a series of afternoon lectures to medical aides. He wanted to help them understand the larger picture—*why* they were taking blood pressure, blood samples, and so forth—so that they might feel more a part of the treatment team. A noble mission, and yet . . . Listen to how it turned out:

"About 40 showed up for the first lecture, and every one of them seemed eager for the information. Many of them gathered around me to ask questions when the lecture was over.

"But only about half of them showed up for the second lecture. Again, they all seemed eager and asked lots of questions.

"Only half of *them,* about ten, showed up for the third lecture. As before, they all seemed eager and asked questions. But I couldn't understand why attendance was cut in half each time. So I asked the head nurse what happened to them."

"They quit!" was the reply.

"Quit? But *why?*"

"Well, when they finally realized the importance of what they were doing, they quit to avoid the heavy responsibility."

––––––––––

Here was an instance in which desired performance wasn't perceived as punishing until the aides learned the "why's" of their work. So never mind whether *you* perceive the consequences as rewarding or punishing—what matters is how the performer perceives it.

Finally, how often, when you have guests, do you rush over to where the kids are playing quietly in the corner and say, "Hey, kids, you're doing a *great* job of playing quietly in the corner"? Or do you, like most of us, wait until they start acting up and then rush over to scold?

One can argue that you are, at best, providing no consequence for desired behavior. There may be favorable results for playing quietly in the corner, but *you* aren't the source of them.

A gloomier view of the situation is this: If *attention from parent* is viewed by your child as desirable, what must he or she do to get it? When you ignore episodes of peace and quiet but attend to the uproars, you strengthen the likelihood that you will be confronted by an uproar. Put a bit more bluntly, you are engineering the situation to give you something you say you don't want.

An old expression fits here: It's the squeaky wheel that gets the grease. Might not this be why people feel that to get action they must do something other than behave in a manner resembling "sitting quietly in the corner"?

We're not suggesting, by the way, that you "spoil" your children by refraining from admonition when they misbehave. We are only making the point that when you forget to "glow after good" and only "growl after bad," you run the risk of making the growl a rosier consequence than you intend.

Summing Up

When you're dealing with a situation where performers seem not to be rewarded or punished for doing it right or doing it wrong, look to see whether there are any consequences at all for performing.

If such consequences do exist, check whether these consequences impinge on the performer. If not, arrange one or more consequences that *do*.

When you want someone to perform in some particular manner, the rule is: **Make it matter.**

What to Do

Determine whether there is a meaningful consequence for the desired performance.

How to Do It

Ask these questions:

- Does performing as desired lead to consequences that are felt by the performer?

- Is there a favorable outcome for performing?

- Is there an undesirable outcome for not performing?

- Is there a source of satisfaction for performing?

- Can the person take pride in this performance as an individual or as a member of a group?

- Is there satisfaction of personal needs from performing as desired?

Part IV
Are There Other Causes?

*Could They Do It if They
Really Had To?*

Needless to say, if people already know how to perform as expected, but aren't performing that way, the solutions you've been collecting will probably make the discrepancy go away.

But if they don't know how to do what they're expected to do, then you need to find out whether or not you'll need to turn to what is usually a more expensive solution, that of training. That's what we'll sort out now.

7

Is It a Skill Deficiency?

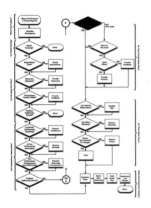

WHERE WE ARE

A performance discrepancy exists, and we have located several possible remedies. The search goes on. We need to know whether the discrepancy exists because of a skill deficiency—because the performers don't know <u>how</u> to do what's expected of them.

Having found clues to the cause(s) of the discrepancy in the most obvious places, it's time to dig a little deeper. So in this step we explore to determine whether the performance discrepancy is due to a *skill deficiency.* In essence, are nonperformers not performing as desired because they *don't know how* to do it? If their lives depended on it, would they *still* not be able to perform?

If a genuine lack of skill is not the problem, then you can forget training as a potential solution. After all, "teaching" people what they already know how to do isn't going to affect the performance discrepancy. When people already know how to do something but don't do it, then the solutions lie elsewhere. On the other hand, when a genuine skill deficiency exists, then something has to be "fixed." You will either need to change an existing skill level by teaching new skills or change what people are required to do. That is, you will either have to teach them what they can't do now, or find ways to simplify or change the size or nature of the task so that it is within their capability.

In actual practice, most of the time it's likely that your problem won't be caused by a genuine lack of skill. Except for performers who are new to their jobs, or the jobs are new to the performers (new processes, procedures, tasks, equipment, etc.), people usually will be able to do what's expected of them and will need little or no training. This is an important discovery that should cause you to rejoice. Training is usually the most costly, time-consuming solution, and it is always exciting to discover that the expensive solution you were asked to provide ("I've got a training problem") can be solved with far less cost and effort. *Convincing* someone that training isn't the answer is another matter.

Examples from Life

The following cases illustrate discrepancies that exist because—or not because—of skill deficiencies.

A Case of Sagging Motivation

The manager of a machine shop complained, "This machinist simply isn't motivated enough to do this job." We asked him what the machinist did that caused him to complain about motivation.

"He just takes forever to get his work done."

"Does he know what's expected of him?"

"Oh, sure. He's got detailed blueprints of every job, and we talk about the deadlines. But that doesn't seem to help. He's still slow."

To make a long story short, it turned out that this machinist was highly skilled, using his tools and machinery to turn out perfect products. And motivation wasn't his problem. He really wanted to do a good job and was rewarded by compliments from his colleagues when he did. So why couldn't he work as fast as expected—as fast as the other machinists? Math. He just wasn't good at translating the mathematical specifications on the blueprints into action. In addition, he had trouble remembering whether .0001 meant one thousandth of an inch or one ten-thousandth of an inch. And this lack of math skill slowed him down. A lot.

The solution was to provide some coaching on decimal numbers, after which he began working nearly as fast as everyone else. What started out as a "motivation" problem ended up as a lack of skill in a small, but critical, part of the job.

The Case of the Candy Caper

The manager of a medium-sized food company announced, "I've got a training problem, and I want you to develop a training program to solve it." We asked him to explain.

> "In our new plant we make only six varieties of our candies; and because we have only six varieties, our sales reps travel around in panel trucks with a supply of each. In a sense, each rep is a traveling warehouse."

> "And the problem?"

> "The reps are pushing only *one* product instead of all six. I want you to teach them to sell all products equally."

> "Do they know they're supposed to sell all six products?"

> "Of course. We've told them many times."

> "Do they know *how* to sell the other five?"

> "Of course. It's no different from the one they are pushing."

"Do they know as much about those other five as they do about the one they're selling well?"

"Certainly they do. We have a good product course, and they have been carefully trained in all of the products."

"So they could sell the others if their lives depended on it?"

"Of course. But they don't."

"Do you have any idea why they don't push those other five products?"

"Well, yes. I suppose it's because they get three times as much commission for the one as they do for the other five. But they ought to want to sell the others *anyhow*."

Aha! What started out to be one of those "I've got a training problem" episodes turned out to be something entirely different. The performance discrepancy was clearly *not* due to a lack of skill. The sales reps *could* sell the products, but they didn't. In this case, training was clearly not the remedy. What would you teach? What would you put into a course? What information could be imparted that the reps didn't already have? True, you could lecture them on the importance of selling the products equally (if they didn't already know that). Or you could explain how their jobs depend on their selling those other five products (if that were really true). But training will not make any difference in their *skill* at doing that which the manager wants them to do. Since they already knew how to do as desired, the answer was not training. It was something else.

A Case of Handwriting on the Walls

A principal complained, "We've got to teach these kids not to write on the toilet walls."

But what would you put into a course on Non-toilet-wall Writing? Can't you just see the curriculum?

Monday: Introduction to Non-Writing

Tuesday: History of Non-writing

Wednesday: Toilet Appreciation

Thursday: Famous Johns and Their Dastardly Defacement

Friday: Pot Power

A Case of It's No Accident

Managers are often heard to say, "If only we could make these people more safety conscious." One interview with a manager went like this:

"Safety is a real problem for you?"

"Yes, it is. Every year we lose two million dollars because of accidents."

"Do you think your employees can recognize a safety hazard when they see one?"

"Oh, sure. Most of them have been around for some time, and they know what's safe and what isn't."

"Do they know how to report a safety hazard?"

"Yes, but they don't. And they oughta wanna do more about safety. It's in their own best interest. We need to teach them to be more safety conscious."

So the manager put safety posters on the walls and insisted that employees watch safety films on a regular basis.

Nothing much happened to the accident rate, as might be expected, for this was another of those cases where people knew how to perform as desired, but didn't. An important performance discrepancy existed, but it was *not due* to a skill deficiency. In such cases the question is not what to teach, but rather how to rearrange things to get the performance that is already available.

Whenever you hear someone say, "They oughta wanna," or some variation thereof (usually accompanied by the waggling of a forefinger), it is almost certain that you are *not* dealing with a skill deficiency. It is almost certain that the people *could* perform as desired if the conditions and the consequences were right.

- The sales reps know how to sell the products, but they don't; they *oughta wanna.*
- Kids *oughta wanna* brush their teeth without being nagged by their parents.
- The legal staff *oughta wanna* settle more cases out of court.

No amount of information, no amount of exhortation, is necessarily going to change an "oughta wanna" situation. What's needed is a change in the conditions or the consequences surrounding the desired performance. "You oughta wanna do it *for your own good*" is not a potent motivator; it is one of the weakest techniques known for influencing anyone to do something he or she already knows how to do.

Loose Language

In thinking about this issue, we wonder if the trouble doesn't spring from the imprecision with which many people so often use our language. They say things like, "I'll *teach* you to sass your mother." But this does not mean that the speaker intends to instruct the sasser in how to sass the sassee. It means that the speaker intends, through the arrangement of conditions and consequences (whap!), to modify the performance of the sasser—to cause that child to do something he or she already knows how to do; namely, to refrain from sassing.

Perhaps this explains the genesis of the expression, "I've got a training problem." It seems that often when a difference is perceived between what someone is doing and what others would like that person to be doing, they conclude that the way to reduce the difference is by training, by instruction. But training is only one of the remedies for a performance discrepancy. In fact, training is only one of the remedies *even when* a genuine skill deficiency exists.

After all, there are different "forms" of skill deficiencies. Sometimes people can't do it today because they have *forgotten* how, and sometimes because they *never knew* how. Solutions for these situations are different. And sometimes people don't do the job because they can't—perhaps they lack the mental capacity or the physical strength. Again, a different solution is called for.

Sometimes you may find it hard to judge whether a skill deficiency is involved, or how much of a deficiency it is. If records don't tell you whether the skill was once present, and you can't tell by watching people as they try to do the thing they are suspected of not doing, then you might try the direct approach. Talk to some of them and ask them whether *they* feel their skill is weak or whether something else is causing the discrepancy.

Summing Up

When you detect an important performance discrepancy, do not automatically assume that it is a "training problem" and that the solution involves teaching/training, even when you are dealing with a skill deficiency. Before taking action, determine whether the performance discrepancy is due to a genuine skill deficiency.

What to Do

Determine whether the discrepancy is due to a genuine skill deficiency.

How to Do It

Ask these questions:

- Could the person do it if really required to do it?
- Could the person do it if his or her life depended on it?
- Are the person's present skills adequate for the desired performance?

If it makes sense, ask the person who's not performing:

- What might you learn how to do that would make your job easier?

8

Could They
Do It in the Past?

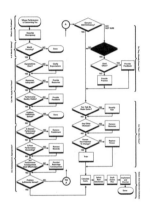

WHERE WE ARE

*A performance discrepancy exists
and is considered important. It has
been established that it is a genuine
skill deficiency. They couldn't do it
if their lives depended on it.*

Shucks," said the elderly gentleman, "I used to know how to do
that pretty good. You just give me a day or two to practice getting the kinks out, and I'll be right in there with the best of 'em."

If he's right, what a waste it would be to start teaching him
the skill from the very beginning. In terms of what has to be
done to get rid of a skill deficiency, there's a great difference
between the skill that *used to be* and the skill that *never was.* Yet
the number of instances in which we make the mistake of trying to teach people something they already know is very large
indeed.

So once you've established that you are dealing with a genuine skill deficiency, the thing to do next is ask: Could they do it in the past? If they could, they should require far less training to get them back up to speed than if they never knew how to perform in the first place.

Determining whether a lack of skill is due to a form of forgetting or to a lack of training is one of the more important decisions in the analysis of performance discrepancies. It's also one of the more neglected decisions.

NOTE: Even when it's plain that a genuine skill deficiency exists and that a person has *never had* the skill, the solution is not necessarily a formal training program. This issue is explored in a coming chapter, but it isn't too early for a cautionary note: *Beware of concluding that a genuine skill deficiency exists.* It's amazing how many courses are given under the assumption that students know nothing whatsoever about the main topic until taught otherwise. All of the students are made to wade through all of the material from the beginning. This can waste a lot of time and may create misconceptions about the effectiveness of a course where the teacher succeeds in "teaching" what the students already knew.

If you have ever gotten involved with children and ended up cricking your back while playing games or bending your ego as you floundered over eighth-grade mathematics, you will agree that time can play havoc with skills that used to exist. It happens in jobs, too. Consider the following example:

The Case of the Reviled Radar Tech

Several years ago, one of us was a member of a team assigned to assess the proficiency of radar technicians who had graduated from a military course designed to teach that occupational specialty. The team traveled to locations around the country to test each technician on his own equipment. While the radar tech waited outside, the team "inserted a trouble" into the radar equipment. The tech was then shown one symptom, much as happens when a radar operator discovers that something isn't working.

One young man tested did an incredibly poor job, even though he had done well during his training that ended some months previously. He hardly knew where things were located, let alone what to do to find the troubles. Here, it seemed, was a performance discrepancy of large proportions. When the results of the test were reported, as was required, his commanding officer exploded.

"Get that man in here," he roared. "I'll teach *him* to make our unit look bad."

Fortunately, he was persuaded to sit still long enough to answer a few questions.

"How long has this man been assigned to your unit?" he was asked.

"About six months."

"What has he been doing during that time?"

"He's been assigned as an oiler."

"How much time has he spent inside the radar van?"

"Well, none. I just told you he's been assigned as an oiler."

"So he hasn't had any practice or experience in radar maintenance since he joined your outfit?"

". . . No, I guess not."

Here, then, was a technician who had spent several months learning a rather complex skill; but for the following six months had had no opportunity to practice that skill. No wonder his test performance was poor. No wonder there was a difference between what he could do and what he was expected to be able to do.

The battery commander also saw the point. Instead of chastising the man, he assigned him immediately to maintenance duty (under the watchful eye of a more experienced man).

———————

This was an instance in which:

- There was a genuine performance discrepancy.
- It was important to remedy.
- It was due to a skill deficiency.
- The skill was once there but had been forgotten.

It was a classic case of a skill withering away for lack of exercise. Other examples are not hard to find.

Some capabilities fade with age. On a physical level, it's unlikely that you can still suck your big toe. But it's conceivable that although you can still throw a ball, you can't throw it as hard and straight as you once did. Can you do the splits, or dash a speedy 100 meters? Or, if we look at mental tasks, how about naming the gods in Vulcan mythology, reciting Hamlet's soliloquy, proving Pythagorean's theorem, diagramming a sentence, using a slide rule? Well, you get the point. Skills you once had fade away unless kept alive by practice. But if they are not completely dead, they may be revived with something much smaller than a formal course.

A Case a Little Closer to Home

Getting a little personal now . . .

RFM: Peter, didn't you used to live in San Francisco?

PP: Yes.

RFM: Then how come you get lost when you drive there?

PP: Come on, now. I don't always get lost. Just most of the time.

RFM: Why?

PP: Well, it all seems so familiar that I don't bother with maps—and then I find I've forgotten some of the streets. I don't get much practice any more. Haven't you ever forgotten anything from lack of practice?

RFM: Not very much. Only most of what I learned in school.

PP: Wastrel!

RFM: Wait a minute! I remember from seventh-grade biology that the esophagus has a pyloric valve on the end of it.

PP: How nice. What else do you remember?

RFM: Ah-h . . . mmm . . . well. . .

PP: Didn't you used to be good at math?

RFM: Not actually good, but I used to know how to solve calculus problems and how to do things like analysis of variance. But I couldn't do them today. Never needed to after I left graduate school.

PP: But you could relearn them, don't you think?

RFM: Sure I could. And in less time than it took the first time around.

PP: Exactly the point. You used to be able to do things you can't do now, but you could relearn them in less time than it took first time around.

In none of these cases would we propose the expensive route of formal courses of instruction. If we want to sustain these once-known skills at an acceptable level, then the need is probably for a "skill maintenance program" of the kind described in the next chapter.

Summing Up

In this chapter we've called your attention to the importance of those questions that help you decide whether a skill deficiency is due to some form of forgetting or to the fact that it never existed. If it never existed, there's a good chance that training will be indicated. But if it once existed and now is lost, strayed, or stolen, training from scratch would be a more expensive remedy than you need. More likely, practice and feedback will be all that is needed.

Whether you answer "yes" or "no" to "Could they do it in the past?" (Did each person once know how to perform as desired?), there's another question to answer before you will know what remedies to suggest or select. We'll consider that question next.

What to Do

Determine whether the skill once existed.

How to Do It

Ask these questions:

- Did the person once know how to perform as desired?

- Has the person forgotten how to do what needs to be done?

9

Is the Skill Used Often?

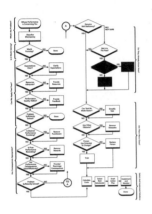

WHERE WE ARE

An important performance discrep-
ancy exists, and it is a genuine skill
deficiency. We have discovered that
at one time the person was able to
perform as desired.

It is not uncommon for people to discover that, even though they once knew how to do something well, they've either lost their "edge" or lost entirely the ability to do what once they did with ease. When a skill fades or disappears, an appropriate remedy to consider is a skill maintenance program. Skill maintenance programs come in two major forms.

Periodic Practice

One kind is meant to help someone "stay in practice." It is a systematic honing of an important skill or state of knowledge that has to be used only occasionally. The police departments of the country recognized long ago that though police officers rarely use their weapons, they must be able to do so quickly and accurately when the need arises. To keep their accuracy at an acceptable level, officers are required to practice regularly on a pistol range—an example of a performance maintenance program.

The concert pianist practices and practices between concerts, not only to increase his or her skill, but to maintain it. Pianists know that the fine edge of an existing skill can deteriorate rather quickly.

Both of these examples are cases in which performance (and peak performance, at that) is required only occasionally or infrequently. In these cases, periodic practice is the useful remedy. The more critical the skill, the more important that this practice be provided.

Practice with Feedback

The second kind of skill maintenance program—practice with feedback—is needed in a different situation. This is the case where:

- A skill deficiency exists.
- The person used to be able to perform the skill well.
- *The skill is in constant use.*

These are situations in which, paradoxically, performance deteriorates *despite* constant practice. And this is a totally different problem from situations where performance withered away because of *lack* of practice.

But isn't it true that "practice makes perfect"?

Unfortunately, that ragged old adage is misleading. Practice makes perfect *only* when you have information about how well you are practicing. In fact, if you have no way of knowing how well you are doing, practice may serve merely to entrench poor or imperfect actions. Your marksmanship will not be improved if you merely shoot at the moon. Your pronunciation of a foreign language will not improve unless you can hear the difference between your way of speaking and a native's way of speaking. Practice without feedback is of little value.

The Case of the Slipping Solderers

In an electronics assembly plant, high precision was demanded of women soldering components together. On joining the company, they were taught to solder, and they were not allowed on the production line until they could consistently make acceptable solder joints. On the job, it was found that the quality of soldered joints tended to fall off after a few weeks, even though the women made hundreds of joints each day. Why?

It was hard to get feedback about the quality of each soldered joint as it was made. You couldn't necessarily tell just by looking. It wasn't practical to make immediate mechanical and electrical tests of each connection. Faulty work in a subassembly may not have been discovered until many joints had been made by many operators. Tracking down the faulty connection and the operator concerned was possible, but costly.

Once again, a performance maintenance program was useful. This time, though, practice was not the primary need, because the soldering task was "practiced" hundreds of times a day. Here it *maintained* skill level by providing the operator with periodic feedback about the quality of her work. All operators were required to renew their certificate of competence every six months. If they checked out, fine; if not, they were given some brief brush-up training. This, it was found, was enough to keep them up to snuff.

The Case of the Diminishing Driver

A friend complained, "That's the *third* traffic ticket I've had in a month. I've been driving for ten years and never had a citation—and all of a sudden they start picking on me!"

Hmmm. Wasn't it more likely that his driving skill had slipped somewhat, even though he got plenty of practice? After all, you don't find out about (get feedback for) every infraction, for every display of poor or dangerous car handling. There is no one there to inform you each time you forget to use a turn signal, or cut another driver short, or make a turn from the wrong lane, or follow another car too closely. When people do get feedback in the form of a traffic citation, they seldom recognize this as an indication of slipshod driving; instead, there is the tendency to point that ever-ready finger— in someone else's direction. (If fingers were as lethal as 45s, we'd all be dead by now.)

The Case of the Perpetual Performers

"But I interview more than a dozen people a day," grumped the manager, "and now you tell me I don't do it right? I get more practice at interviewing than anyone in the plant."

She was right. She interviewed more people than anyone else around. And yet . . . and yet there was something about her performance that rubbed people the wrong way. Here was still another instance in which the performance was less than adequate, even though the skill was exercised frequently.

What was happening? No feedback. She never found out that she was irritating some of her interviewees. The people interviewed certainly wouldn't tell her, and those who heard them grumble only commented among themselves. So why should this manager behave differently when there was no feedback to suggest that the performance was less than satisfactory?

It Happens All the Time

Isn't this something we all experience in everyday living? We spend a lot of time interacting with others, and hence get a lot of practice at it. Yet how often does someone take us aside and offer real honest-to-goodness feedback that would help us do it better? Practically never, right? When was the last time you got feedback on your table manners? Or on our business etiquette? How often do you wonder about whether you said "the wrong thing" because everyone is too polite to tell you?

Summing Up

Any time performance is something other than what is desired, and there is reason to believe that the desired performance could be within the person's capabilities, check to see whether he or she is receiving regular information about the quality of the performance.

If a *frequently* used skill slips, look for lack of feedback as the probable cause. If an *infrequently* used skill slips, look for lack of practice as a probable cause. Perhaps it would help to see the situation graphically.

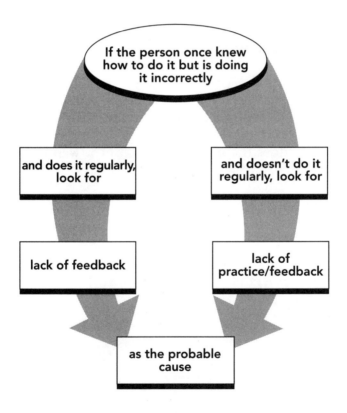

If the person once knew how to do it but is doing it incorrectly

and does it regularly, look for

and doesn't do it regularly, look for

lack of feedback

lack of practice/feedback

as the probable cause

What to Do

Determine whether the lost or deteriorated skill is used frequently or infrequently.

- If the skill is used **frequently** but has deteriorated despite regular use, maintain the level of performance by providing periodic feedback.

- If the skill is used **infrequently**, maintain the level of performance by providing a regular schedule of practice with feedback.

How to Do It

Ask these questions:

- How often is the skill or performance used?

- Is there regular feedback on performance?

- Exactly how does the person find out how well he or she is doing?

10

Can the Task Be Simplified?

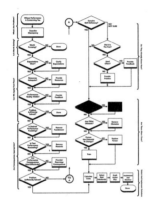

WHERE WE ARE

A genuine performance discrepancy exists, and we have determined that it is a genuine skill deficiency. In the job as currently defined, there is something the person cannot do. Before concluding that formal training is needed, we should give some thought to whether the task itself might be simplified.

W e are still only exploring possibilities. By now, you may have several ideas on how to close the gap between the desired performance and what is now being done. And any of those ideas may be enough to solve all or part of the problem. In forming those ideas, however, we have assumed that the job must be done in its existing form. Nothing wrong with that if our final solution(s) are easy to put in place. But it's always worthwhile—and particularly if the solution calls for significant time and effort—to see if the job itself can be modified so that the person performing will be more likely to succeed. In other words, can we change the skill requirements to more closely fit the current capabilities of the performer(s)?

Changing the Skill Requirement

Changing the requirements of the job is often much simpler and less expensive than almost any other solution. Those who don't have the skill to perform the job as presently defined can become more productive when the job can be changed to fit their capabilities. Four ways of changing the skill requirements include:

1. Changing the criteria of successful performance.

   Do the present standards for the job call for a higher level of perfection than is really needed? If the standards for accuracy, speed, completeness, neatness, and the like were eased off a little, would it really make an unacceptable difference?

2. Helping with mental tasks.

   Instead of requiring someone to memorize lists and sequences, particularly when the information is not used often, could you substitute an "aid to recall"—a list pinned on the wall, a checklist of the sequence of steps to be performed? Could you do away with the need to remember by simply controlling the order in which materials or information arrive? Could you control the flow of work with something like the single-queue, first-come/first-served system widely used in banks and post offices?

3. Helping with physical tasks.

   Could you provide a machine for lifting heavy loads? Redesign a tool that's hard to use? (That's how Phillips head screwdrivers came to be invented.) Is it possible to rearrange the workplace, lessening the distance that has to be reached, or re-orienting a computer screen so that it doesn't put a crick in a neck?

4. Redesigning the job itself.

   Would it be possible to allocate some part of the job to another person? Maybe you could reshuffle duties so that fewer different tasks or different combinations of tasks have to be handled by each person concerned?

Some of this probably sounds obvious, particularly since we used similar thinking back in Chapter 3, "Can We Apply Fast Fixes?" In practice, the need and place for some of these changes may be less obvious—which may explain why these problems have persisted in the first place! Practices in the workplace, be it shop floor, office, or anywhere else, get nailed in place for all sorts of reasons, making it sound as if there's one, and only one, way of doing things. Those reasons include:

- Time-hallowed precedent.
  "That's the way we've always done it."

- Myths about what's accepted in high places.
  "That's what the boss wants."

- Physical or mental elitism which sorts the tough from the softies, the intellectuals from the ignorant.
  "I don't need a back support to lift heavy weights."
  "If you knew chemistry, you'd see why X comes before Y."

Now we're not saying that any of those "reasons" are necessarily wrong. But "the way we've always done it" can survive as part of the corporate mythology even in the face of serious efforts to make a change. "What the boss wants" may have been an off-hand, misunderstood remark, filtered down through the levels until it became a mythical policy statement (e.g., "Policy won't let us put authors' and contributors' names on reports."). The strong-backed elitist may not just be a blow-hard giving bad advice (he lifts his body weight at the gym every evening and has the body to prove it), and the walking fount of knowledge could be right (she does "know the chemistry" and can explain why Y before X is wrong). But making others like that could still be unnecessary. So any time you bump into such a statement, test it out. Simplifying the required performance is usually better than teaching someone to do the more complicated version of the task.

Let's look at some examples under each of the four major headings. As you read, see if you can think of a parallel example from the problems you have to deal with.

Changing the Criteria

No matter how the present standards of competent performance came into being, look at each of them and ask: "Why do we have this standard? Are we demanding more than we need in terms of rate of working, accuracy, finish, completeness, etc.?"

The first, rate of working, is always worth probing. Unacceptable errors can creep into the picture whenever someone must keep on rushing to deliver according to an arbitrary definition of "on time." You know the old question: "Why not get it right the first time, rather than taking time to fix it later?" What does it cost to repair those "Hurry up" mistakes?

Several other questions may help change your viewpoint about the way job and/or task criteria are currently defined.

Change the questions as needed to fit the task you're looking at:

Do we really need to finish this surface to one-ten-thousandth of an inch?

Is it true that the colors or pattern must match precisely?

Does the layout of the letter have to exactly match the style book?

Will it matter if the cherry is off-center on the whipped cream?

Can we accept a few daisies in the lawn or must it be daisy-free?

Do these videotapes really have to conform to network production standards?

A word of warning: It may take both courage and diplomacy to start probing issues of this sort.

Helping with Mental Tasks

Examples abound where "know-how" is needed, but where nobody would think of providing a training course as a solution. That notoriously difficult task of programming a VCR—assuming you don't have a young teenager on hand—should be handled by looking at the instruction book. Bought a new car and unsure of how to work the windshield washer or set the radio buttons? Just read the manual. It's simpler than a course.

Even in a case where "doing it right, no errors" is critical because nasty consequences follow incorrect performance, a similar solution works well. Using a fire extinguisher, for example, requires a small but critical amount of knowledge. Rather than try to store information in everybody's head by presenting a course on fire fighting, you put instructions where they can be seen, right on the side of each extinguisher.

If you need an extinguisher in a hurry but have forgotten how to use it, it takes only a second or two to refresh your memory.

In the best of all possible worlds, every household might have available at all times a person able to render first aid for all conceivable cases of poisoning. Even now, most of us take care of that problem adequately by fastening a list of poison antidotes to the door of the broom closet. (And maybe some do the on-line equivalent by hitting computer keys to summon the information onto their screens.) Whatever the method, storing accurate information where it's readily available may be preferable to trying to remember what to do in the panic of an emergency.

The captain of a jetliner, no matter how grizzled and wise, must use a checklist to ensure that all items are checked during the pre-flight inspection. There's nothing unprofessional about using such an aid; in fact, the unprofessional is the one who tries to get away without using the memory aid.

And imagine the chaos if every person who prepared airline tickets had to remember all the information there is to know about fares, flight times, destinations, flight numbers, days the flights are operative, and a gaggle of other details. Even if such were possible, the problem would be multiplied every time there was a *change* in ticket prices and schedules. With the information stored in a computer instead of stuffed into someone's head, it is easily and accurately available and easy to change.

Prompting works even when it's not as complete as a manual or checklist. In fact, "shorthand" is desirable in some cases: "In an emergency, dial 911." Or even "Emergency 911." Labels on controls help prevent errors by the new or infrequent user.

Snappy rules and acronyms work well, too: Which way to screw the canister onto a gas mask? "Righty-tighty, lefty-loosey." The "rule of the road" when passing the colored buoys which mark the channel as you sail your yacht in and out of harbor is: "Red right returning." And everyone remembers: "i before e, except after c." (That's the rule, as someone noted, that raises spelling to a sceince.)

The Case of the Meter Readers

Consider the case of the meter readers. Women at the end of a production line making electronic products recorded the electrical characteristics of each product so that an accept/reject decision could be made. To do so, they took about six readings from as many meters, and wrote down the numbers on a card.

In an ordinary day, each woman made hundreds of readings; and many of them had had months, even years, of experience. But when their meter-reading accuracy was measured one day, it was found to be only 40 percent! Interestingly, a group of women with no special training in reading meters performed at the same level. But when the analog meters (with pointers showing the readings along one or another scale) were replaced by digital meters that displayed the readings in numbers, performance instantly shot up to near perfect accuracy. The meter-reading task was made considerably easier simply by eliminating the need for careful interpretation of often difficult-to-read scales.

Color Coding

Aids to performance don't have to be in words, even. A useful way of helping people "distinguish one from another," widely used because it lessens the need for remembering, is color-coding. Color-coded pathways on the floor tell forklift operators where to travel and where to store items in a warehouse, or guide patients to hospital departments, or travelers to trains. Color-coding indicates what gas is stored in a cylinder; colored bands tell the value of the resistors used in electrical circuits; at the gas station, color on the pumps tells octane ratings. Colored price tags in clothing stores are often coded to indicate size or to denote sale items.

A note of caution: Color-coding is not always well used. Picture one of us in the control room of an anonymous nuclear power plant. On one side of the room is a twelve-foot shelf filled with large red binders.

Us:	What are those binders for?
Them:	Oh, they're guides for procedures we have to follow.
Us:	Any reason they're colored red?
Them:	Yes, those are emergency procedures.
Us:	Covering all sorts of emergencies?
Them:	Yes. We have to refer to them and "do it by the book" any time we have an emergency.
Us:	Since they all look alike, how do you know which binder to use for a particular emergency?
Them:	Well . . . uh . . . you . . . just know.

Shapes

Using different shapes is another useful aid in sorting "this one" from "that one." The control that puts the wheels down in an aircraft has a round end, the one that works the flaps has a square end. You can tell by feel which handle is which, without distraction from the important task of looking where you're going. On an assembly line, the hole or socket into which a part is fitted has a distinctive shape (square pegs and round holes, remember) so that nothing goes together unless you have the right part, properly aligned. The three prongs on the end of your power cords make it impossible to plug them in upside down.

The Case of the Careless Copier

Take this example we ran into at a large company that makes copying machines. People in the marketing department had noted that an unusually large number of customers were having difficulties with one model of copier.

"They just don't know how to insert the toner bottle." (That's a plastic bottle filled with the black powder that makes the printed image.) "All they have to do is slide it along IN the track, but they slide it ON TOP of the track instead. That creates a mess as the toner spews all over the machine, and the customer calls the maintenance people. It's damned expensive."

As you might expect, the first solution proposed was to train the customers. Analysis showed, however, that the performance discrepancy was a "sort-of" skill deficiency; the operators could sort-of do it if they really had to, but they found it hard to do it correctly without paying a great deal of attention. The solution? Further analysis revealed that the task could be simplified by painting a red stripe on the machine where the toner bottle was to be inserted, and a similar stripe on the bottles themselves. The instruction could then be simply, "Line up the stripes when inserting the bottle." The cost of this proposed solution was about $15,000. Compared to what it might have cost to train customers to perform the task more accurately without the performance aid, it was a good solution, indeed.

Helping with Physical Tasks

This is the "ergonomic" area, making the job easier to handle by changing the environment in some way.

When heavy objects have to be lifted, plainly you need a performance aid such as a crane or forklift. Less obvious is the case where a not-so-heavy object has to be lifted many times, in which effort is exerted over time. In such a case, performance may improve if the height or distance of lifting can be reduced, or conveyor rollers provided. In the office, poor performance on the word processor is often attributed to carpal tunnel syndrome, which, in turn, is often tied to poor positioning of hands and keyboard—a sort of domino effect. Changing something earlier in the chain (the hand position) eases the strain, which eases the damage to the wrist, leading to better typing.

Other ways in which work can be simplified include providing better access to what has to be done. Improving visual or physical access to the task—making it easier to see or get to the things that need doing—and clarifying the information to be used are examples. Plumbers, for example, find it much easier to install food disposers under a sink before all the carpentry work encloses the space. Electricians find it much easier to get to the places where they need to string wire before the open spaces are covered by the wallboard.

Redesigning the Job

The most obvious example is to allocate some part of the job to someone else. If the pace of work is such as to invite mistakes, or if the attention of the performer has to be directed in several directions at the same time, or if doing it right takes three hands, consider splitting off some part of the operation.

If there's great variability in the job, with each variation calling for different skills, maybe you should split the job, making each person a specialist and limiting the range of problems to be dealt with by each. Perhaps part of one performer's job can be swapped for another's?

Finally, performance can often be improved simply by allowing workers to periodically swap jobs—"You do my job for awhile and I'll do yours." Where job swapping is feasible, it helps reduce the boredom of repetitive tasks and increases worker ability to pay attention to key aspects of their work.

Summing Up

Even when a genuine skill deficiency exists, any solution to the problem should be weighed against the possibility of changing some aspect of the job, thereby overcoming the effect of the skill deficiency, at least in part.

Opportunities to incorporate one or more kinds of performance aid (checklists, instruction sheets, signs, labels, color-coding, and the like) can almost always be found.

If training seems to be the only remedy, on-the-job training may be easier and cheaper, and just as good as the formal variety. As one of the sages of the business, Thomas Gilbert, put it, "Show-how is cheaper than know-how."

What to Do

See if you can find a solution simpler than performance maintenance or formal training. Try to reduce the difficulty of the job.

How to Do It

Ask these questions:

- Can I reduce the standards by which performance is judged, particularly the "Hurry Up" demands?

- Can I change the job by providing some kind of performance aid? Can I store the needed information in a more reliable and permanent way (in written instructions, checklists, etc.) than in someone's head?

- Can I provide help with the physical demands of the job, including redesign of the workplace to allow for more efficient work?

- Can I reduce the pressure by parceling off part of this job to someone else? Or arrange for workers to swap jobs for specific periods of time?

11
Any Obstacles Remaining?

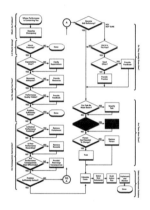

WHERE WE ARE

Before we finish sleuthing for clues and begin deciding on solution(s), we want to know whether we've missed anything. In particular, we want to know whether there may be some remaining obstacles that are a little less obvious than those we discovered in Chapter 3.

In Chapter 3, "Can We Apply Fast Fixes?", we encouraged you to look for three kinds of "sore thumb" problems, namely (1) invisible expectations which left workers in the dark about what was required of them, (2) physical obstacles that made performance unnecessarily difficult, and (3) inadequate feedback that starved people for information by which to improve what they were doing. Then in Chapter 10, "Can the Task Be Simplified?", we suggested that instead of "changing the worker," you should consider whether it might be better to "change the job."

Here the emphasis will be a little different. With likely causes and remedies in mind, you should make one last check to
ensure you haven't been lured off course by any unrecognized
assumptions, biases or myths—or by obstacles that may be
somewhat less visible than those considered in Chapter 3.

First, we'll give you examples of how conflicts, arising from
the job itself or from dealing with people, can confuse the
issues. After that, we'll offer more examples of problems that
can arise when standing too close to a problem.

Conflicting Demands from the Job

Let's begin with this business of conflicts.

The Ever-Ringing Telephone

Have you ever said to yourself, "I could do this job perfectly well if only the !?#$%# telephone would stop ringing so that
I could concentrate for five minutes at a time!"

That's a perfect example of a situation in which a job would
get done more efficiently if the conditions were changed
(without, please note, the need for instruction). It's a typical
problem; the victim is capable of doing what has to be done
and would do an acceptable job if only he or she could get at
it. You can easily identify obstacles of this kind by the direct
approach; ask the performer to tell you what gets in the way of
performing.

We know that in industry it is courting inefficiency, if not
disaster, to organize in a way that gives a person more than one
boss. Inevitably it happens that in trying to please one, he or
she must neglect the interests of others. Though multiple-
bossism is recognized as poor management practice, that
doesn't keep it from happening, as when two or more people
are required to "share" a secretary.

The Non-Teaching Teachers

Consider our schools. Politicians, the public in general, and parents in particular grumble about schools. Teachers, they say, should get in there and teach. Yet all too often teachers find themselves swamped in non-teaching activities—collecting milk money, keeping interminable records, and otherwise burning up time on chores just as well handled at a clerical level. College teachers, expected to use visual materials and computers freely, complain that the materials and help they need are available only from a remote (but oh-so-central) location, hedged about by a flurry of paperwork administered by an office that is not always open when the teacher can go there.

Apply this to your own experience: How often have you been dismayed at the way something takes a lot longer than it should because of paperwork, or the number of approvals required, all apparently justified as "the way it's done here"? Or because some functionary is "responsible for" the equipment and therefore resists tooth and nail letting the intended users use it?

Multiple Agendas

We've referred elsewhere to the problem of "multiple bossism." It's not a new problem—it's right there in the Good Book: "No man can serve two masters." No worker should be put in a position of being told on the one hand, "Do this," and on the other, "Do that." That, plainly, is bad management.

But this obstacle to good performance can be sneaky; the problem can exist even without having two people involved. For instance: Policy says one thing but what's rewarded is another (talking safety but rewarding production is the classic example). It also happens when you have a single individual who says one thing one day and something else the next.

The Case of the Multiple Assignments

Back to schools again. Typically, students have as many "bosses" as they have teachers. Each "boss" demands time and attention from the students, and often each imposes different rules. As a result, three lots of homework all have to be done the same night when they could easily have been spaced out through the week. But the students who fail to deliver all the assignments when due find themselves with unfavorable consequences. They may end up saying, "I hate school." That's not what schools say they are about, and it is an outcome that can be avoided. This is not to say that students don't goof off. But it does indicate that we might get more from students (and who might get more satisfaction from school) if we paid more attention to the conditions under which they are expected to perform.

Even worse than the problems of voices that do not sing in harmony is the problem of the "secret agenda." It takes many forms.

The Case of the Hidden Hatchet

A large company took a look at its course for management trainees. When the course was analyzed for effectiveness, it was noted that some trainees were let go at the end of instruction even though their technical performance was good or adequate. When we asked why, we were told it was because these trainees manifested some personal characteristics considered inappropriate for an executive.

Had these characteristics ever been brought to the attention of the trainees so that they might have a chance to change them? No. Why not? Because it is hard to tell a man that you don't like the color of his ties, or a woman that her blue jeans are offensive. It is easier to tell people that they are not suitable for the job, or to mumble something about performance, and drop the hatchet.

The course now includes a "personality" checklist that the training supervisor must fill out and show the trainees each month. In this way, trainees who exhibit behaviors considered objectionable by management will have an opportunity to change if they so desire.

The Case of the Elusive Evaluation

The faculty of a medical school once complained, "These students of ours will argue for hours over half a point on our *written* exams. Yet it isn't the written exams that are important. We've got to teach them to be less concerned with those darned paper-and-pencil tests." The rest of the conversation went like this:

"Do students really care about their performance on the written tests?"

"Yes. And they shouldn't. It's the *subjective* evaluations the staff makes of the students that are important."

"When is this evaluation made?"

"All day and every day our staff members are noting and evaluating each student's actual performance. We note how he or she performs with patients in the clinic, with other students, and with staff, as well as noting performance in the lab."

"How do you consolidate the results of these subjective evaluations?"

"We compare notes."

"Who does?"

"The staff. We get together and discuss the progress of each student."

"Is the student present?"

"Certainly not!"

"So the results of the *written* exams are *visible* to students, but the results of *subjective* evaluations are *in*visible to them?"

"Yes. But visible or not, it's the subjective evaluations that are really important; and that's what students really ought to be interested in."

You can imagine how difficult it was to refrain from asking point-blank, "If they're *that* important, why keep them such a big secret?"

The Case of the Masticating Menace

We met a man highly competent and creative in his field who, we were told, was avoided by friends and business associates alike. Associates dreaded having to take him along to meet clients if a meal was involved, because he chomped his food with his mouth open—and talked while doing so. He had done it for years, and for years people avoided taking him to business meals. Nobody had the nerve—or the consideration—to tell him about it.

So why should he change? *Would* he change if aware of the hidden agenda?

How many executives have been fired, kicked upstairs, or retired because their superiors had the authority but not the guts to tell them about an offensive but easy-to-correct habit?

How many teachers must there be who return test results to students days, even weeks, after the test was taken (too late for the feedback to serve much purpose), and who then complain that student performance isn't any better than it is—and that the students don't seem to care?

Might your relations with others improve if you could know how they really feel about your present words and actions? Would you be willing to give up using a particular expression, or a gesture, if you knew it was offensive to someone you cared about?

The Case of the Unappreciated Frankness

Closely related to not knowing that you are expected to do something is not knowing *when* you are expected to do it. For example, a physical scientist working in the laboratory of a rather large corporation confided that he had been rated down by his manager because of what the manager referred to as an "undesirable characteristic." The conversation went like this:

"My boss said I didn't know how to keep my mouth shut."

"And can you?"

"Of *course* I can. Discretion is the name of the game in the lab I work in. If I couldn't keep my mouth shut, I'd have been out of a job long ago."

"Then what do you suppose your manager is complaining about?"

"Well, every once in a while he calls me into a meeting and asks me to tell them what I *really* think about something or other. And I do."

"And that's bad?"

"Only sometimes. Occasionally there is someone sitting in the meeting from another division, or even from a customer's company, and I'm not aware of it. *Then* when my manager asks what I really think, he seems to want me to say something to make the company look good rather than to tell him what I really think. Trouble is . . . I can never tell when to do which."

———————

Thus, if a person is unable to tell *when* to perform in a particular way, if the signal isn't recognizable, somebody might conclude that the person doesn't know *how*. Another subtle obstacle to performance.

A Final Check on Assumptions

By now you've seen that the cause of a problem is not always what someone says it is. Assumptions may be made about the origin of a performance discrepancy, and it can sometimes take a lot of probing to learn what's truly happening. Take a look at these examples.

———————

The Case of the Sleepy Workers

The training director of a dynamite factory overseas told of an instance where all the training in the world would have been useless in solving the problem.

He was called by a plant manager. "I've got a training problem," said the manager. "These people are lazy. Many fall asleep on the job, and they don't come to work regularly. I want you to come up here and teach them their jobs. I want you to teach them to be motivated."

The training director was too smart to fall into the trap of taking a statement like that at face value, especially since it began with the usual confusion of problem with solution. Knowing his human relations, he replied, "I'll come and take a look around so that I can see more clearly what needs to be taught." (It doesn't get you very far to tell a client that his or her diagnosis is probably wrong. It works better to agree that there is a problem and then do your analysis out loud, hoping that *the client* will spot the difficulty.)

The training director went to the site, looked around, talked to people, and reviewed employee records. All the while, he was asking himself whether he was dealing with a skill deficiency—and, if not, why the men were not performing as expected.

He found the answer in an unexpected place—the medical office. Better than 60 percent of the employees in question were suffering from a disease that shows up in symptoms of sleeping sickness. *Of course* these men were falling asleep on the job. *Of course* their attendance was spotty.

But there wasn't anything wrong with their skill or with their motivation. They were simply sick. Once cured, all was well. Until those medical records were checked, though, no one even guessed that the obstacle to performing as desired was physiological.

Again, all the training in the world would not have done much good. Had the training director simply done what he was asked, his training program would have failed. Then the plant manager might have said, "Why spend all this money on a training department? We'd be better off without 'em." And what's more, if the training department continually used training as a solution for the wrong problems, he'd be right.

––––––––

Thus, if performance discrepancies appear *not* to be due to a lack of skill or motivation, one thing to look for is the *obstacle.* "I can't do it" isn't always just an alibi; it can be an accurate description of the situation. And if you will look around to see what might be obstructing performance, you will find the solution to at least some of your performance problems.

––––––––

The Case of the Parisian Training Problem

Not all performance problems arise so neatly from a single, major cause, underlining the caution not to leap in and proclaim, "Aha! That's the problem!"

Imagine yourself being called in by the personnel director of a French department store and being asked to solve a training problem. Specifically, you are asked to develop a sales course for clerks. At this point you have no information about *why* the course is needed (you don't know whether there are performance discrepancies, and if so, how large they may be), and so you don't yet know whether instruction is needed. Clearly, more information is needed.

On questioning, the director reveals that he wants sales training because "gross receipts are not what they should be."

Now the amount of money taken in by a store is only partly related to the skill of its salesclerks. Since further questioning fails to elicit information directly related to salesclerks and their abilities, you begin to wonder if the cause of the problem might be elsewhere. You ask to be shown around the store. Within a few minutes, you note several clumps of people gathered around cash registers, trying to give the clerks money to complete transactions. Why was it so difficult to buy something? The amount of paperwork the clerks had to put up with was daunting.

Next, you find that some merchandise was placed on the counters according to manufacturer rather than according to type. Someone wanting to look at transistor radios, for example, might first have to go to the Phillips department (on the main floor) to see what they had and then walk to the Telefunken department (one floor up at the other end of the store) to see what merchandise was available there. (And there were more than twelve departments in the store that sold some form of rubber hose.)

In some ways, this is typical of the situations wrongly labeled "training problems." Basically, what is wrong is that management has rushed to a solution without first looking at other elements of the problem. Here, as in most situations involving those infinitely variable entities called people, there is probably no perfect solution to yield a perfect answer. But there are usually some solutions that are superior to others in terms of return for effort expended.

It's not too much to say that the management of this store singled out the element that was most visible (the salesclerks) and most under its control and made it the scapegoat for an important discrepancy. They then identified a solution that involved changing the salesclerks in some way.

The trouble with premature identification of solutions is that it blocks off exploration of other problem elements. We tend to say to ourselves, "Well, that's that. We've nailed down what we're going to do. Now let's get on with doing it." Because we feel, "We're doing something about it," some of the burden of the problem has been lifted from our shoulders.

It's probably clear, however, that other elements contributed to the store's problem. In studying the procedures, it became plain that the store's merchandising policies almost seemed designed to prevent customers from buying; or, having once bought, to discourage them from coming back again. It was hard to find what one wanted; it was hard to complete a purchase. Once the merchandising procedures were revised and the time to complete a transaction was reduced, sales increased.

The Case of the Frustrated Shopper

Sometimes the obstacle blocking performance is not caused by entangling procedures; rather, desired performance is hampered by a shortage of resources. Let's say that your "job" is to go to the store to buy something. When you get there you find that there isn't anyone to answer questions or help you find what you're looking for. Doesn't this make your shopping "job" harder than need be? Will the frustration cause you to avoid this store next time around? Aren't stores like this shooting themselves in their collective feet with a performance discrepancy based on a misguided attempt at economy?

The world of retail selling has given us many other examples. For instance, way back when, in the days when the first retail computer stores opened, the sales staffs consisted largely of computer programmers. Someone had decided that programmers were the only ones who knew enough about the products to sell them. The result, though, was largely exasperating to the customer. Customers could stand there waving a fistful of money until closing time and never be noticed, because the "sales" staff was busy playing at the terminals. The customers knew how to give clerks money, so there was no skill deficiency involved. They wanted to buy the products, so there wasn't a motivation issue. What there was, though, was a large obstacle preventing the customers from performing (buying) the way they wanted to perform.

Update: If you can't speak the buzzwords of computing—which seem to change every week—have you tried to get advice from someone working in a present-day computer store? (The more things change, the more they stay the same.)

The Case of the Timid Golfer

One of our colleagues tells this story:

"I'd always wanted to play golf, so I took a golf course in college. They taught me how to hold a club, how to swing, and I was all set. And yet, after the course ended, it was seven years before I actually played on a public course."

"What stopped you?" we asked.

"They didn't teach me how to *get onto* a golf course, and I was embarrassed at the thought of not knowing the ropes."

It may seem like a small impediment to you, but it kept our friend from enjoying the sport he's enjoyed ever since.

The Case of the Diffident Dancer

PP: Bob, didn't you have a similar experience with your dancing lessons?

RFM: Yes. When I decided to take tap lessons when I turned 55, it was six weeks before I could screw up the courage to call a dance studio.

PP: What prevented you?

RFM: It wasn't skill—I knew how to look up a number and use the phone. It was the thought of this gray-haired man clomping around amongst a bevy of leotard-clad little girls that stopped me. When I did finally look in the phone book, it was another six weeks before I selected a number to call.

PP: And when you finally gathered the courage to call?

RFM: Once I called it was smooth sailing. But not knowing what to expect was a real obstacle, and the way the ads were written just made it worse.

It's no good to just sit there thinking, "That was no obstacle, that was just stupidity. All he had to do was call and get the information he needed." Remember Cram's law:* People don't do things for the damnedest reasons.

———————

Those last two examples are both about obstacles caused by reluctance to step through a door to new experiences (unjustified, as it turns out, since both came out with happy endings) of looking foolish in an unfamiliar situation. If lack of information keeps people from approaching situations in which they would like to be involved, it doesn't help to charge them with "stupidity" or to write off their doubts to "poor motivation." Since we're in the business of getting rid of obstacles to performance once they've been identified, our task is to address the obstacle and try to close the gap between what we've got and what we need. Most of us will not always "boldly go" into new experiences. Just as the golfer needed a lesson on "how to get on the golf course," there's a need in other situations for a similar transition easing the anguish of that first step into uncharted territory. It's always wise, therefore, to wonder if there isn't something subtle preventing the performer from getting started on the tasks at hand.

* Periodically muttered by Dr. David Cram, who also *does* things for the damnedest reasons.

The Case of Sagging Production

These impediments to performance can take many forms and may appear in unlikely places. A few years ago, one of us was asked to review a division of a company and make whatever recommendations for improvement seemed appropriate. Things were going pretty well, so this was not one of the instances that begins with "I've got a training problem." Production was down a little, but it was not a matter of panic proportions, although puzzling.

As is customary, two or three days were spent soaking in the activities of the division, working from inspectors of incoming material toward the loading dock.

It was learned that though production was sagging, nothing else had changed. There was no new product that people had to learn how to build. The same employees were still on the scene. There were no new, complicated machines to master. There seemed to be no morale or personality problems of any significance. Parts were flowing smoothly to the supply bins located at one end of the production floor. Tools were plentiful and in good working order.

Then what? The answer, the ridiculous answer, was discovered while sitting with some spot welders at their workbenches. It was noticed that they were rather slow in getting up to refill the empty parts bins on their benches. Why? They were one stool short on the production floor! Getting up meant that a welder's stool might be gone when she returned. So each woman dawdled when her bins were empty, and each spent time carving her initials or taping identifying marks on "her" stool.

For want of a stool . . . Clearly this was an obstacle to desired performance, but one not easily spotted with the naked eye.

Summing Up

In summary, before settling on solutions, look for subtle impediments to performance. Look for things that might be getting in the way of their performing as desired. Look for:

- Lack of authority, lack of time, or lack of tools.
- Poorly placed or poorly labeled equipment.
- Bad lighting and uncomfortable surroundings.
- Lack of *direct* information about *what* to do and *when* to do it.
- Competition from secondary tasks within the job itself and from the actions (or inactions) of other people.
- The "nobody told me" problem. There's usually no excuse for secret agendas or conflicting policies.

Above all, keep in mind that if they can do it but aren't doing it, there is a reason; only seldom is the reason either a lack of interest or a lack of desire. Most people want to do a good job. When they don't, it is often because of an obstacle in the world around them.

Be aware that the assumed cause and effect are not always accurate and that the true origins of problems are not always obvious. Problems often surface downstream from the place where they originate.

Any time it seems that there's no cause for a discrepancy— that is, it doesn't seem due to a lack of skill or motivation— keep looking; you still haven't found the obstacle. Widen your search.

Finally: First you state the problem *and the cause,* then you devise solutions. Having a "solution in search of a problem" is not a recommended approach.

What to Do

Determine whether there are subtle obstacles preventing expected performance.

How to Do It

Ask these questions:

- What prevents this person from performing?

- Does the person know what is expected?

- Does the person know when to do what is expected?

- Are there conflicting demands on this person's time?

- Is there competition from secondary tasks?

- Are there restrictive policies that ought to be changed?

- Can I reduce "competition from the job"—phone calls, "brush fires," demands of less important but more immediate problems?

- Could the problem be caused upstream from where the consequences are being felt?

12

Do They Have What It Takes?

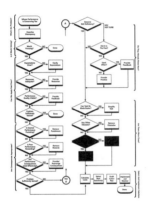

An important performance discrepancy has been identified, and it has been discovered that it is a genuine skill deficiency. Before moving on, however, we need to know whether the performers in question are "right" for the job.

By this point in the analysis, you may have several ideas about how to tackle the different causes of genuine deficiencies in performance. Keep them on "hold" until you have explored another issue by asking: Do the non-performers have the potential to benefit from this change? In plain language, do they have what it takes to learn what they don't now know?

You can make all the changes you like; but if an individual doesn't have what it takes, either mentally or physically, to do the job, the changes are a waste of time.

Any time someone cannot handle an existing job, you're stuck, inevitably, with the two universal alternatives to all of the solutions proposed in this book: Change the job or change the person. The first alternative was discussed in previous chapters. The second is the subject of this chapter.

"Changing the person" means, of course, to substitute another individual (or a machine) for the apparent non-performer. Sometimes it's quite plain that this is inevitable, as when physical limitations prevent performance. The decision to transfer or fire, however, is not always as straightforward as it may seem when your patience is running out. In fact, to look at a problem with anger or impatience is to look at it through a distorting lens.

The Case of Getting an Eyeful

On a production line making very tiny products, for example, a foreman complained that one woman made considerably more mistakes than anyone else. Like the others, she peered through a binocular microscope to see the tiny parts and to assist with their assembly. She assembled the same product as the others, and under the same conditions. But she was considerably "clumsier" than the others. The foreman wanted to get rid of her—that was his solution.

This case came to the attention of the department concerned with training and performance, and its members looked around and asked questions. They quickly discovered that this worker was not looking through the microscope with both eyes as she should have been. She looked with only one eye at a time. She didn't know that looking with both eyes at the same time made any difference when the instrument was properly adjusted. But without the depth perception that comes with using both eyes simultaneously, she could not see well enough to assemble accurately. Hence, she was labeled "clumsy."

After only two or three *minutes* of instruction in the proper use of the microscope, the woman's work was the equal of all the others in the department. She wasn't clumsy, or unmotivated, or incapable of learning. She was simply prevented from doing the job well by lack of information. In this example, "transfer or terminate" was not the remedy—a little bit of training was.

The remedies of transfer and termination are used more often than they should be. They are the crude hatchets of those unsophisticated in their knowledge of the limits of human performance, a sign of failure to locate less traumatic remedies. They should be considered a last resort rather than a first.

The issue of "potential to perform" should be approached in two stages: Could the person learn the job? Does he or she have what it takes to do the job?

If people can learn a job, they can do it, can't they? Not necessarily. It sounds contradictory, but some people become under-performers because they are overqualified for the job.

Some companies court trouble without realizing it by following a policy of over-hiring. "We always hire the best people available," they boast; then they go on to set people to work at jobs that are beneath their abilities. College graduates are put to work as glorified typists or given simple tasks on a production line; engineers find themselves working in the drafting department. Managers who succumb to this temptation are bewildered when dissatisfaction appears in its many guises—low morale, absenteeism, edginess, uncooperativeness, and so on.

The Case of the Expensive Interpreter

In a company we know, inspectors tested some complex electronic devices at the end of assembly. They did so by connecting the devices to their test equipment and checking readings on dials. The day-shift inspector was an older woman who had little idea of why she was doing these things. She did what she was trained to do and hooked up the devices and recorded the readings. If the readings deviated from those specified, she rejected the device.

The night-shift inspection, on the other hand, was handled by a young woman who was a doctoral candidate in the arts at a nearby university. She found an intellectual challenge in any task. To counteract her boredom with the job routine, she worked hard at finding out all she could about the how and why of the manufacture of the devices. Eventually, she was able to hold an intelligent conversation about the devices with engineers. Because of her increased knowledge, she began to *interpret* the readings on her test equipment. She no longer adhered to the strict accept/reject instructions of her training. As a result, she began to accept devices that should *not* have been accepted and to send others back for expensive reworking when they *should* have been accepted.

It's always a temptation to put the "best" available person into a job. But when that person is much overqualified, the rewards can be short-lived. A more realistic matching of skills with jobs will avoid the boredom and lack of challenge that lead to performance discrepancies after the first rush of enthusiasm.

The Case of the Reluctant Garbage Carrier

The problem of over-qualification can arise at home, too. Take the case of the teenager assigned to the carrying-out-the-garbage detail. The young are notoriously (and perhaps rightly) impatient of activities they consider boring. So the teenager fights carrying out the garbage.

"I'm his father/mother," you say. "Why should I get stuck with this chore when I have this son/daughter sitting around? Isn't it boring for me, too?" Yes, of course. But emotional issues aside, the teenager is bored and wants to be involved in something more exciting. Garbage-carrying loses out when it competes with doing, or even dreaming about, most other activities. The rewards of garbage-carrying have to be competitive with those real or imagined delights—a good trick. The least this tells you is that those who work at tasks for which they are overqualified need some extrinsic reward to take the place of "satisfaction in the job."

Following the lead discussed in the previous chapter, you may wonder whether the task can be simplified or made more interesting. Why is there so much garbage? Could the amount be reduced? (Eat your spinach!) If it could, that might make for fewer trips to the can. How about installing a disposal or a trash masher? That might reduce the number of trips still further.

How about making the task more interesting? One father we know claims he hasn't had any trouble at all getting the kids to mow the lawn—since he bought a motorized lawn mower that they can sit on and drive!

Are They Right for the Job?

Meanwhile, back to the point of this chapter. "Do they have the potential?" refers only in part to intellectual capacity, as mentioned earlier. *Appropriateness* for the task or job is another facet to consider. A person may have all the mental and physical qualities needed to do the job and still be wrong for it.

"I suppose I could learn to fill out that evil tax form, but I'll hate it."

"Sure I can do the job, but I just don't like to work in cold weather. You just might as well not send me there in the first place."

"I can do the job OK, but I just hate doing it with that music blaring all day long."

"No, I don't *want* to do that job, no matter how good I might get at it."

"I love photography, but I'm a little too claustrophobic to work in a darkroom."

In each case the person is wrong for the job, whatever it may be. There's a lack of inclination. When people so plainly announce themselves to be square pegs, they lack the potential for sustained performance.

Summing Up

In summary, it is useful to determine whether someone has the capacity to do the job required, and whether he or she would "fit" the job mentally and motivationally, even if the performance in question were brought up to standard. If the answer to both questions is "yes," go ahead with your analysis. If not, replace the performer with someone more suited to the job.

What to Do

Determine whether the person has the potential to perform as desired.

How to Do It

Ask these questions:

- Could the person learn the job (is the individual trainable)?

- Does this person have the physical and mental potential to perform as desired?

- Is this person over-qualified for the job?

- Is this person right for the job?

Part V
Which Solutions Are Best?

What should I do now?

Now that you've collected all the clues and potential solutions, it's time to decide which solution mix will come closest to solving the problem.

To do that, you'll need to think seriously about the cost of the problem, and about the cost of each of the best solutions, before making the final solution decision and drafting your action plan. This section will help you to do that.

13

Which Solution Is Best?

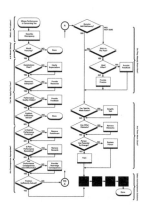

WHERE WE ARE

One or more solutions or remedies for a performance discrepancy have been identified. We need to find out what each solution would cost, so that we can select the most cost-effective combination.

Isn't this the end of the line? By now you probably have what looks like one or more relevant solutions, so why not put them to work? Because there's one more question to ponder before racing for the finish line: Will the results be worth the trouble? This can be a tougher question than it seems, and all too often it doesn't get the attention it deserves.

If you have followed the procedure we've described, you'll have concentrated on finding potential solutions for your problem, without too much regard for whether the solution is the most practical or feasible in your situation. As a result, one or more of the remedies you have generated may be inappropriate simply because they are beyond the resources you can bring to bear. Perhaps it's plain that you would not be able to get the money, perhaps it violates policy, or maybe you don't have the organizational "muscle" to implement it. Here's how to proceed.

1. Check the Feasibility of Each Solution.

As the first step in deciding which solution is best, ask these questions of each one:

- Is this possible solution clearly inappropriate or impossible to implement?
- Is this possible solution plainly beyond our resources?

When the answer to either of the questions is "Yes," put the solution aside for the moment. Don't discard these possibilities, though; someone may be able to show you how to put that "unworkable" solution into practice. Too many "It can't be done" and "It's against company policy" assertions have been shown to be untrue, so avoid being hasty about scrapping solutions that look impossible at first glance.

2. Determine the "Cost" of Each Solution.

The next step is to determine the "cost" of each remaining solution. Just as you affixed a value to each of the consequences of the discrepancy, now determine what it would cost to adopt each of the tentative solutions you developed during the analysis.

Why bother with each one? For two important reasons:

a. All too often, perhaps without realizing it, people lock onto a solution without giving "equal time" to other potential answers. The selected solution may be one they had even before doing the analysis; or it may be one that, on the face of it, is more "obviously" right than others. That's not to say that either of these types of solutions will never be the right one. But plunging too quickly for an answer without considering the cost of all alternatives deprives you of another advantage—the other important reason.

b. As you ponder costs, you will probably find yourself generating even more solutions, compromises, and combinations that are often more innovative and more appropriate than the original answers.

Solutions Aren't "Free"

Don't jump too quickly, either, to the conclusion that any solution comes free of cost. Consider, for example, the common problem of instructors who insult or humiliate their students in one way or another (such as forcing them to participate in ill-conceived role-plays). Someone notices and says:

"There's a discrepancy between what these instructors are doing and what they should be doing. We've got to do something about that."

"Fine. How will you get them to stop doing it?"

"Why, we'll tell them to stop."

So "telling" is proposed as the solution. And, on the face of it, this solution doesn't cost anything at all. All you have to do is to tell. But it isn't as simple as that, is it? Even if telling worked—which it seldom does—someone has to decide how the telling should happen. Will someone prepare a memo for all instructors? Will someone sit down with them in a group and tell? Or meet with them individually and tell? It is clear that when you think about the proposed solution in terms of "cost," it isn't as free as it looks. It may be quick and easy to do; but even for a solution of such dubious effectiveness, there is likely to be a "cost" in terms of someone's time, at the very least.

It's that way with most solutions. It "costs" somebody something to "do something." Perhaps not much, but something. When considering solutions, then, it is useful to estimate the cost of each tentative action. It will help prevent you from rushing off to implement a solution settled on before the analysis; it will help you to put the "obvious" solution into perspective; and it will help prevent you from implementing solutions that are more massive than the problem. After all, you wouldn't want to find yourself in the position of implementing hundred-thousand-dollar solutions to ten-thousand-dollar problems, or requiring ten people to involve themselves in a solution when a checklist would do as well.

Doing Nothing Can Be Expensive

Clearly, money is an important measuring instrument in decisions regarding solutions for performance discrepancies. After all, if you can't afford a particular solution, or if a solution costs more than the results are likely to be worth, plainly there is further analysis to be done. A less obvious case, perhaps, is that of doing nothing. The cost of the solution should be weighed against the cost of maintaining the status quo. What looks at first like an "unreasonable" cost may look considerably more attractive if the true cost of the present situation is examined. You proved this when you calculated the cost of the discrepancy back in Chapter 2. Calculating the size or "cost" of a discrepancy is the same as calculating the cost of doing nothing.

There's a tendency to say that an existing state of affairs "costs nothing" and that any solution that entails an added outlay of money therefore has to be more expensive. But the "hidden cost" of "doing nothing" about a performance discrepancy can be considerable—in inefficient performance, overly long or unnecessary courses, scrap piles larger than they need be, lost or angry customers, employee turnover and absenteeism, and varying degrees of frustration.

Intangible Costs

The paragraphs above may make it sound as though we are talking only about money when estimating solution costs. Not so. There are cost dimensions other than monetary ones, as a proposed solution will often require time, talent, people-dedication, hard work, and so on. These intangibles must not be ignored; and when included in the sum total of the solution requirement, the solution may not be worth the expected results.

Consider for a moment the "problem" of getting people to buckle their seat belts when driving. "People really oughta wanna wear their seat belts," goes the cry. What happens if they *don't?* Statistics are trotted out to "prove" that a certain number of people will die. And how much is a life worth? How much should we be willing to spend to prevent people from dying as a result of their own folly? Clearly, there are intangible costs incurred by letting the problem alone, and some intangible costs incurred by "solving" the problem (costs such as the loss of freedom to act as one wishes and belt-burn on the necks of shorter drivers, to mention only two).

In the United States, millions of dollars have been spent on bells, buzzers, interlocks, and widespread exhortation to "buckle up." This expensive "solution" hasn't worked very well. Elsewhere, better results have been achieved almost at the stroke of a pen. Australia, for example, has passed a law requiring a fine whenever, and for whatever reason, anyone is caught driving without a fastened seat belt. The result is better than 85 percent compliance, a far more successful solution than that of "throwing money at the problem."

But how to evaluate intangible costs? Most of the time it is easier than it looks. The procedure for evaluating intangible solution costs is threefold:

1. Name the intangibles;

2. Describe the components of people and effort that would be required to implement the solution; and

3. Describe the implications of implementation, whether they be political or personal.

The use of this procedure may not provide you with precise numbers, but it will put you in a better position to rank solutions in terms of total cost.

By the time you have identified an area of intangible costs and have described the amount of effort that will be involved, the practicality of the solution may be obvious. For example, once you see that cleaning up the neighborhood will take the efforts of 50 volunteers, and that it would take more organizing and bell-ringing and telephoning hours than you have to offer, the solution of "get the neighbors to do it" looks pretty unlikely, even without thinking about monetary aspects of the cost.

The Case of the Thieving Loan Officers

Intangible costs can come from any direction. Consider the plight of the training director of a large bank:

"We lose about a half-million dollars a year through bank robberies!"

"Sounds like a lot. What do you do about it?"

"Plenty. We hire more guards, we buy cameras and miles of videotape, we teach people complex defensive routines, and we buy other special equipment."

"How much does that cost?"

"Don't ask."

"You mean it costs more than half a million a year?"

"It sure does."

"Why do it if it costs more than the problem?"

"Well, it has value other than just deterring robberies. Our customers are reassured by knowing we have all the latest gadgets, and we look 'up-to-date' in the eyes of our peers. We feel that those results, unmeasurable though they may be, make it important to spend more on a solution than the problem is costing."

"Sounds like a wise decision."

"Well, it is and it isn't."

"Oh?"

"Well, we lose half a million a year in robberies, but we lose twenty-four million a year in loan losses."

"Wow! What do you do about that?"

"Nothing."

"Nothing?"

"Nothing. Most of that loss is caused by vice-presidents who fail to follow established loan procedure. They make loans against the better judgment established by policy, the loan goes sour, and we lose a bundle."

"Why isn't something done about the problem?"

"Ahh, it's called clout. The board or the president could do something about it, but my department doesn't have the clout. So we concentrate our efforts on preventing robberies."

Here was an instance in which a solution (preventing robberies) cost a lot more than the problem itself (the robberies), and in which a much bigger problem (the loan losses) was ignored. Isn't there an old saw having to do with goring oxen? (By the way, if you think we invented this episode, you're wrong.)

You can probably think of several instances in which the intangible (unmeasurable) costs of the solutions played a large part in the decision on just *which* solution would be tried. Once the intangible costs have been evaluated, the monetary aspect often pales in comparison.

3. Evaluate Solutions.

Which solution (or combination of solutions) is best? What action should you take? By now it's possible that one solution will stand out clearly as being better than the others you considered. The value of implementing the solution will clearly be positive. The solution will be:

- *economical* (considerably cheaper than the problem);
- *practical,* in that the means for implementing it are available to you; and
- *feasible,* in that it will be acceptable to the people affected and not harmful (politically or otherwise) to you or others.

Divide and Conquer

But what happens if all of your potential solutions are rejected because they were plainly beyond your resources? Or because, on close examination, they proved unfeasible or impractical?

The answer is the same for both. You will have to re-examine the problem and the solution to see if one or both can be scaled down. Ask:

- Can the problem be attacked in parts?
- Can a portion of the solution be used to solve a portion of the problem?

Sometimes it makes good sense to settle for less than the ultimate solution. If you shoot for something less than perfection, you may be able to get acceptable results for a good deal less effort. Or, when problems and solutions seem out of reach, it often makes sense to ask: What will give us the most result for the least effort? Which aspect are we best equipped to tackle? Which part of the problem interests us most? Which part of the problem is the most "visible" to those who must be pleased? So . . .

- If you can't afford to train 50 people, can you train five and have them provide on-the-job training for their colleagues?
- If you can't afford to hire all the guards indicated for plant security, can you shore things up sufficiently with closed-circuit TV?
- If you don't have room in the house for a piano, could your child learn to play the piccolo? Or an electronic keyboard?
- If you don't have the room or the teachers in your school to provide vital vocational training, can you persuade local industry to provide some space and know-how?
- If you can't provide the service to all, can you find a quick way to tell who needs the service most?
- If you can't find a foolproof way of telling whether ammunition is in working order other than by firing it, can you use a random-sampling technique that will be almost as good?

4. Draft an Action Plan.

A good way to test the feasibility of your solutions is to draft a simple action plan. For each possible solution, this plan briefly describes the answers to these two questions:

a. Who will be expected to implement this solution?

b. How will you get that person or persons to do what it will take to make the implementation happen?

It isn't enough simply to expect someone else to "change the policy," or "provide training," or "arrange feedback," or "get a law passed." Unless you say *who* will do it and *how* you will get that person to do it, your solutions may never be put into practice. Without an action plan, you might not cause yourself to think about what happens next. In addition, you would deprive yourself of an opportunity to test the cost of each solution. Here's an example.

Suppose you've analyzed a discrepancy having to do with engineers who seem totally uninterested in completing their paperwork by the allotted deadlines. During the analysis you discover that there are no significant consequences *to the engineers* whether or not they meet these deadlines. Obviously, one solution will be to arrange consequences, and arrange them in such a way that meeting deadlines leads to a favorable consequence *to the engineers,* and not meeting the deadlines leads to consequences that are considered unfavorable *by the engineers.*

How will you make that come to pass? Will you storm into the office of the manager and demand that consequences be arranged? Will you draft a description of some of the possible consequences that might be useful, and then send a memo to the engineers' manager outlining the cost of the problem, as well as your suggestions for a solution? Will you present the substance of your memo in person? What do *you* need to do to get this particular solution implemented? Your answer to this question will form a piece of your action plan. You would repeat the process for each of the solutions you intend to recommend.

Summing Up

In summary, answer the "What do I do now?" question by doing the following:

a. Collect all the potential solutions that address the issues revealed by your analysis (such as the need to reduce punishment of desired performance or the need to eliminate obstacles);

b. Determine or estimate the cost of implementing each solution;

c. Select the solution(s) that will add the most value (solve the largest part of the problem for the least effort); and then

d. Draft a brief action plan that describes, for each solution, how it will be put into practice and who will do the work.

What to Do

Estimate the cost of each potential solution, select the solution or combination of solutions that is most practical, feasible, and economical, and draft an action plan that describes who will implement each solution and how each solution will be implemented.

How to Do It

Answer these questions:

• Have all the potential solutions been identified?

• Does each solution address itself to one or more problems identified during the analysis (such as skill deficiency, absence of potential, incorrect rewards, punishing consequences, distracting obstacles)?

- Have all the problems identified been addressed?

- What is the cost of each potential solution?

- Have the intangible (unmeasurable) costs been assessed?

- Which solution (or combination of solutions) is most practical, feasible, and economical?

- Which solution will add most value (solve the largest part of the problem for the least effort)?

- Which solution are we best equipped to try?

- Which remedy interests us most? (Or, on the other side of the coin, which remedy is most visible to those who must be pleased?)

- Have I drafted an action plan that describes how each solution will be implemented and who will do the implementing?

Part VI

Quick-Reference Checklist & Final Thoughts

Now that the steps of our performance analysis procedure are familiar to you, we can summarize them for you in a Quick-Reference Checklist. Use the checklist as a guide, or as a way to help others see why they really oughta wanna re-evaluate solutions they have already decided upon.

We also offer a few final suggestions for applying the performance analysis procedure in the world around you.

A
Quick-Reference
Checklist

I. Describe the Problem

1. What is the performance discrepancy?

- Whose performance is at issue?
- Why is there said to be a problem?
- What is the actual performance at issue?
- What is the desired performance?

2. Is it worth pursuing?

- What would happen if I let it alone?
- Are our expectations reasonable?
- What are the consequences caused by the discrepancy?
- Is that cost enough to justify going on?

II. Explore Fast Fixes

3. Can we apply fast fixes?

- Do those concerned know what is expected of them?
- Can those concerned describe desired performance? Expected accomplishments?
- Are there obvious obstacles to performance?
- Do these people get feedback on how they are doing?

III. Check Consequences

4. Is desired performance punishing?

- What are the consequences of performing as desired?
- Is it actually punishing or perceived as punishing?

5. Is undesired performance rewarding?

- What rewards, prestige, status, or comfort support the present way of doing things?
- Does misbehaving get more attention than doing it right?

6. Are there any consequences at all?

- Does desired performance lead to consequences that the performer sees as favorable?

IV. Enhance Competence

7. Is it a skill deficiency?

- Could they do it if their lives depended on it, i.e., could they do it if they really had to?

8. Could they do it in the past?

- Could they once perform the task but have forgotten how?

9. Is the skill used often?

- How often is the performance displayed?
- How often is the skill applied?
- Is there feedback on how things are going? Is the feedback available regularly?

10. **Can the task be simplified?**

   - Particularly for "hurry up" demands, can I reduce the standards by which performance is judged?
   - Can I provide some sort of performance aid?
   - Can I redesign the workplace or provide other physical help?
   - Can I parcel off part of the job to someone else or arrange a job swap?

11. **Any obstacles remaining?**

   - Does something get in the way of doing it right?
   - Lack of knowledge about what's expected?
   - Conflicting demands?
   - Restrictive policies?

12. **Do they have what it takes?**

   - Is it likely that this person could learn to do the job?
   - Does this person lack the physical or mental potential to perform as desired?
   - Is this person over-qualified for this job?

V. Develop Solutions

13. **Which solution is best?**

   - Have all potential solutions been identified?
   - Does each address one or more parts of the problem(s)?
   - Have estimates of any intangible costs of the problem(s) been included?
   - What is the cost of each potential solution?
   - Which solution(s) are most practical, feasible, and economical?
   - Which yields most value, solving the largest part of the problem(s) for least effort?

B
In the Real World

In this book we've described a way to analyze a particular kind of problem—those involving discrepancies between desired and actual human performance. Though it may seem to have taken a long time to describe, it doesn't take nearly as long to *do*. After a little practice, you will find yourself quickly ticking your mental way through the key questions, sometimes taking only a few seconds to see a problem in a new light—and to identify a likely solution. You will find, too, that after you've practiced the analysis a few times, you won't be able to keep from looking at the world through your performance analysis lenses.

To survive, however, you'll have to remind yourself that people usually don't do apparently dumb things on purpose, that they actually believe their way of doing things is pretty good. That's one reason you'll run across many situations which, for one reason or other, are so obviously out of whack that you'll wonder how anything ever gets done.

For example, you'll hear executives say they want their products to be user-friendly, yet they won't seek input from human-factors specialists until the product has been manufactured. You'll hear them talk about the need for boosting productivity, all the while soaking up thousands of employee hours with purposeless meetings. You'll find CEOs pitting one division against another in a race for results, only to wonder why, as a consequence, there is no communication among them. You'll run across managers who squeeze out their most experienced employees (often referred to as early retirement), then wonder why new-hires aren't as competent as the people just discarded. (For a crystal-clear picture of how the world actually works, there's a book that contains all the wisdom of the ages. It's called *The Dilbert Principle,* by Scott Adams.)

You'll notice schools that give diplomas to people who can't read, write, or make change, causing industry to spend millions to right this wrong. And you'll notice that the consequences are felt by industry and by the graduates, not by those causing the problem; no consequences, in other words, to those turning out the non-functional adults.

But there's a brighter world at the end of the tunnel, because there is growing realization that people act as they do for reasons other than malicious intent. Those in charge are learning that it's possible to attack performance problems by methods other than by finger-pointing, exhortation, and threats. They're learning that training isn't always the magic solution when unsatisfactory performance is detected. And they're learning that it's OK to ask for help.

As time goes by, therefore, you'll be more and more likely to be asked to help with problems of human performance. Typically, you'll be asked to solve one performance problem— the one the client recognizes—that probably lives in a sea of others. Navigating these waters successfully requires somewhat more than performance analysis skill. So in closing, we'd like to offer some thoughts to help you on your road to blazing success.

Handholds Along The Walk Of Life

- Control your face and words. Performance analysis skill will allow you to see disjoints and mismanagement in the world around you. When working with clients you will be well served to control your snickers and your words when your understanding of the situation allows you to see solutions invisible to the client.

- Expect and look for hidden agendas; they're everywhere. Rarely will people begin by telling you either the true problem or the real reason they want it solved. As you've learned, most people can't distinguish between problems and solutions (e.g., "I've got a training problem."). So keep asking questions, keep on observing, until you're confident that you've learned how things are and why they are as they are.

- Respect the client. There are reasons why things are being done the way they are. They may not be good reasons—or even rational reasons. Nonetheless, your clients may have a great deal of themselves invested in the *status quo;* they may not take kindly to an implication that their way isn't the best way or to the thought that for years they've been doing it wrong. Remember, too, that when you propose a solution to a problem, you're also proposing that someone needs to do something differently—to *change.* And willingness to change may not increase in proportion to the size or seriousness of the problem.

  Before proposing your solutions, therefore, ask yourself how you would feel if someone proposed to you what you are about to propose to them. And ask yourself whether your proposed changes are realistic in light of what you know about the situation. Tell yourself that you're in the business of making things better than they were, and the struggle for perfection may not be realistic or feasible. Then treat them as you would be treated, i.e., do unto others . . .

- Respect client values. People aren't necessarily wrong because their values differ from your own, and their habits and practices don't necessarily have to be "fixed" because they don't match your own ideas of goodness and efficiency. When you enter your clients' territory, tell yourself that you're visiting someone's home. Though you may be there to solve a specific problem, you won't have been invited there to solve *all* the problems. So be a good guest. Think about the destitute plumber who, when asked to fix a leaky toilet, couldn't refrain from offering advice on how to improve the customers' child-rearing practices. Similar behavior can make you destitute, too.

- Allow your client to save face. For example, never blurt out the solution to a performance problem until you've walked through the analysis together. The client has lived with this problem for some time without seeing the solution(s). If, in your excitement, you verbalize these solutions too early, your client may feel belittled and insulted. Enjoy your ability to make sense out of things, but try not to offer solutions until you understand the environment in which the problem lives.

- Let your client solve the problem. Do your analysis "out loud," asking questions and reflecting answers; often, the client will suddenly make the connection between problem and solution. When that happens, you won't have to "sell" the solution or work as hard to get it implemented. (And there's nothing wrong with allowing a bit of social banter into your analysis discussions, relaxing the mood and allowing time for insights to spring forth.)

Epilogue

If you analyze *your* performance problems systematically, you may even come to view some of the larger problems of the world from a new vantage point and understand why some of the "tried and true" solutions are so ineffective. You may, for example, find new ways of thinking and responding to such comments as:

"Politicians oughta wanna reduce government spending."

"Posters hung in public places will help reduce the incidence of traffic deaths."

"People should take more responsibility for their own health."

"The government oughta wanna get off our backs."

"People oughta wanna make the government obey the Constitution."

"More people oughta wanna take responsibility for their own health."

Our checklist won't help you to understand *everything* about why people behave as they do. But if each of us could perceive more clearly the nature of just *one* important human problem—and throw his or her weight behind a solution related to the cause—we might just move bigger and more important things than mountains. It's worth a try.

We leave you with this final thought: Those who work to *solve* problems are more highly valued than those who merely label them.

Part VII
Appendices

C
Reprisal!

Every book should have a little corner from which authors are allowed to strike back. After all, several dozen individuals have had a go at our thoughts and at our manuscript—picking and probing, suggesting this, trampling on that, or just staring blankly at a mangled explanation they really should have understood.

Such knavery cannot go unsung—so sing we will. We wave the banner of acclaim for all those who so patiently allowed themselves to be battered by earlier, more primitive explanations of the concepts presented herein, and who were magnanimous enough to batter back.

More pointedly, we skewer with the lance of laud and commendation these generous souls who took pains to try on one or another of our later drafts and tell us just where it pinched and how the fit could be improved: John McCann, Rodney Cron, Randy Mager, Maryjane Rees, Vernon Rees, Andy Stevens, Walter Thorne, and Tom Watts.

And we hurry to lance (and laud, of course) those who so generously hacked and slashed their way through this new edition:

David Cram, Dan Raymond, Bonnie Abney, Ennis Pipe, Eileen Mager, and Paul Staples, as well as our favorite editress, Slash-'n-Burn Mary Kitzmiller.

Long may they dangle!

Robert F. Mager
Peter Pipe

D
For Further Reading

Gilbert, T. F.   *Human Competence: Engineering Worthy Performance,* ISPI Tribute Edition. International Society for Performance Improvement, 1996.

Kerr, S.   "On the Folly of Rewarding A, While Hoping for B," *Academy of Management Executive,* Volume IX, Number 1, February, 1995.

Zemke, R.   *Figuring Things Out.* Reading, Mass.: Addison-Wesley Publishing Co., 1982.

Zigon, J.   "Rewards and Performance Incentives," *Performance & Instruction,* International Society for Performance Improvement, Volume 33, number 10, 1994.

Index

MORE GREAT BOOKS FROM DR. ROBERT F. MAGER!

Dr. Robert F. Mager has authored one of the most extensive and renowned collections of books and resources on issues of human performance in existence today. These books are considered to be *the* reference library for anyone serious about educating others and improving human performance. You'll find everything you need to learn how to:

• develop successful instruction,
• find realistic solutions to performance problems,
• measure the results of your instruction,
• generate positive attitudes in learners,
• and much more!

Order your copies today and get resources you'll use for a lifetime.

	Quantity	x Price=	Total
Measuring Instructional Results *How to determine whether your instructional results have been achieved*		x $19.95=	
Preparing Instructional Objectives *A critical tool in the development of effective instruction*		x $19.95=	
How to Turn Learners On... without turning them off *Ways to ignite interest in learning*		x $19.95=	
Analyzing Performance Problems *How to figure out why people aren't doing what they should be, and what to do about it*		x $19.95=	
Making Instruction Work *A step-by-step guide to designing and developing instruction that works*		x $19.95=	
Goal Analysis *How to clarify your goals so you can actually achieve them*		x $19.95=	
The How to Write a Book Book		x $17.95=	
Troubleshooting the Troubleshooting Course		x $17.95=	
What Every Manager Should Know About Training		x $19.95=	
Subtotal			
Shipping & Handling*			
GA & TX residents add 7% sales tax to the subtotal plus shipping and handling			
Total Order			

* *Please add $6.00 for the first book, plus $1.50 for each additional book. Please allow four weeks for delivery by UPS Ground Service.*

Name _____

Phone _____ Fax _____

Organization _____

Address _____

City _____ State _____ Zip _____

☐ My check or money order for $ _____ is enclosed

Charge my ☐ Visa ☐ Mastercard ☐ AmEx   Exp. Date _____

Card Number _____

Name on Card _____

Please send this form and your check, money order, or credit card number to:

CEP
P.O. Box 102462
Atlanta, GA 30368-2462

Call 1-800-558-4CEP for volume discount information.

Call for shipping charges on international orders.

For credit card orders, fax this order for faster delivery: (770) 458-9109 or use our website at: www.cepworldwide.com

Preparing Instructional Objectives

A critical tool in the development of effective instruction

Third Edition

Robert F. Mager

CEP PRESS
A division of
The Center for Effective Performance, Inc.
Atlanta, Georgia

Books by Robert F. Mager

Preparing Instructional Objectives, *Third Edition**

Measuring Instructional Results, *Third Edition**

Analyzing Performance Problems, *Third Edition**
(with Peter Pipe)

Goal Analysis, *Third Edition**

How to Turn Learners On ... without turning them off, *Third Edition**

Making Instruction Work, *Second Edition**

Developing Vocational Instruction (with Kenneth Beach)

Troubleshooting the Troubleshooting Course

The How to Write a Book Book

What Every Manager Should Know About Training

* Sold as a six-volume set (The Mager Six-Pack)

WORKSHOPS BY ROBERT F. MAGER

Criterion-Referenced Instruction (with Peter Pipe)

Instructional Module Development

The Training Manager Workshop

For more information, contact:
The Center for Effective Performance, Inc.
2300 Peachford Road, Suite 2000
Atlanta, GA 30338
(770) 458-4080 or (800) 558-4237

ISBN 1-879-618-03-6 (PREVIOUSLY ISBN 1-56103-341-3)
ISBN 1-879-618-15-X (SIX-VOLUME SET)

Library of Congress Catalog Card Number: 96-072449
Printed in the United States of America

05 04 03 02   10 9 8 7 6 5 4 3 2

Contents

Note

Much of this book has been put together differently from most books you have read. On many pages you will be asked a question. When this happens, select the best answer, and then turn to the page referred to beside the answer. This way, you read only the material that applies to your needs, and you can proceed without being distracted by unnecessary explanations.

Another Note

Every once in a while you'll find some "boxed" material on·a left-hand page. This is adjunct material that you may find interesting or useful. Read it as you go, or, if you find that distracting, save it for a rainy day.

Preface

Once upon a time a Sea Horse gathered up his seven pieces of eight and cantered out to find his fortune. Before he had traveled very far he met an Eel, who said,

"Psst. Hey, bud. Where ya' goin'?"

"I'm going out to find my fortune," replied the Sea Horse, proudly.

"You're in luck," said the Eel. "For four pieces of eight you can have this speedy flipper, and then you'll be able to get there a lot faster."

"Gee, that's swell," said the Sea Horse and paid the money, put on the flipper, and slithered off at twice the speed. Soon he came upon a Sponge, who said,

"Psst. Hey, bud. Where ya' goin'?"

"I'm going out to find my fortune," replied the Sea Horse.

"You're in luck," said the Sponge. "For a small fee I will let you have this jet-propelled scooter so that you will be able to travel a lot faster."

So the Sea Horse bought the scooter with his remaining money and went zooming through the sea five times as fast. Soon he came upon a Shark, who said,

"Psst. Hey, bud. Where ya' goin'?"

"I'm going to find my fortune," replied the Sea Horse.

"You're in luck. If you take this short cut," said the Shark, pointing to his open mouth, "you'll save yourself a lot of time."

"Gee, thanks," said the Sea Horse. He zoomed off into the interior of the Shark and was never heard from again.

The moral of this fable is that if you're not sure where you're going, you're liable to end up some place else.

It's true, isn't it? If you don't know where you're going, the best-made maps won't help you get there. Without a blueprint, the finest materials and the most skilled artisans wouldn't be able to create the house of your dreams. Similarly, without a way to communicate your instructional objectives to others:

- You wouldn't be able to decide which instructional content and procedures would help you to accomplish your objectives.
- You wouldn't be able to create measuring instruments (tests) that tell you whether your students had become competent enough to move on.
- And your students wouldn't be able to decide for themselves when to stop practicing.

A clear statement of objectives, on the other hand, will help you avoid these and other problems, because they will give you, and others, a sound basis for selecting instructional content and procedures, as well as the means for finding out whether your important outcomes have actually been accomplished. Objectives will also provide you with a communication tool through which you can let others know what you, or someone else, has decided is worth teaching.

This book is about the characteristics of usefully stated objectives. It will show you how to draft objectives that communicate your instructional intent, and it will show you where objectives fit in the larger scheme of the instructional enterprise.

This book is NOT about who should select objectives, nor is it about how one goes about deciding what is worth teaching. These are critical issues, but they are beyond the scope of this book.

Specifically, the objective of this book is this:

Given any objective in a subject area with which you are familiar, be able to identify (label) correctly the *performance*, the *conditions*, and the *criteria* of acceptable performance when those characteristics are present.

Once you recognize the presence or absence of the characteristics of well-stated objectives, you will be able to prepare your own.

If you care about developing and/or delivering instruction that will give your students the skills and knowledge important for them to have, this book is for you.

Robert F. Mager

Carefree, Arizona
January 1997

1
Objectives

Instruction is effective to the degree that it succeeds in:

- changing students
- in desired directions
- and not in undesired directions.

Instruction that doesn't change anyone has no effect, no power. If it changes students in undesired directions (that is, if it has unwanted side effects), it isn't called effective; instead, it is called poor, undesirable, or even harmful instruction. Instruction is successful, or effective, to the degree that it accomplishes what it sets out to accomplish.

Once you decide to teach someone something, several kinds of activity are required if your instruction is to be successful. For one thing, you must assure yourself that there is a need for the instruction, making certain that (1) your students don't already know what you intend to teach and (2) instruction is the best means for bringing about the desired change. For another, you must clearly specify the outcomes or objectives you intend your instruction to accomplish. You must then select and arrange learning experiences for your students in accordance with the principles of learning and must evaluate student performance according to the objectives originally selected. In other words, first you decide where you want to go, then you create and administer the means of getting there, and then you arrange to find out whether you arrived.

The steps for accomplishing this arrange themselves into these four main phases:

Analysis

Design/development

Implementation

Evaluation/improvement

A number of procedures and techniques are available through which to complete them. The analysis phase, for example, should answer questions such as these:

Is there a problem worth solving?

Is instruction a relevant part of the solution?

If so, what should the instruction accomplish?

After all, instruction is only one of several possible solutions to problems of human performance. Unless a suitable analysis is performed before instruction is developed, it is quite possible to construct a magnificent course that doesn't help anybody at all. It is possible to construct a course that nobody needs, either because instruction is unrelated to solving the problem that gave rise to it or because it "teaches" things the students already know. Techniques such as performance analysis[1] and goal analysis[2] can help avoid such wasteful practices.

---

[1] See *Analyzing Performance Problems,* Third Edition, R. F. Mager and Peter Pipe (1997).

[2] See *Goal Analysis,* Third Edition, R. F. Mager (1997).

If analysis reveals that instruction is needed, objectives are drafted that describe the important outcomes intended to be accomplished by that instruction. In other words, objectives are drafted that answer the question "What is worth teaching?" Instruments (tests) by which the success of the instruction can be assessed are then drafted.

Only after the preceding steps have been completed is the actual instruction drafted, tested, revised, and then put into use. And, please note, only after the analysis phase is complete or near completion are objectives drafted. This is an important point, because when you read or hear that "the first thing you do is write objectives" or "objectives are written before instruction is designed," you should translate that into "*after* the analysis is completed, then objectives are prepared *before* the instruction is designed."

What Is an Instructional Objective?

An instructional objective is a collection of words and/or pictures and diagrams intended to let others know what you intend for your students to achieve.

- It is related to intended outcomes, rather than the process for achieving those outcomes.
- It is specific and measurable, rather than broad and intangible.
- It is concerned with students, not teachers.

The Objective of This Book

This book is concerned with the *characteristics* of a usefully stated objective, rather than with its derivation or selection. The purpose of the book is limited to helping you specify and communicate those instructional intents you or someone else has decided are worth achieving. If this book achieves its objective, you will be able to recognize the characteristics of well-stated objectives when they are present. Once you can recognize desirable characteristics, and after a bit of practice, you will be able to prepare your own objectives by modifying your drafts until they are well stated.

Specifically:

*Given any objective in a subject area with which you are familiar, be able to identify (label) correctly the **performance**, the **conditions**, and the **criteria** of acceptable performance when those characteristics are present.*

To help you reach this objective, I will describe some of the advantages to be gained from the careful specification of objectives, describe and illustrate the characteristics of a usefully stated objective, and give you some practice in recognizing such objectives. At the end, you will have an opportunity to determine just how well our efforts have succeeded.

Before we begin, it will be useful to look in some detail at the difference between instructional process and instructional results.

Outcomes vs. Process

An objective is related to an intended outcome of instruction, rather than the process of instruction. For example, when a chef adds seasoning to a soup, that is part of the process of cooking. But it isn't the result of the cooking. The soup itself is the outcome, or result, of the cooking.

Lecturing is something an instructor does to help the students to learn; it is part of the process of instruction. But a lecture is not the purpose of the instruction. The purpose of instruction is to facilitate learning. So when teachers teach (process), they do it because they hope that students will learn (the result or outcome). Therefore, statements such as the following are descriptions of instructional process, rather than of intended results.

- To provide a lecture series on phrenolationism.
- Be able to perform well in a role-play situation.
- This course provides extensive practice exercises.

Because recognizing the difference between process statements and outcome statements is critical to the effective use of objectives, it will be useful to check your ability to spot the difference. Following are two statements. Turn to the page number shown beside the outcome statement.

Be able to sing. *Turn to page 9.*

Develop confidence. *Turn to page 7.*

Uh, oh. What are you doing here? Nowhere in this book are you directed to this page.

In this kind of book, when you are asked a question, you are to select what you think is the correct response, and then turn to the page number indicated beside that alternative.

You see, I'm trying to tailor my comments to your needs so that you won't have to waste your time reading about things you already know. By answering the periodic questions, you'll be able to test yourself through the book a lot faster than if you had to read all the pages.

Don't miss this note!

> Every once in a while you'll find some material boxed on a left-hand page. This is adjunct material that you may find interesting or useful. Read it as you go, or, if you find that distracting, save it for a rainy day.

Please return to the page from whence you cometh.

You said that "Develop confidence" is an outcome statement.

Let me try again. Think of your instruction as being like a train that takes your students from one place to another. The question to be answered by an objective is, "What are students expected to be like when they arrive at their destination?"

It might help to think of the difference between statements describing the process of building a house and those describing the characteristics (outcomes) of a completed house. For example, here are some process statements about the construction process:

- The foundation is laid before the walls go up.

- Walls are to be constructed of crushed tin cans.

- Scaffolding will be used when installing the roof.

In contrast, the following statements describe characteristics (outcomes) of the completed house:

- The house contains three fireplaces.

- The front of the house faces south.

- All windows are constructed of double-pane glass.

Outcomes are the results we get from processes.

Turn to page 5 and select the correct response.

Right on! "Be able to sing" is an outcome statement. It describes something we might want our students to be able to do. Keep this up and you'll fall out of the back of the book in no time.

Specific vs. General

Another characteristic of an objective is that it is specific, rather than general, broad, or "fuzzy." If objectives are fuzzy, they don't do us any good and we might as well not bother with them. We want them to be specific, so they will help us to make good instructional decisions.

Here are a few examples of specific and fuzzy statements. Put a check mark beside the specific statements, and then turn the page to check your responses.

Understand logic. _____

Know your enemy. _____

Thread this needle. _____

Reassemble this cat. _____

Think. _____

Smile when addressing a customer. _____

Turn the page to check your responses.

The items checked are specific; the others are fuzzy.

Understand logic.   _____

Know your enemy.   _____

Thread this needle.   ✓   _____

Reassemble this cat.   ✓   _____

Think.   _____

Smile when addressing a customer.   ✓   _____

As you will see, specific statements are precise; you can immediately determine whether or not you have met the objective. If you have not met it, the specific statement indicates what you must do to meet it. On the other hand, general or abstract statements (fuzzies) leave you in the dark. They must be reworded until they say exactly what is expected.

Measurable vs. Unmeasurable

An objective is considered measurable when it describes a tangible outcome. For example, objectives that describe intended outcomes that you can see or hear are measurable.

For example, an objective that says, "Be able to tie a knot," is measurable, because we can see knot-tying behavior and therefore assess whether it meets our expectations.

On the other hand, a statement that says, "Be able to internalize a growing awareness of confidence," is not only not measurable, it can't even be called an objective. What would you measure? What would you watch a student do to decide whether or not the internalizing had occurred to your satisfaction? The statement doesn't say.

Students vs. Instructors

"Instructional" objectives describe the student's performance rather than the instructor's performance. Objectives that describe the instructor's performance are called "administrative" objectives. Instructors help students to accomplish the instructional objectives.

For example, some of the following statements relate to what instructors might do, and some relate to what students might be expected to learn to do. Put a mark beside those that relate to student performance.

————— Lecture on the theory of tail wagging.

————— Be able to draw a duck.

————— Arrange field trips.

————— Arrange role-playing exercises.

————— Be able to write a business letter.

————— Explain the importance of the bottom line.

————— Be able to make change without error.

Turn to page 12.

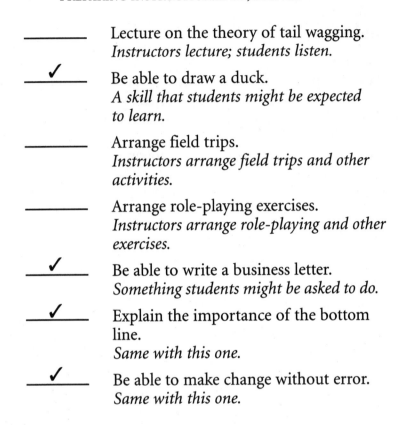

_____ Lecture on the theory of tail wagging.
Instructors lecture; students listen.

✓ _____ Be able to draw a duck.
A skill that students might be expected to learn.

_____ Arrange field trips.
Instructors arrange field trips and other activities.

_____ Arrange role-playing exercises.
Instructors arrange role-playing and other exercises.

✓ _____ Be able to write a business letter.
Something students might be asked to do.

✓ _____ Explain the importance of the bottom line.
Same with this one.

✓ _____ Be able to make change without error.
Same with this one.

This might have seemed like a trivial exercise, yet there are many instructors who cannot yet distinguish between statements about *instructor* activity and *student* performance. (If you're unlucky, you'll run into hundreds of so-called "objectives" that begin something like, "Seventy percent of the class must be able to _____." Such statements relate to teacher goals, not intended student outcomes.)

For now it's enough to know that if an objective is going to be useful, it needs to contain *specific and measurable student outcomes*.

2
Why Care About Objectives?

To wonder why we should care about instructional objectives is like wondering why we should know:

- where we're going before buying a bus ticket
- what we're intending to manufacture before turning on the factory
- whom we intend to hit before throwing the pie

After all, instruction is only successful to the degree that it succeeds in changing students in desired ways, rather than in undesired ways. If instruction doesn't change anyone in desired ways, it isn't any good, regardless of how elegant the lectures are or how complicated the hardware used to present it is.

Simply, if instruction is to accomplish desired outcomes, it is imperative that those designing the instruction, as well as the ones doing the instruction, have a clear picture of those desired outcomes.

Because objectives are tools for describing intended outcomes, they provide a key component for making instruction successful and are useful in several ways.

Materials/Procedure Selection

When clearly defined objectives are lacking, there is no sound basis for the selection of instructional materials and procedures. If you don't know where you're going, how will you know which road to take to get there? (Or, as Yogi Berra said, "When you reach a fork in the road, take it!")

After all, machinists and surgeons don't select tools until they know what they're intending to accomplish. Composers don't orchestrate scores until they know what effects they are trying to create. Too often, however, one hears instructors arguing the relative merits of books versus lectures, computers versus video, self-pacing versus group-pacing—without ever specifying just what results they expect these things to achieve. Instructors simply function in a fog of their own making unless they know what they want their students to accomplish as a result of their instruction.

Instructor Ingenuity

Once the important outcomes of instruction have been derived and clearly stated, it is then possible to say to instructors, "Here are the objectives you are expected to achieve. Now go use your best wisdom, experience, and ingenuity to achieve them." In other words, the existence of the objectives can free instructors to be creative and flexible.

With objectives in place, it is no longer necessary to expect all instructors to be doing the same thing at the same time during a lesson. It's like a football game, where the quarterback selects the best play to get his team where he knows it has to go. You can imagine what a game would be like if all quarterbacks had to use the same sequence of plays and have to succeed or fail "merely" on the basis of how well each play was executed.

Consistent Results

Objectives provide the basis for achieving consistent instructional results. With the instructional goal posts clearly visible, it is possible to provide enough instruction and practice so that all students learn to perform at least as well as the objectives require. Some will learn more or reach a higher performance level than the objectives require, of course, but everyone can be expected at least to accomplish each objective.

With objectives, it is possible to achieve desired results without requiring consistency in the process for getting those results.

Measurable Results

How many courses have you taken in which the tests had little or nothing to do with the substance of the instruction? No surprise there. Unless objectives are clearly and firmly fixed in the minds of both instructors and students, tests are likely to be at best misleading; at worst, they will be irrelevant, unfair, or uninformative. Without clear objectives it simply isn't possible to decide which measuring instrument will tell you what you want to know.

She: Why are you waving that meter stick around?

He: I wanna know how windy it is.

Clearly stated objectives provide a sound basis for selecting the means by which to find out whether they have been achieved. Suppose part of an objective said, "Be able to make a low-altitude parachute jump . . . " How could you find out whether your students can actually do what they were supposed to learn to do? How about a multiple-choice test? After all, they're easy to score, and you could even claim to be using an "objective" test. No? What about something in a true-false variety? You could have lots of fun dreaming up wrong answers.

True/false: Parachutes always come in pairs.

True/false: Red parachutes are heavier than white ones.

How about an essay test? Students should be able to describe how a parachute works and how they are packed, shouldn't they?

No doubt you saw right off that the only way to test whether someone can make a low-altitude jump is, in effect, to say, "Lemme see you make a low-altitude jump." And how did you know that? Because the objective clearly stated the intended outcome of the instruction. With clear objectives you don't have to be an expert in test construction to select and create measuring instruments that will tell you whether your objectives have been accomplished.

Goal Posts for Students

Clearly defined objectives also can be used to provide students with the means to organize their own time and efforts toward accomplishment of those objectives. When the instructional intent has been clarified—and revealed to the students—it is no longer necessary for them to guess what an instructor might have in mind for them to accomplish.

He: Think we should memorize the chapters?

She: Don't bother. This one's a footnote fanatic.

As you know too well, many students are required to spend considerable time and effort learning the peculiarities of their instructors when those instructors fail or refuse to let them in on the secret of what they're expected to learn. Unfortunately, such knowledge can be useful in helping students breeze through a course with little more than a bagful of tricks designed to rub the instructor the right way. Clear objectives in the hands of the students eliminate the need for such time-wasting and anxiety-producing activity.

Which leads to the final point: With clear objectives, it is possible to organize the instruction itself so that instructors and students alike can focus their efforts on bridging the gap between (a) what each student can already do and (b) what each needs to be able to do to accomplish each of the assigned objectives.

Instructional Efficiency

We have seen time and time again that when good objectives have been derived, existing instruction often can be drastically shortened. In fact, instruction can sometimes be eliminated altogether when the objectives help reveal that inadequate job performance is due to factors other than lack of knowledge or skill.

This "miracle" is effected by comparing information about what people need to be able to do (as described by the objectives) with information about what they already know how to do (as provided by target-population descriptions and/or performance tests). When there is no difference between the "should be able to do" and "can already do," it is clear that more instruction won't help; it is clear that the source of inadequate performance must be found elsewhere. (There are many reasons why people don't do what they already know how to do: Unclear performance expectations; absence of tools, space, or authority to perform as expected; and so on.)

Objectives are also useful in helping organizations respond to the pressures of downsizing and the resulting need to do more with less. With such pressures operating, it is critical for workers to become competent as quickly as possible. At the

Here is an example of how, when objectives aren't stated carefully, activities in the classroom can hinder the student's efforts to achieve an objective.

At a large training establishment operated by the government, a course was once offered in which students were to learn how to operate and repair a big, complex electronic system. The goal of the course was simply stated: To be able to operate and maintain the *XYZ Electronic System.*

Since it was impossible (because of the exorbitant cost) to provide each student with a separate system to practice on, it was decided to increase the amount of troubleshooting students did during the course by giving them some "practice" in the classroom as well as in the laboratory.

During the classroom troubleshooting exercises, the instructor would pose various problems for the students to solve. He would point out a component on one of the many schematic diagrams of the equipment and ask, "What would happen if this component were bad?" Students would then trace through the circuitry (on paper) in an effort to divine the *symptoms* that would appear as a result of the instructor's hypothetical trouble. The students, in other words, were given a trouble and asked to induce symptoms.

This procedure, however, was exactly opposite to that which was expected of the learners on the final examination or on the job. There they were typically shown a *symptom* and asked to locate the *trouble.* The instructors were expecting learners to run forward by teaching them how to run backward.

Thus, for want of a specific statement of objectives, students were not only learning the wrong thing, but the habits they were developing in the classroom were in conflict with those they were expected to use on the job.

same time, it is important that they not be removed from their job sites any longer than absolutely necessary to attend training. Objectives not only allow the training to be streamlined to the needs of the individual trainee, they often allow instruction to be delivered a module at a time, at more convenient locations, and during short periods that do not disrupt the flow of work.

Summary

Objectives are useful for providing:

- A sound basis for selection of instructional materials and procedures,
- Room for instructor creativity and ingenuity,
- Measurable instructional results,
- Tools for guiding student efforts, and
- A basis for realizing instructional efficiency.

There are additional advantages, not the least of which is that the act of drafting objectives causes one to think seriously and deeply about what is worth teaching. When objectives are drafted for courses already in existence, they can serve to spotlight opportunities for instructional improvement.

A Basic Distinction

Before practicing to recognize the characteristics of a usefully stated objective, we should make sure we're beating on the same drum. So far, we've noted that objectives are statements describing intended instructional outcomes, rather than the processes or content that will be used to achieve those outcomes. They describe ends rather than means. Therefore, there is a significant difference between course descriptions and their intended outcomes.

Course descriptions tell what a course is about, e.g., "Includes study of all the great philosophers, from Aristotle to Berra."

Objectives describe what students are expected to be able to do, e.g., "Given a stick, be able to beat a dead horse to oblivion."

Now read the following statement and the questions at the end of the statement. Then turn to the page number shown beside your answer to those questions.

A general survey of the organizing and administration of elementary- and secondary-school libraries, with emphasis on methods of developing the library as an integral part of the school. Includes functions, organization, services, equipment, and materials.

What does the above statement represent? Is the statement an *objective* of a course or a *description* of a course?

An objective of a course.   **Turn to page 23.**

A description of a course.   **Turn to page 27.**

Some years ago, the chief instructor of a 32-week military course noticed the peculiar fact that students were doing rather poorly on every *third* examination. Scores were low on the first exam and then considerably better on the next two, low on the fourth and high on the next two, and so on. Since scores were consistently low and then high even for the brighter students, the instructor correctly concluded that this peculiarity was not because of student intelligence or the lack of it. He then decided that he was so close to the course he probably wasn't seeing the woods for the trees, so he called in consultants.

During their analysis of the situation, the consultants noticed that the course was divided into five sub-courses. Each sub-course was taught by a different team of instructors, and during each sub-course the students were given three examinations. They discovered that students did poorly on the first test because they hadn't been told what to expect; they had to use the first test as a means of finding out what the instructors expected. Once they had learned what the objectives were, they did much better on the next two exams of that sub-course. But then another team of instructors took over. Believing the second team's examinations would be similar to those of the first team, the students prepared themselves accordingly, only to discover that the rules had been changed *without their knowledge*. They then did poorly on the fourth test (the first test given by the new instructor team). And so it went throughout the course. Objectives were vague, and the students were never told what to expect.

Once these conditions were made known to the chief instructor, the problem was easily solved.

You said the statement was an objective of a course. Apparently I didn't make myself clear earlier, so let me try again.

A course *description* tells you something about the content and procedures of a course. A course *objective* describes a desired outcome of a course.

Perhaps the sketch below will help make the distinction clear:

INSTRUCTION
(course)

PREREQUISITES	DESCRIPTION	OBJECTIVES
What a learner has to be able to do to qualify for a course.	What the course is about.	What a successful learner will be able to do at the end of the course.

Whereas an objective tells what the learner will be able to do as a result of some learning experiences, the course description tells only what the course is about.

The distinction is quite important, because a course description does not explain what will be accepted as adequate accomplishment. Though a course description might tell students which field they will be playing on, it doesn't tell them where the boundary lines are, where the goal posts are located, or how they will know when they have scored.

It is useful to be able to recognize the difference between an objective and a description, so try another example.

Which of the following statements looks most like an objective?

*In at least two computer languages,
be able to write and test a program
to calculate arithmetic means.*

Turn to page 29.

*Discusses and illustrates principles and
techniques of computer programming.*

Turn to page 31.

College catalogs frequently mislabel the content. For example,

Course Objective: To cover the military strategies
                     and tactics of the Civil War.

Statements such as these may say something about the objective of the instructors, but nothing about what the students should be able to do at the conclusion of the course. Calling it an objective doesn't make it one.

WHY CARE ABOUT OBJECTIVES?

You said the statement was a description of a course. And right you are! I'm sure you recognized the statement as a course description lifted from a college catalog.

One final word about course descriptions before moving on. Though a description sometimes tells us a good deal about what a course includes, it does not tell us what the course is supposed to accomplish. More important, it does not tell us how to determine when the intended outcomes have been achieved.

So, though a course description may be perfectly legitimate for a catalog, here we are interested *only* in the intended *results* of that course.

Zip ahead to page 33.

You said "In at least two computer languages, be able to write and test a program to calculate arithmetic means" was a statement of an objective.

Correct! The statement describes an intended outcome—something the student is expected to be able to do—rather than the procedure by which the student will develop that skill.

Since you can tell the difference between a course description and a course outcome, it's time to move on.

Turn to page 33.

Well . . . no. The collection of words that led you to this page is a piece of a course description—and not a very good description, at that. Look at it again:

Discusses and illustrates principles and techniques of computer programming.

Notice that the statement seems to be talking about what the course covers or what the instructor will be doing. There isn't a word about what the student will be able to do as a result of the instruction. I hope you are not being misled by the fact that college catalogs are full of statements like this one. They are not statements of learning outcomes, and they are not what we are concerned with here.

Let me try to explain the difference this way. A course description outlines various aspects of a *process* known as instruction. A course objective, on the other hand, is a description of the intended *results* of the instructional process. It's sort of like the difference between bread and baking. Baking is what you do to get the bread, but it isn't the same as bread. Baking is the process; bread is the result. Similarly, instruction is the process; student competence is the result.

Turn to page 5 and read the material again.

3
Where Objectives Come From

Instructional objectives come from many sources. Some of these sources are rational, systematic, and useful; others are egocentric, disorganized, and astonishingly haphazard. Systematic derivation procedures lead to objectives truly worth accomplishing. The "I know what's best for students" approach, on the other hand, often leads to objectives that describe outcomes of little value to the student. This is because "I know best" decisions can so often be totally disconnected from any real need for instruction. Such questionable decisions can be derived from prior experience which may be out of date, from biases inspired by the chapters that happen to be included in a textbook, from instructor preferences about what they *like* to teach, or from inertia—"I've *always* taught it this way."

When derived from any of these non-systematic "methods," the resulting instruction can prove totally useless to the student, regardless of the importance of the subject matter to the instructor. Unfortunately, people embedded in the middle of an educational system can easily lose sight of the fact that good objectives are ultimately derived from the real world. (That's another way of saying that the purpose of instruction is to help someone learn to do something of value—to someone other than the instructor.) Instructors can get so engrossed in "teaching points" that they forget that the purpose of the enterprise is to get beyond the "talk about" to the "DO about."

Properly derived objectives—all genuine objectives—are ultimately about *doing*. They describe the desired results of instruction, rather than the activities of instruction. They provide descriptions of instructional destinations, thus allowing us to derive components of the instructional process that will be truly relevant to reaching those desirable destinations.

Most instructional objectives are derived from two general sources:

1. Personal desires
2. External needs

Personal Desires

People often decide that they want to accomplish something on their own, with or without formal instruction. New Year's resolutions, for example, often describe personally selected objectives:

"I will lose ten pounds by June 1."

"I will be out of debt by the end of this year."

Self-selected goals that involve *learning* might include the following:

"I'll learn to play the harp so that I can wow my neighbors at the block party next month."

"My spouse is leaving me, so I'm going to the bookstore to learn everything I can about how to handle a divorce."

"My boss returned my monthly report with all the spelling errors circled. I'd better learn how to spel."

Having decided, they are the ones who must take action to accomplish their goals. Those who prefer a systematic approach will take steps to decide as precisely as they can just what it is they hope to accomplish through their learning. They will, in other words, establish a list of objectives. Having done that, they are in a much better position to decide what actions they need to take to accomplish them.

External Needs

Suppose, though, that you have decided to become a licensed Zamboni driver, so that you can get paid for tooling around an ice rink while waving at the cheering throngs. In this instance, it doesn't matter much what you may want to learn, because the learning need will be defined by what it takes to accomplish the task. In other words, the instructional objectives for your learning will be derived not from your personal preferences, but from what other people have determined to be the tasks that any Zamboni driver has to be able to perform.

If you sign up for instruction, the objectives will be derived and established by the coach or instructor. But how do they derive these and other objectives? They do it by analyzing various levels of needs. The analysis might begin by reviewing the needs of an entire organization, or it might begin at a lower level, such as a division or department. At the end of the process, the analysis finally reveals needs that must be fulfilled if the desired goals are to be achieved. "Need" here refers to a performance "hole" that must be filled if an expected or planned accomplishment is to be realized. For example:

"To qualify for enrollment in Algebra II, students need to be able to perform these tasks." (List would be added here.)

Because traditionally most instruction has been done in classrooms, we sometimes forget that we often use those very same classrooms for things other than instruction. For example, here are the kinds of activities for which classrooms are often used:

Information sessions:	"Let me explain the benefits package."
Sales sessions:	"Let's begin by singing the company song."
Motivation sessions:	"You really oughta wanna get out and sell."
Orientation sessions:	"Here's an overview of this course."
Bull sessions:	"Let's knock some new-product ideas around."
Instructional sessions:	"Here's how to do it."

Notice that only the instructional sessions tend to change behavior in carefully specified ways. Therefore, instructional objectives are appropriate only for teaching sessions. The fact that "it" is done in a classroom shouldn't stampede you into deriving and drafting objectives. Create objectives only when there are things that people don't yet know how to do and also need to know how to do.

"To perform your job competently, you need to be able to solder well enough to meet military specifications."

"An analysis reveals that 50% of our sales force can't speak English well enough to communicate with our customers. We need to correct this problem as soon as possible."

"We're planning to make significant changes in the organization, and people will need to have these listed skills and knowledge to function successfully." (List would be added here.)

Once these performance needs have been derived, they are compared against what individuals can and cannot now do. Those things that people cannot now do, *and* need to be able to do, become objectives for instruction.

Systematic Derivation of Instructional Objectives

Those responsible for meeting external performance needs (e.g., performance analysts, instructional developers) use a systematic procedure to derive objectives and to decide what is worth teaching. This procedure follows some version of the following steps:

1. *Task listing.* Any job, position, profession, or hobby consists of a collection of tasks. This collection names the things that people do when carrying out their work or play. (Note: A task is a series of steps leading to a useful/meaningful outcome.) Here are the names of some tasks that people might have to perform:

Here is an example of a skill hierarchy, or pyramid, showing the relationships between the skills involved in making a pizza.[1]

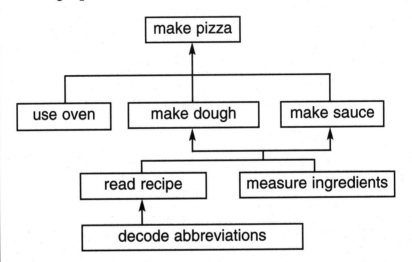

Read the hierarchy this way: Before students can practice the main skill (making pizza), they need to be able to use an oven, make dough, and make sauce. These skills are subordinate (prerequisite) to the terminal skill in that they must all be learned before the terminal skill can be practiced in its entirety. But these three skills are independent of one another; *they can be learned in any order.*

Before the skills of making dough or making sauce can be practiced, students will have to be able to read a recipe and measure ingredients. These skills are both subordinate to the sauce-and-dough making but are independent of one another. Either could be learned first. Finally, to read a recipe, the learner first has to learn how to decode abbreviations.

[1] Hierarchy courtesy of Diane Pope.

- Prepare a lesson plan
- Take spinal X-rays
- Change a tire
- Interview an applicant
- Write a report
- Write correctly spelled letters
- Play a song
- Send/receive Morse code
- Drive a golf ball at least 200 yards

If the job is new, or if there is some question about whether the current tasks being performed are appropriate, a "higher" level of analysis will be indicated. In other words, first we'll decide what the job should consist of, and then we'll list the tasks that will be required to do the job.

2. **Task analysis.** Once the tasks have been identified, the next step is to draw a picture for each task describing the steps and key decisions that make up the task. This procedure, called task analysis, reveals the components of the task by describing what a competent person does when performing the task. It gives the reason for starting to perform the task; it describes the steps followed and decisions made during completion of the task; and it indicates how to tell when the task has been completed, i.e., when to stop doing the task.

3. **Skill derivation.** With a task analysis in hand, it is possible to answer the question, "What would anyone have to know or be able to do before being ready to practice this entire task?" For example, before being ready to practice the task of interviewing a job applicant, anyone would have to be able to (a) interact tactfully, (b) speak

the applicant's language, and (c) complete an interview form. To complete the interview form may in turn require that the interviewer be able to (d) write legibly and/or (e) make computer entries.

In this way all of these skills that anyone would need to have are systematically derived from what competent interviewers actually do.

4. *Objectives drafting.* Now that the required skills have been derived from the task analyses, the next step is to draft objectives describing the limits—the "amount"— of skill that anyone would need to perform the various tasks. The objective describes the performance desired, the conditions under which the performance should occur, and the level of skill required.

The objectives describing the skills needed for performance of all of the job-related tasks provide the basis for development of a curriculum, a course, or coaching sessions.

The beauty of this procedure is that instructors who have derived objectives in this manner are able to prove that what they are teaching is relevant to the fulfillment of an important need.

5. *Skill-hierarchy drafting.* The next step is to draw a skill hierarchy that shows the prerequisite relationships between the objectives. A hierarchy looks a good deal like an organization chart and shows which skill needs to be mastered before another can be profitably practiced. For example, one needs to learn to speak a language before learning how to interact tactfully; one needs to be able to write before practicing writing reports or filling in forms. (See example on page 38.)

6. ***Curriculum derivation.*** To this point, the focus has been on what anyone would have to be able to do to perform competently in the target area (job, assignment, hobby, etc.). With objectives and hierarchy in hand, it is now possible to derive an efficient curriculum for each student or trainee by comparing the objective with what a given student can already do. If a given student can already do what one or more objectives require, these objectives are deleted from that student's curriculum.

Trainers expecting to work in business and industry must at the very least be able to perform the systematic objectives—deriving steps just described.

Now that we've taken a brief look at where objectives come from, it's time to consider the anatomy of an objective, so that you will be able to recognize a useful one when you see one and to draft your own.

4

The Qualities
of Useful Objectives

Experience during recent decades has shown that instructional objectives are extremely important tools in the design, implementation, and evaluation of instruction. They are useful in pointing to the content and procedures that will allow instruction to be relevant and successful. They are useful in helping to manage the instructional process itself, and to point to the means for assessing instructional success.

Objectives in the hands of the students prevent the students from having to guess at how they might best organize their time and effort.

But what are the qualities of a useful objective? What characteristics would make one objective more useful than another?

Simply put, a usefully stated objective is one that succeeds in communicating an intended instructional result to the reader. It is useful to the extent that it conveys to others a picture of what a successful learner will be able to do; and to the extent that the picture it conveys is *identical to the picture the objective writer had in mind.*

Now, any number of combinations of words and pictures and symbols might be used to express an intended outcome.

What you are searching for is that group of words or symbols that will communicate your intent exactly as YOU understand it. For example, if you provide other instructors with an objective and they then teach some students to perform in a manner that *you agree* is consistent with what you had in mind, then you have communicated your objective in a meaningful manner. If, on the other hand, you "had something more in mind" or they didn't "grasp the essence" of your intent, then your statement failed to communicate adequately, regardless of how that statement was worded.

A meaningfully stated objective, then, is one that succeeds in communicating your intent; the best statement is the one that excludes the greatest number of possible meanings *other than* your intent.

Unfortunately, there are many slippery words that are open to a wide range of interpretation. (If you have tried to write more than a few sentences that say what you mean, you know how exasperating those little devils can be.) It isn't that such words aren't useful in everyday conversation. After all, you wouldn't want to be skewered with a "What do you mean by that?!" every time you said something like "It's a nice day," or "I really appreciate you," or "I'm fine." But if you use *only* such broad terms (or "fuzzies") when trying to communicate a specific *instructional* intent, you leave yourself open to *mis*interpretation.

Consider the following phrases in this light:

WORDS OPEN TO MANY INTERPRETATIONS	WORDS OPEN TO FEWER INTERPRETATIONS
to know	to write
to understand	to recite
to *really* understand	to identify
to appreciate	to sort
to *fully* appreciate	to solve
to grasp the significance of	to construct
to enjoy	to build
to believe	to compare
to have faith in	to contrast
to internalize	to smile

What do you mean when you say you want learners to know something? Do you mean you want them to recite or to solve or to construct? Just to tell them you want them to "know" tells them little—because the word can mean many different things. Until you say what you mean by "knowing" in terms of what students ought to be able to DO, you have said very little at all. Thus, an objective that communicates best will be one that describes the student's intended performance clearly enough to preclude misinterpretation.

How can you create this type of objective? What characteristics might help an objective to communicate and be useful? Several schemes might be used in stating objectives, but the format described on the following pages is known to work, and it is the one I have found easiest to use.

Three Characteristics to Include

The format includes three characteristics that help an objective to communicate an intent. These characteristics answer three questions:

- What should the learner be able to do?
- Under what conditions do you want the learner to be able to do it?
- How well must it be done?

1. **Performance.** An objective always states what a learner is expected to be able to do and/or produce to be considered competent.

    Example: Be able to ride a unicycle.

    (The performance stated is *ride.*)

    Example: Be able to write a letter.

    (The performance is *writing;* the product of the performance is a letter.)

2. **Conditions.** An objective describes the important conditions (if any) under which the performance is to occur.

    Example: Given a product and prospective customer, be able to describe the key features of the product.

    (The performance is to occur in the presence of a *product* and a *customer;* these are the conditions that will influence the nature of the performance, and so they are stated in the objective.)

3. **Criterion.** An objective describes the criteria of acceptable performance; that is, it says how well someone would have to perform to be considered competent.

> *Example:*   Given a computer with word-processing software, be able to write a letter. Criteria: All words are spelled correctly, there are no grammatical or punctuation errors, and the addressee is not demeaned or insulted.
>
> (In this case the criteria of acceptable performance are labeled as such; often they are not.)

Sometimes there will be no special conditions to include, and sometimes it is impractical or useless to include a criterion (as when the criterion is obvious). But the more you say about your desired intent, the better you will communicate.

Characteristics That Should NOT Be Included in Objectives

It would be possible to add other features to objectives, such as instructional procedures, descriptions of the target audience, or format requirements.

Instructional procedure. For example, it would be possible to include a description of the procedure by which the objective will be accomplished, as in:

"Given six lectures on the subject of _____ . . ."

This feature would not serve a useful purpose, and it could be extremely limiting. What about an instructor who could accomplish the objective with only two lectures? Or with no lectures at all? Or could succeed by some other means? And what about the students who need no instruction at all? The objective should mention only outcomes, so that those charged with accomplishing those outcomes will be free to use their best wisdom and experience in doing so.

Imagine what would happen if industrial blueprints included information about how the products described should be manufactured. Aside from cluttering the blueprints and making them difficult or impossible to read, it would hamper those who had better ways to proceed than those described in the blueprint.

Target audience. Some people also describe the target audience for which the objective is intended, as in:

"First-line supervisors will be able to interview applicants . . ."

Such a feature would also get in the way. While it may be true that first-line supervisors need to be able to interview applicants, that might also be true for other groups. Should you have a different objective for each group, even though each of those objectives would say exactly the same thing?

In attempting to answer that question, I remember a school system whose teachers were required to write classroom objectives, course objectives, school objectives, district objectives, and county objectives. All those objectives described exactly the same performance, but the teachers went nuts trying to make them look different. In short, the answer is no.

Format. It would also be possible to insist that all objectives conform to a specific form or format. For example, one could expect all objectives to be written in a single sentence, or to begin with the conditions, or to not exceed a certain number of words. This again would be lunacy, as it would be another way to defeat the purpose of the objective, which is to describe a desired outcome.

I once visited a school in which teachers were expected to write their objectives on a form printed by the principal. His form had a line printed every two inches down the page, the implication being that every objective was no more than seven inches long and two inches high. Would you be surprised to learn that the teachers were hostile to the idea? But you are not looking for objectives that are a particular size and shape. You are looking for objectives that are *clear,* that say what you want to say about your instructional intents as concisely as possible. And that is all. So, anybody who says that an objective must be no more than two inches high and seven inches wide or who says an objective must or must not contain certain words should be reminded that the function of an objective is to communicate. If it does, rejoice. If it doesn't, fix it! You don't work on an objective until it matches someone's idea of "good looks"; you work on it until it communicates one of your instructional intents, and you write as many objectives as you need to describe ALL instructional results you think are important to accomplish.

The following chapters are intended to help you to do just that.

5
Performance

A useful objective includes these characteristics:

1. **Performance.** It describes what the learner is expected to be able to DO.

2. **Conditions.** It describes the conditions under which the performance is expected to occur.

3. **Criterion.** It describes the level of competence that must be reached or surpassed.

In this chapter we will investigate the first of these characteristics, that of performance. Performances may be visible, like writing, repairing, or painting; or invisible, like adding, solving, or identifying.

Visible (Overt) Performance

To be useful, an objective must state what it is that learners must do to demonstrate their mastery of the objective. This is easy to do when the main intent (the primary object of the objective) is visible or audible. For example, if the objective calls for students to be able to dance, or to interview, or to draft a report, the objective will state those visible/audible performances:

Be able to dance . . .

Be able to interview . . .

Be able to produce a report . . .

Can you tell directly when someone is dancing? Of course. Interviewing? Yes. Producing a report? Yes again. These are directly observable performances. In each of these instances the objective clearly states what it is that students are expected to be able to do, and each intended performance is directly visible and/or audible; you can see or hear someone doing it.

If a statement does not include a visible performance, it isn't yet an objective.

Many statements, however, only pretend to describe a performance. For example, consider the following:

To develop a critical understanding of the importance of effective management.

Though this may be an important goal, the statement doesn't tell you what someone would be doing when demonstrating mastery of the "objective." What would be your guess? Writing an essay on the importance of management? Answering multiple-choice questions on the history of management? Preparing a production schedule?

The statement not only doesn't say, it doesn't even provide a clue. In such cases it is highly unlikely that two or more people could agree on what the statement means; it is open to far too many interpretations. As an "objective" it is useless because it doesn't clearly communicate an intent.

Worse, the words "To develop . . ." suggest that the statement is referring to the *process* by which someone might come to have an understanding of the importance of effective management. Since you already know that objectives are about intended outcomes, you can see yet another defect in the above statement.

Now try this statement:

Given all available engineering data regarding a proposed product, be able to write a product profile. The profile must describe and define all of the commercial characteristics of the product appropriate to its introduction to the market, including descriptions of at least three major product uses.

What's the performance stated in the objective? Draw a circle around the words that tell you what the student will be doing when demonstrating achievement of the objective.

Check your response on the next page.

Given all available engineering data regarding a proposed product, be able to (write a product profile) The profile must describe and define all of the commercial characteristics of the product appropriate to its introduction to the market, including descriptions of at least three major product uses.

The student will be writing a product profile. Can you tell when someone is doing that? Yes. Therefore the statement includes a visible performance and so meets the first requirement of an objective.

The way to write an objective that meets the first requirement, then, is to draft a statement describing one of your intended instructional outcomes and then modify it until it answers the question:

What will the learner be DOING when demonstrating achievement of the objective?

Let's apply this test to some examples.

Which of the following statements is stated in performance terms? Turn to the page shown beside the answer you select.

Be able to write a news article.   *Page 57.*

Be able to develop an appreciation of music.   *Page 59.*

You said "Be able to write a news article" is written in performance terms. You've got it!

You remembered to apply the key question. What must people DO to demonstrate mastery of the objective? Why, they must write a news article. You can tell directly when they are doing that, so writing qualifies as a visible performance. You don't know whether the writing must be done by hand or on a keyboard, such as the one I am flogging at this very moment, but you do know that the main intent of the objective is writing. (NOTE: If the instrument of writing is important, that will be described as one of the conditions under which the performance is to occur.) For now, be content with performance.

Try another one. Turn to the page shown beside the statement that contains a performance.

Be able to understand mathematics. **Page 65.**

Be able to sew a seam. **Page 67.**

You said "Be able to develop an appreciation of music" was stated in performance terms. Gadzooks!

Maybe you thought so because the importance of the goal overshadowed the murkiness with which the goal was stated.

Ask the magic question: "What would someone be doing when demonstrating mastery of this goal?" Writing an essay on the meaning of opera? Sighing in ecstasy when listening to Bach? Answering multiple-choice questions on the history of music? Buying records? Stomping feet? The statement doesn't say. It doesn't give us a clue.

Let's consider performance a little more closely.

A performance is described by a *doing* word. If the word describes something you might be able to DO, then it describes a performance. If it only describes something you can BE, then it is not a *doing* word.

Here are some examples of *doing* words (performances):

> running
>
> solving
>
> writing

Here are some examples of *being* words (abstractions):

> happy
> understanding
> appreciating
> knowing

Turn to page 61.

You can see someone *running, solving,* or *writing.* Therefore those words qualify as performances.

But *appreciating* and *understanding* describe abstract states of being. That is, they describe states of being whose existence can only be *inferred* from performances. You can find out whether people understand something only by watching them act or by listening to them. You can tell whether they have a certain attitude only by watching them say or do something from which the existence of the attitude may be inferred.

See if you can tell the difference between performances (*doing* words) and abstractions (*being* words). **Circle the words below that describe performances:**

stating

writing

valuing

drawing

listing

appreciating

internalizing

smiling

When you have finished, turn to page 63.

Check your responses with mine. The performances are circled.

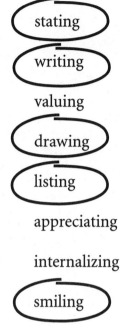

stating

writing

valuing

drawing

listing

appreciating

internalizing

smiling

The circled words describe things that people might do. The words not circled describe internal states of being. Valuing, for example, is not something that someone does; rather, it is something that is felt.

Now let's look at some statements and practice recognizing which ones include *performances*. Read the statements below, and turn to the page referred to beside the statement containing a *performance*.

Be able to understand mathematics. **Page 65.**

Be able to sew a seam. **Page 67.**

You said "Be able to understand mathematics" included a performance. Not for a minute.

What would people be *doing* when demonstrating their understanding? Defining mathematics? Writing an essay on Einstein? Solving problems? Correcting problems? Devising problems? The statement doesn't say anything about what someone might be expected to be able to do.

While *understanding* is a fine word for everyday conversation, it is open to far too many interpretations to be useful in an objective.

Try not to be trapped by the fact that the above statement begins with "be able to," as those words can be followed by sheer nonsense. Consider these slippery things:

Be able to develop an increased appreciation and sensitivity.

Be able to internalize a growing awareness.

What would someone be doing when internalizing a growing awareness? What would anyone be doing when developing an appreciation and sensitivity? I dunno. The statement doesn't say.

What we are looking for is the word or words that describe an intended action, whether that action be directly observable (running, writing, editing) or invisible (solving, recognizing, recalling).

Try another one. Turn to the page referred to beside the statement that contains a *performance:*

Be able to apply scientific knowledge.   **Page 69.**

Be able to stain slides.   **Page 71.**

You said "Be able to sew a seam" describes performance.

Yes. What are people doing when demonstrating their achievement of this objective? They are sewing something—that's what they are doing. We don't know whether there are any special conditions under which the seam sewing must occur, and we don't know how well someone would have to sew to be considered acceptable, but we do know that they have to sew seams (or so it seems). Thus, this statement meets the first requirement of an objective—it includes a performance.

Try another.

Turn to the page referred to beside the statement below that includes a performance:

Be able to apply scientific knowledge.   *Page 69.*

Be able to stain slides.   *Page 71.*

Well, I suppose I can understand how you might say that "apply scientific knowledge" states a performance. After all, the word *apply* sometimes DOES describe a performance. If the objective were about applying paint or applying makeup to a face, I would agree that I could tell when someone was doing the applying. But "applying scientific knowledge" is rather like "applying oneself with a proper attitude." You don't have the faintest idea of what the student would be doing. Singing a song? Taking out an appendix? Mixing a solution? Constructing a still? The statement doesn't give us any clue.

A statement ought not be called an objective unless, at the very least, it tells us what someone would have to do to demonstrate achievement of the objective. So, when you are looking for the performance, ask the question "What is the *doing* word?"

Turn to page 65 and reread.

You said "Be able to stain slides" includes a performance. Of course!

You can tell whether the stainer is staining the stainee. Therefore you can tell whether someone is doing what the objective says it is important to be able to do.

One final example. Which of the following statements includes a performance?

Develop a knowledge of food-service equipment. **Page 73.**

Be able to add a column of numbers. **Page 75.**

Come on!

How can I help you to internalize your growing awareness of infinite feeling states and consciousness levels if you keep slipping off to pages like these, "just to find out what is printed on them"?

As long as you're here, though, we might as well share a word or two about the topic at hand. *Develop* is one of those words which by itself doesn't tell you if it is describing a performance. All sorts of things might be developed—theses, neighborhoods, or triceps. But none of these is a performance; none describes anything anyone does. *Develop* is one of those words that depends on the words that follow it for its meaning, like "apply" and "demonstrate." Worse, it usually describes instructional *process,* and we want an objective to describe *outcome.*

There are other such sneakies. *Acquiring an attitude* is not at all the same as *acquiring a wallet.* The latter is a performance; the former is not.

Enough of diversion. Let's get back to work.

Read page 75.

You said "Be able to add a column of numbers" includes a performance. Yes.

What would someone be doing when demonstrating mastery of the objective? Adding a column of numbers. So the statement meets the first requirement of an objective.

Covert (Invisible) Performance

"Wait a minute," I hear you screaming, "something's fishy here. Someone could add while standing perfectly still! Or ogle, even. How can you call those performances when nobody can see them?"

Good point. As you've noted, some performances are not visible to the naked eye, such as solving, discriminating, and identifying. In these cases, statements that say:

Be able to solve . . .

Be able to discriminate . . .

Be able to identify . . .

are inadequate because they don't describe a visible performance. Though these and other invisible (covert) performances are often important, statements that describe only the covert performance are not yet objectives. Why? Because they don't tell us what someone must DO to demonstrate mastery of the objective.

Why not solve this problem simply by demanding that objectives describe only visible performance? Because a lot of the important performances we intend to nurture are covert (invisible), and to ignore them would prevent us from talking about a large part of our intended outcomes. As we are often interested in having students learn to solve problems, recognize specific characteristics, recall procedures, etc., the exclusion of this important part of our instruction would legitimately cause too many people to have a cow.

What to do? Simple, really. Whenever the main intent of your objective is covert, just add an indicator behavior to reveal how the covert performance can be directly detected. (Huh? Whut's an indicator?) An indicator behavior is one that will tell us directly whether a covert performance is happening to our satisfaction. An indicator is simple, direct, and always something that every trainee already knows how to do.

For example, if the objective is about an ability to discriminate counterfeit money, you would think it through as follows.

Hmm. The main intent of this objective is to be able to discriminate counterfeit money. But because I can't see anyone discriminating, I'll need to think of a way to find out whether the discriminating is happening. I know. I'll have them sort a pile of money into two piles. If they can do that correctly, I'll have a direct indication of their ability to discriminate. So all I have to do is to add the word "sort" to the objective, like this:

Be able to discriminate (sort) counterfeit money.

So we can write about covert performances in objectives as long as there is a direct way of finding out whether the performance is in good shape. "Direct way" means that there is a single act or behavior that will indicate the presence of the covert skill. The rule is this:

Whenever the performance stated in an objective is covert, add an indicator behavior.

That way, everyone will know what you mean when you use slippery words such as "identify." Just make sure the indicator you add is the simplest and most direct behavior you can think of, and make sure that it's something every trainee already knows how to do. Common examples are circle, underline, point to, write, say.

Occasionally I hear from someone who is disturbed about the use of the words "be able to" in an objective.

"I don't want them to be *able* to do things," goes the complaint, "I want them to DO them. Therefore, I think it's inappropriate to use those words in an objective."

Hmm. I can understand the source of the concern. But the purpose of an objective is to describe a capability you want them to carry around with them so that they can use it when they need or want to.

So I use "be able to" to describe the desired capabilities that should be available on demand.

When I want the capability actually demonstrated, I do so with a test. A test is a set of commands. "Answer these questions," "Interview this customer," and "Here's a symptom; locate the trouble," are examples of test items that ask for performance. If my objectives are couched in "demand language" rather than "capability language," they might confuse their users.

But if "be able to" pushes you into a psychic trauma, don't use it. Use whatever words will best communicate with your student populations.

Below are a few expressions, some of which describe covert performance and some of which describe overt performance. Here's what to do:

1. Place a check mark beside those expressions that describe performances that you can see or hear directly (overt).

2. Then, for those expressions describing covert performances, write the simplest, most direct indicator behavior you can think of that would tell you whether the covert performance existed.

Drive a bulldozer. _____

Identify transistors on
a wiring diagram. _____

Recognize tactless
statements. _____

Discriminate between
normal and abnormal
X-rays. _____

Paint a trombone. _____

Dissect a politician. _____

When you are ready, turn to page 80.

1. Drive a bulldozer.   _____✓_____

2. Identify transistors on   Circle
   a wiring diagram.   _____

3. Recognize tactless   Point to;
   statements.   underline
                               _____

4. Discriminate between
   normal and abnormal   Sort
   X-rays.   _____

5. Paint a trombone.   _____✓_____

6. Dissect a politician.   _____✓_____

1. You can watch someone driving a bulldozer, so you don't need an indicator to tell you that the performance happened.
2. But "identify" is a slippery word, and you need an indicator to let people know what you mean.
3. The same is true for "recognize." How do you want me to let you know that I have recognized to your satisfaction?
4. "Discriminate" usually means "be able to tell one thing from another," and you need an indicator to discover whether the covert discriminating occurred.

5, 6. You can watch people painting trombones and dissecting politicians, so no indicator behaviors are needed.

You see the point. When you can observe the main intent of the objective directly, just state the performance. But when the main intent is covert, add an indicator. The simplest way to do it is to write the indicator right after the performance, in parentheses, like this: "Be able to identify (sort) . . ."

Always State the Main Intent

Sometimes you will stumble over some objectives that state perfectly good indicators whose main intents are missing. For example:

> *Given completed Form 31s, be able to circle erroneous entries.*

What's the performance stated in the objective? Circling. But is circling what the objective is about? Hardly. The objective is about being able to *discriminate* (tell the difference between) correct and incorrect entries. So the objective should state that main intent:

> *Given completed Form 31s, be able to recognize erroneous entries.*

Because "recognize" describes a covert performance, it is useful to add an indicator behavior by which the presence of the covert performance may be detected. The simplest way is to state the main intent and then to follow it with the indicator in parentheses. Like so:

> *Given completed Form 31s, be able to recognize (circle) erroneous entries.*

Here's another example:

> *Given the brand names of products currently available to the cosmetologist, be able to underline those considered safe to use as shampoo.*

What's the performance stated in the objective? Underline. That's what it says. But do you suppose the writer of the objective is burning to have his/her students go through life underlining brand names? Doesn't seem likely, does it? Though the objective *says* underline, it's pretty clear that the objective writer has something more important in mind. In this example, it's easy to guess that the intent is for students to be able to discriminate—tell the difference—between safe and unsafe shampoos (or real poos, for that matter).

(Objectives like these—those that fail to state a main intent—are likely to be branded as trivial.)

Simply put, objectives aren't about indicators; they're about main intents. It's the main intent that students are supposed to learn. If they have to *learn* an indicator behavior, that behavior has absolutely no business being used as an indicator.

Summary

1. *An instructional objective describes an intended outcome of instruction, rather than the procedures for accomplishing those outcomes.*

2. *An objective always states a performance that describes what the learner will be DOING when demonstrating mastery of the objective.*

3. *When the main intent of an objective is covert, an indicator behavior—through which the main intent can be detected—is added.*

4. *Indicator behaviors are always the simplest, most direct behaviors possible, and they are always something that every trainee already knows how to do well.*

6
Conditions

By the time you have written an objective that says what you will expect your learners to do, you will have written a far less ambiguous objective than many which are in use today. Rather than expecting your students to guess what you have in mind when using such ambiguous words as *understand, know,* or *appreciate,* you will have at least revealed what you want them to accomplish. Regardless of how skimpy the statement may be, it will exhibit the most important characteristic of all—*it will be written down.* If it isn't written down, it isn't anything. If it is written down, it can be improved. And if it states a performance, it can be called an objective. Therefore, by the time your statement identifies a desired performance, you are more than halfway toward developing a useful objective.

But simply specifying the performance may not be enough to prevent serious misunderstanding of your intent. For example, suppose you are the master of ceremonies at the annual awards' night of the Whyners Club. As part of the program, you call me up from the audience and bet me a carload of broccoli that I can't lift the 500-pound barbells sitting on the stage.

I agree to the bet and then quickly get two burly types from the audience to help me, and we lift the barbells with ease.

"Where's my broccoli?" I ask.

"Wait a minnit," you reply. "You were supposed to lift those barbells by yourself."

"Oh? You didn't say that there were any *conditions* attached to this performance," I reply. "Why didn't you say so?"

"You should have *known* that I meant for you to do it by yourself."

"Sorry. My crystal ball hasn't come back from the cleaners. You'll just have to *keep* your broccoli," I say, snickering all the way back to my seat.

You can see how risky it can be to assume that others know what you are thinking. (If they *did* know what you were thinking, you'd have a lot more to worry about than the broccoli police.) You've had any number of experiences such as these during your school career: instances in which you were taught one thing and tested on another, for example, because the objectives weren't clear (if there were objectives at all).

To avoid surprises when working with objectives, we state the main intent of the objective *and* describe the main conditions under which the performance is to occur. An objective that says, "Be able to hammer a nail . . . " is different from one that says, "Given a brick, be able to hammer a nail . . . " If it just says, "Be able to hammer a nail . . . " you might assume that it means hammering with a hammer. That might be the logical assumption in the absence of any other information. But think how dismayed you would be if you practiced hammering with your hammer; but when it came time to demonstrate your skill, you were asked to hammer with a brick—or a stone—or a stapler. You would no doubt feel betrayed, tricked, and deceived—and you'd be right.

At the same time, you can imagine the writer of the objective looking up in total surprise, saying, "How could you *not* know I meant for you to hammer with a brick? You know perfectly well there are no hammers where you're going to be working." An objective such as "Be able to run the hundred-yard dash" may be stated in enough detail to prevent serious misunderstanding, provided the runners are not tricked by unexpected conditions such as having to run barefoot up a slippery slope—as the instructor shouts, "Hey, now. *Anybody* can run on level ground. That's no challenge."

Miscommunications such as these can be avoided by adding relevant conditions to your objective. How? Simply by describing the conditions that have a significant impact on the performance. By telling people what they will have, and not have, to work with when performing, and by telling them of special circumstances in which the performance must occur. In other words, by describing the givens and/or limitations within which the performance is expected to occur. Here are some examples:

Given a standard set of tools and the TS manual . . .

Using your service revolver . . .

Given a matrix of inter-correlations . . .

In the presence of an irate customer . . .

Without the aid of references . . .

With only a screwdriver . . .

On an obese patient, be able to . . .

On a fully functioning wrist computer . . .

How Much Detail?

How detailed should you be in your description? Detailed enough to describe each of the conditions that would be needed to allow the performance to happen; detailed enough to describe the conditions that would make a significant difference to the nature of the performance.

Here are some questions you can ask yourself to guide you in identifying key conditions.

1. What will the learner be expected to use when performing (e.g., tools, forms, etc.)?

2. What will the learner not be allowed to use while performing (e.g., checklists or other aids)?

3. What will be the real-world conditions under which the performance will be expected to occur (e.g., on top of a flagpole, under water, in front of a large audience, in a cockpit, etc.)?

Here is an example. Look at the objective below, and then turn to the page referred to under the part of the sentence that describes the conditions.

Given a list of factors leading to significant historical events,

Page 95.

be able to identify (underline) at least five factors

Page 89.

contributing to the Crash of 1929.

You said the phrase "be able to identify (underline)" describes conditions.

No, you selected the performance. Perhaps you're still thinking about the first important characteristic of an objective, the performance. If so, I'm glad you remembered it, but now we're attempting to identify (underline) the conditions under which the performance will be expected to occur.

Maybe it will help if you ask the question, "With what, or to what, will the learner be doing whatever it is he or she will be doing?"

Here's another example. Turn to the page number shown under the conditions.

Given a list of chemical elements,

Page 91.

be able to recall (write) the valences of each.

Page 93.

You've got it. "Given a list of chemical elements" is a condition that announces what will be provided during the expected performance, that of recalling valences.

Now identify (there's that sneaky word again) the conditions stated in the following objective. Turn to the page number shown under what you select as the conditions.

While blindfolded, and presented with wine samples, be able

Page 99.

to recognize (say) which samples were aged in oak casks.

Page 97.

No, you selected the performance, "be able to recall (write)," rather than the conditions, "Given a list of chemical elements."

Let me explain it this way. Suppose I said that you need to be able to recall the symbols and valences of chemical elements. With only that much information as a guide, you might go off to memorize all the symbols and their valences, only to discover that when it came time to perform, you would be provided with a list of the elements and asked to write their valences.

You might feel a little betrayed or deceived, because you spent all that time memorizing the symbols when, in fact, you would be provided with a list of them.

This can be an important point, because while doing your job you may often be provided with job aids in the form of checklists, procedures, lists of key steps, etc. These are intended to prevent you from having to memorize mountains of information. If you didn't know that these aids would be provided to help your performance, you might break your brain memorizing information that would, in fact, be provided to you.

Try this one: Turn to the page number shown under the conditions.

While blindfolded, and presented with wine samples, be able

Page 99.

to recognize (say) which samples were aged in oak casks.

Page 97.

You chose "Given a list of factors leading to significant historical events" as the words describing the conditions or situation under which the selecting behavior was to occur.

Correct. These words tell you that students will not be expected to choose factors from a library of books or from an essay on history or from their memories. The statement tells them that a list will be provided and that they will be expected to recognize rather than to recall.

Here is another example. Turn to the page number shown under the stated conditions.

Given a list of chemical elements,

Page 91.

be able to recall (write) the valences of each.

Page 93.

No, you chose the performance (recognize wine sample) rather than the conditions.

Maybe it would help to think of it like this. Imagine the performer standing in an empty field. With what would you have to provide this person before he or she would be able to do what the objective asks? Paper and pencil? A device or object? Another person?

The easy way to approach this task is like this:

1. First, circle the performance stated in the objective.

2. Then, look for conditions that would make a difference in how the performance is shaped.

Follow those two steps on this example. Circle the performance, and then underline the conditions.

Given a bag full of folded newspapers and a neighborhood street,

be able to throw a paper onto the roof of each house.

Now turn to page 101.

Got it! You correctly selected the conditions that were stated, "While blindfolded, and presented with wine samples."

Whenever you're not sure which is which, start by circling the performance (the DOING) words, and only then look for the conditions that might affect the performance. Of course, if no performance is stated, you'd be wasting your time to go any further. If it doesn't state a performance, it isn't an objective at all.

Try this example. Circle the performance, and then underline the conditions.

Without references, be able to recall (write) at least seven patient characteristics to which the therapist should respond and at least five characteristics to which the therapist should withhold response.

Turn to page 105.

Given a bag full of folded newspapers and a neighborhood street,

be able to throw a paper onto the roof of each house.

As you can see, circling the performance makes it a lot easier to decode the objective. If there is no performance stated, you're not dealing with an objective, so you can stop right there (or run screaming to the objective writer for more information).

Once the performance has been circled, it is easier to answer the question, "What are the conditions under which the performance will occur?"

Here's another example. Circle the performance, and then underline the conditions.

Given a malfunctioning DC motor of ten horsepower or less, a kit

of tools, and references, be able to repair the motor.

Turn to page 103.

An objective need not consist of only a single sentence. On the contrary, quite a few sentences might be required to communicate your intent clearly. This is often true, for example, when you are describing objectives requiring creative activity on the part of the learner. Here is one such example:

> *Be able to write a musical composition with a single tonal base within four hours. The composition must be at least sixteen bars long and must contain at least twenty-four notes. You must apply at least three rules of good composition in the development of your score.*

Here is another example, this one from a workshop designed to prepare participants to design performance-based instruction.

Given: *A list of ideal course characteristics, learning-environment description, skill hierarchies, objectives, skill checks, and the course procedures for this course.*

Performance: *Be able to draft a list of procedures by which your course will operate.*

Criteria:
a. *The procedures are as consistent with ideal characteristics as constraints will allow.*
b. *The list at the very least includes procedures describing how students are to proceed in regard to (1) course attendance and working hours, (2) module completion, (3) location and use of resources, (4) skill checks, and (5) module sign-off.*
c. *The procedures are written to be understood by your target population.*

Given a malfunctioning DC motor of ten horsepower or less, a kit

of tools, and references, be able to repair the motor.

If your work matches the above, you're doing fine. If it doesn't, here's another question to ask when hunting for conditions:

What would it take to make this performance possible?

Here's one last example before we move to the third characteristic of a useful objective. Circle the performance, and then underline the conditions.

Without references, be able to recall (write) at least seven patient

characteristics to which the therapist should respond and at least

five characteristics to which the therapist should withhold

response.

Turn to page 105.

Without references, be able to recall (write) at least seven patient

characteristics to which the therapist should respond and at least

five characteristics to which the therapist should withhold

response.

About the only special condition mentioned here is "without references." Everything else tells you what the students are to do and how well they have to be able to do it.

QUESTION: If the objective doesn't _say_ the students can use references, can't you presume that they will have to work without them? Can't you _assume_ that "no references" is intended? Isn't it a fair inference? Since I can't tell what is in the mind of the objective writer, I can't tell whether it is a fair inference or not. But when you're writing an objective, why take a chance on having your objective misinterpreted when you don't have to? Why not simply add a few words to say what you mean? Then the reader will know for sure, rather than for maybe.

Turn to page 106.

How Many Conditions?

How finely should conditions be described? Should every objective state conditions?

The answers to these questions are: Add enough description to an objective to make it clear to everyone concerned just what you expect from the learner. If what you expect is made clear just by stating the desired performance and the degree of excellence you desire (the criterion), then don't add conditions arbitrarily. How can you tell whether the conditions are defined clearly enough? Give your draft objective to a couple of students, and ask them what they think they would have to do to demonstrate their mastery of the objective. If their description matches what you have in mind, then you have done well. If it doesn't, then a little patching here or there is in order. But remember the ironclad rule of objective writing:

If there is disagreement about the meaning, don't argue about it—fix it!

For now, you have had enough practice with identifying conditions to have the basic idea. There will be more practice later on to sharpen up your skill, so let's move on to the final characteristic of a useful objective, the criterion of acceptable performance.

Summary

1. *An instructional objective describes an intended outcome of instruction, rather than the procedures for accomplishing those outcomes.*

2. *An objective always states a performance describing what the learner will be DOING when demonstrating mastery of the objective.*

3. *When the main intent of an objective is covert, an indicator behavior—through which the main intent can be detected— is added.*

4. *Indicator behaviors are always the simplest, most direct behaviors possible, and they are always something that every trainee already knows how to do well.*

5. *To prepare an objective:*

   a. *Write a statement that describes the main intent or performance expected of the student.*

   b. *If the performance happens to be covert, add an indicator behavior through which the main intent can be detected.*

   c. *Describe relevant or important conditions under which the performance is expected to occur. Add as much description as is needed to communicate the intent to others.*

7
Criterion

Once you have described what you want students to be able to do (the performance) and the circumstances in which you want them to do it (the conditions), you will have given them far more information about your intents than they are accustomed to receiving. With performance and conditions made clear, it will no longer be necessary for them to wonder how best to focus their efforts.

There is something else you can do, though, to increase the communicating power of your objective: Add a criterion of acceptable performance. This will tell students how well they will have to perform to be considered competent. By adding information about the yardstick by which accomplishment of the objective will be measured, you will enormously strengthen the usefulness of your objectives. You will have gained several advantages.

1. You will have a standard against which to test the success of the instruction.

2. Students will know how to tell when they have met or exceeded the performance expectations.

3. You will have the basis for proving that your students can, in fact, do what you set out to teach them.

Those are powerful benefits in the quest for improved performance.

What you must do, then, is complete your objectives by adding information that describes the criterion for success. Remember that if it isn't measurable, it isn't an objective. What we are now turning our attention to is the issue of just what should be measured.

Before you proceed, however, turn to the page that best describes your feeling at this moment.

Many of the things I teach are intangible and CANNOT be evaluated.   *Page 113.*

Show me how to describe criteria of acceptable performance.   *Page 115.*

Occasionally someone asks, "Why bother with objectives? If you have good test items, aren't objectives redundant?"

It is a question that deserves comment.

Perhaps I can clarify the relationship between objectives and test items by rephrasing the question this way: "If you have a ruler with which to measure the dimensions of a building, why do you need a blueprint?" Answer: So that anyone will know whether the completed building looks the way it was intended to look and so that similar buildings can be constructed if desired.

The same is true of objectives. If you had only test items, you wouldn't know what critical characteristics were important to develop, you wouldn't know how to determine whether the main intent had been achieved, and you wouldn't know how to tell whether students were competent enough to be considered acceptable.

Thus, the objective describes where you are going, while the test items are the means by which you find out whether you got there.

Well . . . all right . . . but if you are teaching things that cannot be evaluated, you are in the awkward position of being unable to demonstrate that you are teaching anything at all. Though it is sometimes appropriate for a course to be aimed at providing opportunities for students to explore or debate ideas (process), our concern here is with instruction whose purpose is to accomplish important learning results (outcomes).

The "My subject is intangible" approach is risky for at least two reasons. First, it lulls people into thinking they are saying something when they are not. For example, how would you know whether this "objective" was achieved?

After having studied a variety of forms of non-verbal communication, the student is able to demonstrate an ability to send and receive non-verbal messages.

To cast "objectives" in such vague language serves only to confuse students, as well as those charged with development of the instruction. It is the lazy approach to instruction.

Second, the "My subject is intangible" conviction simply isn't true. You already make decisions about whether or not students can or cannot perform to your satisfaction, and with a little effort you can describe the basis for that satisfaction. In other words, you can say what students would have to say or do for you to agree that they had accomplished the "intangible" result. If it is important that your students learn something of consequence, it is important to find out whether or not you have succeeded in teaching them. Hiding behind the "intangible" myth won't help.

Turn to page 115.

Perhaps you have had academic experiences similar to this one. During class periods of a seventh-grade algebra course, a teacher provided a good deal of skillful guidance in the solution of simple equations and made sure that all students had enough practice to give them confidence in their ability. When it came time for an examination, however, the test items consisted mainly of stated (word) problems, and the students performed rather poorly. The teacher's justification for this "sleight of test" was that the students didn't "really understand" algebra if they could not solve word problems.

Perhaps the teacher was right. But the skill of solving equations is considerably different from the skill of solving word problems; if he wanted his students to learn how to solve word problems, he should have taught them how to do so.

Don't expect a learner to be able to exhibit Skill B simply because you have given practice in Skill A.

All right, let's consider some of the ways to add criteria of acceptable performance to your objectives.

Note that we are not looking to specify a *minimum* or *barely tolerable* criterion. We are looking for ways to describe the *desired* or *appropriate* criterion. Sometimes that means a low performance level is OK, and sometimes it means that only perfect performance is OK. Sometimes it means that considerable error can be tolerated, and sometimes it means that no errors can be tolerated. For example, while it might be acceptable for a shipping clerk to tie an occasional knot that slips, surgeons are expected to tie knots that don't slip. Ever.

Speed

One of the common ways to describe a criterion of acceptable performance is to describe a *time limit* within which a given performance must occur. Such a time limit is often implied when you tell students how long an examination period will be. If the speed of performance is important, however, it is better to be explicit about it; then no one will have to guess at what you have in mind for them to do. When time is of the essence, it is only fair to communicate that criterion to the learner. For example, consider this:

Instructor: You flunk!

Student: But I ran the hundred-yard dash, like you said.

Instructor: True. But you were too slow.

Student: But you didn't say how fast we had to run.

Instructor: Would I ask you to run if I didn't want you to run fast? You should have known that speed was important.

You might also write the objective on page 117 by using this format:

Conditions: *Dry, level track.*

Performance: *Run the hundred-yard dash.*

Criterion: *Within fourteen seconds.*

This format is especially useful for more complex objectives.

If speed is important, say so in the objective, and more people will perform as you intend.

If you do NOT intend to evaluate a performance on the basis of its speed, you need not and should not impose a time limit. The rule is to impose only those criteria that are important. If it is important that the running be done to a speed criterion, then the objective might better read:

Be able to run the hundred-yard dash on a dry, level track within fourteen seconds.

Then all the students would know what they should do, where they should do it, and how fast they should do it.

Let's try a little practice in recognizing criteria in an objective. Read the following objective and then turn to the page below the words that describe the criterion of acceptable performance (the words that tell how well the learner must be able to perform the task).

Given tools, references, and a malfunctioning centrifugal pump, be able to clear the malfunction within fifteen minutes.

Page 119.   **Page 121.**

Turn to the page number that brackets the criterion.

You said that "be able to clear the malfunction" is a criterion of acceptable performance. No, I think you may still be thinking about performance rather than about quality of performance. Performance is critical, of course, but the words you chose tell what the learner is expected to do, not how well it is to be done.

When looking for criteria, look for the answer to the question, "How well does the learner need to perform to achieve the objective?"

When the criterion relates to speed, look for words that tell you how fast something needs to be done (e.g., within five seconds), words that tell you what has to be done before another event begins (e.g., before the red light comes on), or words that tell you how often something must be done per unit of time (e.g., must fire at least three rounds within two seconds).

Turn to page 117 and read the item again.

You said that "within fifteen minutes" is the criterion. You've got it.

For this objective, it doesn't matter whether the performer uses a wrench or a hammer to get the job done; what matters is that the malfunction is cleared within fifteen minutes. How will you find out whether someone has met this criterion? Simple. Provide the student with a malfunctioning pump, some tools, and references; ask him or her to fix it within fifteen minutes, and time the performance. If the pump is fixed within fifteen minutes, the criterion of acceptable performance will have been met.

How Many Pumps?

You may be thinking, "I wouldn't consider them competent if they repaired only one pump. I'd want to see them repair a range of malfunctions before I'd be willing to stamp them US Choice." Good point. It makes a lot of sense to expect people to perform under the range of conditions described in the objective before agreeing that they have achieved the objective. But though this is good practice, it relates more to how you test rather than to how you write the objective. If you're not careful, you can find yourself writing test items and calling them objectives. For example:

Given five malfunctioning pumps, be able to fix them . . .

smells like a test item. Why? Because the main intent is for people to be able to repair malfunctioning pumps. Not five pumps or two pumps, but however many malfunctioning pumps come along. To include, "Given five pumps . . ." in the objective will confuse the objective (what they need to be able to do) with the test situation (how you will find out whether they can do it).

Accuracy

Speed is only one way to determine a criterion of success. Sometimes the accuracy of a performance is more important than its speed, and sometimes both speed and accuracy are important.

Here's an example of an accuracy criterion:

Be able to state the time shown on the face of any clock to within one minute of accuracy.

Since the rapidity of the performance is unimportant, no speed criterion is shown.

Or your objective might include criteria like these:

. . . and solutions must be accurate to the nearest whole number.

. . . with materials weighed accurately to the nearest gram.

. . . correct to at least three significant figures.

. . . with no more than two incorrect entries for every ten pages of log.

. . . listening carefully enough that no more than one request for repeated information is needed for each customer contact.

. . . with all surfaces finished to a 64 smoothness tolerance.

Use whatever word or means that will communicate how well your students must perform before you will agree that they have achieved the objective.

Now answer this question. Which of the following includes an accuracy criterion? Turn to the page number shown beside your selection.

Given a yard of baloney and a sharp knife, be able to cut the baloney into slices no more than one centimeter thick.

Be able to visualize with 90 percent accuracy.   *Page 127.*

You said that "Be able to visualize with 90 percent accuracy" included an accuracy criterion. I can see how you might think so. After all, the sentence actually includes the word "accuracy."

But just what is it that someone would be doing? Visualizing? Visualizing *what*? Angels on the head of a pin? Electrons in a cyclotron? How your amour might look in iron underwear? Don't be deceived by the fact that a percentage is stated. If the description of accuracy doesn't make any sense— that is, if it doesn't tell you clearly how well you must perform—it isn't a criterion. Here are some other silly non-objectives.

Be able to internalize a growing awareness with 90 percent accuracy.

Be able to dramatize an increasing sensitivity. Criterion: nine out of ten dramatizations must be correct.

Be able to compose a sonata with 90 percent accuracy.

As you can see, it's not a criterion just because it contains a number. The number has to make sense, which means it has to refer to a genuine performance and it has to describe a limit to that performance.

Return to page 125 and read the item again.

Let's split a hair.

As you work with objectives, you will notice that while the performances stated therein tell you what people are expected to be able to DO, the criteria often may describe the characteristics (or shapes) of the PRODUCTS of that doing. When, for example, objectives ask that someone be able to:

- write a report
- construct an amplifier
- repair a word processor

the criteria will describe the desired characteristics of the products of those performances. The criteria will say something about the characteristics of the *final* report, the *completed* amplifier, or the *repaired* word processor, rather than about *how* those products were produced (the shapes of the performances).

"So what?" I hear you muttering. So not a whole lot. It's just that, in these instances, you determine whether the performance is adequate by looking at the product of the performance rather than at the performance itself. And you make darn sure you don't allow people to be elevated on the shape of their *performance* when it is the shape of the *product* that is important. Don't allow the sort of evaluation that says, "Oh, sure, her report is terrific in all respects, but she wrinkles her nose when she types, so we'll have to take ten points off."

It's "nice to know" the distinction between performance and its product, because sometimes your criteria will need to describe performance or product, and sometimes some of both. But your attention should be directed toward describing the criteria that matter, regardless of their labels.

Yes. The objective you selected has an accuracy criterion, and that's no baloney. The objective tells you that the baloney must be cut accurately enough so that no slice is thicker than one centimeter.

Given a yard of baloney and a sharp knife, be able to cut the baloney into slices no more than one centimeter thick.

It doesn't matter how long you take to do it or how many slices you ruin or drop on the floor. Performers will have achieved the objective if they meet the single accuracy criterion stated.

Quality

Many times the speed or accuracy of a performance is not critical. Instead, something about the quality of the performance must be present if the performance is to be considered acceptable. For example, in our Criterion-Referenced Instruction (CRI) Workshop, one module requires trainees to learn to answer questions on their feet about CRI, so that they'll be able to handle themselves well in a give-and-take discussion about the subject.

But what does that mean? How much give and how much take? Clearly a speed criterion is not appropriate, because in real life it doesn't matter how fast one speaks. The first criterion listed is an accuracy criterion, but the others refer more to the quality of the responses. Here's how we wrote this objective:

In an interview, and without references or notes, be able to respond correctly to questions relating to criterion-referenced instruction. Criteria:

    a. All information offered is factual.
    b. Information is pertinent to the questions.
    c. Questioners are treated courteously (they are not insulted or demeaned).
    d. Jargon is defined when it is first introduced.

You can see that it would be possible to clutter this objective with criteria referring to many other aspects of the performance, none of which would make a difference to the quality of the responses. The trick is to confine oneself to describing only those criteria that are important to the way the performance will be expected to occur after the instruction is ended.

Where Do Criteria Come From?

How will you know whether a criterion should require that a performance be completed in ten minutes or twenty minutes? Or that it should demand brushing your teeth with more than one pound of pressure rather than less than a pound of pressure? Or that the objective should call for ten customer calls per day rather than five? In other words, where do (or should) criteria come from? There are four general sources from which criteria may be dictated or derived.

Job Requirements

Those who derive objectives from real world needs will observe and interview competent and/or exemplary performers and describe what the performers do and how well they do it. They will then use this information as the basis for deriving objectives and the criteria that should be attached.

For example, if competent pie-throwers actually hit their targets at least eight times out of ten throws, an "80% hits" criterion might be added to the pie-throwing objective. Why not make it 100? Because any idiot can write an objective that says, "Be able to do this or that with 100% accuracy." That doesn't mean it's a better criterion, and it doesn't mean it's a realistic criterion. Remember, perfection costs money; the tighter the criteria, the costlier the training. It's like smoothness; the smoother you want the surface machined, the more it will cost. Any time you see an objective that calls for perfection (i.e., "100% accuracy"), attack it. Make the objective writer defend that as a realistic criterion.

Sometimes the criteria will be set at entry level. In these instances the criteria will be set to reflect what employers require in the way of entry-level skill (what it will take to get the job in the first place), rather than what the employee will be like after extensive experience and practice. When a manager says, "I can't hire tellers who can't count," it is wise to find out what "can't count" means and then set a criterion accordingly.

Improvement Requirements

Another source of criteria can be the requirements that must be met if performance improvement is expected to occur as a result of practice alone. What this means is that criteria are set to reflect the answer to the question:

"How much entry-level skill does someone need in order for practice alone *to lead to improvement?"*

For example, if someone leaves the training environment able to solder three joints per minute correctly and *without supervision,* that person has all the skill needed to improve with practice. If someone is willing to hire this person at that skill level, the employer will know that the skill will improve with practice (provided that the employer gives *opportunities* for practice before the skill deteriorates).

If, however, the criteria are set so low that improvement would require more than just practice (e.g., coaching), then the skill will either deteriorate or the performer will learn to do it wrong.

Academic Requirements

Derivation of appropriate objectives and criteria in the academic environment is easier. (It's technically easier, but it's often a nightmare politically—because of turf battles.)

Suppose, for example, that you are assigned to teach Algebra I and set out to derive objectives for that course. (No, no. Don't go to the textbook; use a more rational approach.) One source of objectives for your course would be the prerequisites of Algebra II. So you would go to whomever is teaching the advanced course to find out just what the entry-level expectations are for that course. If that instructor gives you a list of objectives, and tells you, "These are the things I expect students to be able to do when they enter my course," you will have a good idea of what your students should be able to do when they leave *your* course. Thus, the prerequisites for the next course(s) will tell you a lot about what objectives and criteria should be for the preceding course.

This isn't the only source from which your criteria may be derived. For example, if one of the consumers of your students will be the local community, you can take steps to answer the question, "What do these students need to be able to do, and how well, to function successfully in their community?" and set your criteria accordingly.

Personal Experience

Another guide to criteria (but not always the best) comes from personal wisdom and experience. People who are actually performing the skills described by the objectives in real-world settings are likely to have good insights into the performance quality needed to do the job well. Thus, if you are drafting objectives and are at the same time living the skills you're writing about, your judgments about appropriate criteria would be valuable. If, however, you don't actually do the things the objectives describe, then don't rely on your judgments; go to competent performers and derive the criteria from their performances.

Pointing to the Criterion

There are at least three ways to indicate a criterion without actually describing the criterion in the objective. All are ways of pointing to the criterion:

1. If an intended criterion has been made *explicit* in some document or other, the thing to do in the objective is to add words that tell where to find the criterion. For example:

   . . . according to the Standard Chart, 2023 edition.

   . . . Criterion: manufacturer's specifications, *Repair Manual, Corrugated Soap,* 2023 edition.

   . . . according to the criteria described on p. 33, *Manual* 27-10.

This procedure should be used, however, only when the criteria are clearly stated in the reference you are pointing to and only when that reference is readily available to the performers.

2. If the desired performance consists of a number of steps and if an evaluation checklist exists, you might point to that checklist as a description (or partial description) of the criteria. For example:

   . . . Criterion: All steps to be performed as well as, and in the sequence described by, the Cheeky Checklist of Proper Kissing.

   . . . with each action to compare in quality (sequence is not important) with the Performance Checklist of Turgid Terpsichore.

3. On rare occasions you might find it appropriate to point to competent performance shown on a piece of film, videotape, CD, etc., saying, in effect, "Do it like *that.*" This might be useful if the performance involves

complex movements difficult to describe, such as dance steps, diving, or underwater maneuvers. I hesitate to mention this method, however, for fear that someone will take it as a license to use *only* the dynamic media without also describing the key characteristics of the desired performance in the objective itself. Such a practice would be almost as uninformative as that other false criterion, "to the satisfaction of the instructor." Refer to film, videotape, or documents only if they help in making the desired criteria clear to all concerned.

Condition or Criterion?

Sometimes it is not easy to read an objective and tell whether a phrase describes a condition or a criterion. Sometimes the two rather blend together. For example:

Be able to do consecutively thirty push-ups, thirty sit-ups, and thirty pull-ups without the use of mechanical aids.

What is the criterion? The *number* of acts that must be performed? Yes, but some would call it a condition. Some would say that "without the use of mechanical aids" also is part of the criterion. Their argument would go this way: A criterion tells how good a performance must be, and in this case the performance must be good enough to be done without aids. Who is right?

Doesn't really matter, as long as the intent of the objective is clear. The problem here is caused by the wording. If the objective had been worded like this:

Without the use of mechanical aids, be able to do consecutively push-ups, sit-ups, and pull-ups. Criterion: thirty each push-ups, sit-ups, and pull-ups.

or like this:

Performance:	Do consecutive push-ups, sit-ups, and pull-ups.
Conditions:	Without the use of mechanical aids.
Criterion:	Thirty each.

there would be no question about which is a condition (something that influences the shape of the performance), and which is a criterion (something that tells how much performance is required). What is important is that an objective be refined until it communicates the intent of the writer. If it answers the following questions, I would consider it a useful objective, regardless of whether everyone agreed on the labels for the phrases:

- What is the main intent of the objective?

- What does the learner have to do to demonstrate achievement of the objective?

- What will the learner have to do it with or to? And what, if anything, will the learner have to do it without?

- How will we know when the performance is good enough to be considered acceptable?

If you cannot specify a criterion with as much clarity as you would like, or if you can't even *begin* to decide what the critical criteria are for an objective, use the "Hey, Gofer" ploy. That is, you first think to yourself, "Hey, Gofer. I want you to find out whether these people have, or have not, achieved this objective . . . and here's what I want you to look for." Then jot down the instructions that will tell Gofer how to decide whether the learners have or have not achieved the objective. This ploy is especially useful when your head is stuck in the "It's intangible" mode.

Summary

1. *An objective is a collection of words, symbols, and/or pictures describing one of your important intents.*

2. *An objective will communicate your intent to the degree you describe what the learner will be DOING when demonstrating achievement of the objective, the important conditions of the doing, and the criterion by which achievement will be judged.*

3. *To prepare a useful objective, continue to modify a draft until these questions are answered:*

   • *What do I want students to be able to do?*

   • *What are the important conditions or constraints under which I want them to perform?*

   • *How well must students perform for me to be satisfied?*

4. *Write a separate statement for each important outcome or intent; write as many as you need to communicate your intents.*

5. *If you give your written objectives to your students, you may not have to do much else. Why? Because often students are already able to do what you are asking them to do and will be happy to demonstrate their ability, now that they know what is wanted of them.*

8
Pitfalls and Barnacles

O ver recent decades, those of us involved in the systematic design and implementation of instruction have seen many ways in which objectives have been used—and misused. On the one hand, we've seen objectives used as a tool for tailoring instruction to the needs of the individual student and for delivering instruction in ways that minimize learning time. On the other hand, we've seen the most ludicrous statements parading as objectives, we've seen statements with confusing phrasing and useless words, and we've seen profound-sounding statements that couldn't be of any use whatsoever. In short, we've seen objectives used in highly productive ways, and we've seen them used in ways that impeded the progress of instructors and students alike. This chapter describes the most-frequently seen troublesome objectives.

False Performance

This point was made earlier, but its importance warrants some repetition. One of the most pervasive defects of statements that are mistakenly called objectives is that they have the appearance of objectives but contain no performances;

therefore, they are not objectives at all. Here are some examples:

- Have a thorough understanding of particle physics.
- Demonstrate a comprehension of the short-story form.
- Be able to relate to others in a demonstration of empathy.
- Be able to think critically and analytically.
- Be able to understand individual differences in patients.
- Know how to conduct a sales interview.
- Know how to appreciate the importance of corporate strategy.

Expressions such as these may describe some important goals in very broad terms. However, they are not objectives, because they do not state what someone would have to do to demonstrate mastery of the unstated main intent.

When statements without performances are thought of as objectives, they lead to a variety of confusions. People are likely to argue about which instructional procedure is suitable for accomplishing the vaguely stated intent and are frustrated when the statement offers no firm guidelines. They cannot agree on methods for assessing achievement of the intent and may complain that all objectives are useless. The instructor is at a loss in understanding why the *students* are at a loss in understanding what they are expected to be able to do. Little wonder, as broad statements provide few clues to action.

When interpreting or drafting an objective, you must first look for the performance. Draw a circle around it. If there isn't a performance to draw a circle around, it isn't an objective— yet. Fix it or forget it.

False Givens

Another common error (in the sense that it does not help in

communicating an instructional intent) is the inclusion of false givens. These are words or phrases that may follow the word *given* in an objective but that describe something *other* than specific conditions the learner must have or be denied when demonstrating achievement of the objective. Most typically, the words describe something about the instruction itself, such as the following:

Given three days of instruction on . . .

Given that the student has completed six laboratory experiments on . . .

Given that the student is in the category of gifted . . .

Given adequate practice in . . .

Here are other examples, actually labeled as conditions in the objective:

Conditions: Pre-course reading material that overviews the managerial leadership process.

Conditions: Discussion group.

Conditions: a) Competent instructors.
b) One's own knowledge of regional organization.

Because none of these items has anything to do with describing the conditions affecting the performance stated in the objective, they are ripe for the charge of "false givens."

As indicated earlier, an objective is useful to the degree that it communicates an intended outcome. If you allow it to describe instructional procedure, you will restrict all concerned in using their best wisdom and experience to help accomplish that outcome. Make sure that the conditions described in your objectives tell something about the situation in which you expect the student to demonstrate competence.

Teaching Procedures

Related to the false givens is the error of writing an objective to describe a teaching point, a practice exercise, or some other aspect of classroom activity. For example, consider this:

Be able to choose an art print or photo that illustrates a theme of your choice and explain how it illustrates that theme.

Why would you want a student to do such a thing? Certainly it isn't because a meaningful thing to do in the world is to go around explaining to people the theme that's illustrated by a photo you have chosen. Presumably, the reason for wanting students to engage in this activity is that it will help them learn to do something that *can* be considered a meaningful skill. For example:

Givens: *A theme.*
                         Collection of art prints and/or photos.

Performance: *Identify (point to) the prints/photos that illustrate the theme.*

Criterion: *At least 60% of your choices match the choices of a panel of art experts.*

The argument is not with the usefulness of having students practice selecting prints and explaining themes; the argument is with writing descriptions of such activities and calling them objectives. There are two practical reasons for this argument: 1) if you describe all instructional activities or teaching points and call them objectives, you will be up to your . . . er . . . a . . . well, you'll be drowning in verbiage (this is why some teachers complain that there are too many objectives); 2) the main function of an objective is to help course planners decide on instructional content and procedure. If the objective describes a teaching procedure, it will fail to perform its primary purpose, because it will be describing instructional practice rather than important instructional outcomes.

You can avoid this problem by asking yourself *why* you want students to be able to do what you've described in each objective you draft. If your answer is "Because *that* is one of the things they need to be able to do when they leave here," then the objective can probably stand. If, however, your answer is "So that they will then be able to _____," and you fill in the blank with something *other* than what the draft objective describes, then that draft objective may describe a teaching procedure. If so, it should be modified to describe the desired outcome, instead. Here is another example:

Be able to discuss in class the case histories handed out by the instructor.

Why did this instructor want students to be able to discuss written case histories in class? Her answer was something like this: "Because if they are going to be able to solve problems, they need to be able to tell the difference between statements of fact and statements of opinion. The discussion of case histories gives them practice in doing that." Ah so. Her response made it clear that her original objective described a teaching procedure rather than an intended outcome, a means rather than an end. She would find this objective more useful, therefore, if she modified it to describe the reason for the practice activity of case discussions:

Given written descriptions of problem situations involving interactions, be able to identify (label) statements of fact and statements of opinion.

Write your objectives about things you want your students to be able to do when they leave you, and you will avoid drowning in trivia.

Gibberish

A problem similar to that of the false performance is that sometimes the so-called objectives either contain, or are composed entirely of, phrases with little or no meaning. The following are examples of worthless expressions:

Manifest an increasing comprehensive understanding ...

Demonstrate a thorough comprehension ...

Relate and foster with multiple approaches ...

Have a deep awareness and thorough humanizing grasp ...

When such words are followed by a description of desired performance, they are not disastrous; they just get in the way. If they are not so followed, the danger is more substantial. The danger is that people will be lulled into thinking something meaningful has been said and then may question their own sanity or intelligence because they fail to perceive the meaning that isn't there. For example, "Demonstrate the ability to make practical application of information in a creative way." What in the world would someone be doing when demonstrating mastery of such a fogged intent? When you see an entire statement like that, which consists of a meaningless combination of words and symbols, you can understand why some people complain that objectives are useless. Consider the following:

Embark on a lifelong search for truth, with the willingness and ability to pose questions, examine experience, and construct explanations and meanings.

Develop a thorough understanding of the corporate culture, to include policies on harassment, ethnic diversity, and equal access to individual counseling.

The student must be able to demonstrate an ability to develop self-confidence and self-respect.

Verbiage such as this may seem impressive, but it is of little use in communicating instructional intents. Nor can I offer an improved version of these statements, as I don't know what their writers were trying to convey. Fortunately, there is a simple solution.

The best way to degibberize an objective is to give it to a couple of students and ask them what they think it means. While their utterances may sometimes be a little hard on the ego, those utterances will usually show the way toward a cleaner, simpler statement of your intent.

And don't forget editors. A good editor can make miraculous moves toward simplicity and clarity by changing just a few words here and there, and I am continually amazed at how helpful they can be. (You have to watch them, though, for many are slaves to their style manuals and are sometimes willing to sacrifice meaning in their push for conformity.)

Instructor Performance

Another practice that interferes with the usefulness of an objective is that of describing what the instructor is expected to do rather than what the student is expected to be able to do.

The instructor will provide an atmosphere that will promote the development of self-esteem, confidence, and security.

The teacher will help the student recognize natural consequences of behavior.

The instructor will assist the student in the development of . . .

Demonstrate to students the proper procedures for completing Form 321.

Phrases such as these might properly describe an instructor objective or an administrative objective, but they say nothing about what results are to be expected insofar as student competence is concerned. Similarly, statements that begin:

Each student will . . .

Eighty percent of the students will . . .

have no meaning to a student, either. What can a student do about an "objective" that says "70 percent of the students must be able to demonstrate an ability to read"? Such statements may provide the basis for instructor objectives, but they are of no help to students.

An instructional objective describes student performance; it avoids saying anything about instructor performance. To do otherwise would unnecessarily restrict individual instructors from using their best wisdom and skills to accomplish the objective.

When reviewing your draft objective, ask whether it is referring to student performance. If so, rejoice; if not, revise.

False Criteria

A more insidious defect is to state a "criterion" that tells the students little or nothing that they don't already know. Consider these:

To the satisfaction of the instructor.

Must be able to make 80 percent on a multiple-choice exam.

Must pass a final exam.

Students know they have to satisfy the instructor. What *would* be news would be a description of what they have to do to produce such satisfaction. If instructors do, in fact, make judgments about whether students are or are not competent, there is no reason why those instructors cannot reveal the basis for their judgments. Of course, it might take some thought and effort. So what? That's what professional instruction is all about.

The second and third examples above tell the student a little something about the administrative aspects of the criterion situation but tell them nothing about how well they will have to do whatever the objective demands. That is, "80 percent on a multiple-choice exam" does not describe the desired quality of performance. We all know how easy it is to manipulate the difficulty of an examination by varying the wording and the choice of items. The 80 percent isn't the problem; it is the *substance* of the 80 percent that is the problem. If you were told, for example, that you were expected to be able to shoot well enough so that 80 percent of your shots fell within the bull's-eye, you would have a description of competence level that you could do something about. But to say that you had to earn 80 percent on a multiple-choice exam or 90 percent on an essay exam or that you had to reach an 80/90 criterion is to tell you little that could help you to guide your own efforts. The same is true for the designer of the instruction—such "criteria" do not help in deciding the type and amount of instruction for accomplishing the objective.

If you want to see how bad things can get, read the following, which warrants exposure but not comment:

> *Given twenty problems dealing with three operations in decimals and two types of percent and percentage problems; 90 percent of the students whose chronological ages range from 11.0 to 11.11 and who have given evidence, by the Lorge-Thorndike or other ability test, that they will achieve above the third quartile, will solve the problems and write solutions at 92 percent accuracy as evidenced by scores on a teacher-devised test administered by May (!!!!).*

To test the criterion in an objective, ask whether the criterion (1) says something about the quality of performance you desire, (2) says something about the quality of the *individual* performance rather than the group performance, and (3) says something about a real, rather than an imaginary, standard.

Related Issues

Five issues on which I would like to comment still remain. They don't have to do with the actual wording of the objectives, so they do not fall strictly within the limits of this book. But since they're common problems relating to objectives, they deserve a mention.

Irrelevant Test Items

A common bad practice is that of teaching one thing and then testing for another; that is, of using test items that ask for performance other than that called for by the objectives. Such a practice is deceitful, regardless of the rationalizations offered for its use. For example, though an objective may make it clear that students need to be able to *make change,* irrelevant test items might look like these:

1. Define money.

2. Name the President on the fifty-dollar bill.

3. Describe the risks of not being able to count.

None of these items ask the student to do what the objective asks, namely, to make change. As a result, no one will discover whether or not a student can perform as required, and no one will learn what remedial actions, if any, should be initiated. But that doesn't stop people from rationalizing this bad practice:

"They can't make change if they don't know what money is."

"They can't really appreciate money if they don't know whose faces are on the bills."

"I like to vary the type of items I use to make my tests interesting."

"I'm teaching for transfer."

"I want my tests to be a learning situation."

"Trainees should learn by discovery."

Regardless of the excuse, the use of irrelevant test items in assessing achievement of an objective poses several dangers. For one thing, it models deceit for the students. It tells them that it doesn't bother the instructor to teach one thing and then test for something else. It confirms the instructor as the enemy. For another, with irrelevant test items you will never know whether the student has learned to perform as desired. A well-written objective will prescribe the form of the test items by which the objective can be assessed.

Wrong Objectives

The charge that certain objectives are trivial is usually made for one of two reasons, neither of which has anything to do with how the objectives are worded. The triviality charge is usually aimed at objectives that look less potent than they really are and at those that are, in fact, trivial because they don't relate to anything of importance.

First, you can't tell whether an objective is trivial just by reading it; you have to compare it with the world around it—with the consequence of not achieving the objective. If it wouldn't matter to anyone or anything whether the objective was or was not accomplished, then it may indeed be trivial. If, on the other hand, some significant consequence would result from non-accomplishment of the objective, then it isn't trivial, regardless of how simply it may be worded or how "small" the performance described is.

For example, suppose an objective for a bank teller says, "Be able to smile visibly when serving a customer." That sounds pretty Mickey Mouse until you learn that grouchy tellers lose customers and sometimes lose their jobs. There's nothing trivial about losing customers, and there's certainly nothing trivial about losing your job.

Another example: An objective for bartenders says, "Be able to serve customers without spilling or slamming." (They're supposed to be able to serve without slamming bottles or glasses on the bar or table.) Now you've got to admit that sounds pretty trivial as an objective. But when compared to the consequences of not accomplishing the objective, a different picture emerges. In this particular hotel chain, bartenders who slam glasses or spill drinks on customers are fired. Is that trivial? So objectives that lead to meaningful consequences are not trivial, regardless of how they may sound to the casual reader.

Objectives are also charged with triviality when they are incorrectly derived. Objectives ought to come from somewhere to serve meaningful, rather than merely cosmetic, purposes. Suppose you're visiting your brother Flatson at the school where he teaches, and this conversation takes place:

You: Hi, Flat. What are you up to?

Flat: You wouldn't believe it! I've got to trump up a bunch of #*$*&^ objectives.

You: What in the world *for?*

Flat: Oh, the principal just came by and ordered us to write objectives for all of our courses. Said that the new district policy requires everybody to have objectives.

You: So where are you getting these objectives?

Flat: Heck, I'm just writing some to describe what I'm already doing in my courses.

Unfortunately, this scene has been played out in too many school districts and corporate training departments. As I said, objectives ought to come from somewhere if they are to be worth drafting, and writing them to reflect existing instruction is putting the cart before the horse. Why bother to construct blueprints after the house is built, other than for cosmetic reasons intended to convince someone that you constructed your instruction in a rational manner? (For information about how to derive objectives in a systematic manner, review Part III in *Making Instruction Work*, by R. F. Mager.)

False Taxonomizing

A taxonomy is a way of classifying things according to their relationships. If you have never heard the term before, you should skip this section, as it does not describe a problem that relates to you. You won't miss a thing.

Every now and again we bump into someone who claims to be having unusual difficulty in drafting objectives. They feel their objectives are unsatisfactory, even though review of their work reveals objectives that are quite well stated. Then why the discomfort? Taxonomitis. For some reason these troubled souls are trying to distort their objectives to fit some sort of taxonomy (classification system). Just because it is *possible* to write objectives that reflect different levels of a classification scheme, they seem to feel it is therefore *necessary* to do so. "All our objectives are at the same taxonomy level," they complain. "We need some at other levels," they assert. One person even felt that objectives had to conform to a normal distribution of classification levels to be considered satisfactory. What in the world for? I don't know where such an idea originated, but I wish it would go away.

If you have derived your objectives from a real need and have described what you want your students to be able to do, why change the objectives just to conform to a taxonomy?

Now, a taxonomy, or classification scheme, can be useful in reminding you of the range of objectives you might write or select, the words you might use in describing your intents, or the kinds of test items that might be appropriate for assessing your objectives. But to deliberately write objectives to fit a classification system rather than a need seems a gross misuse of these thinking tools.

Orphan Objectives

One of the strangest and most wasteful practices in relation to objectives is that of writing some and then putting them on the shelf—unused. People who engage in this ritual then complain bitterly that objective writing is a waste of time. And for them it is. If they don't know what to do with objectives once they have them, or if they don't intend to find out what to do with them, then they are clearly wasting their time in writing them.

Why would anyone write objectives who didn't intend to do something with them? Mostly because some well-meaning administrator or manager ordered them to. But to order people to write objectives without making sure they know *how,* and *why,* is to invite dissension and frustration. After all, drafting objectives is only one of a series of steps in the analysis, design, and implementation of instruction. To order that it be carried out in a vacuum is a wasteful practice; at the very least, it will produce objectives that do little more than gather dust.

"Attitude" Objectives

Sometimes you will see statements like the following:

Be able to appreciate the importance of customer service.

Have a favorable attitude toward reading.

Develop a positive attitude toward safety.

Have an appreciation for literature.

Have a professional attitude.

Where is the performance? There isn't any. Therefore *they aren't objectives.* They are not specific descriptions of intent. Statements like these describe *states of being;* they do not describe *doing.* While such statements may address areas of extreme importance, it is misleading to refer to them as "attitude" or "affective" *objectives.*

The risk in doing so is that the readers of such statements may be lulled into thinking these are objectives merely because the topics are important; and objective writers may be lulled into thinking that when they have written such statements, they have finished their work. On the contrary, they have just begun. You see, statements about the affective (feeling, attitude) are *always* statements of *inference,* not of performance. They are predictions about future behavior that are inferred from the circumstantial evidence of what people say and do. Thus, if you see me stuffing myself with popcorn, you might infer that I have a favorable attitude toward popcorn and will eat popcorn when the opportunity presents itself. You may or may not be correct, but the behavior is the only basis you have for the inference.

If we're serious about accomplishing one or more of our affective and other abstract intentions, how, then, can we describe them in the form of objectives? We perform a goal analysis. Here's how.

1. Derive the performances that would satisfy you that the intent had been achieved.

2. Write a complete sentence to describe each of the performances.

3. Check-mark those performances that are already in the repertoire of your target audience. In other words, mark the ones your target people already know how to do.

4. Write an objective describing each of the performances left unchecked during the previous step. (You need write objectives for only these items, because these are the only ones you'll need to teach. The remaining performances will be included in your list of expectations but won't need to be turned into complete objectives.)

Here's a quick example. A manager was concerned that employees "be safety conscious." But what did that mean? How would he recognize someone who was acceptably safety conscious? Clearly, his first step was to say what he meant by "safety conscious" in terms of performance before he could find out (a) how many people already met the expectations and (b) what he would have to do to get the rest of the people to meet the expectations.

After some thought, the manager decided that people who were safety conscious:

a. Wear their safety equipment when appropriate.

b. Follow safety rules at all times.

c. Report safety hazards to the proper person(s).

Once the meaning of "safety conscious" was described in terms of expected human performances, it was easy to decide what to do next. He quickly determined that everybody already knew how to do the second and third items listed above, but some didn't know the proper way to put on and/or use some of the safety equipment. To accomplish his goal, then, the manager needed only to write one or more objectives describing the expectations regarding safety equipment and to arrange instruction for those who could not yet perform to the objectives' criteria.

Note that the objectives were written to describe the performances rather than the abstract state (safety consciousness) they represented as it would have been useless to describe the intent in such vague terms as these:

Be able to demonstrate safety consciousness in all appropriate situations.

That isn't an objective as it includes no DOING word. The words "be able to" don't turn gibberish into objectives.

Whenever you need to write objectives to describe states or conditions that are essentially abstract (understanding, knowing, attitude, motivation, feeling, appreciation), first use the goal analysis or similar procedure to help define those abstractions in terms of the performances that would represent their accomplishment. Once you've done that, you'll be in a position to decide which of those performances you'll have to teach, i.e., the things that your trainees cannot already do.

(Hmm. If statements about abstract states such as attitudes can't be called objectives until the performances which define them have been derived and described, wouldn't it be fair to say that there's no such thing as an "affective" objective?)

The checklist on page 166 can help you review your draft objectives. But try not to be constrained by form and format. State what you want your students to be able to do, what they will be doing it with or without, and how well they will have to do it for you to consider them competent.

And now, what's your pleasure?

A little more practice wouldn't hurt.   *Turn to page 155.*

I'm ready to test my skill.   *Turn to page 173.*

9

Sharpen Your Skill

The old saw about practice making perfect has about as much truth in it as the one about experience being the best teacher. Practice will improve a skill, and experience can improve one's competence—but *only* if there is feedback regarding the quality of the performance. If you don't find out how well you are doing while you are practicing or experiencing, your skill is not likely to improve. Therefore, while practice is important, practice with feedback is essential if the practice is to serve its purpose. Which may be the long way around the barn to tell you that this short chapter offers some guided practice in recognizing useful characteristics of objectives and a wee bit of practice in editing a few that are in need of repair.

"Wait a minnit," I hear you saying. "How come the objective of the book wants me to be able to *recognize* useful characteristics and now you want me to do a *repair* job?" Good question. Answer: This is a practice chapter to help you sharpen your discrimination skill. Asking you to repair a few objectives will cause you to pay closer attention to what you are learning to discriminate.

So sharpen your pencil and have at it.

Practice Items

Read the statements below. Place a check mark in the appropriate column to the right if a statement includes a performance, conditions under which the performance is to appear, and/or a criterion by which successful performance of the objective can be assessed.

HINT: Always begin decoding an objective by circling the performance. If no performance is stated, it isn't an objective and you need go no further.

	PERFORMANCE	CONDITIONS	CRITERION
1. When you complete this section, you will know the history of money as a medium of exchange.	___	___	___
2. Without references, be able to describe (write) the key conditions that promote learning and those that retard or interfere with learning.	___	___	___
3. On a live patient undergoing laparoscopy, be able to locate (point to) the following structures: ovary, ligaments of the ovary, fallopian tube, uterus.	___	___	___
4. Given twenty minutes of instruction and a lab exercise, be able to develop an understanding of the difference between igneous, metamorphic, and sedimentary rocks. Criterion: 80% correct.	___	___	___
5. Given a progressive discipline situation (where an unjustifiable lack of performance improvement follows the initial corrective discussion), be able to conduct a progressive discipline discussion using the key actions listed in the PDS Discussion Guide.	___	___	___

Turn to page 158.

	PERFORMANCE	CONDITIONS	CRITERION
1. When you complete this section, you will know the history of money as a medium of exchange.	—	—	—
2. Without references, be able to ⟨describe (write)⟩ the key conditions that promote learning and those that retard or interfere with learning.	✓	✓	✓
3. On a live patient undergoing laparoscopy, be able to ⟨locate (point to)⟩ the following structures: ovary, ligaments of the ovary, fallopian tube, uterus.	✓	✓	✓

Comments

1. This statement is pretty much useless as a statement of intended outcome. For one thing, it doesn't state a performance ("knowing" might be a state of mind, but it isn't a performance).

   You didn't get caught on the false given (condition), did you? "When you complete this section" tells you something about the learning experience; it doesn't describe a condition that will affect the desired (unstated) performance.

   Finally, no criterion is stated—or even implied.

   Statements such as these may be useful as course descriptions, but they should not be confused with objectives.

2. Here a performance (describing) and an indicator behavior (writing) are both stated, providing good information about what someone will be expected to be able to do.

   "Without references" is the conditon stated. Performing without references would be different from performing with references available.

   A criterion is implied rather than clearly stated. We are told that we must describe conditions (whatever they are), but we aren't told anything about the quality of the expected performance. This objective could be improved by a clearer description of the criterion.

3. Here again, both a covert performance (locate) and suitable indicator (point to) are stated. The key condition, "On a live patient," is also described.

   In this objective, a criterion is clearly implied. The objective says to be able to locate four specified items. If less than the four are located, the objective hasn't yet been achieved. (If you disagree, don't argue—fix the objective.)

	PERFORMANCE	CONDITIONS	CRITERION
4. Given twenty minutes of instruction and a lab exercise, be able to develop an understanding of the difference between igneous, metamorphic, and sedimentary rocks. Criterion: 80% correct.	____	____	____
5. (Note: The following objective is intended for managers.) Given a progressive discipline situation (where an unjustifiable lack of performance improvement follows the initial corrective discussion) be able to conduct a progressive discipline discussion using the key actions listed in the PDS Discussion Guide.	✓	✓	____

4. You didn't get caught on this false given, did you? It describes instructional procedure; it does *not* describe the conditions under which the performance is to occur. No performance is stated. And if it isn't, what possible meaning could there be to saying "80% correct"? It's rather like saying "Be able to understand the problems of the world. Criterion: 80% correct." Just labeling something a criterion doesn't make it one.

5. The performance is clearly stated (. . . be able to conduct a progressive discipline discussion . . .).

   Two conditions are also clearly stated (even though we may not have the background to understand the meaning of the first one). The first is "Given a progressive discipline situation . . . ," and the second is "using the key actions listed in the PDS Discussion Guide."

   The second item should be thought of as a condition rather than as a criterion. Why? Because it tells us something about what we will be doing during our performance, i.e., using the key actions in the Discussion Guide, but it doesn't tell us what to look for to decide whether the performance meets the intended standards. This objective would be a lot easier to read if it were cast in the form:

   Performance: Conduct a progressive discipline discussion.

   Givens: PDS Discussion Guide.
                  Progressive discipline situation (where an unjustifiable lack of performance improvement follows the initial corrective discussion)

   Criterion: (missing)

Practice Items

Try a few more. If a statement includes a performance, conditions, and/or a criterion, place a check mark in the appropriate column to its right.

	PERFORMANCE	CONDITIONS	CRITERION
1. The student will learn the basic sanitary standards in the food industry, according to local and state codes.	____	____	____
2. Students will gain knowledge of the structure of the molecule and briefly describe how the structures can be demonstrated.	____	____	____
3. <u>Given:</u> A need or assignment to conduct a performance appraisal, appropriate forms, and an interviewee, <u>Performance:</u> Conduct an appraisal interview. <u>Criteria:</u> Interviewee reports satisfaction with the discussion and states an intent to achieve the agreed-on work targets for the upcoming period. The interviewer and interviewee are willing to sign the form as accurate.	____	____	____
4. <u>Condition:</u> A three-hour discussion of the merits of a flat tax. <u>Performance:</u> Present (verbally) the advantages and disadvantages of a flat-tax system. <u>Criterion:</u> 90% accuracy.	____	____	____
5. <u>Given:</u> A functioning Meltdown Six computer terminal, be able to log on and send a message of your choice to any specified address. <u>Criterion:</u> All messages are received by their addressees.	____	____	____

Turn to Page 164.

	PERFORMANCE	CONDITIONS	CRITERION
1. The student will learn the basic sanitary standards in the food industry, according to local and state codes.	—	—	—
2. Students will gain knowledge of the structure of the molecule and briefly (describe) how the structures can be demonstrated.	✓	—	—
3. Given: A need or assignment to conduct a performance appraisal, appropriate forms, and an interviewee. Performance: (Conduct an appraisal interview.) Criteria: Interviewee reports satisfaction with the discussion, and states an intent to achieve the agreed-on work targets for the upcoming period. The interviewer and the interviewee are willing to sign the form as accurate.	✓	✓	✓
4. Condition: A three-hour discussion of the merits of a flat tax. Performance: (Present (verbally) the advantages and disadvantages of a flat-tax system.) Criterion: 90% accuracy.	✓	—	—
5. Given: A functioning Meltdown Six computer terminal, be able to (log on) and (send a message) of your choice to any specified address. Criterion: All messages are received by their addressees.	✓	✓	✓

Comment

1. This is another of those nothing statements. So the student will learn. How nice. But what about the result of that learning? You haven't been let in on the secret. No performance, no need to look further.

2. Yet another nothing statement. Again, this statement might be useful as part of a course description, but is worthless as a description of an important outcome to be achieved.

3. Here is a good objective. After reading it, you know what you're expected to be able to do, the conditions under which you'll be doing it, and the criteria by which the performance will be evaluated. Use this one as a model for your own drafts.

4. Uh, oh. Here's another of those cosmetically nifty statements—nice format, but no substance.

    The item listed as a condition is merely a description of part of the instructional process, and the "criterion" isn't. Remember: Calling it a criterion doesn't necessarily make it one. In the context of this statement, "90% accuracy" has no meaning.

    About all we can say in favor of this item is that a performance is stated. True, that's more information than a lot of "objectives" provide, but not enough.

5. This is another good example, even though the performance was stated in the objective as part of the "Givens."

    Performance: Send messages to specified addresses.

    Conditions: Given a functioning computer terminal.

    Criteria: All messages get to where they're sent.

Now try your hand at fixing objectives in need of some repair.

Objectives Checklist

Your objectives will communicate better if you can answer "YES" to the following questions:

Performance

1. Is your main intent stated?

2. If the main intent is covert (mental), is an indicator behavior stated?

3. Is that indicator behavior the simplest and most direct one you can think of?

Conditions

4. Have you described what the learner will be given, or be deprived of, during performance of the objective?

5. Have you described all of the conditions that will influence the shape of the performance?

Criteria

6. Have you described how well the learner must perform to be acceptable?

7. Do those criteria describe some aspect of the performance, or the product of the performance, rather than instructional process or meaningless percentages?

8. Where a percentage is included in a criterion, does it reflect a realistic expectation?

Editing Practice

Here are some objectives in need of repair. Strike any unnecessary or confusing words, and add indicators where performances are covert (mental, cognitive). Where useful characteristics are missing, add them. If you are not familiar with the content, make something up. The checklist of the facing page may be of help. (Hint: It will be easier to rewrite these on another piece of paper or on your word processor.)

1. Given a potential customer, be able to describe the features and benefits of your product.

2. Having completed as much practice as you feel necessary, be able to type a business letter. Criterion: Satisfaction of the instructor.

3. Know how a personal pager works.

4. In a classroom environment, be able to make a five-minute presentation on a topic of your choice. The presentation should show good form.

5. After studying the text and discussing it with colleagues, identify examples of ethical and unethical conduct.

When you have finished your repairs, turn to the next page.

How'd You Do?

1. *Given a potential customer, be able to describe the features and benefits of your product.*

   This one needs only minor repair. A performance is stated, and so is one of the key conditions that would influence that performance. What's missing is a criterion that would suggest how to judge the product—describing performance.

   If you were asked to demonstrate accomplishment of this objective, however, you might have some questions about the conditions. "Wouldn't I have an actual product handy while I'm explaining features and benefits?" "If not, wouldn't I at least have some product literature to refer to?" Taking questions such as those into consideration, your objective might look like this:

   Given a potential customer, a product, and related literature, be able to describe the features and benefits of the product. Criteria: All key benefits and features highlighted in the literature must be described; all information presented must be factual; customer must not be insulted, demeaned, embarrassed, or ridiculed.

2. *Having completed as much practice as you feel necessary, be able to type a business letter. Criterion: Satisfaction of the instructor.*

   The verbiage before the comma represents a false given; it talks about instructional practice rather than about conditions that would affect the performance of typing a letter. Add the conditions under which the typing is expected to occur. On a 1912 Remington typewriter? Using a computer keyboard?

   The performance is fine, but the "criterion" stinks. We already know that we need to satisfy the instructor. So those words tell us nothing. What would be useful would be to learn just *what* would satisfy the instructor. A box of candy? A case of beer? Here's one way to re-write this objective:

Given a legible handwritten letter and a functioning computer, be able to type the letter in accordance with the standards described in Manual 12-21.

3. *Know how a personal pager works.*

This objective states no performance, no conditions, and no criteria, so fixing it will require more crystal-balling on your part. What is "know" supposed to mean in this context? Be able to describe what a pager does? Trace the signal flow through the circuits? Describe the theory of pagers? What? You'll have to decide. (Remember: When someone asks you to deal with "fuzzies" such as these, they abdicate to you the power to decide what they mean. Take advantage of it.) I arbitrarily decided that the objective-writer wants me to be able to repair pagers, and so modified the statement this way:

Given all necessary tools, spare parts, and reference materials, be able to repair any brand of pager. The repaired device must function to manufacturer specifications described in the Service Manual.

Your objective will look different, of course, depending on what meaning you decided to select.

4. *In a classroom environment, be able to make a five-minute presentation on a topic of your choice. The presentation should show good form.*

Hooray! An objective with a nicely stated performance . . . but that's about all. Is "in a classroom environment . . ." a condition or a description of the place where the practicing will occur? If the objective-writer intends for us to learn to make presentations in classrooms only, then the words before the comma are a condition. If the intent is for us to make presentations in other environments as well, the words before the comma should be deleted.

The only words that smell like a criterion here are "The presentation should show good form." But what does "good form" mean? Standing up straight, chin in, chest out, tummy sucked in? Fingers extended and joined? What? This is clearly an instance where the objective-writer should have completed a goal analysis on this "fuzzy" before inflicting it on us to divine its meaning. To fix this statement, you'll have to decide what "good form" means and add any conditions you think are relevant to the performance. Here's one possibility:

Given visuals of your choice and a topic of your choice, be able to make a five-minute presentation. Criteria:

a. *Didn't turn back to audience,*

b. *Wrote legibly when using flip chart or board,*

c. *Removed visuals from view when not in use, and*

d. *Used gestures and movement to emphasize points made.*

It's anybody's guess what the objective-writer meant by "good form," so almost any definition you used would be appropriate, so long as it is described as clearly as possible and is written down.

5. *After studying the text and discussing it with colleagues, identify examples of ethical and unethical conduct.*

Things are getting stickier. In dealing with this one, it would help to know from which course the objective was taken; it was swiped from a nursing course. At least that helps pinpoint the subject.

The first problem here, of course, is that the words before the comma describe instructional procedures rather than an outcome. Delete them. The second problem is that we don't know which of the several possible meanings of "identify" is intended. Add an indicator behavior. Finally, there is no criterion. One needs to be added.

To fix this objective, it helps to ask the question, "Now how could I find out whether a practicing nurse can identify ethical and unethical nursing behavior?" Here's one way to do it.

Given videotaped scenes depicting a nurse carrying out various duties, be able to identify (describe) instances of unethical behavior. Criterion: All instances of unethical behavior (as defined by the NP Ethical Handbook) are described.

10
Self-Test

On the following pages is a short skill check with which you can check your skill at discriminating (pointing to) the characteristics of objectives. Answer all the questions, and then check your responses on pages 176–179.

The self-test consists of twenty items. In the first ten, you are asked whether or not each statement contains a performance. In the last ten, you will need to make three discriminations for each item (whether or not it contains a performance; whether or not it contains a condition; and whether or not it contains a criterion). If you make no more than one error in the first ten items and no more than six errors in the next ten, color yourself competent. Otherwise, you may want to review the chapter(s) dealing with the characteristic(s) on which we disagree.

Notice that a perfect score is not expected. Why not? Because you may not be familiar with the content of some of the objectives. In such cases it may be difficult to recognize conditions or criteria that aren't clearly labeled as such.

Have at it!

SELF-TEST

A. Do the following statements include performances? Does each at least tell what the learner will be doing when demonstrating achievement of the objective?

	States a Performance	
	YES	NO
1. Understand the principles of power grids.	___	___
2. Be able to write correct examples of the logical fallacy of the undistributed middle.	___	___
3. Internalize the meaning of Ohm's Law.	___	___
4. Without the use of memory aids, be able to name the bones of the body.	___	___
5. Know the needs for nursing care associated with the stresses of life situations and with common aspects of illness.	___	___
6. Demonstrate a *deep* understanding of the plays of Shakespeare.	___	___
7. Be able to identify *(circle)* objectives that include a statement of desired performance.	___	___
8. Develop an ability to recognize that the practical application of democratic ideals requires time, adjustment, and continuous effort.	___	___
9. Appreciate the ability of others, and perform as an intelligent spectator.	___	___
10. Be able to describe the log-on procedure for your own computer.	___	___

B. Read the statements below. Place a check mark in the appropriate column to indicate any characteristic of a useful objective you find in each.

	PERFORMANCE	CONDITIONS	CRITERION

11. Without memory aids or other assistance, demonstrate a knowledge of the rules of grammar.

12. Be able to write an essay on evolution.

13. Using any reference materials, be able to name correctly every item shown on each of twenty blueprints.

14. Be able to write a description of the steps involved in making a blueprint.

15. On the 25-yard range, be able to draw your service revolver and fire five rounds from the hip within three seconds. At 25 yards, all rounds must hit the standard silhouette target.

16. Be able to know well the cardinal rules of good manners.

17. Given an oral description of the events involved in an accident, be able to fill out a standard accident report.

18. Be able to write a coherent essay on the subject "How to Write Objectives for a Course in Law Appreciation." Course notes may be used, as well as any references.

19. Be able to develop logical approaches in the solution of personnel problems.

20. Without reference materials, be able to describe three common points of view regarding racial inferiority or superiority that are not supported by available research.

Solutions for Part A

Performances are circled.

	States a Performance	
	YES	**NO**
1. Understand the principles of power grids.		✓
2. Be able to (write) correct examples of the logical fallacy of the undistributed middle.	✓	
3. Internalize the meaning of Ohm's Law.		✓
4. Without the use of memory aids, be able to (name) the bones of the body.	✓	
5. Know the needs for nursing care associated with the stresses of life situations and with common aspects of illness.		✓
6. Demonstrate a *deep* understanding of the plays of Shakespeare.		✓
7. Be able to (identify (circle)) objectives that include a statement of desired performance.	✓	
8. Develop an ability to recognize that the practical application of democratic ideals requires time, adjustment, and continuous effort.		✓
9. Appreciate the ability of others, and perform as an intelligent spectator.		✓
10. Be able to (describe) the log-on procedure for your own computer.	✓	

Comments for Part A

1. A goal analysis would be in order here to determine the meaning of "understand."

2. You can tell whether someone is writing, so it qualifies as a performance.

3. Same problem as with Item 1.

4. Naming is a performance; you can tell when it is being done.

5. Same problem as with Item 1. An important goal, perhaps, but no performance is stated.

6. Underlining doesn't make words more specific—and that's <u>really true.</u>

7. Identifying is a covert performance that can be directly assessed by a single indicator behavior such as circling, underlining, or checking.

8. Again, perhaps an important thought, but what would you be doing when recognizing that application of ideals requires time?

9. You didn't get caught on the "perform as an intelligent spectator" part of this, did you? What would you be doing when performing? Shouting? Throwing bottles at an umpire? Sitting quietly? We are given nary a clue.

10. Describing is a performance. We are not told whether the describing must be oral or in writing, but either way the describing is a performance.

Solutions for Part B

Performances are circled.
Conditions are underlined.
Criteria are in italics.

	PERFORMANCE	CONDITIONS	CRITERION
11. <u>Without memory aids or other assistance,</u> demonstrate a knowledge of the rules of grammar.		✓	
12. Be able to (write) an essay on evolution.	✓		
13. <u>Using any reference materials,</u> be able to (name) *correctly every item shown on each of twenty blueprints.*	✓	✓	✓
14. Be able to (write) a description of the steps involved in making a blueprint.	✓		
15. <u>On the 25-yard range,</u> be able to (draw) your <u>service revolver</u> and (fire five rounds from the hip) <u>within three seconds.</u> *At 25 yards, all rounds must hit the standard silhouette target.*	✓	✓	✓
16. Be able to know *well* the cardinal rules of good manners.			
17. <u>Given an oral description of the events involved in an accident,</u> be able to (fill out) a standard accident report.	✓	✓	
18. Be able to (write) a coherent essay on the subject "How to Write Objectives for a Course in Law Appreciation." <u>Course notes may be used, as well as any references.</u>	✓	✓	
19. Be able to develop logical approaches in the solution of personnel problems.			
20. <u>Without reference materials,</u> be able to (describe) *three common points* of view regarding racial inferiority or superiority that are *not supported by available research.*	✓	✓	✓

Comments for Part B

11. *Demonstrate* is that trap word that often leads us to believe we are saying something specific.

12. Though you may read an implication that the writing must be done without reference materials, that condition is not stated. Neither are we told how the essay will be judged competent.

13. This one says something about performance, conditions, and criterion. It may be an objective that would appear at the bottom of an objectives hierarchy—that is, it may be a very low-level skill—but it is an objective.

14. Here you may feel that a criterion is implied. It says to write the steps, and that could be read to mean "write all the steps correctly." And then, again, it might mean something else. If a few words will make the criterion clear, it is better to add them than to rely on inferences.

15. You may not agree with the purpose of the statement, but it is a good objective.

16. Italicizing *doesn't* make it so—or specific.

17. Again, you may read an implication of "without error." I wouldn't, because I never assume that perfection is demanded unless it is explicitly specified. Perfection is seldom a realistic expectation.

18. What does coherent mean? How would we recognize coherence if we saw it? We are not told.

19. Ah, well. Another nice-sounding statement, but not an objective. Besides, the word "develop" usually means that the statement is talking about the process of acquiring the intended competence, rather than about the result of the acquiring.

20. This one is tricky. How well must the describing be done? Well, it has to describe three points of view not supported by research. Not much of a criterion, I'll admit, but a start.

Scoring

To compare your responses against the criterion, do the following:

1. In items 1 through 10, circle every incorrect check mark.

2. In items 11 through 20, circle any space that you left empty but that should have a check mark. Circle the spaces you checked that you should have left empty.

3. Total the circled spaces (errors). If there are seven or fewer, AND if they include no more than one error in recognizing the presence or absence of a performance, consider yourself competent to recognize the presence or absence of the characteristics of a useful objective.

If you have more errors than specified in the criterion, you may want to review the chapter(s) dealing with the characteristic(s) on which we disagree.

> NOTE: When there is disagreement about the meaning of an objective, it is always faster and easier to fix it than argue about it.

One final thought.
You are now ready to begin
drafting your own objectives.
May you be as picky with *them*
as you have been with mine.

The Stoner
and the Stonees

Professor, professor," cried the second-assistant digger-upper. "I think I've found something."

"Oh," replied the professor, raising his archeological head from the archeological dirt. "What is it?"

"It's a large stone with writing on it," enthused the excited assistant. "Maybe it's another part of the *Great Recipe of Life.*"

"Let me see," said the professor as he raised his magnificent magnifying glass. "No, no, I think you're mistaken. See these markings? These are the names of people."

"People?" queried the assistant. "What people?"

"Hmm," replied the great one, profoundly. "It looks as though these are the names of people who contributed to the shaping and the fixing of a book."

"Why would anyone put their names in stone?" asked the assistant.

"Well," replied the professor, "it says here that the author didn't want anyone to forget just who it was that beat and bashed his words into presentable shape. He wanted the world to remember each and every one for what they did to his work."

"What did they do to it?" asked the assistant, edging closer for a better look.

"A number of things, according to these hieroglyphics. For example, it says here that Dave Cram, Margo Hicks, and John Warriner had something to do with making sure the manuscript hung together. Continuity check is the term he used.

"Then he lists some people who helped test to make sure the book accomplished what it was supposed to. He called that his outcome check. The names are Maryjane Rees, John Alston, Joe de Hazes, Jeannette Hanne, Grant Bodwell, Michael Hanau, Jerry Tuller, and Jean White.

"After that he lists those who participated in a . . . an attitude check, apparently to make sure the book didn't contain any accidental turnoffs. Their names are Billy Koscheski, Elizabeth Epperson, Pauline Stone, Ann Redl, Dick Niedrich, Andy Stevens, Jane Kilkenny, and Marilyn McElhaney.

"Diane Pope is mentioned in deeply chiseled letters because she contributed a special example. Jeanne Mager is named as chief chiseler."

"Look at this!" cried the assistant. "Here are some words with a box chiseled around them. What do they say?"

"These," continued the professor as he tried to push his nose through his magnifying glass, "are the names of those who helped to test the cover design of the book. They are Frank Sedei, John Gray, Karen Schwartz, Sue Markle, Jim Straubel, Mike Nisos, Roger Kaufman, Margo Hicks, Bob Morgan, Al Collins, Joan Fleetwood, Stephen Daeschner, Bob Reichart, Harold Stolovitch, Wally Stauffer, and Jan Kaufman.

"And," continued the professor pomporiously, "here is a clump of names of those who tested other cover designs. Looks like Clair Miller, Bill Valen, Dan Piskorik, Letitia Wiley, Carol Valen, Eileen Mager, Johan Adriaanse, Bob White, Jim Reed, Ethel Robinson, Fahad Omair, Phil Postel, Gérard

Conesa, David Heath, and Paul Guersch."

"That's amazing!" wowed the assistant.

"Help me topple this big boulder! We must leave no stone unturned." Which they did.

"Aha!" amazed the professor. "There are even more names here. Look. These are people who helped shape the third edition."

"What did they do?" queried the assistant.

"Several things. Good and bad samples from their vintage objectives collections were generously offered by Paul Whitmore, Richard Lookatch, Kay Newell, Ann Parkman, Ken Fackler, and James T. McGoldrick.

"Initial trampling was kindly undertaken by that virtuoso manuscript bashist, David Cram. Following the revision, another group of miscreants gleefully added their footprints: Carl Winkelbauer, Al Wilson, Marianne Hoffman, Hilton Goldman, Jerri Shold, Ann D. Demonet, John R. Criswell, Diane Wardrop, Lee Alderman, Wayne Seamans, and Eileen Mager."

"Gee whiz," exhaled the assistant. "That author didn't seem to know how to do anything by himself."

"Perhaps not," was the reply. "But it says here—you see these large chiselings—it says that those who would do unto others should care what those others prefer. That's why these people were asked to try on the manuscript. They helped to make it communicate better . . . and that's why they were stoned."

Index

CEP WORKSHOPS

CEP offers *the* industry-standard Mager Workshops for training and performance improvement professionals. Our workshops don't just tell you about CRI-based instruction; we teach you how to *apply* the methodology to training projects.

Criterion-Referenced Instruction by Robert F. Mager and Peter Pipe
The CRI Methodology Part 1: Analysis, Design and Evaluation

The Criterion-Referenced Instruction workshop will give you immediately applicable, practical skills in analysis, design and evaluation necessary to succeed in a state-of-the-art training and performance improvement department. You'll learn how to:

- Conduct in-depth analysis (including goal, performance and task analyses)
- Edit and derive clear and measurable objectives
- Draft effective procedural guides, skill checks, course scenarios and course maps
- Plan course evaluations
- Quickly evaluate existing materials and plan course improvements

Instructional Module Development by Robert F. Mager
The CRI Methodology Part 2: Development

In the follow-up workshop to CRI, you build on your CRI skills to:

- Draft, try out and revise at least two modules of instruction for a course you are developing
- Test modules with other participants
- Experience firsthand the tryout process from the student' point of view
- Learn by seeing instruction in a variety of formats and subject areas

The Training Manager Workshop by Robert F. Mager

Learn how to support the achievement of your organization's strategic goals by providing employees with the skills and motivation to perform their jobs to management's expectations. During the workshop, you will work on the following modules:

- Evaluate instructors' performance
- Evaluate proposals for services
- Plan course evaluations
- Review training development progress
- Assess media choices
- Review training modules
- Solve performance problems
- Identify job tasks
- Create effective objectives
- Identify prerequisite skills

For more information and a schedule of public workshops, visit www.cepworldwide.com or call us at 1-800-558-4CEP

Making Instruction Work

or Skillbloomers

*A step-by-step guide
to designing and developing
instruction that works*

Second Edition

Robert F. Mager

CEP PRESS
A wholly owned subsidiary of
The Center for Effective Performance, Inc.
Atlanta, Georgia

Books by Robert F. Mager

Preparing Instructional Objectives, *Third Edition**

Measuring Instructional Results, *Third Edition**

Analyzing Performance Problems, *Third Edition**
(with Peter Pipe)

Goal Analysis, *Third Edition**

How to Turn Learners On . . . without turning them off, *Third Edition**

Making Instruction Work, *Second Edition**

Developing Vocational Instruction (with Kenneth Beach)

Troubleshooting the Troubleshooting Course

The How to Write a Book Book

What Every Manager Should Know About Training

* Sold as a six-volume set (The Mager Six-Pack)

WORKSHOPS BY ROBERT F. MAGER

Criterion-Referenced Instruction (with Peter Pipe)

Instructional Module Development

The Training Manager Workshop

For more information, contact:
CEP Press
2300 Peachford Road, Suite 2000
Atlanta, GA 30338
(770) 458-4080 or (800) 558-4237
www.ceppress.com

ISBN 1-879-618-02-8 (PREVIOUSLY ISBN 1-56103-467-3)
ISBN 1-879-618-15-X (SIX-VOLUME SET)
Library of Congress Catalog Card Number: 96-072447
Printed in the United States of America

05 04 03 02 01   10 9 8 7 6 5 4

Contents

Kneedimples (A Magerfable)

Kneedimples

(A Magerfable)

Once upon a time in the land of Upsyde Downs, the Keeper of the Wisdom said to the next in line, "Doodly, you are soon to become of age, so it is time for you to enter the world and learn to Trip the Light Fantastic. It is time for you to become the best that you can."

So Doodly hurried off with his heart in his hand and a spring in his step, for he was truly eager to become all that he could.

When he finally arrived at what he believed to be the Greatest Learnatorium in all of Upsyde Downs, he was ushered to an audience with the Keeper of the Knowing.

"You have truly come to the right place," intoned the Keeper. "We have all of the Knowing there is to Know. So if you will learn what you are told, you will surely become all that you can."

Doodly was mightily impressed. He was sure he had found the Right Place. After all, didn't they have Starbright Projectors and Redeye Comblabulators with shimmering screens? Of course they did! Weren't the instructors the greatest stars of the Light Fantastic? Of course, they were! So, convinced of the soundness of his choice, Doodly applied himself in earnest. He listened keenly and wrote down what he heard. He put a mark beside all the right answers and wrote the most masterly essays. Inevitably, he rose to the top of the class, because there simply wasn't anything about Tripping the Light Fantastic that Doodly couldn't tell you about.

Finally the appointed day burst over the horizon. Doodly was handed his three-dimensional holographic diploma, along with as much pomp as could be arranged under the circumstances. He was so proud that he showed it to everyone in sight. But when at last the oohs and aahs abated, he tucked his diploma under his arm and went off to find . . . a Position. Naturally, he went first to Upsyde Fantasies, the most magnificent theater in all of Downs.

"Here is my diploma," he said proudly to the Keeper of the Entertainment. "I am ready to Trip the Light Fantastic and show that I have become the best that I can."

"Well, well, well," said the Keeper, with a lift of his eyebrows. "Anyone with a diploma as shiny as yours certainly deserves respect. And as we happen to have an opening for tonight's performance, you're hired."

So within hours it came to pass that Doodly faced his first Opening Night. He was so excited that his synapses literally twanged in anticipation. Then, just as he was giving his shoes a final sparkle, he heard the fanfare and the great clashing of cymbals—his cue for his first Grand Entrance. And he rushed onto the Stage of Life.

But the Glorious Triumph was not to be. For hardly had he approached the center of the stage before he got all tangled up in his own feet and fell flat on his face. Kersplat!

"Oh, my," said Doodly to the sweet young partner twiddling on her toes and trying to swallow a horrendously loud giggle. "They certainly taught me the tripping part of it, but I wonder what happened to the Light Fantastic? I could do this well before I started."

And wonder he might. Because try as he did, and he *did* try, all he could ever manage was a very ungainly but hilarious squat that caused everyone to roar with laughter whenever he walked upon the stage.

And from that day on, whenever people heard that Doodly was on the program, they would come from miles and miles and miles around to watch. Oh, not to watch him Trip the Light Fantastic, of course, because he hadn't actually been taught how to *do* that. If truth be told, they came to watch Doodly squat.

And the moral of this fable is that . . .

SKILL DOES NOT BLOOM FROM WORDS ALONE.

Or, in somewhat less poetic terms, telling isn't the same as teaching. Though it is a remarkable accomplishment to have developed the skills and knowledge needed to be considered competent in one's craft, those skills are not the same as those needed for teaching that craft. Just as an ability to *make* a tuba is not the same as an ability to *play* one, an ability to *play* one is not the same as an ability to *teach* someone else to do likewise.

Therefore, those who would like to share their competence with others will take steps to learn the skills by which that end is accomplished.

Robert F. Mager

Carefree, Arizona
January 1997

Part I

What It's All About

1
What It's All About

The world of instruction has changed from the days when instruction followed the lecture-in-the-morning-lab-in-the-afternoon approach and the only tools in the instructor's tool kit were the lecture, the lab, and on-the-job training (OJT). It has changed from the days when instructors were selected because they were good at their specialty, whether or not they knew anything about communicating that specialty to others. It has changed from the days when instructors were allowed to teach as much about a subject as time would allow, regardless of the relevance of the content to the need of the individual student. It has changed from the days when those who "winged it" in the classroom were held in awe.

Now, there is a craft of instruction rich in procedures and techniques for assuring that students develop important skills, and for sending them away with a desire to apply what they have learned and an eagerness to learn more.

This book is about that craft. It isn't about all the bits and pieces of the craft. It's only about those pieces that will ensure that (a) instruction is the correct solution to a problem, (b) the objectives of the instruction are derived from demonstrated needs, (c) the substance of the instruction is adjusted to what each student needs, and (d) instructional practices contribute to, rather than detract from, student eagerness to learn more. It's about how to make instruction work as well as possible with the tools at hand. Fortunately, those tools are within the grasp of those with even the most limited instructional resources—they need no special approval or budget to make them work.

Who It's For

This book is for those vitally important people who teach in an environment where the outcomes of their instruction are of serious consequence to both student and sponsor alike—who teach, in other words, where it matters whether the instruction accomplishes its announced goals and objectives. It is for those who teach so that others may achieve intellectual and economic independence, as well as self-respect, in their own worlds.

What It's For

The purpose of this book is to describe and illustrate the key components of the instructional craft. But just as there are far more words in the English language than you will ever need or use, there is far more to know about the craft of instruction than you can, or need to, put to practical use. This book is about those practical pieces—the pieces that will make your instruction lean, on target, motivating, and effective.

Though the chapters of this book cannot send you away highly skilled in the procedures being described, they will point you to those procedures that, if applied, will increase the elegance (effectiveness and efficiency) of your efforts.

> **NOTE:** Many instructors are literally dropped into a course, given a textbook, and told to "Go teach." Though this situation may not be ideal from either an instructor's or student's point of view, it often cannot be avoided. But even though you have to "hit the ground running," you

can still apply—immediately—some of the course improvement procedures described in this book.

ANOTHER NOTE: If, at any point, you find yourself thinking that it is impossible to apply any of the techniques described in this book because you are "stuck with the 50-minute hour," or because you "just don't have the time," skip ahead to the last chapter, "Course Improvement." Read the chapter and then apply the "Course Improvement Checklist" *to the course you are teaching or are preparing to teach.*

2
The Performance World

Why Instruct?

The only justification for instruction is that one or more people cannot yet do something they need or want to be able to do. Unless these two conditions exist, there is no valid reason to instruct.

That may sound like a trivial idea, until you consider the amount of time you've spent in classes thinking or saying, "But I already *know* that," or "I don't *need* to know that." Such thoughts indicate the waste of student time and motivation, not to mention the waste of instructional resources caused by thoughtless insistence on instructional ritual when no sound reason for it exists.

The Goal

Our primary goal as instructors should be to make our students as successful as possible while at the same time imposing ourselves as little as possible on their lives. Just as the ethical physician treats only those in need of treatment, for only so long as that need lasts, our goal is to instruct as effectively as possible for only as long as the need exists; that is, until each student can perform as desired.

And because we are humane and because our job is to help people to grow, our intent *during* instruction should be not to hurt, belittle, bore, frustrate, humiliate, insult, waste the time of, or otherwise demean, our students. In other words, in addition to fulfilling our instructional mandate, our goal should be to *do no harm.* To accomplish these intents, we seek out procedures and practices that will give our students the skills they need, as well as the motivation to use them and the eagerness to learn more.

The World of Human Performance

But accomplishing these goals requires us to use more tools than are available within the confines of good instructional practices. In fact, the world of human performance is a whole lot bigger than instruction. Before venturing into specifics, therefore, I'd like to offer some perspective on this larger performance world.

Instructional Technology

When we set out to help people to do something that they cannot now do but need to do, we dip into a bag of procedures currently referred to as "instructional technology." These are the techniques and procedures by which we influence what people *can do.* When there is a skill or knowledge deficiency to be eliminated, one dips into this bag and selects one or more remedies to solve the problem.

TERMINOLOGY NOTE: Though the current rubric is "instructional technology," we're talking about the craft of instruction, about the best procedures currently available for modifying human capabilities *through instruction.* Figure 2.1 names some of these procedures.

Figure 2.1

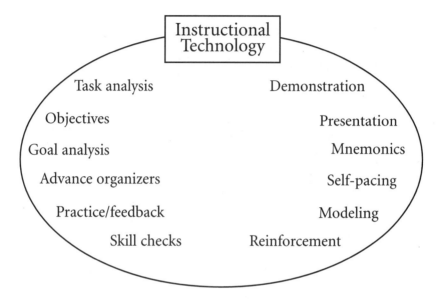

Mission:
To change performance capability,
or what people can do.

Performance Technology

Instructional technology, however, is a subset of a larger collection of procedures and techniques known as "performance
technology." When people *already know how* to perform but are
not performing as desired, more instruction *won't help.* Let me
say that again, and louder. ***When people already know how to
perform, but are not performing as desired, more instruction
won't help.*** Such situations call for application of different

techniques aimed at modifying not the "can do," but the "do do" (sorry about that); techniques that encourage people to do what they already know how to do. For example, if students already know how to study but don't, more *instruction* on study skills won't help. What will help is the management of consequences that will increase the likelihood that they will do what they already know how to do.

As you are well aware, people often don't do what they know how to do, usually because of one or more of these reasons:

- They don't know what they are expected to do.

- They don't have the tools to perform as desired.

- They aren't given the authority to perform as desired.

- They're never told how well they're doing.

- They are punished for performing as desired.

In these instances, remedies other than instruction are needed; for example:

- information (manuals, policies, notices, etc.);

- authority to perform as desired;

- feedback for present performance;

- tools, space, equipment;

- performance management (arranging the environment so that desired performance is allowed and rewarded, rather than punished);

- performance (job) aids;

- task redesign (to simplify the desired performance);

- process improvement;
- interface redesign (to make the human/machine interface more logical, easier to deal with).

Some of these strategies for modifying the "do do" as well as the "can do" are identified in Figure 2.2.

Figure 2.2

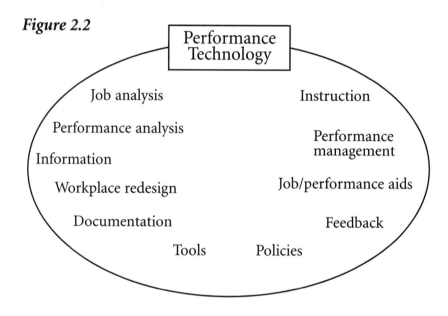

Performance Technology

Job analysis

Instruction

Performance analysis

Performance management

Information

Workplace redesign

Job/performance aids

Documentation

Feedback

Tools

Policies

Mission:
To facilitate desired performance, or what people do do.

Management

Both instructional and performance technologies are subsets of an even larger domain referred to as "management." Management involves the *allocation and control* of available resources toward the accomplishment of goals and objectives. That's as true of the management of a giant corporation as of the management of a ship, a church, a family, a classroom, or our own personal lives. When we are allocating and controlling available resources to accomplish goals and objectives, we are managing. Some of the resources usually available to corporate managements are shown in Figure 2.3.

Figure 2.3

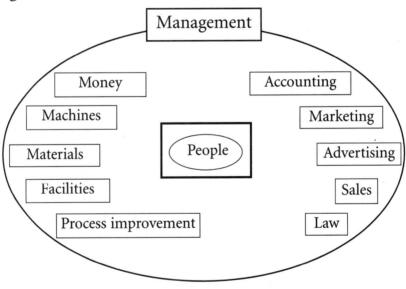

Mission:

Allocate and control resources
to accomplish goals and objectives.

Any corporation, for example, has a variety of resources available with which to accomplish its goals: machinery, money, production procedures, research information, marketing, advertising, law, accounting, and so on.

One of the key resources is *people*. It takes people to do many of the things that need doing. To get things done in a way that helps rather than hinders the accomplishment of the goals, however, people have to do things in a productive rather than an unproductive way. The function of the performance technology procedures is to make that happen. It reaches for the tools of that technology when people already know how to perform, and reaches for instruction when they don't.

Figure 2.4

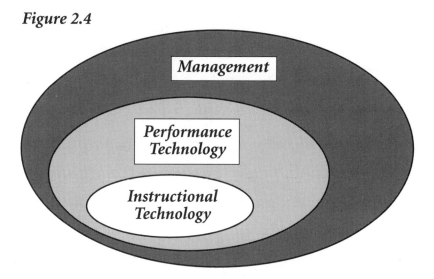

You can see by the model shown in Figure 2.4 that while instruction is an important tool for improving human performance, it is only one of the ways of doing so. For this reason we say, "We're no longer in the training business; we're in the *performance* business," and why we say, "Instruction is a last resort."

Instruction Is a Last Resort

In the past, we've been accustomed to using instruction as the remedy of choice for almost any problem involving human performance. They're not doing what they're supposed to be doing? Well, teach 'em. They don't have the right attitude, or aren't motivated? Teach 'em some more. Instruction was our magic bullet, probably because instructing was our goal. But no longer. Now *performance* is the target! The focus has changed from instruction (a process) to performance (the desired outcomes of a process). Within the instructional process itself, the focus has changed from presentations by the instructor to practice by the students.

Once the focus shifted to performance, it became clear that we already had a number of tools available to make that performance happen, and that instruction was only one of them. We also came to realize that almost every one of the non-training tools was faster and cheaper to implement than instruction. That's why we think of instruction, like surgery, as a last resort. When it's the remedy of choice, it's important that it be done—and done right the first time. But when it isn't needed, it shouldn't be done at all.

As you work through the chapters to come, therefore, remind yourself that in real life there will be many, many instances in which you won't have to complete all the steps involved in the design and development of instruction; in fact, sometimes you won't have to complete any at all. Why? Because by the time you've concluded the analysis steps, you'll have discovered how to get the performance you want or need—without the need for instruction.

To Learn More: See Resources #12 and #19. (The "Useful Resources" list can be found at the back of this book.)

3

Strategy of Instructional Development

Now that we've considered the big picture, it's time to get more specific. This chapter will present a brief description of the phases of the instructional process, as well as a description of the main techniques and procedures through which we develop instruction that works. The chapters that follow this one will describe each procedure in more detail, describe how to carry out the procedure, and offer one or more examples. Though some of the procedures may be new to you, the overall strategy will be familiar, simply because it asks you to do in your instruction what you already do in other aspects of your life: decide what you want to accomplish, apply the tools and techniques needed to accomplish it, and then determine how well you did.

The Instructional Design/Development Sequence

The procedures through which instructional design and development are carried out are often clumped into four broad phases: analysis, design/development, implementation, and evaluation/improvement. Some practitioners prefer to clump the components into five or six phases, while others prefer to think of them as fitting into three such "buckets." Don't be distressed by these preferences. After all, there are any number of ways to package a baloney; what matters is the quality of the meat. No matter which general headings are

Figure 3.1

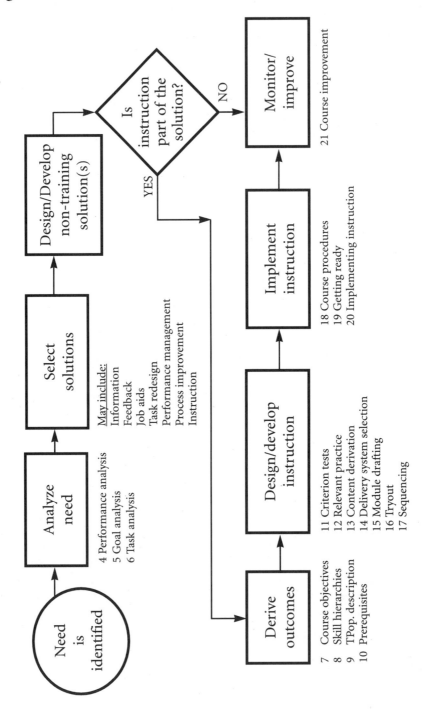

used to group the procedures, all are important to the success of the instruction.

To provide a picture of how the chapters of this book fit into the overall process, I've grouped the major steps in the process under seven general headings (See Figure 3.1). (Chapter titles and numbers are shown under the activities to which they pertain.) This diagram deliberately emphasizes the *instructional* part of the process because, after all, that's what this book is mostly about. Often, however, instruction plays only a small part in solving human performance problems. Here is a brief tour of the diagram, starting at the upper left.

Quick Tour of the Process

Analyze the need and select solutions. The process begins when a need is identified. This generally happens when someone decides that instruction is needed, or that one or more people aren't doing what they should be doing. The need is then analyzed so that appropriate actions (remedies, solutions) may be selected.

Design/develop non-training solutions. Because actions other than—or in addition to—instruction are almost always part of the solution mix, development and implementation of these non-training solutions is initiated. These remedies usually include information about performance expectancies, feedback, job aids, task simplification, and so on. (Implementation of these actions usually provides immediate benefits—whether or not instruction is ultimately included in the solution mix.)

Derive the instructional outcomes. If instruction is part of the solution, the intended outcomes (objectives) of the instruction are derived and stated, skill hierarchies depicting the relationship between those objectives are drafted, the intended student audience (target population) is described, and prerequisites are established.

Design and develop the instruction. The instruction is then designed and developed, tested, and revised, and the modules (lessons) are put into a suitable sequence for delivery to the students.

Implement the instruction. Before the course is delivered, however, course procedures are drafted so that students and instructors alike will know the rules by which the instruction will proceed. Instructors make sure they are prepared with the skills that will allow them to instruct effectively and efficiently—without detracting from the learning or from student motivation. The course is then ready for the students.

Monitor and revise. Once the course is implemented, it is periodically checked (evaluated) to make sure it still does what it was designed to do, and improvements are made where they are indicated.

That's the fast tour. Here now is a brief description of each of the chapters that follow.

NOTE: The procedures described in this book appear in the approximate order followed when a *complete* instructional development project is undertaken, that is, when all the procedures are used. But it is *not necessary to apply them in the exact order shown,* nor is it always necessary to use *all* of them to accomplish your mission.

You may want to refer to Figure 3.1 as you read the chapter descriptions that follow. Before doing that, however, read the note just above one more time.

Analyzing the Need (Part II)

The moral of one of my fables says that if you don't know where you're going, you might wind up someplace else—and not even know it. That seems pretty obvious. But how can you decide where to go in the first place? How can you decide on a worthy destination?

The analysis procedures available to the instructional developer are intended to deal precisely with these issues. They help to answer questions such as these:

- Is instruction called for in this situation?

- If not, what remedies should be applied?

- If so, what is worth teaching?

- Who is the target audience for this instruction?

- What should this instruction accomplish, i.e., what does exemplary performance look like?

The answers to these questions make it easy to prepare instruction that will teach people the things that will add value to the individual student, and to avoid teaching things that won't.

Performance Analysis (Chapter 4)

Though it often seems hard to believe, instructors are frequently asked to develop courses intended to teach people what they already know, or to use instruction to solve problems that can't be solved by instruction.

The performance analysis procedure helps to prevent these instructional errors by revealing the differences between what people are actually doing and what they should be doing, by detecting which of those differences can be eliminated by instruction, and by pointing to solutions that will help solve the problem, whether the solution is instruction or something else. This procedure is an important tool in the arsenal of those oriented toward improving performance by the best means available.

Goal Analysis (Chapter 5)

The goal analysis procedure is useful in revealing the important components of performances usually described in abstract (fuzzy) terms. Thus, a goal analysis is called for when it isn't easy to say what students should be able to do when performing competently.

If, for example, students will be expected to be "personable," or "self-starters," or "good leaders," a goal analysis will reveal exactly what a person would have to do to be worthy of that label.

Rather than be found at a particular point in the process of instructional design and development, goal analyses are completed whenever and wherever fuzzy intentions appear.

Task Analysis (Chapter 6)

The task analysis (sometimes referred to as a job/task analysis) is one which results in a step-by-step description of what a competent person does when performing a relatively sequential task, whether the steps of that task are mainly cognitive (mental) or psychomotor (physical). It is a way of making competent performance visible, much as a blueprint provides a way to make the components of a finished product visible. After a task analysis has been completed, it is possible to derive the skills that *anyone* must have before being ready to practice the entire task. In this way it is possible to make sure that all important skills and knowledge are taught.

Deriving the Outcomes (Part III)

When the analysis procedures reveal a need for instruction, the next activity is to specify the important results that the instruction will need to accomplish for it to fulfill the need. This is done by stating the instructional objectives, by depicting the prerequisite relationships between the objectives, and by determining which skills must be in place (i.e., prerequisites) before a student will be able to profit from the instruction.

Course Objectives (Chapter 7)

Instructional objectives are statements that describe the desired instructional outcomes (results); they describe what students must be able to do to be considered competent (Note: Correctly implemented instruction continues until the student can perform as the objectives describe). Objectives are derived from the skills that anyone would need before being able to practice tasks described by the analyses. They describe instructional targets, much as blueprints describe the components of a finished product.

Skill Hierarchies (Chapter 8)

Skill hierarchies are simple diagrams showing the dependency relationships between the skills that must be in place before a larger, more comprehensive, skill or task can be practiced. They are useful in determining which skills *must be learned* before others can be addressed. They also provide the substance from which course maps are derived, and with which decisions can be made about the most efficient use of limited practice materials and equipment.

Target Population Description (Chapter 9)

The target population (TPop.) description summarizes the key characteristics of those who will be the recipients (the targets, the audience) of the instruction. By knowing their characteristics, it is possible to better mold the instruction to each student: to select objectives, examples, terminology, media, and procedures that will best allow each student to accomplish his/her goals. It is one of the key techniques for making instruction work. (Note: TPop. descriptions are sometimes drafted after the instructional outcomes have been derived and stated.)

Course Prerequisites (Chapter 10)

Prerequisites describe what students must be able to do before they can profit from your instruction (they are *not* course descriptions). Prerequisites are derived from the TPop. description and from decisions about what will and will not be taught during the course.

Developing the Instruction (Part IV)

The design/development phase includes the drafting of measuring instruments (tests), as well as development, tryout, and revision of the instruction itself. Though some consider one or more of these steps to be part of the analysis phase, it is a hair unworthy of splitting.

Criterion Tests (Chapter 11)

More commonly referred to as "performance checks" or "skill checks," criterion tests are the instruments by which students and instructors can determine whether the instruction works; that is, whether a student, after instruction, can perform as an objective demands. They are the instruments by which students and instructors alike can determine whether the student is ready to move to the next unit of instruction. They are not intended to determine how well a student performed in comparison with other students, but to determine how well the student performed in comparison with the objective.

Relevant Practice (Chapter 12)

This is a description of what must be provided—the "stuff" it will take—to make it possible for students to practice the substance of the objective. The description lists tools and equipment needed as well as environmental requirements. It also lists any other *persons* that may be required for practice to occur under realistic conditions. Since practice is essential to making instruction work, it is important that the practice be crafted correctly.

Content Derivation (Chapter 13)

With objectives, criterion tests, relevant practice, and Tpop. descriptions in hand, instructional content can now be derived to facilitate accomplishment of each objective. The procedure used ensures that students will learn what they need to know, while not having to attend to irrelevant content or to study what they already know.

Delivery System Selection (Chapter 14)

This procedure determines the combination of media, resources, and other items that will be most useful in delivery of the instruction. It identifies the means by which learners will be taught what they need to know *before* they can practice, and it identifies the things that will be needed to provide the practice itself. Media decisions are made after content has been derived and are usually easy to make and take little time.

Module Drafting (Chapter 15)

Modules (lessons, instruction units) are drafted according to a "floor plan" that assures (a) practice in the objective of the module and (b) feedback regarding quality of the practice. The module also includes the knowledge that must be acquired before a student can profitably practice the objective. Performance-based rather than time-based, a module includes the instruction needed to accomplish a given objective, rather than instruction that fills a unit of time. If the previous steps have been completed (which is easier and more quickly done than it looks at this point), the instruction will practically draft itself.

Tryout (Chapter 16)

Tryouts are a key step in instructional development. They provide information about whether the instruction is working and about where improvements need to be made before they can be considered ready for delivery to the students. Those who are serious about instructional quality will always insist on at least one tryout before putting a course "on line." Instructors who must do their own development should always consider their first delivery of the course as a tryout.

Sequencing (Chapter 17)

Sequencing refers to putting the modules (instructional units, lessons) into an order that (a) maintains and enhances student motivation, (b) builds new or complex skills onto existing ones, and (c) provides periodic practice of things already learned.

Implementing the Instruction (Part V)

Delivering instruction at the state of the art means instructing in a way that will help students learn what they don't already know, as efficiently and as humanely as possible. As most instructors work under somewhat less than ideal conditions, compromises have to be made. Implementation, therefore, means instructing in a way that applies the state of the art as well as the situation will allow.

Course Procedures (Chapter 18)

Course procedures are derived from ideal characteristics and local constraints. These are written down so they may be given to the students and used as guidance by both students and instructors. A course "map" may be derived from the course procedures and the skill hierarchies; the map shows students how the course modules are related to one another and which modules must be mastered before others can be attempted, and is used to help students to decide what to do next.

Getting Ready (Chapter 19)

Before instructing, instructors need to know how to facilitate, rather than to impede, the instructional process. This includes being able to define the components of instructional success, to apply and control the favorable consequences that will be used to strengthen desired performances, to apply the modeling principles that facilitate or impede performance, and to strengthen student self-efficacy (self-judgments about the level of one's abilities).

Implementing the Instruction (Chapter 20)

The instruction is then made available to the students. For each module, students review the objective and decide whether they need instruction or practice before attempting to demonstrate their competence. If they decide they need instruction, they work through the instruction, practice until they feel ready, and then demonstrate their mastery of the objective. If they decide they don't need further instruction, they simply demonstrate their mastery of the objective. In either case, if they meet or exceed the criteria, they are encouraged to advance to the next unit. If they don't meet the criteria, the instructor (person, computer, other) diagnoses the weakness and prescribes a remedy (usually more instruction and/or more practice).

Improving the Instruction (Part VI)

Because needs and jobs change, because new technologies, materials, and devices become available, and because the characteristics of incoming students change, professional instructors take steps to keep their instruction up-to-date.

Course Improvement (Chapter 21)

Course improvement consists of, first, identifying opportunities for improvement and, second, taking the necessary steps to capitalize on the opportunities. The procedure involves comparing existing instructional practices to those that would be in effect if the instruction were functioning at the state of the art; that is, comparing *what is* with what *could be.*

Summary

- The analysis procedures will help ensure that the instruction is *worthy* of working (because it teaches the "right stuff");

- The development procedures will make sure the instruction *can* work;

- The implementation procedures will ensure that the instruction *does* work; and the

- Evaluation and improvement procedures will ensure that the instruction *continues to work* as well as possible.

What Next?

The chapters that follow describe each of the tools and procedures named above, and provide an assortment of examples. Though the descriptions are offered in the approximate order in which they are usually accomplished, it should not be implied that any step is completed and then forgotten. Instructional development always involves modification of earlier steps in light of what develops later. Further, the decision to develop instruction is discontinued whenever it is discovered that the desired performances can be achieved in other ways.

The procedures for systematic development of instruction are not limited to any subject matter, profession, or vocation. Regardless of the intent of the instruction, the procedure for its development is basically the same.

A final word before proceeding. Though the content of this book must be presented in some sort of order, you should not believe that you can reap benefits only by applying all of the techniques, and in the order presented. Your instruction can be improved by the application of almost any one of these procedures, whether or not others are applied as well. The final chapter will suggest a priority for improvement of existing instruction—a sort of "bang-for-the-buck" list that will provide clues about what might be the most productive next step.

To Learn More: See Resources #12, #15, and #19. (The "Useful Resources" list can be found at the back of this book.)

Part II

Analyzing the Need

4
Performance Analysis

Situation: Someone has suggested that you either create a course, modify an existing course, or locate and purchase a course. You want to be sure that instruction is really needed in this situation, and if not, what else should be suggested.

Or, you have noted that one or more people aren't doing what they're expected to do; that is, that there is a difference between their actual and desired performance. You want to know what you can do about it.

Suppose someone came to you and said, "Look. These students aren't coming to school on time. I want you to develop a course to fix that." What would you teach? The history of time? How to read clocks? The importance of promptness? Pendulum appreciation? You see the point. Students already know how to get to school on time. If they don't do it, it's because of some other reason. If there is a solution to the problem, it has to be something other than instruction.

Like a hammer, instruction is only one possible tool for getting a job done. It is usually the tool of choice when people (workers, students, managers) cannot now do something they need to be able to do. But what about those instances in which students already know how to do what they need to do? Or part of what they need to know? That is, what can you do when people can already perform as desired, but aren't doing it for reasons having nothing to do with skill? Clearly, a procedure is needed for sorting through these problems and to locate solutions that will work. Enter the performance analysis.

The performance analysis is the tool of choice when people aren't doing what they should be doing. It is a way of finding out whether the differences between what they're doing and should be doing can be eliminated by instruction, or whether some other action is called for. This procedure is especially crucial for those who are expected to develop instruction *at the request of other people.* It is needed—desperately—by all instructors who are told:

- "We need a course."

- "Improve their motivation."

- "Fix their attitude."

- "They don't understand the fundamentals."

- "We have a training problem."

Unfortunately, many administrators and managers don't yet know how to analyze problems having to do with people performance. So when they see a symptom—someone doing something they shouldn't, or not doing something they should—they jump to the conclusion that the person *doesn't know how* to do it. So they ask their trainers to provide instruction. In thousands of instances, that instruction is then used to "teach" people things they already know. A total waste. If only a small amount of time (often a few minutes will do) had been taken to find out *why* people weren't performing to expectations, a proper—and less expensive—remedy could have been selected. Hence the importance of the performance analysis.

To make sure that instruction is used only when it will teach people what they don't already know, and that solutions are found that will solve the problem, you need to begin by describing the performance discrepancy in performance terms. You need to describe:

a. what they should be doing, and

b. what they are now doing.

If a performance discrepancy exists, then you need to determine whether the difference is due to a skill deficiency or to something else. If they aren't doing what they should be doing because they don't know how, then instruction *may* be a useful remedy. But if they already know how and aren't doing it, then some other remedy needs to be applied.

With the performance analysis you will be able to:

a. identify discrepancies between what people are now doing and what they should be doing,

b. determine the causes of the discrepancies, and

c. point to remedies that will solve the problem.

Figure 4.1 Performance Analysis Flowchart

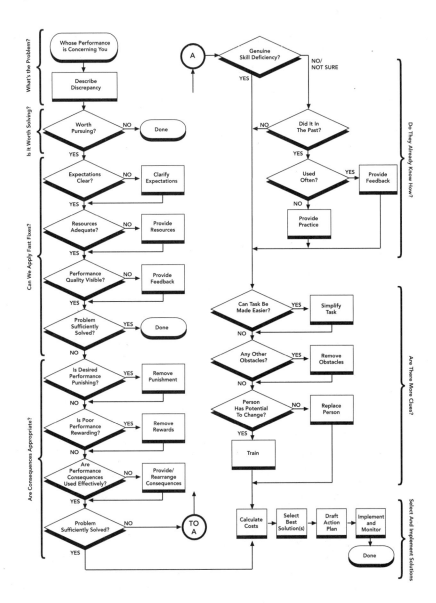

How to Do It

Here's a brief description of the steps in the procedure. Figure 4.1 offers a visual picture of the procedure in the form of a flowchart.

1. Name the category (job title) of the person or people whose performance is at issue.

2. Describe as specifically as possible what it is they *should* be doing.

3. Describe equally specifically what it is the performers *are* doing that causes someone to say there is a problem.

4. Estimate what the discrepancy is costing in aggravation, frustration, turnover, scrap, insurance rates, time lost, money lost, equipment damage, customers or good will lost, accidents, cost of a supervisor's time to fix the problem, and so on. Decide whether the discrepancy is worth doing something about.

5. If the estimated cost of the discrepancy is small, stop. In other words, if it's only a problem because you say it is, and it isn't having any impact on the rest of the world, stop.

6. Next, explore fast fixes. There are several reasons why people don't perform as expected, and some of them are so common and so easy to fix that they should be considered early in the procedure. So check to make sure that people (a) know what's expected of them, (b) have the resources (tools, equipment, supplies, etc.) needed to perform as desired, and (c) can recognize *when* they're performing to expectations. Make necessary fixes before proceeding.

7. Has the problem been sufficiently solved as a result of the previous step? If so, stop. If not, find out what happens *to the performers* when they do it right and when they do it wrong. Explore the consequences to the performers for desired and undesired performance. Answer these questions:

   a. What happens to them when they do it right?

   b. What happens to them when they do it wrong?

   c. Are there any consequences at all for performing in the expected way?

   NOTE: These questions precede the next step because consequences are almost always in need of adjustment and therefore almost always suggest actions that will solve the problem without the need for more analysis.

8. If the problem is sufficiently solved as a result of adjusting consequences, test your solution(s) and devise an action plan. If not, determine whether the performance discrepancy is a genuine skill deficiency. Answer the question, "Could they do it if their very lives depended on it?" In other words, could they do it if they really had to?

9. If they could, it's not a skill deficiency, so you know that instruction will not solve the problem. You've already eliminated the high-probability causes of the problem; now you need to sort among the remaining causes.

10. Answer the question, "Did they *ever* know how to perform as expected?"

If so, and if the skill is used often, then feedback is likely to be the remedy (they aren't performing as expected because they aren't getting any information about how well they're doing).

If the skill is not used often, then review and practice, and/or provide performance (job) aids (e.g., checklists, color coding, interlocks, etc.).

11. Check whether there are obstacles getting in the way of the performer (e.g., they don't have the authority to do what's expected of them, resources aren't available when they're needed, etc.). If so, you've detected another source of the problem.

12. If you are dealing with a genuine skill deficiency, and the performers never did know how to do it in the past, then explore whether the task(s) can be simplified—made easier. This can often be accomplished by changing the task itself or by supplying checklists, procedures, diagrams, manuals, color coding, etc., to aid the performer.

13. If the problem persists, determine whether the performer has the potential to learn to perform as desired. If not, then you'll need to replace the performer with someone more likely to succeed.

14. If the performer does have the potential to learn what's needed, then consider instruction as a solution.

15. If you're doing a complete performance analysis, that is, going through all the steps without stopping to apply solutions, then you're ready to sort through the solutions and select those that will be most appropriate and cost-effective. During the analysis you will have identified

several possible causes, and now you should calculate how much it would cost to fix each of them.

16. Select the best solution(s)—those that will impact the problem, are within your power to apply, and cost less than the problem itself.

17. Draft an action plan. This simply means to say specifically who will implement each solution and how you will get them to do it.

18. Implement the solutions and check on the results.

A performance analysis usually takes less time to complete than to describe, simply because the solutions to performance problems are usually easy to spot once you begin asking the right questions. For example, why don't students ask questions when they don't understand? In many instances it's because they get punished when they do—because the instructor insults and embarrasses them in public. Why don't salespeople behave in a customer-oriented way? Because nobody has told them what that means. Why don't workers solve problems themselves, rather than asking the boss to do it? Because they haven't been given the authority to do it. And so on.

Yes, it's often that simple to solve problems of human performance. Sometimes it's a little more difficult, but usually only because information has to be collected before the analysis questions can be answered. Here's an example.

Example: In this example, an instructor who teaches computer repair in a technical school is approached by the Dean.

> *Dean:*   We need to beef up your course on trouble-shooting.

Inst: I'm certainly willing to do that. What seems to be missing?

Dean: Well, I've had calls from a couple of companies who are complaining that their troubleshooters won't use the hotline when they're supposed to.

Inst: What do you mean?

Dean: If they can't clear up a problem within 22 minutes, they're supposed to call the hotline and talk to the "hotshot" about it. But they don't do it.

Inst: What do they want me to do about it?

Dean: They think you should beef up your course.

Inst: Don't the troubleshooters know how to use the telephone?

Dean: Of course they do.

Inst: Do they know the procedure for calling the hotline?

Dean: Of course they do. But they don't use it.

Inst: So they know what's expected of them, they have the necessary tools and procedures, and they already know how to do what they're supposed to do. That tells us that instruction isn't going to help. Would it be OK for me to talk to a couple of their troubleshooters?

Dean: I don't see why not.

(Two days later.)

Inst: I think I've got a handle on this problem.

Dean: What did you find out?

Inst: Well, when troubleshooters call the hotline, they're likely to get some verbal abuse—sarcasm—from the hotshot on the other end of the line. Comments like, "What? You *still* haven't learned to solve that simple problem?"

Dean: That would hardly encourage anyone to call a second time.

Inst: There's more. If the hotline is called, and then the troubleshooter fixes the problem alone, the hotline gets credit for the fix.

Dean: Good grief.

Inst: There's even more. Troubleshooters are expected to stay on the problem until it's fixed. If they don't fix the problem by the end of the working day, they're supposed to stay with it until it is fixed. Of course, they get overtime pay for staying late.

Dean: Some system.

Inst: Yep. It's another case of performers being soundly punished for doing the very thing they're expected to do, and rewarded—with overtime pay—for doing what they aren't supposed to do.

Dean: No wonder they don't do what they're supposed to do—and know how to do. What do you suggest?

Inst: I suggest you talk with the managers who brought this up, and gently ask them the questions that will make it clear to them that company policy is getting in the way of desired performance. I'd suggest you try to lead them to see that the solution to this problem isn't instruction, but a change in the way performers are treated when they do what's expected of them.

As pointed out earlier, everyone who is concerned about the performance of others needs to be able to use the performance analysis procedure.

To Learn More: See Resources #4, #6, #7, and #17. (The "Useful Resources" list can be found at the back of this book.)

5
Goal Analysis

Situation: *While deriving the important outcomes of your instruction, you've run into some abstract expectations, such as "They should be motivated," or "They should be more safety-conscious," or "They don't have the right attitude." You want to know how to handle those abstractions and learn what, if anything, you'll need to teach to better accomplish those goals.*

Suppose that you've just completed a job analysis and shown your work to someone whose opinion you value who says, "This is great. This is just what these people are supposed to do," and then adds, "But we also want them to be conscientious about their work and more thorough in their reporting. And it's important that they be professional." Since you can't watch people conscientiousing, or thoroughing, or professionaling, what to do?

The fact is that not everything we want people to be able to do can be described in terms of tasks—not everything can be directly observed. Sometimes, rather than being expected to carry out tasks, people are expected to exhibit certain characteristics, states, or traits.

For example, you may decide, or be told, that students should:

- be motivated,

- demonstrate courtesy to _____,

- be safety-conscious,

- value total patient health,

- have good analytical ability,

- be problem-solvers,

- be self-starters,

- exhibit good leadership characteristics,

- be empowered,

or any of hundreds of other possible states. When expectations are stated as "fuzzies"—vague terms—a task analysis, which you'll read about in the next chapter, won't help. Since there is no task to watch anyone perform (you can't watch people leadershipping or attituding), a different tool is needed.

Enter the goal analysis. The purpose of the goal analysis is to determine what it would take in the way of observable human performance to be able to say that the goal had been accomplished. The purpose is to say what someone would have to do to be considered "safety-conscious" or "competent"—to say what someone would have to do to be worthy of being labeled as having achieved the goal. In other words, the goal analysis will show you how to recognize one when you see one.

When to Do It

Frankly, it would be nice never to have to do a goal analysis. But alas, people (including ourselves) don't always say what they mean. That being the case, we need to have a procedure handy (like a fire extinguisher) that we can throw into the breach when the need arises. When does the need arise? When there is an important goal to achieve that hasn't yet been described clearly enough to let you select the means of achieving it. The goal analysis procedure is used whenever you have to answer questions like these:

How can I help them to understand?

What do they mean by "fundamentals"?

How can I make them more motivated?

How can I teach them to be diligent?

What do I do about the "affective domain"?

How can I help them to be more "safety conscious"?

There isn't any one point along the development trail where you stop to do a goal analysis; you do it whenever the fuzzies creep out of the woodwork—that's when you take a little time out for some fuzzy-slaying.

© Dilbert reprinted by permission of United Feature Syndicate, Inc.

When Not to Do It

Everything called a goal is not suitable for goal analysis—only those which focus on some desired human attribute and lead to a description of *desired human performances.* Analysis of goals such as "provide good customer service," "be professional," and "speak pleasantly," deserve goal analyses because they refer to something you want people to do and because the analysis will result in a list of desired people performances. Organizational goals such as "Let's double the market share," or "We need to go global," on the other hand, refer not to people characteristics but to corporate characteristics. Goal analysis in these situations is not appropriate because the results lead not to descriptions of human performance, but rather to descriptions of organizational performance.

How to Do It

There are five steps to the procedure. The steps are repeated as needed. Here they are.

1. Write down the goal, using whatever words best express your intent. Be sure your statement is described in terms of outcomes rather than process. For example, make it say, *"Have* a favorable attitude toward _____," rather than *"Develop* a favorable attitude toward." That will help keep you out of the trap of thinking about *how* you are going to accomplish the goal before you know what the achieved goal should look like. In other words, it will help keep you from fussing around with bows and arrows before you've constructed the target.

2. Think about what would be happening if the goal were achieved. Think in terms of people performance. What would people have to do or say, or refrain from doing or saying, before you would be willing to say that they had

achieved the goal? List as many performances as you can think of. Don't edit. Just list.

3. Sort the list. Many of the items you listed will be as fuzzy as the one you started with. That's okay. Put a mark beside the fuzzies, write them on another piece of paper, and apply Steps 1 and 2 to these new fuzzies.

   Continue until you have a list of performances that collectively represent the goal. Continue until you can say, "Yes. If people did these things and refrained from doing these other things, I would say they had achieved the goal."

4. Expand the words and phrases on your list into complete sentences that tell when or how often the performance is expected to occur. This will help you to place limits around the expected performances. It will help to say "how much" performance will satisfy you (or someone else). For example, a goal analysis on security-consciousness included the item, "No unattended documents." When expanded into a complete sentence, it read, "Employee always locks sensitive documents in safe before leaving the room."

   This step will also help you to weed out statements that, on second thought, don't say what you mean.

5. Test for completeness. Review the performances on your list (there will usually be from one to seven items and only occasionally more), and ask yourself, "If someone did these things, would I be willing to say that he or she is _____ (goal) _____?" If so, you are finished with the analysis. If not, return to Step 2 and add the missing performances.

Example #1: A shop instructor I once knew completed a list of tasks he wanted his students to be able to perform when they left his course. But he was uneasy about the list.

> "There's something missing," he said. "There's more to it than just these tasks."

> "Oh," I said. "Can you give me an example?"

> "Sure," he replied. "I want them to be safety-conscious."

> "That sounds reasonable," I said. "Can you tell me how to recognize a safety-conscious person when you see one?" And we were off into a goal analysis. Not long after, we had a list of "performances" (Step 2) that included these items:

> - Understands the need for safety practices.
>
> - Wears hard hat in designated areas.
>
> - Sweeps shavings from work area.
>
> - Wears safety goggles while performing designated tasks.
>
> - Uses saw guard on table saw.
>
> - Appreciates safety equipment.

> "How can you tell when someone understands the need for safety practices?" I then asked.

> "Well, they follow the safety rules," was the reply. So we replaced the fuzzy with "Follows safety rules."

"How can you recognize someone who appreciates safety equipment?" I asked next.

"Easy," he said. "They take good care of it."

So we deleted that fuzzy as well and replaced it with a performance. Our list then looked like this:

- Follows safety rules.
- Wears hard hat in designated areas.
- Sweeps shavings from work area.
- Wears safety goggles while performing designated tasks.
- Uses saw guard on table saw.
- Keeps safety equipment in good working condition.

Since we could tell whether these items were or were not happening, we moved on to the fourth step. When we were done, our items looked like this:

1. Follows all posted safety rules whenever in the shop.

2. Wears hard hat each time a designated area is entered.

3. Keeps lathe area clean by sweeping shavings into the bin provided.

4. Wears safety goggles while performing the tasks posted.

5. Does not remove saw guard without permission while using table saw.

6. Keeps personal safety equipment in good working condition.

7. Reports faulty shop safety equipment.

Your definition of safety-consciousness would be different, of course, because your situation and environment are different. But that doesn't matter. What matters is that you describe what it would take for the goal to be accomplished. Only then will you know what action to take to accomplish it.

The final step was simple. When my friend said, "Yes, if people did those things on the list, I'd be willing to say they were safety-conscious," we were done with the analysis.

Example #2: While working with the training staff of an automobile manufacturer, I was told that one company goal was to improve customer service over the coming year.

> "No," the training director said after thinking about it, "that isn't quite it. What we want to do is to provide quality service."
>
> "Where?" I asked.
>
> "In auto service," was the reply.

It was important to determine just what part of the business he was talking about, because the definition of "provide quality service" would be different in the bookkeeping department (or most anywhere else) than it would in auto service.

After working through the first four steps described above, we had a list of performances that looked like this:

- Customer complaints are written down.

- Service reps refrain from arguing with customers.

- Service reps smile when talking with customers.

- Service reps listen carefully (i.e., do not have to ask customers to repeat things they have already said).

- Repaired autos are ready when promised.

- Repaired autos are returned to customers without dirt or grease, either inside or outside the car.

- Causes for the complaints have actually been remedied.

- There is less than one percent return (cars returned because the repair was not properly completed).

"If these things happened," I then asked, "would you be willing to say that you were providing quality service?"

"Well . . .," was the cautious reply, "I guess so. But we want to provide the quality service without the mechanics using up more parts than they need."

"I can understand that. But does the number of spares used have anything to do with how you would recognize quality service?"

"I guess not directly. But it's important."

"Tell you what. Let's focus on quality service until we're sure we can recognize it when we see it, and then we'll move on to the spares issue."

Which we did.

Example #3: Believe it or not, the following flowchart was developed as a result of a goal analysis. An instructor was asked to develop instruction that would teach students to use "good judgment" when deciding which criterion level to assign to each (military) task to be taught. She saw immediately that it would be impossible to decide what, if anything, to teach until she knew what "good judgment" meant in terms of human performance. After her goal analysis was completed, she saw that it would be easy to convert the results into the following flowchart. In effect, the flowchart says that performers will be using good judgment when they follow its steps.

Figure 5.1

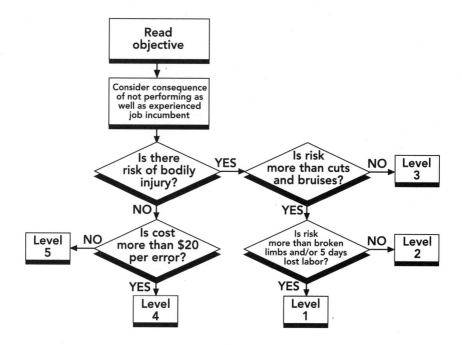

Example #4: While conducting a recent workshop in Beijing, China, one participant explained how important it was for American expatriates to have a "working knowledge" of Mandarin. "If they can't work in Mandarin," he said, "we can't hire them." Because it was unclear just what "working knowledge of Mandarin" meant, he carried out a goal analysis. Initially, his list looked like this:

- Can communicate in Mandarin.

- Can understand the Chinese.

- Can read Mandarin.

- Can write in Mandarin.

Not bad, but the list still contained four fuzzies. After further work, his description of "working knowledge of Mandarin" looked like this:

- Can express themselves verbally in Mandarin well enough to be understood by Chinese business people.

- Can repeat accurately what was said in Mandarin.

- Can read work-related reports and Chinese newspapers; i.e., can accurately describe what is read.

- Can write reports and correspondence well enough to be understood by Chinese business readers.

As you can see, the purpose of the goal analysis is to reveal the meaning of vague terms and expressions so that you can decide what to do to get more of what's wanted.

NOTE: When trying to determine the meaning of some-one *else's* fuzzy, there's a right way and wrong way to go about it. The wrong way is to ask someone to write down what they mean by the fuzzy. This is intimidating and threatening and won't get you very far, because they won't know how to do what you've asked. They won't know what they mean by their fuzzies without some serious thought. The right way is to do it yourself. Write out what you think the vague terms mean, and then show it to the other person while asking, "If _____ did these things, would that satisfy you?" It's a lot easier for people to fix things than to create them.

Remember that when someone speaks to you in fuzzies, they are abdicating to you the power to say what they mean. Grab it! Say what *you* think the fuzzy should mean, and then offer it for approval.

ANOTHER NOTE: Don't do goal analyses in a group— it'll take forever. If you must get the agreement of others on the meaning, work with one person at a time. Other-wise, you may be "grouped" or "teamed" to a frazzle. Besides, working one-on-one helps spare the loss of face when the fuzzy-utterer discovers how simply the fuzzy can be defined.

What to Do with It

Once the goal has been analyzed into the performances that represent its meaning, it's easy to see what to do next.

1. Put a check-mark beside each of the things that students can already do. If they can already do it, you won't get more of it by "teaching" it. If they know how to do it but *aren't* doing it, complete a performance analysis to find out why they aren't doing what they know how to do.

2. Consider the items not checked. If they can't do it and need to be able to do it, you or someone else will need to teach them to do it. Decide who will teach what.

3. Complete a task analysis for each of the tasks that must be taught. (See Chapter 6, *Task Analysis.*)

4. Write objectives to describe the main outcomes you need to achieve, and then follow as many development steps as needed to facilitate the performance you need.

To Learn More: See Resources #3 and #9.

6
Task Analysis

Situation: You suspect there are things people should be doing that they cannot now do. To verify whether instruction will be needed, you want to paint a picture of what competent people do when performing the way you need others to perform.

One of our goals is to develop and deliver instruction that prepares people to perform in a useful manner in a "real world" situation, whether that "real world" happens to be a job or another course. Another goal is to make sure that the instruction itself teaches those useful skills with as little wasted motion and effort as possible. To accomplish those goals, we need to know what people have to be able to do before they can begin practicing the tasks to be performed. Enter the task analysis.

Task analysis is the name given to a collection of techniques used to help make the components of competent performance visible. It's a set of ways to draw a picture of what competent people actually do, or should do, when performing a task. From this picture it is then possible to derive the skills that anyone would have to have before they, too, can perform the task competently. It is a way to visualize the steps and decisions involved in carrying out a procedure.

There are several ways to go about a task analysis. Some of the approaches break desired performances into microscopic detail; and others, only into moderate detail. In practice, one uses the procedure that provides the level of detail needed to get the job done; that is, the level that will make the analysis serve its purpose. That means using the analysis procedure that will best answer the questions, "What do competent people do when performing this task?" and "What would *anyone* have to know before he or she could begin practicing this entire task?" The procedure described below will be useful in most of the situations you will encounter.

What's a Task?

A *task* is a series of steps leading to a meaningful outcome. There. That's the standard definition, but it's only helpful once you know what it means. Think of it this way: Every job is made up of a collection of tasks, things that you do during the course of a month that you refer to as "my job." (Note that these tasks are not necessarily related, that your job does not necessarily consist of a *coherent* set of tasks. For example, you may find yourself answering the telephone one minute, filling out a form the next, and dictating a letter the next. At home, you may find yourself making a meal one minute, rebuilding your car the next minute, and taking out the garbage the next. These are tasks that are all part of the "job," but are not related to one another.) These tasks have a beginning, a middle, and an end.

You are referring to a task whenever you ask someone to "Go and _____": take out the garbage, tie off an artery, change a tire, set a bone, interview a prospective employee, write a report, analyze a report, sell a product, make a verbal report, cut a head of hair, do a pre-flight check, adjust your computer printer driver, and so on. Each of these tasks has a beginning and an end, with a series of steps in between.

A *step* in a task, on the other hand, would be something like tighten a nut, pick up a scalpel, select a component, ask a question, press RETURN, enter name in box 3, remove the cover, or take a deep breath. Each represents *one* of the actions that need to be taken in order to accomplish the meaningful outcome. Here are some other examples of one step in each of several tasks.

Task	Step in the task
Disassemble a device	Disconnect power
Make a dress	Pin pattern to fabric
Pick a lock	Select picks
Play a part (in a play)	Speak lines
Cash a check	Verify endorsement
Apply at bank for a loan	Grovel

Who Should Do It?

Who should carry out the task analysis? That's easy. If there isn't anyone else to do it, and if it hasn't already been done, then you're elected. Fortunately, that doesn't mean you'll be saddled with an impossible or time-consuming chore. In fact, you may find it rather enjoyable. All you need to do is locate, observe, and interview a competent performer (who may be yourself).

"Wait a minnit," you may be shouting. "I can't spend time going to where people are performing the job or profession I'm teaching. Besides, I don't teach the entire curriculum. My students don't go directly to the job; they go to other courses."

Good point, and I understand your predicament. Analysts in industry have little difficulty deriving their instruction from observation of exemplary performers. Those analysts are able to observe (or study descriptions of) exemplary performance so that they can say, "Aha. *This* is what we want people to do on the job; *those* are the things they don't yet know how to do; so here are the things we will have to teach them."

Those teaching in educational institutions, however, are working in a "cottage industry" environment where instructors often behave as though they were in "business" for themselves. This is an environment where each instructor decides what to teach and how much of the subject to include in the time allotted; where five instructors teaching a course with the same name are likely to be teaching five different courses; where the objectives of one course in a series are seldom derived from the prerequisites of the next one in line; where the objectives of the last course in line are seldom derived from any aspect of the real world where the learned skills are expected to be applied.

But all is not lost. You can use yourself as one source of information for the task analysis. Then again, you must know some people who do this thing in the "real world." You can talk to them, and maybe observe them as they work. And you can find out from the instructors of the next courses in the sequence what they expect students to be able to do when they enter those courses, because their prerequisites should be, at least in part, your objectives.

How to Do It

The task analysis involves: (a) drafting a task list (an activity sometimes referred to as job analysis) and then (b) describing the steps in each of the tasks listed.

Task Listing

The first step is to list all the tasks that make up the job. It makes no difference that one task may be considered critical and another trivial. They are *all* to be listed, so that a complete snapshot of the job can be studied. If those performing the job are expected to perform a task, write it down. You will decide later which tasks will need to be learned and whether you will be the one to teach them.

For example, nearly every job involves some sort of paperwork. People are expected to complete forms, write reports, read job tickets, fill out requisitions, write letters, and so on. If paperwork is expected, those tasks should be included on your list.

Many jobs also require people to interact with other people. Sometimes it is with customers, sometimes with patients or victims, sometimes with superiors, with colleagues, or with spouses. Appliance-repair people are expected to "instruct customers" on how to avoid certain problems in the future. Managers are expected to "conduct exit interviews," and police officers are expected to "interview witnesses." Whatever its nature, if the competent job performer is expected to do it, add it to your list. Here's an example of a task list.

Example: Electronic Technician.

1. Troubleshoots to locate troubles.

2. Clears troubles from equipment.

3. Completes parts-requisition forms.

4. Reads schematic and/or wiring diagrams.

5. Uses test equipment to make measurements.

6. Calibrates test equipment.

7. Interprets test results.

8. Records test data.

9. Solders components.

10. Applies first-aid procedures.

11. Cleans and sharpens tools.

12. Cleans work area.

13. Disassembles equipment.

14. Assembles equipment.

15. Elicits symptoms from customers.

Notice that each of the items on this list begins with a verb, a "doing" word. This is one way to tell whether the item being described is a task or just a piece of subject matter. For example, if an item reads "anatomy" or "measurement," you would know instantly that subject-matter is being described rather than tasks. If a subject-matter item cannot be described in "doing" terms, it should not be included in the task list.

Task Detailing

The second step in the analysis is to list the steps and decisions involved in performing each of the tasks on the list. For each task, answer these questions:

1. When is the task performed (what triggers initiation of the task)?

2. How is the task performed (what are the steps followed and decisions made while performing the task)?

3. How would you know when you're done (when the task has been satisfactorily completed)?

There are two common ways to analyze a task, by listing and by flowcharting.

Listing. One way to make the components of a task visible is to simply list them as you would build a shopping list. Here are two examples:

Example #1: Task: Start an IV.

When initiated? When patient's chart says to do it.

1. Read patient's chart.

2. If IV is not called for, stop.

3. If IV is called for, collect equipment.

4. Get material to be administered.

5. Locate patient.

6. Verify that correct patient has been located.

7. Prepare patient psychologically for the procedure.

8. Sterilize site where needle is to be inserted.

9. Locate vein.

. . . and so on.

When completed? When IV is running according to requirements.

Example #2: Task: Clean spark plugs.

When initiated?   a. Plugs are dirty.
                      b. Customer asks.

1. Open hood.

2. Locate spark plugs.

3. Cover fender with protective material.

4. Remove ignition wires.

5. Remove plugs.

6. If plugs are cracked or worn out, replace them, and then go to Step #12. If not, go to Step #7.

7. Clean the plugs.

8. Check gap in each plug.

9. Adjust gap as necessary.

10. Test the plugs.

11. Replace plugs.

12. Re-connect ignition wires.

13. Check engine performance.

14. If OK, go to step 16.

15. If not OK, complete the designated steps.

16. Clean tools and equipment.

17. Clean any grease from car.

18. Complete required paperwork.

When is task complete? Engine runs smoothly.

Even though these examples described relatively simple tasks, you will note that it is somewhat awkward to show *in a list* the decisions to be made and just how the actions resulting from those decisions should be handled.

Flowcharting. There is a better way, called flowcharting. A flowchart is easy to read and clearly shows the alternatives to be followed when decisions are involved. Furthermore, it reveals where information is still missing.

To flowchart a task, you need only two symbols to depict the steps of the task: a rectangle to depict actions and a diamond to depict decisions (see Figure 6.1). Other shapes, such as ovals and squares, may be used to depict various outcomes, but the rectangle and the diamond are all that are needed to show the components of the task itself.

Figure 6.1

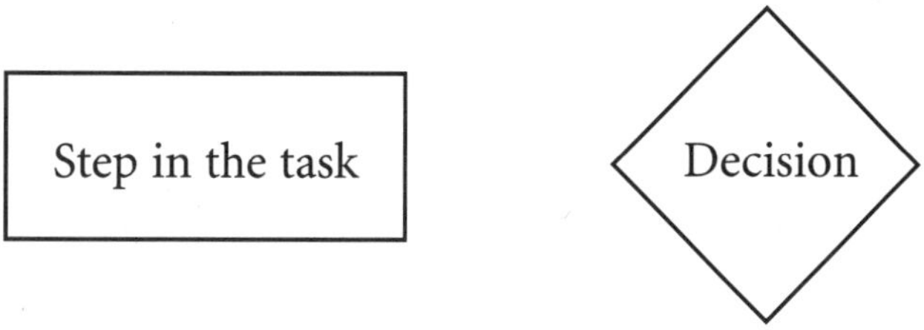

Begin by writing down the event that causes the task to be performed. Here are a few example events that initiate tasks:

- Phone rings.

- Customer asks _____.

- Red light comes on.

- Grinding sound is heard.

- Screen shows error message.

- Patient screams.

Then write down what happens next. If it's an action, write it in a rectangle. If it's a decision, write it in a diamond, and draw lines from the diamond to the different actions that would result from the decision. Sometimes there are several actions that might be taken as a result of a decision. For example, if the pressure is less than 10 lbs., do thing A; if the pressure is between 10 and 50 lbs., do thing B; if the pressure is more than 50 lbs., run! Usually, though, there are only two alternatives: Do thing A if the decision is yes, and do thing B if the answer is no. For example, if I were to flowchart the spark plug cleaning example, it would look like this:

Figure 6.2   **Clean Spark Plugs**

When initiated?   a. Plugs are dirty.
                      b. Customer asks.

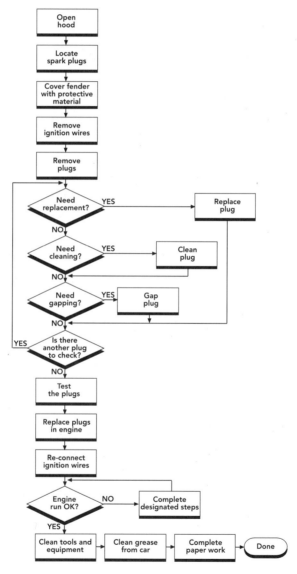

When terminated?   Engine runs smoothly.

NOTES:

a. Don't include instruction in the analysis. The purpose of the analysis is to visualize competent performance so that better decisions can be made about how to get more of it. Putting "how to learn it" comments in the task analysis puts the cart before the horse and defeats its purpose.

b. Statements such as "Select a screwdriver" or "Select a lipstick" are not considered decisions and don't belong in a diamond; no matter which screwdriver or lipstick is selected, the action that *follows* is the same. Use a decision symbol only when one decision would lead you to a different *action* than would another decision.

c. Don't be concerned if one part of your analysis seems to be more detailed than another. The purpose isn't to produce some tidy document for display; the purpose is to help answer the question, "What would *anybody* have to be able to do before practicing this entire task?" When the analysis is detailed enough to answer that question *for each* step, consider it finished.

d. The quality of the analysis is unrelated to the straightness of your lines. So don't waste time with a ruler. Do your flowcharting on a large piece of paper, and do it with a pencil. If you prefer, flowchart the task using a computer-based flowcharting-application program.

The following examples provide three additional flowcharts.

Example #1: This flowchart depicts the main actions followed by someone troubleshooting equipment at the customer's location.

Figure 6.3   **On-Site Troubleshooting**

When initiated? Malfunction report received.

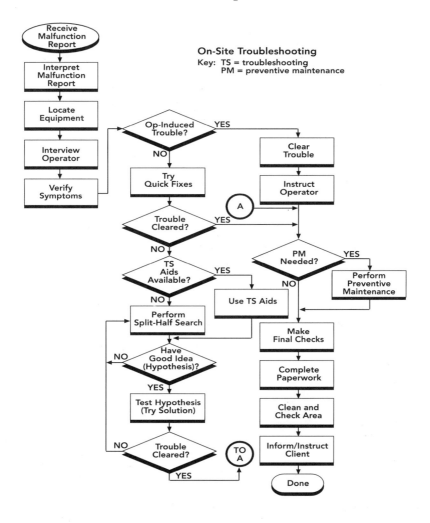

When terminated? Equipment functions according to
                    specifications.

Example #2: This flowchart shows the steps followed when conducting a performance analysis.

Figure 6.4   **Performance Analysis**

When initiated?   Someone's performance is less than adequate.

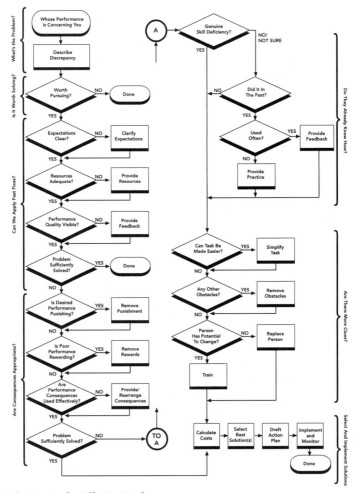

© 1997 The Center for Effective Performance

When terminated?   Cause(s) and remedies have been identified.

Example #3: Here is a flowchart showing the key steps in conducting a task analysis when the information is to be obtained from a subject-matter specialist.

Figure 6.5 **Conduct Task Analysis**

When initiated? The details of competent task performance need to be described.

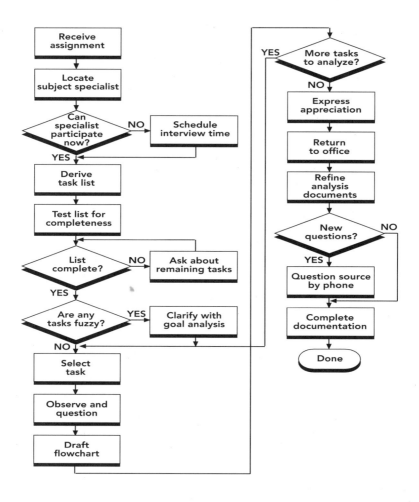

When terminated? All key actions and decisions are described in the sequence in which they are performed.

Sometimes, when products are so new that subject-matter specialists do not yet exist, the task analysis has to be done by analyzing the available documentation (e.g., engineering drawings) to answer the question, "What do we *imagine* someone will be doing when performing this task?"

Deriving Skills

Once the task analysis shows the components of competent performance, you can then derive the skills that *anyone* would need to have before practicing the entire task. To do this you need to forget about students for the moment (though you'll think a great deal about them later). At this point you are interested only in naming the skills that *anyone in the world* would have to have before practicing the task step you are considering.

How to Do It

1. Consider each step of your analysis in turn.

2. In a column to the right of the step, write the skills that anyone would have to have before they could practice that step. Note: Lots of steps won't require you to write anything beside them because they are simple or have no sub-skills, such as, "Pick up wrench," or "Locate Box 3." Don't make it harder than it is.

3. When you have finished, delete the duplications from your list of skills. For example, it is likely that you have written "Read English" beside several of the steps, because, among other things, someone would have to be able to read to perform that step. If the reading skill required for each step is the same, delete the duplications. If, however, different levels of reading skill are required for the various steps, they do not represent duplications and should not be deleted.

4. Later on, you'll draft an objective to describe each of the remaining skills.

Example #4: This example shows the skills that anyone would need to perform three of the steps in the troubleshooting task shown earlier. (Initiating and terminating cues are not shown.)

Figure 6.6   **Troubleshooting Skill Requirements**

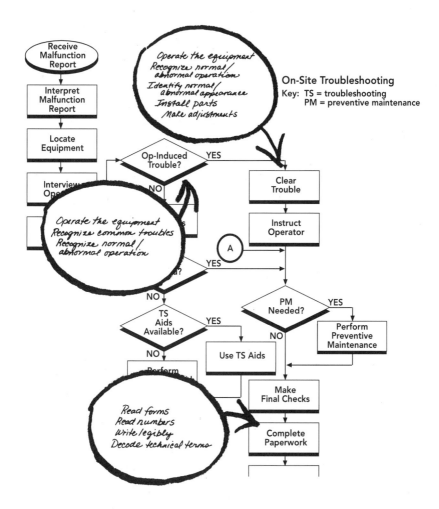

To Learn More: See Resources #1, #4, #12, and #15.

Part III

Deriving the Outcomes

7

Course Objectives

Situation: *You want to draft descriptions of the important outcomes of the proposed instruction.*

Your analysis has revealed that there are things your intended students (a) can't yet do that (b) they need to be able to do. Now it's time to describe the instructional outcomes (the need to do's); it's time to construct a verbal picture that will help guide you in developing the instruction and help guide your students in focusing their efforts. (This is not to suggest that you should avoid writing out your objectives until you have completed the analysis steps. Even if you do no analysis at all, it is still useful to reveal in writing what you want students to be able to do when they leave the instruction.)

What Are Objectives?

Objectives are a little like blueprints. They provide the guides that will guarantee that you are teaching what needs to be taught. And, because objectives describe *outcomes* rather than instructional process, they free developers and instructors alike to use all their ingenuity and creativity toward accomplishing those outcomes.

NOTE: Statements describing intended instructional outcomes are called objectives because their accomplishment can be measured. *Goals* are broad (fuzzy) statements of intent; *objectives* are measurable statements of intent. In plain language, if an outcome statement isn't precise enough to measure whether the outcome has been achieved, it isn't an objective.

Characteristics of Objectives

Here's an example of an objective to which you can refer as you read the characteristics described below:

Objective: Given an accident report form and an accident scene, be able to complete the report.

Criteria: a. All entered information is correct and legible.
              b. Report is completed within 15 minutes.

1. An objective describes student performance. It doesn't say anything about what the instructor will do or try to accomplish. It doesn't describe course content or the textbook.

2. An objective is about ends rather than means. It describes a *product* of instruction rather than the *process* of instruction. It describes what students will be able to do when they are competent, rather than describing how they will be made competent.

3. An objective describes the key conditions under which the performance occurs on the job; i.e., the tools, equipment, environment, and circumstances that will influence the performance.

4. An objective describes the standard of acceptable performance; it tells how well someone must perform before being considered competent *on that objective.*

Each objective, then, will describe the (a) do what, (b) with what, and (c) how well:

      a. what someone should be able to do,
      b. the conditions under which the doing will occur, and
      c. the criteria by which the performance will be judged.

How Many Objectives?

You will need as many objectives as it takes to describe the important things you want students to be able to do. There will be one objective to describe each of the tasks you want students to be able to perform and one to describe each of the key skills they will need to learn before being ready to practice those tasks.

(There will be *no* objectives describing course content or the intended instructional process. To write objectives about anything but meaningful *outcomes* would swamp you in an unmanageable quagmire and would defeat the purpose of the objective. Objectives describe the ends. Items such as instructional content and practice material are means to the ends and go into the instruction rather than into the objectives.)

Each objective will be written in enough detail so that another professional instructor could turn out students who could do what you want them to do at the proficiency levels you prescribe.

Warning: Jargon Ahead

Over the past 25 years or so the notion of objectives has picked up jargon like a ship collects barnacles. They have been called behavioral objectives, competencies, outcomes, and performance objectives. Worse, the same objective has been labeled at one and the same time a classroom objective, a course objective, a school objective, a district objective, and a county objective.

But if you describe a measurable outcome important to accomplish, that is an objective.

Keep this in mind: they're not called behavioral objectives, because many describe the *product or result* of the behavior rather than the behavior itself. They're not called competencies, because competency means skill rather than intended outcome. The word *objective* doesn't need to be modified by the word *class, course, school,* or *county,* unless *different* outcomes are intended for those different entities.

If you describe an intended outcome specifically enough to tell whether it has been accomplished, call it an objective. Period.

How to Do It

1. Collect all the analysis documents drafted to this point.

2. While reviewing the task flowcharts, write an objective to describe the performance of each task.

3. Now look at the list of skills that anyone would have to have before practicing the entire task. Write an objective to describe each of those skills. In other words, write a statement to describe the limits of those skills, one that tells how much of each skill is needed by someone intending to perform the task. (Note: If you are an

experienced developer, write objectives only for those skills you are certain your students do not already possess.)

How much detail should you use? Just enough so that someone else reading the objective would understand it the way you do. How to find out? Show your draft to one or two people and ask them to tell you what they think it means. It doesn't matter if they don't understand the technical content of the objective. If they don't say what you want them to say, don't argue. Fix the objective.

4. Test your objectives for completeness. Each one will be good enough when you can answer yes to the following questions:

   a. Does it say what someone will be doing when demonstrating accomplishment of the objective (e.g., writing, solving, disassembling)?

   b. Does it describe the important conditions that will exist while the performing is being done (e.g., "given a wiring diagram"; "from memory"; "given an irate customer"; "using the tools available in the Happy Hair Styling Kit")?

   c. Does it tell how to recognize when the performance will be considered satisfactory (e.g., "it operates to within plus or minus two degrees"; "all customer objections have been addressed"; "correct to within one decimal"; "polished to a 63 finish")?

5. If you have completed one or more goal analyses during the task analysis, and if you listed one or more performances that students cannot now do, write an objective to describe each performance that will need to be taught.

6. If, as you draft your objectives, you find yourself writing one or more fuzzies, such as *understand, comprehend, appreciate, know, demonstrate,* or any other abstraction, complete a goal analysis for each fuzzy. Mark the performances that represent things students cannot yet do, and write an objective describing each of those performances.

Examples

Here are some examples of objectives. Note that though their form differs (some are written in a single sentence, others in two or more, and so on), they all say something about desired student performance, about the conditions under which the performance will be expected to occur on the job, and about how to tell when the objective has been accomplished (the criterion of acceptable performance).

Objective #1: Given any instructional objective, be able to identify (circle) the stated performance, the main intent, the conditions under which the performance will occur, and the criterion of acceptable performance, when these characteristics are present.

Objective #2: Given: A prescribed confined space, standard equipment, and two other team members.

Action: Carry out a confined-space entry and exit.

Criterion: Entry and exit will meet ATA-7 Safety Practices.

Objective #3: Given: A Model XXX System, standard tool kit, spares kit, and at least one symptom of a common malfunction.

Performance: Return the system to normal operation.
Criteria: The system functions within specs. There is no cosmetic or structural damage to system or to immediate area. No more than one unnecessary spare was used. No complaints were filed by client personnel.

Objective #4: Given a patient of any weight, be able to start an IV using no more than two needle punctures.

Goofing Off with Objectives

If it were not for the obfuscators, the preparation and use of objectives would be relatively simple. We would simply say what we want students to be able to do and then get on with developing instruction that teaches them to do it. Unfortunately, there is a gaggle of folks who like to make things harder than they are, who like to hang all sorts of danglies on the dashboard of their instruction. "Oh," you hear them saying as they look over your perfectly wonderful objectives, "now that you have written your classroom objectives, you must write course objectives, and then school objectives, and then the county objectives." Huh? They can't be serious! But yes, they actually do try to propagate the fiction that it is actually meaningful to say that a shovel is not only a shovel, but also a spade, a digger, a scooper, and a dirt-remover. I've seen dozens of honest instructors faced with this ridiculous task of rewriting the same objective to fit different jurisdictions. And I've seen them become frustrated, and then furious, as well they should.

There are other ways to goof off with objectives. One is to create a "taxonomy" of performance levels, so that instead of saying how well a person must perform, the objective simply says, "Level B3," or "Criterion level A2." This looks very precise, until you look at the definitions of these "levels." Then you discover that the criterion is still being kept a secret. Here's an example from one of these "criterion taxonomies." This one is called TPL-2 (Task Proficiency Level). This is how it is defined: "Can do most parts of the task. Needs help only on hardest parts. May not meet local demands for speed or accuracy." How well should a student be able to perform a task with this alleged criterion? You still don't know.

When you write an instructional objective, you are simply trying to communicate something about what you want students to be able to do when they leave you. That's all. If you want them to be able to unscrew a light bulb while rubbing their tummies, say so and be done with it. Don't let the bedazzlers drape your objectives with ornaments that are neither useful nor pretty.

Oh sure, you may find yourself having to conform to some bureaucratic demand to write your objectives in peculiar ways. If so, bend a little. Write a clean set that will be useful for your own instruction, and then rewrite them according to the "guidelines" you are expected to follow. Send those on up the line where they will do little harm.

To Learn More: See Resources #5, #11, and #12.

8

Skill Hierarchies

Situation: *You have drafted objectives that describe what you want students to be able to do at the end of your instruction. Now you want to know which objectives must be taught before others can be usefully attempted.*

Before plunging into development or improvement of the instruction itself, it will be useful to arrange your objectives into a picture that will show you how the objectives relate to one another.

Why Bother?

Suppose that you come to my class in brain surgery and, after offering an overview of the course, I anesthetize a couple of volunteers and ask you to show the class how to do a brain transplant.

"Wait a minute," you might scream in protest. "How can I do a brain transplant when I don't even know which instruments to use—or even how to get into the head—or how to get the brains out once I *do* get in? Hey, I'm not even sure where the brains *are* in these two numbskulls!"

Now, now, don't get excited. You've made your point. You noticed right off that the order in which things are taught can make a big difference in how well (and how quickly) students will reach mastery of the objectives. That's exactly why the hierarchy is so useful.

But there's more. Sometimes the order in which things are taught *doesn't* matter, and that can be even more valuable to know than where a specific learning sequence *must* be imposed. When the learning difficulty isn't impacted by the order in which the skills are taught, you can safely leave the sequencing decisions in the hands of your students (gasp!) so that they can attack the one that's best for them at the time.

Better yet, when some lessons require practice equipment, and, for example, you don't have enough atom-smashers to go around, your hierarchy will tell you how each student can be productively engaged while one is smashing a few atoms. So the skill hierarchy is a useful tool.

What's a Hierarchy?

A skill hierarchy is a picture that shows the prerequisite relationships between skills. It shows which are subordinate to others; that is, which must be learned before others can usefully be attempted. It also shows which are independent of one another; that is, which can be learned in any order. Just as the task flowchart visualizes the key steps and decisions involved in performance of a task, the hierarchy visualizes the *relationships* between the skills needed in performance of a task.

The task analysis *flowchart* says, "This step is followed by that step, which is followed by that decision, which is followed by that step." Thus, the flowchart describes a *process.*

In contrast, the *hierarchy* says, "This skill must be *learned* before that one can be learned," and "This objective is unrelated to that objective, and so these two objectives can be taught in any order." Thus, the hierarchy describes *relationships.*

Why Now?

Since you won't be sequencing your lessons (modules) into a course until after you've drafted them, why draft a skill hierarchy now?

Good question. Because you've just been thinking about, and drafting, the objectives of your instruction, you've got objectives on the brain. So it will be a little easier to simply go the next step and draft your hierarchy while you're hot.

There's another reason. Once you've drafted your hierarchy and TPop. (target population) description, you'll be able to decide on the prerequisites for your course. In other words, you'll be in a position to decide which skills you will teach in your course and which you will require students to bring with them when they arrive. This type of intellectual baggage is referred to as prerequisites and means, "I'm not going to teach it here; so if you want to benefit from my instruction, you'd better learn to do it before you come." Because you'll want to make the prerequisite decisions shortly after you draft your hierarchy, now is a good time to see what the hierarchy will look like.

What Does a Hierarchy Look Like?

A skill hierarchy looks very much like an organization chart (ugh!), except that instead of depicting the relationships between people, departments, and divisions, it depicts the relationships between skills. Here's an example.

Example #1: This hierarchy shows the skills that must be in place before someone can practice the entire task of baking a cake.

Figure 8.1

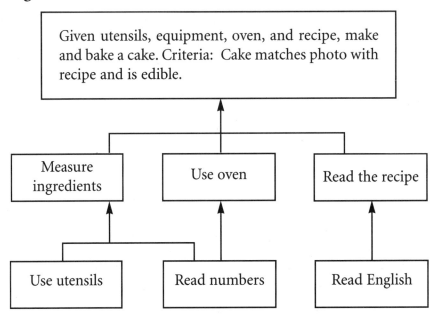

Read it from the top down, like this: Before being ready to practice the entire objective (baking a cake), anyone would have to be able to measure ingredients, use an oven, and read the recipe, and these three skills can be learned and practiced in any order. Before they can practice measuring ingredients, they need to be able to use utensils and read numbers, and these two skills can be learned and practiced in any order. And so on.

As we have all been victims of those who have *not* had the appropriate sub-skills in place before practicing the entire task, we should applaud the existence of the hierarchy and vigorously promote its use in the design of instruction.

Example #2: Before I show you another example, you may want to take a small Valium. I don't want to lose you to a bad case of hierarchy-shock. This next example is rather comprehensive and contains quite a few boxes and lines. So before looking at it get a blank piece of paper so that you can instantly cover all but a small piece of it. Got it? Okay, then, refer to the fold-out hierarchy at the back of this book.

This hierarchy shows the relationships between all the skills needed to troubleshoot a piece of electronic equipment. Don't let the apparent complexity of this hierarchy blow your socks off. Just look at it a piece at a time, just as you did the first one, reading from top to bottom.

> **NOTE:** The dotted lines shown at the right of the hierar-
> chy identify skills that may or may not have to be learned,
> depending on the location of the job assignment.

Notice that the hierarchy does not say anything about any individual person. It shows what *anyone* would have to be able to do before being ready to practice the entire task. Once we know what *anyone* would have to be able to do, then we can match that picture with the existing skills of a particular individual and derive a curriculum for that person from the difference.

How Are Hierarchies Constructed?

It's really easier than it looks.

Suppose that on reviewing your task analyses, you find that students are going to have to learn to fill out certain forms in the performance of the job (whatever it may be). You note also that they are going to have to be able to read English.

Does one of these two skills—"fill out forms" and "read English"—have to be learned before the other can be learned? Or could you teach them in any order? Could students learn to fill out forms if they couldn't read them? Obviously not. So in this case the reading skill must be in place before the form-filling-out skill can be practiced. The little hierarchy would look like this:

Figure 8.2

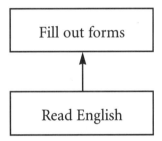

This tells us that all the skills shown leading into the box to which the arrow points should be mastered before that skill can be usefully attempted. We say that the reading skill *is subordinate to,* or *prerequisite to,* the "form-filling-out" skill. This does not mean that the reading skill is less important than the other. It means only that it must be in place before the other is attempted. It also tells us something else: It doesn't matter what an instructor alleges to be a preferred style of teaching, or a student professes to be a preferred style of learning; the hierarchy shows that one skill *must* be learned before the other—because one is part of the other.

Now let's consider another pair of skills. In reviewing your task analysis, you find that your sales students will have to be able to (a) describe product features to customers and (b) operate the product—let's say a car.

Would one of these two skills—"describe product features to customers" and "drive car"—*have to* be learned before the other could be attempted? That is, would I have to learn to describe the features of the car before I could learn to drive it? Or could I learn to drive without learning how to describe features to customers? I could, couldn't I? Both skills are important, but it wouldn't matter which was learned first. This hierarchy would look like this:

Figure 8.3

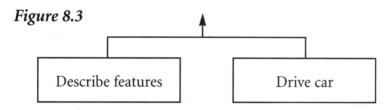

If you know which skills are independent of one another, you also know which sequencing options you could leave to the student if you so desired. In addition, you have information that will allow you to maximize course efficiency when you don't have enough practice equipment to go around. When practice equipment is limited, you can let your hierarchy tell you what students can *productively* work on while waiting their turn for the equipment.

How to Do It

1. Refer to the skills you derived from your task analyses. These are the skills you wrote to the right of the task steps that require them.

2. Delete the duplications from that list of skills. For example, it is likely that you will have written "Can read English" or "Can interview applicants" several times. If the *same* reading skill or interviewing skill is referred to in each instance, delete all but one of them. It makes no sense to "teach" a skill once it's learned.

3. Consider any pair of skills. Answer the question, Can these two skills be *learned* in any order? If so, draw them

side by side on your hierarchy. (A neat trick is to use those little pads of paper that are gummed on one end. Write each skill on one of the "stickies" and then move them around until you are satisfied.) If one must be learned before the other, the subordinate skill (the one that must be learned first) should be drawn below the other and connected to the one above it by an arrow.

4. Answer the same question for each pair of skills.

5. Draft a hierarchy; i.e., draw lines between the skills showing how they relate to one another.

6. Test your hierarchy.

   a. Make sure that every box on your hierarchy describes a skill rather than content. How? If you can put the word *can* in front of each item, it is probably describing a skill. For example, "Disassemble" makes sense when you add *can*—"Can disassemble." "Algebra," however, makes no sense at all when written, "Can algebra." Delete algebra and replace it with the skills that are relevant to the performance of the task in question. The subject matter won't get lost; it will go into your lessons. But subject matter has no place on the skill hierarchy.

   b. Starting at the top of the hierarchy, put a finger on each box that has one or more arrows leading into it and ask, "Is it true that students cannot practice this skill (the one you are pointing to) before they learn the skills shown as subordinate to this skill?" If the answer is "yes," go on to the next box and repeat the process. If the answer is "no," make the necessary correction.

c. Stand back and look at your hierarchy. If it is longer than it is wide, that is, if there are more levels from top to bottom than there are from side to side, it's likely that you have fallen into the trap of identifying process (steps in a task) rather than relationships (how skills relate to one another). Retest the hierarchy by repeating step 6b.

There is more to the matter of deriving hierarchies than can be described here. But the steps above provide the essence of the procedure.

To Learn More: See Resources #12, #15, and #16.

9

Target Population Description

Situation: You are ready to describe the key character-istics of the intended audience of your instruction, so that you can decide where the instruction should begin.

No doubt about it. "Target population description" is a piece of jargon right out of the late-night horror flicks. But not to worry. It means nothing more than "the students at whom your instruction is aimed." It could be called "audience description," but the word *audience* is generally reserved for a clump of people expecting to be entertained. Since we are not in the entertainment business (well, not officially, anyway), the word *audience* has misleading implications. As you run into the *target population description* verbiage below, just keep in mind that it refers to that particular gang of people for whom your instruction is intended, whether they are all alike or all different. So having swept the mystery aside, onward!

To this point in the string of analysis events, we have been considering procedures that will help us describe the end point, or outcomes, of instruction. With the information derived from the task, goal, and performance analyses, it will be possible to write objectives that describe what students should be able to do at the time they leave the instruction. (This is the topic of Chapter 7.) Now it will be useful to think about the "raw material" for the instruction, the students themselves. Just as the objectives will help determine where the instruction should end, the characteristics of the entering students will help determine where the instruction should begin.

Think of it this way: Instruction takes students from where they are to where they need to be, from their present state to a desired state. Thus, the instruction for any individual student should close the gap between actual and desired competence.

What they need to be able to do
– <u>What they can already do</u>
= The instruction

You can see from this simple formula why the importance of a target population description cannot be overemphasized. Without it, the entry point for any student can only be arrived at by guessing.

What's in It for Me?

Target population information not only will help to reveal a useful starting point, it will help to shape the course itself. It will help determine which examples are most likely to fit, what vocabulary to use, and even what media and procedures to adopt. For example, if you learn that your students are active people, you won't make them sit passively for long periods of time. If you know they find reading difficult, you'll want to minimize the reading load by using other ways to present information. If they tend not to be interested in sports, you'll want to avoid examples from that area. If yours is a required course being attended by students who are "kicking and screaming" all the way, you'll want to make a special effort to ensure that students understand why they're there, and to motivate them to dig into the activities of the course.

BABY BLUES

© Reprinted with special permission of King Features Syndicate

If you spend even a tenth as much time thinking about and describing your students as you do thinking about your subject, you will develop a powerful tool for ensuring the effectiveness of your instruction. And you'll find some new ideas for increasing student interest in your subject.

"Wait a minute," you may be saying. "Does anybody actually do this target population thing?" You bet they do. Look in the folder of any accomplished instructional developer and you'll find several pages of prose describing the audience for the intended instruction. And the more diverse that audience, the more detailed the description. There's gold in them thar words (translation: detailed knowledge of the target population is one of the fastest roads to improved instructional efficiency and student motivation).

Like the other procedures described in this book, the target population description is yet another procedure that you can apply without requiring special permission or changes to policy.

How to Do It

1. Begin by reminding yourself that your TPop. description will be a working document that will not be published or seen by others. Remind yourself that it is not necessary to organize the content into categories unless that activity helps you to think.

2. Think about the students who will be entering your course, and write down everything you think you know about them. Write the items in whatever order comes to mind. Let one thing remind you of another. If you need help getting started, use these questions as triggers:

    What are their interests?

    Why are they taking this course?

    Do they want to be in this course?

What is their age range?

What will be the likely male-female split?

Do they have families?

What attitudes and biases do you expect them to bring?

What training and experience have they had in relation to the subject you teach?

Which of the skills listed on your task analysis do they already have?

What tools and equipment do they already know how to use?

What can you say about their physical characteristics?

What other responsibilities will continue during the course (i.e., are they expected to continue doing their job while learning)?

While they're in training, are they away from home, living in a hotel? How do they feel about their accommodations?

3. Describe the range of a characteristic wherever you can. For example, if you write, "Some will have graduate degrees, and some will be new to the subject," or "Some will have 20 years of experience while others will be new hires," you will know immediately that you will have to treat students differently if you are to be helpful to all of

them. To treat them all alike would be to bore some and frustrate others, and that's not your goal.

4. When you have said all you can say, keep the document handy. Add to it as items come to mind (while you're completing other steps in the development process). This is a working document that should grow as you go.

If you're thinking, "But I don't *know* anything about them because I never know who will enroll," you're kidding yourself. You may not know their exact characteristics, but you surely know a lot about the people who *won't* be coming to your course. Will you be teaching kings? Foreigners? Ph.D.s? Veterans? Opera singers? Come on. Sit down and say what you can about them. And if you *really* don't know anything about them, take a little time to find out. Talk to the registrar. Get some names and call them on the phone. Talk to them. They'll be delighted to tell you about themselves. And they'll be overwhelmed at the thought that an instructor actually cares.

When you can write two to eight pages that answer the questions on the checklist at the end of this chapter, you can conclude that you know enough about your students to design instruction for them.

NOTES:

- Describe them as they are, rather than as you wish they were. Write what they can actually do rather than an idealized version of those skills, e.g., "They're not all high school graduates," rather than, "They *should* be high school graduates."

- Describe people rather than institutions or policies. Say what people are like, rather than what the course will or should be like, e.g., "Most like to drink beer," rather than, "Company policy requires regular beer-drinking."

- If you think your students are all different, describe the ways in which they differ. Sure, they're all different. But most of those differences won't have anything to do with how you design instruction. Others will matter a lot. You spot the important differences by asking yourself whether the *same* instructional approach will fit for the entire *range* of the characteristic you are thinking about. For example, will the same approach work for baldies as well as for bush-heads? Sure. But will the same approach (treatment) work for readers as well as non-readers? For experienced as well as inexperienced? Less likely.

- Don't bother to organize what you write, and don't fret if you say the same thing more than once. Nobody's going to see this document.

Example #1: This example is organized under headings; the second one is more of a mind-dump. Both formats are equally useful.

TPop:	Sales Personnel
Course:	Computer Order Entry

Physical Characteristics

- These people range in age from 25-40.

- About half are male and half female.

- There are no apparent physical limitations.

- Most will be away from home, and the younger ones will be bleary-eyed from too much carousing the night before.

Formal and Informal Training

- All of the new hires will have at least a master's degree.

- The older reps will have more varied training. Some will have a degree, and others only a year or two of college.

- They will have 5-20 years of experience with the company.

- All are facile with English, and all are used to writing reports.

- All can read quite well.

- All are familiar with order-writing; they know company procedures and policies. They just don't know how to enter orders onto a computer terminal.

- The younger engineering grads will be familiar with computers; the older reps will not.

Anticipated Attitudes

- Many of the older reps are apprehensive that they will show up poorly against the younger people who use computers better than they do. They worry that they are old dogs who won't be able to learn the new tricks.

- The older reps will be somewhat resentful about being away from their territory for the duration of the course. They feel they could be making money instead of sitting in a classroom. Some feel that the computer will make order-writing take longer than it does now.

Interests

- Many students play golf with business colleagues—especially the older males.

- The majority are married, have families, and spend significant time socializing within the family network.

- They have a lot in common and tend to socialize within

the group as well. Though the older ones are apprehensive about learning to use computers, everyone hates the paperwork associated with writing orders.

- Most of the recent college graduates have had extensive computer experience and play with computers as a hobby. In particular, they spend time "surfing the net."

Sources of Reinforcement

- Many of the older "career" reps just do their jobs to collect a paycheck and receive little self-fulfillment from the job. They know they will never be promoted and no longer want to be.

- They are very protective of their territory—nobody's going to tell them what to do.

- The younger "flow-through" reps are enthusiastic about doing a good job and are pleased with themselves when they know they have done so. They will be promoted, and they know it.

- They are looking forward to the computer automation program. They are not wedded to the existing method and are eager to rid themselves of paperwork.

Example #2:

TPop:	Field Service Reps
Course:	Appliance Repair

- About 95 percent are male, and all are married.

- They range in age from 25 to 60.

- They are all strong enough to do the lifting and bending

required by the job. None have disabilities that would get in the way.

- They are not diet freaks, though some take regular steps to stay fit.

- All have completed high school, and a few have had a little college.

- Some have been in the military and received some electronics training there.

- Others have learned something of electricity or electronics through home-study courses or while working in dad's shop.

- Only a few have had appliance training before joining this company.

- Their interests include sports (football, bowling, basketball, fishing), TV, gambling, and ham radio.

- They don't jog or play tennis, golf, or chess.

- They are interested in computers, though many of the older ones are skeptical about their ability to learn much about programming.

- They are likely to have mechanically-oriented hobbies. These include ham radio, auto or motorcycle repair, and repairs around the house. They are all mechanically inclined and can handle hand tools with ease.

- They are not likely to read for pleasure, though they are not poor readers. They'd rather talk about "the trouble that got away" than read.

- They truly enjoy having control of their day. They like to decide how they will spend their time. They would much rather be on the road than in the classroom.

- They enjoy handling customer complaints, and they especially enjoy having a satisfied customer ask for them by name. They like to solve customer problems, but some aren't too skilled in customer interaction.

- Many like to tell themselves that they will soon start their own business, but few understand the implications of that challenge.

- They do not like to use test equipment or wiring diagrams in the presence of the customer, because they feel the customer will conclude they don't know what they are doing and that the repair will take a long time. They prefer to "wing it" rather than use test equipment.

- They prefer their training be "hands-on" rather than theoretical, and they badmouth any course that includes as much as 50 percent lecturing.

- About 20 percent will say they don't know why they've been sent to the course. These either think they are competent enough already or don't want to learn to handle a wider range of products. These are the reluctant dragons.

NOTE: The descriptions in these two examples contain several items that should influence the shape of instruction (content as well as procedures) designed for these students. If you find it hard to spot these cues, try this: Write a brief description of *your* own personal characteristics and then compare it to the characteristics of any course you've taken. The discrepancies between the way the course was run and the way it should have been conducted to maximize your learning reveal things the course developers should have taken into consideration before developing their course.

Goofing Off with Questionnaires

Questionnaires are *not* a useful source of information about your students. Why izzat, you may wonder? It's because it takes a great deal of skill and time to prepare a questionnaire that will elicit the type of information you may want. Items have to be drafted, and they absolutely must be tested and then revised, and maybe tested again, before one can have any assurance at all that the questionnaire tells you what you want to know. And people with this specialized skill are rare. If they are skilled in questionnaire development, they are not likely to be working in a training department.

If you just slap a questionnaire together, you aren't going to find out what you want to know, because it's hard to write items that aren't ambiguous. And when faced with ambiguous questions—or questions they think may be dangerous to their job—people will simply tell you what they think you want to hear. What you will do is create a great deal of paperwork for somebody—reproducing multiple copies, locating mailing addresses, affixing postage, and so on. You will also create work for someone who has to tabulate and/or analyze the "results." But those results will be mostly "garbage in—garbage out."

So unless you are looking for a way to expand your empire, consider the questionnaire as an impractical method for finding out about a target population. And don't use a questionnaire just because someone is bedazzled by data gleaned from large samples. It is far more productive, as well as faster and cheaper, to talk to a few people directly, either by phone, e-mail, or in person.

A Helpful Checklist

Check your target population description against the following list. Does it include information about:

1. age range?

2. sex distribution?

3. nature and range of educational background?

4. reason(s) for attending the course?

5. attitude(s) about course attendance?

6. biases, prejudices, beliefs?

7. typical hobbies and other spare-time activities?

8. interests in life other than hobbies?

9. need-gratifiers (i.e., what would reward them)?

10. physical characteristics?

11. reading ability?

12. terminology or topics to be avoided?

13. organizational membership?

14. specific prerequisite and entry-level skills already learned?

To Learn More: See Resources #2, #15, and #16.

10
Course Prerequisites

Situation: You have a clear picture of what students should be able to do when they leave you (objectives) and a picture (skill hierarchy) showing which skills must be learned before others can be attempted. You also have a good description of your target population. You can now derive the point at which it would be most appropriate to begin your course.

Here's another neat way to save development time while making sure that the finished course will do what you want it to. Just as you were systematic about deciding where the course should *end*, you want to be just as systematic about deciding where it should *begin*. Do it by using the procedure described in this chapter to answer the following questions:

Who will be qualified to enter my course? What, if anything, will they need to be able to do before they can benefit from my instruction? How can I select the least amount of content that will take students from their current skill level to mastery of the objectives?

Obviously, the *fewer* the restrictions on the entering student, the larger the number of people who will qualify for your course (and the more likely it will be that students will differ from each other in important ways). The *more* restrictions placed on the entering student, the *less* likely you will be to find people who meet your requirements (and the more likely they will be similar to each other). The trick is to write prerequisites that are realistic.

Let's Get One Thing Straight!

But let's get one thing straight. "Algebra 101" and "Abnormal Psych" are *not* prerequisites. They may be the names of a couple of courses, and they may be required for administrative reasons before someone may enter your course, but they don't qualify as prerequisites to your course. *A prerequisite is a skill that someone must have in order to benefit from your instruction.* If your course is taught in English, then students must be able to handle that language before they can benefit from your instruction. If you don't intend to teach in English, then an ability to understand the language is a prerequisite. If your course assumes that students already know how to solve algebraic equations that have one variable, then they will be less likely to benefit from your instruction if they enter it without that skill. If you don't intend to teach that skill, then it will have to become a prerequisite.

The *name* of a course tells nothing about the skills that students will have when completing the course. A course name describes only an administrative requirement that must be fulfilled; it says nothing about what students should be able to do before entering your course.

Where Do They Come From?

Prerequisites are derived during course development. Whenever you decide to *assume* that entering students will be able to do this or that, you are establishing a prerequisite. Why? Because prerequisites are formalized assumptions.

For example, when you say to yourself, "I'm not going to teach the math they should have learned last semester," it means you are going to *assume* that those math skills are already in place. If students who do *not* have those skills will be less likely to profit from your instruction, a rule should be established that says, "No one may enter this course without the following skills: . . . e.g., solve an equation; lift at least 50 pounds; climb a pole with climbing irons; name the bones of the body."

Be Realistic

You can see why it is important not to be arbitrary about the prerequisite skills you demand. On the one hand, if you make too few demands and allow everyone in, you will have to begin your instruction at square one. That may be impractical. On the other hand, if you require that too many prerequisite skills be brought to your course, you may not find anyone at all who qualifies. The goal is to be realistic.

Prerequisite skills should be demanded only when necessary. If you have no control over your incoming students and are expected to accept everyone who enters, it is silly to make demands about prior knowledge and skill. The realistic approach is to accept the students who appear on your doorstep and then begin your instruction where they are when they arrive. Sure, you'd rather teach the advanced stuff. But if the students don't have the basics, and if there is no one else to provide them, and if they need them before they can learn the advanced material, you have three choices:

1. Turn up your nose and say, "I'm not going to teach them what they should have learned elsewhere," and plow into the advanced material, wasting both your time and theirs.

2. Teach them the basics.

3. Find another way for them to learn the basics while you teach the advanced material.

So set up screening criteria (prerequisites), only when:

a. there are one or more things students should be able to do before entering your course, and

b. you have decided it's reasonable to expect them to be able to do them, and therefore you won't need to teach those things in your course.

How to Do It

1. Review the task analyses and the list of skills that anyone would have to have before practicing those tasks.

2. Review your target population description.

3. For each skill answer the question, "Is it reasonable to expect that entering students will already have this skill?"

4. If so, add that skill to your list of prerequisites, and design your course on the assumption that the skill will already be in place.

5. If it is not reasonable to assume that entering students will have this skill, decide how it will be taught—in your course or by some other remedial means?

6. Then, as you develop or modify your course, keep an *Assumption List* handy. Whenever you decide to assume that students will know something or be able to do something when they enter your course, add it to the list.

7. Write the prerequisites in the form of objectives.

8. Review your prerequisite objectives and make sure that each describes a skill rather than a course name (you are well aware of the wide variations in the way that any course can be taught by two or more instructors).

A Simpler Way

1. Review your skill hierarchy. (Remember that the hierarchy shows all the skills that *anyone* would have to have before practicing the skill shown at the top.)

2. Starting at the bottom, ask yourself whether it is reasonable to assume that your entering students will be able to perform the skill you are pointing to. For example, ask yourself whether it is reasonable to assume that they already can "Read English" or "Use hand tools" or "Add/subtract." (Refer to your target population description for guidance.)

3. If so, draw a circle around that skill.

4. If most or all of your incoming students can be assumed to have a given skill, consider that skill a prerequisite. That is, say to yourself, "I will assume that students can do this when they arrive and therefore I won't have to teach it in my course." Then decide what you will do about those few who do not have that skill—such as provide remedial material.

5. If you have been *told* what skills you must teach, but some of those skills don't *need* to be taught, tell yourself that you will only provide instruction in them for those who may need it.

6. Draw a line across the bottom of the hierarchy that expresses the rule: Skills above the line will be taught in

my course (or somebody else's course); skills below the line will be assumed to be brought by entering students and will therefore be considered prerequisites.

Example #1: After reviewing your TPop. description, you find that it is reasonable to assume that most or all incoming students will be able to use a computer word-processing application to write letters. So you base your instruction on that assumption. You decide not to teach students how to use the application. Instead, you will teach only the more advanced applications, and you will turn your assumption into a prerequisite objective, as follows:

> Given a Spelgud word-processing application and one or more draft letters, enter and save the letters in the application.

Example #2: Refer to the fold-out hierarchy on the last page of this book. The target population for a course in troubleshooting consists of people who have had experience in working with a variety of equipment. Though their experience varies, it is reasonable to assume that all of them can perform the skills shown below the heavy line. Those skills, therefore, will not be taught. Instead, they will be considered prerequisites and entering students will be so informed.

To Learn More: See Resources #1, #5, #12, #15, and #16.

Part IV

Developing the Instruction

11
Criterion Tests

Situation: You have drafted objectives, a hierarchy, and a target population description. Now you want to develop the tools by which you can find out whether those objectives have been achieved—by which you can find out whether the instruction worked.

If it's worth teaching, it's worth finding out whether the instruction was successful. That sounds reasonable, doesn't it? After all, we weigh ourselves to find out whether we have achieved a weight target, and we test products to find out whether they are ready to ship to customers. In the same way, we measure the performance of our students to find out whether our instruction is doing what it's supposed to be doing.

The most direct measure of instructional success is to determine how many objectives were accomplished by each student. Enter the criterion test. The name is derived from the criteria stated in an objective. In practice, largely because the word "test" has such anxiety-producing connotations, criterion tests are usually referred to by labels more acceptable to the people using them. Skill checks and performance checks are common examples.

The purpose of the criterion test (skill check) is to determine whether an objective has been achieved, so that both student and instructor can determine what action to take next. If the criteria have been met, the student is encouraged to move to the next instructional unit. If the performance is weak, the problem is diagnosed and a remedy is suggested (usually more explanation or more practice). This use of a test is very different from the practice of "give 'em a grade and be done with 'em." The purpose is to help rather than to label.

When to Draft Skill Checks?

The time to draft skill checks is soon after you have drafted the objectives, but before you draft the instruction. There are two good reasons for this. First, drafting the skill checks soon after drafting the objectives will help you to clarify the objectives. Whenever you find yourself having difficulty drafting items that are correct for an objective, it will almost always be because the objective isn't yet clear enough to provide the necessary guidance. Clarify the objective, and the skill check items will fall into place.

Second, drafting skill checks soon after the objectives will also help you to focus your test items on the outcomes to be measured, rather than on the instructional process. It will help you to focus on writing items that will find out whether the outcomes have been achieved rather than on whether students can recognize or recite material that was covered during the instruction (except, of course, in those rare instances where recognizing and reciting are legitimate objectives).

"But three chapters ago you said I should draft my *hierarchy* after I drafted the objectives," I hear you screaming. "Which is it?" Easy there. Calm down. You can draft skill hierarchies or skill checks in any order; just make sure you do both things before you begin drafting relevant practice descriptions (which will be described in the next chapter).

Characteristics of Criterion Test Items

Test items that tell you whether an objective has been mastered have these two main characteristics: The test items match the objectives in both performance and conditions.

1. Each item matches the objective in *performance*. That is, the performance called for in the test item is the *same* as that called for by the objective; i.e., the item asks students to do what the objective says they should be able to do.

2. Each test item matches the objective in *conditions*. That is, it asks the student to perform under the same conditions spelled out in the objective.

The results of the test are evaluated by comparing the actual performance of the student with the criteria stated in the objective. This means that the student performance must achieve the same criteria as stated in the objective for that performance to be considered acceptable.

Why insist that a test item match the objective in performance? Let me answer that with another question. Why test at all? Your answer should be that you want to predict whether students will be able to do what you have taught them when they leave you. The best way to do that is to observe a sample of the *actual performance* you are trying to develop. Anything less than that won't tell you what you want to know. Think about it this way: Suppose your surgeon were hovering over you with gloved hands and the following conversation took place.

Surg: Just relax. I'll have that appendix out in no time.

You: Have you done this operation before?

Surg: No, but I passed all the tests.

You: Oh? What kind of tests?

Surg: Mostly multiple-choice. But there were
           some essay items, too.

You: Good-bye!

In practice it isn't *always* possible for your test items to duplicate the conditions called for by the objective. In such cases one approximates those conditions as closely as possible.

But it *is* always possible for a test item to demand the same performance as that described in the objective. For example, if an objective asks students to be able to repair equipment under water or to splice cables on top of a pole, it may not be possible to provide the water or the pole. In those instances you would provide the closest approximation to those conditions that you can. But you would *always* ask them to *repair,* and you would *always* ask them to *splice.* The rule is this: If you must, approximate the conditions, but *never approximate the performance.*

How to Do It

Prepare a criterion test for *each* objective whose accomplishment you want to measure. Many of those tests will consist of only one item (question), and the rest will need only three or four. How do you know how many items to include? The rule is this: The test will contain as many items as are needed to sample the range of conditions called for in the objective. Here are the steps for preparing a criterion test (skill check).

1. Read the objective and identify the performance (what it wants someone to be able to do).

2. Draft a criterion item that asks students to exhibit that performance.

3. Read the objective again and note the conditions under which the performing should occur (i.e., tools and equipment provided, people present, key environmental conditions).

4. Write those conditions into your test instructions.

5. For conditions you cannot provide, describe approximations that are as close to the objective as you can manage.

6. If you feel you must have more than one item to test an objective, it should be because (a) the range of possible conditions is so great that one performance won't tell you that the student can perform under the entire range of conditions, or (b) the performance could be achieved accidentally. But be sure that each item calls for the performance stated in the objective.

Example: For example, suppose I am teaching selling and my objective is that students will be able to follow the steps for closing a sale. And suppose I want that performance to occur in the presence of seven different kinds of customers (e.g., calm, angry, hostile, stupid, and so on). I would write an item to test performance involved in closing a sale that would be something like this:

a. Go to video room A, where you will find a product and a "customer."

b. Read the information sheet he or she hands you.

c. When you are ready, turn on the video recorder.

d. Using the product provided, try to close a sale.

Then I would talk to myself like this: "How many times would I want to see that performance before I would agree that students had accomplished the objective? Well, if they could do it once, I'd know they could *do* it, but if they did it only in the presence of a calm customer, I wouldn't know whether they could do it with a hostile one. I think if I had three samples of performance, I'd be satisfied they could handle the skill under the conditions specified."

Then I would write three criterion test items, *each of which calls for the same performance* under a different part of the condition range specified in the objective. In the example above, the items would all read the same, but the person playing the customer would be different. One would be hostile, one would be angry, and one would pretend to be a little dull. Most of the time, writing test items is simpler than the above paragraph implies. Here are some more examples.

Example #1: Suppose an objective reads:

Objective: Given a Model 12 keyboard, and a standard tool kit, be able to disassemble the keyboard down to the frame within ten minutes.

Let's follow the steps listed above.

1. What's the performance called for by the objective?

   Disassembling.

2. Draft a criterion test item.

   Disassemble this keyboard in ten minutes.

3. What are the conditions stated?

   The student is given a Model 12 keyboard and standard tool kit.

4. Add the conditions to the test item.

   On table 3 you will find a Model 12 keyboard and a standard tool kit. Use the tool kit to disassemble the keyboard down to the frame. You will have ten minutes.

5. Can all the conditions be provided as called for by the objective?

   Yes. No changes needed in the item.

6. Are additional items necessary?

   No. There is no range of conditions and little likelihood the performance could be correct by chance.

Example #2: Let's try another one. The objective says:

Objective: Given a malfunctioning Model 239 atomic bomb, one symptom, and a standard tool kit, be able to repair the malfunction within 30 minutes.

1. What's the performance called for by the objective?

   Repairing.

2. Draft a test item.

   Repair that atomic bomb.

(Example #2, continued on next page)

3. What conditions are stated?

    *A malfunctioning bomb, one symptom, and a standard
    tool kit.*

4. Add the conditions to the test item.

    *You will find a Model 239 atomic bomb in room 10.
    The problem is that the detonator is showing an
    intermittent short. Use the standard tool kit provided
    to repair the malfunction. You will have 30 minutes.*

5. Can all the conditions be provided as stated in the objec-
    tive?

    Not on your life, they can't.

I can hear you shouting, "I am *not* going to give students *any*
kind of bomb to be tested on no matter *what* the objective
says!" Good for you. But while I can appreciate your feeling,
you'd be only partly right. True, it would be impractical to provide the real thing here, even though trainees will be working
on the real thing on the job. But that should never mean that
you will ask for anything less than the performance called for
by the objective, in this case, repairing. No matter what else
you choose to do, you should ask the students to demonstrate
repairing behavior, rather than talk-about-repairing or write-
about-repairing. No multiple-choice exams, please. Only by
having them perform per the objective can you find out
whether the objective has been achieved.

It's the conditions you will modify, not the performance. So
find the closest approximation to the real thing you can, and
then ask for the actual performance on that. How about a
wooden bomb of some sort? How about a real one that has
had the oomph taken out of it? What's your best offer?

NOTE: If you write your test items according to the above procedure, and find yourself saying, "But the test items look pretty much like the objective," you need to have a little chat with yourself. Remember that the object of instruction is to bestow competence just as elegantly as you can manage to do it. The object of testing is to check to see if you've succeeded. The object of testing is not to use trick questions just to make it harder, or to spread people on a curve, or to find out whether students "really" understand. If your test items look similar to your objectives, rejoice. That's the whole idea.

The Multiple-Choice Trap

There is often a temptation to want to use multiple-choice and true-false items for testing competence. After all, didn't we spend an academic lifetime answering this type of item? Yes, we did. And aren't multiple-choice and true-false items easily scorable by scanners? Yes, they are. And isn't that a useful type of item for spreading students on a curve? Yes, indeed.

But all of that is irrelevant. The most reliable way to find out whether learners can change a tire is to ask them to do it. If you used multiple-choice or true-false items, you might find out what they *know* about tire-changing, but you won't find out whether they can do it. And if you wanted to use those types of items, who would write them? You? Who would do the item tryouts? You? Writing multiple-choice items is a specialty; it isn't easy to dash off a few items that are unambiguous and that test exactly what you want to test; without training in this skill you will be very likely to write items that don't follow good item-writing practice.

And who would do the scoring? You? If not, who will see to it that the test papers get to the scoring machine, and back again—in a timely manner? You see the trap. Just because someone refers to multiple-choice items as objective—which they are not—that doesn't make them useful, appropriate, or convenient. Worst of all, they practically never tell you whether your objectives have been actually achieved. Remember the surgeon who passed all the *written* tests on appendectomies?

Examples

Here are some examples of objectives, along with several possible test items for testing achievement of each. The test item that would be appropriate for testing achievement of the objective has been checked. The items not check-marked may tell you whether students can perform some part of the objective, but only the check-marked items will tell you whether they can perform as the objective demands.

Objective #1: Given your own computer terminal loaded with word-processing software, be able to type a business letter in accordance with the standards described in Company Manual 10A (page 23).

Test Items:

1. *Describe the five elements of a business letter.*

2. *On the attached letters, circle the typos and items not corresponding to company policy.*

3. *Tell how you would instruct a secretary in the preparation of business letters in accordance with company standards.*

✓ 4. *From the attached copy, type a business letter on your own terminal in the form described in Company Manual 10A (pg. 23).*

Objective #2:

Conditions: Given a Model 5 computer, standard tool and spares kits, a VOM, and at least one symptom of malfunction,

Action: Clear the malfunction.

Criteria: Computer is returned to normal operation and functions within specifications.

              There is no cosmetic or structural damage to the computer or surrounding area.

              All paperwork is correctly completed.

Test Items:

1. *Draw a block diagram of the Model 5 computer.*

2. *Explain how you would troubleshoot a Model 5 computer.*

3. *List the five most common troubles that happen to the Model 5 computer, and check those that are operator-induced.*

✓ 4. *The Model 5 computer in room 156 will not boot. Use the tools and spares that are in the room to clear the trouble. When you are finished, complete the Standard Trouble Call Report in the envelope labeled "STCR."*

Objective #3: Having written a goal you feel is worthy of achievement, be able to derive (write) the performances that, if exhibited, will cause you to agree that the goal is achieved (i.e., write an operational definition of a goal you feel is important to achieve).

Test Items:

1. *Describe the steps in completing a goal analysis.*

✓ 2. *Select a goal for your course and complete a goal analysis.*

3. *Review the completed goal analyses in the attached envelope. Circle the items that have been incorrectly described as performances.*

Objective #4: Given a disassembled M-16 rifle, be able to correctly assemble it, while blindfolded, within five minutes.

Test Items:

1. *List the parts of an M-16 rifle.*

2. *Describe the action of the M-16 rifle. Also state the history of the rifle and three combat situations for which it is the weapon of choice.*

✓ 3. *On the table in front of you is a disassembled M-16 rifle. Put on the blindfold and assemble the rifle. You will have five minutes to make the rifle completely operational.*

Objective #5: When approached by a prospective customer, be able to respond in a positive manner (i.e., by smiling, offering a suitable greeting, and by asking how you might be of service).

Test Items:

✓ 1. *Go to the videotaping room. When the instructor turns on the recorder, provide a suitable greeting to each of the "customers" who will enter the room.*

2. *Tell how you would respond in a suitable manner to a customer.*

3. *Write a description of a typical customer.*

Summary

To find out whether objectives have been accomplished,

1. Make sure your test items ask students to do what the objective asks them to be able to do, and

2. Ask them to do it under the conditions stated in the objective.

3. Then, when reviewing the performance, consider the objective achieved only when the performance matches, or exceeds, the criteria described in the objectives.

Finally, remind yourself that if you are going to the effort of using techniques intended to make instruction work, it is worth the effort to find out whether you've succeeded.

To Learn More: See Resources #10, #11, #15, and #18.

12
Relevant Practice

Situation: Before drafting instruction, you want to know what it will take to provide practice in the objectives.

As the trumpets tootle to the rumbling of the kettle drums, I enter to center stage and begin:

Me: Ladeeees and gentlemennnnn. Introducing the world's greatest magiciannn ... YOU ... ably assisted by the world's most handsome assistant ... ME. (At which point you, wearing a flowing black cape and red tights, enter stage center ... and proceed to look befuddled.)

You: *(Stage whisper to me)* Where's my magic apparatus?

Me: I left it in the garage.

You: You did what?

Me: I didn't think you'd need it.

You: *(Shouting in stage whisper)* And just how do you expect me to do my tricks without my magical apparatus?

Me: Hey! You're the magician!

All right, so maybe I lost my head to make a point, but the fact is that many things simply cannot be done without the "right stuff." And the right kind of practice is one of the most important "stuff" of all. After all, you can't practice making an elephant come out of a hat if you don't have a hat. Similarly, you can't practice the tuba if you don't have one, nor practice your golf if you don't have the balls for it.

Of course, most instructors know that practice makes perfect. They know that one learns to play the piano by practicing on the piano, rather than by talking about the piano or by answering multiple-choice questions about music. They know that the way to learn to interview or solve problems or to dance is to practice interviewing, problem-solving, or dancing. They know that practice is one of the powerful activities that makes their instruction work.

Less well understood is that the *nature* of that practice influences its usefulness.

Practice Makes Perfect, But . . .

Practice is a powerful way to develop skill, and a key component to making instruction work. But practice by itself is not enough! Practice without information (feedback) to the student about the quality of the practice can be worse than no practice at all. You already know why. Because students may spend a great deal of effort practicing and learning and getting better at the *wrong thing*. Therefore it is an instructional error (some call it fraud) (1) to withhold practice opportunities and (2) to allow students to practice without a suitable source of feedback.

Sources of Feedback

Feedback can be provided either by external or internal sources. Either you can build into the students' heads the ability to recognize correct from incorrect performance, or you can have another person or device do it. If you are going to build the performance criteria into the students' heads, then you must *prevent them from practicing until this is done.* Plainly put, unless you're going to provide an external source of feedback, they must not practice until they know how to evaluate their own performance.

If you will have an external source provide the feedback, you must be sure that the person or mechanism providing the feedback knows the performance standards. If another person is to provide feedback, that person must know more than just how to recognize correct and incorrect performance. That person must also be able to offer the information in a way that will not destroy the motivation or self-esteem of the student.

Practice Isn't Practice Unless . . .

Suppose you saw me practicing the tuba and said, "Hi there. What are you doing?" And suppose I replied, "Why, I'm learning how to dance." What would you think? Suppose I then said, "Y'know, I've been working hard at this, but my dancing doesn't seem to be improving. Got any ideas?" I think your reply would be obvious: "If you want to learn how to dance, you need to practice dancing." And of course you'd be right—and I'd thank you for not using saltier language in your reply.

That is an obvious example of wrong (useless) practice. Other examples are a little harder to decode. Suppose while learning to be a policeman you are expected to learn when and when not to shoot (a rather important skill). And suppose the instructor had you practice reciting the law that pertains to shooting. Would that practice help you get better at making the shoot/no-shoot decision? You see that it isn't as easy to decide in this case. Actually, knowing the law may be useful information, but it won't improve your ability to make the instant decisions that shooting situations require. It wouldn't, in other words, provide *relevant* practice of the skill in question.

Before deriving the content of your instruction, therefore, you should describe the "right stuff" that will be needed for practice of each objective. Not only will that make it easier to derive the instructional content of the lessons (modules), it will make the actual development process go faster.

How to Do It

Here's how to describe relevant practice for an objective. Once you've done it for six or so objectives, it will only take a minute or two to do it from then on.

1. *Performance.* Write down what the student would be doing when practicing the essence of the objective.

   Example: If the objective says, "Be able to assemble schlorks . . .," you would write "Assemble schlorks."

   Example: If the objective says, "Be able to write a computer program," you would write "Write computer program."

2. *The right stuff.* Write down the things (the right stuff) that you would have to provide in order to make the practice happen. (The objective will tell you.)

   Example: If the objective says, "Given a set of parts and a standard tool kit . . . ," you would list "Set of parts" and "Tool kit."

   Example: If the objective says, "Given a prospective customer and a product to sell . . .," you would write "Prospective customer," and "(insert the name of the product)."

3. *Adequacy feedback.* Write down how you will provide feedback (information) about the adequacy of the practice performance (whether it's OK or not OK).

   Example: If the performance can be compared against a list of right answers, write "Answer key."

   If the performance can be evaluated against a checklist that describes the key characteristics of the performance, write "Checklist of criteria or key points."

   Decide whether, given the right answers, or checklists, or modeling, or descriptions of desired performance, students could decide for themselves whether their performance is OK or not OK (adequacy feedback). If they could, let them. If they couldn't, you will have to decide how to provide an external source of feedback (e.g., another person).

4. *Diagnostic feedback.* Now you need to think about who or what will diagnose performance that is not yet OK. That means thinking about who or what will determine what's wrong with the performance, and how the diagnostic feedback will be provided to the student. Answer this question:

   If the student knows that the performance isn't yet good enough, could the student decide what is wrong with it?

   If so, you're done with this step. If students can't be counted on to decide what's wrong with their performance, you will have to provide an external source of diagnostic feedback (e.g., another person).

5. ***Corrective feedback.*** If students know what's wrong with their practice performance, will they know what to do to fix it? If so, that's all you need to do. If not, you'll need to provide an external source of information about how to correct the performance (e.g., another person; written description of common problems; checklist of probable remedies).

6. The final step is simply to take your answers to Items 1-5 and draft them into a short description of relevant practice for each objective. This description may be as short as one that says, "Provide tools, schematics, faulty thermostat, list of tolerances of adequate operation. Student will practice repairing. Instructor will provide diagnostic and corrective feedback." Sometimes more "right stuff" will have to be provided to make the practice relevant to the objective, possibly including an instructor or other student to supply feedback by observing the practice while making marks on a checklist.

Whatever the result, the importance of practice—*relevant* practice—cannot be over-emphasized. As you well know, *doing is the key to competence.* Since the conditions under which the doing takes place can be critical to student improvement, it pays to complete this step in the development process with care, no matter what or where you are teaching. It usually takes only a few seconds after some practice.

> **NOTE:** Sometimes you will need little or nothing to provide the conditions for relevant practice. When this happens, you may tend to feel as though you've done something "wrong" or forgotten something. When that happens, try this: Imagine your student in an empty room and then ask yourself what you will need to provide to make it possible for that student to practice the objective. If it's only a pencil and a piece of paper, so be it. If it's only a musical score, so be it.

RELEVANT PRACTICE CHECKLIST

PERFORMANCE

1. What will trainees be doing when practicing the objective?

Replacing parts

2. What do the criteria in the objective talk about?

- • Product of performance → | Save the Product | ✓
- • Shape of performance → | Record the Performance | ✓

CONDITIONS

3. What cues/conditions must you provide to make the practice possible (i.e. to meet the conditions stated in the objective)?

R-bander engine   manual
bench   parts
tools

FEEDBACK

4. How will you let trainees know their performance is OK or not OK (i.e. meets the standards of the objective)?

(Check as many times as needed.) → | • Description of correct responses |
| • Modeling of desired performance |
| • Checklist of criteria or key points | ✓
| • Description of desired performance |
| • |

5. Given those standards, can you rely on trainees to decide if their performance is OK or not OK?

(YES) ↓   NO → | Have somebody (or something) provide the comparison of performance with standards |

6. If the work is NOT OK, can you rely on them to decide what is wrong with the performance?

(YES) ↓   NO → Could they tell what's wrong if you model the performance and/or describe common problems?

If YES . . . | Provide modeling and/or description of common errors (problems) |

If NO . . . | Have somebody diagnose the performance |

7. If they know what is wrong with their performance, can you rely on them to know what to do to improve?

(YES) ↓   NO → Would they know how to improve if you modeled the performance and/or described typical remedies or solutions?

If YES . . . | Provide modeling and/or description of typical remedies or solutions |

If NO . . . | Have somebody provide the remedies or solutions |

8. Describe relevant practice. Account for all the checks made above, and include all items needed to provide the cues/conditions listed in item 3.

ADEQUACY

DIAGNOSTIC

CORRECTIVE

© The Center for Effective Performance. From *Instructional Module Development,* by R. F. Mager. 2nd Edition, Revised 1996.

Here are some examples:

Example #1:

> *Objective:* Be able to replace any component in an R-Bander aircraft engine. Conditions: shop environment, tools and manual available. Criterion: No damage to tools or engine; replacements are made according to R-B procedures.

Thinking it through: (The checklist on the following page is a job aid often used in the preparation of relevant practice descriptions.) The numbered items below refer to the numbered items on the checklist.

1. "Let's see. The performance called for is that of replacing parts.

2. "The criteria talk about the performance itself (replacements are made according to R-B procedures) *as well as the product of the performance* (correctly replaced parts as well as undamaged tools and engine). That means I should record (e.g., videotape) the performance so that it can be reviewed later.

3. "To make practice possible, I'll have to provide an engine on a bench, some tools, some replacement parts, and the manual. Oh, yes; I'll also need a video recording setup. That way students can evaluate their own practice performance.

4,5. "Now about adequacy feedback. How can I provide the basis for letting students decide whether their performance is OK or not OK? Hmm, I can provide a checklist of key items. That way they can review their videotape to see whether their work matches the checklist items.

6. "Now about diagnostic feedback. If their work is not OK, will they be able to recognize what's wrong with it? Yes, I'm sure they will.

7. "And finally, corrective feedback. If they know what's wrong with their performance, can I count on them to know what to do about it? Yes, in this instance I can."

And that's it. My relevant practice description will look like this:

Relevant Practice Description:

Provide: R-Bander engine
Bench conditions
Tools
Manuals
Replacement parts
Checklist of key points
Video recording setup

Procedure: While being video-recorded, students will be asked to replace a series of parts. For feedback, they will review the tape and match their performance to a checklist of key points.

NOTE: The procedure is the same for any objective, regardless of whether it requires practice with hardware, various forms of human interaction, problem-solving, creativity, etc. Because relevant practice is the key to the development of competent performance that will endure in the face of adversity and the ravages of time, it is important to use a systematic procedure in the description of relevant practice. That way you won't leave out any of the key ingredients.

RELEVANT PRACTICE CHECKLIST

PERFORMANCE

1. What will trainees be doing when practicing the objective?

Writing relevant practice descriptions

2. What do the criteria in the objective talk about?

- Product of performance → | Save the Product | ✓
- Shape of performance → | Record the Performance |

CONDITIONS

3. What cues/conditions must you provide to make the practice possible (i.e. to meet the conditions stated in the objective)?

*Objective
Checklist
Something to write the description on*

FEEDBACK

4. How will you let trainees know their performance is OK or not OK (i.e. meets the standards of the objective)?

(Check as many times as needed.) →

• Description of correct responses	
• Modeling of desired performance	✓
• Checklist of criteria or key points	✓
• Description of desired performance	
•	

5. Given those standards, can you rely on trainees to decide if their performance is OK or not OK?

(YES) ┐   NO → | Have somebody (or something) provide the comparison of performance with standards | ☐

6. If the work is NOT OK, can you rely on them to decide what is wrong with the performance?

YES ┐   (NO) → Could they tell what's wrong if you model the performance and/or describe common problems?

If YES . . . | Provide modeling and/or description of common errors (problems) | ✓

If NO . . . | Have somebody diagnose the performance | ◯

7. If they know what is wrong with their performance, can you rely on them to know what to do to improve?

(YES) ┐   NO → Would they know how to improve if you modeled the performance and/or described typical remedies or solutions?

If YES . . . | Provide modeling and/or description of typical remedies or solutions | ☐

If NO . . . | Have somebody provide the remedies or solutions | ◯

8. Describe relevant practice. Account for all the checks made above, and include all items needed to provide the cues/conditions listed in item 3.

ADEQUACY | DIAGNOSTIC | CORRECTIVE

© The Center for Effective Performance. From *Instructional Module Development*, by R. F. Mager. 2nd Edition, Revised 1996.

Here is one more example.

Example #2: For an example of a totally different sort, let's use the skill of writing relevant practice descriptions.

Objective: Given an objective and a checklist, be able to write a description of relevant practice. Criteria: The description includes (a) the performance required, (b) critical cues and conditions under which the performance is expected to occur, and (c) sources of adequacy, diagnostic, and corrective feedback.

Thinking it through:

1. "Let's see now. The performance called for is that of *writing* a relevant practice description (#1 on the checklist on the preceding page).

2. "All the criteria describe the product of the performance, so there would be no need to record the performance for later review; that is, the objective calls for a written description rather than for the behavior that leads to that description. I'll save the product (the written description).

3. "To make practice possible, I'll have to provide one or more objectives for students to practice on and some checklists. That's about all.

4. "How can I provide the basis by which they can decide if their descriptions are OK or not OK? I can provide a model of a description. It would also help them decide whether their description is OK or not OK if I provided a completed checklist.

5. "Could students compare their descriptions with those two items and decide whether their performance is OK or not? Yes, they could.

6. "There's no problem about diagnostic feedback. If their performance is not OK, they can decide what's wrong with it, provided that I provide them with a model of a well-written relevant practice description and a description of the common errors.

7. "Would they know how to correct their work, given the model, the checklist, and the description of common errors? Yes, I know for certain they could do that. Therefore I don't have to provide an instructor or someone else to do it for them. And that's it. I'm now ready to write a brief description of what it would take to provide relevant practice."

Relevant Practice Description: To make practice possible, I need to provide (a) objectives, (b) checklists, and (c) something to write the description with and on. For feedback, I need to provide a model of the correct descriptions, completed checklists for each objective, and a description of common errors.

> **NOTE:** Though it takes only minutes to prepare brief relevant practice descriptions for a batch of objectives, it is a key step in the development process. Without it, it's just too easy to provide wrong practice, partial practice, or no practice at all in the important skills that need to be learned.

To Learn More: See Resources #13 and #16.

13
Content Derivation

Situation: You have derived objectives and know what it will take to provide relevant practice in those objectives. Now you want to derive the content that will bridge the gap between what students can already do and what they will need to know or do before being ready to practice the objective.

Content derivation is about closing gaps; it's about closing gaps between what people can already do and need to be able to do. Obviously (I hope), if there is no gap—no difference—between what they can do and need to be able to do, then there's no need for instruction. There's no need to impose on their, or your, valuable time to "teach" them what they already know.

That's a pretty powerful idea, because if it were actually put into practice, the amount of instruction in the world could be reduced at least by half. (Remember all that time you spent in classrooms expected to "learn" what you already knew?) So why don't we put it into practice? Two main reasons.

Why We Don't

Mostly for administrative convenience, we've traditionally clumped our instruction into "lessons" spanning a
pre-determined amount of time, usually fifty minutes. This
fifty-minute burst of instruction is usually referred to as a
"period." Because of this fixed-time lesson period, we've been
snookered into filling it with instruction, whether it was needed or not. You remember how it went:

> "I need to teach my students how to fill out these
> forms."

> "How long will that take?"

> "Not more than ten minutes, so I'll have to think of
> something else with which to fill the rest of the
> period."

> "Why don't you just dismiss them and let them get
> on with their lives?"

> "Hey, I can't just let them go after they've learned
> what they need to know."

> "Why not?"

> "Well, if somebody caught them wandering in the
> halls, or found out I was letting them go 'early,' I'd
> probably be fired." (Note: Some people refer to this
> situation as Adult Day Care.)

> "Oh."

There is another reason for excess instruction. Traditionally,
courses have been content-driven. That is, they have been
designed to teach as much content as the allotted time would
allow. As there is never any shortage of content, there is always

enough to fill the periods. ("Hmm. I'll include the first three chapters . . . leave out the fourth one . . . but be sure to include Chapter 7. That's my favorite topic . . . and besides, that topic has always been included in this course . . .")

Instruction Fills a Gap

Now instruction is designed to fill a need; rather than being designed to fill time, instruction is designed to accomplish important outcomes. This change in approach has changed the definition of a lesson:

Then: A lesson consisted of whatever amount of instruction filled a fixed time period. Thus, one student may need ten minutes to accomplish one objective, and another may require two hours, but what they got was a fixed time period. During a traditional lesson period, then, a student might master one or two objectives or only part of an objective. Time was fixed, and performance levels achieved were variable.

Now: A lesson consists of all the instruction and practice required to accomplish an objective. Thus, a lesson consumes whatever time it takes to reach mastery of an objective. To avoid confusion, this kind of lesson is called a "module" and includes all the stuff (instruction, demonstrations, practice) needed to promote mastery.

Selecting Content

Knowing that there is more to know than time to teach it— or interest in learning it—we are led to the conclusion that some content must be selected in, and some selected out; that choices will have to be made. How shall these choices be made? Actually, it's relatively easy.

You know what the important outcomes of the instruction should be, and you know more or less what your students will be able to do when they arrive. You know what "stuff" is available to you in the place where learning will occur, and the restrictions under which you will have to work. And you know what you will need to do to make relevant practice possible.

Deriving content for your instruction, therefore, amounts to reviewing the requirements for relevant practice, your target population description, and your hierarchy, and answering the question:

"Why aren't they ready to practice this objective NOW?"

What prevents them from being ready to practice as soon as they "enter" the module? The answer to that question will tell you what needs to be done to fill the gap between what students can now do and what they need to be able to do before being ready to practice the entire objective of the module.

The secret to deciding what to put in and leave out is to think about module content as the difference between what is already known and what needs to be known.

 What needs to be known
– <u>What is already known</u>
= What needs to be taught

Why Aren't They Ready to Practice Now?

Usually, when students aren't prepared to practice as soon as they enter a module, it is because there is something they don't know, such as *how* to do what they're expected to do, or because there are some safety precautions to learn or common errors they should be able to avoid, or because they don't yet know how to recognize what the desired performance looks and feels like (you don't want them to practice until they can monitor their own performance).

Sometimes, they aren't ready to practice now because they don't believe that what they're supposed to learn is valid; they don't believe it will work. For example, those who don't believe that self-managed work teams work aren't ready to practice working in such an environment. Something needs to be done before initiating practice exercises to convince them that such work teams do indeed work. (Perhaps a demonstration or a game would be appropriate.)

The Hard Part

The *procedure* for deriving content is relatively simple. The hard part is getting used to the idea that the current lesson probably contains quite a bit more content and activities than needed to accomplish the objective. (Not long ago my colleagues and I found that a group of manager trainees would become better performers if a well-tabbed three-ring binder of information were used to replace the *entire* 18-week course they were required to attend. This is not to suggest that any or all of *your* courses should or could be replaced by a job aid; it is only to remind you that efficient instruction often requires that at least some content in an existing course be dropped. Or saved for another course.)

You know how it goes. We all have our favorite topics, war stories, anecdotes, and demonstrations. We like the subject we are teaching, and we are all wrapped up in it. That being the case, discovering that some or all of what we do in the classroom can be better done *without* can be something of a blow to the ego. But if we are serious about making our instruction work, and work as efficiently as we can make it, then we need to think of those "extras" as obstacles rather than as necessities.

Module Components

Before being ready to practice content derivation, you need to have a list of module components. This list can be used as a job aid to remind you of the components that you should almost always include in a module and those that you might include. In the list of module components that follows, the items you should almost always include are shown in bold italics:

Prepare to Practice

These are components used to get students to the point where they are ready to practice the objective:

- ***Objective***

- ***Skill check description***

- ***Description of relevance (to the student)***

- Modeling (demonstration) of competent performance

- Instructional content (e.g., explanations, demos)

- Alternate resources

Relevant Practice

- ***Practice***

- ***Feedback***

Directions

- *Labels (e.g., module name and/or number)*

- *Directions to students (e.g., Go get . . .).*

- Directions to other instructors (e.g., To teach this unit you'll need the following materials, etc . . .).

Evaluation

- Self-checks

- *Skill check*

- *Self-evaluation explanations*

As you can see, the basic "floor plan" of a module is one that, at the front end, always informs students of the purpose and relevance of the lesson, and at the back end, always provides practice, feedback, and evaluation. In between, it offers whatever instruction is needed to get them from where they are to where they are ready to practice.

How to Do It

Now we're ready to consider the content-derivation procedure.

1. Review the objective.

2. Review your description of relevant practice for that objective.

3. Review your target population description and hierarchy, and note what students can already do when they enter this module.

4. Now answer the question, "Why aren't they ready to practice this objective *now*, at the time they begin work on the module?"

Imagine that a student has read the objective of the module and understands the importance of learning what the module has to teach. Why would that student not then be ready to practice that objective right then and there? That's the question to answer. To make it easier, break the question into smaller ones:

a. Do you believe they aren't ready to practice because they don't yet know *how* to do what they need to do? If so, what do they need to know how to do?

b. Do you believe they aren't ready to practice because there are one or more common errors they are likely to make in their present state of readiness? *Which* common errors?

c. Are they not yet ready to practice because they haven't yet been taught how to avoid certain dangerous situations? *Which* situations?

d. Are they not ready to practice because they don't yet know how to tell when their practice performance is OK or not?

The answers to these questions will tell you what content to include. Of course, if there is some "standard" content that isn't needed for answering these questions, **leave it out.** If you happen to leave something out that should be in, you'll find that out when you test the module. (Note: The reverse is not true. If you put something in that should be left out, testing may not expose it. So it's always better to start "lean" and add content and activities where necessary.) So there's little need to worry about making your instruction too skimpy.

NOTE: Here's an important tip on how to complete this step in the development process. Think of yourself as constructing a *summary* of lesson content, rather than an outline of content. Sure, your content will be presented in an organized manner when the module is *finished,* but it can be an obstacle to begin outlining before you have any substance to outline. So just list the content of the module as you answer the questions above. And when you find that for some objectives you will need only to provide practice and feedback, reward yourself. Your students will thank you for refraining from boring them with things they already know, and, if they're an enlightened lot, your administrators will thank you for getting the job done with a minimum of wasted motion.

"But I couldn't let my students out early," I hear you gasping. Of course not. After all, we're not *that* enlightened. But you *can* provide a menu of optional activities that students would find interesting and productive if they reach competence before the time is up. Or, you could teach them how to do a performance or goal analysis. *Everybody* ought to know how to do *that.*

Warning: Danger Ahead

The technique described in this chapter is a powerful one. Use it for the course that you develop, but be cautious about applying it to someone else's. Though you will be able to identify all sorts of unnecessary instruction once you've learned this technique, you would be wise to share that knowledge with great care. Nobody likes to be told that there is no need for some—or all—of what they are teaching.

Examples

Below are two examples of the content derivation procedure. The first contains a subject with which you're not likely to be too familiar, so you won't already be expert at the skills involved.

Figure 13.1

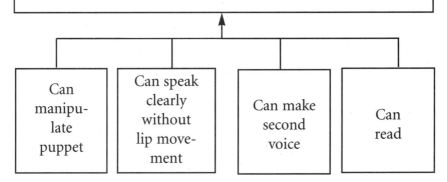

Given a script and a puppet, be able to act out the script. Criteria: The voices originate from the correct source, both vent and puppet react appropriately to the other's lines, and the vent does not anticipate (i.e., turn toward the puppet before the puppet begins to say a line).

| Can manipulate puppet | Can speak clearly without lip movement | Can make second voice | Can read |

Example #1: Ventriloquism involves a blending of the skills of manipulation (operating the puppet), voice, and lip control. Assuming students can read a script, once these three sub-skills are mastered they're ready to learn how to act out a script. Here's the objective, along with the hierarchy to show which skills must be in place before they enter this module. (By the way, ventriloquists often refer to themselves as "vents.")

Relevant Practice Description: Students will be provided with:

- a script,

- a puppet, and

- video equipment.

For feedback, they will review (with a coach) a videotape of their performance.

Content derivation: Having completed modules involving practice in the sub-skills, students now enter the module that will teach them to act out scripts. Why aren't they ready to practice as soon as they enter the module? They already know how to read, how to produce a voice for the puppet, how to speak using lip control, and how to manipulate the puppet's controls. So why aren't they ready to practice acting out a script?

They're not quite ready to practice because they may not know how to recognize correct performance when they see and hear it; that is, they may not yet be able to recognize a properly acted script. Any other reason they aren't ready to practice? None whatever. This is what a module to teach this objective would contain:

List of Module Content:

- The objective
  This is what you should be able to do . . .

- Performance-check description
  Here's how we'll check your competence . . .

- Description of relevance (rationale)
  This is why this skill is important to you . . .

- Demonstration of correct performance
  Here's what it looks and sounds like when done correctly . . .

- Practice in recognizing correct performance
  This will help keep you from practicing the wrong thing . . .

- Practice in performing, with feedback
  Now it's your turn . . .

- Skill check
  Let's find out how well you're doing . . .

(Ironically, ventriloquism provides a good example of how the *absence* of a critical piece of information can slow development of the skill. The critical information missing from every course I've seen is this: *The ventriloquist can never hear the illusion!* No matter how much they may practice, they will never "hear" the puppet's voice coming from the puppet, because they themselves are making that voice. Once this fact is known by the students they don't feel nearly as silly "talking to themselves;" they're more likely to practice, and they develop confidence in their skills much faster.)

Example #2: Let's use one of the same examples we used for relevant practice. Here's the objective again and the description of relevant practice for that objective:

> ***Objective:*** Given an objective and a relevant practice checklist, be able to write a description of relevant practice. Criteria: The description includes (a) the performance required, (b) critical cues and conditions under which the performance is expected to occur, and (c) sources of adequacy, diagnostic, and corrective feedback.

Relevant Practice Description: Students will be provided with:

- practice objectives,

- checklists, and

- paper to write on.

They'll be asked to write a relevant practice description.

For feedback, they'll be provided with:

- a model of a correct description,

- completed checklists for each practice objective, and

- a description of common errors.

Content derivation: Assume that the target population consists of people who have learned the skills described in the earlier chapters of this book. Now they are entering a module that intends to teach them how to derive descriptions of relevant practice from any objective. What should that module include? Without batting an eye, you should answer, "Practice." Right. No matter what else it includes, it will include practice in the objective and feedback (information) about the quality of the practice performances.

What else? Why can't these people practice the minute they walk into the module? Let's see . . . they already know how to use the relevant practice checklist. But they may not understand the importance of the procedure. Second, they may not know when to do it.

Anything else? No-o-o-o . . . wait. Common errors. Without some help they are likely to decide that they will need an instructor to provide feedback, when a less-expensive medium would do as well or better. Some practice examples using the checklist will prepare them to describe relevant practice effectively. And that's about all.

So here is what the module should include:

List of Module Content:

- The objective
  This is what you need to be able to do . . .

- Skill check description
  Here's how we'll check your competence . . .

- Description of relevance (rationale)
  This is why this skill is important to you . . .

- Explanation of the procedure and examples of the final product of the performance (i.e., some relevant practice descriptions)
  Here's how it's done . . .

- Practice with a series of objectives
  Now it's your turn . . .

- Skill check
  Let's find out how well you're doing . . .

The easiest way to learn the skill of content derivation is to practice by applying the procedure to someone else's objectives (quietly and discreetly). That way you'll get to practice the skill without having your ego bruised at the same time.

To Learn More: See Resources #5, #15, and #16.

14
Delivery System Selection

Situation: Having summarized the content for the modules, you are ready to decide how the instruction will be made available (delivered) to the students.

Now we arrive at what is probably the easiest part of instructional development, that of deciding what combination of things we will use to present the instruction and practice to the student. Though there is a priesthood that advocates charts and diagrams and that would have you believe this is a complicated affair, it isn't, for two main reasons. The first one is that you won't have so many choices available to you that you need a chart to help you decide which to use. Bluntly, if you only have two pairs of socks, it isn't hard to decide which to wear. The second reason is that by the time you have listed the things (materials, media, equipment) you need in order to provide practice and feedback, you'll seldom need anything more.

Why Delivery Systems?

So let's think a little about delivery system selection. First off, instructional technologists talk about delivery system selection rather than about media selection. That may seem as though they're using big words when smaller ones will do, but there is a reason. Media are message carriers: overhead projectors, chalkboards, computers, books, telephones, etc. They are the things on which you "write" the information you want to get to your students.

That's fine, except that we use more than those media to present instruction to our students. We often use people, either to present information, to participate in practice requiring one or more other people, or to assist in providing feedback. In addition, we often use "job things," such as machinery or equipment, to assist with instruction and practice. We use real automobiles for practicing auto mechanics and driving, real heads when practicing barbering, and real rifles when practicing marksmanship. Though these are critical requirements for proper presentation of the instruction, they are not media in the usual sense of that word. Hence the preference for "delivery system selection" rather than "media selection."

Features vs. Benefits

You already know most of what you need to know to select a suitable delivery system for the pieces of your course. You know the features of most of the available media, and you know what they are used for. That's a big leg up. Before we move on, though, it would be useful to think a moment about delivery system benefits.

One feature of hydrochloric acid is that it will eat through metal and cloth. Is that a benefit? Depends on what you're trying to accomplish. If you're trying to etch metal, it might be an advantage. If you're trying quench your thirst, it is definitely a disadvantage.

One feature of a lathe is that it can make round things. Is that an advantage? Depends on what you're trying to accomplish. If you're trying to make a table leg, it's an advantage. If you're trying to make a tin box, it's a useless feature.

One feature of a videotape is that it can call up a picture or motion sequence instantly. Is that an advantage? Depends on what you're trying to accomplish. If you're trying to present an illustration or demonstration, it can be an advantage. If you're trying to give students practice in tying knots, it is of little value.

So a feature of a delivery system is a characteristic. A feature becomes a benefit *only* when it will help accomplish a purpose. (If you keep that in mind, it will help you cut though the razzle-dazzle pitches of the bedoozlers and help keep your instructional costs down.)

Delivery System Selection Rule

Having said that, I can tell you that the rule in delivery system selection is to *select the most readily available and economical items that will provide the features called for by your objectives.* If you don't have any objectives, you'll be easy pickins for those who want to sell you more media hardware than you need. (Watch out for people who come to you with the direction, "We need you to do a video," or whatever the delivery system of the day is.)

> **NOTE:** A common error is to decide on a delivery system for a course, rather than for a single objective or module. This is an error because a *course* could easily consist of pieces that could be learned by computer or other "distance learning" method in combination with one or more classroom pieces where instructor support is available. The mistake is to think that a course has to be delivered by one medium or another, rather than by a *delivery system* consisting of a combination of methods and media.

How to Do It

Complete the following steps for each of your objectives. Believe me when I say it won't take long.

1. List the things that will be needed in order to provide relevant practice of the objective. To do this you would look at the things you listed while describing relevant practice requirements. Underline or circle the items that are *things* (e.g., disassembled crankshaft, drill press, computer keyboard, tool kit, head of hair).

2. Check that the items selected for practice are those that will allow students to make the most responses (get the most practice) per unit of time.

3. Then, if you have other items on the list, decide how you will provide them. For example, if your list says, "List of examples," or "Descriptions of problem situations," write a word or two beside it to say how you will present these items. Will the examples be presented in print? If so, what's the most convenient way to present that print? On paper? On film? On a video or computer screen? If your list says you need a person to assist with the practice, write who that person will be. A student? You? Someone else?

4. If the module will require content in addition to practice, review your content summary and say how you will present the content. Pick something that has the feature needed for the content involved.

5. Now think about your target population. Are the items you selected appropriate for them? If not, select something else with similar features. For example, if you have decided to present information in print but your audience can't read too well, pick a way to present the information that demands less reading.

6. Are the items you've listed available to you? If not, select something that is.

7. Are the items you selected easy for students to use, easy for them to get, and easy for them to operate? If not, try to find something more practical.

8. Finally, can you think of items that will give you the feature you need but that are less expensive to buy and to maintain? If so, change your original selection. For example, although you initially decided to present information by computer, second thought may convince you that a series of explained photos placed in a binder would be cheaper to produce and easier to maintain.

And that's it. Sure, there are times when a decision can be a little trickier to make, as when students to be trained are scattered around the world. But most of the time it will be a simple matter of selecting the things you will need (1) to provide relevant practice and feedback and (2) to present information, demonstrations, and examples. Try not to make it harder than it is.

Example #1: **TPop:** Machinist apprentices

Objective: On a metal lathe, be able to turn brass round stock to blueprint specifications.

Relevant Practice Description: Practice will require a lathe, brass round stock, blueprints. Feedback by instructor or assistant.

Delivery System: Metal lathe, brass round stock, blueprints, instructor or assistant. Micrometer for measuring finished practice work. Instructor to present content (to minimize reading load), supervise practice, and provide feedback.

Example #2:   **TPop:**   Instructional technology students

Objective: Given any objective, be able to prepare a skill check item to match that objective. Criteria: Each item calls for (a) the performance stated in the objective, under (b) the conditions described by the objective.

Relevant Practice Description: Students will be given objectives and asked to write test items. Feedback: model of correct or acceptable items; checklist of key features.

Delivery System: Sample objectives, checklist, and instruction presented in print.

Example #3:   **TPop:**   Sales trainees

Objective: Given product information and the product, be able to describe all key features and benefits to a customer. Criteria: All information presented is factually correct, and customer is not insulted or humiliated.

Relevant Practice Description: In private, another student will role-play a customer and the trainee will use product information and the product itself to practice describing features and benefits. The session will be videotaped. Feedback: Student and instructor will view tape while applying a checklist of criteria.

Delivery System: A student to role-play a customer; videotaping and playback equipment; product information in print; the product itself; instructor to provide information and feedback.

Example #4: **TPop:** Medical students

Objective: Given a functioning computer terminal with the Medical Information System application installed and running, be able to enter medical records and orders. Criteria: All entered data are correct and assigned to the correct patient.

Relevant Practice Description: In private, students will practice entering data into a computer terminal.

Delivery System: A computer terminal loaded with the MIS application system; sample records and data. Feedback to be provided by computer.

To Learn More: See Resources #4, #15, and #20.

15
Module Drafting

Situation: You have all your analysis documents, and you know what will be needed to provide students with practice. You are ready to draft instruction.

Once you have your TPop. description, objectives, relevant practice description, and content summary, your module will practically write itself. Well, all right, maybe that's a slight exaggeration, but not much. Think about it. Every module includes an objective, a skill check description, a description of relevance, practice, and feedback. You've already got those components, with the exception of the description of relevance. So you're almost ready to draft. True, instruction is as much art as science, but the components you already have will take a lot of the guesswork out of module drafting.

How It Goes

The way you actually put pencil to paper (or fingers to keyboard) when drafting a module will depend mainly on how the instruction will be delivered to the students. For example, if the instruction will be delivered by audio tape, you would draft the module in the form of a script. If it will be delivered

Figure 15.1 Basic Module Floor Plan

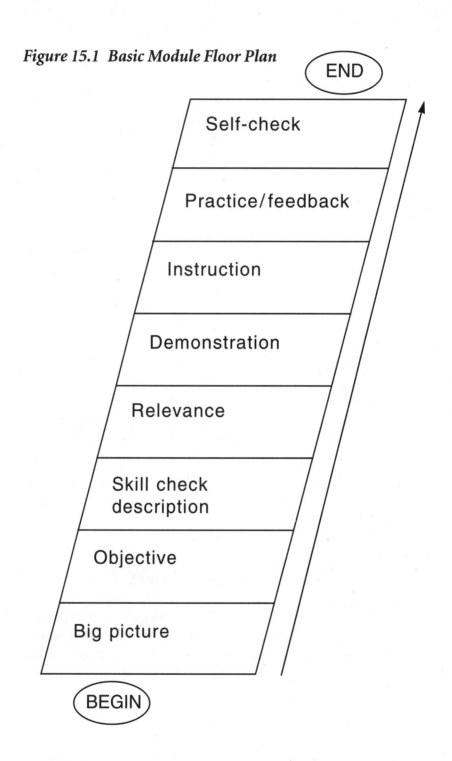

in print, you would write the instruction in a form intended to be read by students. If it will be delivered by computer, you will draft the individual screens that will be viewed by the students. If you will be the primary medium through which much of your instruction will be presented, you will most likely draft the module in the form of a lesson plan. But no matter how the instruction will ultimately be delivered, it begins with words on paper or screen.

The Floor Plan

Whether stated or not, every lesson or module has a floor plan. Something happens first, then something else happens, followed by something else. (How's that for profound?) The kind of floor plan you should be aiming for is one that includes the following components, in approximately the order shown in Figure 15.1.

Big picture: Reminds or shows students where they are in the larger scheme of the course. (Always included.)

Objective: Shows them the objective they are to accomplish, in terms they can understand. (Always included.)

Skill check description: Describes what students will have to do to demonstrate mastery of the objective.

Relevance: Explains and/or demonstrates why the accomplishment of this objective is important to *them.* (Always included.)

Demo: Shows what students will look like when performing the objective. (As needed.)

Instruction: Teaches students what they need to know before they can practice the objective. (As needed.)

Practice/feedback: Provides practice in the objective, along with timely information about performance and progress. (Always included.)

Self-check: Provides students a way to check whether they are ready to demonstrate their ability to perform as the objective requires. (As needed.)

NOTE: The skill check is not listed here as it is not contained in the body of the module.

Notice that the floor plan is not media specific; that is, it can be followed no matter who or what presents the instruction. No matter how the instruction is delivered, students should know at all times why they are doing what they're doing and how to tell when they're doing it satisfactorily, and they should be afforded an opportunity to practice until they *can* perform as desired.

Different lessons will have somewhat different floor plans, simply because the objectives are different and need different module components to accomplish them. Where one module will contain nothing but practice and feedback, another will have considerable guided presentation with information, examples, and demonstrations. Where one can be self-paced, another will need to be group-paced.

The goal is to let students in on the secret of what they will be expected to do, teach them whatever they need to know before they can practice the objective, provide practice and feedback, and then offer a skill check that will assess whether the objective has been accomplished. Use whatever combination of module components are needed to get you there.

Using Existing Material

It is a waste of time to "reinvent the wheel," so save time by locating existing material that can be used as part or all of the instruction. If it already exists, save your time and use it.

But use only those portions that are relevant to accomplishing the objectives. If you make students sit through an entire 30-minute video, for example, when only 3 minutes of it are relevant to the objective, you're not only wasting their time, you're squandering their motivation to learn. The same is true if you make them read an entire chapter of text when only one page will help accomplish an objective. The object is to locate potentially useful material and identify those pieces that will be directly useful in helping someone toward an objective.

When potentially useful materials include a textbook, you will seldom need to include the entire text. Textbooks are written in a sequence that makes sense to the author, or in a sequence that offers a "logical" presentation of the subject matter. They are seldom written in a sequence that is logical from the students' point of view. Further, they always contain a good deal more content than is needed to accomplish the objectives you have on hand. Therefore, when a textbook includes material useful for accomplishing one or more objectives, portions of that text will usually be used in a sequence other than the one in which it was written.

This is not a problem, of course, except when an accrediting agency wants to know why you are using the text "out of sequence" or not using a text at all. If your objectives have been derived from a good analysis, however, you will be able to show the rationale that caused you to select the content that you did. "Or," said one of the kindly souls who helped test the manuscript for this book, "you can always send them an 'approved' course outline and teach another."

How to Do It

Here are some suggestions about how to draft your modules:

1. Review the items on your relevant practice description, along with the module objective.

2. Locate existing instructional materials that might be useful, and compare them with the objective of the module they will be intended for. Mark those pieces or passages that will be relevant. Put the name or number of the objective on the appropriate passage (you should be able to associate each instructional action with the objective it is intended to accomplish).

3. Begin by writing the objective itself as it will be presented to the students; i.e., use language the students will understand at this point in their development.

4. Write the practice/feedback section (the back end) of the module. Say where students should get the practice equipment (if any) or other practice items they will need; tell them what to do with these things, and tell them how to evaluate their practice performance.

5. Write a description or describe a demonstration that will show why it is important *to the student* to develop the competence described by the objective. Remind students of where this objective fits into the larger scheme of things. (Note: Sometimes the importance of the objective is so obvious that little or nothing need be done here. You can't make a dead horse deader by beating it.)

6. If you will need to instruct before students will be ready to practice, and if you will be presenting the instruction

mainly by lecture, draft a lesson plan. Outline the content you will present in one column, and say what students will be doing in another column. List the examples you will use and any practice items that will be needed to teach students how to recognize competent performance of the objective. Make sure that students are active (doing something other than listening or taking notes) during at least two-thirds of the instructional period.

7. Regardless of the delivery system used to present the instruction to the students, be sure to include the directions that will tell them what to do. Include directions such as:

   - View videotape V-34.

   - Check your answers on the next page.

   - Click on the best response.

   - Have an instructor review your findings.

   - Read pages _____ before practicing.

   - Get the performance check and do what it says.

   - Ask an instructor to set up the equipment so that you can demonstrate your mastery of the objective.

   - When you need an instructor, click on the black icon.

   - Complete the following practice exercise.

   - Ask another student to fill out Checksheet W as you conduct the practice interview.

- Ask a student to role-play a customer as you practice the selling skill.

- Complete pages 5-8 in the workbook.

- Ask an instructor to demonstrate _____.

- Give your practice videotape to an instructor for review.

- Sign up for the group practice session.

- Sign up for the brazing demonstration.

In other words, make sure that the module directs the student to the instructional sources and to the practice. When few instructional resources exist, they will either have to be created and included in the module or presented by you. In the latter case the module would indicate to students when they should be ready for your instruction on the topic being studied.

8. Finally, write what students should do to demonstrate their achievement of the objective. If this will be in the form of a written test, tell them where to get it and how it will be administered. If a demonstration of skill on a machine or with a process is in order, tell them where to go and what to get. In other words, state what they will have to do to be eligible to begin another module.

If You're Stuck

Sometimes our pencils go limp or our brains turn to mush. In other words, sometimes we get stuck. Fortunately, there is a simple solution. Write the practice section of the module first.

You already have a description of relevant practice, so drafting the practice section should be easy and help get you started. Say what equipment and supplies students will have to get, say where to get them and what to do with them, and describe how feedback will be made available. Once you've done that, you will have a much clearer picture of what the remainder of the module should be like.

To be perfectly honest, you might consider writing the practice section first for all the modules you develop. Here's why: Just as the writing of a criterion test item is a good way to find out where the objectives need sharpening, writing the practice section is a good way to sharpen your understanding of what else, if anything, will need to be added to the module in the way of content. Just as the result (the objective) tells you what kind of practice you need, the practice will suggest the additional content you will need.

The Lesson Plan

A lesson plan is an instructional prescription, a blueprint describing the activities the instructor and student may engage in to reach the objectives of the course. Its main purpose is to prescribe the key events that should occur during the module. If the instructor finds it necessary to deliver most or all of the instruction through lectures, the lesson plan is the guide to the instructor's actions. When a module is put into the hands of the student, it performs a similar function: it tells the student what to do, where to locate the instructional resources, how to practice, and how to demonstrate competence when ready.

The precise format of the lesson plan is less important than making sure it performs its important functions. As you have already listed or summarized the content of each lesson, the task of preparing a module will be relatively simple. Whatever the format used, however, make sure it emphasizes what *students* will be doing rather than what the instructor will be doing. That way you won't be likely to fall into the trap of developing a course principally on the basis of what you *like* to do rather than on the basis of what students need to do to accomplish the objectives.

Example #1: **Hairstyling.** This example is a module written in the form of a lesson plan for use by someone delivering the instruction by lecturing.

Objective: Using hair-shaping implements and supplies, be able to cut the client's hair to the requested hairstyle.

Instructor Activity	Student Activity
1. Explain purpose of the skill and when it is used. Describe objective and hairstyles to be learned. Describe skill check.	
2. Demonstrate use of each hairstyling tool.	
3. Hold up hairstying tools and ask students to name each.	Respond with names of tools. Ask questions during demo.
4. Demonstrate and explain first hairstyle.	Ask questions during demo. Students practice on each other.
5. Explain and illustrate common errors and how they are avoided.	
6. Correct student errors.	
7. Demonstrate and explain second hairstyle.	Ask questions during demo.
8. Correct student errors.	Students practice on each other.
9. Describe common errors and how to avoid or correct them on second hairstyle.	Students ask questions.
10. Initiate individual performance test.	Students claiming to be ready are tested first, while others continue practicing.
(Continue with additional hairstyles, if any.)	

Sometimes it may be appropriate to add an "Equipment and Materials" list somewhere in the lesson plan. This will provide a ready checklist of the items that will be needed for completing the lesson. Some instructors prefer to add this list near the top of their lesson plans, while others prefer to add a third column to the lesson plan itself. This third column is used as space in which to list items (things) needed for each of the lesson components.

The main thing to keep in mind in lesson planning is to adopt a format that will help you rather than get in your way. And remember: There is no *instructional* reason why all your lesson plans should look alike. Though you may have a bureaucratic mandate to adopt a particular format, you can always fulfill that requirement and then build a lesson plan in a format that will help you *and* meet the needs of the objectives to be taught.

Examples #2 and #3

The next two examples are from a criterion-referenced module (i.e., instruction is designed to accomplish specified objectives). The first may be partly self-paced; the second is entirely self-paced. The module was borrowed from the nine-module course entitled "Instructional Module Development," by R. F. Mager. It is intended for the population of students learning how to be instructional developers and shows them how to prepare the instructions that will be needed when their course will be taught by someone *other than themselves.*

Example #2: Prepare Implementation Instructions.

This example shows the module in lesson-plan format for use by someone delivering the instruction by lecture.

Objective: Given a module of instruction that accomplishes its objective, be able to prepare the directions and instructions that will enable the module to work when administered by another instructor.

Instructor Activity	Student Activity
1. Explain importance of the activity.	
2. Hand out example module.	Read example module. List information needed in preparation for teaching the sample module.
3. Ask students to list the items and information they feel they would need before they could teach the sample module.	
4. Ask students to volunteer the information on their lists, and ask other students to add items or to comment.	Discuss the lists.
5. Hand out Implementation Checklist. Answer questions about the items.	Ask questions.
6. Ask each student to draft the implementation items and instructions needed by another instructor expecting to teach the module.	Write implementation material.
7. Have student give his or her module and implementation instructions to another student. Ask student to list missing items.	Review someone else's module and implementation material and list missing items.
8. Discuss results of the practice.	
9. Administer criterion test.	Prepare implementation material for a second module the student has already drafted.

Example #3: Prepare Implementation Instructions.

Here is the same module as in Example #2, but written in a form to be handed to students who are working through a criterion-referenced, self-paced course in which they are learning to develop modules for similarly conducted courses. In these courses students work at their own pace until they can demonstrate achievement of an objective, and then they move on to the next module.

As you read through the module, see if you can identify the following components (remembering that the skill check itself is not part of the body of the module):

- Objective

- Criterion test description

- Description of relevance

- "Prepare to practice" content

- Practice

- Source of feedback for the practice

- Directions to the student

- Job aid to guide performance

Here is the module in its entirety:

Module: Prepare Implementation Instructions.

Objective: Given a module of instruction that accomplishes its objective, be able to prepare the directions and instructions that will enable the module to work when administered by another instructor.

Criteria: The directions and instructions answer questions about (a) what to collect in the way of materials, supplies, equipment, resources; (b) how to prepare the equipment, materials, and space for use; (c) how to answer common questions and handle common problems; (d) how and when to suggest alternative resources and activities, if any; and (e) how to review performance.

Skill Check: To demonstrate your competence, you will be asked to prepare the directions and instructions that would be needed to allow your module to be administered by someone else. You will be asked to: Locate two participants willing to assist, give one of them your module and additional materials, and ask him/her to serve as instructor. Ask the other to serve as student. You'll observe the session (without interrupting) and make notes of any assistance you need to offer to make the session work.

(**NOTE:** Here's where the instruction for this module begins.)

Why Are Implementation Instructions Important?

The most terrific and fantastic machine in the whole world is useless unless someone knows how to operate it. Unless someone knows what to do with it, it will just sit there gathering dust. Worse, without good operating instructions, people

Example #3, continued:

are likely to misuse those wonderful devices. They may even damage themselves or others in the process.

Modules of instruction are like that. It's one thing to make them work while they are under *your* control. It's something else to be able to make them work when they are under *someone else's* control. It's one thing for you to be able to smooth the path of the learner by offering a resource here or by anticipating a problem there. It's something else to be able to get others to do likewise.

You have done the first part . . . the big part; you've created modules. You've tested them and revised them and you've made them work. Now it's time to add whatever is needed so that someone else can make them work. And if there is one thing you can believe, it's this: Murphy's Law lives; if anything can go wrong, it will. People will administer your module at the wrong time, in the wrong way, without providing the necessary materials or supplies or space. But it's even worse than that. Unless you provide instructors with all the information they need to implement the module correctly, they won't administer it incorrectly . . . *they won't use it at all.* It will go right up on the shelf. After all, the instructor "knows" how to teach the material in your module, and since that way is familiar, it will take precedence over your module . . . unless you make the process of module administration clear and complete, put the words into their mouths that they will say to their students, and tell them exactly what they need to do to prepare and to administer the module.

But what else is there, you may be wondering? After all, you have created modules that are self-contained in that they only need an instructor to provide feedback for practice. What else is there? Think about it this way.

Example #3, continued:

The Slot in the Wall

Imagine that you will slip your module through a slot in the wall, to be administered by an instructor on the other side. You can peek through a little window to see what is happening, but you can neither talk to the instructor nor use body language to signal what should be done next. All you can do is to slip your package through the wall and watch.

What would happen? The instructor picks up the package and fingers through the pieces. What will he or she do then? Would this instructor know whether there are some preparations that need to be made before giving the module to a student? How would this instructor know what to read or look at first? Would this person know:

- what to collect in the way of equipment, supplies and materials, or resources?

- what sort of environment to arrange?

- how to prepare equipment for practice?

- how to schedule students for practice on scarce equipment or other resources?

- how to anticipate and handle common problems or questions?

- how to review practice exercises, if any?

- how to review skill check performance?

- when and how to suggest alternative resources and activities?

Example #3, continued:

If the answer to any of these questions is "No," then something is missing and needs to be added. Usually, this will consist of a "Note to Course Manager" in the self-evaluation material or in the Course Manager Manual. Sometimes it will mean drafting a list of supplies that need to be collected. When students will have to be scheduled for time on equipment or for use of a room, it may mean drafting a sign-up sheet or informing instructors on how the scheduling should be done and how it should be used. And unless you prepare and provide the answers to the above questions, you should expect that your module will be laid aside rather than used as you intend.

You see, you are now dealing with a target population different from the one for which your module was created. You are dealing with the audience of instructors, rather than of students. You are now trying to package your module in such a way that the instructor population will know how to implement the instruction you created for your student population. Quite a different matter from "packaging" a module that will teach an objective. It's the difference between creating a highly flexible computer and creating the instructions that will allow someone to use it. It's the difference between creating a gourmet dinner and creating the recipe that will enable others to re-create that same gourmet dinner. It's the difference between creating a fantastic jazz solo and writing the sheet music that will cause others to play it the same way you do.

So to make your module usable by others, it will need to be accompanied by whatever directions/instructions that will allow others to follow the same implementation steps that you do. And those instructions and directions will need to be just as specific as you can make them. If you are writing instructions for a role-play, for example, rather than simply suggest that the instructor "Give the participants a little pep talk to get

Example #3, continued:

them in the mood," tell them exactly what to say. Put the words right in their mouths.

"Say to the participants the following . . ." Whenever you have to provide directions or instructions for someone else to give to students, be as precise as you can.

Here's an example:

For the Instructor:

1. Get the practice envelope marked R-1, and check to see that it contains the five drawings labeled 1 through 5.

2. Set the controls on the white print machine to accept a medium-density drawing.

3. Hand the envelope to the student, and say to the student: "Here are five typical jobs to be run on your white print machine. Tell me how you would set up the machine to run ten copies of each drawing."

4. Write the student's response in the space provided on the response sheet.

5. If the student's response for the first drawing is correct, say "Good." If it is not correct, tell him or her what the correct response is. (This is a practice session, not a test.)

6. Provide this type of feedback as each item is completed.

Though you may not have to do this sort of thing often, when you do, be precise. Before drafting your own implementation material, it will be useful to look at a few other examples.

Example #3, continued:

Here Is What to Do

1. Ask the course manager to lend you a copy of the *Course Manager Manual* booklet for this course.

2. Review the table of contents to note the types of information contained in the manual.

3. Read the section labeled "Module Notes." Note the types of information and comments included there.

4. Review your own *Course Control Documents* booklet. What type of information included there would help an instructor to administer your module?

5. Borrow the module of a colleague who is also working through this course. Pretend that you will be teaching that module as part of your own course. List the types of additional information that you would want to have before administering the module to a group of students in *your* learning environment.

6. If you have followed the steps described above, you should be ready to tackle the instructor directions for your own module. It may be easier to do if you break the task into four sections and deal with them one at a time.

   a. *Materials Collection*

   In a large number of instances, a module will simply need to be made available to students; not only is the module self-contained, but all the items needed to

Example #3, continued:

make the module function are enclosed within it. Others require the use of equipment or materials or resources. Someone has to be directed to collect these items before the module can be used.

Is everything the student will need contained within the module itself, within the package of print or tapes or disks you have drafted?

Does the student need to use something, fix something, adjust something, fill out something? List those somethings as the items that will need to be collected before the module can be attempted.

b. *Preparation*

If you only have one Limpmobile for each ten students, and if each student has to practice replacing the In-law Ejector, someone is going to have to schedule the practice time. Can it be accomplished by a simple sign-up sheet hung on a door or wall? Will another method be needed? However it is to be accomplished, an instructor or someone will have to prepare the mechanism by which the practice will be scheduled.

Will students need to fill out forms? Will they need to travel to where the equipment they are learning about is located? If so, where will the forms be placed? How will students get to the equipment location?

Will students be expected to practice troubleshooting equipment? If so, what kind of practice "bugs" (troubles) should the instructor insert? In what order? Clear directions will need to be prepared for the instructor preparing to administer the module.

Example #3, continued:

c. *Implementation*

Sometimes the instructor will have a role to play while the module is being attempted by a student. It may be that the course manager will be expected to review a practice exercise or perhaps to demonstrate a procedure. If so, the course manager should be prepared for these activities; instruction on how to handle these activities should be made available.

Are there typical questions that students will ask, common problems to watch out for? Are there typical errors during practice? If so, draft some comments designed to help the course manager implement the module the way you would like to have it implemented.

d. *Evaluation*

When a skill check involves responding to a number of questions for which there are right or wrong answers, students are encouraged to compare their responses with those that are contained in the self-evaluation materials. But what about all those instances in which a skill check asks for original or creative responses or asks students to write something, draft something, make something, say something? The course manager will be expected to review the work and to determine whether the performance is OK or not yet OK and provide diagnostic, and perhaps corrective, feedback.

The skill check for this module, for example, asks you to prepare the directions and instructions that may be needed to implement your module and to take that material along with your module to a course manager for review. Two things have been done to prepare the course manager to handle this review: (1) A Module Note in

Example #3, continued:

the *Course Manager Manual* describes the activity and offers hints in handling typical omissions; (2) A checklist of items to look for is included in the self-evaluation material.

  Do you have self-evaluation material written for your skill check? Is it self-explanatory, or would a course manager benefit from some directions or comments from you about how to proceed?

Your Turn

If you have followed the instructions on the previous pages, you should be ready for the Skill. It will ask you to prepare the items that will be needed before the module can be implemented by someone other than yourself. You will be expected to hand your module and the instructions to a colleague, who will in turn be expected to administer the module successfully to another workshop participant ... *without help from you.* Use the *Module Implementation Checklist* as a guide.

Module Implementation Checklist

1. If materials are used in the module, is there a materials list for the course manager?

2. Are there instructions on how materials should be set out or prepared for use?

3. If equipment is involved, are there instructions about how to locate and set up the equipment?

4. If troubleshooting practice is involved, are there instructions on exactly what practice troubles to use and in what order? Are there instructions on how to set up the practice session?

Example #3, continued:

5. If equipment or space must be shared, is there information on how to schedule the time?

6. Is there information on how to handle common questions or problems?

7. Are there directions on how to handle practice exercises?

8. Is there information about how and when to suggest the use of alternate resources and activities?

9. Are there suggestions on how to review criterion test performance?

This was an admittedly long example, but I feel that you deserve to see what a complete example of a criterion-referenced module might look like. Other such modules may be presented by different combinations of media, but all would contain the necessary module components.

You should now have all the knowledge you need to use the Module Checklist on the next page.

MODULE CHECKLIST

Use this checklist to assure that your modules include all the components they need for facilitating the performance you want.

<u>DOES THE MODULE:</u>

1. Have a title or label? _____
2. Show the student the objective in terms he or she can understand? _____
3. Describe what the student will have to do to demonstrate competence? _____
4. Describe or illustrate the place or relevance of the objective in the larger scheme of things (if needed)? From the student's point of view? _____
5. Demonstrate or show what the student will be like when performing the objective (if demonstration is needed)? _____
6. Prepare the student to practice? _____
7. Include relevant practice of the objective? _____
8. Provide the tools, items, objects needed for relevant practice? _____
9. Provide relevant feedback for the practice? _____
10. Practice what it teaches? Is it free of modeling errors? _____
11. Show trainees exactly what to do or where to go at each point in the module? i.e., are there adequate directions? _____
12. Help trainees decide when they are ready to demonstrate their competence? _____
13. Use the simplest possible delivery system? _____
14. Flow from beginning to end? Does it have continuity? _____
15. Contain no unnecessary obstacles between the student and the learning? _____
16. Have a criterion test and associated self-evaluation (feedback)? _____

If you follow the how-to-do-it steps described in this chapter, you will find the job of drafting your instruction greatly simplified.

NOTE: This procedure will in no way restrict your ability to make your instruction interesting and motivating. On the contrary, students always seem more interested in instruction they perceive as being relevant to their needs or desires. So don't be concerned that "lean" development will take the heart out of the instruction. No matter how tight you make your instruction, there will always be some slack in it for transitions, extra examples, war stories, humor, and anecdotes. But with properly constructed instruction, you will always know that no matter how much or how little you embellish, the instruction will do what it is supposed to do.

To make your instruction work, make sure you teach things not yet known, provide the instruction needed to get students ready to practice the objective, provide practice and feedback, and then take steps to find out whether the student can perform as desired.

To Learn More: See Resource #16.

16
Tryout

Situation: Modules are in the process of being drafted or have already been drafted. You want to know how well they work and what to do to improve them.

Unless you've got a license in mind reading, tryout is the touchstone to instructional success. Oh, sure, I know there isn't time for "that sort of thing." I know that lead times are usually short and instructors don't have much time for course development. But that doesn't change the fact that tryout is the key to success. I know you would agree with me if I were talking about products other than instruction—in many instances you wouldn't even touch the product if you thought it *didn't* go through tryout.

"Has this airplane been tested?"

"What?"

"Has this plane gone through tryouts to make sure it works?"

"We don't have time for that. We consider the maiden flights the tryouts."

"Oh."

Or,

"Has this medicine been through clinical testing?"

"What?"

"Has this medicine been tested on humans?"

"No need for that. We'll know it works if nobody dies from it."

"Oh."

You see the point. No matter how good we are at instructional development, we still don't know for sure whether, or how well, the instruction will work until we try it out. If there is no time for a tryout before a full class of students shuffles in, then the maiden course will have to be considered the tryout. But don't set the materials in concrete until the results of at least one tryout are in. Make only enough copies of things to take you through the first cycle. Believe me, you will want to fix some things before anyone else sees or experiences it. I'd rather have the errors and opportunities for improvement pointed out *before* "going public" rather than after, wouldn't you? Wouldn't you like to know what the critic will say *before* opening night, rather than after—so you can have a chance to smooth out the lumps?

How to Do It

You already know how to conduct a course, so there's little to learn before being ready to conduct a tryout. The main thing you need to know is that the answers to your tryout questions are readily available. Whatever you may want to know about how well your module is working or how well it fits your audience, your students will be your best source of information. And why not? The instruction is being developed for their benefit, so they should be consulted on how well the job has been done.

After all, when your physician whacks you on the back and asks, "Did that hurt?" he or she is asking you for information. When a shoe salesclerk asks you how the fit feels, information from the customer is being requested. So be sure to include your students as the key source of information about how well the instruction fits and about how well it works.

There are two kinds of tryout. The first is a check of the individual module or lesson plan during the development process. It involves trying it out on one person at a time, until all the major kinks have been removed. The second is a tryout of the entire course. Here's how.

For Self-Paced Courses

Try out each module on at least one person before you test the entire course. Find someone (*one* person at a time; if you use large samples at this point, you'll be wasting your time and theirs) as close to your target population as possible. If a member of your target population is available, fine. But it isn't necessary. As long as you find someone similar to your TPop. who cannot perform the objective, that person will be a big help. But do a tryout even if the person most available cannot understand the technical language of the module or doesn't fit the TPop. in other ways. That individual will still locate oversights and errors that you will want to correct before you let anyone else see your work. Here are the steps:

1. Locate someone who is willing to work through the module. (We will refer to this person as the "tester.")

2. Write out your instructions to that person. Explain that this is a test of the instruction rather than of the person, and that you are looking for ways to improve the module. Explain that he or she should make a mark on any part of the material that is difficult or that is a turnoff, or that is bothersome for any other reason. If the material is being presented by a computer or other device, or by an instructor, ask students to make notes (on the pad you provide) of their comments as they go.

3. Let the person read the instructions, and answer any questions that might arise.

4. Give him or her the materials, show where things are located (if appropriate), and then back away.

5. Sit in the corner and *do not interfere* with the tryout. Don't do anything that might be distracting, such as practice your golf swing or tap your pencil. Do not offer information when you see that the tester is in trouble. Instead, make a note on your pad.

6. If you are asked a question, answer it and then *make a note of it*. Always make a note about the reason for your interventions. These notes will tell you what you will need to do to smooth out the instruction. If the tester turns to you and asks a question, one of my colleagues suggests saying, "Do what you think the module is telling you to do," and then noting what he/she does.

7. When the tryout is over, *listen* to the comments of the tester. You can always ignore the suggestions if you choose; you cannot ignore suggestions you don't have.

8. When the tryout is finished, thank the tester profusely, and be sure to add the tester's name to the list of those who helped in shaping the instruction. Be sure to spell the name correctly.

For Instructor-Led Courses

If yours is mainly an instructor-led (lecture-driven) course, the tryout pattern is somewhat different.

1. Find a colleague willing to help.

2. Ask the colleague to compare each of your lesson plans to its objective and answer the following questions:

   a. Will students be shown the module objective in terms they will understand?

   b. Will the importance of the module be explained or demonstrated?

   c. Is practice offered in the objective? Is feedback offered?

   d. Does there appear to be more content than needed? Less? About the right amount?

   e. Will students be doing something other than listening to the instructor for more than 50 percent of the time?

Notice that this procedure does not ask your colleague to dictate or in any way interfere with your style or method of instruction. It merely provides an external pair of eyes that will help you to spot the holes you may have missed while putting the modules together.

Technical Review

It is always helpful to have a colleague or two look through the material to make sure there are no technical errors. If you really need help with the technical accuracy, you might consider a colleague review before the module tryout. If you are the technical expert and just want to make sure you haven't made any big boo-boos, then do it after the tryout. The procedure is the same as that described above for the self-paced course, except that you would not need to watch the review. You would hand, or send, the materials to the colleague along with appropriate instructions and request for assistance. And you would be certain to follow Step 8 in the previous instructions (i.e., thank profusely and record the person's name, correctly spelled).

Caution #1: Though asked for comments on technical accuracy, your colleague may feel compelled to make comments on your instructional approach: "That's not the way I teach"; "It's never been done that way"; "You've left out some of the theory." Your response should be to smile, thank the individual for the assistance, and then feel free to ignore all but those comments that relate to technical accuracy.

Course Tryout

When each of the modules has been tried out at least once and revised on the basis of the information collected, and you have sequenced the individual lessons into a course, you will be ready for a full-course tryout. Here's how.

1. Collect all the things you will need to conduct the course. Refer to the modules; they should each begin with a list of the items required for the instruction. If you don't have everything you need and that you think is reasonable to expect, or that you were counting on, use

the professional approach to procurement: Hold your breath, throw a tantrum, throw yourself at the feet of your department head or manager, and plead for the items you need. If you're in the military, the term "midnight requisitioning" may be appropriate here.

2. Duplicate enough materials for the first run-through. Not more. Get a large stamp that says DRAFT and stamp all the materials.

3. If other instructors or assistants will participate in the tryout, walk them through the procedures. If they are going to assist with the instruction itself, give them some practice in handling the portions they will be assigned.

4. Make a copy of the course procedures (described in Chapter 18) for each student.

5. Put everything in its place, and then check your preparation.

6. Get a notebook (five by eight inches or larger) and in big letters write on it, "Comments and Suggestions."

7. Place this book in a prominent place in the classroom (your desk is fine for this).

8. When the students arrive, welcome them, tell them which course this is (in case they thought they were waiting for a bus to Fresno), hand out copies of the course procedures, and explain them briefly.

9. Tell them that this is an update of an existing course, or a new course, whichever is true. Then tell them that you are sincerely asking their help in improving it. If it's an update, assure them that what they're getting is at least as

good as it used to be. Show them the comments book and encourage them to write their comments in it. If they make suggestions directly to you during the course, thank them and then suggest they write in the notebook. They will feel more rewarded for daring to make a suggestion.

10. Conduct the course—according to the procedures you have given the students.

11. If the course is more than one day long, and more than one instructor is conducting the course, schedule end-of-day debriefing sessions.

12. When it is over, review the comments in the notebook, along with the notes you made yourself.

13. Make the indicated revisions. If there were a lot of revisions, then consider the next cycle a second tryout and repeat the procedure. Go to press only when the indicated revisions are minor or cosmetic in nature, rather than substantive.

14. Provide feedback to those who helped with the tryout(s). When possible, give each an autographed copy of the final product (or at least some part of it).

Cosmetic vs. Substantive Comments

What's the difference between cosmetic and substantive revisions? *Substantive* comments suggest changes to the content or the sequence of the content. Suggestions that you should move this chapter from here to there, or to delete unneeded material, or that you correct technical errors, are suggestions to make substantive changes. Keep testing until the number of substantive comments drops to zero.

Cosmetic comments refer to style. When testers pick at your choice of words, or at your manner of writing, or your "political correctness," you are hearing comments about the cosmetics of your course. These are comments you may or may not want to do something about.

One mark of the professional is the insistence on tryouts before "going public." Just as plays are tried out off-Broadway, night-club acts polished in the smaller lounges, and products tested until they meet specifications, instruction (as well as job aids, questionnaires, and surveys) is put through tryout before being considered ready for regular consumption. The time you spend on tryout is time you will never regret.

To Learn More: See Resource #16.

17
Sequencing

Situation: Modules have been drafted, and you want to determine the most efficient sequence in which they should be devoured by your students.

Since not everything can be learned at once, instruction must be offered in some sort of sequence. One thing must come before another. How shall we decide on the order in which the students should address the individual lessons? By trying to determine what the most beneficial sequence of events would be from the *student's* point of view.

Sequence and Order

It would be useful to begin by considering the nature of sequence and order. Think about it this way. Imagine yourself sitting at a table that has a box of children's blocks on it. Your task is to make a single stack of blocks. Obviously, you must place them one at a time; first you must put down one block, then you set another one on top of it, and so on. But you don't necessarily have to pile them in any order. As long as one block is on top of another, it doesn't matter which block comes before some other block.

If, on the other hand, you were asked to pile them up alphabetically, then the order in which you piled them *would* matter. You'd have to put down the A before the B, and the B before the C.

So What?

What does this have to do with instructional sequencing? Just this. There is always a sequence of lessons; that is, one lesson always follows another. But there doesn't always have to be a *prescribed* order; that is, they don't always have to be studied in the same sequence by each and every student. To understand this point, look back to the example skill hierarchy in Chapter 8. Notice how many of the skills are independent of one another—that is, shown side by side. Though all of these skills must be learned before the terminal objective (the one at the top) can be practiced, the *order* in which they are learned doesn't matter—any one of them could be productively learned before any of the others is attempted. And when the order doesn't matter, it is better to let the students decide on the sequence in which they will do the learning. Having some control helps their motivation to learn.

Traditionally, the only guidelines for sequencing instructional activities have been, "Teach your lessons in a logical sequence," and "Teach from the simple to the complex." That's about as helpful as telling someone to "be good." Those rules are just too vague and have too many possible meanings. After all, *everyone* believes they teach in a logical sequence. But if you look to see what they are in fact doing, you will find that some use a historical sequence, teaching that which happened first, what happened next, and so on. Others teach "theory" before practice. Others claim to teach from the simple to the complex, but usually use a sequence that is opposite to the one they would use if guided by the *students'* definition of simple to complex. And so on.

Fortunately, we can now take most of the guesswork out of sequencing. Here's how.

How to Do It

The goals are to inflame the students' interest in the subject, keep their motivation high, and make sure they have accomplished the course objectives by the time they leave.

1. Begin the course with the topic of highest interest to the students, regardless of where the full treatment of that topic falls within the course. For example, imagine you have signed up for a course in locksmithing because you want to learn to pick locks like the detectives on TV. You show up for the course ready and eager to get started. You sandpaper your fingertips and get ready to pick your first lock. But the first week is on the history of locksmithing, the second covers the theory of locks, and the third is on assembly and disassembly. By then there are cobwebs under your armpits, mildew on your brain, and you're wondering why you came.

    No matter what the item of highest interest to your students may be, begin there. Jerk them into the course by giving them a taste of the goodies. (As one of the testers of this book remarked, "A picture is worth a thousand words; an experience is worth a thousand pictures.") Spend at least half an hour on that topic, and let them know that there will be more about it later. Then, try to sprinkle the items of high student interest throughout the course.

One instructor I talked with recently couldn't understand why students were uneasy with his course at the
end of the first day. Though it is a well-designed and
well-developed course, they still felt frustrated. "What
they want to do is to share their experiences with one
another," he said. (These were auto dealers attending a
seminar.) "If that's what they really want," I suggested,
"start there. Begin with a session during which they are
encouraged to share. Then let them know there will be
time for more of that, either in the classroom or in the
lounge." Don't keep the good stuff hidden until students
have "learned the basics." It works like magic.

2. Move from the big picture into the details. Since you
   know the subject, *you* can think comfortably about any
   piece of it and understand where it fits into the whole.
   Students don't have that luxury. They don't know the
   territory; they need a map. That's what you're there for.
   So start with the biggest picture and then work toward
   the details.

   If equipment is involved, give your students an opportunity to get their hands on it before they do anything else
   and, if possible, teach them how to operate it before you
   teach them anything about how it works. The rule is this:

   > Don't expect students to think about the
   > abstract until they have something concrete to
   > think abstractly about.

   In other words, give them some experience with the
   "things" they're there to learn about—get the concepts
   into their muscles—before expecting them to be able to
   handle the abstract concepts relating to those things. For
   example, if you're teaching people how to repair engines
   or amplifiers, get them to see and feel and hear those

things before you talk to them about nomenclature or how they work.

3. Give your students as many opportunities as possible to decide for themselves which module to work on at any given time. It will help keep them motivated. Naturally, the constraints imposed by the skill hierarchy and by your environment will dictate how many such options you can offer. The easiest way to let them know what the options are is by means of a course map. Such a map shows the entire course at a glance and shows which sequencing options are available at any given point in the course. Even if you don't have the freedom to provide sequencing options at the moment, you should know how to read and construct a course map.

Figure 17.1

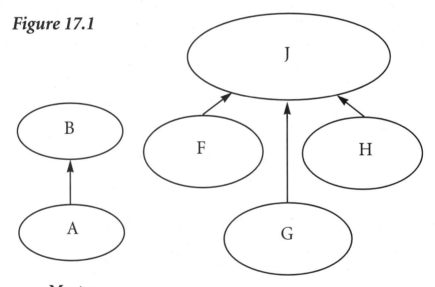

Master Module A before attempting Module B

Master Modules F, G, and H before attempting Module J. Modules F, G, and H may be mastered in any order.

Creating a Course Map

A course map is a simple graphic device through which to communicate some of the course procedures to your students. It shows each of the modules and the dependency relationship between them. For example, an arrow between two units tells students that they should first study the unit from which the arrow leads.

A course map also tells students that they should not study any module that has arrows leading into it before they have mastered *all* the units from which the arrows originate. And it tells them that modules shown in parallel may be studied in any order. Here's how to derive a course map from your hierarchy, your experience, and your knowledge of local constraints.

1. Get out your hierarchy and put the name of each module or skill on a quarter of a three-by-five card or scrap of paper (the little stickies—pads of paper with self-adhesive on one end—are ideal).

2. Push these bits and pieces around on a flipchart-size piece of paper until they depict the same relationships shown on your hierarchy. That's where you begin.

3. If two or three skills are closely related and will take very little time to learn, consider "collapsing" them into a single module.

4. Now think about the flow of the course. For example, if there are two skills that can be learned in any order, but your experience tells you that one of them should be attempted before the other, just move that module an inch or so toward the bottom of the paper. The two skills will still be shown as independent (there won't be a line between them), but the student will be guided to study the one closest to the bottom of the page before starting on the other.

If there are two or more independent objectives that should be accomplished before a third is attempted, draw arrows to show this dependency relationship. Students would then know that they can learn the two independent objectives in any order but that they would have to master both of them before attempting the third.

5. When you have all the items in a position that your experience and knowledge of the learning environment says will work, draw the map on the paper *in pencil.*

6. Explain your map to someone—anyone. Talk them through the map from bottom to top. Try to convince this person that you haven't imposed more sequencing restrictions than your subject matter and circumstances require. And then make the changes indicated.

Figure 17.2

Example #1: Here is a course map showing the sequence of modules to be completed by the students in our self-paced *Instructional Module Development Workshop* (Resource #16). Notice that though a couple of sequencing options are open to the student, the order of the lessons in this course is mostly prescribed. This is because students are expected to apply each skill learned to their own instructional project *in the order* in which these skills are used when developing a course.

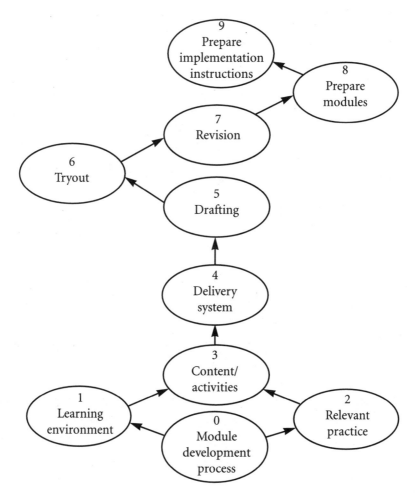

Example #2: Here is a portion of the course map used in the self-paced *Criterion-Referenced Instruction Workshop* (Resource #15). Notice that students have many options in sequencing their instruction. Though it is suggested (but not required) that they begin with modules closest to the bottom of the map, they are encouraged to work on whichever module is of interest at the time and for which they have satisfied the prerequisites.

Figure 17.3

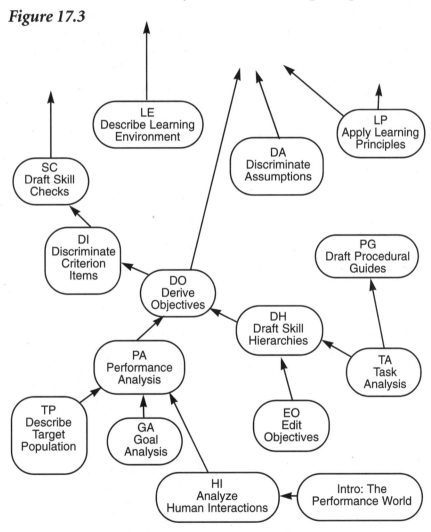

Example #3: This map is from a course called "Developing Performance Aids," created by Peter Pipe. Here the meaning of the horizontally dashed line is: The units below it are to be read, studied, and discussed; but because they are informational only (e.g., Module IN-2), there are no performance checks (criterion tests) associated with them.

The placement of modules DT-1 and ED-1 on the map expresses the best wisdom and experience of the author and says to the student, "While it is true that these modules have no prerequisites and may be studied at any time, you will find it more productive to study them sometime after you have completed module PA-1." Why then didn't the author draw a line between PA-1 and the other two modules? Because he didn't want to falsely suggest that PA-1 *must* be learned before DT-1 and ED-1 can be learned.

Figure 17.4

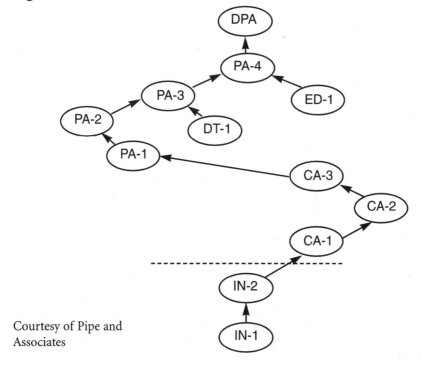

Courtesy of Pipe and
Associates

Example #4: Many years ago, when I taught introductory psychology at a university, all of us on the faculty knew what entering students were interested in. They were interested in sex, ESP, hypnosis, and the behavior of that weird roommate. But where did we begin the course? Why, with the history of psychology. We told them about the good old days when the crazies were chained in dungeons and about how . . . Zzzzzzzzzzzzzzzzz. And then we'd sit around the faculty lounge, grousing about how students weren't motivated like they were when we went to school and scratching for things we could do to wake them up. What incredible naiveté—not to mention arrogance.

What should we have done? We should have started right on the first day with one of those topics of high interest. We wouldn't have had to do much with it, but it would have tugged the students further into the course by starting with something they were known to be interested in, and by promising more on that topic later on.

You don't arouse anyone's interest with the history of anything. Once you *have* aroused interest by helping them develop some skill and thereby some confidence, *then* students may become interested in the history. After all, learning about the history is one of the ways of "experiencing" a subject. But don't ever *begin* a course with history (unless it's a history course). Tell yourself that until students know something about your subject and have developed at least some feeling of competence, history is interesting only to you.

To Learn More: See Resources #8, #15, and #16.

Part V

Implementing the Instruction

18
Course Procedures

Situation: *You want to be sure to deliver your instruction while using procedures as close to the state of the art as your circumstances will allow.*

Suddenly the house lights dim, the orchestra plays a fanfare, and the instructor marches into the classroom bearing—Ta da!—examination papers.

Instr: Today we're going to have a mid-term exam!

You: (Shouting over the pandemonium) Wait a minute! You never said anything about a mid-term!

Instr: Come now. By now you should know that courses come equipped with exams.

You: But a mid-term? At the end of the first week? And without warning?

Instr: Oh, stop your whining. Now come up here and rap out a five-minute description of the theory of relativity.

That dialogue may seem a bit far-fetched, but I'll bet it isn't that far off from some of the experiences you've endured during your own academic career. But you wouldn't do that to *your* students, would you? Of course you wouldn't.

One of the ways to avoid this sort of dastardly deceit is to let students in on the secret of how you intend for the course to function—by giving them a copy of the course procedures up front.

What Are Course Procedures?

Course procedures are the rules by which courses are conducted. Though they may or may not be written down or recognized for what they are, every course operates by a set of rules or procedures. In one course the rule may be, "Tests will be given on the following dates _____," while in another the rule may be, "Take the test when you feel you have accomplished the objective of the module." The rule in still another course may be, "Add your name to the sign-up sheet, and you will be notified when the demonstration has been prepared." In still another course (the kind you've often experienced) the rule is, "I'm not going to *tell* you what the rules are. You'll just have to figure them out yourself." And so it goes. We have rules about when to arrive, when to leave, how to proceed, where to find things, how to get questions answered, and dozens of other things.

Whatever the procedures by which your course will be conducted, *they should be written down and in the hands of the students.* This will tell them what is expected of them and will eliminate their need to waste time "psyching out" the instructor. In addition, the very act of writing the course procedures will help you to derive the most efficient implementation strategy possible for the constraints under which you must function. Whatever you do, prepare a set of course procedures for your students and include them as the number-one item in every student's package of materials.

Where Do Course Procedures Come From?

But where do these procedures come from? How are they derived? After all, you wouldn't just sit down and dream up a set of rules at random. Neither would you write a set of rules that reflects the philosophy of "I'll teach *them* the same way that somebody taught me." That would be the amateur's way out and probably would result in instruction 40 years behind its time.

So how *do* we derive course procedures? We do it by developing rules that put ideal characteristics into practice as closely as local constraints will allow. This means that we compare an ideal or desired course characteristic with our own situation (space, equipment, budget, time, students) and then write one or more rules that will come as close as possible to implementing that ideal characteristic.

These ideal characteristics are derived from research, validated learning principles, and experience; they represent statements that describe what we would be doing if we developed and implemented our instruction in the very best way we know how. Here are some of the main ones.

Ideal Course Characteristics

1. *Instruction exists only where it is a solution or remedy for a problem in human performance.* If they already know how to do it, they don't need instruction. If they don't need to know how to do it, they don't need instruction.

2. *Instructional objectives have been derived from competent performance on the job.* This guarantees that there is a

need for the instruction and answers the question, "How much _____ should I teach?"

3. *Each student studies and practices only those skills not yet mastered to the level required by the objectives.* As a result, you won't waste time and student motivation by teaching them things they already know, but you'll give them enough practice to master the skills being taught.

4. *Student progress is controlled by their own competence.* Application of this characteristic prevents student time and motivation from being wasted by requiring more advanced students to wait while others catch up. It also means slower students won't have to short-change themselves on practice to keep up.

5. *Instruction is directly related to accomplishment of the objectives.* Most or all instruction time will be devoted to teaching what needs to be learned.

6. *Instructional materials impose a minimum of obstacles between the learners and the learning.* Thus, unnecessary impediments to learning are avoided.

7. *Instruction is presented through the simplest delivery systems consistent with the objectives, the learners, and the learning environment.* This saves time and money by ensuring that students will get the instruction they need through the simplest and most direct media that will do the job.

8. *Students are provided with an opportunity to practice each objective and to obtain task-diagnostic feedback regarding the quality of their performance.* (Note: Task-diagnostic feedback is explained in Chapter 20,

"Implementing the Instruction.") Learning is far more effective when students practice what they are learning, and when they receive properly formulated information (feedback) about how well they are doing.

9. *Learners receive repeated practice in skills that are used often or are difficult to learn.* Application of this characteristic ensures that difficult-to-learn and often-used skills will receive periodic refreshment during a course.

10. *Learners receive immediate feedback regarding the quality of their test performance.* This allows a test procedure also to be a learning experience, which is positive and useful. It will also avoid the problems caused by delayed feedback.

11. *Desired student performances are followed by consequences they consider favorable to them.* Because people learn to avoid punishing experiences, this practice will ensure that motivation is strengthened rather than weakened.

12. *Within the limits imposed by content, equipment constraints, and the course map, learners are free to sequence their own instruction.* That is, given the constraints just mentioned, at any given time students may select for study the topic in which they are most interested.

13. *The learning environment itself contains the facilities and equipment needed to implement the above characteristics.* This way neither you nor the student will waste time, become frustrated, or miss important things because of missing items or the need to retrieve items from remote locations (such as regional media centers).

14. *Students will learn to recognize correct and incorrect*

performance before being allowed to practice the skill being learned. This means that students will learn what is needed to make their practice sessions productive.

It is seldom possible to put all of these and other ideal characteristics into practice. There are, after all, time constraints, money constraints, and space and equipment constraints, to name a few. Therefore, course procedures are rules that will implement the ideal as closely as possible. In plain language, we try to derive course procedures that will allow us to say, "I am teaching absolutely as well as constraints will allow."

How to Do It

For each of the characteristics listed above, answer the following questions:

1. Can you implement the characteristic as stated?

2. If so, write a rule that will tell students what to do.

3. If not, say what prevents you from implementing the characteristic.

4. Can you think of a way to get around that constraint?

5. If so, take the action needed to get around the constraint, and then write the rule that will put the ideal characteristic into practice.

6. If not, can you think of a way to get around the constraint even a little bit? In other words, can you think of a way to reduce the obstacle that's preventing you from implementing the characteristic?

7. Take the action needed and then write a rule or rules that will come as close to implementing the characteristic as is possible.

Example: One of the ideal characteristics of instruction is "Student progress is controlled by their own competence." This means that the most efficient instruction is that which allows students to progress to something new as soon as they have mastered what they are learning now. It means that students are not forced to begin new material before they have mastered the old and that they are encouraged to progress to new material as soon as they have mastered the old.

> **NOTE:** Sometimes students will master a skill before developing the confidence needed to actually apply the skill. When this happens, they will often ask if they can practice a little more before moving on. If you can, let them practice. At other times you will find that students are so delighted with their new skill that they want to exercise it—fondle it—before moving on. When this happens, they are literally enjoying the subject matter; it feels good to do something you've just learned how to do. Unless time presses, it is good to allow this to happen.

To show you how to think through the questions above, I'll put some sample "thinking" in the form of a monologue. That way you can see what goes on in the head of someone deriving course procedures.

1. We are considering the characteristic "Student progress is controlled by their own competence." Can you implement the characteristic as stated?

   No way!

2. Write the rules.

   I can't do it.

3. What prevents you from implementing this characteristic?

    This school has always had a 50-minute hour, and instructors are expected to have all students progress at the same rate.

4. Can you think of a way to get around that constraint?

    Well, I suppose I could ask for a policy change, but it seems unlikely it would happen in my lifetime.

5. If so, take the action needed to get around the constraint.

    I can't think of a way around this constraint.

6. If not, can you think of a way to get around the constraint even a little bit?

    Well, I suppose I could make some changes within my own class period without even needing any change in policy. I could give the students the course objectives and the course materials and ask them to tell me when they are ready to demonstrate their skill. When they can perform OK, I could then let them go on to the next objective.

7. Take the action needed and then write the rule or rules that will come as close to implementing the characteristic as is possible.

    Course Procedures: *When you think you have accomplished an objective, you may ask for the test. If you can perform according to the standards (criteria), you may move ahead to the next objective.*

Let me offer a suggestion at this point. Whenever you find yourself saying, "I can't do it because it's against school policy," look a little closer. Many of these "policies" have never been written down, and many of them are fictional. They are only things that everyone believes. Question them.

Another thought. There are many things that you can do differently without ever having to ask for anyone's blessing or approval. After all, you're being paid to exercise your best judgment to get the job done. If you go to your administration or to your management for approval of every change you want to make, you'll soon earn a reputation for being unable to do anything on your own. So think about it. If you can change the color of the paper on which your tests are printed without requiring anyone else's approval, you can change the rules by which you operate your course. And if you can change some of your practices without demanding approval, you can come closer to implementing ideal instruction just by deciding to do it.

A Simpler Way

Here is a simpler way to derive course procedures. Use the model set of procedures listed below as your guide. It is a set of procedures used by those who are in a position to implement most or all ideal characteristics. Imagine that this will be the set of procedures by which you will implement your course. Where you see a procedure that you cannot implement, only then will you need to answer the questions above and make changes. The closer you can come to following these procedures, the closer you will be to applying what is known about making instruction work.

Model Course Procedures

Following are the procedures or rules by which this course is conducted. In general, the procedures tell you to select the module you want to study, to proceed at your own rate, to ask for the Skill Check when you are ready to do so, to work with others as much or as little as you wish, and to use as few or as many resources as you feel you need or want.

How to Begin

1. Read these Course Procedures.

2. Be sure you know the location of the resources, the Skill Checks, the Self-Evaluation material, and the Master Progress Plotter (the sheet that shows which modules you have completed).

3. Begin with Module _____. It is a short introductory unit that will show you the big picture and provide you with a mental map of where you are heading.

4. Use only the resources (readings, practice material) you feel you need to help you develop the skill defined by the objective of the module.

5. Practice the skill at least once before asking for the Skill Check.

6. Take time to muse, to talk to others, and to see how others are applying the skills they are learning. This is not a race. Use the opportunity to sharpen your skills.

Course Map

The Course Map shows how each module of the course is related to other modules and to the course as a whole.

1. Before beginning to study any module, complete all the prerequisites for that module (i.e., all modules shown by lines and arrows leading into that module).

2. The location of a module on the map represents a suggestion as to the approximate point in the course where it will be most meaningful to you. Where no sequence is shown (i.e., where there are no arrows leading into a module), feel free to study those modules in any order you wish.

3. Place an "X" or some other mark on those modules the instructor indicates are optional for you.

Modules

1. Before beginning a new module series, read the introductory comments at the front of the module material. The diagram facing the introduction shows how the modules in that section relate to the rest of the course.

2. Study only one module at a time, but feel free to put that module down and study another that you are eligible to enter whenever you wish.

3. Begin a module by reading the Objective and the description of the Skill Check (or sample test item).

4. When you feel qualified to do so, ask the instructor for the Skill Check. (It's a good idea, however, to read through the entire module so that there won't be any terminology surprises.)

5. Work through the module at your own speed.

6. If you are not sure of your competence, complete all the practice exercises. If you are still not sure, check with the instructor.

7. The instructor will provide a sign-up sheet for those modules that include group practice. Sign up for the session most convenient for you.

Resources

1. There are at least three sources of information for each module: the module itself, other students, and the instructor. Additional resources may also be available. If so, they are listed at the beginning of the module.

2. Consult any of the resources you think may help you, but do not feel compelled to consult them all.

3. When resources are listed in a module, the relevant page numbers are indicated. Feel free to read more widely if you wish, but keep the module objective in mind as you do.

4. Feel free to ask other students which resources they found most helpful; provide the same information for others if they ask.

5. Work with a colleague whenever you wish.

Skill Checks (Criterion Tests)

1. Ask for a Skill Check whenever you feel ready. Before doing so, however, you will save time if you first make sure you can answer "Yes" to these questions:

   a. Did I practice the skill called for by the objective?

   b. Did I get a colleague sign-off, if it is called for by the module?

2. If, after reviewing a module, you feel ready for the Skill Check without further study, go for it.

3. Take only one copy of the Skill Check. Feel free to write on the Skill Check.

4. If you do not perform adequately on a Skill Check, you will be asked, after further study or practice, to complete the same or similar Skill Check again, at the instructor's discretion.

5. When you have completed a Skill Check, check your work against the Self-Evaluation material. The instructor (or whomever else is qualified to do so) will then check your work.

Personal Progress Summary

1. Ask whomever is checking your work to date and initial your Personal Progress Summary next to the appropriate module. This is your verification that you have been checked off on that module and are free to move to another.

Master Progress Plotter

1. When your Personal Progress Summary has been initialed for a module, make sure the instructor makes the proper entry on the Master Progress Plotter. That will be your indication that your mastery has been recorded—and it will provide another reason to feel good about your progress.

End of Model Course Procedures

Optional Course Procedures

You may find a need to write other course procedures, depending on the nature and location of your course, the amount of equipment available, and the time available. Here are some examples:

- Complete all the modules below the line shown on the Course Map before working on those above it.

- When you have completed all the modules below the solid line shown on your Course Map, you will be eligible for the group practice session, minilecture, or demonstration. Sign up for it at that time.

- When a module asks you to complete a practice exercise, write directly on the worksheets supplied.

- Be sure to read the instructions before using the videotape recorder.

- You will find equipment to practice on in Room _____. This room will be open from 10 a.m.–noon, and from 3 p.m.-5 p.m.

- Before you enter the practice room, take one of the tags that is hanging on the door, and then replace it when you leave. Each tag represents an available practice station and will let other students know how many pieces of practice equipment are available at any given time.

- If the work you have completed for a Skill Check is not yet adequate, and if the instructor had to revise or modify it, it will be considered the instructor's work, and you will be asked to repeat the Skill Check after completing some additional practice.

- If, at any time during the course, you feel that there is too much reading, it is probably because you are doing one or more of the following:

  1. Working alone instead of with a colleague when a module suggests it.

  2. Plodding through a resource you consider uninteresting or inappropriate for you instead of putting it down and finding another.

  3. Using printed materials as your primary source of information instead of making use of colleagues and the course manager.

  4. Spending too long with a problem before asking for assistance.

  5. Working through *all* the resources listed in a module, instead of using only those you need to help you develop the desired skill.

To Learn More: See Resources #5, #8, #15, #16, and #17.

19
Getting Ready

Situation: *Your course has been prepared, and you know your subject. Before the course begins, however, you want to make sure that you know how to apply the key motivational techniques that will maximize student eagerness to learn.*

"Good morning. I'm your Geek instructor."
"Ever been to Geekland?"
"No."
"Know how to speak or read Geek?"
"Not yet."
"Know how to dress like a Geek?"
"Don't they wear plastic pen protectors?"
"Know anything about Geek culture?"
"Sorry. I've never met a Geek person."
"Goodbye!"

How's that for beating a dead horse—for trampling the obvious? Of course one needs to know the content of the instruction. How else would one know how to conduct demonstrations, provide clarifying explanations, and answer questions? How else would one gain credibility with the students? How can anyone teach something they don't know?

What may be a little less obvious is that there is more to making instruction work than just knowing the subject matter. Clearly, how you teach can be just as important as what you teach. So before entering the classroom, or computer, or video studio, you'll want to make sure that you can apply at least four of the important practices that have much to do with how well the instruction will work, and with how eager the students will be to learn more; success definitions, performance consequences, modeling, and self-efficacy.

Success Definitions

Recently I questioned several expert instructors individually about their vision of instructional success. I asked each of them, "What would things look like if your instruction were totally successful?" Though they used different words in their replies, the substance was quite similar. Here is a summary of how these instructors visualize instructional success.

1. Students leave the instruction having accomplished the objectives set out for them.

2. They are eager to apply what they learned.

3. They are eager to learn more.

4. They can speak coherently about what they have learned.

In other words, successful instruction sends students away who can do and are willing to do, who have a favorable attitude toward the subject and are eager to learn more. To make that happen you'll need to be especially attentive to what happens to your students *during* their learning. For example, students who are rewarded for arriving late (by having already-covered material explained to them) have no incentive to learn to be prompt. And if you value promptness you will have lost an opportunity to make it blossom.

So how can you arrange things so that students will be most likely to leave with the characteristics you deem valuable? By *learning how to identify desired student performances,* so that you can smile on them when they appear and take corrective action when they don't. Take a few minutes to make a list of the things you consider to be productive (desired) student performances. Answer the question, "What things do I want my students to do while learning, and as a result of learning?" Here is a start on your list of desired student behaviors:

- Arrive prepared to work.

- Ask questions when something is not clear.

- Ask for additional practice material.

- Be willing to practice until the objective has been mastered.

- Offer to help other students.

- Keep trying until they can perform as desired.

- Be willing to spend time maintaining tools and equipment.

- Be anxious to demonstrate their competence and apply their new skills.

- Make favorable comments about the subject they are learning.

(Add your items here)

How does a success definition promote effective instruction? Once you have a clear picture in your mind that tells you how to recognize instances of desired outcomes (evidence of success), and of approximations to desired outcomes, you'll be able to follow those desired outcomes with favorable consequences (to the student). That will make it more, rather than less, likely that you'll get more of those desired outcomes. (As you know, a new skill often looks somewhat shaky—less than wonderful. If you don't recognize it as an acceptable approximation along the road to mastery, you might kill it off.)

Consequences

With a picture of instructional success clearly in mind, you can think about what you will do when the successes (and the approximations toward success) actually occur.

Because instructor behavior is so critical to successful instruction, you must pay careful attention to how you behave in the presence of your students. Whether you like it or not, you are an instrument of reward and punishment, an instrument that will cause students either to want to learn more of your subject or to want to hear no more about it. Whether you like it or not, your own behavior shapes the attitudes of your students. For example, consider the effects of the following instructor statements:

> "Look. This is a dumb video, but I'm supposed to show it, and you're supposed to watch it."

> "I already answered that question three weeks ago."

> "If that's the best you can do, maybe you should be in some other department."

> "Don't try to get ahead of the class."

> "This class isn't as sharp as the one I had *last* year."

"Fifty percent of this class won't be here a month from now."

"I grade on a curve, so no matter how competent you are, some of you will have to get low grades."

"I'm not the one who designed this course."

If you think back over your own academic history, you'll think of dozens of examples of instructor behavior that served only to turn students off. The sad thing is that these events occurred mostly because the instructors were unaware of the effects of what they were doing. Fortunately, there is a way to avoid the accidental turn-offs and to maximize the deliberate turn-ons. Here's how.

Learn to identify the favorable consequences under your control. For example, you can smile or not smile. If you smile on undesired performance, either accidentally or because you don't know any better, you may get more of it. If you offer the equivalent of a pat on the back when a student is goofing off, you may get more of that, too.

If, on the other hand, you frown or somehow insult or demean a student for asking questions or for trying, you'll get less of those positive efforts. So make a list of the things you might do in response to desired performance. And if you're thinking, "There's nothing I can do," you've never been more wrong. You ought to be able to list at least two dozen things that you could do to encourage desired performance when you see it, none of which have anything to do with money. I'll help you get your list started:

- a smile

- a favorable comment

- a little extra attention

- a little time off (even a few minutes works)

- ask the student to explain a concept to others

- applause

Add your own.

-

-

-

Check your own performance. The easiest and most private way to find out whether you are encouraging desired performance and discouraging undesired performance is to set up a video camera in the back of the classroom or lab and just let it record.

Review the tape in private. Look for examples of desired student performance, and then watch to see what you did in response—when the desired performance happened. Did you ignore it? Did you punish it? Or did you pay attention to it, smile on it, say something nice about it? Build on it? This simple review will show you how you might modify your own performance so that you will get more of what you want and less of what you don't want. Your goal should be to "glow" on desired (productive) performances, and to ignore unproductive performances wherever possible.

People See, People Do

Instructional success is also influenced by the quality of the modeling—by what they see and hear the instructor do while they're in the instructor's presence.

Instructors who tell students to do something one way and then do it (model) another will find their students becoming inattentive to their words. Instructors who demonstrate apathy or indifference to what they are teaching will soon find their students doing the same. Instructors who model enthusiasm for their subject and for learning, however, will often find these characteristics rubbing off onto their students.

Few truths have been as well established by research as the fact that most of what we learn during our lives is learned by imitation. We see things done and we try to do likewise. We read about how things are done, our instructors show and tell how they are done, and we try to do likewise. To paraphrase Dr. Albert Bandura, if we learned mainly by trial and error, world population would be a lot smaller than it is; a lot fewer of us would survive adolescence.

Because modeling is such a powerful instructor, it is imperative to instructional success that you do as you want others to do, that you act as you want your students to act, lest you accidentally reduce their interest in the subject you are teaching. Here is a summary of the main modeling principles and an example to illustrate how each might be applied:

1. Observers learn by watching and imitating others; they tend to behave as they have seen others behave.

    Application example: If you want students to follow certain safety precautions, then you follow them—especially when you are in their presence.

2. Observers will be more likely to imitate a model who has prestige in the observers' eyes.

    Application example: Have desired performance demonstrated by someone your students respect: a manager, local hero, football player, rock star. If you have prestige in the eyes of your students, it is doubly important for you to practice what you preach.

3. Observers will be more likely to imitate modeled performance when they see the model being rewarded for that performance.

   Application example: When one student performs to expectations, make sure you respond positively to that performance (e.g., with a smile, favorable comment, token). Other students will be more likely to imitate the desired performance.

4. Observers who see a model being punished will be less likely to imitate the performance that was punished.

   Application example: If a student is punished (demeaned, insulted, ridiculed) for attempting a difficult task and making a mistake, other students will be less likely to attempt the difficult task themselves.

Unhappily, you may not be able to tell when you are accidentally putting students down. (I recall an excellent instructor who took all students' questions seriously. But while he thought about an answer, he would scowl and tug at an eyebrow, which intimidated the other students and made them reluctant to ask their own questions.) Fortunately, there is a simple solution. As previously suggested, put a video camera in the back of your classroom and let it record as you teach. At your convenience you can review the tape while pretending to be a student. You will easily be able to spot the opportunities for improvement.

Self-Efficacy

Instruction that works not only sends students away with the ability to do what the course objectives require, but it also sends them away with the eagerness to apply what they have learned and with the perseverance needed to overcome obstacles. In other words, successful instruction sends students away with high, rather than low, self-efficacy. You influence the strength of your students' self-efficacy whether you like it or not.

What is Self-Efficacy?

Self-efficacy refers to people's judgments about their capability to execute specific courses of action; it refers to their belief in their ability to perform specific tasks or apply specific skills. Self-efficacy isn't concerned with *actual* skills and abilities, but with people's *beliefs* about the strength of those skills and abilities.

People who say with confidence, "I can climb an elephant blindfolded," and then proceed to do so, have high self-efficacy toward elephant-climbing. Because of their strong self-efficacy, they will be more willing to climb elephants in the future, and they will be more likely to brush themselves off and try again when they fall off. Those who are equally skilled at elephant-climbing (or anything else), but who judge themselves to be poor at this critical skill will be less likely to be willing to practice the skill, and will be less likely to persevere in the face of setbacks. You can see the importance of having strong self-efficacy toward the things you can do well.

Self-efficacy is not necessarily related to level of skill, because people may or may not make accurate judgments about the strength of their abilities. Everyone knows someone who is better at something than they judge themselves to be. "Aw, shucks," they may say, "I'm not really very good at that," even though they may in fact be the best in the business.

Because such people are handicapped in their ability to succeed, and because instructors and parents are the most common causes of low self-efficacy, the importance of learning
how to strengthen self-efficacy in your students cannot be
overstated.

How is Self-Efficacy Strengthened?

The goal is to facilitate a match between an actual level of
skill and self-judgments about that level of skill, so that people
really believe they can do what they can in fact do. Here's how.

1. **Performance mastery.** The most powerful action is to
   make sure your students are given an opportunity
   to practice until they achieve mastery, and to help them to
   perceive that they have, in fact, mastered. Help them
   to understand that their mastery came about as the result
   of their own efforts, rather than as a result of the instructor's efforts, or because of a job aid, or because of luck.

2. **Feedback.** Provide task-diagnostic, rather than self-
   diagnostic, feedback for practice efforts.

   Self-diagnostic feedback interprets less-than-perfect
   performance as a personal deficiency. "You just aren't
   motivated enough;" "Maybe you just don't have the
   talent for this work;" "How many times will I have to
   tell you this?" "You're just not good at this." "You're not
   working up to your potential." Self-diagnostic feedback blames imperfect performance on failings of the
   individual.

   Task-diagnostic feedback focuses on the task being performed. Failure is used as information through which
   the performance may be improved, rather than as evi-

dence of incompetence. "If you'll put your hand in this position rather than that one, I think you'll see some improvement;" "If you stand in front of the elephant rather than behind it, you'll have more things to hold onto as you climb;" "If you'll hold a drinking straw between your lips, you'll actually be able to see the improvement in your lip control as you practice." Task-diagnostic feedback focuses on ways in which performance of a task may be improved.

3. **Modeling.** Self-efficacy can be improved when students watch others like themselves performing competently. (Refer to the modeling discussion in the previous section.)

4. **Social persuasion.** Self-efficacy is influenced by the comments of others (we all know the powerful effects that unkind comments can have). Arrange for success experiences and then help students interpret those success experiences as indications of improvement. Your own comments and actions are always influencing the self-efficacy of your students, either favorably or unfavorably. You cannot choose to use or not use social persuasion, so you must be careful about your behavior when in the presence of your students. Keep it positive.

5. **Physiological information.** Sometimes people will make judgments about their ability, or lack of it, from physiological cues: aches, pains, effort, etc. They will confuse the difficulty of a task with their ability to perform it. "Gee, I'm not very good at this—this is hard." Lots of things are difficult to do, but lots of people become very good at doing them. Help your students to understand the difference between hard work and skill

level. Make sure they understand that the need to work hard at something shouldn't be misinterpreted as a lack of skill.

To Learn More: See Resources #4, #12, #13, #15, #17, #19, and #20.

20

Implementing the Instruction

Situation: Everything has been prepared, you're prepared, and students are about to arrive.

Now you're ready to begin the instruction. You may do it primarily through lecture, through a self-paced format, through a "distance learning" format, through computer or video, or through some combination of these formats. These delivery formats tend to clump themselves into two basic variations:

1. *Instructor-controlled,* where the instructor controls the flow of events (e.g., lectures in the classroom, lectures by video), and

2. *Performance-controlled,* where learning activities are controlled by student progress toward accomplishment of an objective (e.g., usually through self-paced formats).

Instructor-Controlled Instruction

In this traditional format the instructor is the primary source of information, usually offered to students in the form of presentations (lectures). The main advantage is that a single instructor can present information to as many students as can be brought within eye- and earshot, which, through the use of television and satellites, can amount to millions.

The main disadvantages are that instructors need to be taught, though often they are not, how to be good presenters; individual attention is difficult (and in some cases, even impossible) to maintain; all students must receive the same instruction in the same way and at the same pace; and students cannot practice individually for as long as they need to become proficient in each of the objectives.

Performance-Controlled Instruction

In this format students' progress is controlled by their own performance. Students exert some control over their learning activities, in that when they have mastered one objective, they are encouraged to move to the next. This is a highly flexible format that can accommodate instructor-led presentations as well as group sessions when they are called for by the objectives. Performance-controlled instruction is usually conducted in a self-paced mode.

The advantages of this format are that (a) each student has the opportunity to study and practice until all objectives are accomplished, (b) students often have some control over the sequence in which they address the modules, (c) instructors can devote most of their time to coaching individual students, and (d) all principles of learning can be applied toward effective performance. Another advantage is that the instruction can be guaranteed to accomplish the objectives that analysis has revealed to be important.

Disadvantages are that (a) instructors require some coaching before they can manage this format, and (b) some instructors find it difficult or impossible to handle this type of performance-oriented structure (they would rather perform than coach). Another "disadvantage" is that lead time is required to prepare the materials. Though this is also true of the instructor-led format, instructors have so often been expected to "wing it" (instruct without preparation) that many people erroneously believe that good instructor-led instruction takes little or no preparation, while a performance-based course takes more preparation time than is reasonable.

Here's how instruction is managed in both instructor-controlled and performance-controlled formats.

Managing Instructor-Controlled Instruction

No matter what the format of your instruction, you will always have occasion to present information by means of the lecture. When this is the case, you are acting as a transmitter, a broadcaster, of information, and your own behavior, as always, is critical. For example, if students cannot easily understand your words, all your preparation and all your expertise will be of little value. If your diction is poor, or your accent difficult to understand, you yourself become an obstacle to learning.

There are other characteristics that a good presenter (lecturer) should have if he or she is to facilitate learning rather than interfere with it. Here is a list. The effective presenter:

1. speaks clearly and understandably,

2. has mastery of the subject matter,

3. models desired student performance,

4. models enthusiasm for the subject and for learning,

5. provides positive consequences for desired performance,

6. can operate instructional equipment,

7. uses visuals in a timely manner and without causing distraction,

8. diagnoses individual student problems and recommends remedies, and

9. can handle a variety of instructional methods (e.g., discussions, question-and-answer sessions, role-plays).

Whether you are experienced or inexperienced, your presentations will benefit from periodic checkups. Because we are prone to picking up distracting mannerisms...er...ah...and gestures over time, the wise instructor periodically reviews his or her presentation behavior at least twice a year. This is done by using one or both of the following procedures:

1. Videotape one of your presentations, and then pretend you're a student and review it in private as you answer the checklist questions found in the "How to Do It" section below, and/or

2. Give your students a copy of the Presentation Checklist and ask each of them to complete it at the end of one of your presentations.

Since the instructor is the key instrument through which instruction is offered in the instructor-controlled format, it is important that that instrument (the instructor) be kept in fine tune.

How to Do It

Though just about everyone can talk, not everyone can deliver a presentation in a way that will teach. To make the presentation accomplish its purpose it needs to have certain characteristics. Here are the basic steps.

1. Before you begin, make sure you and your students have all the material needed for the lesson at hand.

2. Make sure the students are as comfortable as you can make them (temperature, adequate lighting, etc.), and make sure they can see everything that you will be doing.

3. Explain the objective of the lesson—students should have a written copy of their own to refer to. If this isn't the first lecture in the series, spend a minute or two reviewing what came before. (If you are using a course map, refer to it to remind students of the bigger picture.)

4. Explain/demonstrate why what they are about to learn is important to *them*.

5. Follow your lesson plan (described in Chapter 15).

6. Allow students to spend as much lesson time as possible practicing.

7. Then find out how well each student can perform the objective being learned. (This is much more difficult to do in the instructor-led format than the performance-controlled format, but do your best.)

Here is a Presentation Checklist to help remind you of the key features of a successful presentation. This Checklist is worded to be completed by the student. Marks in any but the Yes column represent opportunities for improvement.

Presentation Checklist

	Yes	No	?
1. Was the objective of the session clear to you?			
2. Was it clear *why* the content or skill is important to *you*?			
3. Did the body of the presentation seem organized from your point of view?			
4. Were you "taught" only the things you didn't already know?			
5. Did you have opportunities to ask questions?			
6. Did you get helpful answers to those questions?			
7. Did you have an opportunity to practice what you were taught?			
8. Was your practice followed by prompt and useful feedback?			
9. Was the instructor easy to understand?			
10. Did the instructor seem interested in what was being taught?			
11. Did the instructor avoid doing anything to belittle, insult, or demean you or other students?			
12. Did the instructor avoid distracting mannerisms?			
13. Did you accomplish the objective of the lesson (module)? That is, can you now perform as the objective describes?			

Managing Performance-Controlled Instruction

In this format the instructor functions more as a coach than as a performer. Though the instructor is encouraged to instruct where necessary, the main burden of the instruction is carried by other media, such as audiotapes, videos, CDs, print (manuals, tests, booklets), simulators, or computers. Nonetheless, the instructor provides critical functions: makes resources available when needed, diagnoses student problems, instructs when necessary, and verifies performance progress. Though the course may be self-paced, it is not conducted without an instructor (unless it is designed to be a self-study course). In fact, this format recognizes that instructor time is too valuable to be wasted on matters that can be better handled through other means.

Instructors using this format have a great deal more control over learning progress than those using the instructor-led mode. When students have to demonstrate an ability to perform on one objective before they are encouraged to move to another, the instructor can have constant and instant knowledge of where each student is in relation to course completion and can take immediate remedial actions when needed.

If you have occasion to conduct a performance-controlled course, you will need to think of yourself as a coach or consultant rather than as the main dispenser of information. You will spend most of your time assisting individual students: diagnosing their difficulties and recommending corrective action, providing additional practice opportunities, reviewing performance and offering feedback, and reinforcing (glowing on) student successes and partial successes.

In addition to the skills listed earlier for classroom presenters, you will need only to develop your coaching skill to the point where you can sit with an individual student and calmly provide answers to questions, demonstrate a procedure, let the student make "safe" mistakes, and review performance. Because you will be physically closer to the student than when

you are standing in front of a classroom, you will need to modify your gestures; sweeping gestures are fine when you are lecturing but inappropriate when working with individuals. You
don't want to run the risk of knocking their glasses off or giving them a bloody nose while you're explaining a concept.

For the same reason, you will want to make sure you don't
create other obstacles to learning as would be the case, for
example, if you had bad breath. (We can't use course managers
in our own workshops who are smokers, for example, even
though they don't smoke in the classroom; that's because
almost all of our participant non-smokers try to avoid sitting
close to those who smell of stale tobacco.)

How to Do It

When you are ready to conduct a performance-controlled
course in a self-paced manner, here are the steps to follow.

1. Begin with an orientation session. Explain to students
    what the course will be about, and hand out a copy of the
    objectives. Answer questions so that everyone knows
    what they will be expected to be able to do to be consid-
    ered competent.

2. Hand out a copy of the course procedures and make sure
    everyone understands the rules by which you will be
    operating. They won't believe you at first no matter what
    you tell them, so you will have to repeat this information
    from time to time, and you will have to be sure to follow
    the procedures yourself.

3. Make sure students know where to locate all the
    resources, and explain the items uppermost in their
    minds at this time (i.e., what the hours are, where the
    bathroom is, and information about lunch).

4. Tell them how to begin the course. Make sure they each have a copy of the course map, and explain the options and constraints. Make sure everyone understands any symbols or conventions you have used in drawing the map, and make sure they understand what to do as soon as you end the orientation session.

5. As soon as the orientation session is over, wander around from student to student and remind them again where and how to begin. This may be the first time they have been given an opportunity to have anything to say about their own learning, so give them time to adjust. It may take up to a day or two to get into the flow of things, after which there will be no stopping them.

6. Follow the course procedures.

7. When a participant has accomplished all the objectives, provide a certificate of achievement (which actually means they have achieved, not just that they showed up), and ask the participant to complete a short question-naire intended to identify opportunities for course improvement.

To Learn More: See Resources #13, #15, #17, and #19.

Part VI

Improving the Instruction

21

Course Improvement

Situation: You want to locate opportunities for improving your existing instruction and to discover which changes will give the most benefit for the least effort.

A course is *effective* to the degree that it accomplishes what it sets out to accomplish. It is *efficient* to the degree it accomplishes its purpose with the least motion (time, effort, money). Since nothing is perfect, everything can be improved, including instruction. But just because instruction *can* be improved is not enough reason to go to expensive lengths to do so. If the instruction is doing what it is supposed to do, if it is doing so without undue cost, and if it is sending students away with more rather than less interest in the subject, it should be considered successful. Although you should make improvements when the need or opportunity arises, and you should make efforts to detect opportunities for improvement, a constant (and usually expensive) hunt for *perfection* is not a cost-effective use of your time.

Having said that, let's consider course improvement. This is something you do all the time. You do it when you refine your lesson plans, you do it when you make equipment more readily available to your students, you do it when you make the objectives a little easier to understand, and you do it when you make the instruction more tightly related to the objectives.

Improvement Requires Change

Though it is always necessary to change something in order to improve it, change doesn't always lead to improvement, Madison Avenue and politicians notwithstanding! To improve something means to make one or more of its characteristics come closer to some ideal or desired state. But you can claim that improvements have been made only if you know what you are trying to achieve, if you know the objectives you are trying to accomplish. For example, if you can say, "Hey, there; I gave a thirty-minute talk today and only said 'aah . . .' twelve times compared to yesterday's 'leventy-seven times," *and* if aah-less speech is the goal, standard, or ideal you are trying to achieve, *then* you can say that you have made an improvement.

Think of it this way. Improvement is the last of a four-step process.

1. **Measurement.** The first step is measurement. When you determine the extent of some characteristic, you are measuring. For example, "It's six feet long" is a statement about a measurement.

2. **Evaluation.** When you make a judgment based on a comparison of a measurement with a standard, you are evaluating. For example, "It's too short" is a statement of judgment. The thing measured has been compared against a standard or ideal and found not to match. Without a standard against which to compare a measurement, you cannot tell whether the thing measured is OK or not OK.

3. **Opportunities for improvement.** When your evaluations reveal discrepancies between measurements and standards, you identify opportunities for improvement. For example, "Five percent of my students didn't accomplish *all* their objectives during the time allotted, but they all should have," means that there was a discrepancy between the percent completing and the *desired* percent completing. It also means that an opportunity for improvement has been identified.

4. **Improvement.** Improvement is the result of action taken to cause one or more characteristics to move closer to the ideal or desired condition. For example, "I increased the amount of practice time, and now only one percent of my students don't accomplish all the objectives in the time available" means that action has been taken to successfully reduce the difference between what exists and what is desired.

What Should I Measure?

Depends on what you want to know. With all the statistical techniques that are available, it would be possible to collect mountains of numbers about a course. But most of them would be worthless. Why? Simply because most of that information would be of no use in making practical improvements. Most of it would simply amount to counting angels dancing on the head of a pin (which is a waste of time since we already know the answer is 42). So relax. Course improvement is relatively easy if you keep your eye on the possible.

As I said, what you measure is determined by what you want to know. So what *do* you want to know about your course? As soon as you decide what you want to know, you will know what to measure. There are three main things you should want to know about your course.

1. **Does it work?** Is it effective? Does it do what it's supposed to do?

2. **Is it of value?** Does it fill a need, either of the student or of the institution or organization?

3. **Is it efficient?** Is it up to date? Does it match the state of the art? Does it impose minimum obstacles between the student and the learning?

When to Do It

The first question (Does it work?) should be answered as each lesson or module is completed, and again (if appropriate) at the end of the course.

The second question (Is it of value?) should be answered during the analysis phase, i.e., before instruction is developed, and then periodically after the course has been put on line.

The third question (Is it efficient?) should be answered continually throughout the course, and at the end of the course when you scan the reaction sheets for opportunities for improvement.

How to Do It

Figure 21.1 will help you to visualize the method for answering the three key questions. Read the graphic clockwise like this: We start in the "real world"—from a real need, whether that be to teach someone to perform a job, to be prepared for the next course(s), or to function more successfully in some type of community. Then, through the analysis procedures, we derive the objectives of the instruction. We then develop instruction intended to accomplish those objectives. Through the instruction we develop competent students and then send them off to that portion of the world for which we have prepared them.

Figure 21.1

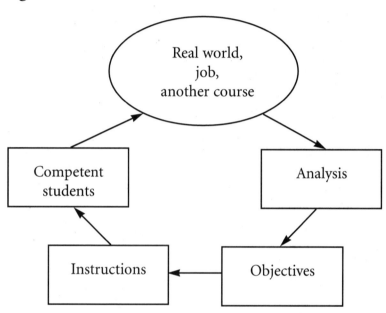

Here's how to think about answering the three key questions:

1. **Does it work?** This question is answered by comparing student performance with the objectives of the instruction (See Figure 21.2). It is *not* answered by looking at the content of the instruction, at the instructional procedures, or at what people are doing on the job. (By now you know that there are several factors that influence what people actually do on a job, or in a classroom, and that skill is only one of them. In other words, there are many reasons why people may not do what they know how to do. That's why it is not possible to assess whether

training works by watching their "real-world" performance.)

For example, if 95 percent of the students accomplished the objectives, then the course is "working" for 95 percent of the students. If 100 percent is the desired number, then there is an opportunity for improvement.

Figure 21.2

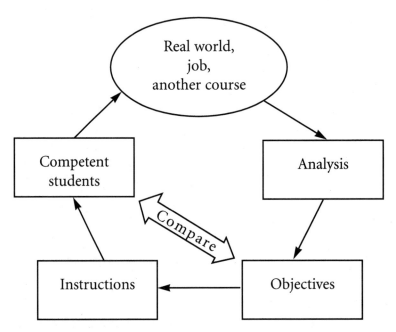

2. **Is it of value?** This question is answered by comparing the objectives of the instruction with the needs that gave rise to them (see Figure 21.3). In other words, this question is answered by verifying the accuracy of the analysis that led to the objectives, by comparing the objectives with the need. It is not answered by looking at the content of the instruction or at the instructional procedures.

If students no longer need to be able to do some of the things taught in the course or need to learn things not currently taught, then the opportunity for improvement lies in adjusting the objectives to meet the current need.

Thus the question, "Does it work?" is answered by determining whether the instruction does what it *sets out to do,* and the question, "Is it of value?" is answered by determining whether the instruction sets out to do something that *needs doing.*

Figure 21.3

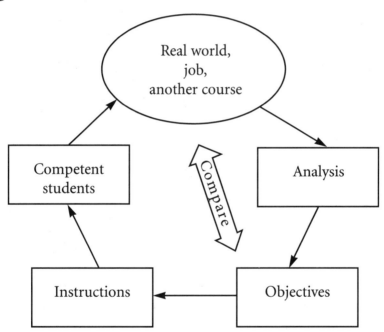

3. **Is it efficient?** This question is answered by comparing the instructional practices against the state of the art (expressed in terms of ideal characteristics), that is, by determining how closely those practices match the ideal

characteristics (see Figure 21.4). For example, if you noted that your tests did not yet match your objectives (for whatever reason), then you would have noted a discrepancy between what you *had* and what you *could* have had if your tests matched the state of the art, and you would have identified an opportunity for improvement. For another example, if you noted that students were not allowed to progress on the basis of their competence, you would have noted a discrepancy between what you were doing and what you should do, and identified another opportunity for improvement.

Figure 21.4

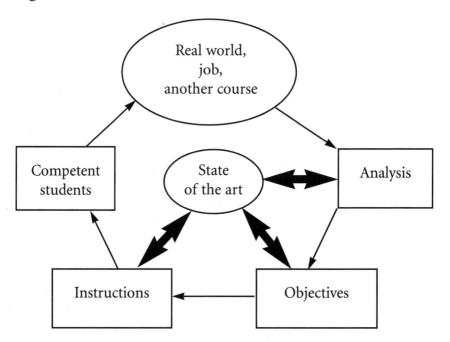

Here is a checklist of some questions that will help you spot opportunities for improvement. (The checklist also works as an excellent tool for auditing or assessing the effectiveness of training courses implemented as part of a quality management system.) You can derive your own list by reviewing the ideal characteristics presented in Chapter 18 and preparing questions that will allow you to determine just how well the course currently implements each of them.

Course Improvement Checklist

A check-mark in any but the "Yes" column represents an improvement opportunity.

Objectives	Yes	No	?
1. Do you have objectives for your course, stated in performance terms?			
2. Are the objectives derived from the job, craft, or vocation being taught?			
3. If your students feed into another course, are your objectives derived in part from the prerequisites of that course?			
4. Were the objectives derived from some part of the real world (i.e., derived to meet a real need)?			

Course Materials			
1. Does each student have a copy of the course objectives?			
2. Is the instructional content confined to what is needed to accomplish the objectives (i.e., includes no irrelevant instruction)?			
3. Are the instructional materials all keyed to the objectives so that students know which materials are relevant to the accomplishment of each objective?			
4. Are the materials understandable to the students? (Ask them.)			
5. Are the instructional materials readily available to students in the learning environment?			

Learning Environment

	Yes	No	?
1. Does each student have a copy of the course procedures (the rules by which the course is conducted)?			
2. Do students report that these procedures are actually followed?			
3. Do students have a course map or similar document showing how all the skills of the course relate to one another?			
4. Do course procedures pose a minimum of obstacles between students and the learning (i.e., do course procedures facilitate rather than hinder learning)?			
5. Are trainees free to move around the learning environment (subject to safety restrictions and group-related restrictions dictated by course objectives)?			
6. Do students have immediate access to course components such as texts, manuals, equipment, parts, diagrams, videotapes?			
7. Is the environment free of avoidable distractions such as noise, interruptions, discomfort, harsh or low lighting, uncomfortable temperature?			

Practice

	Yes	No	?
1. Does each learner practice each key skill?			
2. Is immediate feedback provided for practice exercises?			
3. Can each student practice until the objective has been accomplished?			
4. Is at least half the instruction time devoted to practice?			

	Yes	No	?

Instructor

1. Has the instructor had training in:

    a. Classroom presentation skills?

    If not, have steps been taken to assure that the presentations match the characteristics of the Presentation Checklist on page 244?

    b. Instructional development?

    If not, will he/she promise to make the improvements suggested by this checklist?

2. Does the instructor model the performance expected of the students? (Ask the students.)

3. Does the instructor behave positively toward students rather than belittle or insult them? (Ask the students.)

4. Does the instructor behave positively toward the subject he/she is teaching; i.e., model enthusiasm? (Ask the students.)

5. Does the instructor show pride in the students' growing competence? (Ask the students.)

6. Does the instructor make himself/herself available to assist individual students during the learning session?

Students

	Yes	No	?
1. Do students exhibit a strong desire to learn what is being taught?			
2. Are students encouraged to practice only those skills in which they need improvement?			
3. Are students allowed some choice in the sequencing of their study?			
4. Are students allowed some choice in the method of learning and in the instructional resources they use?			
5. Are students allowed to practice until they have accomplished an objective?			
6. Do students receive individual attention when they need it?			
7. Are students encouraged to move to another unit of instruction when their competence has been demonstrated on the present one?			
8. Does something desirable happen to the students (from their point of view) when they reach competence in all the objectives (e.g., favorable comments, cheers, applause, diploma, time off)?			

Performance Tests (Skill Checks)

	Yes	No	?
1. Are students encouraged to demonstrate their competence (complete the skill check for the unit they are studying) when they feel ready to do so?			
2. Does every test item measure a course skill (i.e., does each item match the objective it is measuring in terms of performance and conditions)?			
3. Do students receive immediate and constructive feedback on their test performance?			
4. When a student's performance is judged to be not yet competent, is the weakness diagnosed and additional assistance given—without belittling the student?			
5. Is the student required to demonstrate competence in each key skill before being considered competent in the skills being taught?			

Opportunities Knocking

Once you've spotted improvement opportunities, you'll want some guidelines for sorting them out. It's one thing to spot an opportunity for improvement; it's something else to decide whether the improvement is worth making. Sometimes an improvement would cost far more than it is worth. For example, suppose you find a way to shorten a course by 10 percent. That would be worth thinking about doing, especially if the shorter course would be just as effective. But suppose the cost of that potential improvement would be far greater than the value of the improvement?

For another example, suppose you note that you could make the course work a lot better (improve the effectiveness) by letting students work for 4-hour stretches over 5 consecutive days, rather than for 50 minutes 3 times each week for **X** weeks. And suppose you also know that you'd have about as much chance of changing local policy as a goose has of running a marathon on a pogo stick. What to do? Look for other opportunities. Here's a way to think about the priority for taking advantage of the opportunities.

Attack Rules

1. *Fast fixes.* Make the easiest changes first, regardless of the payoff. For example, if you spot a dozen opportunities for improvement, and the easiest to implement would be to make your overheads more readable, do that first, even though it may add only a little to the effectiveness of your instruction. Making the easiest fixes first will get you moving and will give you some fast successes about which to feel good.

2. *Independent fixes.* Make the changes that don't require

the assistance or approval of someone else, regardless of payoff. If you can improve the course a little bit today, that's at least as good as improving it a lot next year. For example, if you could make your tests match your objectives without needing approval to do so, that would be a higher priority change than that of trying to get approval to teach your course in a single 40-hour block.

3. ***High payoff fixes.*** Make the fixes that will provide the highest payoff in course effectiveness, even if approval is required. Here is the list of actions that will give you the most return for your efforts, in order of priority:

a. *Make objectives match the need.* Check your objectives against the need from which they were derived to make sure that they describe what students need to be able to do.

b. *Provide outcome information to students.* If you do nothing else, make sure that a copy of the objectives is in the hands of the students. This act will give them a fighting chance of accomplishing what they need to accomplish, even though instructional materials may be scarce or poorly crafted.

c. *Provide a reason to learn.* Once students know what is expected of them, the next best thing to do is to make sure they have a solid reason to learn. So make those changes that will help students perceive how it is important to them to accomplish the objectives, and remember that "Someday this will be important to you" is not a reason to learn. Instead, it is merely a symptom of instruction that hasn't yet been made relevant to the students.

  d. *Provide as much practice time as possible.* Arrange the instruction so that students can practice when they are ready, for as long as they need to achieve mastery of the objective. Make sure they find out how well they are progressing.

  e. *Provide instructional resources.* Give students whatever materials and other resources are currently available, regardless of their quality. When students want to learn, they'll do it in spite of inadequate resources.

4. **Supportive environment.** Once the above steps have been attended to, the best way to improve the quality and efficiency of your instruction is to improve the learning environment itself.

   • Provide easy access to resources. Make sure that as many resources are available in the classroom itself as possible and that access isn't restricted by unnecessary bureaucratic rules.

   • Minimize obstacles such as distractions, whether these are provided by noise, students, instructors, or outsiders.

   • Make sure students know it's OK to practice and perform as desired and that it's OK to make mistakes while learning.

   • Be available to help, but stay out of their way.

   • Offer positive consequences for desired performance, as well as for performances that *approximate* the final desired performance.

- Make your feedback comments task-diagnostic, and gently correct your students when they make self-diagnostic comments.

5. ***Adopt more streamlined procedures.*** Go back to your course procedures and see where you can modify them to more closely approximate the ideal instructional characteristics found in Chapter 18.

6. ***Improve the instruction itself.*** Polish the presentations, hone the examples, and clarify the demonstrations. It may come as a surprise that this item is on the bottom of the priority list. But think about it a moment. What good is it to improve the elegance of the instruction itself if that instruction serves no useful purpose, or if everyone is convinced that it is of little or no value to them, or if students can already perform as desired? How much will it add to the effectiveness or efficiency of a racing car to paint it when the tires are flat and the engine is dead? Sure, it's important to improve the elegance of the instruction itself; smooth instruction helps motivation as well as ease of learning. But until the above items are attended to, improved elegance isn't likely to net you much gain in instructional success.

So work to make the course responsive to a real need before working to improve the elegance of the course materials. Work to provide students with a real reason to learn before working to improve the quality of your slides. Remember the Wacky Watchmaker who worked hard to reduce the number of parts needed for a wristwatch. When asked whether it worked, he replied, "Certainly not. But it doesn't work—*efficiently.*"

And keep in mind that Rome wasn't burned in a day. Make your changes one at a time. And then reward yourself each time you do so.

In Closing

Instruction is an act of humanity. It is an attempt to enrich the lives of others by expanding their ability to deal more successfully with the world in which they live. The measure of our success is the degree to which we can make our graduates employable, self-sufficient, and socially adept. There are few callings more personally rewarding or of greater importance to society than that of contributing to the success of others.

Useful Resources

1. Carlisle, K. E. *Analyzing Jobs and Tasks,* 1986. Educational Technology Publications, Inc. 140 Sylvan Avenue, Englewood Cliffs, NJ 07632.

2. Cram, D. D. "Professor T-Pop." *Performance and Instruction,* July, 1979; pp. 38–41.

3. Cram, D. D. "Advice to the Training-Lorn," *Performance and Instruction,* March, 1983; pp. 26–27.

4. Harless, J. H. "Guiding Performance with Job Aids," *Introduction to Performance Technology,* 1986, pp. 106–124.

5. Hoffman, M. "What to Leave Out When Time Is Short," *Performance and Instruction,* April, 1987.

6. Mager, R. F., and Pipe, P. *Analyzing Performance Problems,* Third Edition, 1997.

7. Mager, R. F., and Pipe, P. Performance Analysis Flowchart and Worksheets (24/pkg.), 1997.

8. Mager, R. F. *How to Turn Learners On . . . without turning them off,* Third Edition, 1997.

9. Mager, R. F. *Goal Analysis,* Third Edition, 1997.

10. Mager, R. F. *Measuring Instructional Results,* Third Edition, 1997.

11. Mager, R. F. *Preparing Instructional Objectives,* Third Edition, 1997.

12. Mager, R. F. *What Every Manager Should Know About Training,* 1992.

13. Mager, E. W. *Classroom Presentation Skills Workshop,* Third Edition, 1997.

14. Mager, R. F. *Applied CRI,* 1987.

15. Mager, R. F., and Pipe, P. *Criterion-Referenced Instruction: Practical Skills for Designing Instruction that Works,* 4th ed., 1994.

16. Mager, R. F. *Instructional Module Development,* 2nd ed., Revised 1996.

17. Mager, R. F. "No Self-Efficacy, No Performance," *Training Magazine,* Lakewood Publications, April, 1992.

18. Schrock, Sharon A., and Coscarelli, William C. C. *Criterion-Referenced Test Development,* 1996. ISBN: 0-9616690-22-0.

19. Tosti, D. T. "Feedback Systems," *Introduction to Performance Technology,* 1986; pp. 166–167.

20. Pipe, P. *Developing Performance Aids Workshop,* Peter Pipe Associates, 1981. Peter Pipe Associates, 962 Chehalis Drive, Sunnyvale, CA 94087.

Resources 6 through 16 are available from:

The Center for Effective Performance, Inc.
4250 Perimeter Park South, Suite 131
Atlanta, GA 30341   (770) 458-4080
               (800) 558-4237

Resources 2, 3, 4, 5, and 19 are available from:

International Society for Performance Improvement
1300 L Street NW, Suite 1250, Washington, DC 20005

Makenzie Mit Der Bookentesting

The house lights dimmed and the orchestra charged into the overture. Cymbals crashed, trombones trombled, and trumpets hootled. Violin bows flashed and bobbled in unison, as though locked together in a frenzy of musical calisthenics.

"That's a pretty enthusiastic overture," said the novice. "What's this opera about, anyway?"

"Well," responded the regular, "it's a tribute."

"Tribute? To what or whom?"

"To a clump of folks who were generous enough to help the hero test his book. The opera opens with the hero sitting at the typewriter, writing a book. He begins by singing and whining about how hard it is to write. It's a very sad aria."

"Sounds like a nut. What happens then?"

"His wife comes in . . . Lola Lollapalooza. She's a soprano played by Eileen Mager. She tells him about her day in the village. Then they sing a duet, with her trying to get him to let her see the book, and him subtly trying to get back to work."

At this point the first act ended and the smokers ran for the exits.

"What happens next?" asked the novice.

"The next act takes place after he's finished a first draft and is ready to try it out."

"Try it out?"

"Yes. Before he sends it to the publisher, he wants to know whether the book has the right content for its audience and whether it's as clear and useful as he can make it."

"Isn't he smart enough to answer that for himself?"

"Well," replied the seasoned one, "he's smart enough to know that his mind-reading skills aren't very good. So to make sure he's headed in a useful direction, he's asked someone to check it for continuity and completeness."

"Aha."

"Here he comes now. The first person to run his mind over the manuscript is Doctor Magic Whizzmore, played by Paul Whitmore."

Just then a dashing figure in flowing robes entered and began to sing in sonorous tones.

"Why is he carrying that box under his arm?"

"That's his computer. He always carries it. It's connected to his oblong medulla. Shhh. Listen as he tells the writer about his findings, about his reactions to the content. It's a very moving aria."

"Now what?"

The soprano had returned and repeated her aria entreating the writer to let her see his work. He bent down to tie his shoelace; while on his knees he begged the question.

"The suggested revisions have now been made and another tryout has been done, this time by the baritone in the purple knickers waving the golf club. This role is being consummately played by David Cram . . . he plays it often. He's singing about how he checked the manuscript for completeness and content, as well as for its integrity in the corporate training environment."

"Does he always carry that golf club?" queried the novice.

"He has to. It's attached to him. His doctor has told him that if he ever unscrews the golf club from his hand, his bottom will fall off."

"This seems like a long opera."

"They all do. The music covers the absence of plot, and the loud singing helps keep the audience awake. But we're nearing the climax. Look. Here come the Teepoppers."

"The what?"

"The Teepoppers. They represent the target audience of the book. They have a great deal of instructional experience, especially in the vocational and technical training environments. They're singing their recommendations. These roles are brilliantly played by Bob Miller and Jim Maxey. This is important stuff. Notice how closely the writer is paying attention and making notes."

"Wait a minnit. Here comes that soprano again. What does she want now?"

"Same thing. Wants to offer her help, but the husband keeps telling her he's saving her for the grand finale. Even so, she's good for his morale."

"How does it come out in the end?"

"Wait and see. Look. Another round of revision has been completed, and the writer has sent out copies for technical accuracy."

"I thought he just did that."

"That was to make sure the content would work for the audiences it is intended for. This check was to make sure that the procedures described are psychologically sound, accurately apply principles of learning, and won't unintentionally turn the readers off."

"Looks like a parade is starting."

"No. It's just that each of the people asked to check technical accuracy sings a recommendations solo in turn. Gives us a chance to see some colorful costumes as we listen to their wisdom."

"Who are playing these roles?"

"Those roles are incomparably played by Marianne

Hoffman, Bill Valen, Carol Valen, and Paul Whitmore."

At this point the soprano returned, the curtain came down on the second act, and the smokers ran for the exits.

"The last act opens with the chorus singing about the title check," confided the veteran. "The writer has asked a number of people to respond to several possible titles. They sing about their choices while the writer sings about the importance of making the title fit the intended user."

"I've just become glad they don't sing this stuff in English."

"If you will think about it, you will see that this is a very important part of the process. How often would you buy a steak that was called dead cow?"

"I see your point. Who are these people?"

"These roles are ably played by Al Wilson, Carol Valen, Lex Danson, John Pate, Skip Wolfe, Millar Farewell, Seth Leibler, Joyce Kelly, Verne Niner, Bill Valen, Alan Steffes, and Eileen Mager."

"The soprano finally got a whack at it?"

"Yes. And now she's into her big scene. She was saved for last, y'know. Loved ones can be the hardest critics, and he didn't want to take a chance on being demoralized before he finished. But she finally got to do her manuscript tryout and is now singing her recommendations."

"Long, isn't it?"

"But beautifully sung."

"Why is that lady in the red mask and black cape slashing at the manuscript?"

"That's the editor, played by Mary Kitzmiller. She's the heavy, acting out how she sliced words and punctured phrases to ready the manuscript for publication."

"Couldn't he write?"

"No matter how well he writes, there are always hundreds of changes that will make the product more readable, more literate, more interesting. Also gives editors a feeling of power."

Just then another group of colorfully-clad singers marched in.

"Now what? I thought it was over."

"Oh, these are the people who tested the new edition. Their chorus is an operatic version of 'Pick a Little, Talk a Little, Pick, Pick Pick.' It's very important and is being very well sung by David Cram, Ann Parkman, Seth Leibler, Lola Lollapalooza (Eileen Mager), John Gaylord, Dan Raymond, Marianne Hoffman, and Paul Whitmore.

"Quite a handsome group, wouldn't you say?"

"Look. Here's the grand finale. The writer has assembled all the contributors into his den . . ."

"Big den."

"Artistic license. He's describing their important contributions to the development of the book and is singing the praises of each in turn. He's imploring the audience to stand in awe at their assistance and to applaud their generosity until their hands turn red. Let's join in."

And so they did.

Index

Goal Analysis

How to clarify your goals so you can actually achieve them

Third Edition

Robert F. Mager

Books by Robert F. Mager

Preparing Instructional Objectives, *Third Edition**

Measuring Instructional Results, *Third Edition**

Analyzing Performance Problems, *Third Edition**
(with Peter Pipe)

Goal Analysis, *Third Edition**

How to Turn Learners On . . . without turning them off, *Third Edition**

Making Instruction Work, *Second Edition**

Developing Vocational Instruction (with Kenneth Beach)‑

Troubleshooting the Troubleshooting Course

The How to Write a Book Book

What Every Manager Should Know About Training

*Sold as a six-volume set (The Mager Six-Pack)

WORKSHOPS BY ROBERT F. MAGER

Criterion-Referenced Instruction (with Peter Pipe)

Instructional Module Development

The Training Manager Workshop

For more information, contact:
   The Center for Effective Performance, Inc.
   2300 Peachford Road, Suite 2000
   Atlanta, GA 30338
   (770) 458-4080 or (800) 558-4237
   www.cepworldwide.com

Copyright © 1997, 1984, 1983 by The Center for Effective Performance, Inc. All rights reserved. No part of this book may be reproduced by any means, transmitted, or translated into a machine language without written permission from the publisher. First Edition 1983, Third Edition 1997.
ISBN 1-879-618-04-4 (PREVIOUSLY ISBN 1-56103-339-1)
ISBN 1-879-618-15-X (SIX-VOLUME SET)
Library of Congress Catalog Card Number: 96-72445
Printed in the United States of America

05 04 03 02 01 00   10 9 8 7 6 5 4 3

Contents

Preface

Once upon a time in the land of Fuzz, King Aling called in his cousin Ding and commanded, "Go ye out into all of Fuzzland and find me the goodest of men, whom I shall reward for his goodness."

"But how will I know one when I see one?" asked the Fuzzy.

"Why, he will be *sincere*," scoffed the king, and whacked off a leg for his impertinence.

So, the Fuzzy limped out to find a good man. But soon he returned confused and empty-handed.

"But how will I know one when I see one?" he asked again.

"Why, he will be *dedicated*," grumbled the king and whacked off another leg for his impertinence.

So the Fuzzy hobbled away once more to look for the goodest of men. But again he returned, confused and empty-handed.

"But how will I know one when I see one?" he pleaded.

"Why, he will have *an empathetic understanding of his self-actualizing potential*," fumed the king and whacked off another leg for his impertinence.

So the Fuzzy, now on his last leg, hopped out to continue his search. In time, he returned with the wisest, most sincere and dedicated Fuzzy in all of Fuzzland and stood him before the king.

"Why, this man won't do at all," roared the king. "He is much too thin to suit me." Whereupon, he whacked off the last leg of the Fuzzy, who fell to the floor with a squishy thump.

The moral of this fable is that . . . *if you can't tell one when you see one, you may wind up without a leg to stand on.*

IF YOU CAN'T TELL ONE WHEN YOU SEE ONE, YOU MAY WIND UP WITHOUT A LEG TO STAND ON.

If your goals—your visions—are important to achieve, then it is essential that you do more than just talk about them in "Fuzzy" terms. And that is just as true for organizational and community goals as it is for personal and family goals. Broad statements of intent can be achieved only to the degree that their meaning is understood, to the degree that you can recognize achievement of the goals when you see it.

And that is what *Goal Analysis* is about. The goal analysis procedure can be very useful in helping you to describe the *meaning* of goals and visions you hope to achieve, whether those goals deal with attitude, appreciation, understanding, success, or profitability. It is a procedure designed to help you determine the important dimensions or components of a goal, so that you will be able to make good decisions about how to accomplish the goal and about how to keep track of your progress toward goal achievement. It is a procedure that anyone will find useful, from techies to homemakers, from students to managers, and will even be useful to those who feel that their jobs are unlike any others and very hard to describe.

It is *not* the object of this book to tell you what to achieve or what you should mean by the words you use. But if you have ever wished that you or the organization with which you are affiliated could be better at accomplishing their goals, *Goal Analysis* will give you the tools you need.

Robert F. Mager

Carefree, Arizona
January 1997

1
What It's All About

Almost everyone wants to be more successful. Regardless of who they are or what they do, individuals want to be knowledgeable, have poise, be able to communicate and listen, and a thousand other things. Organizations want to shape their vision, and they want their employees to provide good customer service, achieve high morale, conserve energy, be responsible, appreciate diversity, and a thousand other things. Members of the clergy want to increase reverence, encourage unselfish devotion, provide merciful ministry, and a thousand other things.

Almost all people want to improve these things either in themselves or in others. "They need to have a better attitude" and "We've got to teach them to be properly motivated" are commonly heard expressions. "We need to improve their self-concept" and "We want them to behave in a professional manner" are others. The uttering of these important intentions, however, is only a beginning step toward their accomplishment. Saying them isn't the same as achieving them.

What to do? What steps should we take to accomplish the many important goals (visions) in our lives? Should we tell people what to do? Should we organize a course and have them attend? Should we establish rules, invent forms, punish offenders, praise the good? The key question is "Exactly what should we do to accomplish our important goals?"

The answer is "There is no way to decide what action to take until we know what we are trying to accomplish." Too often, people would rather do something than think about the purpose of the doing. For them, action is the same as progress.

And when it comes to goal achievement, that action all too frequently takes the form of instruction. "We've got to teach them to have the right attitude," they say. But "attitude" isn't a skill that requires know-how. So what is there to teach? Or "We've got to teach them to improve their citizenship." Again, there's no clue as to what, if anything, needs to be taught.

If there is a real difference between what people can do and what they need to be able to do, and if those people have a genuine need to do what they can't do, then instruction may help. Maybe. But maybe a different action is called for. There's no way to know until the intended outcome is clearly stated. Consider this nutty dialogue between a hypothetical doctor and woman:

Doc: Ah, good morning, madam.

Mad: Good morning, doctor.

Doc: Just a moment and I'll have your prescription all written out.

Mad: Wait a minute. . .

Doc: No time like the present, you know.

Mad: But I haven't even told you why I'm here yet.

Doc: No need. I've been a doctor for seventeen years.

Mad: Don't you even *examine* people?

Doc: What for? I've been trained and licensed to practice, and I know what most people need in the way of treatment.

Mad: You give everybody the same treatment?

Doc: Of course. Saves time.

Mad: That's crazy!

Doc: Not at all. Most patients improve. Some improve more than others, of course, but that's mostly because they try harder.

Mad: What about the ones who get worse?

Doc: No problem. I label them as failures and send them on . . . and on . . . and on. Ah, by the way, why are you here?

Mad: I was the new receptionist. And good-bye!

You see the point. Action is easy. What isn't so easy is relating actions to outcomes. What isn't easy is *purposeful* activity, activity that will get you where you want to go. And if instruction (or any other remedy) is to be successful, there must be a connection between the problem and the solution, between the need for the instruction and the nature of the instruction. Often the connection is obvious. If you want to be able to play the piano, the instruction needs to provide skills and practice in playing the piano. If you want to be able to make a speech, you need to practice speechmaking.

Sometimes, however, the connection between the intention—that is, the intended result—and the actions needed to get the result isn't so clear. Consider this dialogue between a professor and student:

Stud: I refuse to pay you for this course.

Prof: Why? Didn't I teach you how to make the finest buggy whips ever created?

Stud: Yes, you did.

Prof: Well then?

Stud: But I took this course because I wanted to understand history.

Prof: Can you deny that buggy whips were used by some
of the most important people in history?

Stud: I suppose not.

Prof: Can you deny that buggy whips are an integral part
of history?

Stud: I don't know. I never learned any history. I only
learned how to make buggy whips.

Prof: But wasn't I successful in teaching you how to make
good buggy whips?

Stud: Yes. But the fact remains . . .

Prof: Yes?

Stud: You didn't solve my problem.

It seems pretty obvious that if your goal is to improve students' understanding of history, you don't proceed to make
them expert buggy-whip makers. Nor would you instruct
them in welding or weaving. But what *would* you do? Maybe
instructing isn't even the right approach. Maybe some other
action is indicated. Or maybe *no* action at all. How can you
decide how to proceed *until* you know what "understanding
history" means?

To take other examples, how should you proceed if the goal
is to make "better citizens"? What should you do if the goal is
to achieve "good judgment," "perceptive listening," "motivated
workers," or "effective therapists"? Though these states may be
among the most important to achieve—and all goals *sound*
important—*the act of stating them in the abstract does little to
suggest the means of their achievement.*

Shapes and Sizes

Goal statements come in all sorts of shapes and sizes and are wrapped in all sorts of words. Some are stated briefly; others are not. One thing they have in common is that they all sound important.

Some goals refer to us as individuals:
- be a good citizen
- have self-confidence
- be a knowledgeable consumer

Others refer to the organization:
- be technologically innovative
- offer an enlightened workplace
- provide opportunities for personal growth

Still others refer to the environment or the community:
- enhance urban livability
- provide a modern environment
- maintain empathetic public servants

But if a goal is important to achieve, then it is important to do more about that achievement than to simply talk about it in abstract terms. Again, that's just where goal analysis comes in.* (It will help show you just what steps to take to accomplish your goals.)

The Goal of this Book

The goal of this book is to help you "know when and how to do a goal analysis." But that's a fuzzy. It sounds nice, but it doesn't tell you what "know" means. It sort of points in the direction of

*In technical jargon, the goal analysis procedure is called "developing an operational definition."

the desired outcomes, but it doesn't describe them very well.

Aha! This is just the situation that calls for a goal analysis. Having performed one on this very fuzzy statement, I can now be more specific in telling you what the goal of this book means.

The goal, "know when and how to do a goal analysis," means:

1. Be able to tell the difference between statements that describe abstractions and those that describe performances.

2. Having identified a goal that you consider important to achieve, be able to describe the performances that represent your meaning of the goal. In other words, be able to describe specific outcomes that, if achieved, will cause you to agree that the goal is also achieved.

As a test of your success with the procedure, you would select a goal you think important, carry out the procedure, and then answer the question, "If a person exhibited the performances I have described in a way I have described, would I agree that he or she has achieved (represents) my goal?" When you are able to answer "yes," you will be finished with the analysis. If your answer is "no," further analysis would be indicated.

What Next?

The goal analysis procedure is not a procedure that you set out to do because you *want* to; rather, it's something that you do because you *have* to. Let's take a look at the bigger picture to see just where the goal analysis procedure fits in.

2
When To Do It

Where does the goal analysis fit into the larger scheme of things? To answer that, we'll need to take a brief look at the bigger picture, which relates to our intent to improve something.

Executives and managers work to improve the functioning of their organizations; trainers work to improve the ability of their trainees to perform their jobs; teachers want to better prepare their students to cope successfully in the world around them; and parents want to help their children become productive, responsible, and happy adults. And, as individuals, our intent is often to improve some aspect of our lives (e.g., adopt more useful habits) or to strengthen our skills.

There are a number of procedures available through which to accomplish these improvements, and here are very brief descriptions of some of the main ones.

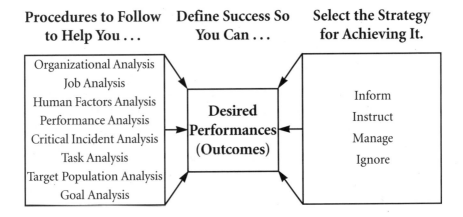

Procedures to Follow to Help You . . .	Define Success So You Can . . .	Select the Strategy for Achieving It.
Organizational Analysis Job Analysis Human Factors Analysis Performance Analysis Critical Incident Analysis Task Analysis Target Population Analysis Goal Analysis	Desired Performances (Outcomes)	Inform Instruct Manage Ignore

Organizational Analysis

An organizational analysis is used to determine just what it is the organization should look like to best accomplish its mission. The focus is on (1) verifying that the various components of the organization (division, departments, sections, etc.) are designed and connected in the best possible way to get the organization where it wants to go and (2) specifying meaningful outcomes that will lead to mission accomplishment. An organizational analysis also looks at all the supports (e.g., policies, equipment, trained people, etc.) that need to be in place to ensure that people can do their jobs effectively.

Job Analysis

A *job* consists of a collection of tasks. Sometimes this is a fixed collection of tasks that can be carefully described, and sometimes the boundaries of the job are intended to be flexible (e.g., "Your job title is Corporate Troubleshooter, and your job is to do what you think needs to be done"). A *job analysis* is intended to identify the tasks that should define a job, to name and describe the tasks that will best serve the organization (as defined by the organizational analysis) in producing the desired accomplishments (outcomes).

Human Factors Analysis

These analyses are intended to find out how best to design equipment so that it will fit the human beings expected to use it. The purpose is to find out how to make the equipment "user friendly," easy to use, and idiot-proof.

For example, a great deal of human factors analysis is done in the design of aircraft cockpits, not so much to make them comfortable for the pilots, but to make information instantly available to them when they need it.

Whatever the specific intent, the general intent is to find ways to improve human performance.

Performance Analysis

The performance analysis is used to determine why people aren't doing something they are supposed to be doing or why they are doing something they shouldn't be doing. It helps one to select solutions that will eliminate a performance discrepancy (the difference between what is happening and what should be happening). The analysis consists of evaluating the size or importance of a performance discrepancy, then determining whether the discrepancy exists because of a lack of skill or motivation to perform a known skill or because of obstacles that prevent the desired performance from occurring.

Critical Incident Analysis

This procedure (sometimes called a *significant incident analysis*) attempts to answer the question, "What isn't happening according to expectation?" By collecting and analyzing incidents of deviations from the expected (accidents, for example), it is possible to determine what actions might be taken to remedy (reduce or eliminate) the incidents. Sometimes the remedy is information, sometimes it is instruction, and sometimes it involves actions such as color-coding equipment or clarifying directions.

Task Analysis

If the performance analysis indicates that people don't know *how* to do what they need to be able to do, instruction is usually, but not always, needed as a remedy. When instruction appears to be a solution, the next question to be answered is "What should the instruction accomplish?" The task analysis is one way to derive the answer to this question. This technique reveals the components of competent performance—that is, it provides a step-by-step look at how competent people perform a task, so that decisions can more easily be made about what *other* people would have to learn if *they* are to perform in the same competent manner.

Target Population Analysis

An act that is wasteful of human motivation, as well as of time and money, is that of "teaching" people things they already know. The target population analysis helps to eliminate this problem. This technique consists of a careful examination of the characteristics (abilities, education, interests, biases, experience) of those for whom instruction is intended. With this information available, it is possible to select instruction for any individual by subtracting what the individual already knows from what the individual needs to know. The remainder can then be prescribed as the curriculum for that individual.

The information revealed by the target population analysis is also useful in adjusting the examples, the language, the media mix through which the instruction and practice are presented, and the speed of the instruction, so that they more closely match the needs of the people for whom the instruction is intended.

Goal Analysis

People are often expected to perform in ways that are not reflected in tasks. In addition to performing certain skills, they are expected to "appreciate music," "show respect for school," "develop a proper customer attitude," or "take pride in their work." Since it isn't possible to watch them developing or appreciating, and if these states are important for them to achieve, how will you proceed? How will you decide *if* instruction will help them to achieve the desired state? And if it will, how will you decide *what kind* of instruction to organize?

A task analysis won't help, because there is no task to observe. A critical incident analysis won't help, because there are no errors or problems to tabulate. A target population analysis is useful mainly as a procedure for adjusting existing instructional objectives, so that is out. Likewise, a performance analysis can't be carried out until the relevant performances are identified.

This is where goal analysis fits. The function of goal analysis is to define the indefinable, to tangibilitate the intangible— to help you say what you mean by your important but abstract goals (or *fuzzies,* as they will be called in this book). *With this procedure, it is possible to describe the essential elements of abstract states—to identify the main performances that constitute the meaning of the goal.* Once you know the performances that collectively define the goal, you will be in a better position to decide which of these performances need to be taught and which need to be managed. Then you can select the most appropriate teaching or management procedures and arrange to measure your progress toward success.

We Use It All the Time

Carpenters may set out to lay a floor and suddenly discover a need to use their tape measure. They may set out to set a window and again have to reach for their tape measure. As a matter of fact, no matter which task they begin, it is likely that they will need to use their tape measure somewhere during completion of the task.

The same is true of goal analysis. While you may sometimes deliberately set out to complete a goal analysis, there are many other instances in which you will discover that you need to complete a goal analysis if you want to get on with the task you are performing.

For example:

When you're engaging in:	*Do a goal analysis when you hear:*
Organizational Analysis	*"The organization needs to be more flexible and resilient."*
Job Analysis	*"They need to be self-starters."*
Human Factors Analysis	*"This gismo needs to be 'user friendly'."*
Performance Analysis	*"They should be more safety conscious."*
Critical Incident Analysis	*"There are too many accidents."*
Task Analysis	*"The next step is to answer the phone in a friendly manner."*
Target Population Analysis	*"They are highly motivated."*

In each of the instances above, and in thousands like them, a goal analysis would be appropriate, because someone has uttered a fuzzy in need of clarification.

When Do We Use It?

So where does the goal analysis fit into the larger scheme of things? *Everywhere!* When do we use the goal analysis procedure? Anytime these two conditions exist:

1. Someone describes an intent in abstract (fuzzy) terms, and

2. The intent is important to achieve.

Who Can Use the Goal Analysis Tool?

Just about everyone. Here are a few examples:

If you are a:	*You would use it whenever you accomplish or define what is meant by:*
CEO	"Maximize shareholder value" or "Create a strong competitive advantage."
Sales Manager	"Use a consultative selling approach" or "Have salespeople exude enthusiasm."
Technical Supervisor	"Be professional" or "Understand troubleshooting."
Quality Engineer	"Be quality conscious" or "Be a competent engineer."
Production Engineer	"Produce a quality product" or "Provide world-class service."
Instructor/Teacher	"Understand gas welding" or "Be a good instructor."
Accounting Manager	"Appreciate investment principles" or "Be a detail person."

What Next?

Now that we know what a goal analysis is and when to use it, it's time to learn the procedure itself. Before we do, however, we need to know just what an abstraction (fuzzy) really represents. Without an understanding (oops—there goes one now) of the nature of an abstraction, it might be difficult to appreciate (there goes another one) just how important the goal analysis can be. So that's where we'll begin.

3

Where's Your Attitude?

What do physicians do when individuals ask, "Am I healthy?" How do they determine a state of health? What do they actually *do?* What they do is to check specifics. They take blood pressure, check eyes and ears, count pulse, check reflexes, and kick tires. And from information about *observable* things, they make statements about an abstract state—health. If the observable indicators look positive, physicians are willing to say that a person is healthy; that is, they are willing to generalize from the specific. But they don't ever check health directly. Health doesn't exist as a thing that can be probed, poked, or weighed. It is an abstract idea, the condition of which is *inferred* from visible specifics. Always.

Every statement about abstractions is inferred from visible or audible specifics. By definition, if an abstract term described something that was visible or audible, it wouldn't be abstract. That goes as much for statements about "attitude" as it does for statements about "motivation." It's as true for statements about "understanding" as it is for statements about "knowing."

Since it is worthwhile to be clear about this matter of abstractions versus specifics, let's think for a moment about "attitude." We might just as easily select any of the other common abstractions that we talk about (such as motivation, understanding, or self-concept), but we'll let attitude represent them all. What is true for attitude is true for every other abstraction.

So let's begin. Just what do we mean when we use the word *attitude?* Is attitude a *thing?*

Well, no. Not a thing like a meringue or a mukluk. *Things* are what you can poke with your fingers or beat with a stick. Attitudes are not that sort of thing. You can't dissect people and take out their attitudes any more than you can dissect them and take out their thoughts. That doesn't mean that attitudes and thinking don't exist; it's just that they aren't directly available for physical examination—or for poking or pinching.

So if attitude isn't a thing, what is it?

Attitude is a word, that's what it is. And words mean whatever their users want them to mean. (This one seems to have more misusers than users.)

By attitude, we generally mean to describe an abstraction, some sort of general state or condition existing inside ourselves or others. When I say, "She has a favorable attitude toward mukluks," I am suggesting that the person will behave in one way when faced with a mukluk rather than in another. I am suggesting that the mukluk-lover will tend to say favorable things about the object, that she will tend to move toward the object when she sees one rather than away from it, and that she will tend to seek out ways to come into contact with the object. Similarly, a person who is said to have a favorable attitude toward music would be expected to say favorable things about the sound, to respond favorably when in the presence of the sound, and to seek out ways of increasing the amount of time that he or she is in the presence of the sound.

It's a Prediction

An interesting thing about attitudes is that every statement about attitude is a statement of prediction. No matter what someone says about the attitude of someone else, he or she is making a prediction about how that person is likely to behave in the future. Based on what you have seen someone do or heard someone say in the past, you predict how he or she will perform in the future. If you see me turn a bowl of fish soup over the cook's head, you might be urged to comment: "He has a negative attitude toward fish soup." Such a comment is based on what you saw me do and is intended to predict that putting me in the presence of fish soup will be followed by some sort of negative act or comment on my part (toward the soup or the soupee). You might be right or wrong, but the statement about attitude is a statement of prediction, a statement that intends to suggest how I might behave in some future time.

Since an attitude is not directly visible, it follows that all statements about attitude are based on circumstantial evidence that takes the form of visible behavior. If you hadn't seen me dump the fish soup on the cook or heard or read an account of the fish story, you would have had no basis whatever for making a statement about how I am likely to behave in the presence of fish soup. You might be wrong in your attitude statement (your prediction); it might be the cook I dislike and not the fish soup. No problem; lots of people make incorrect predictions from the information available to them. The point is simply that, right or wrong, *a statement about attitude is a statement of prediction based on what somebody says or what somebody does.*

Indicator Behaviors

The behaviors on which attitude statements are based can properly be called *indicator behaviors,* for they are used as indicators of attitude. Indicators are common items of our existence. We use thermometers to indicate temperature, speedometers to indicate speed, and voltmeters to indicate voltage. In each case, we use some sort of device to tell us the state or condition of something we cannot see or measure directly.

Some indicators are better than others. A voltmeter is a better indicator of the amount of voltage present in an electrical circuit than the sensation you feel when you grab the wire. The loudness of your "ouch" is not directly related to the amount of the voltage.

The same holds true for attitudes and their indicator behaviors. Some behaviors are better indicators (predictors) of attitude than others, and it isn't always easy to tell which is better.
To make it more difficult, any particular behavior might well
be an indicator of any number of attitudes. When I poured the
fish soup on the cook, he couldn't tell whether that behavior
was indicating a distaste for fish soup, *his* version of fish soup,
fur-lined soup bowls, dirty aprons, or him. In the absence of

some other indicators (behaviors) on my part, he could pre-dict pretty well *that* I found something distinctly not to my lik-ing, but not *what.* He would need to observe more of my behavior if he wanted to be sure. If, while carrying out the deed, I spoke thusly: "Sir, my distaste for fish soup is exceeded only by my distaste for fish stew," he would have a better clue as to how to interpret my soup-pouring behavior.

So, for example, instead of merely noting that a person chews gum when she enters a classroom and then predicting, "She has a poor attitude about my course," it is more prudent to try to find at least several of the indicators that are repre-sentative of the attitude in which you are interested. If you know which performances you will accept as your meaning of an attitude or other goal, you will also know how to assess whether the attitude (tendency to perform one way rather than another) is in the condition you would like. You will also have clues about which performances to change in order to improve that condition; when someone changes what he or she does, others are likely to change the words they use to describe the person.

As an example, if a person has been labeled "hostile" because of his tendency to throw pies in the faces of his col-leagues but later gives up this action, others are likely to stop calling him hostile and begin referring to him as reformed, or mellowed, or as having had a change of heart.

Notice that nothing in this discussion has had anything to do with behaviorism ... or any other sort of ism. The concern with what people do and what they say does not stem from any sort of philosophical base. We are concerned with behavior (performance) because we have no other choice, no other route into the heart or mind of a person. It is the only sound basis we have for judgments about what is happening inside another human being. No matter how deeply we may desire that someone "develop a strong, positive self-concept" or "feel a deep and abiding appreciation for the value of eagles," the only evidence we have of the existence of such conditions is what the person says and does.

Since it is the *doing* that causes us to agree or disagree that some abstract state is present, it is the *doing* that matters most. So if you can figure out how to get people to do the things that represent the *definition* of a goal (abstract state), you will be in a much better position to achieve that goal. And that is the purpose of the goal analysis—to help you determine just what people would have to say or do for you to be willing to agree they had achieved the goal. Once you know what those "say and do" things are, you will find it much easier to figure out how to get them to happen.

Next?

Since knowing when to use a tool is a significant part of knowing how to use it, we'll begin with some practice in recognizing situations in which the goal analysis will help.

4
Recognizing Fuzzies

A manager had just reviewed a task analysis of an important position in his firm. "Yes," he said, "these are the skills we want performed in this job; but we also want the person to *communicate a positive attitude toward the company.*"

Now when we are talking about a skill, whether of the hand or of the mind, we can easily determine whether it exists in the shape we would like, and we can easily determine what to do to make it better. If we want to be better at batting, we would practice swinging a bat. If we want to be better at singing, we would sing. But suppose we want to be more successful or better human beings. Exactly what would we do to improve? Sing? Swing? Smile more? Get into another line of work? Hard to tell, isn't it?

Or suppose, as in the example described above, we want to be better at communicating a positive attitude. Would we study diction? Whistle while we work? Say nice things? We can't tell. It could be any or all of these things and perhaps dozens more.

The truth is that until we know what the person who wants to achieve this or any other goal *means* by the statement, we cannot decide how to achieve the state. Moreover, we cannot decide whether we are making progress or if we have been successful.

But that's not enough reason to use the goal analysis. After all, we spend a large part of our day speaking in fuzzies, and appropriately so.

"Good morning."
"Ah, good morning. Nice day, isn't it?"

That's a common interchange, intended to express friendship or courtesy. But hardly an appropriate time to reply with "Nice? Now *there's* a fuzzy. Just what do you mean by *that?*" Or:

"Ahhh, ma cherie, I loooove you."

Again, "What do you mean by *that?*" is hardly the correct reply. And so it goes. We often speak in generalities, and in most situations these abstractions are perfectly acceptable. But sometimes not. When the manager says, "We *must* improve our company image," or "You perform your tasks well, but you need to work on your attitude," *that's* when the goal analysis is used. When you say, "I must become more assertive," or "I want to be a better person," *that's* when the goal analysis is important. Whenever one of these abstractions (or *fuzzies*) shows up as something important enough to do something about, *then* is the time to use goal analysis. The goal analysis will unfuzzify the abstraction to the point where you can say whether there *is* any useful meaning, and if so, what the essence of that meaning might be.

Fuzzy-Watching Practice

Before reaching for the goal analysis tool, you need to know how to do two things:

1. Be able to recognize an abstraction when you see one, and

2. Decide whether that abstraction is important to achieve.

I can help you with the first; the second you will have to do for yourself. So here we go.

Intents to develop such states as "favorable attitudes," "deep appreciation," or "sense of pride" are examples of abstractions; they do not tell you what a person would be doing when demonstrating the state or condition, nor do they suggest the behavior that would indicate how you can tell that he or she has done it. On the other hand, items such as "writing," "decanting," and "hopping" are examples of performances; they *do* tell you what a person would be doing when demonstrating his or her ability to do it.

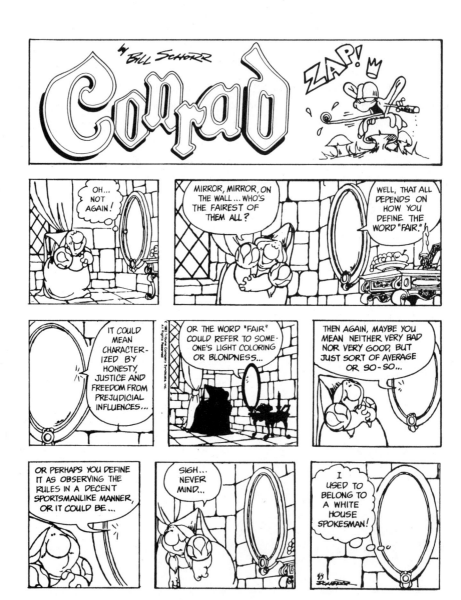

Reprinted by permission: Tribune Company Syndicate, Inc.

Let's check to see if we are thinking along the same lines.

Examine the intents listed below. Some are fuzzies (abstractions), and some are specifics (performances). *Check the fuzzies;* then read on to see how well we agree:

1. ____ interview an applicant

2. ____ appreciate music

3. ____ feel a sense of pride in one's work

4. ____ repair a trombone

5. ____ set a broken leg

6. ____ develop a sense of comradeship in attaining common goals

7. ____ edit a manuscript

8. ____ have a religious dedication to one's profession

9. ____ defend liberties

10. ____ write a report

11. ____ be a good citizen

Compare your responses with the comments on the pages that follow.

1. ____ interview an applicant

Can you tell whether someone is interviewing? Of course. Interviewing is directly observable, so you can call it a performance.

2. _✓_ appreciate music

What is someone doing when appreciating? Sighing? Breathing hard? Reciting the history of music? Playing a piece? The expression doesn't indicate or even imply the performances that constitute the meaning of the abstraction. This is a fuzzy.

3. _✓_ feel a sense of pride in one's work

Mmm ... important, maybe. But in one's work, definitely not a performance. Ask the key question: "What would someone need to do to convince you that he or she had achieved this goal?" Those are the performances; this is a fuzzy.

4. ____ repair a trombone

Since you can see the repairing being performed, this is a performance.

5. _____ set a broken leg

Can you tell whether a person is setting a broken leg? Yes. You can see the steps of the task being performed. You may not be able to tell whether it is being done correctly, but you can tell that it is being done. A performance.

6. ✓ develop a sense of comradeship in attaining common goals

Ah, a beautiful sentiment and perhaps a worthwhile goal to attain, but definitely a goal and not a performance. Can you see people developing a sense of comradeship? Would everyone *agree* that what you see them doing is developing a sense of comradeship? Not likely. Another problem with this goal is that the word *develop* implies process; it implies that we're thinking about *how* the sense of comradeship will be attained, instead of what it will look like when it has been attained.

7. _____ edit a manuscript

This is a performance. You can tell if someone is editing. You may find that different editors behave differently when editing, but you can tell when they're editing. (My editor snickers ominously when slashing and thrusting at my words; others simply shake their heads while tsking.)

8. ✓ have a religious dedication to one's profession

This one is such an abstract abstraction I would even hesitate to give it the label of goal (it's more like a mission). It is of about the same caliber as "get the country moving again." The words have a lovely ring to them, but they don't provide the basis for making decisions about how we would know such a dedication if we saw one. "Having a dedication" isn't at all the same level of specificity as "having a baby."

9. ✓ defend liberties

Again, we have a nice-sounding goal. We can easily nod in agreement about its importance, but we would be hard put to say what to do to increase liberty-defending skills or recognize a liberty defender when we saw one. It doesn't matter that what a person might do to defend liberties is different in different situations; until we know what those things are, we can't make improvements.

10. ____ write a report

We may disagree about the criteria by which a given report should be judged, but there is not likely to be any disagreement about what someone is doing when writing a report. Writing is a performance that is directly visible (and often *audible,* if you find writing as hard as I do).

11. ✓ be a good citizen

This might be number one on the hit parade of fuzzies. It's certainly important, but what's a person doing when he or she is being a good citizen? What would you take as evidence that Sturmun Drang qualifies for the good-citizen award? Would it be different if he were a first grader than if he were a senior citizen?

Overt/Covert Performances

There are a few words that look like abstractions, but which are, in fact, performances. Words such as "identify," "discriminate," and "solve," for example, describe performances which are internal (covert); they describe actions that can be performed invisibly to the outside world. Just because they are invisible (covert) doesn't necessarily mean that they are abstractions.

Visible (overt) performances include behaviors such as hopping, singing, writing, and interviewing. These are things you can see people doing directly; you don't have to *infer* whether someone is doing these things because you can observe the performances directly. The existence of covert (invisible/cognitive) performances have to be inferred from things you see and hear people doing. How could you know someone has *recalled* a list of numbers? Or identified some fuzzies? You would have to ask them to do something visible or audible from which you can *infer* that the recalling or identifying has occurred.

So how can you tell the difference between covert performances and abstractions?

There is a simple test by which you can tell the difference between a performance and an abstraction. Find out whether there is a direct way to determine the nature of the alleged performance by asking this question:

> "Is there a *single* behavior or class of behaviors that will indicate the presence of the alleged performance, about which there would be general agreement?"

If the answer to the question is "yes," you have a performance. If it is "no," you are dealing with a fuzzy.

Let's try the test on a few likely candidates. If you believe an item to be a performance, see if you can jot down an answer to the key question. I've filled in the first one.

	What single act, if any, might you ask someone to perform that will tell you whether the condition exists?	*Is this item a performance?*
1. adding numbers	**Say (or write) the correct answer**	**Yes**
2. identifying piranhas		
3. appreciating values		
4. understanding computers		

Go on to the next page.

I would consider only the first two items to be performances. To find out if someone identified piranhas correctly, you could ask the person to point to the piranhas. That is a single act that would tell you directly if the internal performance occurred. You could also ask an individual to paint a red dot on each piranha or tap his or her finger on each of their heads. There are lots of *indicator behaviors* you could select from, so there is a direct way to sample the existence of the identifying.

But what *single* act would tell you whether anyone was appreciating values? Would everyone agree with the act you might select? Unlikely. And what single act would tell you whether there was an understanding of computers present? Making favorable comments about computers? Writing programs? Answering multiple-choice questions? Designing a computer? All of the above? None of the above? Would there be immediate agreement on the indicator you might select? Again, unlikely. Therefore, we would say of these items: "Value appreciation and computer understanding may be important goals to achieve, but they are not performances. If they *are* important to achieve, we must use the goal analysis to determine what to do to get the results we want."

One way to tell whether a statement is too broad to be considered a performance is to put the substance of the statement into the "Hey, Dad" Test. You simply use the substance of the statement to finish this sentence: "Hey, Dad, let me show you how I can _____!" If the result is absurd and makes you want to laugh, you are dealing with a statement broad enough to be considered an abstraction rather than a performance. For example: "Hey, Dad, let me show you how I can internalize my growing awareness!" (Yeah? Lemme see you!)

Silly, isn't it? That's because we aren't talking about a performance, either visible (external) or invisible (internal). We are talking about an abstraction. Try another example: "Hey, Dad, let me show you how I can be satisfied with my goals!" Not as funny, perhaps, but still rather odd. Now try this one:

"Hey, Dad, let me show you how I can smile!" Aha! Now that one has the ring of sense to it.

Try the "Hey, Dad" Test on the following items and see if it doesn't help you spot the performances from the abstractions:

- ride a bicycle

- add columns of numbers

- appreciate the value of gravity

- be warmed by success

- internalize the decision-making process

If you would like a little more practice in recognizing the difference between performances and abstractions, go to the next page.

Otherwise, go on to page 43.

Here are a few more items to help sharpen your ability to recognize performances and fuzzies. There are the usual three kinds of items on the list:

(1) visible or audible (overt) performances,

(2) invisible (covert) performances, and

(3) abstractions (fuzzies).

Check the fuzzies. Remember the key question: "Is there a single thing a person might do to convince me he or she is demonstrating the condition described in the item?"

1. ___ smiles a lot

2. ___ says favorable things about others

3. ___ feels deeply about others

4. ___ is confident in his or her ability

5. ___ can recognize symptoms

6. ___ is able to appreciate company policy

7. ___ is able to manage with enthusiasm

8. ___ knows how to compare prices

9. ___ can discriminate business trends

10. ___ is able to assemble components skillfully

Compare your responses to those on the pages that follow.

1. ___ smiles a lot

A performance. You can tell when someone is smiling. We don't know what "a lot" means, but that is another issue.

2. ___ says favorable things about others

Can you tell if someone is saying things about others? Yes. So this item can be called a performance.

3. ✓ feels deeply about others

What is someone doing when "feeling deeply?" We don't know and can't tell from the statement. A fuzzy. Perhaps important, but a fuzzy nonetheless.

4. ✓ is confident in his or her ability

Same as the last item.

5. ___ can recognize symptoms

Here is one of the covert performances. You may not be able to tell *whether* a person is recognizing at any point in time (he or she can stand around perfectly still while doing the recognizing), but you can tell whether the results of the recognizing are satisfactory or unsatisfactory. You can tell directly by asking the person to tell you something, point to something, label something, etc. The test is whether you can use a single indicator as evidence that the recognizing has occurred as desired.

6. __✓__ is able to appreciate company policy

I'm sure *you* weren't fooled by the "is able to" opener, but there are still people who think that any sentence beginning with those words is automatically specific enough to be called a performance. That isn't the case at all, as this item illustrates. A fuzzy, not a performance.

7. __✓__ is able to manage with enthusiasm

Same as for the previous item.

8. __✓__ knows how to compare prices

This is a little bit of everything. "Knowing," of course, is an abstraction, but "comparing" is something else. Can you tell if someone compared? You could ask the person, who might reply, "Yes, I compared." But that isn't any better than if he or she said, "Yes, I know." Actually, there are a number of things someone might be doing when comparing—noting those things that are the same, finding the smallest or the largest, etc. Can you name an indicator behavior by which we will know if the comparing is acceptable? If you are not sure, or if there is room for disagreement, better think of this item more as a mini-fuzzy that will have to be defined further.

9. ✓ can discrimi-
     nate business
     trends

Similar to the last one. Again, because of the context, there is room for discussion about what "discriminate" means. Does this mean that someone divines trends, points to trends when they are shown on charts, or senses them during the flow of a business day? By itself, we would have to consider it an abstraction that needs further clarification before we could agree on what the person would be doing when doing it. If, however, there is a single indicator behavior that would satisfy you that a person could discriminate business trends, then you can consider "discriminate" to be a covert performance.

10. ___ is able to
      assemble
      components
      skillfully

Can you tell what someone is doing when he or she is assembling? Yes. The person is putting things together. We don't know what "skillfully" means, but that doesn't matter, because "skillfully" is a word suggesting something about the criterion of acceptable performance, rather than a description of the performance itself.

Summary So Far

A goal is a statement describing a broad or abstract intent, state, or condition.

A goal analysis is useful whenever a goal exists that is important to achieve, or to achieve better than is presently the case. It is used whenever a statement of intent describes an abstraction, when the statement doesn't answer the question, "How will I know one when I see one?"

A performance is an activity that is directly visible or audible (overt), or directly assessable. An invisible or internal (covert) activity can also be considered a performance if it is directly assessable—that is, if there is a single behavior that will indicate the presence of the performance.

5
Getting It Down

It's time to plunge into the procedure itself, step by step. There are five steps, and each will be illustrated with examples from life. In brief, the steps are these:

1. Write down the goal.

2. List performances that exemplify goal achievement.

3. Sort the list and eliminate remaining fuzzies.

4. Describe performances in complete sentences.

5. Test for completeness.

After all the steps have been explained and illustrated, a chapter filled with examples—and a little practice—will follow. Finally, we'll consider some variations on a theme.

Before we begin, however, we should remind ourselves of these important points.

- Most goal analyses don't take very long to complete. When more than a few minutes are required, it's usually because time is needed to complete the list of performances that define the goal, because someone whose input is needed isn't immediately available, or because consensus on the goal meaning has to be reached.

- It is easy to confuse process and results (outcomes). The activities associated with goal achievement are these:

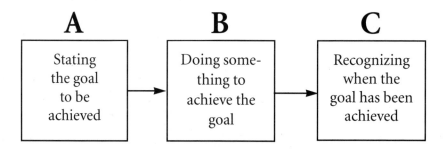

Our concern in this book is with Items A and C, because until we know how to recognize our destination (achievement of the goal), we don't know what to do to get there. The procedure for achieving goals, then, is first to say what the goal is (A), then to describe how goal accomplishment will be recognized (C), and finally to take action (B). Here's how:

Step One

Write Down the Goal.

Use whatever words are comfortable, regardless of how fuzzy or vague they may be. This is the place for such words. The reason it doesn't matter how broad the words are here is that this step is just to get you started and to help you remember what caused you to start analyzing in the first place. For example, you might write items like these:

- The incumbents should have a good attitude regarding their constituents.
- have pride in work
- have an awareness of civic responsibility
- appreciate the legal system
- have a successful marriage
- experience successful industrial relations

Note that the first item looks like a complete sentence, and the others are more like scraps of sentences. No matter. Use the words that make you (or the person for whom you are doing the goal analysis) feel good. If you can make yourself feel good as soon as you begin, you may be more likely to continue.

There is another reason why it is useful to begin a goal analysis by writing down the goal. It is "politically" useful. People can almost always agree with each other on the importance of vaguely stated intentions. They will all tend to agree that things like "good customer relations," "good citizenship," and "ethical conduct" are fine things to have. They will not necessarily always agree on the specific actions that should represent the definition of those things. And if they see only your list of specifics, they may very well accuse you of doing "trivial" things. So write the goal on top of the page. A good place to begin, good window dressing . . . but don't get too attached to the wording, because the process of analysis may show you the sense of taking another direction.

Caution

There is only one caution about how to state the goal. Make sure your statement describes an intended *outcome* rather than a *process*. That way, you won't get bogged down with the problem of means and ends before you get started. Once you know what you are trying to attain, *then* you can think about the best means of getting there. So, make your goals talk about the ends rather than the means of attaining those ends. Make the statement say "*have* a favorable attitude toward barnacles" rather than "*learn* to have a favorable attitude toward barnacles." Make it read "*understand* foreign trade" rather than "*develop* an understanding of foreign trade."

To give you a little practice in making goals describe ends rather than means, here are a few practice items. Each item is now stated in a way that will get the analyst in trouble, because it implies something about how the goal is achieved rather than about *what* the goal state to be achieved is. Fix each item by making it describe ends—that is, cross out the words implying process and replace them with words implying outcomes.

Have appreciate appreciate concept

1. Develop a fuller appreciation of the concept of détente.

2. Grow to discover a yearning for classical music. *has a yearning*

3. Come to see that the pollution problem is important.

Know pollution problem important

4. Develop a sense of humor. *have a sense of humor*

5. Reach the maturity needed to have a favorable attitude toward customers. *have a mature attitude toward custm*

Turn to the next page to see if we agree.

When fixed, this is what the items on the previous page should look like:

1. Appreciate the concept of détente.

2. Have a yearning for classical music.

    or

    Have a favorable attitude toward classical music.

3. Understand the importance of the pollution problem.

    or

    Appreciate the problem of pollution.

4. Have a sense of humor.

5. Have a favorable attitude toward customers.

NOTE: It is always useful to name the "who," the people whose performance is the reason for the goal analysis. For example, the actions representing safety consciousness are one thing for truck drivers and something quite different for accountants. For another example, when managers say, "I want my people to be more responsible," a goal analysis would be far more successful when "my people" is identified. Responsible actions in a laboratory might be quite different from those required by computer programmers.

Before proceeding with a goal analysis, therefore, be clear about whose performance is at issue.

So, the first step in goal analysis is to write down the goal, making sure it describes an intended outcome rather than the means for reaching that outcome.

Step Two

Write Down Everything Someone Would Have to Say or Do for You to Agree He or She Represents Achievement of the Goal.

Without editing or judging, jot down everything that can possibly represent the meaning of the goal. Use only words or phrases and make no attempt to tidy things up as you go. (Tidying will come later.) Just remember this rule: *First you get it down, and then you get it good.*

The reason you must complete this step without being judgmental is that it is the most difficult step to complete, not so much because it's hard to understand, but because it takes time to think through the cloud of fuzzies to the specifics you are searching for. Usually, when we ask ourselves for the meaning of an abstraction, we answer ourselves in yet another abstraction. It just takes a little time to get used to the process of listing performances—instead of abstractions.

So write down everything that comes to mind. We'll sort it all out in Step Three.

Five Strategies

Here are five strategies for getting things down that may help you complete Step Two (describing the meaning of your goal). Use whichever is most productive for you.

1. Answer the question, "What will I take as evidence that my goal has been achieved?" What would cause you to be willing to stamp a person with the label of your goal? If you want a favorable attitude toward school, for example, what would it take to make you agree that the attitude of Jeremy Jimperly is in the shape you would like it

to be? Jot down everything that you can think of, without any concern for the fact that many of the items are just as broad as the one you started with, without any concern for the suspicion that some items may not make the best of sense. If it will help, write the rule on the very top of your page: *First you get it* down, *then you get it* good.

After all, you can't repair what you don't have. You can't cross out things that aren't there. You can't rearrange invisible items. Besides, thinking about what you would accept as evidence of achievement of your goal is hard enough without complicating the matter by having to write down only the things that make sense.

2. Answer the question, "Given a room full of people, what is the basis on which I would separate them into two piles—those who had achieved my goal and those who had not?" After all, you *do* make judgments about whether your students or trainees are acceptable in skill or attitude; you do make statements about their understanding or motivation or feeling. Now is the time to lay on the table the basis for those statements.

3. There is still another way to think about the performances that demonstrate the meaning of your goal. Imagine that someone else will be charged with the responsibility for deciding which of your students will be labeled with the goal and which will not be so labeled, and that you are going to tell this person how to proceed. What will your instructions be? What should he or she look for? *How will the person know a goal achiever when he or she sees one?* Suppose you want people who are conscientious. Never mind for the moment how they get that way or what you might do to achieve that state.

Given a room full of people, how would you separate them into two piles—those who had and those who had not achieved the goal?

Think about the state itself and how you would tell someone how to recognize it. Should your looker look for people who:

- finish their work on time?
- ask for extra assignments?
- work neatly?
- stay until their work is completed?

Jot down all the clues you can think of. (Or, if you are the literate type, all the clues of which you can think.)

4. Think of someone who is one and write down why you think so. That is, think of a person who already has achieved your goal, someone who represents your goal, and write down the things he or she says and does that cause you to be willing to pin the goal label on this person. If, for example, your goal is to have trainees "demonstrate pride in their work," think of someone who demonstrates pride in his or her work and write down the performances that cause you to say this person has your kind of pride. If you can*not* think of anyone who represents your goal, you have a problem. Perhaps your expectations are unreasonable. Perhaps the goal (as you perceive it) is unattainable. If so, then a change in expectation is in order.

   If you cannot think of a real person who represents your goal, ask yourself this question: "Is it reasonable or practical to expect to achieve this goal?" If the answer is "no," revise the goal to one that is reasonable and practical to achieve. If the answer is "yes," and you still cannot think of someone who represents the state or condition described by the goal, you need to think of what a person *might* be like if he or she represented your goal. You are skating on thin ice, though, because when you think of hypothetical people, there is the danger that your expectations will be forever unattainable. It's much better to think of real people and to state why you are willing to point your finger in their direction and say they exemplify your goal. Suppose, for example, you want students "to be able to write effectively." Having written the goal, you would think of someone you know who writes effectively enough to suit you; then you would ask yourself *why* you are willing to say so. What does this person say or do that makes you willing to say he or she writes effectively? Could it be that the person:

- uses good grammar?
- uses descriptive words?
- expresses ideas in the fewest possible words?
- gets desired results?
- gets a reader to repeat his or her ideas with relative accuracy?

BONER'S ARK   **By ADDISON**

Whatever you think might be the basis for your judgment, write it down.

5. Try the back door. If all else fails, here's a sure-fire way to get started. Just write down all the reasons you would *never* point to someone and say, "This person represents the goal." What behaviors, or absence of behaviors, would cause you to say, "This is *not* someone who has achieved this goal, and this is why."

   For example, suppose the goal is "Be a sensitive and caring spouse," and you're having trouble describing what such a person would be like in performance terms. OK. Go in through the back door, and tell yourself what an *in*sensitive clod would be likely to do or not do. Would any of the following behaviors fit?

   - kicks sand in spouse's face.
   - never says, "I love you."
   - pokes fun at spouse's opinions.
   - reads the comics during sex.

   Once you've listed the negatives, it's no trick to turn them into positive statements describing the things a sensitive person does, and doesn't, do. There is an added benefit to the back-door aproach; not only is it a sure-fire way to get started, it will also lead to some giggles—especially if you're doing the analysis with someone else.

Examples from the Positive

Safety Consciousness. This example comes from a group of industry managers whose company had an accident record higher than they thought reasonable. The showing of safety films and the display of safety posters didn't seem to have much effect. The managers decided they wanted to be more successful in achieving safety consciousness in their employees, so they decided to take a closer look at this goal. Following the procedure described in Step One, they wrote the goal on a flip chart: "Be Safety Conscious."

The next step was to remind each other of the things they would take as evidence of safety consciousness, to tell each other the things that safety-conscious people say and do.

"Well," said one manager, "I think of old Joe Carson as being safety conscious, because he reports safety hazards whenever he sees them."

"Yes," said another, "and he wears his safety equipment."

A third then added, "A safety-conscious person is one who follows safety rules, whether they are posted or not. That is, he or she adheres to what is generally considered safe practice."

And so it went. Each item mentioned was written on the flip chart as a potential part of what these managers *meant* by safety consciousness. After half an hour or so, their list looked something like this:

Be Safety Conscious
- reports safety hazards
- wears safety equipment
- follows safety rules (no infractions)
- practices good housekeeping (keeps work area free of dirt, grease, and tools)
- encourages safe practice in others (reminds others to wear safety equipment)
- says favorable things about safe practice
- suggests ways to improve safety record

This, then, was the main basis for deciding whether a person was safety conscious or not. These were the performances that would cause a manager to pin the label of "safety consciousness" on someone. This was therefore the essence of the managers' *meaning* of the goal of safety consciousness.

Pride in Work. Here is an example of a more difficult goal, one that proved harder to define. The faculty of a dental school decided that a very important goal for their graduates to achieve was "pride in work." They explained, somewhat facetiously, that they didn't want their graduates leaning over their patients muttering things like ". . . y'know . . . I never *really* wanted to be a dentist in the first place." Though not meant to be taken seriously, the comment did suggest something about what this faculty meant by *lack* of pride.

After writing down the goal "Have pride in work," the faculty members began to think of the things student dentists might say or do to make their teachers willing to pin this label on them. In this case, as in many others, it wasn't easy to get started. After all, though people often talk to each other in the broad terms of goal language, they seldom think very seriously about just exactly what they mean by those nice words.

After considering that (a) the group was just trying to put down *possibilities* from which to select and (b) there was no need for agreement about what was put down, one of the members offered an opening shot: "Well, at least *I* would never say student dentists had pride in their work if they didn't do their assigned work on time." (If this sounds a little defensive, it is probably because people aren't used to being challenged to expose the basis for their judgment, especially on such affective matters as "pride in work." So, if you are ever in a position to help people define their goals, write down *whatever* is said quickly, and in the old brainstorming manner, refrain from passing judgment on what is said. [That comes later.])

Once the ice was broken, a half-hour of discussion produced the following jottings:

Have Pride in Work (dental students)
- carries out assigned tasks on time
- finishes tasks regardless of the time required
- carries out tasks regardless of whether others carry out theirs
- finishes, or reports, unfinished tasks left by others
- carries out tasks completely, leaving no loose ends
- performs most tasks at maximum personal ability level
- speaks favorably about the profession
- speaks favorably about well-performed tasks
- dresses in a manner befitting the profession

You can see that for this group the essence of "pride in work" had mainly to do with how tasks are carried out. *You* may mean something completely different, and others may have still other meanings (if that were *not* the case, there would be no need to clarify goals). But this faculty has done everyone the courtesy of making *their* meaning visible. *Now* they are in a position to discuss their meaning, to decide whether it is the best meaning for their situation, and to write the objectives that embody the essence of the meaning. And once they've done that, they can act to achieve their goal more effectively than ever before.

Love of Learning. Instructors are frequently heard to say that they want their students to have a "favorable attitude toward learning." This is an admirable intention, provided that instructors then take care to do the things that will enhance such an attitude rather than detract from it. The first step toward such an accomplishment is to make sure that instructors know in detail what students should do or say if they are to be representative of a favorable attitude toward learning.

One group of instructors went about it this way. They first listed the *names* of students they knew who, they all agreed, had a favorable attitude toward learning. Then they began to tell each other what it was these students did or said that qualified them for the "favorable attitude" label. They reminded each other that "anything goes" during this phase of the analysis, and their first list looked like this:

Favorable Attitude Toward Learning
- shows up when expected
- is prepared to work (brings his or her stuff)
- asks questions when in doubt
- does more than the minimum required
- makes suggestions for improvement of the instruction
- helps teach others
- has initiative
- is a self-starter
- is eager and dedicated

Notice that the list trailed off into some fuzzies. This almost always happens, which is why Step Three (the sorting-out step) follows Step Two.

Notice also that even though the goal analysis was not complete at this point, these instructors already had developed some good clues about how to increase favorable attitude. For example, if one of the things they want students to do is to ask questions when in doubt, then the instructors need to make certain that question-asking behavior isn't punished, either intentionally or accidentally. In other words, instructors can increase the number of questions asked by responding to questions in a way that the students consider favorable.

For now, however, the task was to find out just what behaviors (performances) the instructors wanted to see more of and what they wanted to see less of.

Examples from the Negative

As I said earlier, sometimes it isn't easy to get started scratch-papering down the performances that represent the achievement of your goal; sometimes it isn't easy to start describing how to recognize a goal achiever when you see one. Oh, well. If you can't get in the front door, try the back. If you can't get started by describing the positive, try the negative. You can *always* think of several performances that are clearly *excluded* from your meaning of a goal. You can always think of things a person might do or say that would cause you to say, "*That* is certainly *not* representative of a person who _____." For example:

"I would never think of myself as successful if I hadn't stopped smoking."

"I would never agree that people understand the fundamentals of economics if they keep their life savings in a bank."

"Employees with a favorable attitude toward customers don't ignore customers who ask for help."

Once you have started listing the performances that you don't want to see, you can usually turn them into the positive without much difficulty.

Good Personality. Let me illustrate how this works with an example developed with some hotel managers who wanted their bartenders to have a "good personality." If any goal ever qualified as a fuzzy, this is it. Suppose someone handed you a clump of students and said, "Here. Go teach these people to have a good personality." What would you teach them? Where would you begin? How would you know if your instruction had succeeded?

You may not care much about the personality of bartenders, but those who employ them and those who use their services do. (Bars used to be just places to gather for a bit of friendly banter and good cheer; now they seem to be more like group-therapy centers.)

The attempt to think of the performances that would cause the managers to agree a bartender had a good personality left them nothing but blank paper. They couldn't for the life of them get started listing the things that would cause them to point at someone and proclaim "good personality."

So, we tried from the other end:

"Have you ever fired a bartender?" they were asked.

"Have we ever!" was the reply.

"Tell us about them" was the request.

And they did. Within minutes, the hotel managers listed a half-dozen characteristics of the *un*acceptable bartender:

The Acceptable Bartender is Not:
- sour
- humorless
- abrupt
- blameful of customer
- aggressive
- of gloomy appearance

Could you help but notice that all the items on this list are fuzzies? You will often find this to be the case. But first drafts are for getting down, not for getting good. Don't worry about what the first try looks like, because there is a way to handle the problem. Simply put each fuzzy on a separate sheet of paper and start over; repeat the process until you reach the performances that are the essence of your meaning. The hotel managers did that with their negative fuzzies, and they turned them positive as they went. Before long, they had statements like these:

1. Handles glasses with care, without spilling or slamming.

2. Smiles visibly when serving or addressing customers.

And as soon as they had these statements written down, they said, "But wait a minute. Those things don't have anything to do with good personality!" And maybe they were right.

But who cares? Vague terms are interchangeable, and "good personality" was just a place to start. There are any number of other goals they might have started with that would have served as well, such as "friendly person," "empathetic with customers," or even "be a good Joe." The key issue was whether the two statements they came up with represented important performances.

The managers then said, "But wait a minute. Those performances are trivial!" The reply to this charge is that the test of triviality is not in the words *describing* a performance. You cannot tell whether the item is trivial merely by reading it. *The test of triviality is in the consequence of not achieving the performance.* If there is no consequence when the performance is absent, one might well entertain the thought of triviality.

But if there is a consequence, then the performance is not trivial, no matter what words are used to describe it. In the case of the present example, the conversation went something like this:

"What happens to bartenders who spill stuff on hotel customers?"

"We *fire* them."

"What happens if bartenders don't smile regularly?"

"We fire them, too."

What is trivial about being fired? That is really something in the way of a consequence. Since it *matters* whether they are careful and smiley, these performances are not trivial, regardless of how the bartender might feel inside; therefore, the statements that will ultimately describe these intended outcomes will not be trivial either. It doesn't matter whether the words are long ones or short ones; the test of triviality is not in the words but in the consequence.

The Good Teacher. How many times have you heard someone say, "You can't define a good teacher"? Or, "Nobody can say what a good teacher is"? Actually, those are pretty silly statements; they imply that if you can't do something perfectly, you can't do it at all. But try it this way: Can you think of anything that a "good teacher" (whatever that means) *doesn't do?* Of course you can. Lots of things. And if you can list things that are *un*acceptable, you have a good beginning of a description of what is acceptable or desirable. How about these as examples of what good teachers *don't* do:

- keep students in the dark about what is expected of them
- use language or examples that are inappropriate for their audience
- punish students for doing the very things they are expected to do

How about adding a few yourself? Think about the things that turned you off or got in the way of your learning when you were in school. Then add them to my list. Once you've done that and turned the statements positive, you've gone a long way toward describing what many feel is indescribable.

Summary So Far

The first two steps in the goal analysis procedure are these:

Step One: *Write down the goal, using whatever words best describe the intended outcome.*

Step Two: *Write down the performances that would cause you to agree the goal had been achieved, without regard for duplication or fuzzinaciousness.*

6
Sorting It Out

Once you've jotted down the things you think might cause you to agree your goal had been achieved, you will need to go back over your list and do some tidying up and sorting out. Why? Because if your list is anything like the ones I've seen or developed, there will be all sorts of cats and dogs on it. For one thing, you are almost certain to find items that are at least as broad or abstract as the one you started with. Those who begin to say what they mean by "initiative," for example, often write down "is responsible." Similarly, those who begin to say what they mean by "is responsible" write down "takes the initiative."

This is not difficult to understand. In conversation we use lots of words that either say the same thing or nothing at all. Lots of vague terms are interchangeable, you see, so there are bound to be a number of fuzzies making their way onto your list. "We want our students to be conscientious," we say. Oh, and what does that mean? Why, it means we want them to be responsible. And what does "responsible" mean? Well, it means we want them to have pride in their work. And *that* means we want them to be dedicated. And around and around we go, defining one fuzzy with another. Little wonder we don't experience as much success with the so-called affective domain as we'd like.

On your list you may also find redundancies or duplications, things you have said in more than one way. In addition, you may find some items that, on second thought, can be crossed out simply because they don't say what you want to say.

You may occasionally find some items that describe procedure rather than outcomes, means rather than ends. These are to be deleted, for the object of the analysis is to figure out how to know an outcome when you see one, not how to make one happen.

Step Three

Sort the Items Listed in Step Two.

1. Cross out duplications and items that, on second thought, do not represent the meaning of your goal.

2. Place check marks beside the items that do not qualify as performances; that is, check the fuzzies.

3. Make sure all remaining or unmarked items describe outcomes rather than processes.

The checked items (the fuzzies) will each be put onto a separate piece of paper and treated just like a new goal. Performances will be listed and sorted until your entire list consists only of performances—things you can tell if someone is doing or not doing.

Example: Initiative

Here's an example of how it goes. While working toward analysis of a goal described as "demonstrates initiative," a group of managers listed the following items during Step Two (in this case they were referring to first-level supervisors):

- enjoys responsibility
- makes good decisions
- uses good judgment
- is on time

After completing the list, they went through the items for sorting. The first item is a double fuzzy. Both words ("enjoys" and "responsibility") describe general states. Both are inferred from the things you might see someone do or say. Since the managers agreed that this was an important item for further consideration, they labeled it a goal and went to the next item.

They thought about the second and third items. Both were fuzzies, but although good judgment was an important quality, they felt that what they were really interested in was good decision-making. Since good decision-making was the main thing they meant by good judgment, they threw out the latter item as being essentially a duplication of the former.

Finally, they thought about the last item. "Yes," they said, "we can tell directly if a person is on time. One is either there at the appointed hour or one isn't. All we have to do is say what we mean by 'on time,' so that a criterion of acceptable performance will be available." That was easier said than done, however, for there was quite a discussion about just what the limits of "on-timeness" should be. But that was real progress, since they were now discussing the desired shape of a performance rather than arguing about abstractions.

Reworking their list, they now had:

✓ *enjoys responsibility*

✓ *makes good decisions*

   is on time

The first two items, having been checked as goals, were put on separate pieces of paper; a new analysis was begun for each.

The third item, already qualifying as a performance, was shelved until the performances defining the first two goals were identified. Once that was done, the managers were ready for the final steps in the goal analysis procedure.

The list for "enjoys responsibility" looked like this:

- accepts new assignments without complaint
- appears on time for management meetings
- keeps subordinates informed
- meets deadlines
- spends time managing instead of operating

An explanation of the last item is in order. The rule of thumb in industry seems to be: Promote the best operators to supervisory level, but don't teach them how to supervise. As a result, there are thousands of supervisors who are good at their old jobs, whatever the jobs were, but who are totally insecure about managing. The end result is that they tend to spend time doing what they did before they were promoted, because it's what they know how to do.

The list for "makes good decisions" looked like this:

- identifies company goals supported by decisions
- always informs subordinates of decisions, and the reasons for making them
- makes decisions in time to be useful
- keeps well-informed about company goals and plans

Notice that the last item looks more like process than outcome—that is, it looks like one of the things one might do to become a good decision-maker. Once that fact was pointed out, the item was stricken from the list. The two lists were then combined, and further discussion was focused on clarifying the performances.

Example: Honest Reporting

Here is an interesting example of a goal analysis, interesting because it began with a very profound-sounding goal and ended with a list of very measurable performances.

In a large company that employs a substantial number of maintenance people (sometimes called customer engineers, technical representatives, or maintenance crew), management noticed that the information flowing from the field to the company was often erroneous or non-existent. The reports filed after machine repair were used as the basis for several important decisions; but, it was said, those reports were completed in a shabby fashion.

"We need more honest reporting," said management. Suppose you were faced with the assignment of increasing the honesty of the reporting. What would you do? Give lectures on ethics? Extol the importance of company policy? Make examples of those whose reports were not honest? Needless to say, you wouldn't know *what* action to take until you knew the results you wanted to achieve.

In this case two managers sat down to decide just what it was that was wanted. And this is an important point. They didn't sit down to figure out what THE meaning of honesty was, that is, to describe the ultimate definition of honest reporting. They sat down to describe their own desired outcomes. The demand for more honest reporting was what got them started, but they didn't feel enslaved to the words that just happened to be used by those voicing the complaint.

"How would we know if we had honest reporting?" was the question that began the analysis. But before long, the list looked like this:

- accurate
- valid
- complete
- reviewed for corrections

- properly distributed
- promptly filed
- exhibits good report-writing attitude
- legibly written

Notice that what had started out as an analysis of "honest reporting" quickly turned into an analysis of "Proper Maintenance Report." (Thinking does wonders.)

When sorting this list, they quickly deleted "exhibits good report-writing attitude"; they realized that "reviewed for corrections" and "properly distributed" were important but didn't describe characteristics of the report itself. Further discussion clarified the meaning of the performances, after which they drafted their final product. It said nothing whatever about honesty, as that turned out not to be the issue. The issue was the shape of the report. Here's what they ended up with:

The Characteristics of a Proper Maintenance Report

1. All information is recorded in the correct place.

2. All information is true.

3. All information is relevant to the problem
   (no superfluous information is recorded).

4. All information is legible.

5. All boxes are checked or filled.

6. All maintenance actions are recorded.

7. Report is reviewed and signed by the customer.

8. One copy each of the report is:
   a. sent to the district office
   b. given to the customer, and
   c. attached to the failed component, if any.

What began as an alleged problem with morals or ethics was seen, through goal analysis, to be a simple problem of communication. Once the problem description was turned into a checklist and distributed to the maintenance staff, the quality of the reports improved.

Did you notice that one of the items on the list was a negative—that is, it called for the *absence* of superfluous information? Again, I want to repeat that you will often encounter instances in which you expect to determine whether someone has achieved a particular goal by noting the *absence* of behavior. No need to be concerned, now that you are forewarned. After all, there is nothing wrong with defining a goal in terms of the *absence* of behaviors (note how many of the Ten Commandments call for non-behavior) if that is what you intend to mean.

Also, did you notice that this list describes the results of performance, rather than the performance itself? And that the list talks about the characteristics of the completed report, rather than the behaviors (actions) used in preparing the report? Again, no problem. Once again, the purpose of the goal analysis is to help you to describe what things would be like if, in fact, the goal were achieved. If the way to get to that is to describe the products of the behaviors rather than the behaviors themselves, fine.

Sometimes, after completing a goal analysis, people will say, "Wait a minute. We've said what things would be like when the goal is achieved, but is that *right*? Should we adopt a *different* meaning of the goal?" Notice that this question can only arise after you've made the components of goal achievement visible (written down). If that makes you want to "improve" your goal definition, fine. But that is an issue beyond the scope of this book.

Summary So Far

The goal analysis procedure so far, then, is this:

Step One: *Write down the goal in outcome terms.*

Step Two: *Jot down the performances that, if observed, would cause you to agree the goal has been achieved.*

Step Three: *Once a goal has been written and a list has been drafted of the things you think would cause you to agree the goal had been achieved, sort out the list. Delete duplications and the items that, on second thoughts, are unwanted. Check abstractions, and mark performances in some other handy-dandy fashion. Then write each remaining goal (abstraction) on a separate piece of paper. Repeat the process until every item remaining is either a performance or a non-performance: either a "does it" or a "doesn't do it."*

7

Putting It Together

We do goal analyses to help us decide what actions to take to be more successful at achieving those goals. We do it because we want to know what steps to take to get closer to goal achievement, rather than because we enjoy sitting around defining terms. For this reason there are still two steps to complete. These steps will help put boundaries, or limits, around the performances and tell you when you are done with the analysis.

Step Four

Write a Complete Sentence to Describe Each of the Items on Your Final List.

Each sentence will describe an outcome that must be achieved for you to be willing to say your goal is reached. This step will make it easier to test these outcomes to see if they truly reflect what you mean by the goal, and it will help you decide what to do next.

For example, after completing the first three steps of a goal analysis on "good reporting," the manager of a research division came up with this list of performances:

- identifies routing
- determines presentation form
- writes report
- presents report

Though that is a good start, it isn't precise enough to tell us what to do next. Though each item is a performance, it doesn't tell us how to know whether the performance is present or absent. When this manager completed Step Four, his analysis looked like this:

Good Reporting

1. For each report, be able to name the members of senior management to whom copies of the report should be directed.

2. For each report, be able to determine (name) the form of presentation that will most clearly communicate the content to a non-scientific audience.

3. Be able to prepare a written report that summarizes all of the findings, conclusions, and recommendations bearing on the researched issue.

4. Be able to report (orally) to the appropriate members of senior management, providing them with all the information they need to take effective action.

Note that these statements tell us *what* is expected to be done, and they tell us something about *how well* people are expected to do it. With these complete sentences in hand, it was possible for the manager to determine which scientists had the skill to perform each of these items and to decide what action to take in those instances where the skill was lacking. In other words, what might have started as a grumbling exercise about the lack of "good reporting" ended up—through goal analysis—with a blueprint for action.

Take Me to Your Leader

Here's another example, this one from a comprehensive analysis of one of those superfuzzies—"good leadership." One of the items on the original list said something like "Knows how not to reward counter-productive or disruptive behavior." That isn't too bad all by itself, but in this case the analysts went much further. Their Step Four list for this one performance, a mini-fuzzy really, looked like this:

1. Can identify (point to) counter-productive or disruptive behaviors.

2. Can specify and implement techniques for monitoring the occurrence of counter-productive or disruptive behaviors.

3. Can design and implement techniques for eliminating the inadvertent reinforcers of such behaviors.

4. Can modify a reinforcement (reward) program if desired changes fail to occur.

With these descriptions of intended outcomes in hand, they were able (a) to determine whether each of the outcomes was happening to their satisfaction, and if not, (b) to decide what to do about it.

As you read these examples, keep in mind that the analysts were not looking for some sort of supermeaning—some sort

of "one and only" meaning—for their goals. There were looking for what the goal means to them in their situation. Any
search for the one and only meaning is rather like hunting for
a handle on a fog: There is no such thing. It is for this very reason also that it doesn't pay to get too involved with the goal
words you start with. Since there are so many other words you
could have used, and since it is a *practical* rather than an *ultimate* meaning that is being sought, your starting words may
quickly fall by the wayside. If they do, let them fall. And rejoice,
because it means you are getting closer to something you can
do something about.

The task during Step Four, then, is to write as clear a
description as you can of each desired performance. Usually
this will take the form of a single sentence; sometimes it will
require two or more sentences.

Step Five

Test the Sentences for Completeness.

In other words, test your collection of sentences to see
whether you have finished the analysis. This is done by looking at the collection of sentences and asking, "If all these things
occurred as described, would I be willing to say that the goal
had been achieved?" If the answer is "yes," then the analysis is
finished and you are ready to decide what you need to do to
make sure those performances occur as desired. If the answer
is "no," then you need to answer this question: "What else
would have to happen before I would agree the goal had been
achieved?" Add that "something else" to your list, then ask the
first question again: "Now would I be willing to agree the goal
was achieved if the things on this list happened?" If not, you
need to keep searching for the missing item(s). When, at last,
you utter a jubilant (or reluctant) "Yes!" to the key question,
you will be finished.

Here are some examples to show how Step Five works:

A Case of Consciousness

The goal was for production employees to be "more security conscious," because the plant manufactured classified military products. During the second step of the analysis, the managers doing the work quickly discovered that their main concern was with the way in which sensitive documents, such as blueprints, were handled. When they had finished the third step, they had written:

Security Conscious

- does not leave classified documents unattended
- locks up materials

Though these statements describe things you might see a person doing or not doing, they do not answer the question "What will you take as evidence the goal has been achieved?" They do not yet say how to tell when someone does or does not perform as desired. The managers who completed this analysis quickly understood the problem; they asked each other what would be a reasonable expectation with regard to the desired performances. Before long, the following statements were drafted (thus completing Step Four of the analysis):

A person is said to be security conscious when:

1. There are no instances in which he or she has been found to leave sensitive documents unattended.

2. His or her filing cabinet is always found locked when unattended (when the employee leaves for the day or leaves the room in which the cabinet is located).

How will the managers know a security-conscious employee when they see one? They will know one when they find a person who has never left sensitive documents unattended and whose files are always locked during his or her absences. That person will be called "security conscious." Anyone for whom they have counted one or more instances of unattended documents or open files will not be considered "security conscious."

They were then ready for Step Five, the last step in the goal analysis procedure; testing the statements for adequacy. The managers asked themselves if they would be willing to say an employee was "security conscious" if the person locked his or her files and didn't leave classified documents unattended. Their answer was "Well, yes; but only insofar as the care of documents is concerned." Therefore, they were finished with that part of their analysis. If, on the other hand, their answer had been "no," they would have had to find out what was missing in their meaning of the goal. They would have had to find the missing essence of their meaning of the goal.

Now that the managers had a clear idea of what they were looking for, they were in a position to do two things they couldn't do before: (1) determine the current extent of security consciousness (i.e., count the number of employees who were security conscious according to their own definition); and (2) decide what actions to take to increase that number. And *that* is precisely what the analysis is for.

A Case of Gas

This example was developed by a high-school instructor who wanted his students to "understand gas welding." As you might guess, this teacher worked in a vocation area, and he wanted his students to be able to have a comprehensive knowledge (there's a nice fuzzy for you) of the subject. His initial list of items had several fuzzies on it, such as "know how gas is

produced," "understand metals," and "appreciate flame adjustment." Sorting led him to identify and delete the performances
that he was not concerned about. When he drafted statements
about each performance he was concerned about, his meaning
of "understanding" turned out to be:

The student who understands gas welding is able to:

1. Explain production of oxygen and acetylene gases.

2. Explain methods and precautions to be observed while
   handling oxygen and acetylene cylinders and equipment.

3. Assemble gas-welding components to the cylinders.
   Components will include regulators, hoses, blowpipes,
   and tips.

4. Select proper tip and oxygen-acetylene pressures for
   work pieces of the following type (list added).

5. Adjust work piece and blowpipe-tip handle for the flat
   welding position.

6. Light the torch and adjust to a neutral flame.

7. Establish and complete the weld while observing proper
   pattern and ending of the weld.

8. Shut down the welding unit and prepare it for storage.

Carrying out the final step, the test for adequacy, he asked
himself the question: "If students did all these things, would I
be willing to say that they understood gas welding?" His
answer was "yes," so his analysis was finished. Now he was in a
position (1) to determine the number of students who currently understood to his satisfaction and (2) to take steps to
increase that number.

There are any number of things that one might mean by "understands gas welding," as you might guess. One might mean knowing the history of welding, knowing who is who in the welding business, and so on. Some people think that because the subject being taught is vocational, technical, or professional, it is therefore patently obvious what must be taught. This simply isn't true. In any subject area, there are a great many possible answers to the question, "What is worth teaching?"

A Case of Creativity

Some of those who have, in my opinion, done the best job of defining their affective fuzzies are music educators. Not all, but some have made great strides in identifying the essence of some goals generally thought to be absolutely and eternally intangible. What follows is an example of what one group did with the goal "be musically creative." I can't tell you what their initial analysis looked like, since I wasn't present when it was completed; but I can show you the first draft of the sentences they wrote to describe their intended performances. Here is the essence of the skills they will expect of their students if they are to be considered musically creative:

Musical Creativity

1. Given the performance of a song by the instructor, improvise an accompaniment on a rhythm instrument.

2. Be able to improvise vocally a harmony part to a well-known song.

3. Be able to play by ear at the keyboard the melody of a given well-known song.

4. Given the performance of a song by the instructor, be able to improvise an accompaniment on a harmonic instrument other than the piano.

5. Given the performance of a song by the instructor, be able to improvise a harmony line on a melodic instrument.

6. Be able to create a melody and notate it. The melody should have a clear climax and a repose (feeling of resolution) at the end.

7. Improvise at the keyboard an accompaniment for a given well-known song.

8. Be able to compose or arrange music suitable for a brief (32 bars or more) dramatic presentation for performance by fellow students.

There it is. There isn't any question whatever about what students will be doing when demonstrating their musical creativity. Others might have different expectations, of course, but that is irrelevant. What matters is that those who want musical creativity have had the courtesy to say what their goal means.

A Case of Therapy

This next example is interesting because of the way the outcome descriptions compared with the goal. While working on the improvement of their curriculum, a nursing faculty decided that one of their goals was that students "be able to develop a therapeutic relationship with adolescents." This is a very "affective" goal, indeed. It was explained that it was extremely important for each nurse to be able to develop such a relationship with adolescent patients, as it contributed significantly to treatment success. Though an important goal, the faculty was not satisfied with their current success in achieving it. There were lectures on psychology and discussions about adolescents, but the number of students the faculty was willing to certify as having achieved the goal was too small to suit them.

Having written the goal, the next step, of course, was to list the performances that represented the goal. But this led to a heated discussion of several topics that appeared to be only peripheral to the main issue. There was talk of patients who were sloppy in their personal habits and of nurses who left patients unnecessarily exposed while dressing or bathing them. There was discussion of several of the problems of being a nurse in this day and age and of the things that happen in hospitals that make their lives dreary or cheery. But there didn't seem to be much discussion of what was meant by "therapeutic relationship." Finally, something happened. One of the faculty members said, with an air of candor, "Look. Nurses aren't supposed to react to patients just because they're different." And within a short time, two statements that described the essence of *their* meaning of "therapeutic relationship" were drafted. They were:

1. Be able to recognize patient characteristics to which the nurse should and should not respond (list of characteristics added).

2. Be able to respond with the proper skill, and withhold response, as indicated by patient characteristics (list of desired skills added).

In plain words, the first of these statements means that when a nurse sees a patient who is dirty or stinky, he or she isn't supposed to say, "Yechhh!" If the patient exhibits offensive or undesirable characteristics, the nurse isn't supposed to look or speak in a derogatory manner. Thus, the first statement describes an ability to recognize *when* to respond and when not to respond. The second statement means that when a nurse sees a patient to whom he or she is supposed to make a response, the nurse has the skill with which to make that response. Note that the first statement is a pure visual-discrimination item that has nothing whatever to do with feeling (affective) and that the second statement describes some sort of cognitive/psychomotor (knowing/doing) skill that again has nothing "affective" about it.

Thus, the essence of a very affective-sounding goal had nothing whatever to do with feeling; nor do the statements describing the meaning of the goal have any affective words in them.

Nor should they. The basis for statements about abstractions such as "therapeutic relationship" is the things people say and the things people do. When we describe those things we want them to say or do to make us willing to label them with the abstraction, there is little need for fuzzies in our descriptions.

There are two other features of this analysis worth noting. The first feature is that what sounded like a vast and profound expectation—"therapeutic relationship"—was ultimately defined by two sentences. Nurses who knew when and when not to respond and who had the skill to respond when appropriate represented the essence of the goal. Period. The second feature is that the analysts discovered that they didn't want nurses to treat adolescents any differently from the way they treated other people. In short, the process of thinking about their expectations caused the analysts to see that this expectation, at least, was inaccurate. The goal analysis caused them to shift their concern from the treatment of adolescents to the broader category of the treatment of patients in general.

With the meaning in hand, it was possible for the faculty to (a) count the number of people who could perform as desired, (b) count the number of instances in which desired performance actually occurred, and (c) decide what to do to get more of what was wanted.

Was this definition of therapeutic relationship "good" or "right"? Doesn't matter, does it? What matters is that this faculty had the courtesy to think deeply about their expectations and to make those expectations public to all those concerned.

Was their definition "humane" or "inhumane"? The procedure for clarifying goals has nothing whatever to do with humanistic or antihumanistic sentiments. To describe the world is not to change it.

To say what one means by a goal is to reduce neither the importance of the goal nor its profundity.

Though the meaning, when seen on paper, may appear trivial—or even *be* trivial—the act of writing it down means merely that what was once secret is now open for inspection and improvement.

An Ounce of Prevention

This last example offers another instance in which the final goal definition was a lot less complex than originally thought. A large oil company asked me to assist with the development of some instruction. "We need our dockworkers to have a proper spill-prevention attitude," said the manager. "We're getting a lot of flak about oil spills, and we want to make sure everyone who handles the oil has a good spill-prevention attitude."

The goal, then, was to "have a proper spill-prevention attitude," and the method of accomplishment envisioned by this manager was "a course." By now, however, you know that it is fruitless to start any action until you know what the action is supposed to accomplish. So, we entered into a discussion (translation: sneaky goal analysis) so that I could find out what they wanted the oil handlers to do. After a while the manager said, "Look, I don't care *what's* going on in their insides; what I want them to do is to follow operating instructions."

"You mean," said I, eagerly pouncing on this specific, "that if they followed operating procedures, you would be willing to say they had the right attitude about spill prevention?"

"I don't *care* about their attitude," he said firmly. "I want them to follow operating procedures."

And that was it. *All* of it. What started out as "have a proper spill-prevention attitude" ended with a single sentence to define it: "Follow operating procedures." Since the operating procedures were all written down, it was easy to tell when they were and were not being followed.

Sometimes it takes many sentences to describe the meaning of a goal; sometimes only one.

Summary

Once the performances representing the essence of the goal are identified, the final steps in the analysis are to draft statements describing each desired outcome and to test those statements with the question, "If these performances are achieved, will I be willing to say the goal is achieved?" When the answer is "yes," the analysis is complete. The complete goal analysis procedure, then, is as follows:

Step One: *Write down the goal in outcome terms.*

Step Two: *Jot down, in words and phrases, the performances that, if observed, would cause you to agree the goal was achieved.*

Step Three: *Sort out the jottings. Delete duplications and unwanted items. Repeat Steps One and Two for any remaining abstractions (fuzzies) considered important.*

Step Four: *Write a complete statement for each performance, describing the nature, quality, or amount you will consider acceptable.*

Step Five: *Test the statements with the question, "If someone achieved or demonstrated each of these performances, would I be willing to say he or she had achieved the goal?" When you can answer "yes," the analysis is finished.*

8
Some Examples

To some people, examples don't examp unless they are set within their own circumstances. This phenomenon, called the not-invented-here factor (or NIH), implies that unless a procedure was invented or developed for a particular area, it couldn't possibly be useful to that area. But fuzzies are fuzzies no matter where you find them, and you can use the same analysis procedure there as well as here. The circumstances might be different, but the procedure is the same.

No Shortage of Fuzzies

A good place to begin is with some examples of fuzzies I've collected over the years. As you read through the list, you will notice that some are more abstract than others, and that some don't seem to make a whole lot of sense. But I assure you that all of these represent examples of goals that someone was, or is, serious about accomplishing.

From the World of Academe

From a junior high school

Develop a favorable attitude toward school

Develop self-actualizing students

Self-concept

Be a self-disciplined person

Self-worth

Develop self-respect

Appreciate democracy .

Appreciate American culture

Write legibly

From a high school

Good sport

Music appreciation

Good study habits

Art appreciation

Social adjustment

Self-discipline

Leadership qualities

Likes teacher

Love of learning

Shows initiative

Understands minorities

Enjoys school

Self-respect

Respect for others

Is tolerant

From a dental school

Professional attitude

Social consciousness

Relates basic science to clinical practice

Graduates with a feeling that the education was relevant

Has a desire to continue the education

Has an affection for the university

Values total patient health

Thinks like a scientist

Takes pride in his/her work

From a medical school

Applies theoretical concepts in practice

Conducts oneself in a professional manner

Argues effectively

Be interested in continuing education

Establish good rapport with all members of the health team

Communicates effectively

Be a caring physician

Positive self-concept

From a military post-graduate school

Understand the material

Be able to think

Be capable of making original contributions to the field

Be conscious of one's role as manager

Master the fundamentals

No freeloaders

Comprehends the whole picture

Be able to learn on his/her own

Be creative

Develop a proper decision-making attitude

From the World of Work

From an auto manufacturer

Safety conscious

Good diagnostic skills

Handles customer complaints skillfully

Listens to customer complaints

Fixes it the first time

Provides quality service

Sensitive to customer needs

Time efficient

Demonstrates professional attitude

Accepts responsibility

Clearly states customer options

Demonstrates honesty with customers

From a social-welfare department

Ability to accept the client where he/she is

Allows self-determination for the client

Develops good eligibility-worker/client relationship

Be a good eligibility worker

Be an adequate eligibility worker

Know how to close cases

From a supermarket chain

Has pride in work

Customer courtesy

Profit-minded

Friendly

Good front-end service

Clear store ✓

Safe store

Pleasant place to shop

From a marketing division

Cooperative leadership

Cost consciousness

Positive attitude toward the organization ✓

Efficient work organization

Better flow of information

Convince customers ✓

Profit-oriented sales behavior

Good social-political behavior

Knows economic daily news ⌄

Knows how to listen

Knows how to judge himself/herself

From a bank

Bank employees will be treated equally in every aspect of employment in order that all employees may achieve maximum use of their abilities.

All employees will perform their daily operations in a manner contributing to responsible corporate conduct.

All employees will act in a socially responsible manner.

From a chemical manufacturer

Communicates well ✓

Good selling skills

Can use a computer ✓

Good leader

Good analytical ability

Good instructor

Is user friendly ✓

No customer complaints

From a boardroom

Be global minded

Be market sensitive ⌣

Think globally, act locally ✓   BE *global*

Develop empowered employees

From politics

Get the country moving again ⌐

Have a balanced budget

Understand the will of the people ⌐

Have a "Contract with America"

Be hard on crime

Have a clean campaign

Put America first ✓

Have civil rights

As you read through the above lists, you no doubt noticed some repetition from one domain to another. That's inevitable. Why? Vague terms are interchangeable. For example, what is a "good communicator?" Someone who "listens well." Who has a "professional attitude?" Someone who is a "self-starter" and "takes responsibility." Who takes responsibility? Why, someone with a professional attitude.

The inescapable fact is that there are far fewer things that we want people to do than there are fuzzy ways to describe them.

To verify that for yourself, pick any fuzzy from the preceding pages and see how many other fuzzies you can think of that might have just about the same meaning.

Before moving on, there are a couple of ways to make good use of the above lists. Here's what to do:

1. With a pencil, check the goals that describe process instead of outcome. That is, mark the ones that talk about "developing" or "becoming" rather than "being."

2. Then, re-write the checked items as outcome statements. (This should take only a word or two.)

This is a useful exercise, because you'll never want to begin a goal analysis until the goal is stated as an outcome rather than a process. That way, it is somewhat easier to stay focused on describing what goal accomplishment will look like rather than on the process of getting there.

Sample Goal Analyses

Now that you've seen the range of fuzzies with which people grapple, I'd like to show you some examples of the results of that grappling. The following goal analyses appear in various stages of completion. Though all were alleged to represent the performances that would exemplify a goal (Step 3 of the five-step analysis procedure), you will be able to spot a variety of ways in which they can be improved. As you read through them, see if you can spot:

- "performances" that are still fuzzy,
- statements of process rather than outcome, and
- instances where there is a shift in focus; that is, where one item seems to refer to one group of people and another item refers to another group or to an organization.

Once you've had a chance to review these analyses, you'll be offered a chance to practice improving one or two of them.

Good Physical Appearance

This analysis was conducted by a group of trainers in a police department. Here, they said, is how to recognize someone with good physical appearance:

Always wears clean clothing   *Clothing "clean" + well fitted*

Clothing is well-fitting — *wears Clothes that fit well.*

Wears appropriate hair style (according to regulations)

Has the correct height-weight ratio

Leather and brass are shined

This list may seem short and a bit abrupt, but it is complete in that it describes everything the analyst meant by good physical appearance.

Demonstrates Responsibility

Would this description fit into your own work environment?

Carries out assigned tasks on time

Carries out tasks regardless of the time required

Carries out tasks regardless of whether others have completed their own tasks

Offers solutions to problems outside the immediate job

Plays Well in the Sandbox

This is one of the expressions currently heard around the work environment. "She doesn't play well in the sandbox," or "He doesn't even know his sandbox skills are weak," or "We can't afford to hire anyone who doesn't play well in the sandbox," is how the expression is usually used. But what does that mean? Here are two answers to that question. The first is what it means when talking about kids in a real sandbox; the second is a definition from a real organization:

Kids in a Real Sandbox ...

share their toys and information

don't hog the good spots in the sandbox

don't section off territory for their own

don't kick sand on other kids

let everyone play

take turns using the toys

bring toys that everyone can use

don't make messes or pollute the sandbox
(you know what that means)

don't pour sand out of the sandbox

People in a Corporate Setting ...

ask permission before borrowing other people's things

share ideas and information with other people

don't worry about who gets the credit for a good idea

honor written and verbal agreements ⌄

share office equipment, supplies, and resources

don't talk behind other people's backs

don't treat other team members like subordinates

don't belittle others or talk down to them

listen to what others have to say

let others have their say without interrupting

are not abrupt, short, or quick with others ✓

are not subservient to the client ✓

are not sarcastic or negative about other individuals, projects, or the organization

provide constructive task-diagnostic feedback to others

provide feedback in an open, timely, candid manner

openly address conflict

respect other people's race, ethnicity, gender, religion ✓

use badges

sign in and out as required

use correct procedure for taking resources off-site

This second list contains quite a few items about which you are likely to ask, "What do they mean by that?"—indicating that the analysis needs work to make the picture of a good sandbox player clear.

Good Tone of Service

Here is an example from a telephone company:

Telephone operators are expected not only to perform their tasks according to company practice and criteria, they are also expected to perform their tasks with "good tone of service." Now the tasks to be performed were well described in a variety of manuals and documents, and there was fairly good agreement about how to tell whether the tasks were being performed properly. Not so with "good tone of service." Because "good tone" is an abstraction (you can't see anyone good toning), twelve supervisors set out to complete a goal analysis.

After several sessions during which many fuzzies were listed and war stories recounted, an interim list of performances was produced:

Actions
acknowledge requests
express regret
handle requests promptly
discriminate between duty
  and beyond the call of duty
listen attentively
  (criteria: accurate responses, no question repeats)

Must Avoid
swearing at customer
interrupting customer
banging*

Action Should Be Done With:
understandable words
  (vocabulary)
accenting of key words
proper phrase usage

variable pitch
calm voice (under stress
  and normal conditions)
responses tailored to the
  individual

At this point, the supervisors were ready to move to Step 4 of the analysis procedure and clarify their work further by eliminating duplications and writing each remaining item as

---

*"Banging" means to slam hands, books, or equipment in such a way that the customer detects operator irritation or frustration. Should an operator feel tension to the degree that banging something is the only release, he or she should break the connection before "letting go."

complete sentence. Here is the final result of their deliberations:

Good tone of service

1. Answers with proper phrases within two seconds of plug-in.

2. Handles customer requests (i.e., performs operator tasks):

without swearing	with words understandable to the customer
interrupting	key words accented
banging	using prescribed phrases
	using variable pitch

3. Demonstrates an ability to listen attentively by responding to a series of typical calls (a) accurately and (b) without asking the customer to repeat the information he or she has given.

4. Given the following customer situations (list inserted), expresses regret by saying "I'm sorry."

5. Given a series of taped dialogues between operator and customer, supervisor is able to identify those calls in which the operator responded beyond the call of duty.

When the supervisors were asked if they would agree that someone had "good tone of service" if he or she did what the items described (Step 5 of the process), they agreed . . . tentatively. They recognized that there was still a little tidying up to be done. Even so, they created a basis on which they can make sure that each and every operator performs in accordance with the essence of the goal.

Comment

Notice that this last analysis was conducted as a group activity. Should goal analyses always be done in groups? Absolutely not. The optimum number for an analysis is one or two. If you do it alone, it may take longer to think of all the components of the meaning of the goal than if you have another person available to help trigger your thinking. But every additional person will significantly increase the time it will take to get the job done. There will be war stories to tell, anecdotes about people behavior that need to be recounted, and so on.

Suppose a whole basketful of people will ultimately have to agree on the meaning of a goal. Should they *all* be involved in the analysis? No, not in the original drafting. Go ahead and draft the meaning as best you can, then present your draft to the others (individually if possible). Ask them to modify it to their satisfaction. That will take them a lot less time than if you (a) have a large group of people forging the analysis or (b) ask individuals to write their definitions on a blank piece of paper. The rule is: You'll make more progress if you ask people to fix (edit) something already drafted than if you ask them to create it themselves. Criticizing is always easier than creating.

Here's an example: Suppose you have a meeting with your boss and are told, "I want your team to be more quality conscious when they're working." When you ask for clarification, you're told, "Well, you know, pay attention to quality." On that note, your meeting ends. What to do now? Clearly, you will need to define what "be quality conscious" means before you can take any meaningful action to get more of it. The faster approach would be to do the goal analysis yourself and then ask your team to review and improve your initial draft. You would then have something to take to your boss about which to ask, "If my team did these things, would you agree that they were quality conscious when working?" Your boss will find it a lot easier to suggest changes in an existing list of performances, rather than to try to create a coherent definition of the fuzzy from scratch.

9

A Pinch of Practice

It would be useful to practice the steps of the goal analysis procedure while the steps are still fresh in your mind. So this short chapter will provide some opportunities to do just that.

Practice #1. Write the Goals

Modify the following statements so that each describes an outcome (the end result) rather than a process (how to get to the end result):

Develop a high quality of life. *Have high quality of life*

Improve one's health. *HAS HEALTHY LIFESTYLE. lives well*

Become an outstanding musician. *Is outstanding musician*
Knows how

Complete training to become a competent engineer.
TRAINS   trained to be competent engineer. IS COMPETENT ENG

Learn to be a good citizen. *Is A GOOD CITIZEN*

Develop pride in work. *takes pride in their work*
work done well. ON TIME

When you have finished, turn to the next page.

Practice #1 Explanation:

Here's how your goal statements should look:

Develop a high quality of life.

Have a high quality of life.

Improve one's health.

Have good health.

Be healthy.

Become an outstanding musician.

Is (or be) an outstanding musician.

Complete training to become a competent engineer.

Is (or be) a competent engineer.

Learn to be a good citizen.

Is (or be) a good citizen.

Develop pride in work.

Takes pride in work.

Each of these fuzzies now describes the goal in outcome terms rather than in process terms.

Go on to the next page.

Practice #2. Sort a List

Now try sorting a list of performances/fuzzies.

Here is a list of performances from Step 2 of an analysis of the goal, *"takes pride in work."*

Takes pride in work

a. ~~Carries out assigned tasks~~ ok

b. ~~Likes his/her~~ job *[illegible]*

c. ~~Performs tasks well~~ ok

d. Says favorable things about the job *[illegible]*

e. Enjoys his/her work Fuzzy

f. Performs tasks at the level of his/her ability —same as a+c

Here's what to do:

1. Cross out duplications;

2. Place a check mark in front of any item you think is still fuzzy; and then

3. Write a least one performance that might be useful in defining each fuzzy.

Enjoys his/her work   works longer than expected

_____

_____

_____

When you've completed the three tasks,
turn to the next page.

Practice #2 Explanation:

Here is the list again for reference:

   a. Carries out assigned tasks

   b. Likes his/her job

   c. Performs tasks well

   d. Says favorable things about the job

   e. Enjoys his/her work

   f. Performs assigned tasks at the level of his/her ability

1. Cross out duplications.

   Items **b** and **e** seem to be saying the same thing, so either one of them can be deleted.

   Items **a, c,** and **f** all have something to say about carrying out tasks. Item **f** seems to say it best, so I'd delete Items **a** and **c.** That leaves us with:

   d. Says favorable things about the job

   e. Enjoys his/her work

   f. Performs assigned tasks at the level of his/her ability

2. Put a check mark in front of any remaining fuzzies.

   Item **e** is a fuzzy and should be checked.

3. Write at least one performance that might be useful in defining each fuzzy.

There are many possibilities here, such as:

- Works longer hours than expected.

- Performs tasks without urging or prompting.

- Explains tasks to others when asked.

- Whistles while working.

What else might employees do to cause you to infer that they enjoy their work?

Go on to the next page.

Practice #3. Complete an Analysis.

Now try to complete a goal analysis that's already been start-ed. For practice, we'll use an example from a previous chapter.

Demonstrates responsibility

a. *Carries out assigned tasks on time*   ~~*assigned tasks*~~
      ~~*completed within required*~~ *time*

b. ~~*Carries out tasks regardless of the time required*~~
      tasks are completed regardless
      of time required

c. *Carries out tasks regardless of whether others have com-pleted their own tasks* ✓   ② *Tasks are completed*

d. ~~*Offers solutions to problems outside the immediate job*~~ ✗✗
      offers advice to other way   *not right*

Here's what to do:

1. Because goal analysis is useless in the abstract, you will need to select a target for your practice; you will need to say just who is expected to demonstrate accomplishment of the goal. It could be your students, colleagues, admin-istrators, or managers. Whichever target you choose, write the name of that person or group in the space below.

    Target performers: ___General Manager___

2. Read the goal and list of performances given above. Ask yourself whether you would agree that your target audi-ence could be considered "responsible" if they exhibited the listed performances in the environment in which they work.

3. Delete any items that don't apply.

4. Add whatever performances are needed to cause you to answer "yes" to the question, "If these people did these things, would I consider them responsible people?" (You may need more writing space than is provided below.)

5. Convert each of the performances into sentences that describe the intent as clearly as possible. For example, what does it mean to carry out assigned tasks on time? Does it mean they need to be completed by 8 a.m.? By the time a whistle blows? Before the end of the day?

Carries out task.

Completes tasks when required

Demonstrate responsibility

A. assigned tasks completed within regu. time

B. Tasks are completed regardless of time required

C. Tasks are completed regardless of whether others have co

D. offers advice to other mgrs

E. Keeps hotel clean & everything work

F. Staff **When you are finished, turn to the next page.**
Trained to tobe care of guest

Practice Example #3 Explanation:

It's impossible for me to know which group you targeted for your analysis, of course, so I'll have to select one of my own for the feedback that follows.

The target audience for my analysis is a group of technicians who maintain and repair office equipment. For this group, the goal "demonstrates responsibility" was confined to job performance. Here's how I would re-write the items in complete sentences:

1. **Assigned tasks are completed by established deadlines.**

2. **Tasks are completed regardless of the time required.** (This means that the techs keep working until a task is completed, even if they work past the deadline.)

3. **Assigned tasks are completed regardless of whether others have completed their own tasks.** (This means that "It's not in my job description" is not an acceptable excuse for task incompletion.)

4. **Offers advice to other techs when asked.** (I had to decide what this item meant in terms of my target audience, as the meaning as stated was unclear.)

For the target group I selected, I had to add these items to agree that the techs are performing their work "responsibly."

5. **Keeps tools and test equipment in working order.**

6. **Always keeps a full complement of spare parts at hand.**

7. **Completes the expected paperwork at the completion of each repair or maintenance procedure.**

Your completed analysis will differ from mine, of course,

but your final statements should pass the completion test; the collection of performances should be described in a way that will cause you to agree that the goal would be achieved if someone did what the statements describe.

Tact

With the practice just completed, you should be able to tackle the analysis of almost any goal—when you do it by yourself.

You'll need an additional skill, however, whenever you get other people involved in your goal analyses: Tact. You see, when you ask people what they mean by the abstract words they use, when you ask how they would know one when they saw one, you're treading on tender ground (my wife would call it "thin ice"). It's important, therefore, to approach the analysis with care.

How? Tell yourself that most people aren't used to thinking in terms of specifics. Remind yourself that most people think that being specific about the meaning of a goal somehow makes the goal sound less important, less profound. So give them time to talk their way through the steps. Give them time to change their minds about how they perceive things. Let them make some false starts as they zero in on the meaning of the goal.

Above all, remind yourself that you are likely to be asking people to modify long-held beliefs about the meaning of their cherished fuzzies. So be gentle, and provide some talk-think time. And do a draft analysis by yourself, whenever possible, so that you can give others something to shoot at—give them something to fix, rather than create.

10
Surprise Endings

O ne thing you learn from repeated use of the goal analysis is that it doesn't always take you where you think you're going. Sometimes, as we have seen in previous examples, it does lead you to the performances that are the meaning of the goal, to the performances that need to be increased or decreased if the goal is to be achieved better. Sometimes, in other words, the analysis takes you through the five steps of the procedure as described (shown below in Figure 1 as Track A).

Sometimes, however, the analysis causes you to shift direction drastically; and sometimes it all evaporates into thin air.

Figure 1

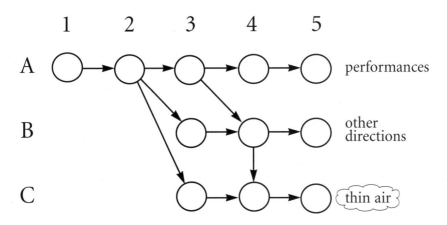

Instead of following Track A, as expected, you may find yourself following Track B or C. This shouldn't be particularly surprising, for it is a common phenomenon in everyone's life. You may go to the doctor with a firm idea of what is wrong with you, only to have his or her diagnosis show the problem to be something entirely different. You may go to the store to buy a new turn-signal light for your car, and later find that what you really needed was a fuse. Fixers of electronic devices sometimes find that their "trouble" disappears once someone remembers to plug in the device. So it goes.

And why not? Nobody's perfect; if we were, there would probably be no need for analysis procedures, especially the kind being described in this book. You start off in one direction, and analysis turns you in another. So? That's what analyses are for!

To help prepare you for the various outcomes you will encounter when analyzing your important goals, I'll provide some examples that show some of the other-than-as-planned things that can happen.

From Welfare to Embarrassment

The first example is from the nursing profession, where there is little question about the importance of accomplishing health goals. While working to identify the specific skills important to the practicing nurse, a faculty noted that they wanted nurses to "show concern for patient welfare." When I asked them to describe the basis on which they would decide if someone did indeed "show concern for patient welfare," the discussion started easily and rolled along merrily. At the beginning, there was a great deal of talk about such things as empathy and sympathy and the difference between these fuzzies. There was discussion about whether it was necessary for nurses to "really like" their patients if they were to give effective treatment, and about the problems of working with doctors and aides. The discussion wasn't exactly pertinent to the problem at hand, but goal analysts learn to allow for some rambling. It seems to help people realize that they normally use quite a few fuzzies during what they consider "technical discussions"; it helps them realize that they don't really know what they are talking about when describing the goals they think important. A little rambling helps clear the air. Asking someone to define a goal in terms of performances *he* or *she* would accept is a little like asking someone to undress in public—if the person hasn't done it before, he or she may need time to get used to the idea.

After ten or fifteen minutes had passed, someone finally said, "Well, no one can be said to exhibit concern for patient welfare if he or she leaves the patient unnecessarily exposed." And the discussion took a sharp turn in a new direction. The participants zeroed in on this topic immediately, and it became clear to those present that concern over "unnecessary exposure" was of more immediate interest than "patient welfare." No doubt items dealing with exposure would be part of what they meant by "patient welfare" (vague terms are interchangeable); but after writing the first item (which was a fuzzy) on their list, they zeroed in on its meaning. Within a minute or two, the faculty had written:

Goal: Shows concern for patient welfare

1. Does not leave patient unnecessarily exposed to:

   fear stimuli

   embarrassment

   treatment

And then, rather than continuing to define this goal, there was strong interest in abandoning it in favor of "unnecessary

exposure to embarrassment." Everyone came up with anecdotes (critical incidents) describing events leading to patient
embarrassment. In each case, the activity or condition leading
to patient embarrassment was jotted down; eventually, the list
looked like this:

Prevents patient embarrassment

1. Controls number of visitors

2. Does *not:*

    a. leave patient exposed physically

    b. treat patient in socially derogatory manner

    c. insult patient's values

    d. insult patient's medical knowledge

    e. bawl out staff in patient's presence

    f. ask more intimate questions than needed to do the job

The remainder of the session was devoted to clarifying the
fuzzies on this list and to testing the list with "the question" to
determine if it represented their meaning of "prevents patient
embarrassment." So, what started out to be an analysis of one
goal (shows concern for patient welfare) ended with the definition of another.

From Listening to Facilitating

This is another example of a change in direction in mid-
analysis. A group of English teachers said that an important
goal in elementary school was to teach kids how to "be better
listeners." When the goal was written on the chalkboard, there
followed a discussion of its importance. After a few minutes, I

reminded the teachers that the next step was to describe what someone might do who represented the goal. But for a time there was only silence.

A lot of thinking . . . but silence.

Finally, one teacher ventured a cautious, "Well, we really can't expect children to listen attentively if they don't have *good hearing.*"

Immediately, somebody wrote "good hearing" on the board.

That prompted another to offer, "And we really can't expect them to listen attentively if it is *too noisy.*"

"Not too noisy" was added to the list.

Then a third said, "Yes, and we really can't expect them to listen attentively unless there is something *worth listening to.*"

"Something worth listening to" was written down. Everyone looked at the board, and then there was a long silence.

And then it seemed as though everyone started talking at once. This happened to be a sharp group of people, and they didn't need any prompting to recognize what had happened. They quickly saw that if they wanted more attention from the kids, they would have to make some changes in their own behavior and in the environment around the kids. A lively discussion followed about just what those changes would be and how they might be put into practice. So, what started out as an intent to decide what to teach children to make them better listeners ended in a description of what the staff would have to do and what the environment would have to be like to make it more likely that students would do what they already knew how to do.

From Responsibility to Effectiveness

Some time ago I had an opportunity to work with the members of a small department charged with improving the "social responsibility of the corporation." These young people had spent a great deal of time trying to decide what the corporation should do to be "more socially responsible," but they succeeded only in pointing fingers and describing what *other* people—government employees, citizens, judge, and vice-presidents—ought to do. The department members were not being deliberately ineffective; they just didn't have a handle on what to do. At this point I was called in to see if I could help. After listening to each member describe his or her understanding of the mission, it quickly became clear that the group's notion of social responsibility was "what *other* people do." A goal analysis was in order.

This time I decided to involve the entire group of six, as I believed it more important for them to struggle with the process together than to individually critique someone's grand definition of the goal. So we began. "How would you recognize a socially responsible person?" I asked. Clearly, that was the wrong approach. They just couldn't get started. So I tried another tack. "Do you *know* a person you can name whom you would consider socially responsible?"

"Yes," was the immediate reply. "Me!"

Though the comment was made in jest, I took it as a starting point and said, "That's a good place to start." With this comment I was signaling that it was OK to horse around with the topic, and that anything they said would be accepted rather than impaled. "What do you do that makes you think of yourself as socially responsible?" I continued, and the discussion blossomed.

"Well, for one thing, I don't steal from the company, like *some* people do."

After writing that comment on a flip chart, I turned to the others and said, "I'm sure you all think of yourselves as socially responsible. What do you do that makes you feel that way?" There was quite a bit of response to that, and it seemed as though everyone wanted to talk at once.

"I come to work on time," offered one.

"I give an honest day's work for an honest day's pay," offered another.

"I make suggestions on how things can be improved," offered a third.

"I try to understand the work of people in other parts of the company," offered a fourth.

After a page of such comments was written, someone said, "Wait a minnit. We're not talking about social responsibility; we're talking about an effective employee."

"That's an interesting observation," I replied. "For the moment, though, let's not worry too much about the goal statement. Let's think about what we think we want people to do."

The point of this example is that what started out to be a discussion of what *other* people ought to be like ended with a discussion of what every employee should be like. In effect, the finger that pointed at others slowly turned back toward the pointer.

From Good Judgment to Accurate Decisions

This example was offered to me by a navy lieutenant who worked in one of the many training groups operating within that organization. She described the situation this way:

"We'd been getting a lot of flak from our management about the so-called poor judgments made by the staff of our training department. We were told that we needed to be better at judgment because we were screwing things up for the commanders who put our graduates to work. When we asked what we were doing wrong, however, all we got was a description of the consequences of the errors. Not the mistakes, but the results of the mistakes.

"Finally, we decided to do a goal analysis on good judgment, and it worked out far better than we expected. What we expected was a list of performances that would tell us how to recognize good judgment when we saw it; what we got was a series of flowcharts and checklists showing *exactly* the steps to follow in the performance of good judgment."

She showed me the initial list they drafted, and it looked like this:

Good judgment
- assign criterion levels
- make field/formal decision
- make field-training/formal-training decision

This list made it clear that *in this context,* good judgment didn't have anything to do with selecting trainees or instructors or with operating ships. It had to do with making decisions related to training. When the analysts completed their Steps Four and Five, their statements looked like this:

1. Given any instructional objective and all available information describing the field situation and trainee quotas, be able to decide whether the objective would best be taught in the field unit or in a formal school environment.

2. For any instructional objective, be able to decide which of five criterion levels should be assigned to it.

(In this example, criterion levels referred to five "levels" of skill, such as "familiarity," "can perform task with supervision," "can perform task without supervision," etc. Each "level" label loosely described the degree of competence required for a given job.)

That was the essence of what they wanted their staff to be able to do regarding good judgment. The interesting thing was that the analysts then moved quickly forward to describing the step-by-step procedure that should be followed when performing each of the above tasks. Figures 2 and 3 show what the flowcharts looked like. You can see how easy it would be to turn the flowcharts into checklists that anyone could follow.

Figure 2

    Job: Training Management

   Task: Make field-training/formal-training decision

Objective: Given any instructional objective and all available information describing the field situation and trainee quotas, be able to decide whether the objective would best be taught in the field unit or in a formal school environment.

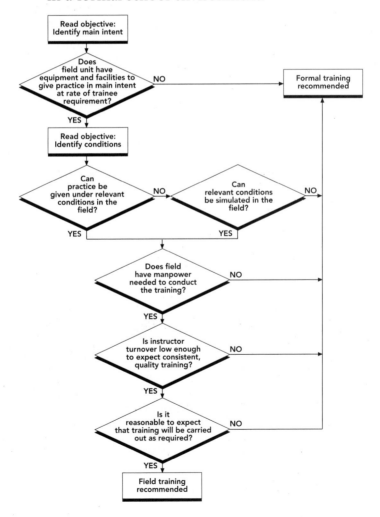

Figure 3

Job: Training Management

Task: Set criterion levels

Objective: For any instructional objective, be able to decide which of five criterion levels should be assigned to it.

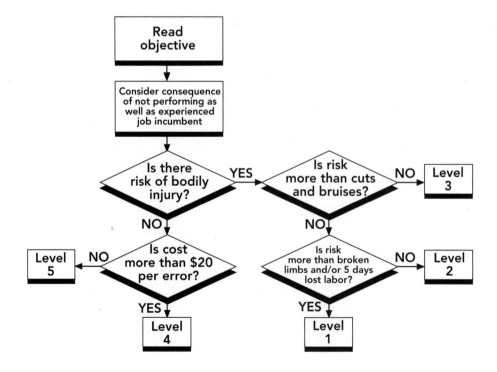

To Thin Air

A few years ago I had a call from a pleasant woman who described a very interesting situation. She said she was a member of a church committee that wanted my help in "establishing an evaluation system by which we can measure the progress of our congregation toward church objectives." Wow! I had never heard of a church that tried to measure the progress of its congregation toward church objectives, and so my ear glued itself to the telephone.

"Do you have any of these objectives written down?" I asked.

"Indeed we do," she replied.

"Would you read me one?" I asked.

"Yes," she said. "Loving service."

Fortunately, I had enough sense to keep my mouth shut while I digested this "objective." Talk about a fuzzy!

Finally, I asked her, "Do you have any more of these—'objectives'—written down?"

"Yes," she replied. "Let me read you the list." And she read:

- loving service
- unselfish devotion
- sincere fairness
- enlightened honesty
- confiding trust
- merciful ministry
- unfailing goodness
- forgiving tolerance
- enduring peace

If you felt a bit overawed while reading that list, I need to remind you that if everyone knew how to be specific about their intentions, they wouldn't need our help. Also, people who have important goals to achieve deserve our best counsel and assistance, regardless of the words they begin with.

I told the woman that there was a series of steps to perform in accomplishing the development of the measurement system the committee was seeking, and that a visit from me wouldn't be profitable until one or two of the steps had already been completed. I explained that she should either work by herself or get her committee together to list the things that people would have to do to be qualified for the labels she listed. We had a long discussion and she took notes to help her memory. She was excited about the activity because she had something very concrete to do.

Alas, when she called back a few weeks later, she sounded defeated. The essence of the problem was that though they talked and talked, no one wanted to talk about specific performances. They wanted to stay at the "merciful ministry" level; they wanted to talk about how to measure *that,* rather than talk about how to measure the *meaning* of that. Too bad, as I was anxious to learn the meaning of those interesting goals.

Summary

Sometimes the goal analysis leads you to a definition of the goal you started with, and sometimes it leads to the definition of another. Sometimes you will be led to give up the analysis in favor of a more urgent activity, and sometimes the content of the analysis will evaporate into thin air. So what? The purpose of an analysis is to give you better information with which to make decisions. If it does that, even by sending you in a different direction, you win!

11
Not for the Casual

This chapter is not for the casual reader or goal setter. It is for those to whom achievement of one goal or another is of the utmost importance or urgency, and who are ready to work toward that end. It is for those who are as interested in accomplishing their goals as they are in defining them.

Additional Steps to Accomplishment

Once you know what successful accomplishment of a goal would look like in terms of what people do, or the results of what people do, you are ready to take some important final steps toward goal achievement. Though these steps are followed *after* a goal analysis is completed, they are included here so that you can see the entire process—from the uttering of a fuzzy that someone says is important to achieve, to accomplishment of that goal.

Step One. *Determine which of the performances revealed by the goal analysis are currently occurring to your satisfaction.* For each of the items on your list of performance statements, determine whether the performance described is already in place. For example, if you want people to show up on time, consult records and people as needed to find out just how many people *do* show up on time; determine the degree to which the actual performance matches the desired performance. If this performance is already within tolerance, go on to the next item. Should you want people to smile while serving customers, determine whether that is now happening to your satisfaction. If not, mark that item for further action.

Once you have determined what is, and what is not, occurring as described by your goal analysis, you are ready for the next step.

Step Two. *Determine which of the non-occurring performances are due to skill deficiencies and which are due to other causes.* In other words, determine if people aren't performing to your satisfaction because they *don't know how,* or for some other reason(s). If they don't know how to perform (or can't perform fast enough or accurately enough or consistently enough), it is likely that they will have to be taught how to perform; that is, if there is a skill deficiency, instruction is probably the remedy. The appropriate items on your list can then be turned into instructional objectives,[1] so that relevant instruction can be organized.

On the other hand, if people *do* know how to perform as desired but for some reason are *not* performing, you will need to find out why they aren't doing what they know how to do before you can decide what action to take to increase achievement of your goal. For example, suppose that as a part of what is meant by "good customer service," you expect your bank clerks to smile when serving customers. Suppose further that you determine that only 50 percent of the customers entering your bank are greeted with a smile. What to do? How can you increase the number of smiles?

---

[1] See *Preparing Instructional Objectives,* Third Edition, R.F. Mager (CEP).

Of *course* people know *how* to smile. Most of them, any-how.[2] If so, why don't they smile as often as expected? To find the answer you will need to carry out a performance analysis[3] that will tell you why people aren't doing what they know how to do and what you can do about it. The performance analysis is likely to reveal that people (a) honestly don't know they are supposed to smile each time they greet a customer; (b) are somehow punished for smiling; or (c) are struggling with an obstacle to desired performance (such as a frantic work load).

At this point you will be ready to take actions that should lead to improved accomplishment of your goal. Arrange for instruction when people don't know *how* to do what they should do, and make the necessary environmental fixes when they're not performing because of other reasons.

Step Three. *If you're really serious about accomplishing your goal, plot your progress on a chart.* And why not? We've seen that an allegedly intangible goal can be defined in terms of the performances that represent it. Since we can tell whether performances occur or don't occur, why can't we plot them on a chart? No reason at all.

And if that goal of yours is as important to achieve as you say it is, then you will surely want to keep track of how you are doing. You will want to compare the steps you take to the results they produce. You may not be able to plot with great precision, and probably wouldn't even want to; but, at the very least, you will want to make sure your actions are taking you in the desired direction.

There is nothing new about the value of indicator charting. Lots of people who care about their effectiveness do it. If you are a manager, you undoubtedly keep tallies and graphs show-ing progress in the events descriptive of company success. If

[2] Some years ago, when a department store chain announced that part of what it meant by "pleasant customer greeting" was that clerks would smile, it was discovered that a small portion of people can't tell when they're smiling in a way that would cause others to agree that they were smiling. The remedy? Have people look into a mirror to see what they look like when asked to smile. A little practice solves the problem.

[3] See *Analyzing Performance Problems,* Third Edition, R.F. Mager and Peter Pipe (CEP).

you are a teacher, you probably keep track of test results and, perhaps, assignment completion and quality. If you are a physician or a nurse, you need no reminders about the importance of charting health (success) indicators. If you are a health-conscious person, you may already be charting your progress in terms of the number of miles walked each day, the number of minutes you exercise, the number of people you can lift above your head, and so on. The only thing that may require a little getting used to is the fact that it is possible to plot the progress of indicators that define some very affective and intangible-sounding states. But it is possible, and it is being done.

A Charting Example:

Let's consider one of the examples used in Chapter 7, that of security consciousness. As you recall, the completed analysis consisted of two performances that indicated an employee's degree of security consciousness.

1. There are no instances in which the person has been found to leave sensitive documents unattended.

2. The filing cabinet is always found locked when it is unattended (when the employee leaves for the day or leaves the room in which the cabinet is located).

Figure 4

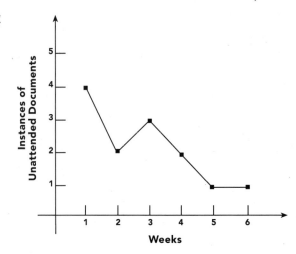

Now then, can you count instances in which sensitive documents have been found unattended? Of course you can. And if you can count them, you can plot them on a graph. In this case, the graph for Susie Schlupopkin might look like Figure 4.

The horizontal line (abscissa) is marked in weeks, and the vertical line (ordinate) is marked in instances. So Figure 4 shows the number of times per week that Susie left sensitive documents unattended. If a weekly count is too insensitive— that is, if it doesn't tell you all you want to know—make a daily count.

As long as the line is moving in the right direction, you can tell yourself that you are moving closer to total achievement of the goal. If it begins to move in the wrong direction, you will need to decide what action to take.

We can plot the second performance of this example in the same way. Here might be the graph of Jeremy Jehumpus:

Figure 5

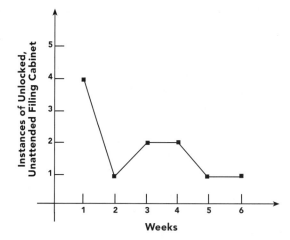

Notice that in Figures 4 and 5, I have plotted instances of *negative* or *un*desired performance. This isn't such a hot idea. You draw attention to whatever you plot, and because attention is highly rewarding, you may get more of the undesired action rather than less. The better approach is to plot the positive whenever you can. Count and plot the number of things that people do right, rather than wrong. In this example, you might plot the number of weeks per month during which there were *no* instances of undesired performance. Better yet, you can plot the percentage of weeks, so that perfect performance will show up as 100% on the graph. Like this:

Figure 6

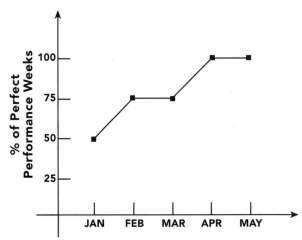

Always accentuate the positive whenever you can. When people find out that you are taking the trouble to plot instances of their performance, you will almost certainly get more of whatever you are plotting. A performance chart is a way of communicating to others the things that are significant to you. When people find out what you consider to be important, you will almost always get more of the performance you want.

Personal Success

More and more people seem to be gearing up to be "more successful" as individuals. They are acting to "take charge of their lives," as the slogan says. "Improve personal success" and "take charge of my life" are fuzzies, of course; so how do these people proceed? What do they do to get more of what they want? By now you know the answer.

First they do what amounts to a goal analysis, to determine just what success would look like if they had it. Then they pick an easy performance to work on, plot how they are doing *now*, and keep track of their progress.

A separate analysis is done in each of the areas (social, family, financial, professional, health, and so on) in which increased success is desired. This method is easier than trying to deal with "personal success" in a single lump. When completing each analysis, it is important to remember that what is important to you is what matters, rather than what the neighbors say or what television projects as important; and it is important to remember that little things count.

I have a friend who constantly tries to improve himself by this method. When he first did a goal analysis, he discovered that the control of his own time was important to him. He hadn't realized it before, but a large portion of his time was controlled by others who came into his office for a variety of reasons—or for no reason at all. Once he learned that time control was important, he decided to find out just how much of his time was currently other-directed. He set up a recorder in his office, and whenever he changed activity, he would say something into the recorder, such as "10:15 Charlie came in to chat," or "10:30 Left for meeting called by boss."

After a month he discovered two things: First, about 60 percent of his time was taken up by things that other people wanted him to do; and second, as soon as people learned he was keeping track of his time, they reduced their demands on his time. They would think twice, for example, before entering his office just to pass the time of day, because they knew this activity would lead to an entry such as "2:45 Mary came in to shoot the breeze."

His plot for this initial analysis looked something like this:

Figure 7

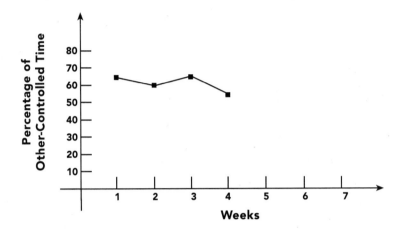

Now that my friend knew how well he was doing in regard to time control, the next thing he had to decide was how well he would have to do to consider himself successful.

Zone of Reason

We are now at a point where the zone of reason becomes a useful tool. After all, *perfection* is seldom a reasonable expectation. But if perfection is unreasonable, what *is* reasonable? The answer to that will always depend on your knowledge of the situation and on the strength of your desire. Consider Figure 7. Would it be reasonable to suppose that anyone can control *all* of his or her time—that is, would it be reasonable to expect *not* to have to spend *any* time doing things that others wanted you to do, or doing things you would rather not do (such as taking out the garbage, writing reports, keeping tax records)? If total time control isn't a reasonable expectation, what is? Ten percent? Forty percent?

How important is it to achieve the goal? How much control can you exert without jeopardizing your job or your friendships? You have to decide what is reasonable. After reviewing his situation, my friend decided that since he was in a business that required a fair number of meetings and conferences, a 40/60 split was a reasonable expectation; that is, if he could reduce the percentage of his time that was other-directed to 40 percent from 60 percent, he would consider that success. So he drew a line across his chart at 40 percent (Figure 8). Any time the plot line dipped to 40 percent or below, he would tell himself he was successful. He wouldn't wait until the line reached zero, since that was unreasonable. The zone of reason was anywhere from zero to 40 percent.

Figure 8

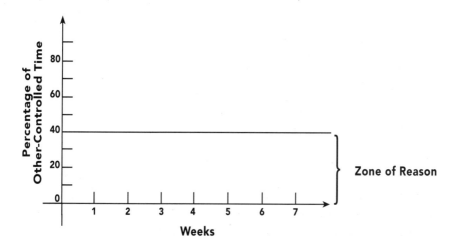

In effect, the line you draw indicates the target you have decided is reasonable to achieve. It is your criterion of success for the item being plotted. Any time your plot line touches or passes that target line, you can tell yourself that you are successful (which is pretty heady stuff).

You might set your zone at different positions at different times. You might begin by noting what you get now in the way of the desired performance and then decide you will determine that your goal for the year is reached if you achieve a five percent increase. You would thus set your zone between five percent above current performance and 100 percent performance. Anything above five percent improvement is considered success and will cause you to agree your goal is achieved, at least so far as that performance is concerned.

In some instances, your zone may be formed not by a horizontal line across the graph, but by a line that angles upward from the origin (the point at which the horizontal and vertical axes meet). Points plotted above that line would fit into your zone of reason; those plotted below the line would not. For example, as I sit here squeezing out one sentence at a time, I look at a chart on the wall before me (Figure 9). This chart plots the number of pages that I produce each day. As my objective is a daily output of at least four pages, I've drawn a

Figure 9

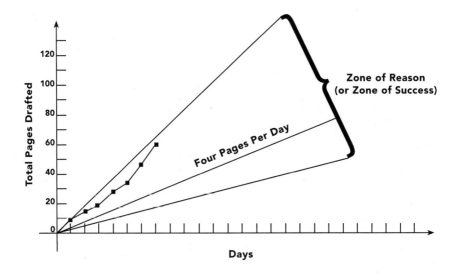

line showing that expectation. That's my zone of reason. I know from experience that with effort I *can* produce four pages per day, and I know I *must* produce that much or more if I am to finish anything within the next century. The chart is useful as a reminder to keep working until I can record progress somewhere within the zone of reason (anywhere on or above the line).

When managing a self-paced course in which students are encouraged to move at their own rates, one finds that some students progress faster than others. But sometimes the slower student is slower because he or she is more thorough and more interested in the course rather than because the student is less capable. Figure 10 shows the progress of three hypothetical students through such a self-paced course. Once experience has been gained with actual students, it is easily possible to set the lower limits of the rate at which the students must progress if they are to complete the course within the time allotted. (Occasionally, there is reason to set an upper limit as well.)

Figure 10

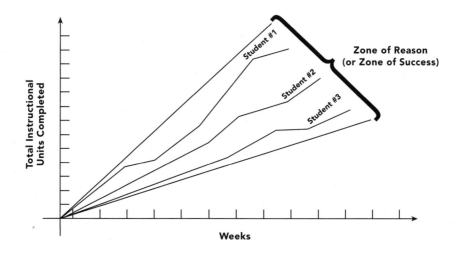

Figure 11 is the Progress Chart used in a two-week performance-based, self-paced workshop called Criterion-Referenced Instruction.[4] The graph line shows the cumulative number of modules (units of instruction) students must complete each day if they are to finish the course in the time allotted. If they have completed at least enough modules to match or exceed the line, they can tell themselves that they will have adequate time to complete the entire course by the time allotted. This line tells students precisely what is meant by "successful completion" of the course.

Figure 11

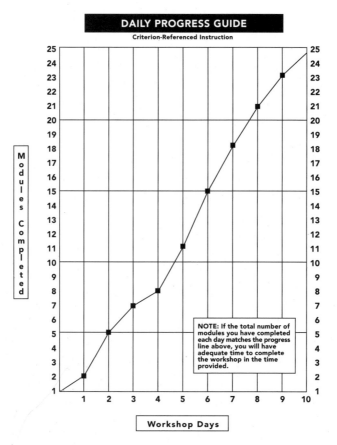

[4] *CRI (Criterion-Referenced Instruction): Practical Skills for Design Instruction that Works,* Fourth Edition, The Center for Effective Performance, Atlanta, GA, 1994.

The Unchartables

Suppose you set out to plot the performances that define your goal and find it difficult to collect the information you want. Suppose it turns out to be impractical to determine whether the performances you are interested in actually are occurring. Then what? Well, one of two things.

If you cannot collect the information you need to plot the performances, you have reason to wonder whether the performances are a reasonable meaning of your goal. If, for example, you define good citizenship in terms of what you expect a person to do ten years hence, you will find it impossible to find out whether you are at all successful in achieving that goal. Sure, you want your employees to vote in every national election, but there is no practical way you can find out if they do. So, wonder if that is a reasonable expectation.

If you conclude that your definition is reasonable but that there is no easy way to collect information to plot . . . for now, that's OK. Nobody said that all fuzzies are easy to define (try a goal analysis of "reverence," for example). If you can't tell how you are progressing, you can't tell. Just make sure you refrain from labeling people as either representing or not representing your goal if you can't tell whether they are performing as you want.

For example, if part of what you mean by "loyalty" is "doesn't badmouth the company," and you can't tell the difference between badmouthing and constructive criticism, just hold off with the snap judgments about who is loyal and who is not. If you have no accurate way to find out what people are saying, or if you decide it would be unethical even to try, either change your expectations or refrain from making inferences about who is and who isn't a goal achiever. But above all, try to remember that it is a highly questionable practice to label someone as having achieved or not achieved a goal state when you don't even know what you would take as evidence of achievement. That is almost as reprehensible as grading students on their "attitudes" when the basis for that grading is unknown and when the basis for the judgment shifts from one student to another.

Mapples and Moranges

Which brings us to a final point. Suppose you are charting two or more performances that collectively define some sort of attitude. It could be that you're charting the components of "favorable attitude toward customers." You have a separate graph for each performance and regularly put a dot on each to show progress.

Now then, if you are charting the performances that are the meaning of your attitude goal, aren't you plotting the attitude? Of course you aren't plotting the attitude directly, as there is no way to get a dipstick into wherever the attitude "is" for a direct reading—by definition. You can, however, plot the basis for your statements and judgments about attitudes; and that is just about as good. Better, in fact, since you can make adjustments as your meaning becomes more sophisticated simply by changing one or more of the charts. Does it matter whether you are *really* plotting an attitude? Isn't taking steps to see if you are moving in the desired direction the real thing that matters (Answer "yes" or "yes")?

Perhaps you are thinking that the indications from each of the charts should be *combined* into a single indicator, and that *that* could be called the attitude chart, if anything is. Perhaps. It is certainly a tempting thought. But if you try it, you are sure to be harassed, bludgeoned, and boiled in oil by the statisticians who understand such things. For one thing, it would be like adding apples and oranges, except worse. You can say that if you have three apples and four oranges, you have seven fruits. But what have you got when you add three apples and four maps? Seven mapples? Seven something, surely; but it just isn't meaningful addition.

There is another problem with combining the content of the various charts into a single number: Most of the charts you want to combine are likely to have intervals of different sizes.

So if you combine your numbers into some sort of total success indicator, you will never know exactly what those numbers mean. But wait a minute. What's the difference? What if a total number has no statistical validity? As long as it makes you feel good to know that you are getting closer to goal achievement, isn't that enough? Well, yes and no. It's enough if you are the only one who sees the numbers and you are *not making judgments about other people* based on those numbers. Otherwise, do not try to combine your charts. Decide what is a reasonable expectation for each performance, mark in the zone of reason on each chart, and concentrate on improving the individual performances. Once you have designated the performances that are important, you can forget about the goal statement that was useful only in getting you started.

12
Let's Pretend

Rather than finish things off with a dreary summary that might send you away with your attitude all wrinkled up, you might find it more useful to check out your ability to explain the topics presented in this book.

Let's pretend you are talking with someone who knows you have just finished reading this book. This person is mildly curious but doesn't know the territory. He or she is the Fuzzy-minded type, whose vague feeling is that only intangibles have "real" value and that anything specific or measurable is automatically base or trivial. He or she seems to believe that those things that are impossible or difficult to understand are somehow profound and that those things that are clear or simple cannot possibly be worthy of his or her respect.

I'll provide his or her side of the interview, and you provide the replies. Afterward, you can compare your sharp and pungent explanations with mine.

Turn to the next page.

Inquirer: Goal analysis, huh? What's that? Do you know
               enough about it to describe it in a sentence or
               two?

You:

Concise, simple, step By step Analysis
of what to do or Achieve

What are we trying to accomplish

procedure for helping define main
goals to the point
where performances are described
& way to discover essence
of what goals mean

Inquirer: Why in the world would you want to do a goal
               analysis?

You:

to get desired results
to understand how to achieve
goal or results in way
that is measurable,
achievable & understandable

help you to describe
what you mean By Success

Inquirer: But how would I know when I should do a goal analysis?

You:

> when you don't have clear cut, concise goal or outcome
>
> you have goals that are not clear, concise
>
> , separate process from result.
>
> Whenever you have a ~~Broad~~ Broad intent of statement That is important to do something about

Inquirer: How would I know one of these broad statements of intent when I saw one?

You:

> how would you recognize one if you saw one
>
> ~~goal~~ generalization
>   - "understand"
>   - "develop"
>   - "achieve"

Inquirer: Can you briefly describe the steps in doing a goal
                analysis?

You:

State goal
do something to achieve goal
Recognize when goal has been achieved

1. write down goal
2. List performances that exemplify achievement
3. sort list, eliminate fuzzies
4 describe performances in complete
                                    sentences
5. Test for completeness

Inquirer: What will I be able to do when the analysis is finished?

You:

> measure outcome
>
> measure performance to desired result

Inquirer: Well, maybe *your* subject is trivial enough to be reduced to a bunch of little performances, but *mine* is intangible.

You:

> how do you know
> if you are
> achieving your goal?

Inquirer: Oh, yeah? Well, let me tell you something. My goals can't be chopped up into little pieces. Besides, you don't think it's necessary to analyze *every* goal to its last ounce of meaning, do you?

You: (Steady now.)

no only those goals that are important to achieve

Inquirer: HMMMmmmmmmmmmmmm . . .

If you'd like to compare your responses with the sort of thing I might say, look at page 147. You might also want to check your accuracy by reviewing the text.

Inquirer: *Goal analysis, huh? What's that? Do you know enough about it to describe it in a sentence or two?*

Me: Sure. Goal analysis is a procedure for helping to define broad goals to the point where their main elements (performances) are described. It is a way to discover the essence of what a goal means.

Inquirer: *Why in the world would you want to do a goal analysis?*

Me: Some goals are quite important to achieve. The goal analysis will help you describe what you mean by success, help you to recognize achievement when you see it. If you know what it is you want to achieve and know what achievement looks like when you have it, you can make better decisions about how to get there.

Inquirer: *But how would I know when I should do a goal analysis?*

Me: Whenever you have a broad statement of intent that is important to do something about.

Inquirer: *How would I know one of these broad statements of intent when I saw one?*

Me: Easy. A broad statement describes an abstraction, such as "understand," "develop," "know," "internalize," or "appreciate." If the statement doesn't answer for itself the question, "How would you recognize one when you saw one?" It's a goal ripe for analysis.

Inquirer: *Can you briefly describe the steps in doing a goal analysis?*

Me: *First,* write down the goal (Step One).

Second, jot down the performances that define the goal (Step Two). Do that by answering whichever of these questions seems more relevant or comfortable to you:

a. What would a person be doing that would cause me to say he or she had achieved the goal?

b. Given a room full of people, what is the basis on which I would separate them into two piles—those who had achieved the goal and those who had not?

c. How would I recognize the goal achievement when I saw it?

d. Thinking of someone who does represent the goal, what does he or she do or say that makes me willing to say so?

Third, go back over the list and tidy it up (Step Three). Cross out duplications and items that, on second thought, don't describe what you want to say. Carry out Steps One and Two for any remaining fuzzies.

Fourth, describe each important performance in a statement (complete sentence) that identifies the manner or extent (or both) of the performance you require to be satisfied the goal is achieved to your liking (Step Four).

Finally, modify these statements until you can answer "yes" to this question: "If someone achieved according to these statements, would I be willing to say he or she had achieved the goal?" (Step Five). Collectively, these statements will represent the meaning of the goal.

Inquirer: *What will I be able to do when the analysis is finished?*

Me: You can do a number of things. You can take steps to find out how things are now going in regard to the performances you want; you can take steps to get more or less of each of the desired performances separately; and you can chart your progress.

Inquirer: *Well, maybe your subject is trivial enough to be reduced to a bunch of little performances, but mine is intangible.*

Me: Perhaps you're right. And if so, it means there is no way to tell whether you are achieving your goals. Therefore, you mustn't claim you are doing so. Unless you perform a goal analysis on your intangibles, you will never know which of them can be achieved, nor by what means.

Inquirer: *Oh, yeah? Well let me ask you something. You don't think it's necessary to analyze every goal to its last ounce of meaning, do you?*

Me: No. Only those goals that are important to achieve. *You don't change the world by describing it, but you put yourself in a better position to move things in your direction if you know what that direction is. So, goal analysis is not for every goal. Only for those that are important to achieve.*

Inquirer: HMMMmmmmmmmmmmm.

BOOK FIXERS EXPOSED!

PRESS RELEASE   **For release upon receipt**

At a hastily called press conference attended by two editors and a clerk-typist, Robert Mager, maker of miniMager-manuscripts, ripped the lid off the secrecy surrounding the development of his three editions of *Goal Analysis*. Not only did he name names, but he identified just who was associated with each phase of manuscript testing. Those present gasped at the revelations.

When asked whether their contributions weren't extremely useful in improving the manuscript, Mager grudgingly replied, "Oh, sure. If it weren't for them, the whole thing would be a shambles. They made me throw out exampless examples and not-so-funny funnies; they choked on things that turned them off and gagged at explanations that didn't explain. Instead of finding a wall to spray on, they scribbled all over my pages with suggestions for improvement and ideas for alternatives. But it all came down to the same thing: Work, work, work!"

"Do you think there is something to be gained from exposing these kindly souls to public glare?" he was asked.

"You bet I do," he replied energetically. "Once they are known, they'll get what's coming to them."

Mager then read the names of those who contributed so graciously to the tryouts, accompanied by blaring trumpets and crashing cymbals. "But I'm not done yet," Mager stammered as someone tried to lead him from the stage. "I'm going to print all their names for the amazement and admiration of the reading public, for Posterity—that's just a few miles from Retrospect, you know—and for raucous cheering by all."

And so it was.

Book Fixers Exposed!

<u>First and Second Editions</u>

1. **Continuity check** (does everything hang together?): David Cram, John Warriner.

2. **Content check** (does it do what it is supposed to do?): Margo Hicks, Ed Krenz, Sue Markle, Sarah Morris, Maryjane Rees, Andy Stevens, Phil Tiemann.

3. **Attitude check** (does it contain unnecessary turnoffs?): Dorothy Carver, Jim Hessler, Bill Hicks, Dan Kratocvil, Frank Moakley, Vernon Rees, Charles Selden, Nancy Selden, Walt Thorne, Jack Vaughn, George Whiting.

4. **Word check** (are there obscure words that can be traded in for common ones?): Brad Mager, Randy Mager.

5. **Cover check** (is the cover design responded to favorably?): Vince Campbell, Jerry Harrison, Jeanne Mager, Debbie Michaels, Sarah Morris, Dick Niedrich, Laura Newmark, Peter Pipe, Oscar Roberts, Bud Robertson, Bill Shanner, Jim Shearer.

<u>Third Edition</u>

Another batch of graffitists contributed to the shaping of the present edition.

Good and bad samples from their goal analysis collections were generously offered by Dan Raymond and Bonnie Abney.

Initial trampling was kindly undertaken by that virtuoso manuscript bashist, David Cram. Once the reeling manuscript was resuscitated, another group of miscreants gleefully added their footprints: Marianne Hoffman, Kay Newell, Dan Lansell, Verne Niner, and Eileen Mager.

Index

How to Turn Learners On . . .
without turning them off

Ways to ignite interest in learning

Third Edition

Robert F. Mager

Books by Robert F. Mager

Preparing Instructional Objectives, *Third Edition**

Measuring Instructional Results, *Third Edition**

Analyzing Performance Problems, *Third Edition**
(with Peter Pipe)

Goal Analysis, *Third Edition**

How to Turn Learners On . . . without turning them off, *Third Edition**

Making Instruction Work, *Second Edition**

Developing Vocational Instruction (with Kenneth Beach)

Troubleshooting the Troubleshooting Course

The How to Write a Book Book

What Every Manager Should Know About Training

* Sold as a six-volume set (The Mager Six-Pack)

WORKSHOPS BY ROBERT F. MAGER

Criterion-Referenced Instruction (with Peter Pipe)

Instructional Module Development

The Training Manager Workshop

For more information, contact:
    The Center for Effective Performance, Inc.
    2300 Peachford Road,Suite 2000
    Atlanta, GA 30338
    (770) 458-4080 or (800) 558-4237
    www.cepworldwide.com

ISBN 1-879-618-18-4 (PREVIOUSLY ISBN 1-56103-337-5)
ISBN 1-879-618-15-X (SIX-VOLUME SET)
Library of Congress Catalog Card Number: 96-72444
Printed in the United States of America

    03 02 01 00   10 9 8 7 6 5 4 3

Contents

There once was a teacher
Whose principal feature
Was hidden in quite an odd way.
　　Students by millions
　　Or possibly zillions
　　Surrounded him all of the day.

When finally seen
By his scholarly dean
And asked how he managed the deed,
　　He lifted three fingers
　　And said, "All you swingers
　　Need only to follow my lead.

"To rise from a zero
To big Campus Hero,
To answer these questions you'll strive:
　　Where am I going,
　　How shall I get there, and
　　How will I know I've arrived?"

RFM

Preface

ONCE UPON A TIME in a little drop of water, King Amoeba decided he wanted to teach his subjects how to have a better life. So he traveled far and wide throughout the Kingdom of Dropland to tell his people how to be better than they were. But nobody listened.

"Psst," said his adviser. "First you have to get their attention. Here. Rub on this magic garlic potion and you will get everyone's attention."

So the king did as he was told and went out to teach his people how to be better than they were. But nobody listened. They swam away . . . and held their noses.

"Psst," said his adviser. "You have to be sure they can hear you. Here. Shout into this megaphone and then everyone will listen."

So the king did as he was told, and went out to spread his wisdom. But nobody listened. They swam away . . . and held their noses . . . and covered their ears.

"Psst," said his adviser. "The people are too stupid to realize what wisdom you have to offer. You have to *make* them listen for their *own good*."

So the king made everyone gather in the Great Solarium while he told them and told them how to be better than they were. But when the Great Doors were opened, everybody swam away so hard and so fast that before they knew it, they had swum right out of Dropland. And henceforth and forevermore they were referred to as Outdroppers.

And the moral of this fable is that . . . *things surrounded by unpleasantness are seldom surrounded by people.*

There is no question that what we *teach* is often different from what we *tell.* Sometimes we teach the beauty and importance of a subject as well as its substance. Sometimes, though, we teach people to dislike, and then to avoid, the very subject we are teaching them about.

How to Turn Learners On . . . without turning them off is about a universal goal of instruction—the intent to send students away from instruction with at least as favorable an attitude toward the subjects taught as they had when they first arrived. It is about the conditions that influence this attitude, about how to recognize it, and about how to evaluate it.

This book is *not* about what to teach. It is simply about a way to help students get the best use of what they have been taught, and about how to influence them to learn more about your favorite subject after they have left you.

If you care whether your students use what you have taken the trouble to teach them, this book is for you.

Robert F. Mager

Carefree, Arizona
January 1997

Part I

Where Am I Going?

1
What It's All About

A thing, to be useful, has got to be used
But hated things, sir, are less used than abused.

How would you like to be able to organize your instruction so that students become so interested and absorbed in what you're teaching that they try to break down your door to arrive early and hang around until you kick them out of the classroom? How would you like to be able to increase the smile count of your students when they enter your learning area? And most importantly of all, how would you like them to leave your instruction eager to think about, to talk about, and to *apply* what you've taught them?

Does that sound too good to be true?

It isn't. Furthermore, it isn't even very difficult to accomplish. Let me tell you a story.

The year was 1967 when twenty-five thirteen-year-olds were selected to participate in a project designed to improve the education in their district. When the project began in this very poor school district, things couldn't have been much worse. These kids, with IQs ranging from 78 to 104, had significant behavior problems. They seldom came to school, were bored when they did, and dropped out as soon as they could. They hated the curriculum.

Then one day, four project teachers said, in effect, "We're going to throw out this boring school curriculum—and we're going to teach you how to *fly*!" Fly? That got their attention.

Why, most of these kids hadn't been out of the neighborhood in which they were born. But fly? Now *that* was interesting.

And, with the help of local private aviation, they did get to fly. All the students got to "drive" the plane for a few minutes on their very first flight (you don't have to know the history of wings to keep a small plane level), and when they returned to earth, became instant heroes in their neighborhood.

To remain heroes and heroines, they had to stay with the curriculum. But a funny thing happened to that "boring" curriculum. The kids discovered that they had to learn to speak clear English—to communicate with the control tower operators. They had to learn math and map reading—to plan fuel supplies. They had to learn geography—to plot their courses. And they became *interested* in learning these, as well as other, subjects. So interested, that they voluntarily built a wind tunnel in the classroom, and both boys and girls eagerly dove into the engines they were given to disassemble. So interested, in fact, that their behavior problems began to evaporate, their attendance increased, and their grades went up. The result? Forty-four percent of the flight group received honor grades in math in senior high school. And not one student dropped out.

"Gosh," you might be thinking. "*We* couldn't do anything like *that*. Where would we get an airplane?" (Actually, that was the easiest part; industry would just love to have an opportunity to provide assistance with projects that make sense.) But it wouldn't take airplanes to get the same sort of results. The teachers could just as easily have said, "We're going to teach you all to be motion picture directors." Or firefighters. Or police officers. Or software developers. Or race-car drivers. Or any of several other things of high interest to students. In each case the students' interest in learning the "boring" subjects of the typical curriculum would increase. Eagerness to learn would improve because the subjects of that curriculum would suddenly have meaning.

There are many similar stories that could be told about how an attitude toward learning was kindled and fanned into a flame so bright that students became not only eager to learn, but eager to apply their learning in the world around them.

You can do it, too; that's what this book is about.

- It's about what you can do to send your students away with a stronger interest in your subject than when they arrived.
- It's about how to send them away not only willing, but eager, to apply what you've taught them.
- And it's about how to avoid sending them away with less interest in your subject than when they arrived.

The Plot

Because the concept of attitudes is an abstraction (a fuzzy) open to several interpretations, we'll need to learn how to say exactly what we mean when we say that our goal is to inspire a favorable attitude toward learning in our students.

Having clarified our perception of what attitudes are, we'll be in a position to describe the attitude outcomes we might be interested in achieving.

Next, we'll learn to recognize approach and avoidance responses (those that indicate favorable or unfavorable attitudes). This skill will help us to recognize progress toward our goals.

Then, because attitudes are shaped, in part, by the conditions and consequences that surround the student attempting to learn, we'll need to explore which of those conditions and consequences work in our favor and which work against us.

By then you'll be ready to learn about a powerful way to make sure that those who *do* have favorable attitudes will actually be willing to put their knowledge and skills into practice with enough confidence to persevere in the face of obstacles and setbacks.

Finally, we'll consider ways to assess the results of our efforts; that is, ways to find out how well we're doing turning our students on, rather than off.

So let's do it.

2
Why It's All About

If telling were the same as teaching,
we'd all be so smart we could hardly stand it.

Why do we teach? Why do we go to the trouble of analyzing, designing, developing, and delivering instruction? What do we hope to accomplish by these efforts?

Don't we instruct because we hope that through our instruction our students will somehow be *different* than they were before the instruction? Don't we teach in order to increase the capabilities of our students?

Consider any of the instruction you yourself may have given. Why did you coach, or tutor, or otherwise assist students to learn? Wasn't it because you hoped they would, as a result of your efforts,

- know more than they knew before?
- understand something they did not understand before?
- develop a skill that was not developed before?
- feel differently about a subject than they felt before?
- develop an appreciation for something where there was little or none before?

If your intent *wasn't* to achieve one or more of these goals, then what in the world were you doing it for?

If they were no different as a result of the instruction, there might have been teaching—but there was no learning. Unless students are changed in some way by the instruction, the instruction cannot be regarded as successful.

Important as that is, it's not enough. After all, we don't go to the bother of teaching just so that students will be able to demonstrate their competence during, or at the end of, the instruction—just so they can go away saying, "Well, that's that. I hope I never hear of *that* subject again. Now I can get on with other things." We want them to go away saying favorable things about the subject and about what they've learned. More, we want them to be willing, and even eager, to actually apply what they've learned in the world around them.

Thus, our primary concern is with influencing how students are able to perform *after* the course is over, *after* our influence is discontinued. We try to instill an appreciation for music now so that students will behave appreciatively *after* our help has been withdrawn. We try to teach them to read, to calculate, to analyze *now* so that they will be able to do those things in the *future.* And whether we are concerned with performance in the immediate future or in the more remote future, we are concerned that our teaching influence become at least as evident *then* as we want it to become evident *now.*

Certainly one of the important goals of education is that the influence of an educational experience will extend beyond the period of instruction. Put another way, we teach so that our students will be able and willing to do something *at some time after our direct influence has ended.* If it's worth teaching, it's worth working toward having that teaching put to use.

How?

There are many things that we can do to influence student attitude toward learning and toward the application of that learning. Some of those things have to do with how the instructional materials are constructed and arranged; some, with how they are presented to the student; some, with what happens to students as they are learning; and some, with what happens to them as a result of their efforts.

Instructors, of course, don't control *all* of the factors that influence attitude toward learning. There are parents, peers, and neighborhoods. There are bosses, corporate policies, and laws. There is the uncle who was admired and the aunt who was there to show the way. And then, of course, there is the mass media.

But we can't pass the buck; we can't avoid facing the responsibility that flows from the fact that *we* influence attitude toward learning. The fact that there are other sources of influence doesn't alter the fact that instructors, as a group, constitute one of those sources. Since this is the case, it is up to each instructor to take whatever steps are available to assure that his or her influence is constructive rather than destructive. But how much does it matter? To answer that, let's try a little metaphor:

Let's Suppose

Let's suppose that everyone in the world had a balloon growing out of his or her head, and let's suppose that the size of the balloon represented the strength of its owner's self-esteem. A larger balloon would mean that its owner had a strong and healthy self-concept, while a smaller balloon would mean that the self-concept was in poor condition.

And let's suppose that as people wend their way through life, their balloons would expand and shrivel in response to the situations they encounter and in response to the things that happen to them. When they find themselves in a situation that is pleasant or nurturing, their balloons would expand. When the results of their efforts lead to a warm or positive feeling, once again their balloons would expand. But each time they met with an unpleasant (aversive) consequence, such as humiliation or embarrassment, their balloons would shrivel just a bit. Many such experiences would shrivel their balloons to nearly empty.

Now, if *you* met someone with a shriveled balloon, you, being a good person, might go out of your way to say or do something intended to help that sickly balloon to expand. And, since you could actually see the state of that person's psyche, you would probably be careful not to do or say anything that would shrivel it even further. At the very least, you might be more thoughtful about how you treated that person and about how you phrased your comments. Rather than barge in with, "Hey. Your fly's unzipped. Are you advertising?" you would probably think about how to communicate this information in a more private and emotionally neutral way.

Now, if we could actually *see* the condition of everyone's self-esteem, and if we could *see* the results of our own words and actions on their balloons, we would quickly learn how to become better at expanding and to avoid shriveling. And we would probably avoid ways of saying things that offend or humiliate others and replace them with words that made them feel better about themselves. In fact, one of the goals of becoming a "better person" might be that of minimizing our shriveling effect and maximizing our expanding effect on those we influence . . . especially on those we care about.

And because it would make *you* feel good when you could see that you had done something to expand someone else's balloon, your *own* balloon would grow as well.

But we can't actually see the size of someone else's balloon, can we? It's all hidden away inside the person. And "hidden" is the right word, because people often work hard to hide the size of their balloons from the eyes of others. You know the words that tell you this is true: "Put on a happy face," "Keep a stiff upper lip," and "Don't wear your emotions on your sleeve." And when we're being polite, or acting like ladies and gentlemen, or being tactful, it is often our intention to hide the shriveling effects that someone else's thoughtless words and acts may have on *us*.

So what to do? After all, we know that whether or not we can see their balloons, our own actions serve to make them grow or shrivel. And we know that our actions affect others whether we intend it or not. We know because the laws of nature tell us so.

So what to do? How can we ensure that we are among the expanders and among those who are expanded in return? And how can we avoid being the shrivelers of others and therefore avoid being shriveled in return?

Since we *know* that our actions affect others, and since we *know* there are laws of nature that influence the strength of this effect, the answer lies in becoming adept at accentuating the positive and eliminating the negative.

The answer lies in learning to recognize, and to apply, those natural laws (principles) in ways that will lead to favorable, rather than to unfavorable—or random—results.

That's why it matters that we take all available steps to make sure that we are expanders, rather than shrivelers, of personal balloons.

Summary So Far

- *Learning is for the* future; *that is, the object of instruction is to facilitate some form of behavior at a point after the instruction has been completed.*

- *People influence people. Teachers, and others,* do *influence attitudes toward subject matter and toward learning itself, whether they want to or not.*

- *One goal toward which to strive is to have students leave your influence with their attitudes as favorable as possible toward your subject. In this way you will maximize the likelihood that students will be willing to use what they have learned and will be willing to learn more about what they have been taught.*

And Now?

We'll begin by exploring the concept of attitude. A certain amount of confusion usually surrounds this topic, and we'll need to sort it out before we can get down to business.

3
Defining the Goal

*If you're not sure where you're going,
you're likely to end up somewhere else.*

Although goals such as "provide good customer service," "appreciate democracy," or "have a favorable attitude toward learning" may be laudable, they are difficult—if not impossible—to achieve when stated in such vague terms. They mean different things—quite possibly equally valid different things—to different people. Though these goals may *name* an important intention, they do not provide us with any information about what the intention would look like if achieved. And if we don't know what successful goal achievement looks like, we have no clues about what to do to accomplish that success. Before proceeding to action, therefore, we must spend a little time thinking about, and describing, the results we expect to achieve.

Let's consider the word "attitude." Although "attitude" is a useful word in everyday conversation—and I have used it myself earlier in this book—it is about as useful as a boot in a bedpan when we are serious about strengthening a favorable attitude.

So let's think about attitude.

Is attitude a thing?

Wellll, no . . . attitude isn't a thing like a nose or a noose. You couldn't dissect a person's favorable attitude toward gumdrops and say, "Aha, madam. *There* is your attitude. Allow me to polish it up just a bit."

But if attitude isn't a thing, what is it?

It's a word. Unfortunately, it's a word that has almost as many meanings as there are people using the word. But there is some agreement about the meaning; no matter what the specifics of the meaning are, people who talk about an attitude are almost always talking about a tendency to behave in one way rather than in another. For example, if we note that a clump of people tend to say "Bleaaaugh!" whenever they are faced with limp string beans, we might conclude that they don't like limp string beans. We might say that they have an unfavorable attitude toward those mushy things. If we note that another gaggle of people tend to fall asleep shortly after the after-dinner speech begins, we might conclude that they have an unfavorable attitude about speakers. It is important to note that whenever we make such observations, we are making inferences *based on visible behavior.*

As a matter of fact, *all* statements about attitude are based on circumstantial evidence: on the evidence of what people say and do.

A good friend of mine has a favorable attitude toward Bach; that is, he likes to listen to music written by Bach. Now this statement is an inference on my part about a tendency, inclination, propensity—or "attitude." It is a conclusion about a general state of affairs based on circumstantial evidence. What kind of circumstantial evidence? Well, he talks about Bach whenever he can slip him into a conversation, and he frequently locates himself where the music of Bach is being played. And he does this for no reason at all . . . by which I mean there is no observable coercion. He simply makes numerous "moving toward" responses to Bach's music. So, from my observations I infer that he has a positive attitude toward Bach.

Attitude Statements Are Predictions. Whenever we make statements about attitudes, we are making predictions about the future behavior of people based on our observations of past behavior. Our predictions, or conclusions, may be right or wrong; but they are predictions nonetheless.

When I say that my friend has a favorable attitude toward Bach, for example, I not only base that statement on things he has said and done in the past, I also predict what that means in the future. I predict that he will take every possible opportunity to put himself into the presence of Bach-like things. I predict he will listen to the music, play it on his piano, go to concerts, etc. If we say that someone has a favorable attitude toward customers, we predict (expect) that rather than avoid customers, this person would approach them, smile at them, ask how he or she may be helpful, provide assistance, and so on.

On the other hand, if we say that someone has a negative attitude about scorpions, we are predicting that this person would avoid the beasties whenever possible, would pass up opportunities to have one as a pet, and would say negative rather than positive things about them.

When we tag someone as having a "favorable attitude," we are predicting some form of *moving toward* responses, and this prediction is based on some "moving toward" behavior already seen. Conversely, tagging a person as having a "negative attitude" is predicting *moving away from* responses, and that prediction is based on some "moving away from" behavior already observed.

Our quest, then, is to increase the strength of approach tendencies toward the subject and to minimize the strength of avoidance tendencies toward the subject; it is to cause the subject to become the object of "moving toward" behaviors rather than of "moving away from" behaviors.

Specifically, we have two goals:

1. Students will exhibit at least as strong an approach tendency (favorable attitude) toward the subject of _____ when they leave your influence as they had when they arrived.

2. When students leave your influence they will be willing to apply what they have learned to the world around them.

These are our goals. And because they should be our primary goals regardless of what we are teaching, or whom we are teaching, they can be referred to as universal goals. No matter what else we accomplish, or fail to accomplish, with our instruction, we should do no harm to student attitude toward learning— and attitude toward what we are teaching.

And Now?

Before we can decide what actions to take to increase an approach tendency (favorable attitude) and decrease an avoidance tendency (unfavorable attitude), we need to be sure we can recognize approach and avoidance responses when we see or hear them. That's what we'll do next.

Part II

How Shall I Get There?

4

Recognizing Approach and Avoidance

A teacher with insight once turned
To a colleague and said, "I've discerned
That if I'm aversive
While waxing discursive
My students detest what
they've learned."

R.F.M.

I'd rather be fishing," says one bumper sticker; "I'd rather be sailing," says another. Both are announcing a preference for one activity over others; both are announcing an approach tendency. Given a choice of activities, those bumper stick*ors* are telling us they would choose fishing and sailing over other activities. And the acts of obtaining and gluing the stickers to the bumpers are examples of approach responses.

Approach Responses

An approach response is an action that indicates a moving

toward an object, activity, or situation. It is a behavior that attempts to get the behaver closer to the target of the approach. It is a behavior that indicates an affinity for the subject of the approach, whether that be sailing, mathematics, or asparagus.

There are several ways in which you could demonstrate an approach tendency. For example, you could physically move toward the target of your affinity (hoping you won't get slapped for moving too close). You could speak favorably about the subject. You could encourage others to become interested in the subject. You could spend time "fondling" or caressing the subject, as people often do when curled up with a good book or when working on a favorite car.

The world around us is filled with approach responses, and a little practice in observation will quickly enable you to spot them by the dozens. To get you started, let's consider some examples from a variety of areas.

Baseball Fans

First, let's take a look at a baseball fan. I'm sure you'll agree that fans have strong approach tendencies toward the target of their fanniness, and that they exhibit any number of behaviors indicating their liking of their favorite activity.

What tells you that someone likes baseball? What does he or she do that causes you to conclude that this person is nuts about the sport?

Suppose you were to observe a fan for a week, and suppose you were to record in your notebook everything he or she did that you consider evidence of a liking for baseball. At the end of the week, your notes might read something like this:

- Talks incessantly about baseball.
- Reads every word about the subject printed on the sports page of both local newspapers.

- Can recite the batting averages of all players of all teams in both leagues.
- During the observation week, watched every game telecast.
- On Tuesday and Thursday, risked losing his or her job by calling in sick in order to attend doubleheaders.
- On Friday, infuriated his or her spouse by watching baseball during a dinner party.
- On Saturday, infuriated his or her spouse by spending the "dinner-out" money on the baseball pool.

This list by no means exhausts the possibilities. You will be astonished at the number of approach responses you will find once you begin to look for them. Some time ago, I ran into an excellent example of approach response toward this very subject. In a letter to one of the personal-advice columns of the old Chicago *Daily News,* a woman wrote:

> "I know men are crazy about sports, but my husband carries this too far. He even took a radio to his sister's wedding so he wouldn't miss the baseball game."

Clearly this man's behavior was intended to cause him to come closer to, or to remain in contact longer with, the subject of baseball; it is an approach response.

Opera Buffs

Next, consider the person who is known as an "opera enthusiast." If you were to observe and record this individual's behavior for a while to see what might have led to such a description, your notes might look something like this:

- Attended all local operas, regardless of cost.
- Talked about opera at length whenever possible.

- Told non-enthusiasts that they "just don't know what they are missing."
- Read books about opera.
- Frequently hums arias from various operas.
- Subscribes to an opera magazine.
- Owns an extensive record collection of favorite operas.

Again, the list of responses that represent an attempt to approach or remain in contact with opera has not been exhausted. Can you think of others?

Enthusiastic Students

Now let's look for approach responses more closely related to instruction. Here's an individual currently enrolled in the second semester of a college biology course. The student's instructor is frequently referred to as "enthusiastic," "inspiring," and "a good teacher." But you don't want to ask about the behavior of the instructor at this point. You are interested in the behavior of the student; more specifically, in discovering evidence from which to predict the nature of this student's future behavior toward the subject of biology. A week-long observation of this student might reveal the following:

- During the week, student went to the library twelve times; used 70 percent of the time spent there reading biology books.
- Tuesday evening, student attended meeting of the university biology club; broke date to attend.
- Wednesday morning, spent $100 on biology texts and dissecting instruments.
- Survey of attendance records shows that student has never missed a biology lecture or laboratory but has cut two or three classes in each of several other courses.

- During the week's three lectures and two laboratory periods, student asked 14 questions, all related to biology.
- Asked to see the course instructor twice in office appointments to discuss points not covered in the course.
- On Thursday, student crouched on the banks of a river for three pre-dawn hours to capture frogs for use as lab specimens.
- Student met with adviser and asked to register for an advanced biology course.

You may object that this list contains exaggerations or that there are omissions, and you may not be willing to accept all the items as relevant to your own situation, but you will surely agree that it contains responses that can be used to make predictions (statements of approach or avoidance tendencies) about the student's future behavior toward biology.

Self-Paced Learners

The biology course just discussed had a lecture format. Let's look at a few of the approach responses commonly seen in courses operated according to a format that is both self-paced and criterion-referenced (competency-based). In these courses, students are given a copy of the course objectives so they know exactly what they must learn to do to be considered competent. They are given a variety of resources from which to learn and practice and are given a great deal of decision-making power over their own instruction. Instructors are available as coaches who assist whenever they are needed. Here are some of the approach behaviors you are likely to see in such a course setting. The students:

- Fix work that is not yet adequate, without urging or pressure.

- Spend time with colleagues (other students) discussing their work or reviewing the colleagues' work.
- Complete more practice exercises than required.
- Come early and stay late.
- Sign up other people at their company for the course.

At one competency-based course in which managers and their team members learn some elements of modern management practice,[1] a number of students were so enthusiastic about what they were learning that they appointed themselves as a task force charged with implementing the techniques of management by objectives back at their organization. They held meetings on their own and developed an action plan. In addition, they drafted and rehearsed a presentation to be made to an executive vice-president upon their return to the company. Finally, they all asked their bosses to be allowed to become certified course managers (instructors) of the course. Strong evidence of approach? You bet.

A word about "comes early/stays late" before moving on. Instructors of lecture courses often complain that students don't get to class on time. Instructors of self-paced, competency-based courses, on the other hand, often mumble about students who want to show up at 7:00 a.m. and who don't want to leave at the end of the workshop day. In our own courses,[2] we have had to establish a policy of simply leaving the students at 4:30 p.m. and going to another room to complete our daily debriefing. Even so, many students continue to work at their learning projects until the doors are locked at 6:00 p.m. This may sound unlikely to you if you have

---

[1] *Blueprint for Performance*®, Fourth Edition, a workshop course on performance management, created by Bonnie MacLean Abney (Abney International, Sebastopol, CA, 1994, 1979).

[2] *CRI (Criterion-Referenced Instruction): Practical Skills for Design Instruction that Works*, Fourth Edition, by R.F. Mager and Peter Pipe (The Center for Effective Performance, Atlanta, GA, 1994).

never experienced this form of instruction; I can assure you, however, that it is not an unusual experience for those who operate their courses in this fashion. In Duluth, Minnesota, for example, soon after the public schools went to a competency-based format, teachers' complaints changed from "We can't get them to show up on time," to "We can't get them to go home in the afternoon." You understand the reason for the complaint— if there are students on the premises, there has to be a teacher there as well.

As you can see by these examples, people who are strongly disposed toward a subject talk a great deal about it, encourage others to participate in it, read about it, buy books about it, study it, publish papers about it, and enter careers about it. Students strongly disposed toward a subject sign up for more courses about it, say favorable things about it, and spend time practicing it.

In general, then, we can say that people with strong approach tendencies toward a subject keep coming back for more experiences with the subject. They seek out experiences with the subject in preference to other desirable experiences. *The more strongly they are attracted to a subject, the more obstacles they will overcome to come into contact with it and stay in contact with it.**

Identifying vs. Weighing

There is a difference between recognizing a thing and putting weight or value on it. It's one thing to say, "That's a stone," and another to say, "That stone weighs five pounds." The same is true for approach and avoidance responses. Identifying them is not the same as interpreting and weighing

---

* One of the most interesting examples of an approach response was this classified advertisement brought to my attention by Peter Pipe:
WANTED: Someone who watches *Love of Life* to fill in an episode missed.

them. Some are stronger indicators of approach, or avoidance, and others are weaker. No matter, as long as you remember that the goal is to maximize the incidence of approach behaviors and minimize the incidence of avoidance behaviors.

Avoidance Responses

Approach tendencies, however, are only half the story. There are also activities that some people tend to avoid. If we can identify responses that lead us to conclude that a person favors an activity or a subject, we should also be able to identify responses indicating a person's tendency to avoid it.

Consider this pithy dialogue:

"Ahh, kiss me, you fool."
"Thank you, but I'd rather not."
"Why not?"
"I never kiss on Wednesdays."

It seems fairly obvious that the second speaker is trying to move away from the first speaker. This is an avoidance response, even though it is verbal. It does not matter *why* the behavior occurred. It doesn't matter whether it was because the first speaker suffered from bad breath or from crumpled toes. It doesn't matter whether it had anything to do with the attraction, or lack of it, of the second speaker for the first. If the response was "moving away from" behavior, it was an avoidance response.

Had you been observing and recording my behavior during the time I was working on the revision of this chapter, your notes might have looked something like this:

- Turned on word processor and typewriter.
- Got up to sharpen pencil.

- Straightened pile of papers.
- Watched bunnies cavorting in desert outside window.
- Typed half a page.
- Watched covey of baby quail stroll by.
- Got up to check thermometer.

Some of those responses look like approach responses and others like avoidance. Whatever my excuse or explanation, those that took me farther away from writing can be called avoidance responses. (I dunno about you, but I find writing to be hard work.)

There are some subjects that may be avoided by people who actually "like" them very much. A dieter, for example, might manage to say, "No, thank you," when offered a favorite dish, or a spendthrift might resist buying coveted new clothes. These are special cases where someone avoids doing something in order to avoid an even more aversive (undesirable or disagreeable) consequence. The dieter avoids getting heavier and more uncomfortable (and possibly, avoids some stern comments from his or her physician); the spendthrift avoids getting a bill that he or she can't afford to pay.

But what about matters closer to the classroom—actions that might be used to infer an avoidance tendency toward an academic subject? The record of a student in his or her second semester of a required college mathematics course might look like this:

- On Tuesday, student tried to persuade mathematics instructor to excuse him or her from the course.
- Student failed to turn in three of four mathematics assignments on time.
- On Wednesday, student spoke with adviser about dropping out of mathematics course.
- On Monday and Wednesday, student was late for mathematics class; on Friday, student failed to appear.

- Told everyone possible that math was useless in the real world and a waste of time to learn.

What other evidence of avoidance have you seen while attending someone else's course? Ever seen these? Ever seen the students:

- Show up late?
- Show up for class unprepared (no paper, no writing tools, etc.)?
- Say unfavorable things about the subject of the course or about the instructional procedures?
- Daydream?
- Disrupt the class?
- Try to discourage others from signing up for the course?
- Try to get by without practicing or studying?

What else can you add? What else have you seen people do, or heard them say, that suggested they would rather avoid contact with the subject, or with the instruction itself, or with the learning, or with the instructor?

What? "SMATs 'n' SMUTs"?

I had an opportunity to witness a hilarious assortment of avoidance behaviors during the original drafting of this book. Since the book was to be about Subject Matter Approach Tendencies, and in a way about Subject Matter Unapproach Tendencies, I referred to the book around the house as "SMATs 'n' SMUTs." When my wife or kids would ask me what I was working on, I'd reply, "Oh, I'm trying to make some progress on 'SMATs 'n' SMUTs.'"

As that became the "name" of the book around the house, I suggested it to the publisher as a title for the book. Well! You wouldn't believe the anguish this caused. Had you been watching, you would have heard and seen the following:

- Publisher recovers from shock and says, "There, there, now (pat, pat), that's a nice little joke ... but you aren't *serious?*"
- Publisher suggests list of alternate titles.
- Editor says, "Well, let's see if it fits after we've worked through the rest of it," hoping it would go away.
- Editor launches into heart-rending lament about the *Fanny Hill* implications of the title, and about how publishing people have a better "feel" for titles (and everything else) than authors.
- Editor melts into a little puddle.

In the face of such grief and pathos, I naturally gave up and settled for a phootnote. Imagine my surprise when, during the crafting of the second edition, the *editor* suggested that we use "SMATs 'n' SMUTs" as a subtitle. What had happened to cause the change of heart? The fact that catchy subtitles are used by readers more often than titles? The fact that readers suggested using it as the main title? An emboldening of the spirit? A mellowing of the psyche? Whatever the cause, there was a gradual transition from avoidance to approach (which should tell you that it is possible to change avoidance to approach).

Meanwhile, back to the subject at hand. Given a choice, people with avoidance tendencies elect to approach something *other* than the subject in question. They will go to varying lengths to prevent contact with the subject. They do not buy or read books about the subject, they do not join clubs relating to the subject, and they do not seek out discussions concerning the subject. When they are faced with the subject, they act to move away from it by changing the topic of conversation, by walking away from the stimulus, or by inventing an excuse to avoid the subject or terminate contact with it.

More importantly, in instructional situations, people often verbalize a conviction that they cannot learn a particular subject matter and that they intend to have as little as possible to do with the subject in the future. *Once such a behavior pattern develops, it is unlikely that they will put themselves in situations where the attitude is likely to be reversed.*

To the extent students avoid experiences with a subject, they will have fewer opportunities to change their avoidance tendencies to approach tendencies. In addition, if students avoid experiences with a subject, it is improbable that they will use, and therefore maintain, whatever skill they had, and almost certain that they will be less willing to learn more about it as time goes by. Each subject that students avoid constitutes the loss of a tool or skill that might have eased their journey through a complex world.

It is for this reason that instruction that teaches students to avoid learning and applying a subject does the student more harm than good.

That good intentions are not enough was clearly demonstrated by an approach/avoidance analysis I conducted for a high-school teacher of mathematics. This teacher is highly motivated to generate enthusiasm and appreciation for mathematics in her students. She likes what she teaches and is anxious that her students share her excitement for the subject. She is courteous and respectful of student questions and makes herself available for questions.

But in spite of her intentions and her initial success at motivation, she managed to *reduce* math interest in about as many students as she managed to increase it.

How? What could such a teacher be doing to diminish subject matter approach tendencies?

It was a classic example of "overkill." She inadvertently spent a great deal of class time presenting material beyond the ability of her students to understand. Her enthusiasm for her subject caused her to try to teach almost everything she knew about math, and that was a lot more than students could understand, regardless of how motivated they were to try. Some students concluded that they could never understand math, and they lost interest.

How to Identify Approach/Avoidance Responses

Here are three procedures that will help you to improve your ability to pinpoint approach and avoidance responses:

1. Think of something that your best friend likes, or dislikes, and ask yourself what that friend *does* or *says* that causes you to conclude that he or she has that like or dislike.

2. When you hear someone say something like "They have a poor attitude toward_____," or "They are strongly motivated to_____," ask that person "What do they say or do that causes you to make that comment about their attitude or motivation?"

3. Carry a small notebook and note each event that leads you to believe that a student is either favorably or unfavorably disposed toward the subject you are teaching. This will help you to get into the habit of observing and identifying clues to approach and avoidance.

The Procedure

The ability to recognize approach and avoidance responses is the key for getting more of the first and less of the second. But how? Here's the procedure. Briefly, the procedure asks you to:

- describe the approach responses you value,
- find out where things stand at present, and then
- take steps to eliminate the negative and accentuate the positive.

In practice, this procedure looks like this:

1. Decide what approach responses you value and write them down. You must have a visible list before you can complete the other steps. For example, do you want your students to:

    -   arrive prepared to work (i.e., with books, manuals, notebooks, pencils, or other equipment)?
    -   begin working on the instruction next in line for study?
    -   practice the material being learned?
    -   willingly correct work that is not yet adequate?
    -   speak favorably about the subject?
    -   ask for discussions about related aspects of the subject?
    -   ask questions when the instruction is unclear?
    -   do more work than necessary?
    -   discuss the subject with other students?
    -   spend time actually performing the skills being learned?

These are only sample items that might be useful in getting your own list started.

2. Check each item on your list to make sure it is reasonable and makes sense. Are these responses that you can observe? Do they represent reasonable expectations (i.e., are you expecting more than they can reasonably be expected to deliver)? When your list is complete (for now), then

3. Determine the extent to which each of the responses is occurring to your satisfaction now. That is, find out where things stand in relation to each of the items on your list. How? Ask people, use questionnaires, count the

number of people who make the desired responses, and so on. I'll have more to say on this topic in a later chapter.

4. Focus on one avoidance response you would like to eliminate, or an approach response you would like to strengthen, and take the appropriate action (to be described in Chapter 5).

Once you have a visible picture of what you expect your students to do—whether that doing is related to approach/ avoidance or something else—you will be ready to think about ways to accentuate the positive and eliminate the negative. We'll do that next.

5

Sources of Influence

If our actions didn't sometimes shout louder than our
words, there would be no call for the expression,
"Don't do as I do, do as I say."

A while ago, Von Haney, a talented graphic artist, created a short animation sequence for an instructional program designed to teach mothers how to increase their success at interaction with those around them. In this scene there are two small boys, one empty-handed and the other holding and sucking a huge lollipop. The empty-handed boy speaks first:

"Hi. Where'd you get the sucker?"

"My mommy gave it to me—as a reward for crying."

"You mean your mommy *wants you* to cry?"

"I guess so. Whenever I cry she gives me a lollipop."

"Gee, I'd cry a *lot* more often if I always got a sucker."

"Of course. It's elementary psychology!"

Most people who have seen this scene just *know* there was something wrong with the way the mother went about trying to reduce crying, although they are often unable to put their finger on exactly what went awry. The sequence makes it obvious that crying behavior is not reduced by following it with a lollipop. But why not? Though the scene doesn't tell us any of the details, it certainly does suggest that there are more successful and less successful ways of interacting and influencing others.

The business/industry version of the lollipop dialogue goes something like this:

"Hey! How'd you get the trip to Paris?"

"My boss gave it to me—as a reward for screwing up."

"You mean your boss *wants you* to screw up?"

"I guess so. Every time my European operation doesn't meet its production schedules, she sends me to Paris."

Sound unlikely? Not at all. It happens every day; if not in these words, then in others.

"Charlie, you did such a good job on that report, I'm going to give you all the *tough* ones from now on. You're just the man for the job."

Would anyone be surprised to hear that Charlie's lost his steam? That he seems less motivated than he used to be? Suppose you had worked hard on an assignment and were then ignored when you presented the results. Worse, suppose you were asked, "Is *that* the best you can do?" Do you think that would affect how you went about completing the next assignment? Do you think your work would be affected if you never found out how well you were doing, or if you were in some way made to feel smaller as a result of your efforts?

The same holds true for students. They, too, are influenced by the things that happen to them. No one is exempt from the laws of nature.

A few years ago a colleague and I implemented a study designed to chart the history of some tendencies toward, and away from, some academic subjects. We interviewed 65 students, currently enrolled in one course or another, who were all adults and who had completed high school and/or college.

The first questions of the interview were designed to identify the most-favored and the least-favored academic subject of each person. Once these subjects were identified, each person was asked a series of questions to determine just how these inclinations got to be that way. These questions were designed to explore each person's feelings about his or her most-preferred and least-preferred subjects and to determine what the individual remembered as the conditions leading to those feelings, as well as to changes in those feelings.

The results of the study were interesting and somewhat unexpected. Almost every person was able to identify the subjects or school activities that were at the top and at the bottom of his or her "popularity scale." What was unexpected were the responses to the questions attempting to discover why and how these subjects came to be rated as they were.

With regard to *favorite* academic subjects, the interviewees discussed the subjects with some facility; that is, they talked as though they remembered something of the subjects. But they seemed to have no clear idea of how they got to be their favorite subjects. Though they always had an answer to the question "How did it get to be that way?" their answers reflected only vague memories. "Oh, I always liked history," they would say, or, "I was born with an interest in art."

When asked about the subject they liked least, however, the story was different. They seemed to remember little about the subject itself and would often come right out and say, "I don't remember a thing about_____, and the less I hear of it, the better." But they *always* remembered just how they learned to dislike the subject . . . at least they *said* they remembered. They were quite capable of pinpointing the events or conditions that they felt were behind their desire to avoid the subject whenever they could. We were perfectly aware that some of the interviewees had faulty memories. What we were looking for, however, were the conditions and consequences they remembered as having an effect, whether or not they were correct, so we would know what they *said* to other people about the subjects they came to like and dislike.

As you read the sampling of interview summaries that follows, dip back into your own academic history to see if you can add other conditions and consequences that may influence approach and avoidance responses toward subjects taught in school.

Case 1

Favorite subject:	Music.
How it got that way:	I've always liked music. It was just a personal liking. No events had anything to do with it.
Least-favored subject:	English.
How it got that way:	None of the teachers could get down to a level where the students could understand what they were trying to get across. They didn't know how to make the subject interesting.

Case 2

Favorite subject:	Art, in high school; psychology, in college.
How it got that way:	I've always liked art. Mother encouraged art by providing lots of materials. In high school the instructor was very good. Had a good sense of humor and worked *with* students. He encouraged us to participate in contests. I still use my art knowledge in my work.
Least-favored subject:	Mathematics.
How it got that way:	I was skipped to third grade after completing only half of second grade. I missed considerable background and felt lost. The third-grade teacher was very impatient and did not believe in individual instruction. She ridiculed me in front of the class. I was above average in all other subjects, but I failed accounting in college.

Case 3

Favorite subject:	History.
How it got that way:	I hated math, wasn't good in English, and so, drifted into history. History interest continued through high school, which is as far as I went. I can't remember anything else that influenced my interest in history, but to this day I continue to study the subject as a hobby.
Least-favored subject:	Mathematics.
How it got that way:	I never could add 2 and 2 and still can't. I changed schools 18 times between first grade and the end of high school. Every time I got to a school, they were studying something for which I had no background, or they were learning something I already knew. Also, there was a grade-school teacher who embarrassed me to death. The instructor once caught me counting on my fingers and took me up to the front of the class to make an example of me. It was humiliating. I hated math.

Case 4

Favorite subject: Spanish.

How it got that way: High-school instructor was tremendous; she spoke Spanish from the first day and taught class to sing Spanish songs. She encouraged special projects and allowed better students to help slower ones.

Least-favored subject: None. (No strong avoidance tendencies toward any subject. In college, this person majored in science. There were two reasons for this: (1) A cousin was taking science and interested the student by talking enthusiastically and by showing homework and experiments. (2) Student had a high-school teacher who had well-organized lectures and a good lab. This instructor checked lab work frequently and showed relevant films and videos that were highly interesting. This instructor was a person to whom students felt they could go with problems. This is an instance where the attitude toward a subject changed over a period of time as the result of events and consequences.)

Case 5

Favorite subject:	Psychology.
How it got that way:	I had a great admiration for the instructor and felt the course was well presented. He did not become angry when students disagreed with him . . . he was willing to be criticized. He did not ridicule. He encouraged his students and had no discipline problems.
Least-favored subject:	Physics.
How it got that way:	I felt I didn't have the mind for it. Also, I had a high-school instructor I liked, but he merely read the text-book to the class and then assigned problems without giving the necessary information that would help in solving them. This instructor couldn't make himself understood.

Summarizing the results of this study, we can say that a favorite subject gets to be that way because the student:

- was comfortable in the presence of the subject.
- admired someone who was competent in the subject or who enjoyed demonstrating or working with the subject.
- found his or her world getting somehow brighter as a result of working with the subject.

A least-favorite subject tends to get that way because the student:

- seems to have little aptitude for it (or feels that way).
- associates the subject with disliked individuals.
- associates the subject with unpleasant circumstances.
- found his or her world getting somehow dimmer as a result of the contact with the subject.

There is no question about the fact that attitudes toward a subject are influenced by factors *other* than those present in the instructional environment. Peers, friends, bosses, and television are just a few of those factors. Our concern, though, is not with whether instructors are the *sole* source of influence, but with whether they are a *positive* source of influence. In other words, if a student is led toward an unfavorable attitude about something being taught, let it not be because of the actions of the instructor or because of the environment created by the instructor.

Try It; You'll Like It

Here's an activity that is always helpful in reminding us of the experiences that cause attitudes toward, and away from, a subject or activity. It follows the study that involved the case just described.

1. First, ask a friend to tell you what his or her favorite and least-favorite school subjects were.

2. Second, ask him or her to tell you how those subjects came to be liked or disliked.

3. Third, ask if your friend has taken a course since starting his or her present job. (Perhaps it was a three-day workshop, a seminar, or a longer course.) If so, ask how your friend felt about that course or seminar.

4. Fourth, ask *why* your friend feels a particular way about this on-the-job course; that is, ask him or her to describe the events that shaped this attitude.

5. Finally, ask yourself this question: "What are the similarities and differences between the attitude-shaping events that occurred in school courses and those that occurred in courses taken while on the job?" Could the events leading to a less-than-positive attitude have been avoided?

Summary

To summarize, sources of influence to approach or avoid subject matter or activities include:

1. *The* conditions *that surround a subject or activity; that is, the conditions that exist while the student is in the presence of, or in contact with, the subject matter or activity.*

2. *The* consequences *of being in the presence of, or coming into contact with, the subject matter or activity; that is, the things that happen as a result of working with the subject.*

3. *The way that others react toward a subject; that is, the attitude* modeled *by others.*

Coming Attractions

Now that we have identified some of the sources of influence, the next step will be to explore just how these sources operate. We'll explore how they should be arranged in order to achieve a desired result.

6
Conditions and Consequences

Exhortation is used more and accomplishes
less than almost any behavior-changing
tool known to man.

Three sets of principles which, for our purposes, influence attitude toward learning are conditions, consequences, and modeling. So far, so good. But the nature of the conditions, the way in which consequences are organized, and the way in which the modeling is done make a difference. When principles are improperly applied, they don't work. Consider this improbable dialogue:

He:	Y'know, I tried that gravity stuff.
She:	You did?
He:	Yeah. But it doesn't work.
She:	What do you mean, it doesn't work?
He:	See that there water trough?
She:	Yes.
He:	Well, the water is supposed to flow along there by gravity. But the principle of gravity just doesn't work.
She:	Well, of course it doesn't work. You're trying to get gravity to make the water run uphill!

Odd, perhaps, but a way to illustrate the point that a principle is no less a principle just because it is misapplied. The principles governing human interaction are no different. Apply them correctly and they will work *for* you. Apply them incorrectly and they will work *against* you. Ignore them and you may never know why things didn't turn out the way you expected. So let's consider the correct and incorrect ways of applying these principles that influence attitude toward learning.

Conditions

Whenever students are in the presence of the subject they are learning, they are also in the presence of conditions. There is temperature, which may be too cold or too hot, and there is furniture, which may be too hard or too soft. Furthermore, there is the psychological environment, which may be hostile and tense or pleasant and supportive.

When naturally unpleasant conditions are paired with a subject being learned—that is, when they are present at the same time—the thing being learned can eventually come to evoke avoidance responses. That is, if a subject that initially has no special significance is presented to someone on several occasions while he or she is experiencing an aversive (unpleasant) condition, that subject may become a signal that triggers an avoidance response. Similarly, if a person is presented with a neutral subject and at the same time is in the presence of positive (pleasant) conditions, that subject may become a signal for an approach response.

Let's examine some everyday examples.

How do you react when a physician moves a hypodermic needle toward your arm? If you are like many people, you tend to back away; if you don't back away physically, you may turn your head to avoid seeing this signal for a forthcoming prick. There is nothing aversive about the sight of the hypodermic needle—the first time you see one, that is. The needle is a neutral object. But after you have experienced pain while in the presence of a hypodermic needle, the sight of the needle itself becomes a signal for an avoidance response.

I came across this magnificent example in a letter that appeared in an Ann Landers column:

> . . . When my mother took me shopping, I soon learned not to express an opinion. My taste was "atrocious." Hers was "elegant." Once when I saw a dress I really wanted, my mother said, in the presence of the saleswoman, "You are as fat as a pig and that dress makes you look like a freak."
>
> From then on I flatly refused to shop for clothes. I told my mother to bring home whatever she liked and I would wear it. I am a grown woman now, but these horrible memories are as vivid as if they had happened yesterday.
>
> I hate clothes and I wear my dresses till they fall apart. *To this day, I cannot pass the dress section where we used to shop without being physically ill* (italics added).*

Yes, neutral objects often turn into those that will attract or repel, and you will find many examples of them if you look. You may not find many that result in the extreme reaction cited above, but they are there nonetheless.

Going back to the study described in Chapter 5, there were several instances where the interviewees responded like this:

> "At first I didn't care much about the subject one way or the other. But the instructor made me feel very

* "Ann Landers" reprinted by permission of San Jose *Mercury* and Publishers-Hall Syndicate.

comfortable, and I began to worry less about a grade and found myself studying the subject more intently than I had planned."

And like this:

"I didn't know what to expect when I first started in the course. But all the instructors were so cheerful that I soon found myself looking forward to learning more about it."

NOTE: Affect feeling is unlike skill in at least two ways. First, nobody has to teach us to have affect. From birth, we all have all the skills needed to express the full range of emotions, both positive and negative. Second, unlike skills, an affect can switch polarity in the blink of an eye— either way. Events can turn a favorable attitude unfavorable, or cause a dislike of something or someone to take a turn toward the positive, in what seems like an instant. A colleague of mine tells this story:

"In college I had put my foot down against Wagner because all the guys were gaga over his music. Finally I *had* to take a required course in Wagner (ugh). I sat there for a couple of weeks, resisting for all I was worth, and then the instructor played a piece of music that changed everything. All of a sudden, like sand castles melting in the surf, my resistance crumbled, and in the space of a minute or so, my attitude changed 180 degrees."

We see, then, that one way of ensuring that we are not the cause of an avoidance tendency toward the subject matter we teach is to arrange our instructional environment so that students who are in the presence of the subject matter are, at the same time, (1) in the presence of positive conditions and (2) in the presence of as few aversive conditions as possible.

BUT. (There always seems to be a but in the ointment.) There is something else you must do to make this principle work for you. What?

You need to make sure that the conditions are considered favorable or pleasant by the students you are instructing. Like trying to make water run uphill, the principle won't work if it is misapplied; that is, if *you* are the only one who considers conditions positive.

The rule, then, is this:

> **When in the presence of the subject you are teaching, students should at the same time be in the presence of conditions *they* consider positive or favorable and in the presence of the fewest possible conditions *they* consider negative or unpleasant.**

A Common Misconception. Does application of this principle mean that instruction must be made "fun" and that students should not be required to work hard?

Not at all! Being in the presence of "work" is not necessarily the same as being in the presence of unpleasant conditions. Consider this dialogue:

"What kind of work do you do?"

"I'm in the sex business."

"The *what?*"

"The sex business. I teach actresses how to kiss."

"And you call that *work?*"

"It's not work, but it's a living."

This may seem an unlikely conversation, but it does serve to illustrate some of the confusion surrounding the word "work." This word has come to have several meanings. Sometimes it is used to refer to an occupation or profession, as in "What kind of work do you do?" When used this way, it seldom carries with it connotations of good or bad, pleasant or unpleasant. But *work* is also often used to refer to an activity that one would prefer to avoid, as in "Oh, that's work," or "I'd rather be enjoying myself, but I've got *work* to do." In these cases, the implication is that the activity referred to is one the speaker finds distasteful.

There is another way in which *work* is given a bad name. The familiar expression, "All work and no play makes Jack a dull boy," clearly implies that *play* is fun and *work* is not. What a horrible fate for a perfectly respectable word.

Were you to check your dictionary, you would find that *work* is "the expenditure of energy directed toward the accomplishment of something." It is engaging in some sort of purposeful activity. Skiing is work, swimming is work, playing the banjo is work, and so is writing. Haven't you ever engaged in purposeful activity that was exciting, engrossing, exhilarating, or just plain enjoyable? Haven't you ever heard anyone say, "I like my work"? Don't you like your work?

There must be something other than the expenditure of energy that causes the word "work" to have an aversive connotation with some activities and not with others. That something is the *conditions* associated with the activity or the *consequences* that follow the activity.

When energy expenditure is associated with aversive conditions, that activity will tend to become aversive; when the energy expenditure is followed regularly by aversive consequences (e.g., punishment), that activity will tend to be avoided.

There is nothing wrong with making students work. There is nothing wrong with making them work hard. But *there are a lot of things you can do to them while they are working* (while they are in the presence of the subject you are teaching) that can make the learning more, or less, attractive.

By all means make assignments, and by all means expect them to be carried out on time. But also do your best to see that these activities are associated with positive conditions and with as few aversive conditions as possible. After all, even under the best of circumstances you will not cause everyone to be wild about your favorite subject. But professional practice demands that you do everything in your power to make certain you don't accidentally destroy whatever interest is already there. *Don't confuse work with unpleasantness.*

Killing Success

There is something even worse than associating neutral subjects (those about which students don't care much one way or another) with unpleasant conditions, and that is to associate *favored* activities or subjects with unpleasant conditions. You'll recognize how this works when you read the following examples:

"All right! Just for that you can practice your piano for an extra hour!"

"OK. For that misbehavior, I'm going to give you twice as many math problems for homework!"

In other words, when an activity (such as studying or practicing) or a subject the student *likes* is used as a form of punishment, that activity may become less of a favorite activity. The rule is: NEVER to use as punishment an activity you would like your students to learn to love.

Consequences

Imagine yourself a student again. When you correctly answer a question posed by your instructor, the instructor smiles and says something like "Good." When you answer a question incorrectly, the instructor makes a comment such as, "Well, let's look at the question again." Wouldn't the probability increase that you will be willing to answer questions and come into contact with the subject matter? In any case, this kind of interaction would not adversely influence your responses toward the subject. Conversely, suppose each time you answer a question incorrectly, the instructor says, "Well, I see old Dumbo is at it again." How long do you think it would be before you stopped raising your hand? How long do you think it would be before you began to think of excuses for not attending class?

When experience with a subject is *followed* by a positive (pleasant) consequence, the probability is increased that the subject will be approached again in the future. When, on the other hand, experience with a subject is followed by aversive (unpleasant) consequences, the probability is reduced that the subject will be approached in the future.

Consider this scene, taken from a practice film intended to help people learn to apply these principles:[1]

> *Worker:*   Hey, boss! I've got the problem solved, and the production run will cost at least 30 per cent less than we estimated.
>
> *Boss:*   John, how many times do I have to ask you not to interrupt me while I'm working on budgets? . . . And will you please get that grubby apron cleaned?

[1] *Who Did What to Whom II?*, a film produced by Mager Associates (Carefree, AZ, 1982).

As you can well imagine, the worker's shoulders sag as he walks out of the scene. Wouldn't yours? After this scene is shown, the following questions are asked. You might try to answer them yourself; then compare your responses with mine.

1. What happened to the worker who solved the problem? (Be careful here. The question asks you to describe the event, rather than to make an interpretation of the event.)

2. Will the worker be more, or less, likely to report his successes to the boss in the future?

3. How could the boss have handled the situation more successfully? (That is, what could the boss have said or done to have caused consequences considered positive by the worker?)

Check your responses on the next page.

1. He was criticized for interrupting and criticized for his appearance.

2. Less likely. His performance led to humiliation.

3. The boss could have:
   - said something nice about the solution.
   - paid attention to the worker's description of a successful experience.
   - asked questions about the solution (another way of rewarding with attention).
   - whooped and hollered with joy.
   - called others and told them the good news.

Can you add five more possibilities?

Though this film example dealt with the workplace, the same principles hold in the classroom. Consider this scene. A student walks into an instructor's office, and this interchange follows:

> *Stud:*   I turned in my extra project a week ago. That was the report that took 40 hours of library research and writing. I was wondering if you've had a chance yet to review it.

> *Inst:*   (Rummaging through a pile of papers on the desk.) Have you seen my calendar? (More rummaging.) I just don't understand why someone would take my calendar and not bring it back.

> *Stud:*   (Walks out of the office, head hanging low.)

Answer these questions about the interchange.

1. What happened to the student who asked for feedback? (Again, the question asks for events rather than for interpretation of the events.)

2. Did the student consider the events to be favorable or unfavorable?

3. How do you know?

4. Will the student be more or less likely to work that hard on a report in the future?

5. How might the instructor have handled the interaction more appropriately?

Turn the page to check your responses.

1. The student was ignored. The instructor spoke of things other than the report being asked about.

2. Unfavorable.

3. The student walked out of the office (avoidance response) with head hung low.

4. Less likely. Actions followed by unpleasantness are less likely to be repeated.

5. The instructor could have:

   - paid attention to the student.
   - said something favorable about the student's report.
   - asked questions about how the report was prepared.
   - smiled.
   - said something nice about the effort.

Can you add a few more possibilities?

Positive consequences, then, make it more likely that students will become favorably disposed toward your subject, and negative or unpleasant (aversive) consequences will make it less likely.

But again we have a but. But there are two things you have to do to make the principle work for you. First, you have to *follow* the behavior with the consequence; the favorable consequence must come *after* the desired performance.

The second thing you have to do to make the principle work for you is similar to what you have to do for conditions—make sure that the consequences are considered favorable by *the students*. It isn't good enough that *you* get pleasure from the consequences; the students must also experience them as positive or desirable. "You did such a good job on that lesson that I'm going to tell you all about how I got started in this field" may provide you with a great deal of satisfaction, but what about the students? Do they care? Or would they consider your story to be an event to endure?

The rule for consequences, then, is this:

Follow subject-matter contact with one or more consequences considered to be favorable by the students themselves.

This doesn't mean that you are expected to say or do something positive *each* and *every time* the students study or practice something. What it does mean is that the consequences should be positive rather than negative and that contact with the subject should lead to the students' worlds getting somewhat brighter rather than somewhat dimmer.

Accentuate the positive and eliminate the negative.

Once again, the correct application of this principle does not imply that you refrain from making your students work hard. It *does* mean that the hard work should be followed by a ray of sunshine rather than by a bonk on the head.

On to Specifics

The third way to increase the likelihood that you will send students away with a favorable attitude toward your subject is to model the performances you expect from your students. We'll consider modeling in Chapter 8.

Right now, let's think about exactly which conditions and events are positive and which are aversive.

Reprinted with special permission of King Features Syndicate.

7
Positives and Aversives

People learn to avoid the things they're hit with.

Although it isn't always possible to know whether an event is positive or aversive for a given individual, some conditions and consequences are universal enough in their effect to provide considerable guidance. In this chapter we will examine some specific examples of positive and aversive conditions and consequences. Remembering that we're concerned with what is positive or aversive from the *students'* points of view, we'll begin with the negative. (That way we can end the chapter on a positive note.)

Aversives

An aversive condition or consequence is any event that causes physical or mental discomfort. It is any event that causes people to think less highly of themselves, that leads to a loss of self-respect or dignity, or that results in a strong anticipation of any of these. In general, any condition or consequence may be considered aversive if it causes a person to feel smaller or makes his or her world dimmer.

There are several conditions and consequences that are avoided by enough people to warrant their being referred to as *universal aversives*. When these conditions or consequences are associated with the subjects we teach, or appear as a result of subject matter contact, then the subject matter, learning, or even the learning environment itself may take on a less desirable hue . . . and no amount of righteous indignation on our part will alter this effect, and no declaiming of how the student "ought" to be more interested will have as much effect toward that end as reducing the aversive characteristics of the learning situation.

Pain

Pain is an acute physical discomfort, as you very well know. Though there are probably few situations left wherein instructors deliberately whop and bop their students, instructional pain is not yet extinct.

I know a violin instructor who, in an angry attempt to get his students' fingers properly positioned, makes those fingers hurt. He makes his students cry with pain and tremble with fear. His claim that this is "good" for the students is nothing more than justification for his uncommon version of educational malpractice.

Some people even believe that pain is good for students and good for learning. For example, you may have heard that idiotic expression, "If it ain't hard, it ain't learnin'." Meaning, "If it doesn't hurt, the instruction can't be any good."

We're talking here of pain inflicted by instructors as part of what they think to be "good instructional practice," rather than the kind of pain that may be an integral part of the subject matter. If you were learning to ride a horse, for example, you

DENNIS the MENACE

"HOW COME I DON'T HAVE A SPECIAL PLACE TO SIT WHEN I DO SOMETHIN' NICE?"

might experience a certain amount of pain in your . . . ah, well, backside. While that is a very real pain, it is horse-inflicted rather than instructor-inflicted. If you were learning to play football, you would experience a variety of kinds of pain that come from the game itself. If an instructor inflicts more pain than necessary to get the learning done, however, he or she is providing you with an example of primitive instructional practice.

When there *is* pain associated with learning the subject, instructors must go to greater pain (I just couldn't resist it) to counterbalance the aversives with positives. That is, instructors must try to make the learning experience net out as a positive one, by doing the kinds of things listed toward the end of this chapter.

Whether the pain is inflicted by the subject matter or by the instructor, pain is a condition people try to avoid. They do this either by learning to deal with the pain or by leaving.

Fear and Anxiety

Fear and anxiety are distress or uneasiness of the mind: apprehension of danger, misfortune, or pain; tension, stress, foreboding, worry, or disquiet; anticipation of the unpleasant.

Fear and anxiety are conditions that people try to avoid. When learning is associated with these states, the learner is more likely to learn to avoid the subject being taught.

Procedures leading to fear and anxiety are those that threaten various forms of unpleasantness. They include:

- Telling students by word or deed that nothing they can do will lead to success, or that contact with the subject will lead to undesirable consequences.
- Telling students, "You won't understand this, but . . ."
- Telling students, "It ought to be perfectly obvious that . . ."
- Threatening the exposure of "ignorance" by forcing individual students to solve problems in front of the class.

role play with emphasizing positive - certificate
follow up - stay AWAY FROM negative - help them to manage others
certificate after - make their job easier

- Basing an attrition rate on administrative fiat rather than on student performance. ("Half of you won't be here a month from now," or "I don't believe in giving high grades.")
- Threatening failure by telling the student, "If you aren't motivated enough, you shouldn't be here." (Translation: "If you aren't motivated enough to learn in spite of my poor teaching, you certainly aren't going to get any help from me.")
- Being unpredictable about the standard of acceptable performance. (For example, a sixth-grade teacher told his students that they didn't have to listen to his discussion if they were having no difficulty with its topic. Five minutes later he berated half the class for "not paying attention.")
- Being unpredictable about the standard of acceptable performance (by telling students one thing and then testing them on something else).
- Letting it be known that the students' general behavior will be reported back to their bosses at the end of the course.
- Basing evaluations on performance unrelated to the skills being taught. ("Oh, sure, you learned it perfectly; but you seldom showed up on time, so I'm going to have to take ten points off for lateness." Or, "Oh, sure, you learned to do it perfectly; but you took more practice swings than most other students.")
- Letting visitors sit in the back of the room.
- Evaluating students by comparing one against the other, rather than by comparing each with the criteria of acceptable performance established in advance; e.g., "I grade on the curve."
- Suggesting that you will be reporting student progress to their supervisors.
- Creating stress unrelated to the learning, usually by making bizarre demands on classroom performance. ("Shine

your shoes"; "sit up straight"; "pick up your pencil"; "put down your pencil"; "stand up and recite the table of random numbers"; etc.)

Frustration

Frustration occurs when goal-directed activities are blocked, when purposeful or motivated activity is interfered with. To frustrate is to interfere with, to check, to make an effort come to no avail, to nullify, to defeat. Practices that can generate frustration include:

- Presenting information in larger units, or at a faster pace, than a student can assimilate. (The more motivated a student is, the greater the frustration when his or her efforts are blocked.) A colleague describes this as the situation where a student came to drink from the fountain of knowledge and somebody turned on a fire hose.*
- Speaking too softly to be heard easily (blocking students' efforts to come into contact with the subject).
- Keeping secret the intent of the instruction or the way in which performance will be evaluated.
- Providing unreadable print, type too small or too ornate, or vocabulary level too high.
- Providing obscure text, or implying more profundity than actually exists, as in, "When two parallel lines are cut by a transversal, the alternate interior angles are equal."
- Teaching one set of skills, and then testing for another.
- Testing for skills other than those stated in announced objectives.
- Refusing to answer students' questions.
- Forcing all students to proceed at the same pace, thus frustrating the slow and boring the quick.

* Courtesy of Jack Vaughn.

- Calling a halt when a student is absorbed with the subject or attempting to complete a project (ringing a school bell, for example).
- Returning work to a student after an unusually long period (several hours or more), thereby preventing the student from obtaining timely feedback on efforts expended.

Humiliation and Embarrassment

Humiliation and embarrassment are caused by lowering an individual's pride or self-respect by making someone uncomfortably self-conscious; by shaming, debasing, or degrading; or by causing a painful loss of dignity. Procedures that lead to these conditions include:

- Publicly comparing a student unfavorably with others.
- Laughing at a student's efforts. When a colleague returned his comments on the original draft of this book, he included the following:

  My own pappy relates his music career thusly: "We had a singing session and the teacher asked me to sing alone. When I did, all the kids laughed. The next day he asked me to do it again. Well, sir, I wouldn't do it. So the teacher made me come to the front of the class, but I still wouldn't do it. So he hit my hand with a ruler. But he could have cut off my fingers and I still wouldn't have done it. I didn't, either. Ever!"*

Another colleague penned the following:

  My creative writing professor at _____ asked if he could read a poem of mine to the class. I was flattered

* Courtesy of Dr. David Cram

until he proceeded to laugh at it, and provided oratory emphasis to emphasize his point. I got a "B" and stopped writing poetry shortly thereafter.*

- Spotlighting a student's weaknesses by bringing them to the attention of the class.
- Making a student wear a badge of his or her "stupidity" (putting him or her in a special seat or section or class, for example, or by requiring the student to keep the "dummy cup" on his or her desk until someone else "earns" the right to the same humiliation).
- Belittling a student's attempt to approach the subject by replying to his or her questions with answers such as "Stop trying to show off," or "Don't try to get ahead of the class."
- Insulting a student for his or her attempt to approach the subject by comments such as "You couldn't possibly understand the answer to that question," or otherwise telling the student by word or deed that his or her questions are considered stupid.
- Repeated failure. It is perfectly appropriate to challenge students enough to cause them to fail on occasion, provided that the *consequence* of failure isn't made deliberately aversive. Repeated failure, however, is sure to lead students to think less highly of themselves and to try to avoid the situations that have come to signify such a shrinkage of self-esteem.

Repeated failure is often engineered into our educational system. One practice is that of grading on a curve. Whenever a performance is evaluated by comparing it with how a number of chance neighbors happen to perform, students with the below-average aptitudes will almost always come out on the lower half of the curve.

* Courtesy of Verne Niner

They might have achieved all the objectives set out for them; they might have learned to work faster or more effectively; they may be exceeding the standard set out by the instructor. No matter. When their performances are compared with those of more talented neighbors, they will always be the losers. This use of the curve is only slightly less reprehensible than the instructor who brags that he or she has a "tough" course because 40 percent of the class "failed." (Has it ever occurred to the braggart that he or she is only 60 percent successful?)

• A common school practice leading to humiliation and embarrassment frequently occurs after a teacher has asked the class a question. In almost every class there seems to be at least one student who is so anxious to come into contact with the subject, so eager to demonstrate competence, that while frantically hand-waving for attention, he or she lets the answer slip out aloud. What is the consequence of this behavior? Does the student's world become a little brighter? Is he or she encouraged to think more highly of himself or herself as a result of this action? Sometimes. Often, however, the consequence is a finger pointed sternly in the student's direction, followed by, "I . . . didn't . . . call . . . on . . . you!" And what the student is learning is that it doesn't pay to get very excited about the things that happen in school, that showing too much interest can have unpleasant results, and that showing excitement can lead to embarrassment, to humiliation. Oh, I know. Students must be taught discipline (and discipline *will* be a problem as long as students are forced to sit in neat little rows listening to lectures). But there are better ways of handling discipline problems, ways that do not embarrass the student while in the presence of the subject matter.

Boredom

Boredom is caused by a situation in which the stimuli impinging on the student are weak, repetitive, or infrequent. Typical avoidance responses are those of leaving the situation and of falling asleep. Procedures leading to boredom include:

- Preventing students from taking an active role in their learning.
- Presenting information in a monotone.
- Rocking rhythmically back and forth while speaking.
- Insisting a student sit through instruction covering something that he or she already knows.
- Using impersonal, passive language.
- Providing information in increments so small that they provide no challenge or require no effort.
- Allowing lethargy-inducing temperatures to exist.
- Using only a single mode of presentation (no variety).
- Pairing students of considerably differing abilities, causing boredom to the faster and frustration and/or embarrassment to the slower.
- Reading the textbook aloud. Consider for a moment the effect on a student of the instructor whose principal technique is to read aloud from the textbook. If a student has prepared for the class by studying the assignment in the textbook, he or she is punished for this effort by having to listen to the same material during class. How can the student avoid some of the boredom? Very simply; by not doing his or her textbook assignments before coming to class. In this way, although the student may suffer through a dull reading of the textbook during the class hour, at least the material read will not be familiar. This is one situation where the student is rewarded for being less, rather than more, diligent. He or she is reinforced for disregarding the assignments of the instructor. Since this situation

is one in which the student's act of entering the classroom is followed by an unpleasant event (boredom), and since people tend to avoid unpleasant events, the student will simply try to avoid attending class whenever possible. And why not? Are *you* eager to place yourself in a boring situation? (Wake up there!)

- Going over material in class that was assigned as pre-reading. Similar to reading the text aloud, this practice promotes boredom. If students do, in fact, follow the instruction to read or study something before attending a class, they are almost certain to be bored during the early portion of the class. This is because most instructors cater to those who may *not* have followed the instructions regarding pre-reading. They go over the material regardless of whether students need it, thereby creating boredom for those who did as they were told. (In other words, following the directions is punishing. Students quickly learn that this can be avoided by not doing the pre-class assignment.)

Physical Discomfort

Physical discomfort is an uneasiness, a hardship, mild pain. Though there are several ways of inducing physical discomfort while the student is in the presence of a subject, many of them are not under the direct control of the instructor. A partial list of those within the instructor's control include:

- Allowing excessive noise or other distractions, such as calling students from the classroom to put out "brush fires" back at the office, allowing students to be interrupted by telephone calls, or requiring students to sit through "guest lectures" unrelated to the purpose of the course.
- Preventing students from moving around at will and from taking care of their personal needs (bathroom, toothache, headache, etc.).

- Requiring left-handed students to sit in those desk chairs that were obviously invented by a right-handed devil.
- Insisting that students be physically passive for longer periods of time than they can tolerate. Here is an example of how discomfort, combined with a reward, led to a most unexpected result:

> A woman had a ten-year-old son who attended Sunday school with some reluctance. She wanted him to feel more positive toward church. But the technique she selected for achieving this goal was to make the boy attend the *regular* service that followed the Sunday-school session. The boy found the regular service a very uncomfortable affair indeed. He had to sit in a hard pew . . . he had to be quiet . . . he had to restrain himself from fidgeting. In addition, he was expected to listen to something he didn't understand at all. Since "sitting in church" was aversive, it was rewarding to *leave* church, because church-leaving led to a turning off of the discomfort. Result: Church became a symbol of discomfort and boredom and was avoided whenever possible.

- Insisting that students pay close attention immediately after a meal.
- Making students travel farther between classrooms than can easily be accomplished in the time allotted.
- Making the classroom too hot or too cold.
- Requiring students to study under poor lighting conditions (such as is found in many hotel meeting rooms), leading to eyestrain and fatigue.
-
-

Using the Subject as Punishment

One school practice that produces aversive conditions and consequences is so common that I want to comment on it separately. This is the practice of using subject matter as an instrument of punishment. You know how it goes: "All right, because you were unruly, you can just stay after school and work 25 arithmetic problems," or "For that, you can just read four chapters tonight instead of the one chapter I was going to assign." Again, the issue has nothing to do with the appropriateness or inappropriateness of punishment. It concerns only the *instrument* of punishment. People tend to avoid the things they are hit with, whether it be a club, a stick, or a subject-matter assignment.

To keep herself from falling asleep while editing my manuscript, the editor will sometimes actually think about the subject she is reading. As she read the following paragraph, she was kind enough to offer the following example:

> "An instructor made an offender stay after class to do extra work, with a paper due at the end of the penalty session. Then, without looking at the paper, he tore it up in front of the student."

No doubt about it. When the subject matter itself is used as a form of punishment, students will quickly learn that the subject is something to be avoided.

So much for the negative side of the issue. Now let's consider the positive side, because that's where we'll find the golden practices through which we can improve attitude toward learning.

Positives

A *positive condition or consequence* is any pleasant event that exists during the time the student is in the presence of the subject matter or that follows his or her interaction with the subject matter. A positive condition or consequence causes the student to think a little more highly of himself or herself and causes the student's world to become a little brighter.

Conditions and consequences that are *universal positives* are just the opposite of the universal aversives. They are the events that lead to success experiences and then acknowledge that success, ensure a variety of stimulation, lead to an increase of self-esteem or improved self-image, and lead to an increase in confidence. Positive practices include:

- Acknowledging students' responses, whether correct or incorrect, as attempts to learn, and following them with accepting rather than rejecting comments ("Try doing it *this* way," rather than "How could anyone make such a stupid error!").
- Reinforcing or rewarding subject approach responses (by a smile, a favorable word, a cheer, a cup of coffee or a lunch, or a little attention).
- Sending a student or three to look at a particularly good piece of work completed by another student.
- Providing a tangible token for successful completion of a particularly difficult or time-consuming piece of work. (In one of our workshops we literally use a large gold sticker, suitably imprinted for the occasion. Though a few of our students—adults—make pooh-pooh comments about the "gold star," they make sure they don't leave without it.)
- Providing instruction in increments that will allow success most of the time.
- Eliciting learning responses in private rather than in public.
- Providing enough signposts so that students always know where they are and where they're expected to go.

- Providing students with statements of instructional objectives that they can understand when they first see them.
- Detecting what individual students already know, and then adjusting the curriculum in order to avoid boring individuals by teaching them what they already know.
- Providing feedback that is immediate and specific to a student's response.
- Giving students some choice in selecting and sequencing of the subject matter (especially if the insructor maintains rigid control over the goals of the instruction), thus making positive involvement possible.
- Providing students with some control over the length of the instructional session.
- Relating new information to old, within the experience of each student.
- Treating students as individuals, rather than as numbers in a faceless mass.
- Using active rather than passive words during presentations.
- Pointing to student progress by comparing today's performance to yesterday's performance (e.g., "You completed twice as many modules today."), rather than by comparing today's performance to perfection (e.g., "You've still got a long way to go before you sing like Pavarotti.").
- For managers only: Allowing only those instructors who like and are enthusiastic about their subjects (and students) to teach.
- Making sure students can perform with ease, not just barely, so that confidence can be developed.
- Expressing genuine delight at seeing each student ("*Delighted* to see you again!").
- Expressing genuine delight at seeing a student succeed.
- Providing instructional tasks that are relevant to the objectives.

- Using only those test items relevant to the objectives.
- Allowing students to move about as freely as their physiology and their curiosity demand.

Positive Practices

In the study described in Chapter 5, interviewees made the following comments about teacher practices that had a positive influence on their interest in the subject under discussion:

"He taught us how to approach a problem so we could solve it for ourselves. He gave us the tools for learning."

"He broke down the subject matter into pieces we could understand. When we couldn't understand something, he tried to find another way of approaching it."

"She made books available at our level. That is, these were books that answered questions we had about the subject at that particular time."

"The instructor reinforced our desire to learn by giving us assistance and by showing a personal interest in what we were doing."

"He led discussions but did not dominate them."

"She had a magnificent manner of presentation; she taught history as though it were a news-analysis course, tying current happenings to historical happenings."

"He was always able to make individual students understand what was expected of them and where they stood."

"She used a lot of variety; she brought in other instructors, used videos and demonstrations rather than pure lecture."

"He asked, and respected, the opinion of students . . . even though he didn't always agree with them."

"She knew her subject and always appeared to have time to help me."

There is nothing revolutionary about the procedures listed in this chapter. Every instructor interested in increasing the capabilities of his or her students uses many or all of them, and others as well.

Then why go into such detail? Simply because *good intentions are not enough.* Though we are generally in favor of sending students away at least as interested in our subject as they were when they arrived, we do little or nothing to *ensure* that this is the case. Such apathy is frightening if one considers that the continuing use of tactics leading to subject avoidance represents an enormous loss of potential skills. Those lost skills may well be one of the greatest burdens our economy will have to carry as we move into an age where a person without economic and social skills will be virtually unemployable.

8
Modeling

People see, people do.

Me: If it is your desire that when instructing, your students confine themselves to an expository style of least complexity consistent with the subject matter and the target population, such an outcome is more probable of accomplishment if your own exposition is isomorphic to that which is desired.

You: Huh?

Me: If you want your students to use plain language when they teach, you should use plain language when you teach.

You: Why didn't you say so?

Me: I just did.

You: Then how come you don't use simple language when you teach?

Me: Don't do as I do, do as I say!

That silly little dialogue should serve to illustrate the essence of the modeling principles, which is—practice what you preach.

While it's true that we learn by practicing, by doing, and by being rewarded for our progress, it is also true that most of what we learn is learned by imitation. Most of what we learn comes from watching others do things that we then try to do—and then become able to do. When we see others do something, there is a tendency for us to imitate their actions. People see, people do.

This means that attitude toward (or away from) learning is strongly influenced by modeling. How does it work?

Modeling influences people mainly by informing them of a way of doing something. When something is demonstrated by a model, the observer sees, or hears of, a way in which that thing can be done. It may not be the right way or the desired way or the safe way, but the way shown is likely to be the way that is adopted.

Suppose you are vacationing overseas and a family asks you to have dinner. As you sit down to the meal, you notice unfamiliar utensils alongside your plate. Since you don't know what they are for, what should you do? One appropriate way to react would be to ask what the utensils are for and how they are used. But it's more likely that you would watch what your host and hostess did and then follow suit, imitating the behavior that they modeled.

Fair enough. But how does this apply to a course? Well, have you ever had a course in which the instructor made unfavorable comments about the subject he or she was teaching?

"This is a required course, and I don't like it any better than you do."

"I don't know why I was assigned to teach this course, but I suppose we'd better get on with it."

"This is terribly uninteresting, but . . ."

"This is a dull video, but I'm supposed to show it."

After reading these comments, a colleague reviewing this manuscript said, "I jumped at the chance to take a course in general semantics from Hayakawa himself. His teaching assistant actually said to me, 'Anybody stupid enough to take this course should get an automatic F.'"

It isn't easy to maintain one's enthusiasm in the face of comments like these. And have you ever attended a course in which the instructor just went through the motions of teaching— never smiled or said anything favorable about the subject being taught, simply recited old notes, and seemed as glad to leave the room as you were? Again, it's hard to maintain a favorable attitude toward anything when apathy is what is being modeled.

Would you know how to hold a knife if you wanted to kill someone? Sure you would. You've seen it modeled on television. Would you know where to kick a man to put him out of business? Sure you would. You've seen that modeled on television, too. Hundreds of times. You've seen a lot of things modeled there, things you now know how to do even though you will never do them. Why do you suppose influence groups try to stop programs from being shown on television? In part, it's because they don't want us to have certain attitudes and skills modeled for us, because they don't want us to see how *others* behave toward one thing or another. They know that television is a powerful modeling medium and that modeling changes behavior. (It's interesting that, on the one hand, the TV people try to convince us that television—and the sex and violence depicted there—*doesn't* influence people; on the other hand, TV people try to sell advertising by convincing their clients that TV *does* influence people.)

Modeling Principles

There are several principles of modeling. The more important ones are listed here, along with an example or two to show you how each principle may be applied to the instructional environment.

1. **Observers learn by watching and imitating others; they tend to behave as they have seen others behave.**

   Application Example. Behave in the classroom the way you want others to behave. If you want students to observe certain safety precautions when handling equipment, then *you* observe those safety precautions. If you want students to do what you tell them to do (whether you do the telling in person or through your writing or other medium of communication), make sure there is no discrepancy between what you tell and what you do.

How *strongly* an observer will tend to imitate modeled performance is influenced by several factors. The following principles describe some of them.

2. **Observers will be more likely to imitate a model who has prestige in the eyes of the observers.**

   Application Example. Have desired performance demonstrated by someone your students respect: a manager, local hero, football player, or movie star. (You can imagine the delight experienced by the students when the teacher invited a local football hero to help her read Shakespeare to the class.) And don't forget that instructors often have prestige in the eyes of students, so it is doubly important that you practice what you preach.

3. **Observers will be more likely to imitate modeled performance when they observe the model being reinforced for that performance.**

   Application Example. Arrange to have a demonstrator of desired performance (the model) applauded, awarded a trophy, given a raise, or praised—in the presence of the observers.

Application Example. A workshop participant offered this personal experience: "My own reports were always very descriptive (also long) until one day I heard my boss being congratulated for being concise in writing a one-page, fully satisfactory report. I now make it a point to be concise, too."

4. **Observers who see a model being punished will tend not to imitate the performance that was punished.**

Application Example. When someone is demonstrating correct performance, be sure he or she is not accidentally punished in the presence of observers. Also, when participants do something wrong, be sure they are corrected; be sure they don't "get away" with it. (If the chief instructor cannot get away with parking in the president's parking place, the students will be less likely to try it.)

Application Example. (Also from a previous workshop participant.) "A colleague was told by our boss that he was too busy to see him. I have since had a tendency to wait until he calls me rather than try to make an appointment to see him. Ever since my colleague was 'put down' when trying to see the boss, I have tried to see him only on matters of utmost urgency."[1]

The research on modeling tells us that *if we would maximize subject-matter approach tendencies in our students, we must exhibit those behaviors ourselves.* In other words, we must behave the way we want our students to behave.

[1] Examples and other material in this chapter are taken from *CRI (Criterion-Referenced Instruction): Practical Skills for Designing Instruction that Works,* Fourth Edition; by R.F. Mager and Peter Pipe (Center for Effective Performance, Atlanta, GA, 1994).

Although a display of interest and enthusiasm is not enough to guarantee that students will come to display similar feelings, the probability is certainly greater that this will happen than if we display apathy and loss of interest. Conversely, a display of apathy on our part doesn't prevent a student from becoming more interested in our topics . . . but it doesn't help. Research confirmed years ago that when you teach one thing and model something else, the teaching is less effective than if you practice what you teach. The father, for example, whose approach is to say, "Stop fighting with the other kids or I'll whip you good," is less likely to be successful than if he were to model the kind of behavior he is interested in teaching. Parents are less likely to teach their kids to love their neighbor when the parents continually fight among themselves than if they were to model the behavior they want to teach. And, as Dr. Albert Bandura suggests, the father who exhorts his children to work hard in school, while he guzzles beer in front of the TV, is less likely to see the desired behavior than if he were to model the beaver instead of the sloth.[2]

What students learn by imitation, however, is not confined to their attitudes relating to various academic topics. For example, one professor who teaches psychology spends a great deal of time teaching students how to read and interpret journal articles. He teaches them how to recognize the difference between data and the interpretation of data and how to recognize the difference between adequate and inadequate controls. At the same time, he is also modeling a certain kind of behavior with regard to criticism. When a student condemns a research report because of a design flaw, this instructor says, "Perhaps. But what is the author trying to say? What is good about the study?" When a student is hypercritical because of the way in which a report is written, the instructor asks, "How could the author have said it better?" In other words, rather

[2] *Social Foundations of Thought and Action,* by Albert Bandura (Prentice-Hall, 1986); see Chapter 2.

than model nit picking criticism, this instructor models positive criticism, and it is likely his students will learn to do the same. If we would like to increase the frequency with which our students think critically or open-mindedly, we have a better chance of succeeding if we demonstrate these qualities ourselves. If we would have our students demonstrate a love for learning, we have a better chance of succeeding if we demonstrate that a quest for knowledge is more important than simply parroting what is in the text.

Are We Models Worthy of Imitation?

There's an easy way to find out. All you have to do is record one or two of your instructional sessions on videotape and then observe the results. (If you manage to sit through the entire playback without falling asleep, you can tell yourself you aren't too bad.) As you watch the playback, ask yourself these questions. Did you:

- spend time looking at the people you were talking to?
- use variety in your voice inflection (i.e., avoid monotone)?
- smile when you talked, at least part of the time? (Do a "smile count." If you don't smile at least once every five minutes, you need some practice there.)
- say something positive about what you were teaching?
- say why others should find the topic of interest?
- refrain from hypnotic movements, such as swaying back and forth?
- refrain from negative comments, such as "This is sort of dull, but . . ."?
- refrain from demeaning or insulting students when they displayed interest in the subject?
- when showing or demonstrating, do it the way you want your students to do it?

NOTE: There are other procedures that are more or less effective in influencing behavior, but a thorough discussion of each is beyond the scope of this book. I will only mention that exhortation, a procedure used regularly for centuries, has seldom been very successful in influencing behavior (e.g., "Pay close attention now, because in several weeks this material will become very important!"). The instructor who does little more than insist his or her students be interested, or insist they be motivated, will certainly have cause for complaining about student apathy.

There are some other things you can do to find out how successful you are in influencing attitude toward learning, and these will be considered in the next chapter.

Where We Are

We have considered three important means by which attitude toward learning, and toward the subject being taught, may be influenced:

- conditions that exist during the learning,
- consequences that occur as a result of trying to learn, and
- modeling of desired performance.

But there's more. Until now we've been concerned with ways to influence attitudes in a favorable way. Now it's time to learn how to make sure your students will be willing to *use* what you have taught them. It's time to learn about the concept of *self-efficacy*.

9
Self-Efficacy

Now you're ready for the big leagues.

You're ready to learn about a powerful technique for influencing whether your students will be willing to use the skills you've taught them and whether they will be able to persevere in the face of periodic failures or other kinds of adverse circumstances. In other words, you'll learn how to help your students turn their favorable attitudes into energetic action. You'll learn how to strengthen their *self-efficacy*. Let me begin with a story or three to set the stage.

The debater. Charlie hadn't even known there was such a thing as a debating course before signing up, but he thought he'd give it a try. He found that he enjoyed the experience. During the course, he enjoyed researching his assigned debate topics and did a good job in presenting his arguments. Even the instructor commented favorably on how his presentations were received.

Soon after the course ended, he was invited to join the varsity debating team. But he declined. He hung back, and no amount of encouragement caused him to change his mind. He just didn't believe his skill was as good as he was told it was.

The scientist. Sharon was a research scientist. She had published several papers in respected journals and was often invited to present papers at professional meetings. She liked her work and was good at what she did. Soon she came to the attention of a prestigious laboratory, which offered her a position of a lifetime: her own lab, lab assistants, a good budget to work with—and all this in a location she liked.

But she turned it down. Why? Her explanation was, "I didn't think I was good enough. I didn't think I could live up to their expectations."

The math student. Some years ago I conducted a learning experiment in a boys' school in Italy. During lunch one day, one of the instructors told me a story about one of his boys. It seems that this boy, who was good at math, took a math test one day, and in answer to the question, "How much is ten divided by one?" wrote *eight.* When asked how he arrived at that answer, the boy replied, "Well, I knew the answer was ten, but our teachers always tell us that when you divide, the answer *has* to be smaller than the number you started with. So I figured if ten wasn't right, the answer must be nine."

"But you wrote down *eight,*" said the puzzled teacher. "Why was that?"

"Well," replied the boy, sheepishly, "everybody always tells me how stupid I am. So I figured if I put down the *right* answer, they would think I was cheating."

What do these three stories have in common? One liked debating, one liked science, and the third liked math. In each case, the person had a favorable attitude toward the subject described. But even a favorable attitude wasn't enough to give them the "courage of their convictions." The debater didn't believe he had the skill for the varsity debating team. The scientist didn't believe she was good enough to accept a "dream" job. And the math student didn't feel confident enough in his skill to write what he knew to be the right answer.

In each case, there was a favorable attitude toward the subject; what was missing was that they didn't *believe* they had the skill that they actually had.

And that's how the concept of self-efficacy differs from the concept of attitude. While it is possible to have a favorable attitude toward a subject or activity, it is at the same time possible to believe that the subject-related skills are weaker or less developed than they actually are. And that causes people to hang back from something they would really like to do. It causes them not to persevere in the face of adverse circumstances.

What Is Self-Efficacy?

Self-efficacy refers to the *judgments* that people make about their abilities to execute particular courses of action—about their *ability to do specific things.* For example, "I know I can give a talk in front of large audiences," "I know I can sew a straight seam by hand," "I know darn well that I can sing this aria skillfully and without forgetting the lyrics."

Self-efficacy isn't about the actual skills that people have; it's about the *judgments* people make about what they can do with those skills. People with low self-efficacy don't believe that they can do the things they actually can do. On the other hand, people with high self-efficacy usually make more realistic judgments about what they can do. When their skills in an area are strong, they judge them to be strong and are willing to act on that judgment.

Why Is Self-Efficacy Important?

The importance of strong self-efficacy cannot be overestimated. Dr. Albert Bandura said it best in "Organizational Applications of Social Cognitive Theory," an article published in the December 1988 issue of the *Australian Journal of Management:*

"People who have a strong belief in their capabilities think, feel, and behave differently from those who have doubts about their capabilities. People who doubt their capabilities shy away from difficult tasks. They have low aspirations and weak commitment to the goals they choose to pursue. Failure wrecks their motivation . . . They give up quickly in the face of difficulties and are slow to recover their confidence following failure or setbacks."

Note that it is possible to have high self-efficacy about a specific performance and, at the same time, expect that it will produce negative results. For example, "I know I can make a terrific sales presentation, but I also know I won't get the contract." Self-efficacy refers to judgments about performing a specific act, rather than to expectations about the consequences or outcomes of that act.

Why Is Self-Efficacy Important to Instructors?

Because people with low self-efficacy are made, not born. Because the actions of instructors can make the difference between a willingness to *try* to apply what was learned and a tendency to quit. Because instructors can make their students less (or more) vulnerable to on-the-job conditions that aren't always supportive and can help them survive rejection and periodic failures.

How Is Self-Efficacy (SE) Strengthened?

There are five types of things you can do to strengthen SE:

1. **Ensure performance mastery.**

    The most powerful way to strengthen SE regarding an ability to do something is to make sure students learn to do that thing well. But mastery is not enough, because mastery is just raw data. Unless students are also taught that the mastery is a result of their own efforts, they may leave you thinking things such as "The instructor helped me," or "I only did it right because of the job aid," or "Other students helped me," or "I was just lucky." For performance to have a maximum effect, students must learn that *they* are the cause of the performance. Here's how:

- Arrange for enough independent practice so that mastery, as defined by course objectives, is achieved or surpassed.
- Break the learning into manageable chunks that have definite end points. That will increase the number of successes that the students can experience.
- Cast your feedback comments in terms of progress achieved, rather than in terms of learning yet to be accomplished.

> *Right:* "Your work shows fewer spelling errors today than it did yesterday."
> *Wrong:* "You've got a long way to go before your spelling will be good enough."

2. Model desired performance.

You've already learned about the importance of modeling, so you need only to be reminded of how to make modeling work for you rather than against you.

- Ensure that you do it (i.e., demonstrate the skills) and talk about it the way you want your students to do it and talk about it.
- Use models (demonstrators) similar to the students, and make sure that the students understand that the modeled behavior is due to the skill of the model, rather than to other factors.
- Have the model make task-diagnostic comments during or after a performance (see task-diagnostic section below).

3. Use task-diagnostic feedback.

We can interpret feedback in either self-diagnostic or task-diagnostic ways, and the way we do it will have an enormous (often life-long) effect on self-efficacy. Here's what these two concepts mean:

Self-diagnostic feedback. When people have been made self-diagnostic, they interpret failure and negative feedback as personal deficiencies, as a reflection of their ability and on their potential to learn more. They may also blame others when they fail. For example, "They didn't give me enough time," or "The boss didn't explain it clearly."

Students develop the habit of thinking self-diagnostically when family or teachers make comments that imply personal deficiencies. Comments such as these, for example, can cause enormous harm:

"You'll never amount to much."

"You're not working up to your potential."

"You're just being forgetful again."

"How can you expect to learn this if you don't pay attention?"

"You just don't have the knack for this."

"You can do better than that."

"Oh, oh. Here comes Clumsy again."

"You could do it if you really tried."

"You'll have to wait till you're older."

Notice that not one of these feedback comments says anything whatever about the quality or accuracy of the performance giving rise to the comment. Not one offers information about how the performance might be improved. Instead, each comment suggests a personal deficiency, something "wrong" with the performer. Each one slaps a label of "not good enough" on the performer. Even worse, the last two comments provide an excuse for not even trying.

Task-diagnostic feedback. In contrast to self-diagnostic feedback, task-diagnostic feedback focuses on the task being performed. This type of feedback comments on characteristics of the performance itself, rather than the performer, and usually offers information about how the performance might be improved. Task-diagnostic feedback interprets failure as information, rather than as evidence of some sort of deficiency on the part of the learner. Examples:

> "If you hold your fingers together like this, it should go better next time."

> "If you use the job aid, it will help keep you from skipping any of the problem-solving steps."

> "This error happened because at this point you added, instead of subtracting."

> "This objective looks good, but you need to add a criterion of acceptable performance."

> "The session recording shows that you provided your students more practice time today than last week. Here's what I think you can do to increase the practice time to at least 50% of lesson time."

Notice that these task-diagnostic comments focus on the tasks rather than on the performers. It's comments such as these that will act to strengthen self-efficacy. Here's what to do in practice:

- Focus feedback comments on characteristics of the performance itself and on ways to improve the performance, rather than on student characteristics.

- Avoid deliberately making students fail in public. For students with low SE, public failure will be more destructive—not only to the performer, but to observers who also happen to be low on SE. For example, don't allow students to perform in front of an entire class until their skill and SE levels are high.

- Arrange for students to experience successes (e.g., mark the *right* answers rather than the wrong ones). Relate student performance to progress toward achievement of the objective.

- Help students interpret their "failures" as being not-yet-competent performance. (As they begin learning a new skill, they are *expected* to make mistakes. If someone labels each and every imperfect practice attempt as another failure, their SE will suffer.)

- Provide students with clear-cut, near-term goals.

- Once a skill has been mastered, provide practice under a range of conditions, so that students can judge themselves competent to handle the actual situations they are likely to encounter.

4. **Strengthen favorable attitude.**

Students who are favorably disposed toward the subject they are learning are more likely to develop subject-related skills. Because skill promotes high self-efficacy, instructors should focus on the development of a favorable attitude toward the target subject. That's what this book is mainly about, of course, so if you apply the techniques described herein, you will go a long way toward strengthening SE in your students. As a reminder:

- Arrange for students to perform successfully, and then be sure to help them interpret their achievements as evidence of increasing capability. For example, "You can see that as a result of your own efforts, you can do that faster (or better) than you'll ever be expected to do it on the job."

5. Interpret physiological information.

People tend to make inferences about their ability from physiological cues such as pain, effort, windedness, emotional arousal, etc. If something is difficult to do, they may very well conclude that they don't have the ability to do it. For example, because I find writing difficult, I've never thought of myself as a writer—even though the writing has proven successful. To me, "real writers" are people whose fingers fly as soon as they sit down at their keyboard (or quill pen), even though they keep telling me I'm wrong. In other words, I confuse the difficulty of writing with my ability to do it. (Having been made aware of the problem, I've managed to invent ways to solve it—for me.)

This is not an uncommon misconception, especially among young students whose self-efficacy may have been damaged at home (e.g., "Why can't you be as smart as your sister?"). Such unfortunates are likely to want to give up as soon as they discover that what they're trying to do requires work.

Your job is to help them understand that the *difficulty* of accomplishing is not necessarily related to their *ability* to accomplish. After all, lots of things require effort; learning to play golf or other sports, learning to play a musical instrument, becoming any kind of a skilled professional, and so on. If students are allowed to conclude that the difficulty of the task defines their ability to learn it, they will lose many opportunities to master what might become highly enjoyable and/or useful skills. What to do?

- Make sure that students do not interpret physiological cues that signify effort (i.e., cues that say, "Hey, there's some hard work going on here!") as a lack of ability.
- Model (demonstrate) finding pleasure in the hard work; e.g., aerobics class instructors who say, "Wow, this is tough," while laughing, smiling, and doing more.
- If experiencing pain, discomfort, or difficulty at a certain point in the learning is normal or a sign of progress (e.g., "no pain, no gain"), say so to the students.

It is critical that the judgments students make about their ability to perform specific tasks (self-efficacy) come close to matching the true level of their skills. With high SE, students will be more likely to try and to persevere in the face of obstacles and occasional failures. It's worth doing all you can to help your students achieve the exhilarating state of high self-efficacy.

And Now?

Now that you know how to develop favorable attitudes and strengthen self-efficacy, let's consider some ways to find out how well your efforts are paying off.

Self-Efficacy Checklist

When you want to find out whether your SE strengthening practices are on track, you may want to use the Self-Efficacy Checklist on the following page as a guide. It includes items specifically relating to improvement of self-efficacy and will help you spot opportunities for improvement.

An Attitude Checklist, included in Chapter 11, is a more comprehensive checklist that will provide reminders about which instructional practices to review when you plan a more complete checkup of your attitude-influencing methods and procedures.

SELF-EFFICACY CHECKLIST

A "YES" answer to the following questions assures that trainee self-efficacy will be strengthened. A "NO" answer represents an opportunity for improvement.

		YES	?	NO
1.	Is each trainee allowed to practice until he/she can perform to the criteria stated in the objectives?			
2.	Does the training arrange for *private* practice (to the degree consistent with the objectives) and feedback?			
3.	Are the conditions under which the practice occurs as close to real world conditions as possible?			
4.	Does the feedback remind trainees that their performance was due to their own skill rather than to other factors?			
5.	Does the feedback focus on performance improvement, rather than on the aptitude of the trainee?			
6.	Does the feedback describe gains (i.e., progress toward the objective) rather than shortfalls (i.e., learning yet to be accomplished)?			
7.	Are trainees provided with proximal (near-term) goals toward which to work?			
8.	After a skill has been mastered, is practice given under the range of conditions described by the objective?			
9.	Are the demonstrations conducted by someone similar to the trainees in attributes (e.g., age, sex, status)?			
10.	Does the model demonstrate the same job or performance that the trainees are expected to learn?			
11.	Does the demonstrator make task-diagnostic comments during or after the demonstration?			
12.	When cognitive strategies are being taught, does the model verbalize those strategies when demonstrating the skills to be learned?			
13.	Have steps been taken to help trainees understand that high effort does not mean a lack of capability?			

Part III

How Will I Know I've Arrived?

10
Evaluating Results

"You can't measure the effects of what I do."
"Why not?"
"They're intangible."
"Oh? Why should I pay you for intangible results?"
"Because I've been trained and licensed to practice."
"Hmmm . . . all right. Here's your money."
"Where? I don't see it."
"Of course not . . . it's intangible!"

Can we talk? In this chapter we're going to consider how you might find out how well your efforts to improve student attitude and self-efficacy are paying off. Before we do, though, we need to put this business of self-review in perspective. It's easier than it may look.

First point. The business of "cleaning up our act" is an ongoing process. We don't apply a set of procedures intended to improve attitudes and then forget about it forever. Improving the effectiveness of our instruction and improving our success at sending students away with favorable attitudes toward the subject of the instruction are things we continue to think about—things we constantly make adjustments to.

Second point. Any self-assessment activity in which we choose to engage is private. Nobody has to see the results of our efforts at self-review. It's like climbing up on the bathroom scale; nobody has to know whether the scale is applauding, laughing its fool head off, or hollering "Help!"

Third point. Because you are looking for indications of progress toward your goal, and because the information you collect will be private, you can relax. Also, because you are looking for progress indicators, rather than looking for scientific data to publish in the *Psychological Journal of Superbly Wrinkled Attitudes,* you needn't be concerned about statistics or any other form of sophisticated mathematical gyrations. You just want to find out whether there are some rough spots in your instruction that you can smooth out and whether you're moving in the right direction. Period.

Since there is something to be learned from earlier attempts to measure so-called intangibles, we will begin here.

Where's Your Intelligence? For many years, there was a serious search for what might be called the single-measure test of intelligence. Scientists measured the length of the forehead or the number and location of bumps on the head and tried to correlate their measurements with something called *intelligence.* But it was all in vain.

For one thing, there is no such "thing" as intelligence in the sense that there is a heart and a brain. Intelligence is not a structure or an organ that can be measured with a pair of calipers or a scale. Intelligence consists of several capabilities or capacities that cannot be accurately predicted by any *single* physical measurement.

Another reason the attempt to find the single-measure test of intelligence failed is that intelligence is a multi-faceted characteristic that can only be inferred indirectly. That is to say, intelligence, like attitudes, is a characteristic that is inferred

> Sometimes it's difficult to remember that the invention of a word, such as "intelligence," doesn't guarantee that there is a descriptive object to go with that word. I can invent a word like "bolguin," for example, or talk about "three-headed Martians," but that doesn't mean that bolguins and three-headed Martians really exist.

from circumstantial evidence. It is a form of prediction about how skillfully someone might handle a given situation, based on what that person has been seen to do.

If we want to measure intangible characteristics such as "intelligence," we must first decide what the concept means, and then we must collect information that will tell us whether someone does or does not have characteristics that conform to our meaning of the concept.

Like the trait "intelligence," "favorable attitude toward _____" is an invisible characteristic. If we want to find out whether students have a favorable attitude toward our subject, we need to collect some items of evidence that will indicate just what "favorable attitude toward _____" is in terms of the things we want students to do or say in relation to that subject.

How can we do that? There are two things we can do to collect information we need regarding student attitude and self-efficacy:

1. We can collect information about how students feel about the subject.

2. We can observe what students actually do as a result of contact with our subject.

Here's how.

How Do They Feel?

If I say to a student, "Hullo, there. How do you feel about my subject?" and get a response of "Phffft," I know that all is not well. On the other hand, if the response is "Gee, it's terrific!," I can be more optimistic. I would want more evidence than that one comment before concluding that this student has a favorable attitude toward the subject, but it's a start.

Similarly, if a student fell asleep in my class, I wouldn't immediately conclude that this behavior was the result of my instruction. After all, there are events not under my control that might lead to dozing off; a hard night before, getting up unusually early in the morning, drugs, illness, etc. (In our workshops, we actually encourage students to drop off for a bit if they feel the need. Since we don't lecture at them, they won't miss anything; and when they awake, they'll be refreshed and ready to pick up where they left off.)

Don't neglect direct questions. Sometimes the direct approach is quickest, least expensive, and most valid. Probably the best way for me to find out whether you like pistachio nuts is to come right out and ask you. If you say, "I like them very much," I have better evidence from which to infer an approach tendency than if I had not asked such a direct question. We can learn a lot about people simply by asking them direct questions.

An experiment was once described to me that bears on the importance of the direct question. The military was reported to have conducted an experiment to find out how they could predict which soldiers would perform well in arctic weather. They gave a large number of soldiers personality and aptitude tests, they measured blood pressure and other physiological variables, and they used questionnaires. After all the data were gathered, analyzed, and digested, they found that the best predictor of whether someone would function well in arctic weather was simply to ask, "Do you like cold weather?" If the reply was "Heck, no!", it was a sure bet that he or she wouldn't do well in the Arctic.

The Questionnaire

The answer to the "How do you feel?" question can be obtained with a questionnaire or by simply asking the student (privately) a question or two that will tell you what you want to know.

Though it would be possible (and scientifically acceptable) to administer a questionnaire at the beginning, as well as at the end, of the instruction, to measure attitude shifts, I don't recommend it. It's awkward, it's intrusive, and it's unnecessary. The last thing you want to do to students when they enter your course is to provide them with an obstacle that will delay their learning. "Good morning. Before we do anything else, I want you to answer the questions on this questionnaire. This will tell us how you feel about the subject of this course, so that we can compare that with your feelings at the end of the course." If they don't run for the exit, you will have at least frustrated their entry into the subject.

So, if you use a questionnaire, use it at the very end of the instruction, when it will be possible to convince the student that honest responses to the questionnaire won't have any influence on his/her grade. (We ask our students to complete a short evaluation form after the student has received his/her Certificate of Achievement. We also ask them during the course to tell us about obstacles and other practices that we can correct or improve on the spot.)

What kind of questions might you use? Consider using those that ask students:

- how they feel about the subject, and how they think they might behave when placed in certain situations or when asked certain questions.
- to make choices involving your subject.

Here are some examples of possibly useful items. As you read through them, remember that there are more sample questions than you will need; four or five of the more appropriate ones should be enough.

Sample Questionnaire Items

Since instructional environments differ in many ways, it is not possible to provide a complete questionnaire that will work in all situations. You will have to consider the items that follow as suggestions. Use the ones that apply, and derive your own from those that don't apply directly. Although the items are numbered consecutively, they are not listed in any order of importance.

1. Do you intend to take another course in _____?
   a. Yes.
   b. No.
   c. I'm not sure.

2. How interested are you in taking another course in _____?
   a. Very interested.
   b. Somewhat interested.
   c. I don't care one way or the other.
   d. Not too interested.
   e. Not at all interested.

3. How interested are you in learning more about _____?
   a. Very interested.
   b. Somewhat interested.
   c. I don't care one way or the other.
   d. Not too interested.
   e. Not at all interested.

4. If I had it to do all over again, I (would/would not) take this course.

5. I find the subject of _____
   a. Very interesting.
   b. Somewhat interesting.
   c. Somewhat uninteresting.
   d. Very uninteresting.

6. List all the subjects you are now taking and then rank-order them from most interesting to least interesting.

There are items (such as Items 7-11) that will bring the student more directly into contact with the subject. Since there may be a difference between what someone says and what he or she does, such "behavioral choice" items are useful. They come closer to requiring a commitment relating to the topic under discussion.

7. If someone suggested that you take up _____ as your life's work, what would you reply?

8. If you were asked to give a short talk about your favorite school subject, which subject would you talk about?

9. What would you reply if, in a casual group discussion, someone said, "_____ is very, very important, and everybody should try to learn as much about it as possible?"

10. Write a paragraph about your favorite school subject. *(Though this is a possible item, it is usually too time-consuming to administer.)*

11. Which of the following subjects would you be most interested in teaching?

    (List your subject and other subjects the student may be studying.)

    a. _____

    b. _____

    c. _____

    d. _____

Another kind of item, generally called the adjective checklist, is shown below. It asks students to circle words that represent their feelings about a subject.

12. Circle each of the words that tell how you feel (mostly) about the subject of _____.

fun	boring	too easy	too hard
useless	useful	exciting	interesting
essential	necessary	worthless	very important

Since it gives the student several quick opportunities to indicate a choice, items modeled after the paired comparison below may also be useful. It is simple to construct. Here's how:

(1) *List your subject and three or four other subjects the student might be currently studying;*

(2) *Make a list of pairs of these subjects, pairing each subject once with every other subject;*

(3) *Reverse the order of some of the pairs so that each subject is listed first about as many times as it is listed second; and*

(4) *Mix up the order of the items.*

With each subject paired at least once with every other subject, the student is asked to consider two subjects at a time and indicate a preference.

For example:

13. On the slips of paper that follow, you are given pairs of subjects. Look at the pairs one at a time and draw a circle around the subject you personally find the more interesting of the two.

   1. algebra   English
   2. history   science
   3. algebra   history
   4. English   science
   5. science   algebra
   6. history   English

A somewhat better index of the student's inclinations is thus gained than if he or she were to comment on each subject by itself. Instructions to the student may vary; they might ask which of the two subjects of a pair the student likes best, which of the two does he or she find more interesting, which of the two would be worth giving up a Saturday afternoon to learn more about, and so on. It is preferable to put each pair of subjects on a separate piece of paper, for later choices might be influenced by the pattern of earlier choices; the student might look back to make sure he or she is "consistent," for example. (A convenient solution is to stack the narrow slips of paper and staple them together on one edge, with one pair of subjects on each slip. This method will make consistency checks more difficult.)

Interpretation of this item is easy, since your interest is confined to a single subject. For each student, count the number of times your subject has been circled. In the above example, each student could circle algebra from zero to three times. If there were 20 students in the class, algebra might be chosen from zero to 60 times, and the "score" might therefore range anywhere from zero to 60. How to interpret the "score"? Well, a "score" near 60 would be as good as you could expect (perfection is an unreasonable expectation), and one near zero should tell you that improvement is possible, that you should ask questions intended to find out why the number isn't larger than it is. Above all, remember that the "score" is nowhere near as precise as the measurement you get from a ruler. Use it as a guide to your next actions, rather than as judgment.

How Long Should a Questionnaire Be?

Your questionnaire should contain as many items as you feel are necessary to give you good evidence about the existence of approach or avoidance tendencies toward your subject.

Which Items Should a Questionnaire Include?

Those that you will accept; those that would cause you to make the instructional changes they suggest. Since you are constructing this instrument for your own use—and *only* for your own use—it makes sense to include only those items that you will accept as meaningful. This is not to say you should not be interested in the *validity* of the items. After all, some items are better indicators than others of how a student is likely to behave in certain situations. But as important as the issue of validity may be, validity should be secondary to self-acceptance. First, develop a set of indicators that you would accept, and *then ask* questions about validity. This way, you can get started now and refine your procedures as you gather experience.

Can You Trust the Responses?

If students know we are asking "attitude" questions, can't they fake their responses? Aren't students merely going to tell us what they think we want to hear?

The honesty with which students will answer the items on a questionnaire depends mainly on how well they trust the person doing the asking. If there is little trust, students will do their best to give what they think are appropriate answers; that is, answers that will do them as little damage as possible. If there is a great deal of trust, students will feel no need to conceal their true opinions, and they will be more likely to respond truthfully.

Suppose I handed out a tendency questionnaire and said, "I am honestly interested in improving my instruction, and I would like very much to know whether I have succeeded in reaching some of my teaching objectives. I'd appreciate it if you would answer these questions as honestly as you can. Your answers will have nothing whatever to do with your grades." And then suppose a small smile turned up my lips in gleeful anticipation. Would you believe my words or my lips?

There are any number of ways in which we can say one thing and clearly communicate something entirely different by our actions, but we *can* get reliable responses to questionnaire items if we ask for responses under appropriate conditions— conditions that convince students that we mean what we say.

If you have been an instructor for any length of time, however, you have probably developed some procedures for administering questionnaires to which there will be only anonymous responses. Perhaps you use items that require checking but no writing. Perhaps you ask a student to collect the papers and shuffle them before handing them to you. These are useful techniques, and you can easily collect others by asking your colleagues. The main thing is to arrange conditions so that students believe their responses will *in no way reflect on them.* Convincing them that there is no way in which you can identify their personal responses may be the best way to succeed. Insist that no names be put on papers, ask a student to collect papers and tabulate responses, ask that the questionnaire be answered outside the classroom and turned in to a student, or ask that papers be put into a box like a voter's ballot box. Whatever procedure you select should indicate to your students your sincerity in wanting to improve the course.

As for instructions to students, I find that I get better results if I tell them I am trying to improve my instruction than if I tell them I am interested in measuring or assessing their attitudes about my subject. Students seem to be more eager to help in response to the first statement than to the second. I asked some students why this might be so, and their answers led me to conclude that it is because the statement "I want to learn something about your attitudes . . ." still has a hint of student grading in it.

What Are They Doing?

Asking people how they feel or how they think they would behave in certain situations is a legitimate way to collect information from which inferences about attitudes may be made. But the adage that says "actions speak louder than words" warrants some thought here. If I tell you that I like to read, and then you discover that I don't own any books and never go to the library, which would you believe—my words or my actions? If I tell you I think comic books are childish, and then you discover that my desk is full of them, would you put more weight on the words or the actions? Right.

All right. If actions speak louder than words, then let's look for action. But not just any action. Let's find out just which actions would satisfy us that our students feel favorably enough about our subject that they will be willing to apply what they've learned. This is a more powerful approach because it focuses directly on desired performances and relieves you of any concern over whether this or that set of performances is or isn't what "favorable attitude" *really* means. You simply describe what student actions would satisfy you, find out how things are going, and then take steps to get more of those actions you consider too infrequent.

Here's how it's done.

1. Describe the things that you would expect students to say or do before you would say they had a favorable attitude toward your subject. Think of someone who does represent the attitude you seek, and list the performances that make you say, "Now *there's* a person with a favorable attitude toward . . ." To help get you started, here's a composite list developed by others. Delete the items that don't apply, and add others that do. Make sure that when your list is finished you can say, "Yes. If students did or said these things, I would say they had a favorable attitude toward my subject."

- ask questions about the subject.
- come early and stay late.
- help other students learn the subject.
- say favorable things about the subject.
- read handouts during breaks.
- ask for more practice.
- practice longer than needed to acquire proficiency.
- ask for related courses.
- encourage others to learn about the subject.
- relate course content to their own job environments.
- do more than the minimum required.
- actually perform the skills being taught.

Again, never mind that some of the items would "fit" better under some category other than "favorable attitude." Just say what you want students to exhibit in the way of "desired performance."

2. When you have finished your draft, make sure that each item on the list is actually something you can see or hear someone do. Then ask yourself this question: "If someone did these things, would I be willing to say that he or she has a favorable attitude toward my subject?" If your answer is yes, then you have completed the list of performances. If your answer is no, then you will need to add the item or items that will cause you to answer in the affirmative.[1]

3. Determine whether each of these actions is occurring to your satisfaction. You can do this by observing whether an action occurs at all, and if it does, count or estimate the frequency with which it occurs. You might also construct a simple questionnaire that asks about each of the actions.

[1] For help with this procedure, see *Goal Analysis*, Third Edition, by R.F. Mager (Center for Effective Performance, Atlanta, GA), 1997.

4. If you find that an action occurs often enough to satisfy you, rejoice. If it does not, you'll want to take steps to find out what you might do to increase the frequency of *that specific action* (without worrying about whether or not it has anything to do with attitude). Suppose, for example, that students are reluctant to ask questions, and you want to decrease that reluctance. Try to find out why they *don't* ask questions. Can it be that they already know the material and don't need further clarification? Or that they're afraid to ask questions for fear of being humiliated? (Think about what happens to students *as a result* of asking a question.)

This procedure will help you learn what is and is not yet happening to your satisfaction and point you in the direction of what to do to get more of what you want. For specific guidance on how to make things better, read on.

11
Improving Results

A poker player down to his last chip was asked,
"How're ya doin'?"

"I dunno," he replied.

"What? You don't know how you're
making out?"

"Oh, sure," said the player. "I know
how I'm making out, but I don't know
how I'm doing it."

If we knew what we were doing that was contributing to success, and if we knew what we were doing that was contributing to failure, we could do more of the one and less of the other. After all, we are dripping with good intentions and want only the best for our students. Sometimes, though, we know how well we are doing, but we don't know exactly what to do to improve.

So this chapter is aimed at showing you how to review various components of your instruction in order to spot those components that may be acting to dampen the enthusiasm of your students. The purpose is to show you how to spot unproductive practices that may have sneaked onto the scene while you weren't looking; the purpose is to identify opportunities for improvement. Once you know what they are, you will know what to do: *Weaken the negatives and strengthen the positives.* You may not have the clout to do anything about some of them, but you will know what should be done about them.

Affect Analysis

The procedure I'll describe has to do with analyzing those conditions and consequences that influence *affect*—that is, the approach/avoidance tendencies related to the subject you are teaching. It isn't difficult to do, but that doesn't make doing it any less important.

Specifically, the procedure asks you to answer three main questions:

1. Are there obstacles that make it harder than necessary for students to come into contact with the subject? In other words, is it somehow difficult for students to get to the place where the subject is being taught or difficult to get the materials they need?

2. Are there unpleasant or aversive conditions associated with *being* in contact with the subject? Is it somehow uncomfortable or humiliating to study the subject?

3. Are there unpleasant or aversive consequences experienced by students as a *result* of coming into contact with your subject? Are students somehow made to feel smaller as a result of studying or applying what they have learned?

Some Examples

Sometimes the conditions and consequences that get in the way of more positive feelings toward the subject are easy to spot; actually, most are easy to spot once you initiate the hunt.

Occasionally, they are more devious. Here are some examples:

Example #1

When I had occasion to teach Introductory Psychology more than 200 years ago, the other faculty members and I knew exactly what incoming students were interested in. They were interested in sex, in hypnotism, in ESP, and in the antics of the weird person living down the hall of the dormitory. We knew all that. We talked about it, and we agreed on it. So how did we start the course? Did we tug on these interests and help them blossom to even greater heights? Did we fan these interests so that we could stimulate interest in other topics as well? Not for a minute! We started with the *history* of psychology. We bored the pants off these eager students with stories of the early eighteenth century, and about how . . . ZZZZZZZzzz. (Stop it! You're putting me to sleep.)

And then we would sit around in the faculty lounge complaining about the attitude of these students. Good grief. One should *never* begin teaching a subject to newcomers by teaching the history of the subject. That's the last thing students care about *at that point.* There's no *reason* for them to care. First, teach them something related to their interests; then, give them some skill in the area . . . along with feelings of competence. Do that, and then—because studying a subject's history is one way of fondling the subject, one way of getting closer to it—students may later *become* interested in the subject's history.

Example #2

A smashing example of the *right* way to begin a course was found in a locksmithing course I took by correspondence, after sending in an ad I found in a magazine. It was apparent that the developers of this course knew exactly why their students were taking this course, just as we knew why our students were taking our psychology courses. People were interested in knowing how to pick a lock. So guess where the course started. Right. Lesson 1 was on how to pick a lock. No history, no preamble; just a lesson on the subject most interesting *at that time* to the entering student. Nobody had to tell students that they weren't experts just because they knew how to pick one little lock; it was perfectly obvious. But oh, what a difference it made in attitude toward the subject! I was eager for the next lesson. Then I discovered that each set of five lessons came in a carton containing about two dozen numbered brown envelopes, about 2 x 3 inches, sealed. When, in the middle of a lesson, I was told "Now open Envelope 23," I would eagerly tear it open. Maybe it was only a key blank or an Allen wrench, but opening the envelope was better than eating peanuts.

In fact, the course was laid out in such an attitude-enhancing manner that I found myself writing an irate letter to my instructor . . . because I had run out of lessons before the next batch had arrived. Now *that's* how to organize a course to improve attitude toward the subject.

Example #3

As I said earlier, it isn't always easy to spot the conditions or consequences acting against you (such as teaching the history of a subject before teaching the subject itself). I once had occasion to conduct an affect analysis for a teacher who couldn't understand the difficulty she was having in her class. She was a fourth-grade art teacher who was very successful in motivating an interest in art activities. She was liked by her students, and they wanted to be able to do the things she could do. But by mid-semester it became clear that interest in art was declining. Many of the children demonstrated increasing apathy toward art and began expressing antagonism toward art class (not toward the teacher, but toward "art *class*"). An affect analysis for this teacher revealed the somewhat subtle cause of this situation. In explaining the project for the day, the teacher used between one-fourth and one-half of the class period. Then, just as the children had organized their materials and were hard at work, the bell rang and they had to stop and go on to another classroom.

There was good motivation in this case and an enthusiastic and skillful teacher. But there was also an event that successfully blocked the motivated activity of the students . . . and frustration resulted. Since frustration is one of the conditions people try to avoid, these students came to associate art class with something unpleasant. Aggravating the situation still further was the fact that the teacher knew time was short, and this caused her to hover over the students and urge them to work faster.

Once this state of affairs was pointed out to the teacher, there was no need to suggest a solution; making her aware of it was enough. Although she had no control over the length of the period and could not change the administrative rules, she was able to get around the restrictive time allocation by reorganizing her activities so more work time (and less teacher-talk time) would be available to the students.

Example #4

Here is an example of how a single situation can make it both difficult to come into contact with a subject and unpleasant to be in contact with it. During one college semester I took a course in a subject that I had looked forward to for some time. But this class was held in a building at the other end of the campus from my previous class. Because we had only ten minutes to get from one class to another, I had to run to get to the second class. Needless to say, I arrived in a sweat and then had to sit through the next class in sweaty (translation: smelly) condition. It was uncomfortable, and it made it difficult to concentrate on the subject at hand.

Example #5

Some years ago, a company that manufactured telephone equipment decided to modernize its training establishment. The first step was to get rid of the ancient lecture-in-the-morning, lab-in-the-afternoon format. This meant that instead of classrooms and labs (where the practicing was done), they would have only combination classroom-labs.

Once reconfigured, each room housed the lab equipment on which students would practice. In addition, there were places where trainees could sit and study, or they could gather around when the instructor wanted to spend a few minutes explaining a concept or demonstrating a procedure.

This arrangement made it easy for students to come into contact with the subject matter, and their interest in the subject, as well as their willingness to work harder, soared. Other companies have since adopted this student-friendly way of organizing the instructional space.

Example #6

Here's an example of an instance in which the consequence of showing an interest in a subject (an approach response) was punished. During an experiment on learner-controlled instruction, one of the engineer/students asked a question of the engineer/instructor. The instructor, who was always interested in answering questions in a thoughtful way, responded in his usual fashion. He walked up to the student, scowled, tugged at his eyebrow, and lifted one foot off the floor. This is what he did when he was thinking. But the student didn't know the meaning of this strange behavior. The result? The session recording showed that the student never volunteered another word for fifty-three minutes. (When the instructor was made aware of his intimidating pose, he immediately vowed to give it up in favor of a more pleasant demeanor. And he did, too.)

Example #7

Because so many computer manuals are still written from the subject matter's, rather than from the user's, point of view, it is more difficult than necessary to find the information needed to eliminate an already frustrating work stoppage. Ask a computer user why he or she doesn't look to the manual and you're likely to hear, "Arrgh! I'd rather ask my cube-mate; it's a lot faster."

What to Observe

When hunting for conditions and consequences that may be getting in the way of a more favorable attitude, or stronger self-efficacy, there are five general areas to explore:

1. The physical environment.
2. The instructional materials and equipment.
3. The instructor.
4. The instructional procedures.
5. Administration policies.

Within each of these areas, you will be interested in looking for opportunities to:

1. Make it easier for students to actually get to the subject matter, to initiate the learning process;
2. Make it less aversive and more comfortable to be in the presence of the subject matter and of the learning process itself; and
3. Make the consequences of learning and of student eagerness to demonstrate their growing competence as positive as possible.

How to Do It

To make it easier to spot opportunities for improvement in the five areas, I've provided an Attitude Checklist that appears on the following pages. Though the questions on the Checklist will suggest what to do to find the answers, here is a short set of general guidelines on how to proceed:

1. Look around your learning environment while answering the questions in Section I of the Checklist.

2. Inspect the instructional materials and actually operate the equipment while answering the questions in Section II of the Checklist.

3. Video-record one or two of your class sessions. If you have lab sessions, discussion sessions, role-play sessions, etc., record one or two of them, too. If you think you can handle it emotionally, put a video camera at the *front* of the classroom pointed at the *students*. That will show you how students are reacting as you present material.

   Review the recordings in private while answering the questions in Sections III and IV of the Checklist.

4. Answer the questions in Section V of the Checklist.

5. Ask a few of your students whether they are experiencing any obstacles to learning. You might give them a copy of the Checklist to prod their thinking.

ATTITUDE CHECKLIST

The items on this Checklist should help you identify changes that will make it easier for students to feel favorably toward what they are learning. If you find yourself placing a check mark in the "?" column, ask a student.

I. Physical Environment	Yes	?	No	Comments
1. Are the classrooms open during the times when students prefer to study?				
2. Do students have adequate work space?				
3. Is the student work space relatively comfortable?				
4. Is the environment too hot? Too cold? Too noisy? Too stuffy?				
5. Do students need to travel long distances to get to the classroom?				
6. Is it easy for them to get to the classroom?				
7. Are students often called away from the classroom?				
8. Can students easily *see* and *hear* the instruction?				
9. Is the lighting good?				
10. Are students allowed to move freely around the learning environment, rather than bolted to the floor in rows?				
11. May students leave the classroom to take care of personal needs?				
12. Are there avoidable distractions? Noise? Activity?				
13. Is there tension, either deliberate or accidental?				
14. Are students anxious to leave the learning environment?				
15. Are students relieved when they leave the learning environment?				
16. Do students find excuses to leave the environment?				

II. Instructional Materials and Devices	Yes	?	No	Comments
1. Is it easy to hear and see the instructor?				
2. Are the materials easy to get at?				
3. Is the reading difficulty appropriate for the students?				
4. Is it easy to see the place or importance of the materials; do students consider them useful?				
5. Are the materials relevant to the learning objectives?				
6. Are the instructional materials interesting?				
7. Are there materials that help the student learn the subject in addition to the instructor's words *about* the subject?				
8. Do type size and style make it difficult to read the material? (Ask a student.)				
9. Is the material organized so that the student can easily find what he or she is looking for? Is it clearly indexed?				
10. Are computer terminals or other equipment available when students need or want them?				
11. Can the equipment be operated easily? Extension cords available?				
12. Is the sound quality of audio materials good enough so that students can hear with ease?				
13. Does the equipment work reliably?				
14. When the equipment breaks down, is there someone there to repair it within a reasonable time?				
15. Are additional supplies (paper, pencils, etc.) readily available?				

III. Instructor	Yes	?	No	Comments
Does the instructor:				
1. Speak loudly enough for all to hear easily?				
2. Speak clearly?				
3. Use a vocabulary level consistent with the subject level? (Does he or she use a freshman vocabulary for freshman subjects?)				
4. Continually orient students so that they always know where they are and where they are going?				
5. Specify instructional objectives clearly? Give students written copies of the objectives?				
6. Allow or encourage questions?				
7. Allow or encourage discussion and allow students to express and develop their own ideas?				
8. Allow or encourage students to pursue some special interest they may have developed in the subject?				
9. Avoid putting students to sleep with a monotone?				
10. Avoid distracting students with annoying mannerisms; e.g., swaying back and forth while lecturing; repeatedly uttering the same phrases, such as "Right?" or "You know what I mean?"; speech mannerisms such as er..ah..um.				
11. Avoid reading the textbook aloud?				
12. Devote minimum time to lecturing?				
13. Avoid rambling?				
14. Appear to be interested or enthusiastic about the subject? How much so?				

III. Instructor (cont.)	Yes	?	No	Comments
Does the instructor:				
15. Avoid requiring students to remain inactive for long periods of time?				
16. Show interest in teaching students, rather than merely keeping order?				
17. Behave as he or she wants each student to behave?				
18. Generate discomfort while talking about or presenting the subject?				
19. Encourage students who are eager to demonstrate their achievement, rather than frighten them or make them anxious?				
20. Respond to student questions?				
21. Answer student questions with interest rather than hostility, insult, ridicule, or disdain?				
22. Respond to student comments or attempts to discuss the subject?				
23. Respond when a student completes a project or turns in an assignment? How?				
24. Return exam results promptly?				
25. Treat student work with respect, rather than hold the work up to ridicule?				
26. Insist that projects or assignments be evaluated promptly? By whom?				
27. Use subject matter as an instrument of punishment?				
28. Insist that assignments be turned in promptly, and then ignore them?				
29. Do anything that convinces the student that he or she could never become competent in the subject? That his or her best efforts aren't good enough?				

IV. Instructional Procedures	Yes	?	No	Comments
1. Do students have a clear idea of what they will be expected to be able to do at the end of the instruction?				
2. Is each student provided with a copy of the objectives at the beginning of the instruction?				
3. Does each student have a copy of the course procedures (the rules by which the course will be conducted)?				
4. Are students required to show up at a certain time and prevented from studying before that time?				
5. Are all students expected to study the same thing at the same time and for the same length of time? (i.e., must they all proceed at the same rate?)				
6. Do the rules make it difficult for students to study a topic when they feel interested in it?				
7. Is the instructor accessible to the students when needed?				
8. Does distance get between students and the subject? How far do students have to travel between the classroom and laboratory? Between classrooms?				
9. Are materials accessible to each student when he/she needs them?				
10. Is the library open when each student is free to use it?				
11. Are library books easily accessible to the student? Are you sure the librarian does not stand between the student and the books?				
12. Is there paperwork (form-filling) between the student and library books?				

IV. Instructional Procedures (cont.)	Yes	?	No	Comments
13. Is there administrative procedure between the instructor and course materials?				
14. Is equipment permanently available where students can use it?				
15. Are films, videotapes, and computer software permanently available where students can use them?				
16. Are students allowed to operate the equipment?				
17. Are visuals permanently available where the instructor uses them?				
18. Does the student spend too great a portion of the period setting up and taking down equipment? Signing in and out?				
19. Are students encouraged rather than discouraged?				
20. Are brighter students prevented from "getting ahead" of slower students?				
21. Are slower students given time to understand the subject?				
22. Are students of considerably differing abilities paired, causing boredom to the faster and frustration or embarrassment to the slower?				

A "Yes" response to Items 1–5 points to an opportunity for improvement.

V. Administrative Policy	Yes	?	No	Comments
1. Must students turn off their interest in one subject when a rigid time block ends (the bell rings) and turn on their interest in another subject? In other words, must student interest conform to administrative policy? Does policy discourage students from working with a subject until they reach a stopping point?				
2. Are classes frequently interrupted by announcements over a PA system or by other intrusions?				
3. Are there conditions that make it difficult for the instructor to maintain interest in his or her students and in the subject?				
4. Is the instructor overloaded with busy work?				
5. Are students who finish their work earlier than others made to sit still until the period is over? Is their diligence followed by some other form of unpleasant consequence, such as cleaning chores or "make work" assignments? ("Since you finished early, you can go out and whitewash those rocks.")				
6. Are grades based on individual student's achievement in relation to course objectives? In other words, is evaluation based on objective-related performance?				
7. Is there recognition or privileges for student achievement?				
8. Do instructors hand out at least as many rewards as punishments?				

V. Administrative Policy (cont.)	Yes	?	No	Comments
9. Regarding the kinds of instructor performance that management rewards: are instructors rewarded on the basis of their interest in, and efforts on behalf of, students? Are instructors rewarded on the basis of the amount of student behavior they have changed? (Are you sure they are not rewarded mostly for committee work, publications, and the amount of equipment they display?)				
10. Does administrative policy *allow* successful instructors to be rewarded more than unsuccessful ones?				
11. Does administrative policy reward unsuccessful teaching by taking from the classroom those students with whom the teacher has failed and giving them to specialists to work with in remote locations?				
12. Do managers take steps to identify how well each instructor is performing?				

What to Do Next

Now that you've collected some information about conditions and consequences that students may consider less than desirable, what should you do about it? That may sound like a silly question, but it isn't, because there are any number of ways you might proceed. Here are my suggestions about what to do—suggestions that will give you the quickest improvement in student attitude for the least amount of effort.

1. Make sure you understand the information you have collected. If you checked any items in the question-mark columns, it means you aren't sure of how to respond to those particular items. Remedy? Ask a student or two how they would respond to the items.

2. Review your responses. Circle every check you made (either in the "Yes" column or the "No" column) that indicates an opportunity for *improvement*. For example, under Section I, a "No" in response to question 2 indicates an opportunity for improvement and should be circled; whereas a "Yes" to question 4 means improvement is needed.

3. Now examine these items that represent opportunities for improvement. Your first move should be to do something about the item that is *easiest* to change. This item may not be the action that will make the biggest improvement, but it will be quick and easy to deal with, and it will help you feel good about making some progress.

   For example, if there are distractions that you can eliminate, that would be a good place to begin. Eliminate visitors or keep the visit frequency to an absolute minimum. Have students turn off their beepers. Tell them not to bring their cellular phones to class. Put a sign on your classroom door that says "Singapore" or "London," so that when someone tries to pry one of your students out of the classroom, you can honestly say, "Sorry; she's in London."

4. One by one, try to do something about the other items that need attention, continuing to make the easiest fix of those remaining. You will find, maybe to your surprise, that you have control over a large number of the needed changes; there will be only a few instances in which you will need either the cooperation or permission of others to remove the obstacle.

5. When you've done all you can, then try to do something about those items over which you have little or no control. Badger the people in charge of keeping the equipment in working order; try to order items that will make your instructional operation work more smoothly.

6. Finally, review the items you did not circle. These describe practices that you are doing right. Look at each item and ask yourself whether it would be possible to make it even "righter" (the editor will kill me for that).

For example, if you have derived the objectives for your instruction from a real need and let your students in on the secret of what they are expected to accomplish, you are doing a good thing. If, however, you haven't yet provided each student with a copy of those objectives at the beginning of the instruction, doing so will be an even better move toward sending students away with a more favorable attitude.

As you can see, the quest for attitude-enhancing practices is a never-ending process of successive approximations. Happily, the process involves skills that you already own. All you have to do is put them to use.

Summing Up

Our attitudes are influenced by the things that happen to us. When good things happen to us while in the presence of another person, we tend to feel more favorable toward that person. When we are made to feel smaller in the presence of that person, we tend to avoid future contact.

The same is true for the subjects we teach. By neglecting student feeling, we can send them away with wrinkled attitudes toward our subject; we can send them away with a tendency to avoid the subject whenever they can. But by making sure that being in the presence of the subject makes them feel good about themselves, by making sure that the results of being in the presence of the subject make them feel good about themselves, by making sure that we model the enthusiasm we would like to encourage, we can send students away feeling good about what they were taught and showing eagerness to learn more.

It isn't difficult. And it's well worth doing.

12
An Awesome Power

As we have seen in this book, people influence people . . . whether they want to or not. That's easy to understand. What may be less apparent is that the *degree* to which they influence others can be awesome to behold. Not only is it possible to influence attitude and self-efficacy for better or worse, it is possible to cause people with mediocre skills to excel, or to destroy the exceptional. Therefore, the importance of how we behave toward others cannot be overestimated. Let me show you just how powerful your actions can be.

We begin by asking ourselves these questions: "What is it that makes Mozart, Joe Montana, Jascha Heifetz, or Arnold Palmer different from the rest of us? Why are they light years beyond the rest of us in the skills with which they apply their specialties? And how did they get that way?"

The common belief, of course, is that high levels of proficiency are the result of "gifts" or of heredity, rather than of experience and practice. You hear people say, "Of course Itzhak Perlman is a super musician. He was born with a silver violin in his mouth." Or "Joe Montana is a superstar because he inherited an enormous talent for football."

But conclusions such as these are the result of superstitious thinking; i.e., if you can't see the cause, attribute it to magic. And if you can attribute it to magic, then you don't have to accept any responsibility at all for your own shortcomings. In other words, if you believe that the super-proficient got that way because of forces beyond their control, then you can tell yourself that there's nothing you can ever do to become like them. You can tell yourself things such as, "I could never learn math," or "I could never be good at public speaking." After all, if you weren't born with the skill, there's nothing you can do to acquire it. (Phootnote: "Talent" is not the same as skill. Skill is an actual ability to do something; "talent" is part of the raw material from which skill may be developed.)

A comfy way to look at the issue, I admit, but wrong. Research results suggest that superstars are *made,* not born. What? How can that be, when everyone knows that "child prodigies" show their excellence at a very early age? How can superstars be made, when some of them have been known to write operas when barely out of their diapers? And if superstars are made, how come we don't make more of them?

To be sure, superstars usually begin with a good dose of talent, but talent is by no means enough. Unless certain things happen, the talent doesn't blossom into skill. Besides, very few child prodigies ever grow up to be adult prodigies. Now why do you suppose that is? Is it because the pool of "talent" was finite and just ran out? Because the "gift" simply evaporated into thin air?

On the one hand, then, we have child prodigies who lose it before adulthood. On the other hand, there are child prodigies who just keep getting better and better as they become adults, and there are people with ordinary talent who have been made into superstars. Consider the work of Shinichi Suzuki, a well-known Japanese musician who gave violin lessons to gymnasiums full of students. A review of Suzuki's students shows that many who began taking violin lessons from him *without any signs of musical talent* attained levels of skill comparable to musical prodigies. What? Students with no obvious talent turning into super-proficient musicians? How is such a thing possible if they weren't born with the "gift"? How indeed? Suzuki's explanation (from his later writings) was that ". . . every child can become highly educated if he is given the proper training." Hear that? His message was that training can make light-years of difference in the level of skill that can be acquired, even among those without a special "gift." *But it has to be the proper kind of training!*

There's even more evidence to support the thesis that superstars are made, not born. A few musicians are blessed with absolute pitch—commonly referred to as "perfect pitch." Play any note, and they can tell you what that note is. Wow! What a "gift." But wait a minute. Research has shown that absolute pitch appears as a consequence of appropriate musical instruction and ample opportunities to interact with a musical instrument. That is, those with perfect pitch had the "right" kind of training and the "right" opportunities to interact with a musical instrument. But here's the interesting part. Absolute pitch can be acquired by anyone, but only if they are between the ages of three and five. But so what? If kids can be taught a skill commonly thought to be the result of a special "gift," then we know that this "superskill" is teachable—regardless of "gift."

Now if anyone between the ages of three and five can acquire perfect pitch, why is it so rare? The answer lies in the definition of "right" kind of training and opportunity. (By the way, most musicians with perfect pitch find it extremely annoying: to them, everybody else is off-key.)

Am I trying to tell you that there is no such thing as a child prodigy or that one person isn't born with more innate "talent" than another? No, no, not at all. But prodigies follow the same sequence of skill-development stages as everybody else. The main difference is that they attain higher levels faster and at earlier ages. For example, Picasso's earlier drawings show that he mastered the same problems the same way as the less gifted do—just faster. Like Picasso, other superstars make the same mistakes and have to solve the same problems as the less talented—they just go through the bumbling stages a lot faster than you or I might.

So if ordinary people can become adult prodigies, how come there aren't more of them? One researcher (Feldman, 1980) answers that question this way: Prodigious performance is rare because extreme talent for a specific activity in a particular child and the necessary environmental support and instruction rarely coincide.

In other words, the number of super-performers might be increased if they could experience the right mix of environmental and training conditions.

How It Happens

Well now, if there is a way to make superstars out of ordinary people and a way for child prodigies to keep from losing their talent, just what are the ingredients of the magic potion by which this is accomplished?

The research summarized from the report quoted above ("Expert Performance," by K. Anders & Neil Chamess: *The American Psychologist*, August, 1994) included several tantalizing conclusions; for example, that many child prodigies don't grow up to be adult prodigies, that many people of ordinary talent grow into exceptional performers, and that people of all levels of talent are shorn of their potential by the conditions and consequences with which they happen to be surrounded. The question that remains is, "Just how do exceptional performers get to be that way?" How do child prodigies get to be adult prodigies, and how do people of "ordinary talent" become prodigious performers? It happens like this:

The process begins at an early age with play. Children try this and that (e.g., mud pies, mandolins, pianos), thus gaining experience with various aspects of their environment. If the play is an enjoyable experience—and if the play isn't punished—they'll get better at it, and one parent or another will ultimately notice "talent."

"Hey. This kid's got talent," they will say and then arrange for the child to take lessons. That initiates deliberate, but limited, practice, with a source of individual coaching, feedback, and reinforcement. It is these conditions—supervised practice, with feedback and reinforcement—that provide the key to development of expert performance.

While this is going on, the parents help the child (help, not nag) to acquire regular practice habits. The parents teach the child that practice has instrumental (practical) value in that practice leads to increments of improvement. The parents point out and reinforce these increments of improvement (e.g., "You handled that movement a lot more smoothly today than you did yesterday."). At the same time, they refrain from dwelling on shortcomings (e.g., "You really look butt-heavy when you skate backward") or comparisons of the child's performance with that of a superstar (e.g., "You've still got a long way to go before you're another Michael Jordan") or such inspiring comments as "I always *knew* you'd never amount to anything."

The next phase begins when the child decides to turn what started as play into a full-time activity. Daily practice periods are then vastly increased, and as the practice leads to visibly improved performance, more advanced teachers are sought out. Improving performance leads to favorable recognition and praise by those other than parents and coaches, and the activity itself takes on rewarding properties; i.e., "doing it" becomes its own reward. Practice becomes self-perpetuating because of the joy experienced by engaging in the activity.

One of two things finally happens. Either the student decides he or she can, and will, make a living at the activity or decides to continue the activity as a hobby or avocation only.

So what begins as enjoyable play ends as enjoyable, highly skilled, productive activity.

It is important to note that *practice alone is not enough* for the creation of superstar performers. No less critical is the careful orchestration (either accidental or deliberate) of environmental and social factors. The opportunity to practice must be readily available (e.g., there's a piano in the house and the child is allowed to use it), and the environment must provide positive reinforcement for practice and improvement (i.e., someone says favorable things about the activity and its results).

To understand why so many people never get to grow whatever talent to the point of expert performance, re-read the previous paragraph. It's because opportunities for deliberate practice are lacking and because the consequences of practice are unpleasant or painful (e.g., hearing "You know you'll never amount to anything," or any of the thousands of other disparaging remarks and acts that can squash forever the motivation to continue). What makes the difference isn't the size of the talent so much as the predisposition to deliberate practice over many years, a predisposition nurtured by a supportive environment.

The tragedy is that if you poke your head out your window, you can almost hear the screams from the ocean of talent being incinerated by thoughtless parents showering disparaging remarks on their offspring and at the same time making sure that practice is anything but an enjoyable event (e.g., "Just for *that,* you can practice *twice* as long today!").

The encouraging fact is that it is within the power of each and every one of us to assist in providing just the kind of environment that will lead to opposite results; that is, instead of slashing deliberately or accidentally at a growing talent, to provide the kind of fertile "soil" in which that person, as well as the talent within, can grow to greater and greater heights.

Though we do not, and cannot, control all the components from which nurturing environments are created, we must accept the responsibility to act in the best interest of those we serve—to help them grow rather than to shrivel. After all, there are enough aversion-producing forces in this old world of ours. As professionals, we must not let it be said that we are among them.

Epilogue

It is easy to teach avoidance ... anywhere in the world you look there is evidence of that. As a species, we do not seem to lack skill in teaching each other to avoid people of other colors, of other ideas, of other religions, and those who might have been born in this country or that. Perhaps there is something about us that makes this inevitable ... perhaps we are not yet civilized enough, or strong enough, to apply what is already known in preventing further spread of aversion. Perhaps it isn't realistic for us to believe we are ready to try to stamp out the game of "you name it and I'll teach you to avoid it."

Perhaps.

Be that as it may, those with the responsibility for influencing the performance of others cannot accept such a defeatist position. To be a professional means to accept responsibility ... responsibility for actions and for results. It is to act in the best interests of those served ... to help them grow rather than shrivel. When we accept the responsibility for professionally influencing the lives and actions of other people, we must do all we can to make that influence positive rather than negative. When we accept the money and the trust of the community, we must accept not only the responsibility for sending our students away with as much knowledge and skill as is within our power to give them, but also for sending them away with the ability and the inclination to use those skills to help themselves and others.

There are enough aversion-producing instruments in this old world of ours. We must not let it be said that we are among them.

A Time for Tribute

"Help, help," I cried. And did they ever!

As you might guess, a book about approach tendencies ought to trigger approach responses toward the subject of approach responses. Accordingly, *How to Turn Learners On . . . without turning them off* was formulated in two loose stages. The first stage consisted of telling the content to members of the intended audience, individually and in groups, and noting their reactions, comments, and suggestions. The object was to find out what it took to get them nodding and to keep them nodding all the way through. (But not nodding off.)

The second stage began when the content was in written form. It consisted mainly of asking instructors and colleagues who tested the various drafts to mark anything that slowed them down, turned them off, or rubbed them the wrong way; to describe what might have caused them to back off; and finally, to describe what might have caused them to move forward.

And did they ever!

They made me change the sequence of topics until it made sense to *them,* and showed no respect whatever for what was "logical" to *me;* ripped out paragraphs I was very fond of and trampled them into oblivion; caused the demise of clever explanations that nobody seemed to understand; bludgeoned me into burning a long chapter (indeed!) on the development of affective objectives (there's no such thing) and half of one on the statistics of attitude assessment (nobody cared); and vetoed examples that didn't examp.

Such impudence cannot go unpunished; such ego batterers must be exposed to public view. Therefore, with ropes of gratitude I tie to the pillory of immortality the 30 teachers who attended the workshop sponsored by the London County Council, the 20 teachers who attended a workshop sponsored by the University of Buffalo, the nine graduate student-teachers of the University of Rochester; and these original culprits, who made marks all over my neat pages:

Albert Bandura; Bruce Bergum; Edith Bryant; David Cram; Anne Dreyfuss; Sister Charlene Foster, S.N.D. de Namur; Arthur Hyatt; Jane Kilkenny; Leon Lessinger; Richard Lewis; Jeanne Mager; Mike Nisos; Judy Opfer; Peter Pipe; Maryjane Rees; Charles Selden; Nancy Selden; Caroline Smiley; Margaret Steen; James Straubel; Walter Thorne; and Jack Vaughn. Especially in need of public exposure are those who offered their artistic opinion and witty remarks regarding cover design drafts. And those are these: Johan Adriaanse, Gérard Conesa, Paul Guersch, David Heath, Eileen Mager, Clair Miller, Fahad Omair, Dan Piskorik, Phil Postel, Jim Reed, Ethel Robinson, Bill Valen, Carol Valen, Bob White, and Letitia Wiley.

Not to be outdone, there were those who couldn't resist sloshing around in the present edition, gleefully pointing to lumps and potholes needing my attention. Folks such as these cannot be allowed to point and snicker behind a veil of anonymity, so expose them I will: **David Cram, Kay Newell, Dan Lansell, Eileen Mager,** and **Verne Niner.** Finally, I must reveal that Mary Kitzmiller was the kindly (!) editress whose sharp eyes and red pencil smoothed the grammatical bumps and tangles.

With music swelling in the background, I raise my glass to all in a burst of thanks and appreciation for their insightful efforts.

RFM

Index

MORE GREAT BOOKS FROM DR. ROBERT F. MAGER!

Dr. Robert F. Mager has authored one of the most extensive and renowned collections of books and resources on issues of human performance in existence today. These books are considered to be *the* reference library for anyone serious about educating others and improving human performance. You'll find everything you need to learn how to:

- develop successful instruction,
- find realistic solutions to performance problems,
- measure the results of your instruction,
- generate positive attitudes in learners,
- and much more!

Order your copies today and get resources you'll use for a lifetime.

	Quantity	x Price=	Total
Measuring Instructional Results *How to determine whether your instructional results have been achieved*		x $19.95=	
Preparing Instructional Objectives *A critical tool in the development of effective instruction*		x $19.95=	
How to Turn Learners On... without turning them off *Ways to ignite interest in learning*		x $19.95=	
Analyzing Performance Problems *How to figure out why people aren't doing what they should be, and what to do about it*		x $19.95=	
Making Instruction Work *A step-by-step guide to designing and developing instruction that works*		x $19.95=	
Goal Analysis *How to clarify your goals so you can actually achieve them*		x $19.95=	
The How to Write a Book Book		x $17.95=	
Troubleshooting the Troubleshooting Course		x $17.95=	
What Every Manager Should Know About Training		x $17.95=	
Subtotal			
Shipping & Handling*			
GA residents add 5% sales tax to the subtotal plus shipping and handling			
Total Order			

* *Please add $4.50 for the first book, plus $1.50 for each additional book. Please allow four weeks for delivery by UPS Ground Service.*

Name _____

Phone _____ Fax _____

Organization _____

Address _____

City _____ State _____ Zip _____

- My check or money order for $ _____ is enclosed

Charge my • Visa • Mastercard • AmEx   Exp. Date _____

Card Number _____

Name on Card _____

Please send this form and your check, money order, or credit card number to:

CEP
P.O. Box 102462
Atlanta, GA 30368-2462

Call 1-800-558-4CEP for volume discount information.

Call for shipping charges on international orders.

For credit card orders, fax this order for faster delivery: (770) 458-9109